THE HIDDEN PLACES OF WALES

By Peter Long

Regional Hidden Places

Cornwall
Devon
Dorset, Hants & Isle of Wight
East Anglia
Lake District & Cumbria
Lancashire & Cheshire
Northumberland & Durham
Peak District and Derbyshire
Yorkshire

National Hidden Places

England
Ireland
Scotland
Wales

Country Living Rural Guides

East Anglia
Heart of England
Ireland
North East of England
North West of England
Scotland
South
South East
Wales
West Country

Other Guides

Off the Motorway
Garden Centres and Nurseries of Britain

Published by: Travel Publishing Ltd, Airport Business Centre, 10 Thornbury Road, Plymouth, Devon PL6 7PP

ISBN13 9781904434900

First published 1997, second edition 2001, third edition 2004, fourth edition 2006, fifth edition 2008, sixth edition 2010

Printing by: Latimer Trend, Plymouth

Maps by: ©MAPS IN MINUTES/Collins Bartholomew (2010)

Editor: Peter Long

Cover Design: Lines and Words, Aldermaston

Cover Photograph: Mount Snowdon from Capel Curig
© Peter Adams Photography Ltd/Alamy

Foreword

This is the 6th edition of ***The Hidden Places of Wales*** taking you on a relaxed but informative tour of a country often referred to as the "Red Dragon". The guide has been been fully updated and in this respect we would like to thank the Tourist Information Centres in Wales for helping us update the editorial content. The guide is packed with information on the many interesting places to visit and you will find details of places of interest and advertisers of places to stay, eat and drink included under each village, town or city, which are cross referenced to more detailed information contained in a separate, easy-to-use section to the rear of the book.

Wales is a country blessed with some of the most dramatic landscapes in Britain. To the north lies Snowdonia, a land of awe-inspiring mountains, wild moorlands and enchanting lakes whilst further south the land is abundant with deep valleys and vast forests. To the west the country has a spectacularly varied coastline of cliffs, coves and sandy beaches. Wales also has a rich cultural heritage full of myths and legends founded on Celtic ancestry but has an equally strong industrial past. We are sure that you will enjoy your visit!

The Hidden Places of Wales contains a wealth of interesting information on the history, the countryside, the towns and villages and the more established places of interest. But it also promotes the more secluded and little known visitor attractions and places to stay, eat and drink many of which are easy to miss unless you know exactly where you are going.

We include hotels, bed & breakfasts, restaurants, pubs, bars, teashops and cafes as well as historic houses, museums, gardens and many other attractions throughout the area, all of which are comprehensively indexed. Many places are accompanied by an attractive photograph and are easily located by using the map at the beginning of each chapter. We do not award merit marks or rankings but concentrate on describing the more interesting, unusual or unique features of each place with the aim of making the reader's stay in the local area an enjoyable and stimulating experience.

Whether you are travelling around Wales on business or for pleasure we do hope that you enjoy reading and using this book. We are always interested in what readers think of places covered (or not covered) in our guides so please do not hesitate to use the reader reaction form provided to give us your considered comments. We also welcome any general comments which will help us improve the guides themselves. Finally if you are planning to visit any other corner of the British Isles we would like to refer you to the list of other ***Hidden Places*** titles to be found to the rear of the book and to the Travel Publishing website.

Travel Publishing

Did you know that you can also search our website for details of thousands of places to see, stay, eat or drink throughout Britain and Ireland? Our site has become increasingly popular and now receives over **500,000** visits annually. Try it!

website: www.findsomewhere.co.uk

Location Map

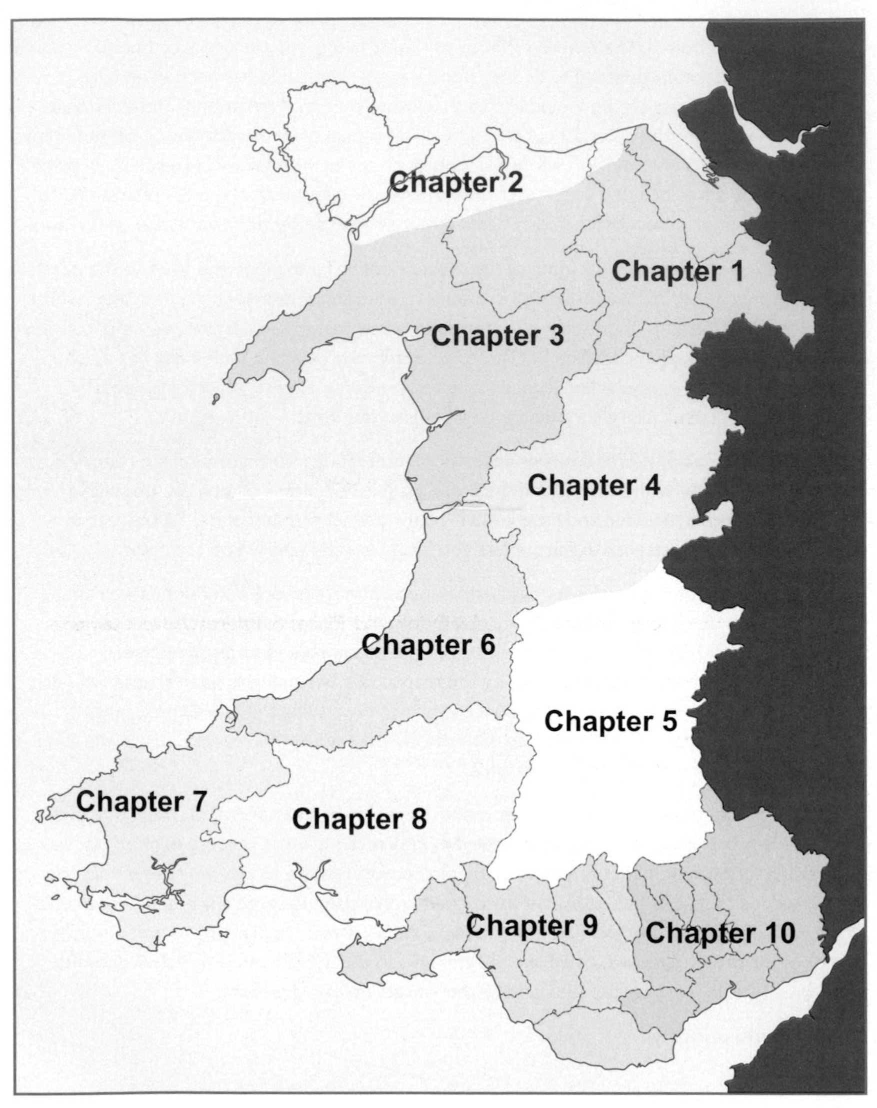

Contents

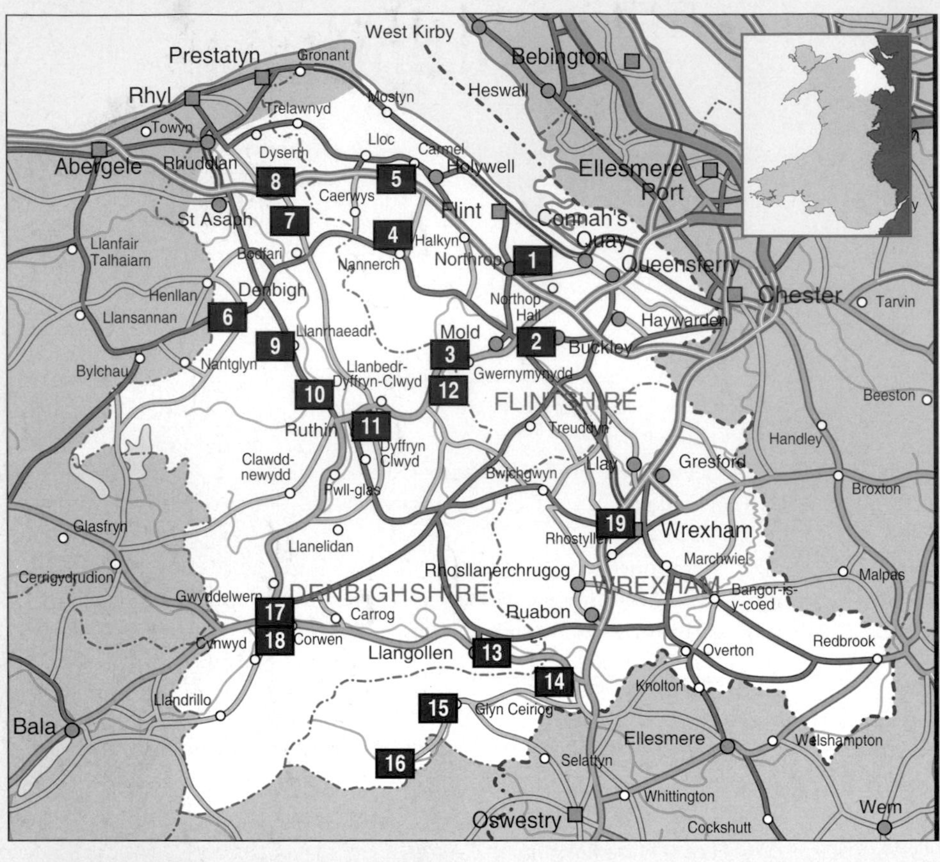

ACCOMMODATION

3	Plas Hafod Country House Hotel, Gwernymyndd, nr Mold	pg 8, 216
6	Castle House Country Guest House, Denbigh	pg 9, 218
9	The Kings Head, Llanrhaedr	pg 14, 220
13	Gales of Llangollen, Llangollen	pg 17, 223
16	The West Arms, Llanarmon Dyffryn Ceirog, nr Llangollen	pg 21, 225
18	Owain Glyndwr Hotel, Corwen	pg 22, 227

FOOD & DRINK

1	The Boot Inn, Northop	pg 5, 214
2	White Lion, Buckley	pg 7, 215
3	Plas Hafod Country House Hotel, Gwernymyndd, nr Mold	pg 8, 216
4	The Crown Inn, Lixwm	pg 8, 216
5	The Rock Inn, Lloc, nr Holywell	pg 9, 217
7	Salisbury Arms, Tremeirchion	pg 11, 219
8	The Smithy Arms, Rhuallt, nr St Asaph	pg 11, 220
9	The Kings Head, Llanrhaedr	pg 14, 220
10	Drovers Arms, Rhewl, nr Ruthin	pg 14, 221
11	Corporation Arms, Ruthin	pg 15, 221
12	The Miners Arms, Maeshafn	pg 16, 222
13	Gales of Llangollen, Llangollen	pg 17, 223
15	The Glyn Valley Country Inn, Glyn Ceiriog, nr Llangollen	pg 21, 224
16	The West Arms, Llanarmon Dyffryn Ceirog, nr Llangollen	pg 21, 225
17	Yum Yums, Corwen	pg 22, 226
18	Owain Glyndwr Hotel, Corwen	pg 22, 227
19	Tastebuds, Wrexham	pg 23, 228

PLACES OF INTEREST

14	Chirk Castle, Chirk	pg 20, 224

North Wales Borderlands

This area of Wales can easily be overlooked by visitors to the country as they speed westwards, but it is a mistake not to stop and explore the towns, villages and countryside, as they are rich in history and scenic beauty. Each of the different areas has its own special character and scenery: the Clwydian Hills, a 22-mile designated Area of Outstanding Natural Beauty; the Dee estuary; the broad, gentle sweep of the Vale of Clwyd with historic towns like Ruthin, St Asaph and Denbigh; Wrexham, the largest town in North Wales, and its surrounds; The Maelor, where the Cheshire Plains transform into the Welsh Hills; Chirk and the beautiful Ceiriog Valley. The Romans certainly forayed into the area from their major town of Chester and there is also evidence of Celtic settlements.

However, it was during the 13th century that Edward I, after his successful campaign against the Welsh, set about building his ambitious Iron Ring of huge fortresses along the Dee estuary and the North Wales coast. Each was built a day's march from the last and the first stronghold was begun at Flint in 1277. Though the great fortresses are now in ruins, the remains of this massive project - the largest seen in Europe - are still very much in evidence today.

The land around the Dee estuary is home to a great number of waders and wildfowl which feed on the mudflats left by the retreating tides. Between the estuary and the Clwydian Range lie small, compact villages as well as the market towns of Mold and Holywell, a place of pilgrimage that became known as the Lourdes of Wales. The range, a grassy line of hills above the Vale of Clwyd, offers fabulous views and exhilarating walks; it is one of the five designated Areas of Outstanding Natural Beauty in Wales (see Anglesey, the Gower Peninsula, the Llyn Peninsula and The Wye Valley in their respective chapters).

Further south lie Llangollen and the Dee Valley. Llangollen is a delightful old town in a picturesque riverside setting which is not only a charming place to visit but is also the home of the annual International Music Eisteddfod (not the same as the National Eisteddfod). An eisteddfod was originally a meeting of bards where prizes were awarded for poetry reading and singing. The event at Llangollen has a true international flavour with such eminent figures as Luciano Pavarotti having graced its stage.

Pontcysyllte Aqueduct, Llangollen

Though this northern gateway to the country is not a particularly large area, it boasts all but one of the Seven Wonders of Wales, wonders which while not quite as spectacular as the more familiar Seven Wonders of the World are nonetheless all interesting in their own right and well worth a visit. They are listed in the famous 19th century rhyme:

Pistyll Rhaeadr and Wrexham Steeple,
Snowdon's Mountain without its people,
Overton Yew Trees, St Winefride's Well,
Llangollen Bridge and Gresford Bells.

•

On the outskirts of Mold lies Clwyd Theatre Cymru, which offers a wide range of entertainment including theatre, music and frequent exhibitions of art, sculpture and photography. It has a bar, coffee shop, bookshop, free covered parking and disabled access.

•

MOLD

The county town of Flintshire, Mold is a pleasant little town with a bustling street market every Wednesday and Saturday. The town's finest building is **St Mary's Church** which was built by Margaret Beaufort, the mother of Henry VII, to celebrate her son's victory over Richard III at Bosworth in 1485. It has some interesting stained glass windows as well as some fine architectural ornamentation. A light and airy building, the church was constructed on the site of an earlier church whose original oak roof, carved with Tudor roses, has been retained in part.

The church stands at the foot of **Bailey Hill**, the site of a Norman motte and bailey fortification which was built at this strategic point overlooking the River Alyn by Robert de Montalt. First captured by the Welsh in 1157 and then again by Llywelyn the Great in 1199, ownership of the castle passed through many hands and today, not surprisingly, nothing remains of the fortress; its site is now marked by a bowling green. Montalt gave the town its English name - a straightforward translation of its Welsh name, Yr Wyddgrug, meaning 'The Mound'.

Mold's most famous son is **Daniel Owen**, the first Welsh novelist of any note. He was born here in 1836 and died here in 1895. Writing only in Welsh, it was Owen's honest accounts of ordinary life that were to make him one of the greatest 19th century novelists and also to gain him the title the 'Welsh Dickens'. His statue stands outside the town library which is also the home of Mold's **Museum** (free), where a room is dedicated to Owen's memory. Another distinguished son of Mold was **Richard Wilson**, an 18th century landscape painter who spent his childhood in the town; dramatic scenes of

St Mary's Church, Mold

River Alyn, Mold

mountainous Welsh countryside were his speciality. Although he was a co founder of the Royal Academy, his work was not valued in his lifetime and he died penniless. His memorial can be seen near the north entrance to the parish church.

The composer Felix Mendelssohn was said to have been inspired by the town's surroundings when writing his opus *Rivulet*. The nearby limestone crags provide panoramic views over the surrounding countryside.

One such scenic area lies three miles west of Mold on the A494 - **Loggerheads Country Park** which is situated on the edge of the Clwydian Range. Classified as an Area of Outstanding Natural Beauty, this large park is an ideal environment for all the family, especially younger members, as there are various trails which are each about one and a half miles long. The trails all start near the late-18th century mill building that used water from the River Alyn to drive a water wheel and two sets of stones to grind corn from the local farms.

Around 200 years ago, Loggerheads was part of the lead mining industry, which was founded in this area of ore-bearing limestone. Many relics of those days remain and can still be seen within the quiet woodland. There is a fine selection of local arts, crafts and souvenirs on display in the Craft Shop at the **Loggerheads Countryside Centre**, where there is also a tea room.

AROUND MOLD

RHOSESMOR

3 miles N of Mold on the B5123

Moel Y Gaer, near this small village, was considered to be a fine example of an Iron Age hill fort until archaeological digs unearthed evidence that suggested this site had been inhabited from as far back as 3500 BC.

To the west of the Rhosesmor lie the remains of a short section of **Wat's Dyke**, a much shorter dyke than Offa's which is thought to have been built by the Mercian King Aethelbald in the 8th century. Just under 40 miles long, the dyke ran southwards from the Dee estuary to Oswestry.

HALKYN

4½ miles N of Mold on the B5123

The village lies close to the long ridge of the **Halkyn Mountains**, which rise to some 964 feet at their highest point and are scarred by the remnants of ancient lead mines and quarries, some of which date back to Roman times.

FLINT

5 miles N of Mold on the A5119

A small and modest town that was once the port for Chester, Flint can boast two historical firsts: it was the first associated borough in Wales to receive a charter (in 1284) and it was also the site of the first of Edward I's Iron Ring fortresses. Dotted along the North Wales coast, a day's march apart, Edward I's ring of massive fortresses

1 THE BOOT INN

Northop

A charming, quality village inn offering the very best in fresh food.

see page 214

•

Linking Holywell with the ruins of Basingwerk Abbey is the Greenfield Valley Heritage Park, a 70-acre area of pleasant woodland and lakeside walks with a wealth of monuments and agricultural and industrial history. There are animals to feed, an adventure playground and picnic areas. In the 18th and 19th centuries this was a busy industrial area which concentrated on the newly established production processes for textiles, copper and brass. Several of the copper works and cotton mills have been restored.

•

represented Europe's most ambitious and concentrated medieval building project. Started after the Treaty of Aberconwy in 1277 and completed in 1284 by James of St George, **Flint Castle**, now in ruins, stands on a low rock overlooking the coastal marshes of the Dee estuary towards the Wirral peninsula. Originally surrounded by a water-filled moat, the remains of the Great Tower, or Donjon, are an impressive sight. Set apart from the main part of the castle, this tower, which is unique among British castles, was intended as a last retreat and, to this end, it was fully self-sufficient, even having its own well.

Flint Castle featured in the downfall of Richard II, when he was lured here in 1399 from the relative safety of Conwy Castle and was captured by Henry Bolingbroke, the Duke of Lancaster and future Henry IV. The imprisonment of Richard here is remembered in Shakespeare's *Richard II*, where, in response to Bolingbroke's, "My gracious Lord, I come but for mine own," the defeated Richard replies, "Your own is yours, and I am yours, and all." At this point even the King's faithful greyhound is said to have deserted him.

During the Civil War, the town and castle remained in Royalist hands, under the leadership of Sir Roger Mostyn, until 1647, when both were taken by General Mytton, who was also responsible for dismantling the castle into the ruins we see today.

St Winefride's Well, Holywell

HOLYWELL

7 miles N of Mold on the A5026

In the town lies one of the Seven Wonders of Wales, **St Winefride's Well**, which was once such a place of pilgrimage it was described as the "Lourdes of Wales". According to tradition, Winefride, the niece of St Beuno, was beheaded by Prince Caradoc after refusing his advances. A well bubbled up at the spot where her head fell. Caradoc was struck dead by lightning instantly but Winefride was restored to life after her uncle replaced her head. Winefride (Gwenfrewi in Welsh) went on to become an abbess at Gwytherin Convent near Llanrwst. After her death in 1138, her remains were given to Shrewsbury Cathedral. Thought to have healing qualities, the well has been visited by pilgrims since the 7th century and still is, particularly on St Winefride's Day, the nearest

Saturday to 22 June. The well, and the Vale of Clwyd, was beloved of the poet **Gerard Manley Hopkins**. He trained as a priest at St Beuno's College, Tremeirchion, and St Winefride's Well inspired him to write a verse tragedy, which contains many beautiful, evocative lines:

The dry dene, now no longer dry nor dumb, but moist and musical.
With the uproll and downcarol of day and night delivering water.

On Wales in general he was equally lyrical:

Lovely the woods, water, meadows, combes, vales,
All the air things wear that build this world of Wales.

St Winefride's Chapel was built by Margaret Beaufort (the mother of Henry VII) around 1500 to enclose three sides of the well. The Victorian statue of St Winifride has a thin line round the neck showing where her head was cut off. Also here is the **Church of St James**, the local parish church which was built in 1770. It is thought that it stands on the site of the original chapel which was constructed by St Beuno in the 7th century.

Basingwerk Abbey was built by Cistercian monks in 1132 and functioned as a self-sufficient community - the Cistercians placed great emphasis upon agricultural labour. Although this was an English house, Basingwerk absorbed Welsh culture and the Welsh bard, Gutun Owain, was associated with the abbey where he wrote *The Chronicle of Princes*, which is also known as the *Black Book of Basingwerk*.

EWLOE

4 miles E of Mold on the B5125

Hidden in a steeply wooded glen area are the remains of **Ewloe Castle**, a fortification which was originally an English stronghold until it fell into the hands of the Welsh in around 1146. Owain Gwynedd set about strengthening the fortress as an ambush castle ready to surprise the soldiers of Edward I on their march through Wales when the battle of Ewloe took place in 1157. Some 150 years later, a tower, two wards protected by a curtain wall and an outer ditch were added. But the castle failed to live up to expectations, particularly after the construction of nearby Flint Castle, and by the late 13th century it ceased to have any military significance.

2 WHITE LION

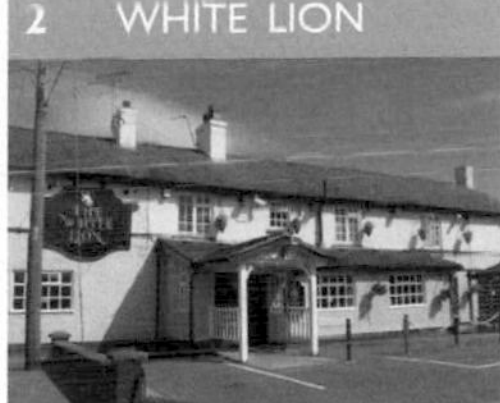

Buckley

Traditional, home cooking and family hospitality is at the heart of this superb public house on the outskirts of Buckley.

see page 215

Ewloe Castle

3 PLAS HAFORD COUNTRY HOUSE HOTEL

Gwernymyndd, nr Mold

One of the finest wedding venues and restaurants in Wales, boasting spectacular views across the hills and valleys of Flintshire.

 *see page 216*

4 THE CROWN INN

Lixwim

A popular inn, dating back to the 17th century and located at the heart of the village of Lixwim.

 *see page 216*

HAWARDEN

5 miles E of Mold on the A550

Mentioned in the *Domesday Book*, this small village close to the English border has two castles, one a ruin dating from the 13th century (the circular keep and hall still stand in Castle Park) and another that was once the home of the Victorian Prime Minister, William Gladstone. He lived at **Hawarden Castle** (private) for some 60 years after his marriage to the daughter of Sir Stephen Glynne in 1839. The house was built in 1750 and enlarged and castellated by Sir Stephen in 1809. The parish church, as well as having stained glass by Burne-Jones, contains the Gladstone Memorial Chapel, where marble effigies of the statesman and his wife, who are buried in Westminster Abbey, can be seen. The village's connections with Gladstone can also be seen in a collection of his books in the famous **St Deiniol's Residential Library**, next to the church.

CAERGWRLE

6 miles SE of Mold on the A541

Once occupied by the Romans as an outpost station for nearby Chester, **Caergwrle Castle**, which stands on a high ridge, probably started life as a Bronze Age hill fort. It was Dafydd, brother of Llewelyn the Last, who constructed the fortification more or less in its present form and it was from here, in 1282, that Dafydd launched his last, and fatal, Welsh attack on the English King Edward I.

CILCAIN

3½ miles W of Mold off the A541

This charming hamlet in the heart of the Clwydian Range has a medieval church, **St Mary's**, with a double nave, a hammerbeam roof and stained glass. To the south lies **Moel Famau** (The Mother of Mountains); a path leads from Cilcain to the summit which at 1,820 feet is the range's highest peak. It is well worth the climb to the summit as not only are there the remains of a **Jubilee Tower**, started in 1810 to commemorate George III's Golden Jubilee (later blown down in a storm in 1860) but the panoramic views are breathtaking. Westwards lies the Vale of Clwyd with the river stretching down to the Irish Sea, while to the east the land rolls gently down to the Dee estuary.

CAERWYS

8½ miles NW of Mold on the B5122

Originally a Roman station, Caerwys grew to become a village of such significance that it received a charter from Henry III. Once an important market town, Caerwys is credited with being the place where, in around 1100, Gruffydd ap Cynan called the first Eisteddfod. This cultural feast was revived in the 16th century following the intervention of Elizabeth I, who gave permission for a competitive festival of Welsh music and poetry to be held here in 1568.

AFONWEN

8 miles NW of Mold on the A541

Another small village in the

Clwydian Range, Afonwen is home to one of the largest craft and antique centres in north Wales. **Afonwen Craft and Antique Centre**, rich in Welsh culture, has a whole host of crafts, accessories and gifts for sale, including furniture, crystal, china and silver, jewellery, pine furniture, clothes and handbags; it also has a licensed restaurant. and holds regular exhibitions and demonstrations.

WHITFORD

10 miles NW of Mold off the A5026

Close to the village of Whitford can be found a curious monument, **Maen Achwyfaen** (The Stone of Lamentation). This Celtic cross, sculpted in the shape of a wheel, is said to have been erected in about 1000 and is the tallest such cross in Britain. The person or event it commemorates is unknown. The renowned 18th century travel writer **Thomas Pennant** is buried in the graveyard adjacent to the grand 19th century church. Born in 1726, he is best known for his book *A Tour in Wales*. Though he travelled constantly throughout the country, he could speak no Welsh and relied on others to translate for him.

DENBIGH

Recorded as a small border town in the 11th century, Denbigh, whose Welsh name 'Dinbych' means a small fortified place, developed gradually round its market place and town square, and by the time of the first Elizabethan era it was one of the largest and richest towns in North Wales, a residence for Welsh princes and a leading centre of Welsh power. Today, it still retains a charm that is enhanced by buildings dating from the 16th century onwards, and most of the centre is now a conservation area. The old town is concentrated around the castle that was built on the site of a Roman settlement and commands good views over the Vale of Clwyd.

Denbigh Castle was one of the biggest and most imposing fortifications in Wales and its ruins are still an impressive sight as they crown the top of a steep hill above the town. It was originally a stronghold of the Welsh prince Dafydd ap Gruffydd, brother of Llewelyn the Last, but when the Earl of Lincoln was given Denbigh by Edward I he began construction of a new castle in 1282. De Lacy removed all traces of the older Welsh fortification and, at the same time, created a new English borough protected by town walls. More than 3,000 labourers worked on the castle and

5 THE ROCK INN

Lloc

A little family-run haven in the village of Lloc, with a fresh and locally-sourced menu.

see page 217

6 CASTLE HOUSE COUNTRY GUEST HOUSE

Denbigh

Elegance, character and luxury all rolled into one historical guesthouse overlooking the Clwyd valley.

see page 218

Denbigh Castle

•

Throughout the centuries Denbigh has been the home to many famous characters including the physician, musician, antiquarian and Member of Parliament, Humphrey Llwyd, who, in the 16th century, made the first accurate maps of Wales; they were published in an atlas of 1573. He is sometimes known as the Father of Modern Geography.

•

•

Born in 1739, Thomas Edwards was another noted native of Denbigh, who went on to become an actor and playwright, under the name of Twm o'r Nant, and was given the nickname the Welsh Shakespeare. After a full, colourful and eventful life, Edwards lived out his last days peacefully in Denbigh and he now lies buried in the churchyard of the splendid 14th century St Marcella's Church.

•

the walls. The walled town was completed by 1311 but it was subject to sporadic attacks during its occupation. In 1402, Owain Glyndwr laid siege to the town and it suffered again during the Wars of the Roses, when the old town was burnt to the ground. In 1645, during the Civil War, Charles I stayed at the castle, which was held for him by Sir William Salusbury (nicknamed Old Blue Stockings because of his flashy taste in hosiery); it later endured a six-month siege before falling, in October 1646, to Parliament forces, after which the castle and the walls gradually fell into disrepair. But an impressive triple-towered Gatehouse and a large stretch of the **Town Walls** still exist and can be walked today. The walk opens up a splendid historic view of the town, particularly the section that includes Countess Tower and the Goblin Tower.

One of the few towns in Wales approved of by Dr Samuel Johnson during his travels through the Principality, Denbigh was also the birthplace of **Henry Morton Stanley.** He was born John Rowlands in 1841, the illegitimate son of John Rowlands and Elizabeth Parry, and grew up partly in the care of relatives and partly in the workhouse in St Asaph. In his late teens he sailed from Liverpool to New Orleans as a cabin boy. There he was befriended by a merchant, Henry Hope Stanley, whose first and last names he took - the Morton came later. He spent the next few years as a soldier, sailor and journalist, and his several commissions for the *New York Herald* culminated in a quest to find the explorer David Livingstone, who had set out for Africa to search for the source of the Nile. At the head of an American-financed expedition, and keeping his intentions hidden from the British, he set out from Zanzibar and struggled to Ujiji, where in 1871 he found the explorer and addressed him with the immortal words "Dr Livingstone, I presume". The two became firm friends, and Livingstone continued his quest after being restocked with provisions. He died a year later. Stanley wrote about his expedition and returned to Africa to take up the exploration where Livingstone left off. He was involved in numerous adventures and enterprises, mainly with Belgian backing, and was instrumental in paving the way for the creation of the Congo Free State. On his return to Britain, he married, spent some years as a Member of Parliament and was knighted by Queen Victoria. He died in London in 1904 and was buried in the churchyard of St Michael in Pirbright; his rough granite headstone bears the one-word inscription "Africa".

Another child of Denbigh was the Elizabethan beauty **Catherine of Berain**, a distant relation of Elizabeth I who married four times and produced so many descendants that she was known as 'Mam Cymru' ('Mother of Wales').

AROUND DENBIGH

BODFARI

3 miles NE of Denbigh on the B5429

Situated in the heart of the Vale of Clwyd, at the foot of the Clwydian Range, Bodfari marks the abrupt change in landscape from arable fields to heath and moorland. Thought to have been the site of a Roman station, the village is famous for **St Deifar's Holy Well**, which can be found at the inn next to St Stephen's Church.

TREMEIRCHION

6 miles NE of Denbigh on the B5429

This small village contains several buildings of interest. The 14th century **Church of Corpus Christi** is the only church in Britain with that dedication. Inside, there's a 14th century tomb-niche containing the effigy of a vested priest while, in the chancel, a tablet commemorates Hester Lynch Piozzi who is better known as Dr Johnson's friend, **Mrs Thrale**. In 1774, Mrs Thrale inherited a house in Tremeirchion she had known in her childhood which was dilapidated and in need of great repair. Following her marriage to the Italian musician, Gabriel Piozzi, the couple rebuilt the house, living there happily until Piozzi's death. In 1567 Sir Richard Clough, a wealthy merchant, built a house near the village. The house is now demolished but the gatehouse still stands. Its unusual architectural style so shocked the locals that they thought the devil must have been the architect and has also supplied the bricks. The local story has it that the devil baked the bricks in the fires of hell; to this day, a nearby stream is known as Nant y Cythraul or the Devil's Brook.

ST ASAPH

6 miles N of Denbigh on the A525

This small town on a ridge between the Rivers Clwyd and Elwy has city status because of its cathedral. Standing on a hill and constructed on the site of a Norman building, **St Asaph's Cathedral** is not only the country's smallest cathedral, it has also had to endure a particularly stormy past. It was founded in AD 560 by St Kentigern (also known as St Mungo), who left his small church in AD 573 in the hands of his favourite pupil, Asaph, while he returned to Scotland. The cathedral was sacked by Henry III's forces in 1245 and then destroyed during Edward I's conquest of Wales some 37 years later. Edward wished to rebuild at nearby Rhuddlan but Bishop Anian II insisted that the new cathedral remain at St Asaph. The building still standing today was begun by Anian and completed by his two successors.

In 1402 the woodwork was burnt during Owain Glyndwr's rebellion (it was subsequently restored by Bishop Redman) and by the 17th century matters were so desperate that many of the possessions were sold and the Bishop's Palace became a tavern. However, St Asaph's Cathedral has

7 SALISBURY ARMS

Tremeirchion

Recently refurbished 16th century coaching inn in pretty Tremeirchion, serving high quality food and real ales throughout the week.

see page 219

8 THE SMITHY ARMS

Rhuallt

Home-made cooking is at the heart of this hidden gem in the peaceful village of Rhuallt.

see page 220

•

Bishop of St Asaph from 1601 to 1604, William Morgan began his mammoth task of translating the Bible into Welsh while he was a rector. During his ministry over the parish of Llanrhaeadr ym Mochnant his congregation grew so upset with his neglect of his pastoral duties for his translation work that he had to be escorted by armed guards to the church. Not only was the finished work of importance to the Welsh churches, each one of which received a copy, but it also set a standard for the Welsh language, which, without being codified, could have been lost forever. Only 19 copies have survived, one of which is on display in the cathedral. A special monument, the Translator's Memorial, commemorates and names those who, under Morgan's guidance, assisted him in translating the Bible.

•

survived and today it holds several treasures including a first edition of the William Morgan Welsh Bible (dating from 1588) that was used at the Investiture of Charles as the Prince of Wales in 1969.

In the 1870s, major restoration work on the cathedral was entrusted to **Sir George Gilbert Scott**, who also worked on the restoration of the cathedrals at Bangor and St David's as well as building many churches and houses throughout the United Kingdom. (The Scott dynasty takes a bit of sorting out: Sir George Gilbert Scott (1811-1878), the most prolific builder and restorer, had two architect sons, George Gilbert Scott Jr (1839-1897) and John Oldrid Scott (1842-1913). John Oldrid's son Sir Giles Gilbert Scott (1880-1960) was responsible for Liverpool Cathedral.)

RHUDDLAN

8 miles N of Denbigh on the A525

Rhuddlan is the site of an early Norman stronghold known as Twt Hill, which today is marked by a prominent earthen mound. Rhuddlan is now overshadowed by its impressive castle ruins. One of the Iron Ring of fortresses built by Edward I, **Rhuddlan Castle**, as one of the most massive and impenetrable of his defences, was the king's headquarters during his campaign. It was from here, in March 1284, that Edward issued the Statute of Rhuddlan that united the Principality of Wales with the Kingdom of England. He also gave the town a Royal Charter when his sovereignty was confirmed. The statute, which lasted until the Act of Union in 1536, was enacted on the site now occupied by Parliament House which bears a commemorative tablet on the wall which is said to be from the original building. Although the castle, like many, was partially destroyed during the Civil War, the town is still sometimes referred to as the Cradle of Wales.

While the castle in its heyday was a magnificent example of medieval defensive building, the most impressive engineering feat in the area was the canalisation of the River Clwyd to give the castle access by ship to the sea some three miles away. The remains of the dockgate, **Gillot's Tower**, can still be seen - this was built by James of St George, who was also responsible for the interesting concentric plan of the castle which allowed archers, stationed on both the inner and outer walls, to fire their arrows simultaneously.

DYSERTH

10 miles N of Denbigh on the A5151

Lying in the foothills of the Clwydian Range, below Craig Fawr's slopes, this village in the scenic Vale of Clwyd boasts a 60-foot waterfall as well as a charming parish church which dates from the 13th century.

Just to the west of the village stands **Bodrhyddan Hall**, the 17th century manor house of the Conwy family who have had their home here since the early 15th century. The hall houses the

Charter of Rhuddlan, and visitors can also see, around the fireplaces in the white drawing room, panels which came from the chapel of a ship of the Spanish Armada that foundered off the coast of Anglesey. Other notable items include Hepplewhite chairs, suits of armour and ancient weapons, a family portrait by Sir Joshua Reynolds and an Egyptian mummy. The **Gardens** here too are of interest, the main feature being a box-edged Victorian parterre designed by William Andrews Nesfield, father of the famous **William Eden Nesfield**, who remodelled the house in 1875. William Eden had a very varied life, being a soldier and a watercolour painter before taking up garden design when he was over 40. He worked on well over 200 estates, among the most notable being the Royal Botanic Gardens at Kew. A much older part of the garden at Bodrhyddan is centred around a well house (bearing the inscription 'Inigo Jones 1612') containing a spring, St Mary's Well, that may once have had pagan significance.

BODELWYDDAN

8 miles N of Denbigh off the A55

The village church, known as the **Marble Church**, was built between 1856 and 1860 by Lady Willoughby de Broke as a memorial to her husband. The landmark white spire is of local limestone, while inside is an arcade made of 14 different types of marble.

Opposite the eye-catching church stands **Bodelwyddan Castle**, a Victorian country house and estate which occupies the site of a 15th century house. The castle is the Welsh home of the National Portrait Gallery, and as well as the wonderful collection of Victorian portraits on display, visitors can see beautiful furniture on loan from the Victoria and Albert Museum and sculptures from the Royal Academy. Anyone tiring of the glorious pieces exhibited here can relax and play one of several hands-on Victorian games and inventions in the gallery, while outside are picnic tables, an adventure playground, maze, terrace café and secret woodland walk. A hands-on science centre is the latest attraction.

18th and 19th century land-scaped parkland surrounds the castle and here, too, is an Arts and Crafts walled garden originally planted by TH Mawson, with some redesign work being undertaken by H Moggridge in 1980.

Rhuddlan Castle

9 THE KINGS HEAD

Llanrhaeadr

A traditional and stylish inn with excellent food, accommodation and real ale to enjoy all year round.

 see page 220

10 DROVERS ARMS

Rhewl

A classy but traditional establishment with a fantastic range of food and drink for all the family.

 see page 221

LLANRHAEADR-YNG-NGHINMEIRCH

3 miles SE of Denbigh on the A525

This pretty little village with its whitewashed Georgian almshouses attracted pilgrims in their thousands in medieval times. They came to drink from the **Holy Well** where a 6th century hermit had invested a waterfall with healing powers capable of curing "scabs and the itch" and even smallpox. St Dyfnog would do penance by standing under the waterfall in his hair shirt, thus transferring his virtues to the water. As late as the 1700s his "mighty spring was still much resorted to" and it was then that the 'bath' was paved with marble which is still in place.

The nearby **Church of St Dyfnog** is entered by a striking timber porch richly adorned with carving from about 1530 but its chief treasure is a marvellous Tree of Jesse window. The Tree of Jesse, most often seen depicted in church windows, details the family tree of Christ down from Jesse, the father of King David. This superb window, made in 1553, was saved from destruction during the Civil War by being buried in a dug-out chest, which can also be seen in the church.

RUTHIN

7 miles SE of Denbigh on the A525

This old market town lies in the Vale of Clwyd, more or less surrounded by a ring of hills, with a layout that appears to have changed little from medieval days. In fact, a description of Ruthin written in Elizabethan times, extols it as "the grandest market town in all the Vale, full of inhabitants and well replenished with buildings". Remarkably, this is as true today as it was then. **St Peter's Square** is a good place from which to view the town; it was here in 1679 that a Catholic priest was hung, drawn and quartered. Situated behind a magnificent set of 18th century wrought iron gates stands the town's splendid **St Peter's Church**. Founded in the late 13th century as a collegiate church, its notable features include an early 16th century oak roof that consists of 408 carved panels while behind the church there are some beautiful buildings in the collegiate close: 14th century cloisters, the Old Grammar School of 1284 and 16th century almshouses.

St Peter's Square itself is edged with many lovely buildings, including the particularly eye-catching 15th century **Myddleton Arms** with its unusual Dutch style of architecture and its seven dormer windows that have been dubbed the 'Eyes of Ruthin'. At one time there were around 60 inns and pubs in Ruthin - one for every 10 men in the town - and nine of these were to be found around the square. On the south side of St Peter's Square stands the impressive wattle and daub **Old Courthouse** which dates from 1401 and was a temporary resting place for prisoners, who were kept in the cells below the magnificent beamed court room. The building is now occupied by the National Westminster Bank but the beam once used as a gibbet still projects from the north-west wall. On Clwyd Street is **Ruthin Gaol**, through whose gates thousands of prisoners passed between 1654 and 1916. Visitors can see how prisoners lived their daily lives – what they ate, how they worked, the punishments they suffered. The cells can be explored and there are hands-on activities for children.

Ruthin Castle, begun in 1277 by Edward I, was the home of Lord de Grey of Ruthin who, having proclaimed Owain Glyndwr a traitor to Henry IV was given a large area of land originally held by the Welshman. After Glyndwr crowned himself Prince of Wales, de Grey was the first to suffer when Ruthin was attacked in 1400. Though the town was all but destroyed, the castle held out and survived the onslaught. During the Civil War, the castle again came under siege, this time surviving for 11 weeks in 1646 before eventually falling to General Mytton. He then had the building destroyed. Partially restored and then owned by the Cornwallis-West family, Ruthin Castle played host, before and during World War I, to many famous and influential Edwardians including the Prince of Wales (later Edward VII), the actress Mrs Patrick Campbell and Lady Randolph Churchill, the mother of Winston Churchill. Today, the castle, with its charming grounds and roaming peacocks, is a hotel specialising in medieval banquets.

Early Morning, Ruthin

In Castle Street of Ruthin, can be found one the oldest town houses in North Wales. Nant Clwyd House is a fine example of Elizabethan architecture although the present 16th century building shows traces of an earlier house. During the reign of Elizabeth I it was the home of Dr Gabriel Goodman, an influential man who was the Dean of Westminster for 40 years. He established Ruthin School in 1595 and built the town's almshouses. Work is under way to open the house to the public in the near future.

LLANARMON-YN IÂL

11 miles SE of Denbigh on the B5431

The capital of the upland Iâl region and occupying an attractive position on the banks of the River Alun, this small village boasts one of Denbighshire's most notable churches. Standing in a spacious churchyard rather like a village green, it is dedicated to **St**

11 CORPORATION ARMS

Ruthin

Popular local pub in the heart of Ruthin known for its lively entertainment and excellent value for money food.

see page 221

12 THE MINERS ARMS

Maeshafn

Set in picturesque woodland and dating back to the early 1700s visitors can enjoy a quality meal or drink in an area of outstanding natural beauty.

see page 222

Garmon, a 5th century warrior bishop who won a great victory in AD 429 against an invading army of pagan Picts and Saxons. The church at Llanarmon became a shrine to the saint thus generating the funds that enabled the building of the double nave. It has a fine timber roof, a well-preserved effigy of a 14th century knight, two old parish chests and a magnificent 18-branched chandelier made in Bruges around 1500. The church was extensively restored during the 1730s and the Georgian influence is apparent in the large round-topped windows, the Classical-style porch and the elegant Georgian font.

LLANFIHANGEL GLYN MYFYR

11 miles SW of Denbigh on the B5103

This sleepy village lies in the fertile vale through which the River Alwen runs. Just to the north lies the **Clocaenog Forest**, Wales' second largest commercial plantation, which covers much of the southern moorland between the vales of Clwyd and Conwy. Managed by the Forestry Commission, it has well-marked forest trails of varying lengths that lead walkers through the mixed plantation of larch, spruce, pine, beech, oak and ash.

On the edge of the forest lies **Llyn Brenig**, a massive man-made reservoir that was completed in 1976 to accompany the smaller **Llyn Alwen**, which dates from the early 1900s. Close to the dam, and reached along the B4501, is a Visitor Centre which explains the local history and ecology of this tranquil Welsh valley as well as acting as a starting point for lakeside walks. By the lake, depending on the time of year, butterflies such as Orange Tip and Tortoiseshell can be seen. Along with the water sports on the lake, fishing is also available.

CERRIGYDRUDION

12½ miles SW of Denbigh on the B4501

This village's name, often misspelt as 'druidion', means 'Place of the Brave' and has absolutely no connection with Druids. There are many tales of fairy cattle to be found in Wales, creatures that are thought to have descended from the aurochs, the wild cattle that roamed Britain in prehistoric times. Cerrigydrudion has it own cow, Y Fuwch Frech (the freckled cow), which lived on nearby Hiraethog mountain. For years she supplied the area with milk and would always fill any receptacle brought to her. One day, a witch began to milk her into a sieve and continued until the cow went insane and drowned herself in Llyn Dau Ychen.

GWAENYNOG BACH

1½ miles W of Denbigh on the A543

During the 19th century **Beatrix Potter** was a frequent visitor to the beautifully situated estate of Gwaenynog Hall, which was owned by her uncle, Fred Burton. It is thought that her sketches of the kitchen garden (which has now been restored) were the basis for *The Tale of the Flopsy Bunnies* and also the working environment of the fictional Mr McGregor the gardener, who wanted to bake Peter Rabbit in a pie.

LLANGOLLEN

A busy and picturesque town set on low hills beside the River Dee, Llangollen is known worldwide for its annual **International Musical Eisteddfod** which has been held here since 1947. For six days at the beginning of July musicians, choirs, folk singers and dancers from all over the world, and many performing in their national costumes, converge on the town to take part in this wonderful cultural event that is centred around the **Royal International Pavilion**, a modern cultural complex which hosts concerts, exhibitions, film shows and craft events throughout the rest of the year. The International Eisteddfod should not be confused with the **National Eisteddfod**, the annual Welsh language cultural festival whose venue alternates between the north and south of the country. The first recorded eisteddfod was held at Cardigan Castle in 1176, and the modern eisteddfod began as a competition between bards at the Owain Glyndwr hotel in Corwen in 1789. It became a truly national event at Llangollen in 1858, when thousands of people came to Llangollen from all over the country. Music, prose, drama and art are included in the festival, which culminates in the chairing and investiture of the winning poet.

Llangollen's history goes back to the late 6th and early 7th century when St Collen, after whom the town is named, founded a church here. The church is still standing but has been much restored and refurbished over the years.

On the north side of the river is **Llangollen Station**, home of the Llangollen Railway Society. Since taking over the disused line in 1975, the Society has restored 8 miles of the railway track and journeys along the banks of the River Dee can be taken on this delightful steam railway. The station houses a museum with a collection of engines, coaches and rail memorabilia. Also along the banks of the Dee lies **Llangollen Wharf**, from where pleasure cruises have started since 1884. Some trips are horse-drawn, while others cross the **Pontcysyllte Aqueduct** in the narrow boat *Thomas Telford* whose name pays homage to the architect of this impressive structure. Eighteen massive columns 126ft high support the huge cast iron trough, 11ft 10in wide and 1007ft long. Those who have a head for

13 GALES OF LLANGOLLEN

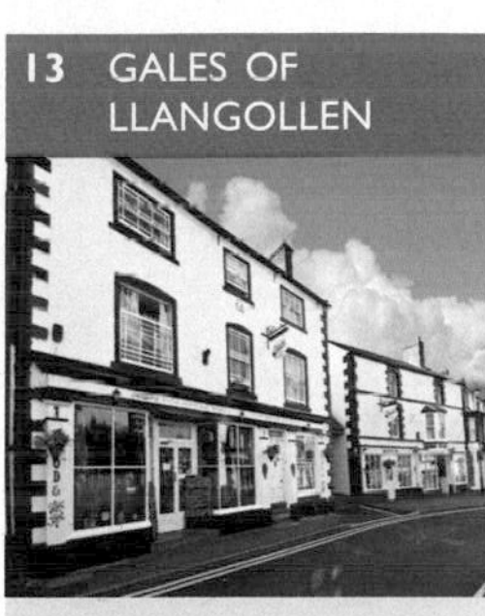

Llangollen

Gales provide a historic setting for a unique family run business for fine wine, great food, fantastic facilities and hospitality all year round.

see page 223

Llangollen Town and River Dee

•

The focal point of Llangollen town is the fine old Bridge over the Dee which is mentioned as one of the 'Seven Wonders of Wales' in the famous poem. Originally built in 1347 with an 8ft breadth by Dr Trevor, who later became Bishop of St Asaph, the four-arched structure was partly rebuilt in 1656, and again in 1863 to allow access to the new railway to pass beneath it. The bridge is still used by today's traffic.

•

•

Overlooking Llangollen are the dramatic remains of Castell Dinas Bran. Originally an Iron Age hill fort, the site was used by Prince Gruffudd ap Madoc to build a castle in 1260. The remains are not extensive, but the climb is well worth the effort as the view over the town and the Vale of Llangollen is quite breathtaking.

•

heights can walk along the towpath where only a lip a few inches high stands between the walker and the river. Opened in 1805, the aqueduct has been recently nominated as a World Heritage Site. **Llangollen Motor Museum** stands close to the town between the canal and the river. Owned and run by the Owen family, it is home to some 60 vehicles describing the motoring past, including a Model T Ford, a Vauxhall 38/93 and what could be the world's oldest motor caravan, the camper van of its day. The Museum also holds a collection of renowned British motorcycles – Nortons, Sunbeams, Triumphs, Sunbeams and BSAs. Call 01798 860324 for opening times.

In the early 19th century Llangollen became famous as the home for 50 years of the "**Ladies of Llangollen**", Lady Eleanor Butler and Miss Sarah Ponsonby. These two eccentric Irish women ran away from their families in Ireland and set up home together in 1780 in a cottage above the town. As well as devoting their lives to "friendship, celibacy and the knitting of blue stockings", the ladies also undertook a great deal of improvements and alterations that turned a small, unpretentious cottage into the splendid house - **Plas Newydd** - that is seen today. The marvellous 'gothicisation' of the house was completed in 1814 . Some of the elaborate oak panels and the glorious stained glass windows were donated to the couple by their famous visitors. These included Sir Walter Scott, William Wordsworth, the Duke of Gloucester and the Duke of Wellington. The ladies were both buried in the churchyard of St Collen, sharing a grave with their friend and housekeeper, Mary Caryll.

The **Gardens** at Plas Newydd are interesting and, while the formal layout to the front of the house was created after the ladies had died and the terraces have been altered since they lived here, they still reflect the peace and quiet the couple were seeking as well as containing more interesting curios from those early Regency days.

The main route north out of Llangollen passes the impressive ruins of **Valle Crucis Abbey**. Situated in green fields and overshadowed by the surrounding steep-sided mountains, this was an ideal place for a remote ecclesiastical house, the perfect spot for the Cistercians, medieval monks who always sought out lonely, secluded places. This abbey was founded in 1201 by Madog ap Gruffyd, the Prince of Powys, and was a very suitable location for the monks of this austere order. Despite a fire, the tower collapsing and the Dissolution in 1535, the ruins are in good condition and visitors can gain a real feel for how the monks lived and worked here. Notable surviving original features include the west front with its richly carved doorway and rose window, the east end of the abbey and the chapter house with its superb fan-vaulted roof. Also to be seen are some mutilated tombs which are thought to include that of Iolo Goch, a bard of Owain Glyndwr. Valle Crucis means 'Valley of the Cross' and refers to **Eliseg's Pillar**, which stands about half a mile from the abbey and was erected in the early 9th century. The inscription on this Christian memorial cross is now badly weather-beaten but fortunately a record was made in 1696 of the words. It was erected in memory of Eliseg, who annexed Powys from the Saxons, by his great-grandson Concenn. The pillar was broken by Cromwell's men and not re-erected until the 18th century.

A little further northwards along this road lies the spectacular **Horseshoe Pass** which affords remarkable views of the surrounding countryside. From the top of the pass can be seen the Vale of Clwyd and the ridge of Eglwyseg Rocks where Offa's Dyke path runs.

AROUND LLANGOLLEN

JOHNSTOWN

6 miles NE of Llangollen on the B5605

On the B5605 between Johnstown and Rhosllanerchrugog lies **Stryt Las Park**, a predominantly wetland area with a large lake and three small ponds. This Site of Special Scientific Interest is home to one of Europe's largest colonies of the Great Crested Newt. The park is open daily, the visitor centre daily in summer, weekends only in winter. In Rhosllanerchrugog, **The Stiwt** is a forum for Welsh language choirs, stage performances and crafts.

Valle Crucis Abbey, Llangollen

BERSHAM

7½ miles NE of Llangollen off the A483

Bersham lies in part of the **Clywedog Valley and Trail** that skirts around the south and west of Wrexham and includes several places of industrial interest. The village was established around 1670 and was the home of the Davis brothers. The fine workmanship of these two famous iron masters can be seen in the beautiful gates at Chirk Park and at St Giles' Church in Wrexham.

The Clywedog Trail passes through Plas Power and Nant Mill, woods that stretch along the River Clywedog between Bersham and Coedpoeth. A well-preserved section of **Offa's Dyke** cuts through Plas Power.

The master and owner of Bersham Ironworks from 1762, John 'Iron Mad' Wilkinson, was himself famous for the cannons he bored for use in the American War of Independence and for the cylinders he produced at the ironworks for James Watt's steam engines. The remains of the ironworks are open in the summer, the Heritage Centre all year round.

CHIRK

5½ miles SE of Llangollen on the B5070

This attractive border town's origins lie in the 11th century castle of which, unfortunately, little remains except a small motte close

14 CHIRK CASTLE

Chirk, Wrexham

An impressive fortress originating in the 13th century, the castle is still inhabited and many of the rooms and the garden are a delight to wander around.

 *see page 224*

•

The early 15th century Welsh hero, Owain Glyndwr, was brought up initially at Chirk Castle before attending the English court of Richard II. Educated as a lawyer, the charismatic Glyndwr rebelled against the English in middle age. Along with uniting the Welsh, he came close to overrunning the English. Finally defeated in 1409, he mysteriously disappeared in 1415 and his death has never been documented.

•

to the town's 15th century church. Today, Chirk is perhaps better known for **Chirk Castle** (National Trust) which lies half a mile west of the village. Begun in the late 1200s on land granted to Roger de Mortimer by Edward I, this still magnificent fortress - with a massive drum tower at each corner - has been rebuilt on several occasions but has managed to remain as impressive today as it must have been centuries ago. The castle is still lived in today by the Myddleton family whose antecedent, Sir Thomas Myddleton, Lord Mayor of London, purchased the castle in 1595 for £5,000. Visitors to the castle see the elegant state rooms, some fine Adam-style furniture, tapestries and portraits. By contrast, the castle's dramatic dungeons indicate that life here was not always so peaceful and genteel.

The parkland surrounding the castle and gardens is very impressive and the estate is entered through a magnificent set of wrought iron gates that were made by the Davies brothers of Bersham Ironworks. **Chirk Castle Gardens** are also well worth taking the time to look around. Much of their layout is based on designs by William Emes that date from the 1760s. Along with the topiary yews, roses and flowering shrubs, the gardens contain a picturesque hawk house. Today's visitors can see conservation in action and discover the new technologies being used to make this splendid old place greener.

Just south of Chirk are two splendid constructions spanning the Ceiriog valley: the first, an aqueduct built in 1801 by Thomas Telford, carries the Llangollen branch of the Shropshire Union Canal, while the other is a viaduct built in 1848 to carry the then new Chester to Shrewsbury railway line over the River Ceiriog.

Viaduct and Aqueduct, Chirk

GLYN CEIRIOG

2½ miles S of Llangollen off the B4500

This former slate mining village is home to the **Chwarel Wynne Mine Museum** which, as well as telling the story of the slate industry that used to support the village, offers visitors a guided tour of the caverns. There is also a nature trail around the surrounding countryside. A narrow gauge tramway, the **Glyn Valley Railway**, once linked the Shropshire Union Canal at Gledrid with the quarries and mines at Glyn Ceiriog. Opened in 1873 and originally horse-drawn, it was later converted to steam and diverted through Chirk Castle estate to meet the Great Western Railway at Chirk station. It carried slate, silica, chinastone and dolerite downstream and returned with coal, flour and other commodities. It also carried passengers, and though it closed in 1935, the bed of the tramway can still be seen here and there. The Glyn Valley Tramway Group was founded in 1974 to conserve evidence of the GVR. The Group has small museums in the Glyn Valley Hotel at Glyn Ceiriog and the former waiting room at Pontafog station, and a GVR Museum and Visitor Centre is to be established in the old locomotive shed and yard at Glyn Ceiriog.

The village lies in the secluded Vale of Ceiriog. Just to the west is the beautiful **Ceiriog Forest** which offers surprisingly pastoral views and vistas along with forest walks and trails.

LLANARMON DYFFRYN CEIRIOG

6½ miles SW of Llangollen on the B4500

This small and peaceful village in the heart of the Vale of Ceiriog was the birthplace of the famous Welsh bard, Ceiriog, whose real name was John Hughes. The 14-mile **Upper Ceiriog Trail** for walkers, mountain bikers and horse riders passes his home, Pen-y-Bryn. In the churchyard at Llanarmon DC are two yew trees certified as over 1000 years old.

LLANTYSILIO

1 mile W of Llangollen off the A5

The **Church of St Tysilio** occupies an idyllic setting surrounded by steep wooded hills. The church dates back to the 1400s and its notable features include a fine medieval roof, a rare oak eagle lectern, a sculpted font and an east window in the pre-Raphaelite style. The poet Robert Browning worshipped here in 1866, an event marked by a brass plaque placed here by Lady Martin, also known as the actress Helena Faucit. She lived in the house next to the church and is remembered at the church by a chapel that was built following her death in 1898.

Below the sloping churchyard, the River Dee cascades over the picturesque Horseshoe Falls and a short distance away is Thomas Telford's **Horseshoe Weir** which was built in 1806 to supply water to the Llangollen Canal.

15 THE GLYN VALLEY COUNTRY INN

Glyn Ceiriog

Renowned for fantastic seasonal food and a selection of real ales, this country inn is ideal for short breaks away with en suite accommodation also available.

see page 224

16 THE WEST ARMS

Llanarmon Dyffryn Ceirog

An impressive and charming establishment nestled in a picturesque village; the award winning West Arms offers the very best in cuisine and accommodation.

see page 225

17 YUM YUMS

Corwen

A small, quality and popular sandwich bar and takeaway business located in the heart of Corwen.

 *see page 226*

18 OWAIN GLYNDWR HOTEL

Corwen

Offering the very best in accommodation food and drink, the famous Owain Glyndwr Hotel is set in the ideal location for those wanting to explore North Wales.

 *see page 227*

GLYNDYFRDWY

4 miles W of Llangollen on the A5

Once the estate of Owain Glyndwr, this village lies on the historic and important A5 and between the Berwyn and Llantysilio mountains. A mound by the road, known as **Owain Glyndwr's Mound**, was once part of an impressive earthwork fortress that was later incorporated into part of the Welsh hero's manor house and estate. Much more recently, Glyndyfrdwy has become known as the home of the Original Butterfly man, Eos Griffiths, who is known worldwide for creating the bright and colourful ornamental butterflies that can be seen adorning homes from Scandinavia to Australia.

CORWEN

9 miles W of Llangollen on the A5

This market town, in a pleasant setting between the Berwyn Mountains and the River Dee, has, for many years, been known as the 'Crossroads of North Wales'. The town's origins can be traced back to the 6th century when the Breton-Welsh saints, Mael and Sulien, founded a religious community here - Corwen's 13th century church still bears their dedication.

Corwen was also once the headquarters of **Owain Glyndwr**, who gathered his forces here before entering into his various campaigns. A steel statue of him stands in the centre of the town. The church at Corwen has an incised dagger in a lintel of the doorway that is known as **Glyndwr's Sword**. The mark was reputedly made by Glyndwr when he threw a dagger from the hill above the church in a fit of rage against the townsfolk. However, the dagger mark actually dates from the 7th to 9th centuries and there is another such mark on a 12th century cross outside the southwest corner of the church. It was in the Owain Glyndwr Hotel in 1789 in Corwen that a local man, Thomas Jones, organised a bardic festival that laid the foundations for the modern eisteddfod. Across the River Dee from the town lies **Caer Derwyn**, a stone rampart around a hill that dates from Roman times. One of Corwen's most impressive buildings is **Corwen Manor**, which was built in 1840 as the workhouse for seven local parishes. It could house up to 150 paupers, with men and women in separate wings.

To the west of Corwen, set in pretty, landscaped grounds is the simple, stone built **Rug Chapel**. A rare example of a private chapel that has changed little over the years, Rug (*'heather'* in Welsh) was founded in the 17th century by 'Old Blue Stockings', Colonel William Salusbury, in collaboration with Bishop William Morgan, the first translator of the Bible into Welsh. The chapel's plain exterior gives no clues to its exquisitely decorated interior. Best described as a 'painted chapel', few parts of the building have been left unadorned. As well as the beautifully carved rood screen, the ceiling beams are painted with rose motifs. However, not all the decoration here is exuberant; there is also a sombre wall painting of a skeleton as a reminder of mortality. The architect Sir Edwin Lutyens acknowledged that his work was influenced by this beautiful chapel and evidence can be seen of this in his most elaborate commission, the Viceroy's House, New Delhi, which was completed in 1930.

LLANDRILLO

12 miles SW of Llangollen on the B4401

The road to Llandrillo from the north follows the Vale of Edeirion and the River Dee as it weaves its way below the northwest slopes of the **Berwyn Mountains**, another mountain range that is popular with walkers and visitors. This small village is a good starting point for walks in the Berwyns and footpaths from the village lead towards Craig Berwyn, whose summit is more than 2100 feet above sea level.

BRYNEGLWYS

5 miles NW of Llangollen off the A5104

Standing on the slopes of Llantysilio Mountain, the large 15th century **Church of St Tysilio**, in the heart of the village is, surprisingly, connected with the family who helped to found Yale University in the United States. Close to the village lies **Plas-Yn-Yale**, the former home of the Yale family and the birthplace of Elihu Yale's father. Elihu himself was born in 1647 in Boston, Massachusetts, and went on to become a governor of India before coming to England. Known for his philanthropy, Elihu was approached by an American College who, after receiving generous help, named their new college in Newhaven after him. In 1745, 24 years after his death, the whole establishment was named Yale University. Elihu Yale is buried in the Church of St Giles in Wrexham.

WREXHAM

The largest town in North Wales, Wrexham has been extensively 'refurbished' in recent years. Its pedestrianised town centre now offers a good mix of small independent shops and boutiques as well as the regular high street names. Wrexham's origins as a market town are reflected in its three indoor markets - the People's, Butcher's and General - the monthly Farmer's Market and the occasional French and Continental Markets. There's also an open air market every Monday in Queen's Square.

For those wishing to find out more about the town and its social, industrial and local history then **Wrexham Museum** (free), housed in the County Buildings that were originally constructed as the militia barracks in 1857, is a very good place to start. The discovery of a skeleton nearby - it became known as Brymbo Man - traces the town's history back as far as the Bronze Age while the Romans are also known to have settled in the Wrexham area. Both Roundhead

•

Another interesting religious building can be found just to the south of Rug, in the direction of Llandrillo. Llangar Church, overlooking the confluence of the Rivers Dee and Alwen, is older than its near neighbour - it is medieval - and, though it was superseded in the 19th century, this small place still retains many of its original features. In particular, there are some extensive 15th century wall paintings and a minstrels' gallery. Both Rug Chapel and Llangar Church are now cared for by CADW - Welsh Historic Monuments.

•

19 TASTEBUDS

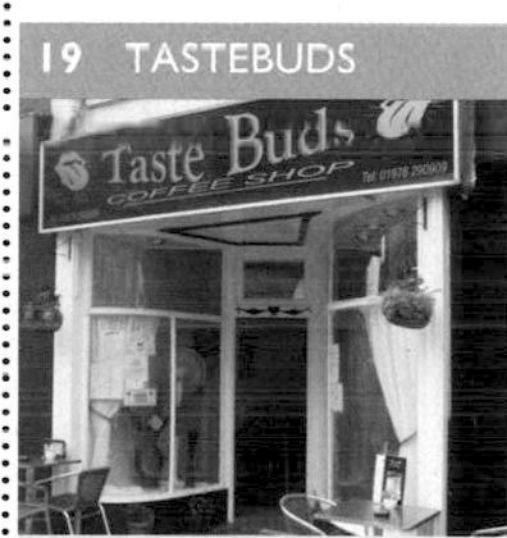

Wrexham

Homemade food and warm hospitality is the order of the day at this delightful little cafe in the heart of Wrexham.

see page 228

•

The Church of St Giles in Wrexham itself is well worth taking the time to look over; its 136 feet pinnacle tower is one of the Seven Wonders of Wales. Begun in 1506 and much restored, this Gothic tower still bears some of the original medieval carvings, in particular those of St Giles, which are recognisable by his attributes of an arrow and a deer. Elsewhere in the church are a colourful ceiling of flying musical angels, two very early eagle lecterns, a Burne Jones window and the Royal Welsh Fusiliers chapel.

•

and Cavalier troops were garrisoned in the town during the Civil War and, in more peaceful times, in the late 19th century, Britain's first lager brewery was built in Wrexham in 1882. The suburb of Acton was the birthplace of Judge Jeffreys, the notoriously harsh lawman who was nicknamed 'Bloody' for his lack of compassion and his belief in swift justice. More recently, Wrexham was central to the early development of football in Wales and the museum houses the Welsh Football Collection.

Perhaps Wrexham's best known building, and one that's a particular favourite of American tourists, is the **Church of St Giles** which dominates the town's skyline. It is famous for being the burial place of **Elihu Yale**, the benefactor of Yale University, who was laid to rest here on his death in 1721. His father had emigrated from Wrexham to North America in 1637 and Elihu was born soon afterwards in Boston. In 1691 Elihu sent a cargo of books and Indian goods from Fort Madras where he was Governor. The sale of the books enabled him to initiate the University of Yale in 1692. The memorial quadrangle at Yale has a Wrexham Tower. Yale's tomb in St Giles was restored in 1968 by members of Yale University to mark the 250th anniversary of the benefaction. It can be found in the churchyard to the west of the tower.

Just to the south of Wrexham and found in a glorious 2,000-acre estate and Country Park, is **Erddig**, one of the most fascinating houses in Britain. Construction on the late-17th century mansion was begun by Joshua Edisbury, the High Sheriff of Denbighshire, who later fled to avoid his creditors. The house passed into the hands of the Yorke family and their descendants, until finally it came into the ownership of the National Trust. Its fabulous state rooms have been restored to their original glory whilst, below stairs, visitors can see the living and working conditions of the many servants a house of this size required. The Servants' Hall is particularly remarkable for its array of portraits of the servants commissioned by the owner. Within the exquisite grounds are restored outbuildings, walled gardens, a yew walk, woodland trails and the National Ivy Collection. New for 2009 are a virtual tour of the house and its collections, accessible horse-drawn carriage rides and cycle hire facilities.

Along with Erddig, which lies within the Clywedog Valley and Trail, is **King's Mill**, a restored mill that dates from 1769 although an older mill has been on the site since 1315.

AROUND WREXHAM

GRESFORD

3 miles N of Wrexham on the B5445

This former coal mining town was the site of a mine explosion in 1934 that killed 266 men. The colliery closed in 1973 but the wheel remains in memory of those who lost their lives in this terrible disaster. The town's **All Saints'**

Church is one of the finest in Wales, with notable medieval screens, stained glass, font and misericords, and a memorial to the mining disaster. It is also home to the famous **Gresford Bells**, one of the Seven Wonders of Wales, which are still rung every Tuesday evening and on Sundays.

Remains of Holt Castle

HOLT

6 miles E of Wrexham on the B5102

The River Dee, which marks the boundary between Wales and England, runs through this village and its importance as a crossing point can be seen in the attractive 15th century bridge.

Holt Castle was built between 1282 and 1311 by John de Warren following an English victory over the Welsh. Built in a quarry, which provided the stone for the building, its prime role was probably to guard a crossing point on the River Dee. Much of the stonework was removed in the 17th century for the construction of Eaton Hall a few miles downstream.

The village of Holt was also the site of a Roman pottery and tile factory that provided material for the fort at nearby Chester.

BANGOR-IS-Y-COED

5 miles SE of Wrexham off the A525

Bangor-is-y-coed, also known as Bangor-on-Dee, is in the area called the Maelor, where the Cheshire Plains turn into the Welsh Hills. The village is well known to race-goers as it is home to a picturesque **Racecourse**, situated on the banks of the River Dee, which stages several National Hunt meetings annually. The village itself has a charming 17th century bridge said to have been built by Inigo Jones. Across the bridge, the **Plassey Craft and Retail Centre** occupies some attractively converted Edwardian farm buildings surrounded by the beautiful scenery of the Dee Valley. There's a wide choice of traditional hand-made crafts on sale, along with a working blacksmith, an equestrian supplier, restaurant and coffee shop.

OVERTON

8 miles SE of Wrexham on the A528

This substantial border village is home to another of the Seven Wonders of Wales - the **Overton Yew Trees**, 21 trees that stand in the churchyard of the village Church of St Mary. Dating from medieval times, these tall, dark and handsome trees have a preservation order placed upon them. Within the church itself there are some interesting artefacts from the 13th century.

•

Bangor was the site of a Celtic monastery founded in around AD 180, which was destroyed in AD 607 by Ethelfrid of Northumbria in what turned out to be the last victory by the Saxons over Celtic Christianity. Apparently, 1,200 monks were laid to the sword as Ethelfrid considered praying against him was tantamount to fighting against him. Those fortunate enough to have survived are thought to have travelled to Bardsey Island. Local legend also suggests that Owain Glyndwr married Margaret Hanmer in the hamlet of Hanmer, just four miles away.

•

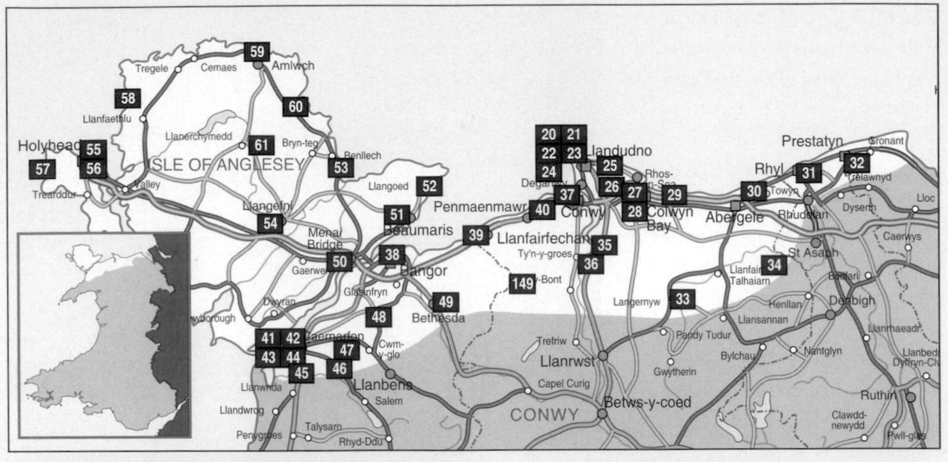

ACCOMMODATION

20 The Lilly, Llandudno pg 28, 228
21 Epperstone Hotel, Llandudno pg 28, 229
24 Bellevue Hotel, Llandudno pg 29, 232
26 The Queens Head, Glanwydden pg 30, 234
28 St Margarets Hotel, Colwyn Bay pg 31, 235
29 The Marine Hotel, Old Colwyn pg 31, 236
30 Morton Arms, Towyn, nr Abergele pg 31, 237
31 The Imperial Hotel, Rhyl pg 32, 238
34 The Hawk & Buckle Inn, Llannefydd pg 34, 241
36 Tal-Y-Cafn Hotel, Tal-Y-Cafn pg 35, 242
39 Min-Y-Don, Llanfairfechan pg 41, 243
40 The Gladstone, Dwygyfylchi pg 41, 245
42 Menai Bank Hotel, Caernarfon pg 42, 245
43 Black Boy Inn, Caernarfon pg 43, 246
44 Gwesty Bron Menai, Caernarfon pg 43, 247
46 Ty'n yr Onnen, Waunfawr pg 44, 247
47 Plas Tirion Farm, Llanrug pg 44, 249
48 Ty Mawr Tearooms, Restaurant and B&B, Llanddeiniolen pg 44, 249
49 The Joys Of Life Country Park, Bethesda pg 45, 250
50 Bulkeley Arms Hotel, Menai Bridge pg 46, 251
51 The Liverpool Arms Hotel, Beaumaris pg 46, 251
52 Tafarn Y Rhyd, Llangoed pg 47, 252
53 The Breeze Hill Hotel, Benllech Bay pg 49, 253
59 The Liverpool Arms, Amlwch Port pg 56, 256
60 Minffordd Self Catering & Caravan Park, Minffordd pg 57, 258
61 Drws y Coed, Llannerch y Medd pg 57, 258

FOOD & DRINK

20 The Lilly, Llandudno pg 28, 228
22 Great Orme 'Rest And Be Thankful', Llandudno pg 28, 230
23 Queen Victoria, Llandudno pg 29, 231
25 Penrhyn Old Hall, Penrhyn pg 30, 233
26 The Queens Head, Glanwydden pg 30, 234
27 The Rendezvous Cafe, Colwyn Bay pg 30, 235
29 The Marine Hotel, Old Colwyn pg 31, 236
30 Morton Arms, Towyn, nr Abergele pg 31, 237
32 Pendre Coffee Shop, Prestatyn pg 32, 239
33 The Old Stag, Llangernwyn pg 34, 240
34 The Hawk & Buckle Inn, Llannefydd pg 34, 241
36 Tal-Y-Cafn Hotel, Tal-Y-Cafn pg 35, 242
37 Fisherman's Chip Shop, Conwy pg 37, 243
38 The White Lion Inn, Bangor pg 40, 244
40 The Gladstone, Dwygyfylchi pg 41, 245
43 Black Boy Inn, Caernarfon pg 43, 246
45 The Newborough Arms,Bontnewydd pg 43, 248
46 Ty'n yr Onnen, Waunfawr pg 44, 247
48 Ty Mawr Tearooms, Restaurant and B&B, Llanddeiniolen, nr Caernarfon pg 44, 249
50 Bulkeley Arms Hotel, Menai Bridge pg 46, 251
51 The Liverpool Arms Hotel, Beaumaris pg 46, 251
52 Tafarn Y Rhyd, Llangoed pg 47, 252
53 The Breeze Hill Hotel, Benllech Bay pg 49, 253
54 Mona House Coffee Shop, Llangefni pg 50, 254
55 Jwmpin Jac's Cafe Bar, Holyhead pg 54, 253
56 Bar2Two, Holyhead pg 54, 255
57 South Stack Kitchen, South Stack pg 54, 256
58 The Lobster Pot, Church Bay pg 56, 257

North Wales Coast & Isle of Anglesey

The coast of North Wales is a perennially popular stretch of British coastline that attracts visitors in their thousands to its holiday resorts. One-sixth of the Welsh coastline is owned and managed by the National Trust, including many popular beaches in this region and also on the Gower, the Lleyn, in Pembrokeshire and Ceredigion.

This very traditional region, where Welsh is often still spoken on a daily basis, has many treasures, both man-made and natural, to discover. Before the coming of the railways, the coastline from Prestatyn to Bangor was sprinkled with small fishing villages. As the hours of mill workers from the industrial towns of Lancashire and others working in the factories of the Midlands were reduced, the concept of an annual holiday, albeit in some cases just the odd day at the seaside, became widespread. Served by the newly built railway network, the fishing villages expanded to accommodate the visitors. Boarding houses and hotels were built for the society visitors coming to take the sea air, and amusements and entertainment were soon a regular feature. Llandudno, always considered 'a cut above', still retains much of its Victorian and Edwardian charm, while other resorts, such as Rhyl, have endeavoured to counter the unsettled British summer weather by the creation of indoor complexes.

Prestatyn, to the east, lies at one end of Offa's Dyke. Built more as a line of demarcation rather than a fortification, the dyke runs from the coast southwards to Chepstow. Still substantially marking the border with England, many sections of the ancient earthwork are visible and can be seen from the waymarked footpath that runs the length of the dyke.

It was also along this coast that Edward I built his Iron Ring of castles. While many are now in ruins, two in particular are exceptional. Conwy Castle, now a World Heritage Site, was built in such a position that the surrounding land provides suitable protection from attack. Caernarfon Castle, as much a royal residence as a fortress, was the place where Edward created the first Prince of Wales when he crowned his own son. Centuries later, in 1969, it was in the grounds of the splendid castle ruins that Queen Elizabeth invested the same title on her eldest son, Prince Charles.

Caernarfon and Bangor lie at opposite ends of the Menai Strait, the channel of water that separates mainland Wales from the Isle of Anglesey. It was not until the 19th century that a bridge was constructed across the strait. Thomas Telford's magnificent Menai Suspension Bridge of the 1820s was joined some 30 years late, by Stephenson's Britannia Bridge.

The Isle of Anglesey, with its rolling hills, fertile farmland and miles of wild and craggy coastline, has attracted settlers from the Stone Age onwards and is littered with evidence of Neolithic, Bronze Age and Iron Age people.

PLACES OF INTEREST

20 THE LILLY

Llandudno

Stylish and elegant, The Lilly caters for all; food, drink and accommodation in a simply stunning coastal location.

 see page 228

21 EPPERSTONE HOTEL

Llandudno

Elegant Edwardian ambience is truly achieved in this historic hotel, offering high quality en suite accommodation, cuisine and award winning gardens.

 see page 229

22 GREAT ORME 'REST AND BE THANKFUL'

Llandudno

This cliff top café offers welcome respite from the 5 mile Marine Drive walk with stunning views across the Great Orme coastline.

 see page 230

LLANDUDNO

Llandudno enjoys a glorious setting overlooking a gently curving bay between the headlands of the Great Orme and the Little Orme, with a second sweep of beach on West Shore which commands glorious views of Snowdonia and Anglesey across the Conwy Estuary.

The largest and one of the most popular of the North Wales coast resorts, Llandudno was developed in the 1850s by the Liverpool surveyor, Owen Williams, and the town still retains an abundance of Victorian features. There's a splendid **Promenade** lined with renovated, redecorated and elegant hotels; a magnificent Pier built in 1878 and the longest in Wales which fortunately survived an attempt in 1914 by Suffragettes to burn it down; a Victorian tramway that still uses the original carriages, and a cable car (Britain's longest) that transports visitors to the top of Great Orme. Nearby is a statue of the **White Rabbit** from Lewis Carroll's much loved story *Alice In Wonderland.* The tribute is to the real Alice - Alice Liddell - who came here on holiday with her family; it was also at Llandudno that her parents spent their honeymoon. Among the visitors to Dean Liddell's holiday home were such notable characters of the day as William Gladstone and Matthew Arnold as well as Lewis Carroll. Though little is known today of Carroll's stay with the family, visitors can be certain that it was on the broad, sandy beaches at Llandudno that the Walrus and the Carpenter "wept like anything to see such quantities of sand" and it was the White Knight who considered "boiling it in wine" to prevent the Menai Bridge from rusting. Off the Promenade towards the Little Orme by the fields, **Bodafon Farm Park** is a

Llandudno Pier

Great Orme Tramway, Llandudno

working farm and also home to the North Wales Bird Trust. Farm attractions include sheep shearing, ploughing, harvesting and collecting eggs. The Trust houses 1000 birds, including eagle owls and falcons.

Although Llandudno is very much a product of the Victorian age, it earlier played host to Bronze Age miners and the Romans and, in the 6th century, St Tudno chose Great Orme as the site of the cell from where he preached. At **Llandudno Museum** visitors are taken through the town's history, from ancient times to the present day, by a collection of interesting exhibits: a child's footprint imprinted on a tile from the Roman fort of Canovium (Caerhun) and objets d'art collected from all over the world by Francis Chardon.

As well as being the home of Llandudno's roots, the massive limestone headland of **Great Orme** still dominates the resort today and also separates the town's two beaches. Two miles long, one mile wide and 679 feet high, its name, Orme, is thought to have originated from an old Norse word for sea monster. In what is now a country park, there are prehistoric sites in the form of stone circles and burial sites, the remains of the Bronze Age mines and **St Tudno's Church**, a 15th century building constructed on the site of the saint's original cell from the 6th century. The summit can be reached by the **Great Orme Tramway**, a magnificent monument to Victorian engineering constructed in 1902 that is Britain's only cable hauled, public road tramway. The **Great Orme Copper Mine** is the only Bronze Age copper mine in the world open to the public. Visitors can explore the

23 QUEEN VICTORIA

Llandudno

Just a stone's throw from the Snowdonia coastline this handsome, traditional pub offers great cask ales and bistro dining throughout the year.

see page 231

24 BELLE VUE HOTEL

Llandudno

Boasting spectacular, panoramic views across Llandudno Bay, the hotel is one of the finest in the area.

see page 232

25 PENRHYN OLD HALL

Penrhyn Bay, nr Llandudno

With a medieval manor house at its heart the Penrhyn Old Hall, nestled in a picturesque, peaceful setting, provides the perfect place to dine out.

see page 233

26 THE QUEENS HEAD

Glanwydden, nr Llandudno

Voted Welsh Pub of the Year the Queens Head hosts a warm welcome, dedicated staff and chefs passionate about creating the perfect relaxing dining experience for you.

see page 234

27 THE RENDEZVOUS CAFÉ

Colwyn Bay

With an experienced chef at its helm the homemade dishes are extremely popular with customers.

see page 235

3,500-year-old passages, see the great opencast mine workings, peer into the 470ft shaft and discover how our ancestors turned rock into metal. The Visitor Centre is open to non-mine visitors, and also at the site are a tea room serving Welsh cream teas and a shop selling a wide variety of books, minerals, fossils and other souvenirs. Outside, look out for the herd of wild goats descended from a pair presented to Queen Victoria by the Shah of Persia.

AROUND LLANDUDNO

RHOS-ON-SEA

3½ miles E of Llandudno on the B5115

Sitting on the western end of Colwyn Bay, Rhos is a delightful little boat haven with plenty of shops and cafés, an award-winning beach 2 miles long, and excellent launch facilities for visiting day sailors. It was from Rhos that **Prince Madoc** set sail in 1170 and is believed to have landed on the north American continent, some 325 years before Columbus made his historic voyage to the New World.

Along the promenade is the small **Chapel of St Trillo**, thought to be the smallest church in Britain with seating for just 6 people. It is dedicated to a 6th century Celtic saint who built his cell here. It stands on the site of an ancient well which provided St Trillo with his drinking water - the well can still be seen in front of the altar. For centuries it supplied the water for baptisms. The chapel is the only surviving building of an abbey that stood here in the 12th century.

COLWYN BAY

5 miles SE of Llandudno on the A55

A more genteel place than the resorts found to the east, Colwyn Bay was built largely during the 19th century to fill the gap along the coast between Rhos-on-Sea and the village of Old Colwyn. As a result, there are many fine Victorian buildings to be seen, and

War Memorial, Colwyn Bay

the beach is served by a promenade along which most of the town's attractions can be found. Colwyn Bay includes among its famous sons ex-Monty Python Terry Jones and a former James Bond, Timothy Dalton. The philosopher Bertrand Russell (1872-1970) was cremated with no ceremony at Colwyn Bay crematorium and his ashes scattered in the sea.

Although Colwyn Bay lies on the coast it is also home to the **Welsh Mountain Zoo**, a conservation centre for rare and endangered species that is best known for the Chimp Encounter, its collection of British wildlife and its feeding of the sea lions. The zoo's gardens, laid out by TH Mawson at the end of the 19th century, incorporate both formal terraces and informal woodlands with paths offering superb views of Snowdonia as well as the Conwy estuary and the North Wales coast. The Tarzan Trail Adventure Playground is a surefire winner with young visitors.

ABERGELE

10½ miles SE of Llandudno on the A548

Along with **Pensarn**, its neighbour on the coast, Abergele is a joint resort which, though more modest than such places as Rhyl, Prestatyn and Colwyn Bay is popular with those looking for a quieter seaside holiday.

Situated on higher ground behind Gwyrch Castle, a ruined Gothic castle shortly to be converted into a hotel, are the natural caverns of **Cefn-Yr-Ogo** whose summit commands magnificent views of the surrounding coastline.

RHYL

14 miles E of Llandudno on the A548

Between them, Rhyl and its neighbour Prestatyn have 4 beaches covering 7 miles of sand. Two of the beaches have been granted the *Seaside Award for Cleanliness and Water Quality*. During the summer months a team of lifeguards patrol the beaches equipped with quad bikes, 4x4s and a rib boat. A more traditional presence on the beaches is the team of donkeys which is owned by a family business now in its 6th generation.

Part of the town's Victorian heritage is **Marine Lake**, a huge artificial lake first opened in 1895 for bathing and boating. Canoeing, water-skiing and windsurfing have since been introduced along with a 15-inch railway which is the oldest in Britain - it opened in 1911 - and one of the oldest anywhere in the world. Visitors can still ride on Joan, the very same train that first arrived here in 1920. The building of a new station, museum and workshop was completed in 2007 and now offers a selection of engines to take you around the 1-mile long track.

As well as the full range of amusement arcades and seaside attractions, Rhyl is home to three large 'fun' complexes. The **Sun Centre** is one of the first all-weather leisure attractions in the country, with indoor surfing and daredevil water slides and flumes. At **SeaQuarium** visitors can enjoy a

28 ST MARGARETS HOTEL

Colwyn Bay

An impressive establishment, standing in its own grounds, The St Margarets Hotel offers a personal touch making it an ideal place to enjoy a relaxing stay away from home.

see page 235

29 THE MARINE HOTEL

Colwyn Bay

With a fantastic reputation for its warm and friendly hospitality the hotel is in the ideal location for exploring the coast and mountains of North Wales.

see page 236

30 MORTON ARMS

Conwy

Lovely family run Inn with chalet-style accommodation, and a menu including delicious Chinese cuisine.

see page 237

31 THE IMPERIAL HOTEL

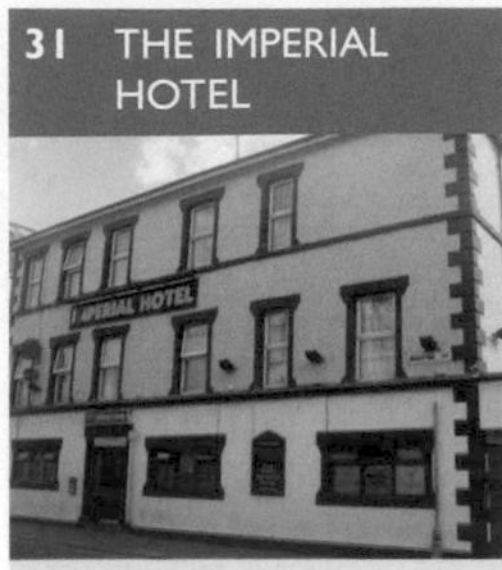

Rhyl

A warm welcome, great hotel facilities and its own bar open to all with good old karaoke at the weekends!

see page 238

32 PENDRE COFFEE SHOP

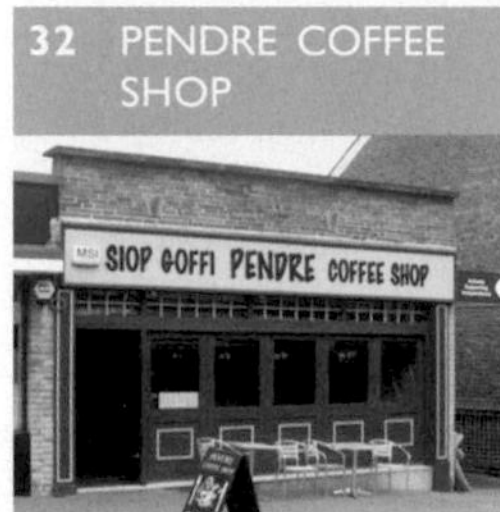

Prestatyn

A warm and friendly coffee shop totally dedicated to good food and great service available for evening hire also.

see page 239

seabed stroll surrounded by sharks, rays and other ocean creatures. The **Ocean Beach Amusement Park** is the largest funfair in North Wales with a huge variety of rides and other amusements. Rhyl's most distinctive landmark is the **Sky Tower**, also known as the Eye in the Sky. Standing 240 feet high, the slender tower dominates the seafront. Its glass bubble, which can accommodate 30 people, rises at an exhilarating speed; once at the top, the bubble revolves to unveil a glorious panorama which on a clear day stretches as far as Blackpool Tower.

PRESTATYN

16½ miles E of Llandudno on the A548

With three great beaches - Ffrith Beach, Central Beach and Barkby Beach - Prestatyn has proved a popular holiday destination over the years. As you would expect, all types of entertainment are available, making the town an ideal centre for family holidays. Although the town undoubtedly expanded with the opening of the Chester to Holyhead railway line in 1848, people were flocking here 50 years before, lured by descriptions of the air being like wine and honey and with the abundant sunshine being deemed excellent for the relief of arthritic conditions and nervous disorders.

However, Prestatyn's origins go back to prehistoric times, as excavated artefacts have shown. While the Roman 20th legion was stationed at Chester, it is thought that an auxiliary unit was based at a fort on what is now Princes Avenue. The discovery in 1984 of a Roman bath house in Melyd Avenue would certainly seem to support this assumption.

Christ Church, Prestatyn's parish church dates from 1863. The churchyard contains the graves of six choirboys who tragically drowned in 1868 as well as

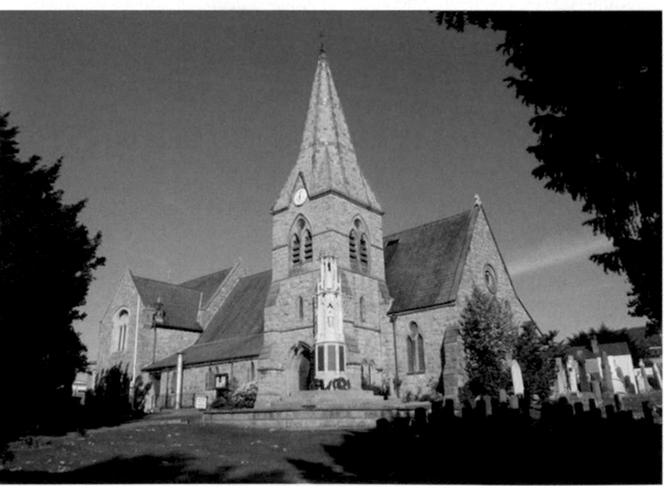

Christ Church, Prestatyn

shipwrecked mariners who were washed up on the shore.

Prestatyn lies at one end of the massive 8th century earthwork **Offa's Dyke**. Although the true origins of the dyke have been lost in the mists of time, it is thought that the construction of this border defence between England and Wales was instigated by **King Offa**, one of the most powerful of the early Anglo-Saxon kings. From AD 757 until his death in AD 796 he ruled Mercia, which covers roughly the area of the West Midlands. He seized power in the period of civil strife that followed the murder of his cousin King Aethelbald and, ruthlessly suppressing many of the smaller kingdoms and princedoms, created a single settled state that covered most of England south of Yorkshire. His lasting memorial is the dyke, which he had built between Mercia and the Welsh lands. With an earthwork bank of anything up to 50 feet in height and a 12ft ditch on the Welsh side, much of this massive feat of engineering is still visible today. The northern end of **Offa's Dyke National Trail** leads up the High Street, climbs the dramatic Prestatyn hillside and wanders through the Clwydian Range. This long-distance footpath of some 180 miles crosses the English-Welsh border ten times and takes in some extraordinarily beautiful countryside. Most people walk the trail in sections; hardier souls take about 12 days to complete it in one go.

A less demanding walk, starting at the southern end of the town, follows the trackbed of the former Prestatyn and Dyserth Railway which closed in 1973.

LLANASA

20 miles E of Llandudno off the A548

Close by the village, whose church has stained glass windows taken from Basingwerk Abbey, stands **Gyrn Castle** which originates from the 1700s and was castellated in the 1820s. It now contains a large picture gallery, and its grounds offer some pleasant woodland walks.

TRELAWNYD

19 miles E of Llandudno on the A5151

Sometimes called Newmarket, this village is well known for its Bronze Age cairn, **Gop Hill**, the biggest prehistoric monument in Wales, which marks the place where, traditionally, Offa's Dyke began, although the town of Prestatyn also claims this honour.

MELIDEN

17 miles E of Llandudno on the A547

Just to the south of Meliden lies **Craig Fawr**, a limestone hill that supports a wide variety of flowers and butterflies, including the Brown Argus, a rare sight in North Wales, whose larvae feed on the Common Rockrose. Nature trails have been laid around the site that not only take in the myriad of wildlife and plants but also an old quarry where the exposed limestone reveals a wealth of fossils deposited here more than 300 million years ago. The short

•

The settlement of Prestatyn is mentioned in the Domesday Book as Prestetone, from the Anglo Saxon Preosta Tun (meaning a settlement in which two or more priests reside). It was Lord Robert Banastre who was responsible for building the Norman Prestatyn Castle; it was of a typical motte and bailey design, but all that remains of the fortification today is one stone pillar on the top of a raised mound that can be found close to Bodnant bridge.

•

33 THE OLD STAG

Llangernwyn

A quality village inn with locally sourced ingredients at the heart of its menu

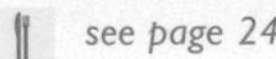

see page 240

34 THE HAWK AND BUCKLE INN

Llannefydd

17th century family-run Inn with a locally sourced menu and spectacular views.

see page 241

walk to the summit is well worth the effort as there are panoramic views from the top over the Vale of Clwyd, the coastline and beyond to Snowdonia.

POINT OF AYR

21½ miles E of Llandudno off the A548

Marking the western tip of the Dee estuary and with views across the river mouth to Hilbre Island and the Wirral, this designated RSPB viewing point is an excellent place to observe the numerous birds that come to feed on the sands and mudflats left by the retreating tide.

LLANGERNYW

10½ miles SE of Llandudno on the A548

This quiet Denbighshire village was the birthplace in 1852 of **Sir Henry Jones**, who became known as 'the cobbler philosopher'. Born the son of a local shoemaker, Henry Jones left school at the age of 12 to become apprenticed to his father but, after the long working day, Henry continued his studies well into the evenings. His hard work paid off and he won a scholarship to train as a teacher and then went on to study philosophy before eventually becoming Professor of Moral Philosophy at Glasgow University. A well-known and highly regarded academic and a widely acclaimed lecturer on social affairs and liberalism, Henry received his knighthood in 1912, and was made a Companion of Honour in 1922. He died in the same year. Though Sir Henry is buried in Glasgow, this village has not forgotten its local hero. In 1934, Jones' childhood home, Y Cwm, was purchased by a fund set up to honour his memory and his work. Today, at the **Amgueddfa Syr Henry Jones** (Sir Henry Jones Museum) visitors can explore the family house including the tiny kitchen and bedroom where the family lived and the shoemaker's workshop where Henry and his father worked. In the churchyard of St Digain's Church stands the **Llangernyw Yew**. The oldest known tree in Wales, and one of the oldest living things in the world, the yew is estimated to be more than 4,000 years old.

DEGANWY

1 mile S of Llandudno off the A546

Just south of Llandudno lies Deganwy, a once thriving fishing village that shares the same stretch of coastline though it has now been taken over by its larger neighbour. Often mentioned in Welsh history, Deganwy was a strategically important stronghold and its **Castle** was the seat of Maelgwn Gwynedd as early as the 6th century. The first medieval castle was probably built here by Lupus, Earl of Chester, shortly after the Norman Conquest. The remains seen today are, however, of a castle built by one of the earl's successors in 1211. Henry II was besieged here by the Welsh and Deganwy was finally destroyed by Llewelyn ap Gruffyd (Llewelyn the Last) in 1263.

GLAN CONWY

3 miles SE of Llandudno off the A470

In Garth Road at Glan Conwy, **Felin Isaf** has two working

watermills and a museum describing the history of the site and the various uses and types of mills.

BODNANT

6 miles S of Llandudno off the A470

Situated above the River Conwy and covering some 80 acres are the famous Edwardian **Bodnant Gardens** (National Trust) laid out in 1875 by the 2nd Lord Aberconwy and still managed by his descendant. Designed in two parts, the upper garden around the house is terraced and the lower, known as The Dell, is formed around the River Hiraethlyn, a tributary of the River Conwy. The pretty Garden House was built in Gloucestershire in the 1730s and was later used as a Pin Mill before being brought to Bodnant in 1938.

CONWY

At Conwy, one of the most magnificent medieval castles ever built towers over one of the world's most complete medieval walled towns. Designated a World Heritage Site, the whole town is in a remarkable state of preservation. Within the walls, the old town is a delight with its tangle of streets and varied shops, pubs and restaurants. A tunnel opened in 1991 carries the A55 under the Conwy estuary and has provided some relief from the heavy traffic that once clogged the town - until then, all traffic had to pass through narrow arches in the city walls.

Conwy Castle is situated on a rock which overlooks the River Conwy and its estuary, and commands wonderful views of the whole area. Begun in 1283, the castle's construction was largely finished by the autumn of 1287. Compared with other of Edward I's castles, Conwy is of a relatively simple design which relies on its position rather than anything else to provide a defence against attack. The town was walled at the same time and they still encircle the vast majority of Conwy, stretching for three quarters of a mile and including 22 towers and three gateways. The castle was also built to be a suitable royal residence. It was used twice by Edward I: once on his way to Caernarfon where his son, the first English Prince of Wales, was born, and again in 1294, when trying to put down the rebellion of Madoc ap Llewelyn.

In 1399, Richard II stayed at the castle before being lured out and ambushed by the Earl of Northumberland's men on behalf of Henry Bolingbroke, the Duke of Lancaster, who later became Henry IV.

As with other castles further east, Conwy was embroiled in the Civil War. A Conwy man, John Williams, became Archbishop of York and, as a Royalist, sought refuge in his home town. Repairing the crumbling fortifications at his own expense, Archbishop Williams finally changed sides after shabby treatment by Royalist leaders and helped the Parliamentary forces lay siege to the town and castle, which eventually fell to them in late 1646.

35 BODNANT GARDEN

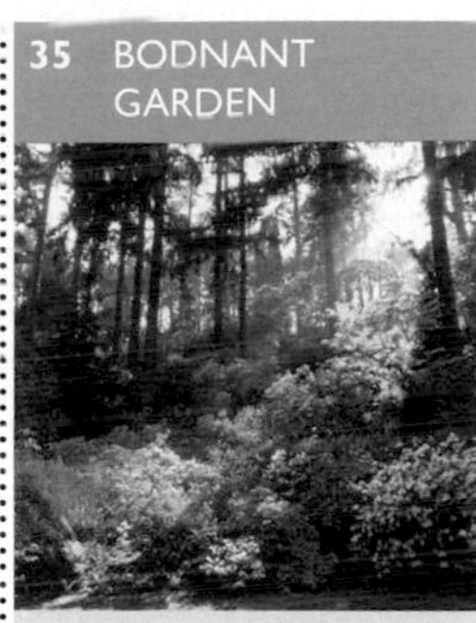

Tal-y-Cafn

One of the most beautiful gardens in the UK, Bodnant has something to interest everyone with plants from around the world.

see page 242

36 TAL-Y-CAFN HOTEL

Tal y Cafn

A former coaching inn with a delightful, spacious beer garden, offering local ales and quality dishes, made from local produce.

see page 242

•

It is not surprising that Conwy and the surrounding area have strong links with the sea, and, like many seaside towns has a traditional mermaid story. Washed ashore by a violent storm in Conwy Bay, a mermaid begged the local fishermen who found her to carry her back to the sea. The fishermen refused even though she could not survive out of the water. Before she died, the mermaid cursed the people of the town, swearing that they would always be poor. In the 5th century, Conwy suffered a fish famine that caused many to believe that the curse was fulfilled. Another fish famine story involves St Brigid. Walking by the riverside carrying some rushes, she threw the rushes upon the water. A few days later the rushes had turned into fish and ever since they have been known as sparlings or, in Welsh, brwyniaid - both meaning rush-like.

•

The town developed within the shadows of its now defunct fortress, and slate and coal extracted from the surrounding area, were shipped up and down the coast from Conwy. Later, as Conwy's trade and links grew with the outside world, the town fathers approached Thomas Telford who planned a causeway and bridge across the River Conwy. Built in 1826, the elegant **Conwy Suspension Bridge** (National Trust) replaced the ferry that previously had been the only means of crossing the river so close to its estuary. At the entrance to the bridge, the Toll House has been restored and furnished as it would have been a century ago. The bridge continued in use until 1958 and is now a pedestrian crossing. The Suspension Bridge was soon followed by the construction of railways. By the side of Telford's bridge stands the **Tubular Rail Bridge** of 1846 designed by Robert Stephenson. Both builders breached the town walls in styles that complemented the town's architecture and the two structures are still admired today.

Bridges, however, are not the only architectural gems Conwy has to offer. **Plas Mawr**, an Elizabethan town house on the High Street, is one of the best preserved buildings from that period in Britain. Built for the influential merchant Robert Wynn between 1576 and 1585, the house has an interesting stone façade and more than 50 windows. Plas Mawr (the name means Great Hall) is particularly noted for its fine and elaborate plasterwork, seen to striking effect in the glorious decorated ceilings and friezes and in the overmantel in the hall. The authentic period atmosphere is further enhanced by furnishings based on an inventory of the contents in 1665. The house came into the possession of the Mostyn family during the 18th century and in 1991 was given by Lord Mostyn to the nation. Close by is **Aberconwy House** (National Trust), a delightful medieval merchant's home that dates from about 1300 and is the oldest house in Conwy. The rooms have been decorated and furnished to reflect various periods in the house's history. The collection of rural furniture on display is on loan from the Museum of Wales.

Just behind Plas Mawr and occupying a converted chapel is the **Royal Cambrian Academy Art** Gallery (free). The Academy was formed to encourage art in Wales and most of the artists featured are Welsh or working in Wales.

Occupying part of the site of a 12th century Cistercian Abbey that was moved to Maenan by Edward I is **St Mary's Church**. This abbey church became the parish church of the borough created by Edward and some interesting features still remain from that time though there have been many additions over the centuries.

On the quayside the fishermen still land their catches, and from here pleasure boat trips can be taken. On the quay, in between terraced housing, can be found what is claimed to be **Britain's Smallest House**, measuring 10 feet by 6 feet; it seems that its last tenant was a fisherman who was 6 feet 3 inches tall - he was presumably also a contortionist!

Conwy was once a famous pearl fishing centre and had a thriving mussel industry, whose history is told in the **Conwy Mussel Centre**, Not on display is the dazzling pearl found in a Conwy mussel in the 1600s - it now forms part of the Crown Jewels. In Bodlondeb Park, just 300 yards from the quay, **Conwy Butterfly Jungle** brings tropical warmth and colour to the town. In the 2,000 sq ft greenhouse visitors can see some of the largest and most beautiful tropical butterflies in free flight, more than 300 species in all. The Jungle is also home to a collection of spiders and insects.

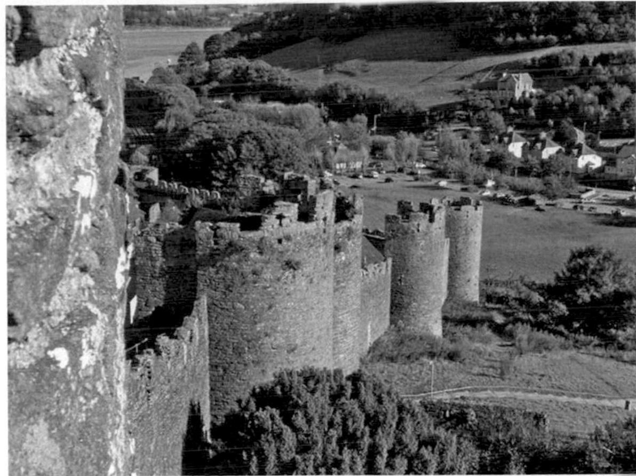

Town Walls, Conwy

AROUND CONWY

ROWEN

4 miles S of Conwy off the B5106

From this very pretty, quiet village a track, which was once a Roman road, skirts by the foot of **Tal-y-fan**, which climbs to 2000 feet at its peak. Roughly six miles in length, the path passes by Maen-y-Bardd, an ancient burial chamber, and eventually drops down towards the coast at Aber. Another, circular, walk of about five miles, one of several in the Conwy Valley devised by Active Snowdonia, passes many impressive cromlechs and standing stones. The route also takes in Caer Bach, where there are traces of a neolithic settlement, the wonderfully unspoilt 14th century St Celynin's Church and the Woodland Trust's Parc Mawr woods.

TREFRIW

8 miles S of Conwy on the B5106

This village, nestling into the forested edge of Snowdonia in the beautiful Conwy valley, was once one of the homes of Llywelyn the Great. He is said to have built a church here to please his wife who refused to climb to the nearest church, which was at Llanrhychyrn.

Once the biggest inland port in Wales, the village today has two main attractions: **Trefriw Woollen Mills** and the local chalybeate springs. The woollen mill has been in operation since the 1830s and it is still owned by descendants of Thomas Williams who purchased it in 1859. It is run by hydro-electric power generated from the two lakes - Crafnant and Geirionydd - which lie to the west of the village.

37 FISHERMAN'S CHIP SHOP

Conwy

If you want to sample Britain's national dish at its very best, a visit to The Fisherman's Chip Shop is highly recommended.

see page 243

While the source of power is modern, the tapestries and tweeds produced here from raw wool are very traditional.

A footpath above the woollen mill leads to **Fairy Falls** where, in the early 19th century, a forge was founded to make hammers and chisels for use in the slate quarries. It closed at the beginning of the 20th century. Sometime between AD 100 and AD 250, while prospecting for minerals in this area, the Romans opened up a cave where they found a spring rich in iron (chalybeate). Covered in later years by a landslide, it was not until the 18th century that the spring was uncovered by Lord Willoughby de Eresby, owner of nearby Gwydir Castle. He went on to build a stone bathhouse. Taking the waters became so popular that by 1874 the original bathhouse was replaced with a pump house and bath, and the bottled water was exported worldwide. Following a decline during much of the 20th century, interest in the natural spring waters has been rekindled. Visitors can take the waters, view the museum artefacts in the tea room and browse in the spa beauty shop.

Lake Geirionydd was the birthplace in the 6th century of the great bard Taliesin to whom in 1850 Lord Willoughby erected a monument. In 1863, a local poet, Gwilym Cowlyd, being dissatisfied with the National Eisteddfod, started an arwest, a poetical and musical event that was held in the shadow of the monument every year until 1922. The monument fell down in a storm in 1976 but was restored in 1994. It lies on one of Active Snowdonia's Conwy Valley walks, which also passes Fairy Falls and old mine workings; it skirts Lake Crafnant and provides memorable views at many points along its route.

LLANRWST

10 miles S of Conwy on the A470

The market centre for the central Conwy Valley owes both its name and the dedication of its church to St Grwst (Restitutus), a 6th century missionary who was active in this area. The town lies in the middle of the Conwy Valley between rich agricultural hills to the east and the imposing crags of Snowdonia to the west. Famous for its livestock fairs and the manufacture of grandfather clocks and Welsh harps, it was also known for its woollen yarn and its sail-making industry. The **Church of St Grwst** with its fine rood screen dates from 1470, though the tower and north aisle are 19th century. It replaced a thatched building from 1170 that was destroyed in the fighting of 1468.

Next to the church lies **Gwydir Chapel**, famous for its richly carved Renaissance interior. This was the private chapel of the Wynn family and among its treasures is an imposing stone sarcophagus of the Welsh prince Llewelyn the Great. This chapel should not be confused with **Gwydir Uchaf Chapel** which lies on the opposite bank of the river Conwy and is particularly noted for its ceiling covered with paintings of angels.

Below the chapel lies **Gwydir Castle**, the Wynn family's lovely Tudor mansion. The dining room is especially fine with its richly carved oak panels, Baroque door-case and fireplace, and rampant gilded Spanish leather. In the grounds are some fine Cedars of Lebanon planted in 1625 in celebration of the marriage of Charles I to Henrietta Maria of France. A short distance from the house is the **Gwydyr Uchaf Chapel** (free), austere on the outside, flamboyantly baroque inside with a jaw-dropping painted ceiling depicting the Creation, the Trinity and the Day of Judgement.

A walk west from the town takes in not only these historic buildings but also the remains of an old crushing mill and the site of the old Hafna Galena Mine.

Back in town, the **Old Bridge** is thought to have been designed by Inigo Jones; it was built in 1636 by Sir Richard Wynn. Next to it stands **Tu Hwnt i'r Bont** (the House over the Bridge), a 16th century courthouse which has since been divided into two cottages and is now a National Trust tea room.

At one point the town was governed neither by the Welsh nor by the English, giving rise to the saying Cymru, Lloegr a Llanrwst – Wales, England and Llanrwst.

CAPEL CURIG

9 miles S of Conwy on the A5

Situated at the junction of the mountain roads to Beddgelert, Llyn Ogwen and Betws-y-Coed, Capel Curig is primarily dedicated to the needs of hikers and climbers who also use the village as a base. A walk south of the village passes by lonely Llyn y Foel and climbs the steep ridge of Daiar Ddu to the top of Mount Siabod; the reward for this expenditure of energy is the most spectacular panoramic view of many of Snowdonia's great peaks. **Plas-y-Brenin**, the National Mountain Centre, is located just to the southwest of the town and provides excellent facilities and training courses for climbing, canoeing, dry slope skiing and orienteering.

BANGOR

A cathedral and university city, Bangor incorporates a wide variety of architectural styles that remind the visitor that this is not only an interesting and stimulating place but also one with a long history. A monastic community was founded here as early as AD 525 by St Deiniol. The town's name is derived

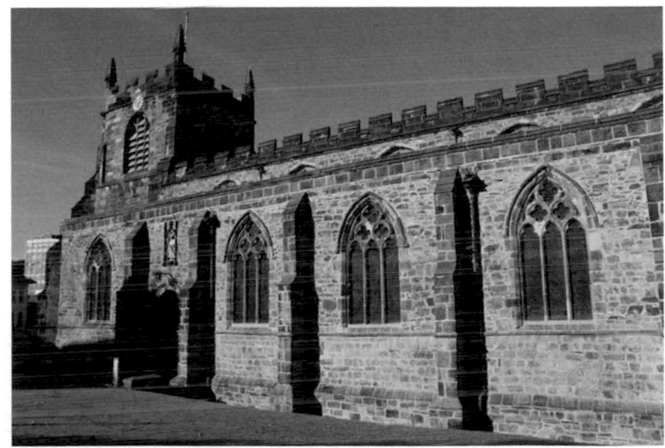

Bangor Cathedral

38 THE WHITE LION INN

Bangor

Offering the very best in hospitality and fine pub food the inn is extremely popular with locals and visitors.

see page 244

from the wattle fence which surrounded the saint's primitive enclosure - the term 'bangori' is still used in parts of Wales to describe the plaiting of twigs in a hedge.

There were settlers in the area long before St Deiniol, including the Romans at nearby Segontium. The **Gwynedd Museum and Art Gallery** (free) is just the place to discover not only the past 2,000 years of history of this area of Wales but also to see reconstructions of domestic life in days gone by. The Oriel Art Gallery exhibits changing displays of work by mostly Welsh contemporary artists.

The mother church of the oldest bishopric in Britain, **Bangor Cathedral** dates from the 13th century and has probably been in continuous use for longer than any other cathedral in Britain. During the Middle Ages, the cathedral became a centre of worship for the independent principality of Gwynedd and when Owain Gwynedd was buried here his tomb became a starting point for pilgrims setting out on the arduous journey to Bardsey Island. Restored in 1866, the cathedral also contains a life-size carving of Christ dating from 1518 while, outside, there is a Biblical garden that contains plants which are associated with the Bible.

Until the slate boom of the 19th century, Bangor remained little more than a village, albeit with an impressive church. Its position on the Menai Strait made this the ideal place for nearby Penrhyn Quarry to build their docks and the town soon flourished in its new role as a commercial centre. Its importance increased further when **Bangor University (o**riginally the University College of North Wales**)** was founded here in 1884. Improvements to the roads and then the coming of the railways to the North Wales coast also saw Bangor grow in both stature and importance. The **Menai Suspension Bridge** was built by Thomas Telford between 1819 and 1826 and was the first permanent crossing of the Menai Strait. Before its completion the crossing had been made by ferry, but cattle on their way to and from market would have had to swim the channel. Not surprisingly there was much opposition to the construction not only from the ferrymen but also from ship-owners worried that the structure would impede the passage of their tall ships. As a result of this concern, the road bridge stands at a height of 100 feet. The **Britannia Bridge**, a mile further southwest from Telford's bridge, is a combined road and rail crossing and was built between 1846 and 1850 by Robert Stephenson. The lions guarding the bridge are by John Thomas, who was responsible for much of the sculpture at the Houses of Parliament. Also jutting out into the Menai Strait from the town is the 1500 feet long **Victorian Pier**, which was built in 1896, almost demolished in 1974 and restored in the early 1980s. It now has original style kiosks and a café at the sea end. As well as being attractive in itself, the pier commands grand views of the Menai Strait, the Great Orme at Llandudno, Snowdonia, Telford's suspension bridge and Bangor itself. Both pleasure and fishing trips can be taken from the pier head.

To the east of Bangor, overlooking the Menai Strait and Beaumaris on the Isle of Anglesey, is **Penrhyn Castle**, a dramatic neo-Norman construction built between 1820 and 1845 by Thomas Hopper with the profits from his slate quarries. It has more than 300 luxuriously appointed rooms and a superb collection of paintings, including works by Rembrandt, Canaletto and Gainsborough. The Castle also has a Dolls Museum, a Victorian walled garden and an Industrial Railway Museum displaying rolling stock once used on the estate's own rail link between the slate quarries and the port. 'Castle and Quarry' is a permanent exhibition exploring Penrhyn's industrial past.

AROUND BANGOR

ABERGWYNGREGYN

6 miles E of Bangor off the A55

To the south of the village, reached by taking a footpath through sheltered woodland, are **Rhaeadr Aber Falls** where the drop of the river is said to be among the steepest in Wales.

Above the village is **The Cross**, a group of trees in the shape of a huge cross. Some people claim it was planted as a memorial to the crew of a German bomber that crashed on the hillside. The reality is more mundane - it was planted by scientists from Bangor University in the mid 1950s as an experiment in sheep management.

PENMAENMAWR

10 miles E of Bangor off the A55

A tiny quarrying village before the arrival of the railway in 1848, this small holiday resort with its sand and shingle beach has changed little since William Gladstone holidayed here in the 19th century, and it still boasts many fine Victorian buildings. Gladstone was a frequent visitor, a fact commemorated by a bust of him on a granite obelisk in Paradise Road. Penmaenmawr has a small industrial heritage park, Parc Plas Mawr.

In the town's steep mountain backed hinterland can be found many prehistoric sites including one of Wales' best known Bronze Age stone circles, **Cefn Coch**. An urn was uncovered here containing the remains of a child as well as a bronze dagger said to be evidence of a ritual sacrifice that once took place here.

CAERNARFON

If you want to brush up your Welsh, Caernarfon is the place to visit. More than 86% of its 10,000 or so residents could speak Welsh according to the 2001 census. Unsurprisingly, it has also been for many years a base for the Welsh nationalist movement.

39 MIN-Y-DON

Llanfairfechan

A B&B of the highest standard in a 19th century building, which boasts spectacular views across the sea at Llanfairfechan.

see page 243

40 THE GLADSTONE

Dwygyfylchi

An award winning, family-run free house serving the very best in homemade food, wines and ales

see page 245

41 CAERNARFON CASTLE

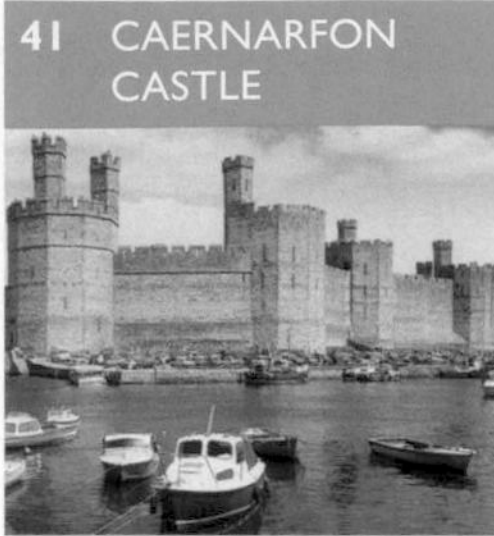

Caernarfon

This magnificent castle was begun in 1283 as a fortress and a seat of government. Now visitors can explore its many covered passageways and wall walks.

 *see page 245*

42 MENAI BANK HOTEL

Caenarfon

A homely hotel offering fantastic breakfasts and incredible sea views.

 *see page 245*

Caernarfon's name simply means 'castle in Arfon' - Arfon being simply the region opposite Anglesey. Situated on the right bank of the River Seiont, near the southwest end of the Menai Strait, the town's history goes back to Roman times when **Segontium Roman Fort** (CADW) was built half a mile from the present town centre. Segontium is the only place in Wales where it is possible to see something of the internal layout of an auxiliary station. Built to defend the Roman Empire against attack from rebellious tribes, the fort dates back to AD 77 when the Roman conquest was finally completed following the capture of Anglesey. Segontium was one of the most important garrisons on the edge of the Roman Empire and was also an administrative centre for northwest Wales. Excavations of the site have revealed coins which show that the fort was garrisoned at least until AD 394. This long occupation can be explained by its strategic position controlling the fertile lands and mineral rights of Anglesey and providing a defence against Irish pirates. The ruins are not impressive, seldom higher than a foot or so, but the displays are informative and the **Museum**, which is run by the National Museum and Galleries of Wales, displays many interesting items, including coins, pottery and weapons which have been uncovered during excavation work.

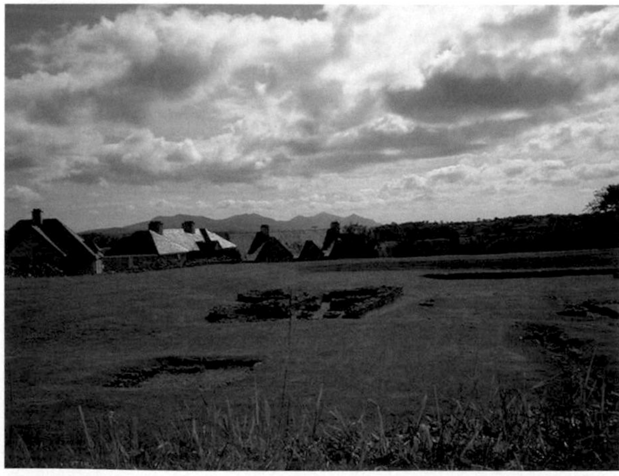

Segontium, Caernarfon

At the other end of the scale of impressiveness from Segontium is the mighty **Caernarfon Castle** which still dominates the town today. The most famous of Wales' numerous great fortresses, the castle was begun in 1283 by Henry de Elreton, who was also building Beaumaris Castle on the orders of Edward I. Caernarfon took some 40 years to complete, built not just as a fortress but also as a royal palace and a seat of government. The design is based around two oval-shaped courts divided by a wall. The outer defences are strengthened at intervals by towers and are, in places, up to 15 feet thick. Over the years, many attempts were made by the Welsh to destroy the castle but their failure is confirmed by the presence of this magnificent building today. It was here that, in 1284, Edward I crowned his son the first English Prince of Wales. Almost 700 years later, in 1969, the castle once again provided the dramatic setting for the investiture of Prince Charles as Prince of Wales. Also at the castle,

Caernarfon Castle

and housed in the Queen's Tower, is the **Museum of the Royal Welch Fusiliers**, the country's oldest regiment - 'Welch' is an archaic Anglicisation of 'Welsh'.

The castle sits where the River Seiont meets the Menai Strait, the expanse of water that separates mainland Wales from the Isle of Anglesey. Close by, the old **Slate Quay**, from where slate was once shipped, is now the place where fishing trips and pleasure cruises depart up the Strait to Beaumaris. **Castle Square**, on the landward side of the castle, holds markets and here, too, can be found statues of two famous Welshmen: the gesticulating, urging David Lloyd-George, once a member of Parliament for the area, and Sir Hugh Owen, the founder of Further Education in Wales.

The Anglesey Hotel and the **Hanging Tower** stand by the castle walls and were a customs house until 1822. The last hanging to take place in the tower was in 1911 when an Irishman named Murphy was executed for murdering a maid. It is said that when he died the bell clapper in **St Mary's Church** fell off. The church itself was founded in 1307 and, though much of it has since been reconstructed, the arcades of the eastern and southern walls are part of the original 14th century building.

Northgate Street is called in Welsh 'Stryd Pedwar a Chewch' - meaning four and six street. Apparently it originates from the time when sailors flocked to this part of town looking for lodgings. four pence for a hammock and six pence for a bed!

From the town, walkers can enjoy a scenic footpath, the **Lôn Las Menai**, which follows the coastline along the Menai Strait towards the village of Y Felinheli and from which there are views across the water to the Isle of Anglesey.

To the southwest of Caernarfon and overlooking

43 BLACK BOY INN

Caenarfon

Historic and atmospheric this lively pub serves fantastic food and well kept ale alongside quality accommodation all year round.

see page 246

44 GWESTY BRON MENAI

Caenarfon

A first class guest house in an ideal location for exploring North Wales.

see page 247

45 THE NEWBOROUGH ARMS

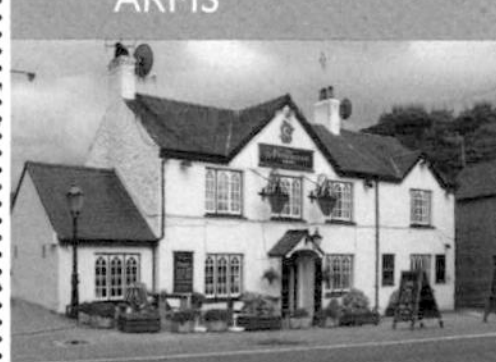

Bontnewydd

True dedication to customer satisfaction can be found here along with fine fresh home cooked food, real local ale and folk nights every other week.

see page 248

46 TY'N YR ONNEN

Waunfawr, nr Caernarfon

Nestled within the spacious grounds of a Welsh hillside farm, this caravan/campsite offers the outdoor lifestyle with all the modern comforts you could want.

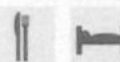 see page 247

47 PLAS TIRION FARM

Llanrug

Fine Welsh country farmhouse hospitality from a B&B located on a working family farm.

 see page 249

48 TY MAWR TEAROOMS, RESTAURANT AND B&B

LLanddeiniolen

Scenic views across Snowdonia in every room of this charming bed and breakfast above a restaurant and tearoom serving home cooked treats.

 see page 249

Caernarfon Bay is **Caernarfon Air World**, located on the site of an RAF station that was built in 1940 and which is also the home of the first RAF mountain rescue team. Pleasure flights are available and there is also the Aviation Museum, housed in one of the great hangars which displays more than 400 model aircraft, has various planes and helicopters on show and also provides visitors with the opportunity to take the controls in a flight trainer.

Caernarfon is the terminus of the **Welsh Highland Railway**, founded in 1955 and is owned and operated by the Ffestiniog Railway. It now runs for 19½ miles: starting near Caernarfon Castle, it climbs up and over the dramatic foothills of Snowdon to reach the village of Beddgelert with a return trip through the awe-inspiring scenery of the Aberglaslyn Pass. Tel: 01766 51600 for timetable and other details.

AROUND CAERNARFON

Y FELINHELI

4 miles NE of Caernarfon off the A487

Situated on the other side of the main road from this village is **Greenwood Forest Park**, a forest heritage and adventure park with something for all ages. Opened in the early 1990s, this centre concentrates on exploring and explaining man's relationship with trees and how, using conservation techniques, the loss of species of trees from the countryside can be halted whether in the equatorial rain forests or ancient temperate forests of Europe. The skills of ancient carpenters and joiners are also on show, particularly in the Great Hall, a building that was constructed entirely using medieval skills and knowledge and is held together by 500 oak pegs.

A couple of miles further east off the A487 and bordering the Menai Strait, **Glan Faenol** (National Trust) comprises parkland and farmland around Vaynol Hall, once one of the largest estates in North Wales. This is an important habitat for wildlife, and there's a pleasant walk leading to the sea and two viewing platforms. The estate has tracts of ancient woodland and several follies, including one built to rival the Marquess Column on Anglesey. The views of Snowdonia and across the strait are memorably depicted in one of Rex Whistler's murals at Plas Newydd.

BETHESDA

9 miles E of Caernarfon on the A5

This old quarry town takes its name from the Nonconformist chapel that was built here and served many of the 2,300 men (and their families) who worked in the quarry at its peak in 1875. The gouged rock of the **Penrhyn Slate Quarries** forms a huge hillside amphitheatre. It was the largest open cast slate mine in the world and still produces high-quality slate 250 years after it was first worked.

From the town, the main road travels through the beautiful **Nant**

Ffrancon Pass which runs straight through and up the valley of the River Ogwen and into the Snowdonia National Park. Five miles south of Bethesda on the A5, **Llyn Idwal** is one of several lakes on the National Trust's Carneddau estate. In 1954 it was declared the first National Nature Reserve in Wales.

ISLE OF ANGLESEY

MENAI BRIDGE

Acting as a gateway to Anglesey, this largely Victorian town developed after the construction of Thomas Telford's **Menai Suspension Bridge**, which connects the island to mainland Wales. Opened in 1826, this was the world's first large iron suspension bridge, stretching 580 feet between its piers and soaring 100 feet above the water to allow large ships to pass beneath. Almost a quarter of a century later, Robert Stepehenson's **Britannia Tubular Bridge** was built to carry both trains and road traffic across the strait. In 1970 it burnt down and only the limestone piers survived. These now support the double-decker A5/A55 road and rail bridge.

The waterfront at Menai Bridge is a popular place for anglers and for people watching the annual Regatta on the Menai Strait held every August. The promenade here is known as the Belgian Promenade because it was built by refugees from Belgium who sought shelter here during World War I.

On **Church Island**, reached by a causeway from the town, there is a small 14th century church built

Menai Suspension Bridge

49 THE JOYS OF LIFE COUNTRY PARK

Bethesda

Scenic country park in the heart of Snowdonia sporting its very own lake and a combination of fantastic bed and breakfast and self catering cottage accommodation.

see page 250

50 BULKELEY ARMS HOTEL

Menai Bridge

A warm Welsh welcome greets guests at this charming pub and B&B, ideally located overlooking the scenic bridge.

see page 251

51 THE LIVERPOOL ARMS HOTEL

Beaumaris

First class food, accommodation and hospitality in one of the area's most atmospheric and historic taverns.

see page 251

on the site of a foundation by St Tysilio in AD 630. The site is thought to have been visited by Archbishop Baldwin and Giraldus when they may have landed here in 1188.

For a place with a difference, **Pili Palas** (**Butterfly Palace**) is an interesting and unusual attraction that will delight everyone. The vast collection of exotic butterflies and birds from all over the world are seen in tropical environments with some wonderful tropical plants. There is also a Tropical Hide, an amazing Ant Avenue and a Snake House as well as a café and adventure play area.

AROUND MENAI BRIDGE

BEAUMARIS

4 miles NE of Menai Bridge of the A545

An attractive and elegant town, Beaumaris was granted a charter by Edward I in 1294 and adopted the Norman name 'beau marais' which translates as 'beautiful marsh'. The lawned seafront with its elegant Georgian and Victorian terraces was once a marsh that protected the approaches to **Beaumaris Castle** (CADW). Often cited as the most technically perfect medieval castle in Britain, Beaumaris Castle was the last of Edward I's Iron Ring of fortresses built to stamp his authority on the Welsh. Begun in 1295 and designed by the king's military architect, James of St George, this was to be his largest and most ambitious project. Regarded as a pinnacle of military architecture of the time, with a concentric defence rather than the traditional keep and bailey, the outer walls contained 16 towers while the inner walls were 43 feet high and up to 16 feet thick in places. It looks as if it would be impregnable to any medieval army, but in fact it was seized in 1403 by Owain Glyndwr who held it for 2 years. Now a World Heritage listed site, Beaumaris Castle is still virtually surrounded by its original moat; there was also a tidal dock here for ships coming in through a channel in the marshes - an iron ring where vessels of up to 40 tons once docked still hangs from the wall.

In later years, the town briefly enjoyed notoriety as a haven for pirates, as well as being a busy trading port. With the advent of steam ships and paddle boats, the resort developed during Victorian times as visitors from Liverpool and elsewhere took the sea trip down to Beaumaris. The town is now a popular place with the yachting fraternity due to its facilities and involvement in the annual Menai Strait Regatta. Beaumaris **Lifeboat Station** is one of seven operated by inshore boats funded by the television programme *Blue Peter*. The station, which has a new weather station, can be visited daily between 10.30 and 4.30.

While having connections with both sea trade and developing as a holiday resort, Beaumaris was at one time also an administrative and legal centre for the island. The

Courthouse, dating from 1614, is the oldest active court in Britain. It is open to the public during the summer and although it was renovated in the 19th century much of its original Jacobean interior remains. It was here, in 1773, that Mary Hughes stood in the dock and was sentenced to transportation for seven years after she had been found guilty of stealing a bed gown valued at six pence (2½p)!

Close by is **Beaumaris Gaol**, which was designed as a model prison by Hansom in 1829. In this monument to Victorian law and order, the last man to hang was Richard Rowlands, who cursed the church clock opposite as he climbed to the scaffold in 1862. Today's visitors can relive those days of harsh punishment, view the cells, the stone-breaking yard and the tread-wheel, and follow the route taken by the condemned men to their rendezvous with the hangman.

An equally interesting place for all the family to visit is the **Museum of Childhood Memories**, a treasure house of nostalgia with a collection of more than 2000 items, all collected over 40 years by one man. There are nine different rooms, each with its own theme, such as entertainment, pottery and glass, and clockwork tin plate toys. The amazing variety of toys vividly illustrate the changing fashions in toys from the 1840s to around 1970.

A popular excursion from Beaumarais is the boat trip around (but not on to) Puffin Island (see below) - trips can be booked at the kiosk at the foot of the truncated pier.

LLANFAES

5 miles NE of Menai Bridge off the B5109

Now a quiet and sedate place, Llanfaes was a busy commercial village long before the establishment of Beaumaris as one of the island's major centres, and travellers from the mainland arrived here after crossing the Menai Strait from Aber and the Lavan Sands.

In 1237, Llywelyn the Great founded a monastery in the village over the tomb of Joan, his wife and the daughter of King John. The tomb can now be seen in St Mary's Church, Beaumaris, where it was moved at the time of the Dissolution. In 1295 Edward I moved the inhabitants of Llanfaes to Newborough so that he could use the stone in the town to build Beaumaris Castle. During World War Two, flying boats were built at the factory on the edge of the village.

LLANGOED

6 miles NE of Menai Bridge on the B5109

In Edwardian times, this historic village was a popular resort with the lower middle classes who came here to stay in boarding houses by the sea. A walk downstream, alongside the river, leads to **Castell Aberlleiniog**, standing in the midst of trees. This was originally a timber castle, built in around 1090 by Hugh Lupus, Earl of Chester, who, along with Hugh the Proud,

52 TAFARN Y RHYD

LLangoed

Vibrant and friendly family run pub and B&B with fine Welsh cuisine, minutes from the coast in Llangoed.

see page 252

•

In Llangoed itself, Haulfre Stables is a small equestrian museum housed in a historic stable block and contains a collection of Victorian harnesses and saddlery, carts and carriages. There's also a garden shop selling fresh local produce.

•

Earl of Shrewsbury, displayed great cruelty to the Welsh. Lupus was later killed during an attack on the castle by Magnus, King of Norway, when he was struck in the eye by an arrow. The ruins of the bailey, which was constructed later, are still visible. Close by is the site of a battle where, in AD 809, the Saxons were, albeit briefly, victorious over the defending Welsh.

PENMON

7 miles NE of Menai Bridge off the B5109

On the eastern tip of Anglesey, this is a beauty spot whose lovely views across the Menai Strait go some way to explaining why it was chosen, centuries earlier, as a religious site. **Penmon Priory** (CADW) was established by St Seiriol in the 6th century. In 1237 Llywelyn the Great gave the monastery and its estates to the prior of Puffin Island. **St Seiriol's Church**, now the parish church, was rebuilt in the 12th century and contains wonderful examples of Norman architecture. A carved cross, recently moved to the church from the fields nearby, shows influences from both Scandinavia and Ireland. The ruins of the priory's domestic buildings include a 13th century wing with a refectory on the ground floor where traces of the seat used by the monk who read aloud during meals can still be seen.

A nearby **Dovecote**, built in around 1600 by Sir Richard Bulkeley, contains nearly 1,000 nesting places. A path, beginning across the road, leads up to **St Seiriol's Well**, which was probably the site of the original 6th century priory. Although the upper part of the building covering the well appears to date from the 18th century, the lower portion is much older and could indeed incorporate something from the priory's original chapel.

PUFFIN ISLAND

8½ miles NE of Menai Bridge off the B5109

Once known as Priestholm and now often called **Ynys Seiriol**, this island is the home of the remains of St Seiriol's sanctuary and is thought once to have been connected to the mainland. The remains of monastic buildings dating back to the 6th century can still be seen here. The island was so named because of the large puffin colonies that nested here. However, the numbers of the nesting birds declined in the 19th century partly due to rats on the island and also because the young birds were considered a delicacy when pickled. Today, the island is again a nesting site for puffins, guillemots and razorbills and there are regular boat trips around it from Beaumaris.

PENTRAETH

4 miles N of Menai Bridge on the A5025

Before land reclamation this sleepy village stood on the edge of Red Wharf Bay, where at low tide the almost 15 square miles of sand supported a flourishing cockling industry. It's now a popular place for a holiday even though it is not ideal for swimming because of the strong tidal currents experienced around this part of the Anglesey coast.

BENLLECH

6½ miles N of Menai Bridge on the A5025

With its excellent beach, Benllech is probably the most popular resort on Anglesey, but those coming here should take care as there are strong tidal currents and the sands can be treacherous. This resort has another claim to fame, as the birthplace of the poet Goronwy Owen.

Traces of a hill fort, **Castell Mawr**, can be found on the west side of Red Wharf Bay, near Benllech. On the evidence of coins found here, the site could once have been occupied by the Romans.

MOELFRE

9 miles N of Menai Bridge on the A5108

This is a charming coastal village with a sheltered, pebbled beach, attractive cottages and sandy beaches to both the north and the south. Fame came to Moelfre in an unfortunate and bizarre way via its lifeboat which, over the years, has been involved in many rescues. Two of them are specially worthy of mention. Returning to Liverpool from Australia in October 1859, laden with cargo and passengers, including gold prospectors coming home after making their fortunes in the Australian Gold Rush, the *Royal Charter* sank. A rigged iron vessel and the pride of the merchant fleet, the ship was all set to make the long passage in record time but, while sheltering from a hurricane in Moelfre Bay, she foundered with the loss of 450 passengers and crew. Only 39 passengers and crew survived and many believe that the gold still lies with the wreck out in the bay. Efforts have been made to recover the lost fortune with varying but not overwhelming degrees of success. It has been said that the larger houses around Moelfre were paid for with gold washed ashore from the wreck. This is despite Customs Officers swamping the village in an attempt to ensure that any salvaged gold ended in the Exchequer rather than in the hands of the locals. Charles Dickens visited the site on New Year's Eve, 1859, and based a story on the disaster in *The Uncommercial Traveller*.

One hundred years later, almost to the day, in October 1959, the coaster *Hindlea*, struggling in foul weather, had eight crew members rescued by the Moelfre Lifeboat. The rescue earned

53 THE BREEZE HILL HOTEL

Benllech Bay

Growing in reputation, it is the ideal place to relax after exploring this holiday paradise.

see page 253

Moelfre Lifeboat Station

54 MONA HOUSE COFFEE SHOP

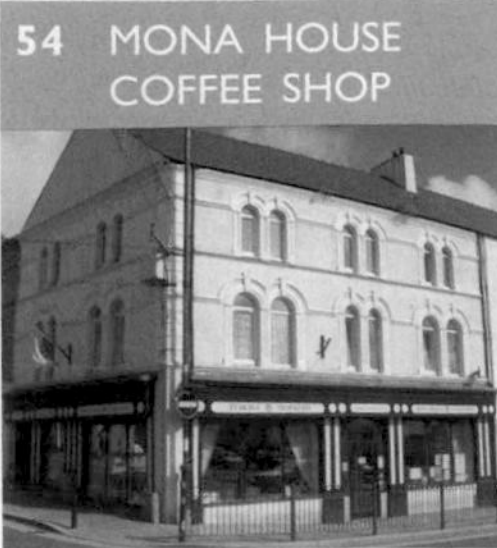

Llangefni

The enticing smell of fresh coffee leads to so much more than a coffee shop with home cooked lunches and tasty treats served throughout the day.

see page 254

Richard Evans, the lifeboat's coxswain, his second RNLI gold medal for gallantry. The **Lifeboat Station** can be visited daily between 9am and 4pm; crew training takes place at 7pm on Wednesdays.

Beyond the station is a small outcrop of rocks, **Ynys Moelfre**, a favourite spot for seabirds. Occasionally, porpoises can also be seen in the bay. About a mile inland from the village, off the narrow road, is the impressive **Lligwy Burial Chamber**, a Bronze Age tomb which has a huge 28-ton capstone supported by stone uprights. It lies half hidden in a pit dug out of the rock. Close by is **Din Lligwy Hut Group (CASW)**, the remains of a Romano-British settlement that covers over half an acre. Certainly occupied around the 4th century AD, after the Roman garrison on Anglesey had been vacated, some of the stone walls of the buildings can still be seen. Excavations of the site have unearthed pottery, coins and evidence of metal working from that period. Nearby are the ruins of the 14th century Capel Lligwy.

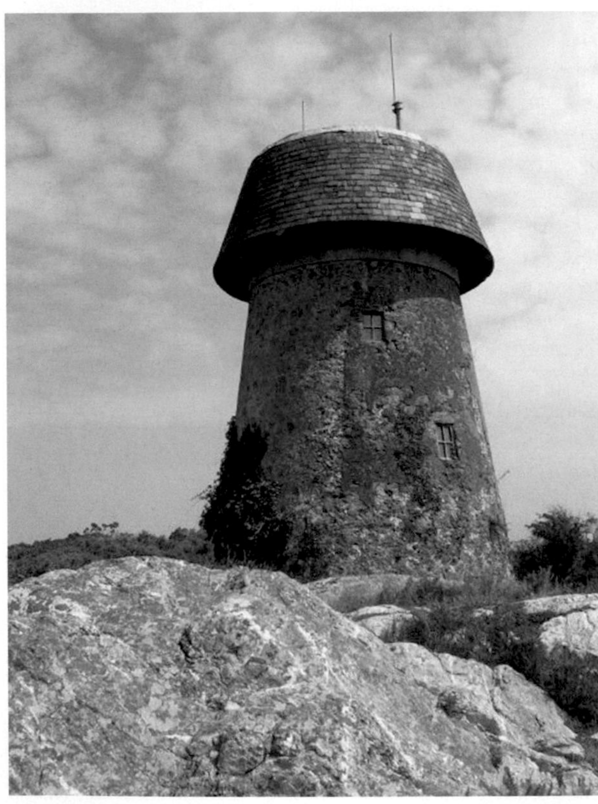

Old Windmill, Llangefni

LLANDDYFNAN

5 miles NW of Menai Bridge on the B5109

To the west of the village lies **Stone Science**, a most unusual attraction that tells the story of the earth from its beginning to the present - a journey spanning 650 million years. The museum illustrates the science with displays of fossils, crystals and artefacts, and there are numerous and varied items for sale in the Stone Science shop.

LLANGEFNI

6 miles NW of Menai Bridge on the B5420

The island's main market and administrative centre, Llangefni is also the home of **Oriel Ynys Môn** (the **Anglesey Heritage Centre**), an attractive art gallery and heritage centre, built in 1991, which gives an insight into the history of Anglesey. From prehistoric times to the present day, the permanent exhibition covers a series of themes including Stone Age

Llanfair PG Railway Station

Hunters, Druids, Medieval Society and Legends.

Llyn Cefni Reservoir to the northwest of the town is an important wildlife habitat and nature reserve overlooked by a hide; it also provides a pleasant picnic area. On the northwest edge of town by the River Cefni, **The Dingle** is a local nature reserve with footpaths through mature woodland. The A5114, which connects Llangefni to the A5, is the shortest A road in the British Isles at less than 2 miles in length.

LLANFAIR PG

1 mile W of Menai Bridge off the A5

Llanfairpwllgwyngyll, often called Llanfair PG, is better known as the village with the world's longest place name. The full, tongue-twisting name is: Llanfairpwllgwyngyllgogerychwyrn-drobwyllllantysiliogogogh and the translation is even longer – 'St Mary's Church in a hollow of white hazel near to a rapid whirlpool and St Tysilio's Church near the red cave' The name is said to have been invented, in humorous reference to the burgeoning tourist trade, by a local man. Whether this is true or not, it has certainly done the trick, as many visitors stop by initially out of curiosity at the name.

The village, overlooking the Menai Strait, is where the Britannia Bridge crosses to the mainland. The **Marquess of Anglesey Column**, 91 feet high, looks out from here over to Snowdonia and the quite splendid views from the top of the column are available to anyone wishing to negotiate the spiral staircase of some 115 steps. The column was finished two years after the Battle of Waterloo, but the statue was not added until 1860, following the death of Henry Paget, Earl of Uxbridge and 1st Marquess of Anglesey, whom it commemorates. Paget fought alongside the Duke of Wellington at Waterloo where he lost a leg to one of the last shots of the battle.

•

The most famous building in Llanfair PG is undoubtedly its railway station - the often filmed station whose platform has the longest station sign and where the longest platform ticket in Britain was purchased. Today, visitors can see a replica of the Victorian ticket office, examine some rare miniature steam trains and wander around the numerous craft and souvenir shops that have sprung up here.

•

Plas Newydd is surrounded by gardens and parkland laid out in the 18th century by Humphry Repton. They command fabulous views over the Menai Strait and also contain a woodland walk, an Australasian arboretum and a formal Italian style garden terrace.

He lived to be 85, having twice been Lord-Lieutenant of Ireland after his military career (see also under Plas Newydd).

The last public toll house, designed by Thomas Telford when he was working on the London-Holyhead road in the 1820s, stands in the village. It still displays the tolls charged in 1895, the year the toll house closed.

ABERFFRAW

12½ miles W of Menai Bridge on the A4080

Though this was the capital of Gwynedd between the 7th and 13th centuries, there remains little trace of those times, although a Norman arch, set into St Beuno's Church, is said to be from the palace of the ruling princes. However, the **Llys Llywelyn Museum**, although modest, has exhibitions recounting the area's fascinating history.

Inland, the **Din Dryfol Burial Chamber** provides further evidence of Iron Age life on the island while, to the north of Aberffraw, on the cliff tops above Porth Trecastell, is the **Barclodiad y Gawres Burial Chamber** (CADW). Considered to be one of the finest of its kind, this burial chamber, along with Bryn Celli Ddu, contains some notable murals. To the west, **Llangwyran Church** occupies a dramatic setting on a small island, linked to the mainland by a narrow causeway. The single-cell church is believed to be 12th century in origin, with a north aisle added in the 1500s.

PLAS NEWYDD

2 miles SW of Menai Bridge off the A4080

Although it is now owned by the National Trust, **Plas Newydd** is still the home of the Marquesses of Anglesey, for the first of whom this splendid mansion was built in the late 1700s. The designers, James Wyatt and Joseph Potter, transformed a 16th century manor house into a flamboyantly Gothic building. Inside, there's a fine Gothic Hall with a fan-vaulted ceiling, a wealth of paintings - mostly family and royal portraits - and a gorgeously decorated Music Room. A former kitchen celebrates the work of Rex Whistler who was a regular visitor to the house. There's a dazzling example of his work in the Rex Whistler Room where a 58 feet long mural incorporates places such as Windsor Castle, Portmeirion and Snowdonia in an imaginary seascape seen from a promenade. Whistler included himself twice - once as a gondolier and again as a gardener. A nearby room houses the Cavalry Museum which contains the world's first prosthetic limb which was made for the 1st marquess who had his leg shot off during the Battle of Waterloo.

BRYNSIENCYN

5 miles SW of Menai Bridge on the A4080

Just to the west of the village is **Caer Leb**, an Iron Age earthwork consisting of a pentagonal enclosure 200 feet by 160 feet encircled by banks and ditches, while, just a short distance away is

Bodowyr Burial Chamber, a massive stone that is, seemingly, delicately perched upon three upright stones. To the south of the burial chamber, and just a mile west of Brynsiencyn, are the earthwork remains of **Castell Bryn Gwyn**, a site which has been excavated and shows traces of having been used from as far back as the New Stone Age through to the time of the Roman occupation of Britain.

Also overlooking the Menai Strait is the fascinating **Anglesey Sea Zoo**, an award-winning attraction that takes visitors beneath the waves and into the underwater world of a wide variety of sea creatures. The imaginative and innovative displays allow visitors a unique view of these interesting beasts, which include sea horses, oysters, conger eels and rays. Down the small road that leads to the shore is **Foel Farm Park**, a working farm with many attractions for all the family.

DWYRAN

8 miles SW of Menai Bridge off the A4080

Just outside the village lies **Bird World**, a popular family attraction set in extensive parkland with views over to the Snowdonia mountain range. Visitors can admire the wide variety of birds on display - more than 1000 of them from all over the world - and picnic in the beautiful surroundings of the lake. There's a Bird of Prey Centre and several ponds that are home to a large collection of waterfowl, swans, rheas and poultry. On site facilities include a refreshment room and, for the children, indoor and outdoor play areas.

NEWBOROUGH

9 miles SW of Menai Bridge on the A4080

Founded in 1303 by the former inhabitants of Llanfaes who had been moved here by Edward I, the village stands on the edge of a **National Nature Reserve** that covers 1566 acres of dunes, coast and forest. Among the many footpaths through the reserve, there are several forest trails that show how the Forestry Commission is constantly trying to stabilise the dunes. **Newborough Warren** is so called because, before myxomatosis, about 80,000 rabbits were trapped here annually. There is a route through the warren to **Abermenai Point**, but the way can be dangerous and advice concerning tidal conditions should be sought before considering the walk.

Llanddwyn Island is also accessible on foot but again tidal conditions should be carefully studied before setting out. Until the 1920s, marram grass, which has been grown for conservation purposes from Elizabethan times, was also a mainstay of the area, helping to sustain a cottage industry in the production of ropes, baskets, matting and thatching materials. A high embankment was built here in the 18th century by Thomas Telford as a defence against the sea which had previously almost cut the island into two.

•

Charles Tunnicliffe, the renowned wildlife artist, had a studio on Llanddwyn Island for more than 30 years. Anglesey Council has purchased a collection of his marvellous work which can be seen at the Oriel (Gallery) Ynys Môn in Llangefni. On the A4080 signposted from Newborough, Newborough Forest is a pine forest with rides, glades and miles of walks.

•

55 JWMPIN JAC'S CAFÉ BAR

Holyhead

Offering freshly prepared food and quality service, fantastic panoramic views of Holyhead Bay can be enjoyed.

 *see page 253*

56 BAR2TWO

Holyhead

An outstanding bar and restaurant, decorated to the highest standard and offering a wide selection of mouth-watering cuisine

 *see page 255*

57 SOUTH STACK KITCHEN

Holyhead

Close to the historic South Stack Lighthouse it is a place all visitors to this scenic island go.

 *see page 256*

HOLYHEAD

Holyhead Mountain (Mynydd Twr) rises to 720 feet behind this town, which is the largest on Anglesey and is itself on an island - Holy Island. A busy rail and ferry terminal, especially for travellers to and from Ireland, Holyhead has all the facilities needed to cater for visitors passing through, although it is also, despite being something of an industrial and commercial centre, a seaside resort. Parts of **St Cybi's Parish Church** date from the 14th to the 17th century and it is situated within the partially surviving walls of the small Roman fort, Caer Gybi (the source of Holyhead's name in Welsh) and on the site of a 6th century chapel. Close to the church is a smaller church, **Egylwys Bedd**, which reputedly contains the tomb of Seregri, an Irish warrior who was repelled by the Welsh chief, Caswallon Lawhir. The town's triumphal arches, built in 1821, commemorate George IV's visit here as well as the end of the A5, the major road from London.

The interesting **Canolfan Ucheldre Centre**, housed in a former convent chapel, is a complete arts centre for northwest Wales. Opened in 1991, it presents film, music and drama events as well as holding all manner of art and craft exhibitions and workshops.

A popular amenity just northwest of the town is **Breakwater Quarry Country Park** which incorporates Britain's largest breakwater. Designed by James Meadow and started in 1845, the structure took 28 years to build and shields an area of 667 acres. From the country park there are many walks along the coast, including a route to **South Stack**. This is a reserve of cliffs and heath teeming with birdlife such as puffins, guillemots and razorbills. The RSPB visitor centre is open daily, the café daily in summer, and the lighthouse is open daily in summer for guided tours. The lighthouse, one of the most impressive in Wales,

Holyhead War Memorial

was built in 1809 and stands on a beautiful but dangerous site reached by a steep stone stairway of more than 400 steps. Above the harbour and breakwater is a memorial in tribute to Captain Skinner who drowned when his packet boat, *Escape*, was lost in 1832. Holyhead's **Lifeboat Station**, winner of 70 awards down the years, can be visited on Sunday mornings, with crew training at 10am.

Between South Stack and North Stack lies **Gogarth Bay**, where the RSPB sea bird centre includes a cavern, known as Parliament House Cave, which is used by a profusion of sea birds such as puffins, guillemots and even falcons. Visitors here can also watch the thousands of cliff nesting birds via live television pictures and enjoy the bracing cliff top walks. **Ellin's Tower Seabird Centre** is another spot favoured by ornithologists with anything up to 3000 birds nesting in the cliffs. The tower was erected by William Stanley in memory of his wife. It was Stanley who did most of the excavation on the Neolithic hut circles, Cytiau'r Gwyddelod, just across the road from the Seabird Centre car park.

AROUND HOLYHEAD

VALLEY

3½ miles SE of Holyhead on the A5

Valley was thought to have gained its name while Thomas Telford was cutting his road through the small hill here. Centuries earlier this was the home of Iron Age man whose weapons and horse trappings found in the area are now on display in the National Museum of Wales.

Valley is perhaps better known today for the nearby airfield established here during World War II as a fighter pilot base. In 1943, the American Air Force expanded the base's capability for use as an Atlantic terminal and now the RAF uses it for training flights and for Air/Sea rescue.

RHOSNEIGR

7½ miles SE of Holyhead on the A4080

This small resort is situated in a quiet spot, close to the sandy beaches and rocky outcrops of **Cymyran Bay**. The beach is popular with wind surfers. The River Crigyll, which runs into the sea by the town, was the haunt in the 18th century of the 'Wreckers of Crigyll' who were famous for luring ships on to the rocks. After being caught and tried at Beaumaris in 1741, the group of desperate men were found guilty and hanged. They became the subject of a ballad, *The Hanging of the Thieves of Crigyll.*

The 1400 acres of gorse and dunes at **Tywyn Trewan Common** are a paradise for botanists and ornithologists.

RHOSCOLYN

4½ miles S of Holyhead off the B4545

With a wide sandy beach that is excellent for swimming and fishing, this scattered but pleasant village was once home to a thriving oyster

•

At the summit of Holyhead Mountain, from where, on a clear day, Snowdonia, the Isle of Man and the Mourne Mountains in Ireland can be seen, the remains of Caer y Twr, a hill fort, are visible. Close by is Cytiau'r Gwyddelod, a hut settlement from the 2nd century.

•

•

St Gwenfaen founded a church in Rhoscolyn in the 6th century and her Well, on Rhoscolyn Head, was said to have properties that cured, in particular, mental illness. The headland is a superb place for cliff walking and there are splendid views northwards over Trearddur Bay and, southwards, over Cymyran Bay. At Bwa Gwyn (White Arch) is a memorial to Tyger, a remarkable dog who, in 1817, led to safety the four-man crew from a sinking ketch. After dragging the cabin boy ashore and returning for the ship's captain, the dog collapsed and died from exhaustion.

•

58 THE LOBSTER POT

Church Bay

Offering the very best in hospitality and fine food the restaurant is extremely popular with locals and visitors.

see page 257

59 THE LIVERPOOL ARMS

Almwich Port

Keg ales and low price/high quality food served daily in a historic environment by the port.

see page 256

industry that is now, sadly, in decline. China clay was also once quarried here, while the local marble was used in the construction of Worcester, Bristol and Peterborough Cathedrals.

LLANFAIRYNGHORNWY

7 miles NE of Holyhead off the A5025

This village, on the approach to **Carmel Head**, has two claims to fame. It was here, in the 19th century, that Frances Williams founded the Anglesey Association for the Preservation of Life from Shipwreck. Along with her husband, who was the local rector, Frances raised funds for lifeboats on the island and through her efforts the first lifeboat station in the area was established.

Lying two miles offshore from the point at Carmel Head are **The Skerries**, a group of windswept islets whose Welsh name, Ynysoedd y Moelrhoniaid, means Island of Porpoises. On the islets stands the last **Lighthouse** to be privately owned - ships had to pay a toll as they passed. When braziers fuelled the light during the 18th century they burnt approximately 10 tons of coal a night! Now automated and owned by Trinity House, its beam is rated 4-million candles.

CEMAES

11 miles NE of Holyhead off the A5025

Boasting two glorious, safe, sandy beaches, **Cemaes Bay** is a popular place on the island that was also once a favourite with smugglers. The most northerly village in Wales, Cemaes is flanked by the elderly Wylfa Nuclear Power Station and a wind farm. Yet it remains picturesque with its small tidal harbour, wonderful walks and abundant wildlife.

The Visitor Centre at **Wylfa Nuclear Power Station** is the starting point for a guided tour of the station and also contains a mass of information about the nature trail surrounding the plant.

Ogof y March Glas - the cave of the blue horse - on Cemaes Bay was named after an incident that took place more than 200 years ago. Following a family dispute, a young man furiously galloped away from his house near the bay on his dappled grey horse. Blinded by rage, he galloped headlong over the cliff; only his hat was ever seen again, although the carcass of his horse was found washed up in the cave.

AMLWCH

14 miles NE of Holyhead on the A5025

South of this seaside town lies the pock-marked **Parys Mountain** which has provided copper for prospectors from as early as Roman times. In 1768 a copper boom helped make Anglesey the copper centre of the world but by 1820 the rush was over as prices fell and the mineral deposits became exhausted. Amlwch had fed off this wealth and swollen in size to become the second largest town in Wales. The harbour, which was built during those more prosperous times, is now used mainly by pleasure craft. In its heyday Amlwch had 6000 inhabitants and

1000 ale houses. The **Amlwch Industrial Heritage Centre** (free) tells the story of the town's rise and fall and distributes a free Heritage Trail leaflet. An oddity worth a look is the **Church of Our Lady Star of the Sea**. It was built of reinforced concrete in the 1930s and its strange design ("like a giant toast rack" according to one visitor) is supposed to represent an upturned boat - with portholes!

DULAS

15 miles NE of Holyhead off the A5025

A once thriving village, Dulas was, in the early 19th century, home to both a brickworks and a shipbuilding industry. Standing at the head of the Dulas River, which runs into the bay, the village overlooks **Ynys Dulas**, a small island which lies a mile or so offshore and is the haunt of grey seals. On the island itself is a 19th century tower built as a beacon and a refuge for sailors; the lady of Llysdulas manor house once had food left there for stranded mariners.

LLANERCHYMEDD

11 miles E of Holyhead on the B5112

To the north of the village lies **Llyn Alaw**, Anglesey's largest lake, well known for its fine trout fishing as well as the abundant wildlife found around its shores. Covering some 770 acres, the lake is actually man-made by the flooding of marshland. It supplies most of the island's industrial and domestic needs.

LLANDDEUSANT

6½ miles E of Holyhead off the A5025

Llanddeusant is home to Anglesey's only stone tower working windmill, built in 1775-76 at a total cost of £529.11s.0d. Four storeys high, with a boat-shaped cap, it ceased milling by wind power in 1924 but was restored and opened to the public in 1984. **Llynnon Mill** not only mills stone ground flour for sale (wind and conditions willing) but also has an attractive craft shop and a popular tea room.

Tradition has it that the green mound, **Bedd Branwen**, near the River Alaw, is the grave of Branwen, the heroine of the Welsh epic, *Mabinogion*. When the mound was excavated in 1813, it revealed a rough baked clay urn containing fragments of burnt bone and ashes. Since the discovery of more funeral urns in 1967, the site has become even more significant.

60 MINFFORDD SELF CATERING AND CARAVAN PARK

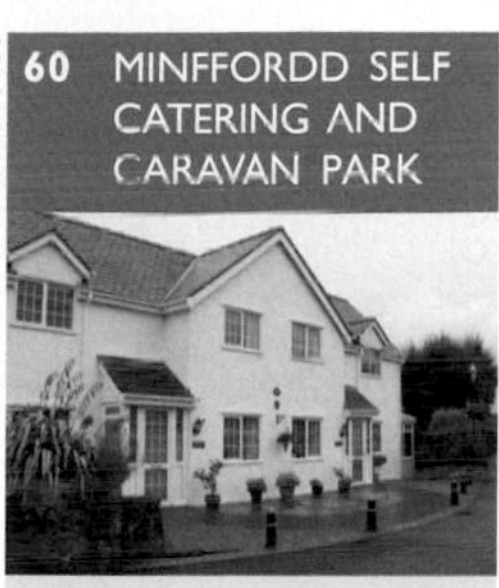

Dulas

Award winning caravan park and self catering cottages provide homely luxury in an area of outstanding natural beauty near the coast.

see *page 258*

61 DRWS Y COED

Llannnerch-y-Medd

A premier farmhouse bed and breakfast surrounded by hundreds of acres of scenic countryside.

see *page 258*

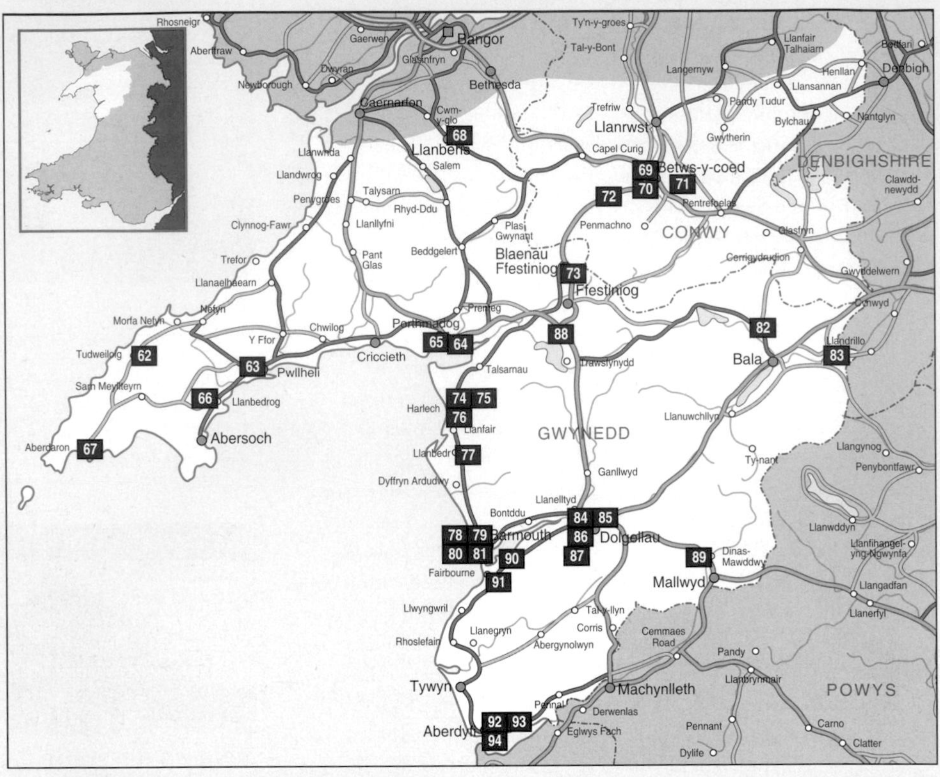

ACCOMMODATION

62	The Lion Hotel, Tudweiliog	pg 60, 259
63	Bay View Guest House, Pwllheli	pg 61, 260
67	Gwesty Ty Newydd Hotel, Aberdaron	pg 67, 263
69	The Gwydyr Hotel, Betws-y-Coed	pg 69, 264
70	Plas Derwen, Betws-y-Coed	pg 70, 265
71	The White Horse Inn, Capel Garmon	pg 70, 266
72	Plas Hall Manor, Pont-y-Pant	pg 71, 266
73	Queens Hotel, Blaenau Ffestiniog	pg 72, 267
75	The Lion Hotel, Harlech	pg 74, 269
77	The Victoria Inn, Llanbedr	pg 75, 271
78	Bryn Melyn Guest House, Barmouth	pg 76, 272
79	Crystal House Hotel, Barmouth	pg 76, 272
83	The Bryntirion Inn, Llandderfel, nr Bala	pg 78, 276
86	Royal Ship Hotel, Dolgellau	pg 80, 279
87	Gwesty Gwernan Hotel, Islawrdref	pg 80, 280
89	Y Llew Coch - The Red Lion, Dinas Mawddwy	pg 82, 281
90	Graig Wen Guest House, Arthog	pg 84, 282
91	Springfield Hotel, Fairbourne	pg 84, 282
92	Cartref Guest House, Aberdovey	pg 85, 283

FOOD & DRINK

62	The Lion Hotel, Tudweiliog, nr Pwllheli	pg 60, 259
66	Glyn Y Weddw Arms, Llanbedrog	pg 66, 262
68	The Peak Restaurant, Llanberis	pg 69, 263
70	Plas Derwen, Betws-y-Coed	pg 70, 265
71	The White Horse Inn, Capel Garmon	pg 70, 266
72	Plas Hall Manor, Pont-y-Pant	pg 71, 266
73	Queens Hotel, Blaenau Ffestiniog	pg 72, 267
74	The Castle Restaurant & Armoury Bar, Harlech	pg 74, 268
75	The Lion Hotel, Harlech	pg 74, 269
76	Cemlyn Tea Shop, Harlech	pg 75, 270
77	The Victoria Inn, Llanbedr	pg 75, 271
80	Goodies, Barmouth	pg 76, 273
81	The Anchor Restaurant & Knickerbockers Ice Cream Parlour, Barmouth	pg 77, 274
82	Hen Siop Frongoch, Frongoch	pg 78, 275
83	The Bryntirion Inn, Llandderfel	pg 78, 276
84	Unicorn Inn, Dolgellau	pg 79, 277
85	The Stag Inn, Dolgellau	pg 79, 278
86	Royal Ship Hotel, Dolgellau	pg 80, 279

Snowdonia Coast & Inland

To the south of Anglesey lies the Llyn (Lleyn) Peninsula, which forms the great curve of Caernarfon Bay. This is one of the most secluded and most beautiful parts of Wales with more than 100 miles of its shoreline designated Areas of Outstanding Natural Beauty. During the Middle Ages, Bardsey Island, lying off the western tip of the peninsula, was a place of pilgrimage, and the ancient route to Aberdaron, from where the pilgrims sailed to their destination, can still in parts be followed. Reminders of the area's early Christian past can be found throughout Llyn, along with more ancient monuments such as hill forts.

The attractive Victorian resorts along the southern shore of the peninsula are sheltered and provide plenty of scope for sailing, swimming and fishing. The birthplace of one of the country's greatest statesmen, David Lloyd George, is a popular place to visit, but the whole region is filled with splendid attractions to see and exciting things to do. Perhaps the most visited of all is the fantasy village of Portmeirion, built from the 1920s to the 1970s by Sir Clough Williams-Ellis.

There are three National Parks in Wales, and Snowdonia, at some 840 square miles, is the largest and certainly the most dramatic scenically. There are several routes up to the summit of Snowdon beginning at various points around its base. Some call for more energy than others, but the least arduous ascent is by the Snowdon Mountain Railway that runs from Llanberis. The most popular walk follows the railway. In and around nearby Betws-y-Coed, the walking is gentler and includes surviving tracts of the vast forests that once covered much of Wales. From the earliest times, this region was mined for its minerals. Gold was mined here long before the Romans arrived, and as recently as the 19th century there were mini-gold rushes in a belt that stretched from Bontddu along the line of the River Mawddach. Copper, lead and slate were also mined up until the start of the 20th century, and the scars left by those industries can still be seen today. Several of the mines have found new roles as visitor attractions, along with the little railways that once carried the minerals from the mines and quarries to the coast.

In the middle of the 19th century, the coastal villages and towns, many of them obscure, quiet fishing communities, were put on the map and changed radically in character with the arrival of the main railway network. As the fashion for sea air grew and communications were made easier, they became popular seaside resorts, and today many of them still retain Victorian and Edwardian buildings constructed to cater for holidaymakers. The scenery throughout the region is truly inspirational, and few would disagree with the verdict of the 19th century traveller and writer George Borrow:

"Perhaps in all the world there is no region more picturesquely beautiful."

PLACES OF INTEREST

62 THE LION HOTEL

Tudweiliog

This great family run establishment is at the historic heart of its village serving fine real ale, choice malt whiskies, home cooked food and quality guest accommodation throughout the year.

  see page 259

THE LLYN PENINSULA

DINAS DINLLE

3 miles S of Caernarfon off the A499

A seaside village at the mouth of the Menai Strait. With a shingle beach and cliffs overlooking Caernarfon Bay, there are many pleasant spots to picnic and enjoy the views down the Llyn Peninsula or across the bay to Anglesey. At the beach's northerly tip lies **Fort Belan**, which was built in the 18th century along with neighbouring **Fort Williamsburg**. It was constructed by the 1st Lord Newborough who felt concern over the threat of invasion by Napoleon; his lordship also raised and equipped his own private army, The Royal Caernarfonshire Grenadiers, which, by the time of his death in 1807, had cost him a quarter of his fortune.

LLANDWROG

4 miles S of Caernarfon off the A499

Llandwrog was built to serve the estate of Lord Newborough at Glynllifon Park, and memorials to the Newborough family may be seen in the mid-Victorian **St Tyrog's Church.**

CLYNNOG FAWR

10 miles SW of Caernarfon on the A499

This typical Llyn Peninsula village on the Heritage Coast is famous for its remarkably large and beautiful church - **St Beuno's** - which stands on the site of the chapel founded by the saint around AD 616. One of the sons of the royal family of Morgannwg, St Beuno had great influence in North Wales and he built his chapel on land which was presented to him by Cadwallon, King of Gwynedd. St Beuno's burial place and his shrine can be seen in this early 16th century building, which lies on the Pilgrims' Route to Bardsey Island. For many years, his tomb was thought to have curative powers.

Nearby is **St Beuno's Well**, whose waters were also thought to cure all manner of illness and conditions, especially if the sufferer had first visited the church. Close by, and virtually on the seafront, stands the capstone and three uprights of **Bachwen**, a neolithic burial chamber.

TREFOR

3½ miles SW of Clynnog Fawr off the A499

This coastal village is dominated by **Yr Eifl** (The Forks) which lies to the southwest and affords stunning views from its 1850 feet summit out over Caernarfon Bay to Anglesey and across the Llyn Peninsula. On the south-eastern slopes of the hill is **Tre'r Ceiri** (Town of Giants), one of the finest Iron Age forts in the country. A stone wall surrounds this once heavily populated circle of 150 huts.

NEFYN

9 miles SW of Clynnog Fawr on the A497

Once a herring fishing village, this resort was granted a charter in 1355, along with Pwllheli, by the

Black Prince. It was here in 1284 that Edward I celebrated his conquest over Wales. Housed in St Mary's church, whose tower supports a sailing ship weathervane, is the **Historical & Maritime Museum**, an excellent place to visit to find out more about this interesting and beautiful part of Wales.

PWLLHELI

Pwllheli is the chief town of the Llyn Peninsula and is often referred to as the 'Jewel' in the Welsh scenic crown. Like Nefyn, it was granted a charter in 1355; a gift by the Black Prince to Nigel de Loryng, who had helped the Prince win the Battle of Poitiers. A popular holiday resort with all the usual amusements, this is also still a market town - it is held each Wednesday. Pwllheli's once busy port, where wine was imported from the Continent, is now home to pleasure craft with a 420-berth marina and an annual sailing regatta. Boat trips are available during the summer to Bardsey Island.

As well as being an ancient town, Pwllheli has played its part in the more recent history of Wales. During the National Eisteddfod in 1925, three members of the Army of Welsh Home Rulers met with three members of the Welsh Movement at the town's Temperance Hotel and joined forces to form the political party, **Plaid Cymru**. The hotel, on the market square, is now a pet shop but a plaque commemorates the meeting. The **Lifeboat Station** at Pwllheli has an all-weather carriage-launched Mersey Class boast and an inshore D Class boat; it can be visited between 10 and 3 daily.

Just to the east of Pwllheli is **Hafan y Mor**, a family-oriented holiday resort, which also encourages day visitors to use its wealth of children's amusements. In complete contrast, just a mile inland from the resort is **Penarth Fawr**, an interesting 15th century manor house with an unusual aisle truss hall.

AROUND PWLLHELI

CHWILOG

1½ miles NE of Pwllheli on the B4354

Close to the village lies **Talhenbont Hall**, an early 17th century manor house that was once the home of William Vaughan. A place of history with its fair share

63 BAY VIEW GUEST HOUSE

Pwllheli

With fine views across the bay and in an ideal location for short breaks, Bay View Guest House makes you feel right at home with great Welsh hospitality.

see page 260

Blue Footbridge, Pwllheli

of ghosts, the hall was used, during the Civil War, as a garrison for Parliamentary soldiers.

LLANGYBI

5 miles NE of Pwllheli off the B4354

Just to the north of the village is **St Cybi's Well** and, behind it, the Iron Age fort of **Garn Pentyrch**. The well was established in the 6th century when St Cybi was in the process of setting up religious cells and a monastery in Holyhead. Sheltered by an unusual building with beehive vaulting which is thought to be unique in Wales, the well had a reputation for curing blindness and warts among many other ailments.

GOLAN

9 miles NE of Pwllheli on the A487

Between the entrances to two wonderful valleys, Cwm Pennant and Cwm Ystradllyn, and a mile off the A487 Porthmadog-Caernarfon road, is **Brynkir Woollen Mill**. Originally a corn mill, it was converted over 150 years ago for woollen cloth production. The waterwheel still turns although the River Henwy is used to generate electricity. Visitors can still see the various machines that are used in the production process: Tenterhook Willey, carders, spinning mules, doubling and hanking machines, cheese and bobbin winder, warping mill and looms. A wide variety of woollen products made at the mill can be bought. The mill is open Monday to Friday; admission is free, and there's ample parking.

Hen Bont - Golan

LLANYSTUMDWY

6½ miles E of Pwllheli on the A497

This peaceful little coastal village is best known as being the home of David Lloyd George, the Member of Parliament for Caernarfon for 55 years and the Prime Minister who, at the beginning of the 20th century, was responsible for social reform as well as seeing the country through the Armistice at the end of World War I. Lloyd George's childhood home, Highgate, is now just as it would have been when the great statesman lived here for the first 18 years of his life. It forms part of the **Lloyd George Museum** which also features a Victorian schoolroom and an exhibition recalling the life of this reforming Liberal politician. When he died in 1945, he won this tribute in Parliament from Winston Churchill: "As a man of action, resource and creative energy he stood, when at his zenith, without a rival. His name is a household word throughout our Commonwealth of Nations. He was the greatest Welshman which that unconquerable race has produced since the age of the Tudors. Much of his work abides, some of it will grow greatly in the future, and those who come after us will find the pillars of his life's toil upstanding, massive and indestructible." The museum is open from Easter to October, and at other times by appointment. David Lloyd George, 1st Earl Lloyd-George of Dwyfor, is buried on the banks of the Dwyfor river, in a tomb designed by Clough Williams-Ellis, architect of Portmeirion. Opposite his grave is a set of **Memorial Gates** presented to the village by Pwllheli in 1952. They feature an elephant and a castle - elephants are part of the town's coat of arms. Visitors to the **Rabbit Farm & Farm Park** at Dwyfor Ranch will meet rabbits of various breeds, along with Shetland ponies, lambs, goats and sheepdog puppies, and also enjoy a pony ride.

Criccieth Sea Front

CRICCIETH

8 miles E of Pwllheli on the A497

This small family resort lies near the northeast corner of Cardigan Bay and enjoys fine views down the Llyn coastline and northeastwards to Snowdonia. Unlike many of the other resorts on the peninsula, Criccieth is more reminiscent of a south coast seaside town rather than one set in North Wales.

An attractive Victorian town, Criccieth is dominated by **Criccieth Castle**, which stands on a rocky outcrop with commanding views over the sea. Built in the early 13th century by Llywelyn the Great as a stronghold of the native Welsh princes, it was captured in 1283 and extended by Edward I; but the core of the structure - the powerful twin towered gatehouse - still exists from the original fortification. Despite Edward's strengthening of the defences, in 1404 the castle was taken by Owain Glyndwr and put to the torch. The castle walls still bear the scorch marks.

TREMADOG

12 miles E of Pwllheli on the A487

This village, developed, like its close neighbour Porthmadog, by William Alexander Madocks, is a wonderful example of early 19th century town planning and contains many fine Regency buildings. Madocks, who was the MP for Boston in Lincolnshire, bought the land in 1798 and built Tremadog

•

One of the best preserved of the 13th century castles that litter the North Wales countryside, the romantic ruins of Criccieth Castle have inspired many artists down the centuries including JMW Turner, who used it as the backdrop for a famous painting of storm-wrecked sailors. The annual Criccieth Festival, held in the third week of June, is renowned for its showcasing of young local, national and international talent.

•

64 PORTMEIRION VILLAGE & GARDENS

Portmeirion

A fascinating village on a peninsula on the coast of Snowdonia, built to illustrate the fact that a beautiful place need not be spoiled by development.

see page 260

on the reclaimed land in classical style, with broad streets and a handsome market square with a backdrop of cliffs. He hoped that the town would be a key point on the intended main route from the south of England to Ireland, but his rivals in Parliament preferred the North Wales route, with Holyhead becoming the principal port for Ireland. The little town of Tremadog, with its well-planned streets and fine buildings, remains as a memorial to Madocks who died in Paris in 1828; he is buried in the Père Lachaise cemetery (see also Porthmadog). The soldier and author TE Lawrence (of Arabia) was born at Snowdon House - now a back-packers' hostel - in 1888 and the poet Shelley is known to have visited on several occasions.

PORTMEIRION

13½ miles E of Pwllheli off the A487

This extraordinary village in a wonderful setting on a wooded peninsula overlooking Traeth Bay was conceived and created by the Welsh architect Sir Clough Williams-Ellis between 1925 and 1972. An inveterate campaigner against the spoiling of Britain's landscape, he set out to illustrate that building in a beautiful location did not mean spoiling the environment. In looks, this is the least Welsh place in Wales: the 50 or so buildings, some of which consist only of a façade, were inspired by a visit Williams-Ellis made to Sorrento and Portofino in Italy and they are mainly either part of the hotel or pastel cottages. In the 1960s the village provided some exotic settings for the cult TV series, *The Prisoner*. Each year, devotees of that series gather at Portmeirion to act out their favourite scenes.

The **Portmeirion Pottery** was established in 1960 by Clough's

Portmeirion

daughter Susan Williams-Ellis and her husband Euan. Susan had studied under Henry Moore and Graham Sutherland, and her classic designs include Botanic Garden (1972) and the recently relaunched Totem from the 1960s. Williams-Ellis' ancestral home, **Plâs Brondanw**, lies some five miles away, up the A4085 northeast of **Garreg**, and the marvellous gardens here make the extra journey well worth while. They are designed to please the eye and also provide some fabulous views over the mountain scenery. Among the splendid plants are charming statues and elegant topiary terraces. Although less well known than the village and gardens at Portmeirion, the gardens at Brondanw are considered by some to be Clough Williams-Ellis' most important creation, and certainly the most beautiful. Sir Clough continued working up until his death at the age of 94 in 1978.

PORTHMADOG

12½ miles E of Pwllheli on the A487

Porthmadog enjoys a stunning setting with Moel y Gest rising almost 800ft as a backdrop and the wide expanse of the Glaslyn estuary stretching to the north and east. A bustling town with many family-run specialist shops and restaurants, and an open air market every Friday from Easter to Christmas, Porthmadog's attractions also include one of the rare cinemas in the area, the **Porthmadog Pottery** and the **Rob Piercy Gallery** featuring works by local artists.

The history of the town and its waterfront is described in the **Maritime Museum** where the importance of the trade in slate and Porthmadog's shipbuilding industry is also told.

Porthmadog is also home to both the recently extended **Welsh Highland Railway** (see also under Caernarfon) and the **Ffestiniog Railway**, the world's oldest narrow track passenger carrying railway. It winds its way up to 650ft to the slate mines at Blaenau Ffestiniog, a journey of some 13 miles passing through some stunning scenery. In the late 1800s, the slate mines were producing some 100,000 tons of slate, all of which was transported by the valiant little locomotives. Harbour Station, Porthmadog, is also home to Spooner's Bar, with its five CAMRA Local Pub of the Year Awards. **Black Rock Sands** southwest of town is one of the few beaches in Britain where you can step out of your car straight onto the sands, which stretch as far as the eye can see. The surrounding dunes are a Site of Special Scientific Interest and provide glorious views across the whole of Cardigan Bay.

LLANBEDROG

3½ miles SW of Pwllheli on the A499

This enchanting village boasts a fine beach and one of the oldest public art galleries in Wales, **Plas Glyn y Weddw**. In 1896, this imposing neo-Gothic mansion was bought by the Cardiff businessman Solomon Andrews who developed

65 FFESTINIOG AND WELSH HIGHLAND RAILWAYS

Porthmadog

Two spectacular narrow gauge steam railways running through the very heart of Snowdonia National Park

see page 261

•

Just over 200 years ago, there was nothing but marshland where Porthmadog now stands. Its transformation was the work of one man, William Madocks, who was also responsible for building neighbouring Tremadog. Member of Parliament for Boston in Lincolnshire and a great entrepreneur, Madocks drained the mud flats that made up the estuary to create land for grazing cattle. The embankment, built to keep the tides at bay, enclosed some 7000 acres of land and re-routed the River Glaslyn to produce a deep water channel that was ideal for the docks. Naming Porthmadog after himself (nearby Tremadog was named after his brother), he saw the beginning of the blossoming of the town in the 1820s.

•

Llanbedrog Church

it into a centre of the arts, complete with pleasure gardens. Inside, there's an astonishing hallway with galleries, an enormous stained glass window and an impressive hammer beam roof. The exhibitions combine items from the gallery's permanent collection with touring works, usually with a Welsh theme. Another attraction here is the delightful conservatory tea room overlooking the sea.

Down on the National Trust-owned beach, multi-coloured beach huts add to the appeal. From the beach, a steepish path leads to the summit of Myndd Tir-y-Cwmwd and some stunning views. Also surveying the vista is the **Iron Man**, a modern sculpture built locally and made of beachcombed material.

66 GLYN Y WEDDW ARMS

Llanbedrog nr Abersoch

A brilliant, homely country inn where locals and visitors alike flock to sample the culinary delights on offer from a wide range of tasty menus.

see page 262

ABERSOCH

6 miles SW of Pwllheli on the A499

A popular family resort with safe beaches, Abersoch lies on each side of the estuary of the River Soch. Its sheltered harbour attracts a wide variety of pleasure craft and it is the major dinghy sailing centre in Wales. Just off the coast lie **St Tudwal's Islands** - so called because the saint founded a religious cell there in the 6th century. Both islands are now privately owned and dedicated as bird sanctuaries.

The site of the 17th century mansion, Castellmarch, in Abersoch, was said to be the home of March Amheirchion, one of King Arthur's knights. Reputed to have the ears of a horse, March (the name is Welsh for horse) kept them hidden and killed anyone who saw them - burying the bodies in a nearby reed bed.

RHIW

11 miles SW of Pwllheli off the B4413

This hamlet lies on a miniature pass and overlooks **Porth Neigwl** (Hell's Mouth), a four mile sweep of beach so called because of its reputation for strong currents; it is a favourite spot for surfing.

Sheltered from strong gales by Mynydd Rhiw, **Plas yn Rhiw** is a small, part medieval, part Tudor, part Georgian manor house which was given to the National Trust in 1952 by the unconventional Keating sisters from Nottingham. The three spinsters, Eileen, Lorna and Honora, purchased the property in 1938 and lovingly restored it after the house had lain neglected for some 20 years. This they did with the help of their friend Sir Clough Williams-Ellis, the architect of Portmeirion.

The house is surrounded by glorious grounds which were also restored by the sisters and provide fabulous views over Porth Neigwl. Visitors can wander through ornamental gardens and, in the spring, the bluebell and snowdrop woodlands. At one time the poet RS Thomas lived in one of the estate cottages where he wrote some of his finest poetry.

ABERDARON

13½ miles SW of Pwllheli on the B4413

Aberdaron, the 'land's end' of the Peninsula, boasts the unusual distinction of being further from a railway station than anywhere else in England and Wales. This small and delightful village features in history books because of a treaty signed here in 1405. The Tripartite Indenture made Wales independent under the rule of Owain Glyndwr. The English later reneged on the deal.

A mile or so from the village lies **Castel Odo**, an Iron Age fort providing evidence that there have been five different occupations of the peninsula dating back to the 4th century BC.

UWCHMYNYDD

15 miles SW of Pwllheli off the B4413

Uwchmynydd stands on the wild and beautiful tip of the Llyn Peninsula, at the point where the first pilgrims set out to Bardsey Island in the Middle Ages. The National Trust is responsible for much of the land towards the tip of the Llyn Peninsula, including the ecologically outstanding coastal heath of **Braich-y-Pwll** where the ruins of St Mary's Church, once used by the pilgrims, can still be seen. This heath is the spring and summer home of a variety of plant life and birds, including fulmars, kittiwakes, cormorants, guillemots and the rare chough. A similar variety of birds populate the tiny islands of Dinas Fawr and Dinas Bach. Five miles east of

Aberdaron

•

Close to the sea in Aberdaron and originally dating from the 6th century, St Hywyn's Church is thought to have sheltered the 12th century Prince of Wales, Gryffydd ap Rhys, from marauding Saxons. During the Civil War, the church once again proved a place of sanctuary as Cromwell's soldiers also sought refuge here. The minister at St Hywyn's for many years was the celebrated poet RS Thomas (1913-2000). He wrote many inspired lines about his beloved country, summed up in this extract:

Every mountain and stream, every farm and little lane announces to the world that landscape is something different in Wales.

•

67 GWESTY TY NEWYDD

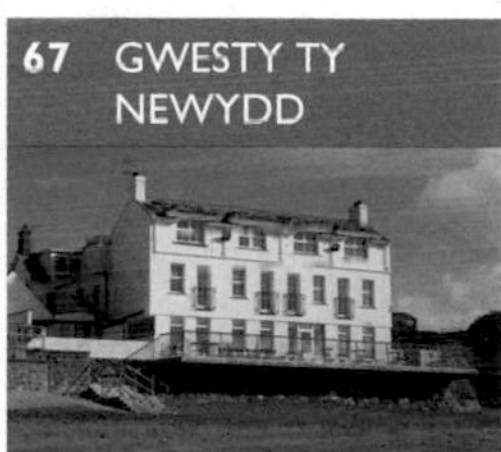

Aberdaron

A delightful hotel with breathtaking views, situated in a unique position on the seashore of Aberdaron.

see page 263

In the rugged setting of Snowdonia, where life has always been harsh, it comes as no surprise to find that it is said that the strongest woman ever to have lived came from Llanberis. Born in 1696, Marged Ifan died at the ripe old age of 105. At 70, it was said, she could outwrestle any man in Wales and could also catch as many foxes in one year as the local huntsmen in 10. After receiving many offers of marriage, Marged is said to have chosen the smallest and most effeminate of her suitors. Tradition has it that she only beat her husband twice: after the first beating he married her and after the second he became an ardent churchgoer!

Aberdaron, on the south side of the Peninsula, Porth Ysgo and Penarfyndd cover 245 acres of beaches and cliffs, while two miles northwest of the village **Mynydd Anelog** is an 116-acre area of ancient common land with the remains of prehistoric hut circles. Here, as in the other National Trust stretches of coastland on the Peninsula, is found our friend the chough, a relative of the crow with a distinctive red bill. Apart from here, this rare bird is usually found only in Pembrokeshire and on part of the western coast of Scotland. The curiously named **Porth Oer** (Whistling Sands), located off the B4417 by Methlem, is worth a visit as at certain stages of the tide the sands seem literally to whistle when walked upon. The noise is caused by the rubbing together of minute quartz granules.

BARDSEY ISLAND

17 miles SW of Pwllheli off the B4413

This wild, whale-shaped island in the Irish Sea has inspired many legends: one says that this is King Arthur's Avalon, another that his magician Merlin sleeps here in a glass castle. Settlement of the island is thought to have begun during the Dark Ages, although it was the death of St Dyfrig on Bardsey that saw the beginning of pilgrimages. At one time it was considered that three pilgrimages to this holy island was equivalent to one to Rome. Little remains of the 12th century monastery, and the island is now an important bird and field observatory. Bardsey is best known for its vast numbers of breeding shearwaters. The Bardsey Island Trust runs a boat from Pwllheli most days and if the weather is favourable also picks up from the hidden fishing cove of Porth Meudwy by Aberdaron.

The island's name is Norse in origin; the Welsh name, **Ynys Enlii**, means Island of Currents - a reference to the treacherous waters that separate Bardsey from the mainland.

LLANBERIS

Llanberis is effectively Base Camp for walkers preparing to tackle the 3560ft high bulk of **Snowdon**, the highest peak in Wales and the most climbed mountain in Britain. On a clear day, the view from the summit is fantastic, with Ireland sometimes visible. Many reach the summit the easy way, with the help of a 1-hour journey on the **Snowdon Mountain Railway**, Britain's only rack and pinion system which was built in 1896 and has carried millions to the top of the mountain over the years. It is not surprising that this mountainous and inhospitable area is also steeped in legend and mystery. The eagles of Snowdon have long been regarded as oracles of peace and war, triumph and disaster, and Snowdon's peak is said to be a cairn erected over the grave of a giant who was killed by King Arthur.

For those wanting another train ride or those who are content with a more sedate journey, the

Llanberis Lake Railway takes a short trip which reveals several different views of the mountain. The railway lies in **Padarn Country Park**, which gives access to 800 acres of Snowdonia's countryside and also includes Llyn (Lake) Padarn. By the side of the lake is Cwm Derwen Woodland and Wildlife Centre with a woodland discovery trail and a time walk exhibition with an audio-visual display. Here, too, is the **Welsh Slate Museum** (free) which tells the story of the slate industry through a variety of exhibitions, a restored slate-carrying incline, a terrace of quarrymen's cottages, audio-visual shows and demonstrations. The De Winton waterwheel is the second largest in Britain and once provided all the power for the mines.

Power on an even greater scale is to be experienced at **Dinorwig Power Station** where bus tours take visitors deep into the mountain to the tunnels and the machinery rooms that control the vast quantities of water of this major engineering project. In Europe's largest man-made cavern the world's most powerful hydro-electric generators are in action.

The **Pass of Llanberis** (along the A4086) is one of the most desolate stretches of road in Wales and is dominated by Snowdon to the south and the curiously shaped **Glyder Fawr's** 3279 feet to the north. Sheep graze beside the narrow road, which in some places is almost blocked by boulders and rocks.

Guarding the entrance to the Pass of Llanberis and overlooking Llyn Padarn are the substantial remains of **Dolbadarn Castle** (CADW; free) which was built by Llywelyn the Great. After the battle of Bryn Derwin, where Llywelyn defeated his two brothers, the victor held Owain ap Gryffydd prisoner here for some 22 years. The last stronghold of the independent princes of Gwynedd, it was from here in 1283 that Dafydd ap Gryffydd fled from the English forces of Edward I. It is a fact known to few that parts of the film *Carry On Up The Khyber* were shot in and around Llanberis.

AROUND LLANBERIS

BETWS-Y-COED

14½ miles E of Llanberis on the A5

A picturesque large village at the confluence of four beautiful forested valleys, Betws-y-Coed lies on the edge of the **Gwydyr Forest Park** as well as in the Snowdonia National Park. The Forest Park offers horse riding, canoeing, mountain biking and over 20 miles of trails through mountain forests. The stone walls in the Park were built by sailors after the defeat of the Spanish Armada to enclose game. The village first came to prominence with the setting up in 1844 of an artists' colony by David Cox and other eminent Victorian countryside painters. Their work inspired others, and the coming of the railway in 1868 brought the tourists to what soon became a busy holiday centre. The 14th

68 THE PEAK RESTAURANT

Llanberis

Host to inspirational chef Angela Dwyer and her signature dishes; this contemporary restaurant sits in the heart of Snowdonia.

see page 263

69 THE GWYDYR HOTEL

Betws-y-Coed

A beautiful and welcoming hotel, with over 12 miles of picturesque fishing rivers for guests to enjoy.

see page 264

70 PLAS DERWEN

Betws-y-coed

Serving the finest Welsh produce the Plas Derwen is a fantastic restaurant and café and offers some of the most elegant rooms in the area.

 *see page 265*

71 THE WHITE HORSE INN

Capel Garmon

Charming rural inn serving real ales and traditional dishes in an inviting family atmosphere in the heart of Snowdonia.

 *See page 266*

century **St Michael's Church**, the oldest building in the village near the railway station, remained the town's major place of worship until it was replaced by the **Parish Church of St Mary's** in 1873.

The village has two small museums. The **Motor Museum** houses a unique collection of vintage and post-vintage cars that includes a fabulous Bugatti Type 57. Next to the railway station is the **Conwy Valley Railway Museum** and shop, a popular place to visit in the summer

As the village is close to the point where the Conwy, Lledr and Llugwy rivers meet, it seems natural that these waterways should play an important role in the development, building and beauty of Betws-y-Coed. Thomas Telford's **Waterloo Bridge**, a marvellous iron construction built in 1815, gracefully spans the River Conwy, while the **Pont-y-Pair**, dating from around 1470, crosses the River Llugwy; further downstream, an iron suspension footbridge spans the river by the church. However, the main attractions that draw people to this area are the waterfalls: the spectacular multi-level **Swallow Falls** on the River Llugwy, Conwy Falls, Machno Falls and Fairy Glen Ravine. The village's most famous, and certainly most curious, attraction is **Ty Hyll**, the Ugly House, which stands close by the River Llugwy. Apparently this building, which looks as though it was literally thrown together from rough boulders, is an example of hurried assembly in order to obtain freehold on common land. The house was often used as an overnight stop by Irish drovers taking cattle to English markets.

The scenery around Betws-y-Coed is truly magnificent, and within minutes of leaving the town centre there are numerous well-marked walks lasting anything from an hour to all day and suiting all energy levels.

CAPEL GARMON

15½ miles E of Llanberis off the A5

Close by the village is the **Capel Garmon Burial Chamber**, which dates from around 1500 BC; the remains of a long barrow with three burial chambers, one with its capstone still in position, can be seen.

NANT PERIS

2 miles SE of Llanberis on the A4086

Once known as Old Llanberis, the village lies at the opposite end of Llyn Peris from its larger namesake and at the entrance to the Pass of Llanberis. The **Well of Peris**, which lies just north of the village centre, was, until relatively recently much visited for its healing powers, as well as for wishing. A successful request was said to be signalled by the appearance of a sacred fish.

DOLWYDDELAN

11 miles SE of Llanberis off the A470

Here can be seen the stark remains of **Dolwyddelan Castle** (CADW) which is unusual among Welsh castles in that it was constructed by a native Welsh prince rather than by the English or the Normans. It was built between 1210 and 1240 by Llywelyn the Great to control a strategic pass through the mountainous region of his kingdom. In 1488, the castle was acquired by Maredudd ap Levan who built the village church that now houses his kneeling brass effigy. After Maredudd's death the castle fell into ruin and the modern roof and battlements seen today were added in the 19th century when the core of the castle underwent restoration. However, the beauty of the castle is very much its lonely setting and from here there are stunning mountain views. A walk starting at Dolwyddelan provides a succession of glorious views over the surrounding mountains, particularly Snowdon and Moel Siabod. The last part of the walk is along paths and lanes and across meadows by the River Lledr.

Dolwyddelan Castle

PENTREFOELAS

19½ miles SE of Llanberis on the A5

Once an upland estate village, Pentrefoelas is now becoming a focal point for the continuation and revival of crafts and skills which were used to maintain the estate; among the attractions is a working **Watermill**.

PENMACHNO

14½ miles SE of Llanberis on the B4406

This delightful village of picturesque stone cottages set in a wooded valley lies on the River Machno, from which it takes its name. Surrounded by glorious countryside, Penmachno lies within an area that is a stronghold of Welsh culture.

To the northwest of the village centre and in the secluded Wybrnant valley lies **Ty Mawr Wybrnant (NT)**, the birthplace of Bishop William Morgan (1545-1604) who was the first person to translate the Bible into Welsh. Now restored to how it probably appeared in the 16th and 17th centuries, the house contains a display of Welsh Bibles, including Morgan's of 1588. A pleasant one-mile walk starts at the house and takes in woodland and the surrounding fields, and wooden animals to spot along the way.

To the northeast of the village and approached by a walk alongside the River Machno, is **Ty'n y Coed Uchaf**, a small farm that gives visitors an insight into the traditional way of life of the Welsh-speaking community in this

72 PLAS HALL MANOR

Dolwyddellan

A perfect country escape, set in four acres of grounds, alongside the River Lledyr, which its guests can enjoy fishing rights to.

see page 266

•

As well as having a main line train service, Blaenau Ffestiniog is the northern terminus of the narrow gauge Ffestiniog Railway, which runs through the vale to Porthmadog. Built to carry slate down to the sea for shipping off around the world, the railway has since been renovated by enthusiasts and volunteers. It now provides a comprehensive service giving passengers the chance to admire the scenery of the vale on their journey to the coast. There are many stopping off points so walkers can take advantage en route of Tan-y-Blwch Country Park and other beauty spots. See also under Porthmadog.

•

73 QUEENS HOTEL

Blaenau Ffestiniog

Newly refurbished to its finer glory, the Queens Hotel welcomes all to stay, drink or dine every day within easy reach of the area's best fishing spots.

see page 267

area. Closed as we went to press: call 01492 860123 for details.

FFESTINIOG

13½ miles SE of Llanberis on the A470

Situated above the Vale of Ffestiniog, there is a delightful walk, beginning at the village church, to **Cynfal Falls**, just below the village. Above the falls stands a rock, known locally as Pulpud Huw Llwyd, that recalls a local mystic who preached from here. Three miles to the northeast, **Gamallt** (NT) is a remote 300-acre moorland that supports a variety of plant life as well as water beetles, sandpipers, ring ousels, wheatears and meadow pipits. Archaeological remains include a large Iron Age settlement, and the important Roman road known as **Sarn Helen** crosses the property.

MAENTWROG

13½ miles SE of Llanberis on the A496

Lying in the Vale of Ffestiniog, this peaceful and attractive village is home to **Plas Tan-y-Bwlch**, where the 19th century terraced gardens provide glorious views of the surrounding area and picturesque walks through woodland. Here, too, among the magnificent trees and rhododendrons, is an oak wood that provides a small reminder of the vast oak forests that once covered much of Wales.

BLAENAU FFESTINIOG

12 miles SE of Llanberis on the A470

This was once the slate capital of the world and the industry still dominates the landscape and economy of this town and the surrounding area. Stretching across from the feet of Manod towards the Moelwyn Mountains, the legacy of the slate industry is visible everywhere - from the orderly piles of quarried slate waste to the buildings in the town.

At the foot of Manod Bach, beside the waterfall at Bethania, **Pant-yr-ynn Mill** is the oldest surviving slate mill of the Diffwys Casson Quarry. Built in 1846, it later saw service as a school before being converted into a woollen mill in 1881. It worked until 1964, when it was closed down and the machinery scrapped. The original part of the building has been preserved and the waterwheel restored; it is now home to an exhibition dealing with Blaenau - the town, the communities, the landscape and the changes to it made by the 20 quarries in the vicinity. The exhibition includes drawings and paintings by resident artist and industrial archaeologist Falcon D Hildred. **Llechwedd Slate Caverns** take visitors underground to explore the world of a Victorian slate miner and man-made caverns of cathedral proportions. The excavations took plave on six leveles and 25 miles of tunnels were carved out of the hillside. One tour includes a short ride on an underground tramway along a tunnel cut in 1846 to the enormous Cathedral Cave.

To the southwest of the town, at First Hydro's power station, is the **Ffestiniog Visitor Centre**, the ideal place to discover the wonders of hydro-electricity. Opened in 1963 by the Queen, the station consists of reservoirs and underwater passages constructed inside the mountains and the displays and exhibitions at the centre explain how the electrical power is generated and also the development of electricity over the years.

BEDDGELERT

7½ miles S of Llanberis on the A498

A winner of both National and European Village in Bloom titles, this attractive village is full of flowers in spring and summer. A conservation village, Beddgelert is surrounded by mountains, including the 2566 feet of **Moel Hebog**, and the whole setting is reminiscent of the Swiss Alps. An unlikely spot one might think for shipping to be an important industry. This was thanks to the River Glaslyn being navigable as far as Pont Aberglaslyn, the stone bridge at the narrowest point of the gorge. Shipping remained a major mainstay of life here until the Porthmadog embankment was constructed in the early 19th century.

The **Pass of Aberglaslyn**, through which the racing waters of the salmon river flow, lies to the south of the village; it is a delightful place with steeply wooded slopes and an abundance of rhododendrons.

The village's name translates as **'Gelert's Grave'** and refers to Prince Llywelyn ap Iowerth's faithful dog Gelert, which he left to guard his little son. When he returned, he found the dog covered in blood and the child nowhere to be seen. He concluded that Gelert had killed his son, so in his fury he killed the dog. Only then did he realise that his son was alive, saved by Gelert from a wolf, whose body lay nearby. It is said that Llewelyn never again smiled, and he buried Gelert with full honours. The reputed grave of Gelert is in a riverside meadow, just south of the village. The land around the grave was bought in 1987 with grants from the Countryside Commission and the Portmeirion Foundation in memory of Sir Clough Williams-Ellis. Beddgelert has another animal connection: **Alfred Bestall**, the original illustrator of Rupert Bear for 30 years from 1935, lived here for the latter part of his life. In his memory, the 'Followers of Rupert Bear' have funded the planting of a picnic meadow near the River Glaslyn.

To the northeast of the village,

Welsh Highland Railway, Beddgelert

74 THE CASTLE RESTAURANT AND ARMOURY BAR

Harlech

Overlooking the beautiful Harlech Castle this unusual restaurant serves up a mix of traditional welsh dishes and Caribbean cuisine for breakfast, lunch and dinner.

see page 268

75 THE LION HOTEL

Harlech

A great cosy, family run pub and bed and breakfast serving real ale and classic pub grub in the heart of Harlech.

see page 269

Harlech Castle

on the road to Capel Curig, lies the **Sygun Copper Mine**, which was abandoned in 1903. The former mine has now been reopened as a remarkable and impressive example of Welsh industrial heritage where visitors can see the maze of underground tunnels and chambers, the massive stalactites and stalagmites and the copper ore veins that also contain traces of gold and silver. Audio commentaries give details of each stage of the mining process, with lighting and sound effects.

Just a short distance further along this road is **Dinas Emrys**, a hill fort that is thought to be associated with the legendary 5th century battle between the two dragons - one red and one white - that was prophesied by the young Merlin. The lake nearby, **Llyn Dinas**, is also associated with the magician and legend claims that the true throne of Britain is in the lake and will only be revealed when a young person stands on a certain stone.

HARLECH

Harlech means Bold Rock and there is no doubting the fact as the town clings to the land at the foot of its spectacularly sited castle, now a World Heritage Site. Another of Edward I's Iron Ring of fortresses, which was begun in 1283, **Harlech Castle** (CADW) is perched on a rocky outcrop for added strength. The castle's situation, close to the sea, has not only proved a great defence but was also useful during its blockade by Madog and his men in 1294, when supplies transported in from Ireland enabled the 37 men inside to hold fast. If the use of power and strength to impress and intimidate an indigenous population was ever aided by architecture then Harlech is a prime example. Situated 200 feet above sea level, its concentric design, with lower outer walls, by the architect James of St George, used the natural defences of its site to emphasise its impregnability. However, in 1404 Owain Glyndwr managed to capture the castle and held it for five years while using the town of Harlech as his capital.

The song, *Men of Harlech*, has immortalised the siege during the War of the Roses when the castle was held for the Lancastrian side for seven years before it finally became the last stronghold to fall to the Yorkists in 1468. The last time Harlech saw action was 200 years later, during the Civil War, when it again withstood attack and was the last castle in Wales to fall to Cromwell's forces. The panoramic views from the castle's battlements take in both Tremadog Bay and the mountainous scenery behind the town.

Outside the castle stands the monumental equestrian **Statue of the Two Kings** representing Bendigeidfran, King of the British, and his nephew, Gwern, heir to the Irish throne who, along with his father, had been killed in battle. The statue, by Ivor Roberts, depicts a scene from *The Mabinogion*, a 14th /15th century cycle of Welsh and Irish legends.

Though not as imposing as the castle, **The Lasynys Fawr** is another building worth a visit while in Harlech. The home of Ellis Swynne (1671-1734), one of Wales' most famous prose writers, the house is an excellent example of one of its period – it dates from 1600. Some of the scenes in the early James Bond film *From Russia With Love* were shot in Harlech. The famous Royal St David's golf course is just outside the town.

Just outside Harlech, to the north, lies **Morfa Harlech**, a nature reserve with woodland trails that occupies the flat land between the town and Llanfihangel-y-Thaethau.

AROUND HARLECH

LLANFAIR

1½ miles S of Harlech on the A496

Between 1853 and 1906, Llanfair was a prosperous slate mining village and the old, deep quarries, the **Llanfair Slate Caverns**, in use until 1906, are now open to the public, who can don miner's helmets and set out on a self-guided tour. During the summer months, there's also a Children's Farm Park with cuddly rabbits, lambs and goats.

LLANBEDR

3 miles S of Harlech on the A496

This village is an excellent starting point for walks along the lovely valleys of the Rivers Artro and Nant-col and into the Rhinog Mountains. At 2,360 feet **Rhinog Fawr** may not be the highest local peak, but from its summit it commands superb views over the Coed y Brenin Forest to the Cambrian Mountains.

The parish **Church of St Peter** (Bedr is Welsh for 'Peter') is

76 CEMLYN TEA SHOP

Harlech

So much more than a tea shop with 28 varieties of tea, coffees, cakes and light lunches are all available here every single thing freshly made with local ingredients in support of fine Welsh suppliers – just taste the difference.

see page 270

77 THE VICTORIA INN

Llanbedr

A historical village inn serving high quality food, ale and guest accommodation all year round in an ideal location for exploring the best part of Wales.

see page 271

78 BRYN MELYN GUEST HOUSE

Barmouth

Located high up on the cliff side, looking down over Barmouth Bay, **Bryn Melyn Guest House** has eight superb en-suite guest rooms.

 see page 272

79 CRYSTAL HOUSE HOTEL

Barmouth

Overlooking the beach this beautiful Victorian bed and breakfast welcomes all to its spacious and inviting family orientated atmosphere.

 see page 272

80 GOODIES

Barmouth

A popular local cafe in the centre of Barmouth serving a wealth of tasty homemade cakes, pies, scones and mains seven days a week.

 see page 273

worth visiting to see the Llanbedr Stone which was brought down to the church from an Iron Age hut circle above the village. It has an unusual spiral decoration.

SHELL ISLAND

3½ miles S of Harlech off the A496

More correctly described as a peninsula that is cut off at high tide, Shell Island is a treasure trove of seashells and wildlife and the shoreline, a mixture of pebble beaches with rock pools and golden sands, is ideal for children to explore. Seals are often seen close by and there is plenty of birdlife; surprising considering the fairly regular aircraft activity from the nearby Llanbedr airfield.

DYFFRYN ARDUDWY

5 miles S of Harlech on the A496

Neolithic remains, as well as the remnants of Iron and Bronze Age settlements, abound in this area and in this village can be found two burial chambers. Perhaps the most interesting is **Arthur's Quoit**, the capstone of which is said to have been thrown from the summit of Moelfre by King Arthur.

BARMOUTH

9 miles S of Harlech on the A496

Occupying a picturesque location by the mouth of the River Mawddach, Barmouth was once a small port with an equally small shipbuilding industry. As the fashion for seeking out sea air grew in the 18th century, the character of Barmouth changed to accommodate visitors flocking here for the bracing sea air - those suffering from scurvy were even fed seaweed, which is rich in Vitamin C and grew in abundance in the estuary. Barmouth today is, like many other seaside resorts, a product of the railway age and the Victorian architecture is still very much apparent.

From the quay, passenger ferries leave for Fairbourne on the other side of the estuary whenever there are enough passengers, and sea angling and sightseeing boat trips are also available. Also on the quay is the **RNLI Lifeboat Museum** with an exhibition of lifesaving equipment. The Lifeboat Station , which has a Mersey Class boat and a D Class inshore boat, can be visited daily between 10 and 4. Nearby, **Ty Gwyn Museum** occupies one of the town's older buildings, dating from the 15th century. The house is now home to a Tudor dynasty exhibition and panels on various local shipwrecks. Ty Gwyn is said to have been built for Henry Tudor, Earl of Richmond, later Henry VII. It was in this house that Jasper Tudor, Henry's uncle, hatched the plot to overthrow Richard III. On the hill behind the museum is **Ty Crwn Roundhouse** which used to be the town's lock-up; it now houses a collection of old photographs of Barmouth.

In late June, the town's harbour is the starting point for the **Three Peaks Race**, a 2-3 day event in which competitors have to sail their monohull yachts to Caernarfon, the English Lake District and Fort

William in Scotland. At each point, they then have to run up the highest peak in each country. At the junction of the Quay and Church Street, **The Last Haul Sculpture** depicts three fishing generations hauling in a catch. The block of Carrara marble from which it is carved from has an unusual history. Back in 1709 a Genoese galleon with a cargo of the famous marble - the stone that Michelangelo had used - sank during a storm a few miles north of Barmouth. About 40 of the 2-ton blocks still lie on the bottom but in the 1980s one block was raised and then carved by local sculptor Frank Cocksey into this striking work of art.

Behind the harbour is **Dinas Oleu**, a small hill that was the first property given to the newly formed National Trust in 1895. It was a gift from the wealthy local philanthropist, Mrs Fanny Talbot, who was a friend of two of the Trust's founding members. **Panorama Walk** is a scenic walk created as a tourist attraction at the turn of the 19th century. There are several viewpoints along its route, the best being the one from the promontory at the end of the path. Built more than 125 years ago and half a mile in length, the **Railway Viaduct** that spans the river mouth has a walkway on the bridge from where there are magnificent views of the town, coast and estuary.

BONTDDU

9 miles SE of Harlech on the A496

Looking at this pleasant village it is hard to imagine that just over a century ago. it was a bustling centre of the Welsh gold mining industry. Apparently, there were 24 mines operating in the area around this village and it was one of these mines that provided the gold for royal wedding rings.

BALA

This agreeable town is a good stopping off point when exploring Snowdonia National Park. Roman and Norman remains have been found here, but the modern town was founded around 1310 by Roger de Mortimer, who was looking to tame the rebellious Penllyn district. The town was by Tudor times a small, and by all accounts not very successful, market town. It later became an important centre for the knitted stocking industry that flourished in the 18th century before the

81 THE ANCHOR RESTAURANT & KNICKERBOCKERS ICE CREAM PARLOUR

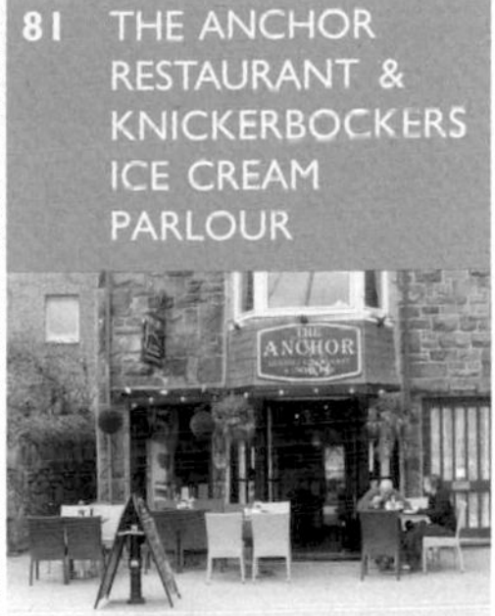

Barmouth

A traditional pub serving fine home cooked meals goes arm in arm here with an impressive ice cream parlour with over 50 flavours – sat right on the quay.

see page 274

Aran Ridge, Bala

82 HEN SIOP FRONGOCH

Frongoch

The embodiment of Welsh hospitality and fine home-cooking, it is no surprise how popular it is with locals and visitors alike.

Ymgorfforiad o'r Croeso Cymreig a choginio cartref graenus,nid yw'n ddim syndod mor boblogaidd yw gyda'r ardalwyr a'r ymwelwyr fel ei gilydd.

see page 275

83 THE BRYNTIRION INN

Llandderfel

Llandderfel's fine village inn has cosy guest accommodation, real ale and an ever changing menu of fine cuisine to suit every taste to reflect the best in seasonal and local produce.

see page 276

inventions and factory systems of the Industrial Revolution put paid to this established cottage industry. Today, though tourism is certainly an important part of the town's economy, it has remained a central meeting point and a market place for the surrounding farming communities. In recent years it has also become a major centre for water sports.

However, it is perhaps as a religious centre that Bala is better remembered. The **Reverend Thomas Charles**, one of the founders of the Methodist movement in Wales in the 18th century, first visited Bala in 1778 and moved here in 1783 after marrying a local girl. Working for the Methodist denomination, Charles saw the great need for Welsh Bibles and other religious books. He joined forces with a printer from Chester to produce a series of books and pamphlets. The story of Mary Jones, who walked some 25 miles from Llanfihangel-y-Pennant to buy a bible from Charles was the inspiration for the foundation of the Bible Society. Notable sons of Bala include Thomas Edward Ellis, a Liberal Member of Parliament who worked hard for Welsh home rule, and Owen Morgan Edwards, who was a leading light in the Welsh educational system. There are statues to both these worthies in Bala. The son of Owen Morgan Edwards, Sir Ifan ab Owen Edwards, established the Welsh Youth Movement, which has a camp at Bala Lake. To the southwest of the town, **Llyn Tegid (Bala Lake)** is the largest natural lake in Wales and feeder of the River Dee. Four miles long, nearly three quarters of a mile wide and up to 150 feet deep, the lake is a popular centre for all manner of watersports. It is also the home of Tegi, the Welsh version of Scotland's Nessie. Formed during the Ice Age, the Lake is an important site ecologically and has been designated a Site of Special Scientific Interest and a Ramsar site (Wetlands of International Importance). Many uncommon wetland plants flourish on its banks, and the birdlife includes coots, mallards, pochards, widgeons and great crested grebes. The fish life is interesting, too, and Bala is the only lake in Wales which is home to the gwyniad, a white-scaled member of the herring family that feeds on plankton in the depths of the lake.

Along the eastern bank of the lake runs the narrow gauge **Bala Lake Railway**, which provides the perfect opportunity to catch a glimpse of the Tegi.

AROUND BALA

FRONGOCH

2 miles N of Bala on the A4212

Just to the west of the village lies the reservoir **Llyn Celyn** on whose banks is a memorial stone to a group of local Quakers who emigrated to America to escape persecution. The modern chapel close by, **Chapel Celyn**, was built as a reminder of the rural hamlet which was drowned when the reservoir was created in the 1960s. Overlooking Llyn Celyn is **Arenig Fawr**, which has, on its 2800 feet summit, a memorial to the crew of a Flying Fortress that crashed here in 1943.

After the Easter Uprising of 1916 in Ireland, a former German prisoner of war camp near Frongoch was used to hold 1600 Irish prisoners, among them Michael Collins. It earned the nickname of the 'Sinn Fein University' because impromptu lessons on guerilla tactics were given to some of the prisoners. When Lloyd George came to power later that year he closed the camp down.

LLANUWCHLLYN

4 miles S of Bala on the A494

This small village at the southern end of Bala Lake is the terminus of the **Bala Lake Railway** which follows the lake for four miles with various stops where passengers can alight and enjoy a picnic or a walk. Spreading up from the eastern banks of the lake is the **Penllyn Forest**, which can be reached and passed through via **Cwm Hirnant** on an unclassified road that weaves through the forest to moorland and eventually reaches **Llyn Efyrnwy** (**Lake Vyrnwy**).

Llanuwchllyn has long been a stronghold of Welsh tradition, and has statues of two eminent Welshmen, Sir Owen Morgan Edwards and his son Sir Ifan ab Owen Edwards, both closely involved in preserving Welsh language and culture.

DOLGELLAU

Meaning 'meadow of the hazels', Dolgellau is the chief market town

Dolgellau Bridge

84 UNICORN INN

Dolgellau

This olde worlde inn offers friendly, traditional service with real ales and great home cooked pub favourites.

see page 277

85 THE STAG INN

Dolgellau

A fantastic welcome accompanies a fascinating history and good old pub grub at this popular traditional pub in central Dolgellau.

see page 278

86 ROYAL SHIP HOTEL

Dolgellau

An attractive ivy clad façade conceals 23 excellently furnished rooms and an atmospheric bar and restaurant serving up a vast variety of award winning menus.

 see page 279

87 GWESTY GWERNAN HOTEL

Islawrdref

A fine family run hotel set in picturesque grounds with its own well stocked fishing lake, superb restaurant and bar lounge with roaring log fire to relax in front of.

  see page 280

for this southern area of Snowdonia and used to be the county town of Merionethshire. Its grey stone buildings are pleasantly situated beside the River Wnion, with Cadair Idris rising in background. The town is very Welsh in custom, language and location, all very evident when the outlying farmers come to town on market day.

Owain Glyndwr held a Welsh parliament here in 1404, later signing an alliance with France's Charles VI. Now, the town's narrow streets can barely evoke those distant times and few early buildings remain. One of the oldest buildings is the seven-arched bridge over the river which dates from the early 1600s. The **Church of St Mary** has a magnificent roof supported by unusual wooden pillars from trees dragged over the pass of Bwlch Oerddws from the forests of Dinas Mawddwy. One of the treasures is an effigy of a 14th century knight, Meurig Ab Ynvr Fychan, while outside in the churchyard is a monument to the Welsh poet Dafydd Ionawr (1751-1827).

Before much of Dolgellau was built in an attempt to lure Victorian holidaymakers to the delights of Cadair Idris, there was a small rural Quaker community here. The **Quaker Heritage Centre** in Eldon Square tells the story of this community and also of the persecution that led them to emigrate to Pennsylvania. Also in Eldon Square, in one of the town's grandest buildings, is Ty Siamas, the **National Centre for Welsh Folk Music**. Opened in 2007, it is named after Elis Sian Siamas, a renowned Welsh harpist, who allegedly served for some years as the harpist to the court of Queen Anne. It stages a year-round programme of musical events and also has interactive exhibitions, meeting facilities, a shop, café and bar. Call 01341 421800 or see website www.tysiamas.com for more details. Rising to some 2927 feet to the southwest of Dolgellau, **Cader Idris** dominates the local scenery and on a clear day a climb to the summit is rewarded with views that take in the Isle of Man and the Irish coast as well as, closer to home, the Mawddach estuary. Much of the area around the mountain was designated a national nature reserve in 1957. The name Cader Idris means 'chair of Idris' after the great poet and warrior. An old legend asserts that anyone who sleeps on the mountain summit will wake up either mad, or blind, or with the ability to write great poetry.

AROUND DOLGELLAU

LLANELLTYD

2 miles N of Dolgellau on the A470

This is the point at which the Rivers Wen and Wnion, boosted by other waters further upland, meet to form the Mawddach estuary. Close by, just across the River Wen, stand the serene ruins of **Cymer Abbey** (CADW; free), which was founded by Cistercian monks in 1198. This white-robed order was established in the late 11th century in Burgundy and they arrived in Britain in 1128 to seek out remote places where they could lead their austere lives. Cymer was one of two Cistercian abbeys created in the Snowdonia region during the Middle Ages - the other is Conwy Abbey - and Cymer held substantial lands in this area. Despite their holdings, the abbey was poor and it also suffered badly during the fighting between England and Wales. In fact, by the time of the Dissolution in 1536 the abbey's income was just £51. Visitors to the site can see the remaining parts of the church, refectory and chapter house set in particularly picturesque surroundings.

LLANFACHRAETH

3 miles N of Dolgellau off the A470

Near the village is **Nannau Hall**, the ancient seat of the Vaughan family, who owned much of the land in this area. It is said that an earlier house on the site belonged to Howel Sele, a cousin of Owain Glyndwr. During a dispute with Glyndwr over Sele's Lancastrian sympathies, the latter shot at but missed his cousin while out hunting. Glyndwr was so enraged that he killed Sele and hid his body in a hollow oak. This hiding place was later to receive a mention in Sir Walter Scott's *Marmion* as "the spirit's blasted tree".

GANLLWYD

5 miles N of Dolgellau on the A470

This hamlet gives its name to the attractive valley in which it is found and which is, in turn, surrounded by the **Coed y Brenin Forest Park**, an area of some 9000 acres around the valleys of the Rivers Mawddach, Eden, Gain and Wen. Originally part of the Nannau Estate, founded by Cadougan, Prince of Powys, in 1100, the forest was acquired by the Forestry Commission in 1922, when extensive planting of conifers took place. Ganllwyd was once a centre for gold mining and, during the 1880s, the nearby mine at Gwynfynydd was prosperous enough to attract some 250 miners. The mine had produced around 40,000 ounces of gold by the time it closed in 1917; it re-opened from 1981 to 1989. The mine is on the route of one of the four waymarked trails, which also takes in waterfalls, forest nature trails and an old copper works. Orienteering is a good way to explore the park, which also offers some of the best mountain biking in the UK. Bikes can be hired at the Visitor Centre, which has a café, shop and exhibitions. There are also riverside picnic sites and a children's adventure play area.

Broadleaved woodlands once covered the land and some of these woodlands still survive at the National Trust's **Dolmelynllyn** estate. On the slopes of Y Garn, a path through this expanse of heath and oak woodland leads to **Rhaeadr Ddu** (the **Black Waterfall**), one of the most spectacular waterfalls in Wales. Also in the heart of the forest are a series of hundreds of steps, known as the **Roman Steps**, which climb

88 BRYN ARMS

Gellilydan

In the idyllic hamlet of Gellilydan sits this great family run pub, which offers local brews, good food and great facilities throughout the year.

 see page 281

89 Y LLEW COCH – THE RED LION

Dinas Mawddwy

Mother and son team welcome you to their historic and lively pub offering homemade food, real ale and fine guest accommodation in the heart of Dinas Mawddwy.

 see page 281

up through the rocks and heather of the wild Rhinog Mountains. In spite of their name they are certainly not Roman; they are thought to have been part of a late medieval trade route between the coastal region around Harlech and England.

TRAWSFYNYDD

10 miles N of Dolgellau off the A470

To the west of the village lies **Llyn Trawsfynydd**, a man-made lake developed in the 1930s as part of a hydro-electric scheme. On its northern shore stands the now defunct **Trawsfynydd Nuclear Power Station** which opened in 1965 and was the country's first inland nuclear station, using the lake for cooling purposes.

Down a minor road close to the power station are the remains of a small Roman amphitheatre that also served as a fort.

ARDUDWY

In the village centre is a statue in honour of Hedd Wynn, a poet and shepherd who was awarded the bardic chair at the 1917 Eisteddfod six weeks after he had been killed in Flanders.

DINAS MAWDDWY

8½ miles E of Dolgellau on the A470

During the Middle Ages, this now quiet village was a centre of local power but the only surviving building from those days is a packhorse bridge, **Pont Minllyn**. A gateway to the upper Dyfi valley, it was once alive with quarries and mines but all that today's visitors can see of past industry is the traditional weaving of cloth at **Meirion Mill** which is known as the 'Mill in the Mountains'. There is also a visitor centre, café and a shop stocking a wide range of beautifully designed craftware and clothing, including a tremendous selection of woollen items, Portmeirion Pottery and Welsh Royal Crystal.

MALLWYD

9 miles SE of Dolgellau on the A470

This small village's inn, **The Brigand**, recalls the days during the 16th century when this area was menaced by a gang known as the Red Robbers of Mawddwy. Eighty gang members were finally caught and executed in 1554 but the survivors exacted revenge by murdering their prosecutor, Baron Lewis Owen, at the nearby town of Llidiart-y-Barwn.

CORRIS

6 miles S of Dolgellau on the A487

This small former slate-mining village, surrounded by the tree-covered slopes of the Cambrian Mountains, was home to the first narrow-gauge railway in Wales. It was constructed in 1859 as a horse drawn railway, then steam locomotives were introduced in 1878 and passenger service began in 1883. After finally closing in 1948, the Corris Railway Society opened a **Railway Museum** that explains the railway's history and also the special relationship with the slate quarries through displays, exhibits and photographs.

Industry of a different kind can be found at the **Corris Craft Centre**, which is home to a variety of working craftsmen and women. An excellent place to find a unique gift, the craft centre is also home to the fascinating **King Arthur's Labyrinth** - a maze of underground tunnels where visitors are taken by boat to see the spectacular caverns and relive tales of the legendary King Arthur.

The legend of King Arthur is first told in **The Mabinogion**, a collection of stories which evolved over 1000 years. Passed from generation to generation from the 4th century onwards, they were not written down in a surviving manuscript form until the 13th century. The *White Book of Rhydderch* and the *Red Book of Hergest* between them contain 11 stories, five of which centre round the exploits of King Arthur and his contemporaries. In these tales we meet Gwenhwyfar (Guinevere), Cei (Sir Kay), Bedwyr (Sir Bedivere), Myrddin (Merlin) and Gwalchmei (Sir Gawain). In the *History of the Britons*, written by the Welsh cleric Nennius around AD 830, we first read of Arthur's battles, some at least of which took place in Wales, from about AD 515 onwards. The last great battle, against his nephew Mawdred and his Saxon allies, marked the end of a phase of Celtic resistance to the Saxons; this battle has been dated to AD 537 and is located by some historians on the Llyn Peninsula. In Welsh tradition Merlin and the great bard Taliesin took the dying King Arthur to the

Corris

magical Isle of Avalon, which recent research has identified as Bardsey Island, where St Cadfan established a monastery and where 1000 Welsh saints are buried. The caverns of King Arthur's Labyrinth are the workings of the Braich Goch Slate Mine, which was operational between 1836 and 1970. At its peak, the mine employed 250 men and produced 7000 tons of roofing slate annually. Just south of Corris, at Pontperthog, the **Centre for Alternative Technology** is one of Europe's leading Eco centres. Seven acres of interactive displays demonstrate the power of wind, water and the sun, and the buildings manifest the latest in eco-friendly materials and design. A visit begins with a ride up the sheer 180ft hillside on a unique water-balanced railway from which there are dramatic views of Snowdonia.

TAL-Y-LLYN

5 miles S of Dolgellau on the B4405

This tiny hamlet lies at the southwestern end of the **Tal-y-llyn**

90 GRAIG WEN GUESTHOUSE

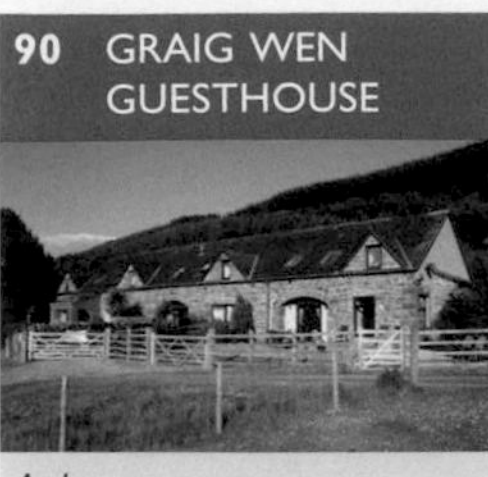

Arthog

Stylish B&B, campsite and self-catering cottages nestled in the heart of Snowdonia National Park overlooking the estuary.

 see page 282

91 SPRINGFIELD HOTEL

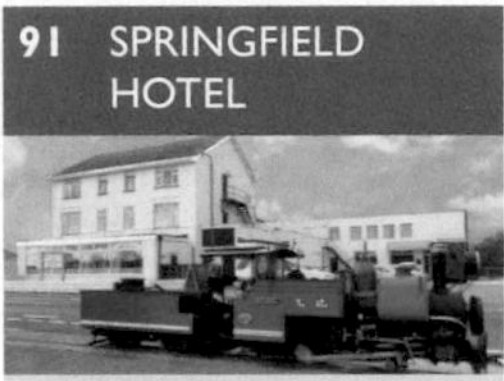

Fairbourne

A great family run hotel with bar, restaurant and great entertainment just minutes from the mountains and seconds from the sea.

  see page 282

Lake, which is overshadowed by the crags of Cadair Idris to the north. The lake is a great favourite with trout fishermen. In the village itself, the 15th century **Church of St Mary's** has an unusual chancel arch painted with alternating red and white roses and studded with some fanciful bosses.

LLANFIHANGEL-Y-PENNANT

7 miles SW of Dolgellau off the B4405

Just to the northeast of this small hamlet lie the ruins of **Mary Jones's Cottage**. After saving for six years for a Welsh Bible in the early 1800s, Mary Jones, the daughter of a weaver, walked to Bala to purchase a copy from Thomas Charles. As Charles had no copies of the Bible available, he gave her his own copy and the episode inspired the founding of the Bible Society. Mary lived to a ripe old age (88 years) and was buried at Bryncrug, while her Bible is preserved in the Society's headquarters in London.

Close by stand the ruins of **Castell y Bere** (CADW), a hill top fortress begun by Llywelyn the Great in 1223. Taken by the Earl of Pembrokeshire on behalf of Edward I in 1283, the castle stayed in English hands for two years before being retaken by the Welsh and destroyed.

ARTHOG

6 miles SW of Dolgellau on the A493

Overlooking the Mawddach estuary, this elongated village is a starting point for walks into Cadair Idris. Beginning with a sheltered woodland path, the trail climbs up to the two **Cregennan Lakes** from where there are glorious mountain views. The lakes are fed by streams running off the mountains and they have created a valuable wetland habitat that is now in the care of the National Trust. Down by the river mouth, there is an **RSPB Nature Reserve** protecting the wealth of birdlife and wildlife found here.

FAIRBOURNE

8 miles SW of Dolgellau off the A493

This small holiday resort lies on the opposite side of the Mawddach estuary from Barmouth and was developed in the late 1800s as a country estate for the chairman of McDougall's flour company. From the ferry that carries passengers across the river mouth, runs the **Fairbourne Railway**. Originally a horse-drawn tramway, now steam-hauled, this 12¼ inch gauge railway runs from Fairbourne to the mouth of the Mawddach estuary. Its midway halt was given an invented name that outdoes the 59 letters of LlanfairPG by eight. Translated from the Welsh, it means "Mawddach Station with its dragon's teeth on North Penrhyn Drive by the golden sands of Cardigan Bay". The dragon's teeth are anything but mystical: they are concrete tank traps left over from the Second World War.

LLWYNGWRIL

10 miles S of Dolgellau on the A493

The village is named after the giant

Gwril, who was supreme in this part of the coast. A 'llwyn' is a bush or grove in Welsh, so the name means Gwril's grove. A mile south of the village is the wonderful medieval **Church of St Celynin** at Llangelynin, more than 600 years old and largely unrestored. Its treasures include wall texts, a rare set of pews named after local families and the grave of Abram Wood, King of the Welsh gypsies.

TYWYN

14 miles SW of Dolgellau on the A493

This coastal town and seaside resort on Cardigan Bay has long sandy beaches, dunes and a promenade, as well as being the start (or the end) of the famous **Talyllyn Railway** which, from 1866 to 1946, was used to haul slate from the inland quarries. The line stretches 7 miles inland and passes at a maximum speed of 15 mph through the lovely wooded Talyllyn Valley. This area inland from Tywyn is also wonderful walking country. The way-marked walks include the new **National Trail** that runs between Machynlleth, Welshpool and Knighton. One of the stations on the Talyllyn line is Dolgoch, from which a walk takes in three sets of magnificent waterfalls. Four walks of varying lengths and difficulty start at Nant Gwernol station and provide an opportunity to enjoy the lovely woodlands and to look at the remains of Bryn Eglwys quarry and the tramway that served it.

ABERDOVEY (ABERDYFI)

16 miles SW of Dolgellau on the A493

This resort at the mouth of the River Dovey (or Dyfi) was once one of the most important ports along the Welsh coast. Shipbuilding flourished here alongside the busy port, whose records show on one particular occasion having 180 ships unloading or waiting for a berth. The town has been attracting holiday-makers since Edwardian times. Today Aberdovey has the highest proportion of holiday homes on this coast and also some of the highest prices. It is a gentle, civilised spot, with all the best attributes of a seaside resort and none of the kiss-me-quick tat of many larger places. Aberdovey has given its name to a Victorian ballad called *The Bells of Aberdovey*, recounting the legend that the sea drowned a great kingdom here and how on quiet summer evenings the bells can be heard ringing out from beneath the waves.

92 CARTREF GUEST HOUSE

Aberdovey

A stunning 100 year old bed and breakfast, combining period features with contemporary 21st century styling in a relaxed environment.

see page 283

93 MEDINA COFFEE HOUSE

Aberdovey

Much more than a coffee house, serving tapas, cakes and desserts, breakfasts and light lunches with a beautifully sun kissed hidden courtyard to the rear.

see page 284

94 MONTY'S CARVERY

Aberdovey

A gem of traditional home cooking serving up a classic carvery and other wholesome traditional dishes each night from 6pm, with convenient guest accommodation above.

see page 285

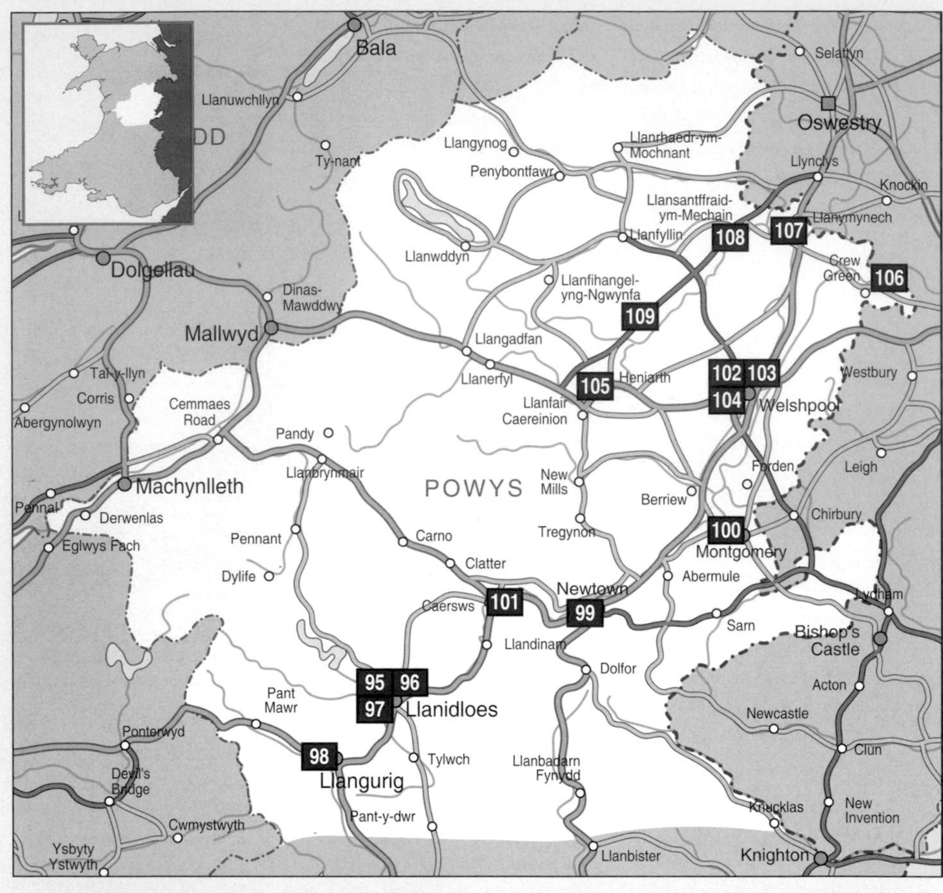

ACCOMMODATION

FOOD & DRINK

PLACES OF INTEREST

North Powys

Once part of the old county of Montgomeryshire, this northern region of Powys is an area of varied landscape and small towns and villages. Situated between the high, rugged landscape of Snowdonia and the farmland of Shropshire, this is a gentle and pleasant region through which many rivers and streams flow. As well as being home to the highest waterfall outside Scotland, Pistyll Rhaeadr, one of the Seven Wonders of Wales, the region has another landmark in Lake Vyrnwy. Built in the 1880s to supply the expanding city of Liverpool with water, this large reservoir is a splendid feat of Victorian engineering that later found fame as a location for the film *The Dambusters*.

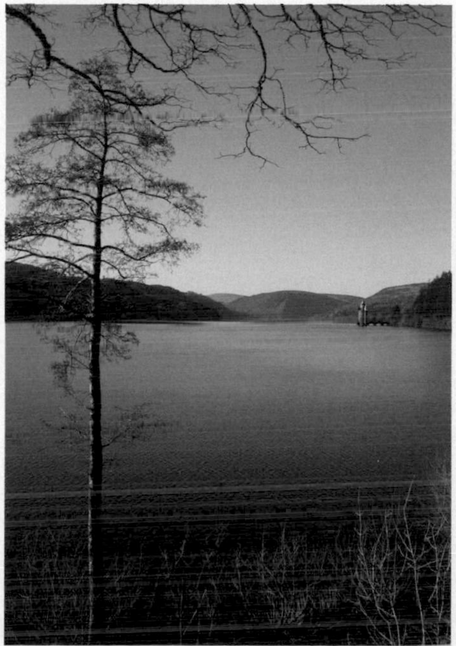

Lake Vyrnwy

The major settlement here is Welshpool, a town situated on the banks of the River Severn close to the English border. Originally known as Pool, the prefix was added to ensure that the dispute regarding its nationality was finalised once and for all. From the town leisurely canal boat trips can be taken along the Montgomery Canal but there is also a narrow gauge steam railway running westwards to Llanfair Caereinion. Near the town stands the splendid Powis Castle, which is famous for the many treasures it houses and also for its magnificent gardens.

Montgomery has a splendidly situated ruined borderland castle and is also close to some of the best preserved sections of Offa's Dyke. Nearby Newtown, which despite its name was founded in the 10th century, is another interesting and historic market town where the famous High Street newsagents, WH Smith, had its first shop. The associated museum tells of the company's growth from its humble beginnings in 1792. Also in Newport is the Robert Owen Memorial Museum commemorating the social reformer and founder of the Co-operative movement.

To the west and beyond the quaint town of Llanidloes lies Machynlleth, the home of Owain Glyndwr's parliament in the 15th century. A visit to the Welsh hero's centre, which is found in the part 15th century parliament house, tells the story of Glyndwr and his struggle against the English.

North Powys is great walking country that takes in some of the finest scenery in Wales. The many marked established trails and walks include a large part of Offa's Dyke Path and Glyndwr's Way, a 123-mile walk that follows a circular route across dramatic landscapes from Welshpool to Knighton by way of Machynlleth.

MACHYNLLETH

This small town is a popular but not overcrowded holiday centre in the shadow of the Cambrian Mountains. It was here that Owain Glyndwr held one of his parliaments in around 1404. On the site today, stands **Parliament House**, a part 15th century building, which contains an exhibition about this legendary hero. Revered as the last native prince of Wales, Glyndwr's aims were independence for Wales, a church independent of Canterbury and the establishing of a Welsh university. After being refused redress when Lord Grey of Ruthin seized some of his land, he laid waste the English settlements in northeast Wales and spent the next few years in skirmishes. He established other parliaments in Dolgellau and Harlech, and sought alliances with the Scots, the Irish and the French. He resisted many assaults by Henry IV's armies, but eventually Henry V seized Aberystwyth and Harlech. Glyndwr soon disappeared from the scene, dying, it is thought, at the home of his daughter Anne Scudamore. It was while presiding over the parliament that Owain was nearly killed by his brother-in-law Dafyd Gam. The plot failed, and Dafyd was captured. He was granted a pardon by Owain and later fought at the Battle of Agincourt.

Clock Tower, Machynlleth

Opposite the house is the entrance to **Plas Machynlleth**, an elegant mansion built in 1653 for the Marquess of Londonderry. In the 1840s, in order to improve his views, his descendant bought up the surrounding lands, had the houses demolished and re-routed the main road away from his mansion. This space is now filled with attractive gardens open to the public and was given to the town by Lord Londonderry.

At the centre of the town is an ornate **Clock Tower** dating from 1872 which was built by public subscription to mark the coming of age of Lord Castlereagh, heir to the Marquess of Londonderry.

Machynlleth's Tabernacle Chapel is now the **Museum of Modern Art, Wales** with six different exhibition spaces, including a constantly changing exhibition featuring leading artists from Wales. The complex also contains a 350-seat auditorium ideal for chamber and choral music, drama, lectures and conferences. Every year in late August, the auditorium is the focal point for the week-long **Machynlleth Festival.**

AROUND MACHYNLLETH

CARNO

10 miles E of Machynlleth on the A470

The dress and interior designer **Laura Ashley**, who was born in Wales, and her husband moved to Machynlleth in 1963 and later settled at Carno, which became the site of the headquarters of the Laura Ashley empire. It was in the churchyard of St John the Baptist, close to the factory, that she was buried after her death due to a fall in 1985. In the hills of Trannon Moor, with access from the A470 at the northern end of Carno village, is the **National Wind Power's Centre for Alternative Technology**, a former slate quarry containing dozens of turbines that generate enough electricity to meet the needs of many thousand homes.

LLANBRYNMAIR

8½ miles E of Machynlleth on the B4518

Set on the banks of the River Twymyn, this village was the birthplace of **Abraham Rees** who published an edition of *Ephraim Chambers Cyclopedia* between 1778 and 1788 after having added more than 4500 new pieces of information.

DYLIFE

8½ miles SE of Machynlleth off the B4518

Apart from an inn and a few houses, there is little left of this once prosperous lead mining community which provided employment for some 2000 workers in the mid-1900s. A footpath from the settlement passes close to a grassy mound which was once a Roman fort, built, it is believed, to guard the nearby lead mines. The path continues past more redundant lead mines that were last worked during the late 17th century before it meanders through a woodland, following the banks of River Clywedog, and on towards Staylittle. The final part of the route lies close to Bronze Age tumuli which suggest that mining occurred in the area even before the Roman occupation.

Close to the village is **Glaslyn Nature Reserve**, a 540-acre tract of heather moorland that is the breeding site for the wheatear, golden plover, ring ousel and red grouse.

STAYLITTLE

11 miles SE of Machynlleth off the B4518

A one-time lead mining village, Staylittle is said to have derived its name from the village's two blacksmiths who shoed horses so rapidly that their forge became known as Stay-a-Little. Situated in a remote area high in the

•

In the former village hall of Llanbrynmair is Machinations, a museum of mechanical magic devoted to automota - figures driven by clockwork, electricity, wind or turned by hand. The collection is housed in an open plan café and each model is operated by a token. The models are fascinating and it's possible to take courses on constructing, painting and carving them.

•

95 THE RED LION HOTEL

Llanidloes

Traditional town centre hotel serving honest-to-goodness pub grub and real ales with a games room and en suite rooms for all the family.

 see page 286

96 THE ROYAL HEAD

Llanidloes

Combining period features with modern styling, this atmospheric inn serves great pub grub and real ale with bed and breakfast accommodation.

 see page 287

97 THE GREAT OAK CAFÉ

Llanidloes

Popular vegetarian whole food, fair-trade café with great homemade food and friendly service.

 see page 288

Cambrian Mountains, Staylittle is on the edge of the **Hafren Forest**, which has several waymarked trails through the forest, along the banks of the upper River Severn and up to Plynlimon, which rises to 2500 feet.

LLANIDLOES

16½ miles SE of Machynlleth on the A470

One of the great little market towns and the first town on the River Severn, Llanidloes is an attractive and friendly place with lots of small, family-run shops of character, including Laura Ashley's first fashion shop and a vintage fashion shop. The town is also home to more than a dozen art and craft outlets, including three sculptors, a jeweller working in crystal, and four painters of stained glass windows. There are also four galleries and the **Minerva Arts Centre** which is the home of the Quilt Association and displays a unique collection of antique Welsh quilts.

In front of the town's picturesque black-and-white **Market Hall**, which dates from circa 1612 and stands on wooden stilts is a stone on which John Wesley stood while preaching here three times in the mid-1700s. The upper floors of the building now house the **Llanidloes Museum**, where there are displays and information on the textile and mining industries that thrived in the area during the 18th and 19th centuries. There is also a natural history exhibition and a red kite centre.

In 1839, the town was a focal point of the bitter **Chartist Riots** after the Reform Bill of 1832 had failed to meet demands that included universal suffrage and social equality. Cheap labour, cheap wool and efficient new machinery had led to a boom in the wool and

Market Hall, Llanidloes

flannel trade in Llanidloes, as in Newtown, Machynlleth and Welshpool. Workmen flooded in, and in 1858 the population was more than 4000. But the boom did not last, the factories closed, and unemployment inevitably ensued. Chartist propaganda reached the town and the Llanidloes unions adopted the Charter. The crowds started to gather and to arm, the police moved in, the Chartist leaders were arrested then released by the crowd, the magistrates fled. The Chartists then ruled for a few days: mills were re-opened and the prices of goods fixed. Then the Montgomeryshire Yeomanry came on the scene, 32 arrests were made and the Chartist ringleaders put on trial at Welshpool. Three were transported, the rest served terms of hard labour.

The Severn Way and Glyndwr's Way cross in Llanidloes, and an interesting waymarked 5-mile walk covers sections of each. To the northwest of the town lies **Llyn Clywedog**, a reservoir that developed in the mid-1960s to regulate the flows of the Rivers Severn and Clywedog. Roads go around both sides of the lake, with the B4518 curving round the slopes of the 1580 foot Fan Hill where the chimneys of the now disused **Van Lead Mine** are still visible. It was once one of the most prosperous mines in this area of Wales, producing 6850 tons of lead in 1876. The deserted houses and chapels of the village that grew up around the mine add a sombre, evocative note.

NEWTOWN

The name has not been appropriate for centuries since Newtown's origins date from around AD 973. But the town only came to prominence after being granted a market charter by Edward I in 1279. This was a centre for textiles and weaving and by the 19th century, Newtown was the home of the Welsh flannel industry that led it to be referred to as the 'Leeds of Wales'. Some of the brick buildings were built with a third or even fourth storey with large windows to let in light for the looms. **Newtown Textile Museum** is a typical example of an early 19th century weaving shop. It consists of six back-to-back cottages on the ground and first floors, and two rooms on the second and third floors running the whole length of the building. The displays include a re-created weaver's cottage and working area from the 1830s.

The museum gives a very good impression of the working conditions of the people which Newtown's most famous son, Robert Owen, devoted much of his life to changing. Born in Newtown in 1771, Owen grew from a humble background to become a social reformer and the founder of the co-operative movement who lobbied vigorously for an improvement in the working conditions specifically within the textile industry. He is particularly associated with the New Lanark mills in Scotland which he ran and

98 THE BLUE BELL INN

Llangurig, nr Llanidloes

A friendly village inn offering a warm welcome and great home cooked food

see page 289

99 ROBERT OWEN MUSEUM

Newtown

Museum dedicated to one of the most successful mill owners of the industrial revolution and a pioneer for social reform.

see page 288

•

Two miles east of Newtown is Pwll Penarth Nature Reserve, a feeding and nesting site for many species of wildfowl. The reserve has a nature walk and two hides, one accessible to wheelchairs.

•

partly owned. The workforce at New Lanark numbered 2000, including 500 children, and Owen provided good housing, cheap goods and the first infants' school in Britain. His remarkable life is told at the intimate **Robert Owen Memorial Museum** (free) which occupies the house where he was born in 1771. Following his death at Newtown in 1858, Owen was buried by the river in the churchyard of St Mary's. His monument depicts the man with his workers and is surrounded by magnificent Art Nouveau iron railings,

Another interesting visit to consider while in Newtown is to the **WH Smith Museum**, where the shop has been restored to its original 1927 layout and devotes much of its space to the history of the booksellers from 1792 onwards. Tel: 01686 626280.

The people of Newtown must certainly be an enterprising lot as it was here that the first ever mail order company was begun in 1859 by a man called Pryce-Jones. The business started in a small way with Welsh flannel but expanded rapidly, and Pryce-Jones even obtained the Royal seal of approval by having Queen Victoria on his list. Sadly, his successors were not as enterprising and the business was sold in 1935. The huge warehouse it used to occupy is now a lacklustre shopping centre, the **Royal Welsh Warehouse.**

W H Smith Museum, Newtown

AROUND NEWTOWN

LLANFAIR CAEREINION

9 miles N of Newtown on the B4385

This village is the western terminus of the **Welshpool and Llanfair Railway**. Passengers at Llanfair can enjoy reliving the days of steam and also relax in the Edwardian style tea rooms at the station. The narrow-gauge railway was originally opened to carry sheep, cattle and goods as well as passengers. It now travels, without the animals and the goods but with happy passengers, along the delightful Banwy Valley, its carriages pulled by scaled-down versions of steam locomotives from Finland, Austria, Sierra Leone, Antigua and Manchester. The railway is one of the nine members of the narrow-gauge **Great Little Trains of Wales** group. The others are: Bala Lake Railway, Brecon Mountain Railway *(Merthyr Tydfil);* Ffestiniog Railway *(Porthmadog);* Llanberis Lake Railway; Rheilfford Eryri *(Caernarfon);* Talyllin Railway *(Tywyn);* Vale of Rheidol Railway

(Aberystwyth); and the Welsh Highland Railway.

MONTGOMERY

7 miles NE of Newtown on the B4385

An attractive market town with a pleasant Georgian character, and also some surviving Tudor and Jacobean buildings that are worthy of note. Above the town, the ruins of **Montgomery Castle** stand in affirmation of this borderland region's turbulent history. The first castle was built in around 1100 by the Norman, Roger de Montgomery. Stormed over the years by rebels, it was rebuilt in 1223 as a garrison as Henry III attempted to quell the Welsh, a consequence being that the town received a charter from the king in 1227. During the Civil War, the castle surrendered to Parliamentary forces but was demolished in 1649 in punishment for the then Lord Herbert's Royalist sympathies. The remains of the castle are open at all times and entrance is free; access is up a steep path from the town or by a level footpath from the car park. The visit is worth it for the views alone. A well-preserved section of **Offa's Dyke** passes close by and is another reminder of the military significance that this area once held.

Housed in a quaint 16th century inn, the **Old Bell Museum** in Arthur Street has 11 rooms of local history including features on civic and social life, Norman and medieval castles, the workhouse and the Cambrian Railway.

Montgomery Castle

The 13th century **St Nicholas' Church** has some interesting features, including wooden carved angels, carved miserere seats and the magnificent canopied tomb of Richard Herbert, Lord of Montgomery Castle. In the churchyard is the famous Robber's Grave: John Davis, hanged in public in 1821 for murder, proclaimed his innocence and swore that the grass would not grow above his grave for at least 100 years!

To the west of the town the Iron Age hill fort **Fridd Faldwyn** tops a 750-feet hill that also provides stunning views to Cadair Idris and eastwards into England.

BERRIEW

7½ miles NE of Newtown on the B4390

Over the years, this picturesque village of black and white half-timbered houses beside the River Rhiw has been a frequent winner of Best Kept Village awards.

Like a number of other places

100 MONTGOMERY WILDLIFE TRUST

Montgomery

Wildlife Trust dedicated to preserving wildlife habitats and protecting endangered species.

see page 288

in Wales, Berriew is associated with St Beuno who apparently heard English voices while communing by the river and warned the villagers of the imposing threat. A large glacial boulder here has been named Maen Beuno after him. Berriew's **Church of St Beuno** contains fine marble effigies of Arthur Price, Sheriff of Montgomeryshire in 1578, and his two wives, Bridget and Jane. The memorial cross of 1933 in the churchyard is by Sir Ninian Comper, whose work can be seen in churches all over Britain.

Close to the bridge, the **Andrew Logan Museum of Sculpture** celebrates the art of popular poetry and metropolitan glamour. Logan's inventive use of whatever was to hand and the flamboyant results make this possibly the most cheerful museum anywhere. It contains examples of Andrew Logan's sculpture, mirrored portraits, watercolours, photgraphs and jewellery from the mid-sixties to the present day. Logan achieved some notoriety in the 1970s as the instigator of the Alternative Miss World Contest which introduced the world to the infamous drag queen, Divine. A 'Divine Shrine' is dedicated to her memory and the Alternative Miss World Crown is also on display. Tel: 01686 640689 for opening times.

A mile outside the town, the gardens at **Glansevern Hall**, entered from the A483 by the bridge over the River Rhiew, were first laid out in 1801 and now cover 18 acres. Noted in particular for the unusual tree species, they also have lovely lawns, herbaceous beds, a walled garden, rose gardens, a lovely water garden and a rock garden complete with grotto. In the Old Stables are a tea room, a garden shop and a gallery with regular exhibitions of paintings, sculpture and interior design. A wide variety of herbaceous plants, all grown at Glansevern, can be bought. Surrounding a very handsome Greek Revival house, the gardens are themselves set in parkland on the banks of the River Severn. Built for Arthur Davies Owen, Glansevern was the seat of the Owen family from 1800 until after the Second World War.

CHURCH STOKE

10½ miles E of Newtown on the A489

This attractive village lies right on the Welsh-English border; just to the west can be found some very visible and well preserved sections of Offa's Dyke. At Bacheldre, two miles along the A489, **Bacheldre Mill** is a fully restored watermill producing award-winning organic stoneground flour. Visitors can enjoy a guided tour and even mill their own flour.

ABERMULE

4 miles NE of Newtown on the B4386

Across the Montgomery Canal and River Severn from this village, which is also known by its Welsh name Abermiwl, lie the scant remains of **Dolforwyn Castle**, which was built in 1273 by Llywelyn the Last (he was the last native ruler of Wales). This was the last castle to have been built by a native Welsh prince on his own soil. Llywelyn also tried to establish a small town around the castle to rival that of nearby, and much anglicised, Welshpool. However, the castle was only a Welsh stronghold for four years before it was taken by the English and left to decay into the haunting ruins of today.

River Severn, Abermule

KERRY

2½ miles SE of Newtown on the A489

Situated on the banks of the River Mule, a tributary of the River Severn, this village lies in the heart of sheep rearing country and has given its name to the **Kerry Hills Breed of Sheep** characterised by distinctive black spots on their faces and legs. Small, hornless and usually white apart from the markings, the Kerry Hills have very dense fleeces that are particularly suitable for dyeing in pastel shades for knitting yarns. This breed is one of several variants on the Welsh Mountain Sheep; others include Black Welsh Mountain, Badger-faced Welsh Mountain, Beulah Speckle Face, Lleyn and Llanwenog.

The village church in Kerry has a chained Welsh Bible of 1690. There was, in former times, a custom at the church that the sexton would 'patrol' the congregation during services and would ring a bell if he found anyone asleep.

LLANDINAM

5½ miles SW of Newtown on the A470

This quiet village with its black and white half-timbered houses was the home of **David Davies**, an industrialist who was instrumental in founding the docks at Barry in South Wales. Davies' bronze statue, made by the same Sir Alfred Gilbert who was responsible for Eros in Piccadilly, stands in the village.

CAERSWS

4 miles W of Newtown on the A470

The village is built on the site of a 1st century Roman fort that was strategically positioned here by the Rivers Severn and Carno. To the north, the remains of an earthwork fort can still be seen. In more recent times, Caersws was the home for some 20 years of the poet **John 'Ceiriog' Hughes**, who was then the manager of the local Van Railway. Born at Llan Dyffryn

101 THE RED LION

Caersws

A great, traditional family run inn, with log fires and a warm welcome to match; a true ale lover's paradise.

see page 290

102 RAVEN INN

Welshpool

Serving top quality, fresh food made to order the Raven Inn is situated next door to one of Welshpool's most popular attractions – the Llanfair light railway.

 see page 291

103 REVELLS

Welshpool

A beautifully restored art deco cinema offering dishes made from the finest, locally sourced produce.

 see page 292

Ceiriog in 1833, he took employment on the railways in Manchester when he was 17. In 1865 he became stationmaster at Llanidloes and six years later took over at Caersws, managing the six-mile railway that ran to the Van lead mines. It is said that many people came to Caersws just for the delight of having a chat to the affable poet. Hughes lies buried in the graveyard at the nearby village of Llanwnog. Near Caersws, signposted off the A470 Machynlleth road, **Llyn Mawr Reserve** is a 20-acre lake with wetland habitat noted for wetland birds such as the great crested grebe, tufted duck, snipe and curlew.

WELSHPOOL

This bustling market town, which was granted a charter in 1263 by the Prince of Powys, was for a long time known as Pool - the Welsh prefix was added in 1835 to settle the long running dispute concerning its nationality as it is so close to the border with England. As is typical with many places in the upper Severn Valley, Welshpool has numerous examples of half-timbered buildings among its other interesting architectural features.

Housed in a former warehouse beside the Montgomery Canal is the **Powysland Museum** which was founded in 1874 by Morris Jones. Earlier, many of the artefacts that formed the museum's original collection had been put together by the Powysland Club - a group of Victorian gentlemen who were interested in the history of mid-Wales. The museum covers various aspects of the region: the development of life in Montgomeryshire from the earliest times to the 20th century; local agriculture and farming equipment; and the building of the first canals and railways in the area. There are also some remains from Strata Marcella, the Cistercian abbey founded around 1170 by Owain Cyfeiliog, Prince of Powys; the abbey was all but destroyed during the Reformation.

Along with the museum, the old warehouse is also home to the **Montgomery Canal Centre** where the story of this waterway is told. Completed in 1821, the canal carried coal and food from Welshpool to the upper reaches of the River Severn. Though, as with other canals, its decline came with the arrival of the railways, the section of the canal around Welshpool is once again open, now for pleasure cruises.

Welshpool is home to two

Canal Bridge, Welshpool

Canal Wharf, Welshpool

interesting buildings, the **Cockpit** and **Grace Evans' Cottage**. The only surviving cockpit on its original site in Wales, this venue for the bloodthirsty sport was built in the 18th century and remained in use until the sport was banned in Britain in 1849. Grace Evans is certainly one of the town's best known citizens as she was instrumental in rescuing Lord Nithsdale (who was in disguise as a lady) from the Tower of London in 1716. As Lady Nithsdale's maid, Grace fled with the couple to France but she returned to Welshpool in 1735 and lived at the cottage, which is said to have been given to her by a grateful Lord Nithsdale

From the town, the narrow gauge **Welshpool and Llanfair Railway** takes passengers on an 8-mile steam train journey through the Powis estates and the delightful Banwy valley to the quiet village of Llanfair Caereinion. Welshpool's original railway station, an impressive listed building, has been ingeniously converted into a shopping centre and restaurant.

Just to the southwest of the town lies one of the best known places in the area - the magnificent **Powis Castle** (National Trust) Originally built by the Welsh princes, it later became the home of Edward Clive, son of Clive of India. One of the Clive family's legacies is the superb display of Indian treasures on display in the **Clive Museum**. The castle is renowned for its collections of paintings and furniture. Perhaps the finest room is the magnificent Long Gallery with its family portraits and statuary.

The castle is perched on a rock above splendid terraces with enormous clipped yew trees overlooking the world-famous gardens. Laid out in 1720, these

104 THE ANGEL

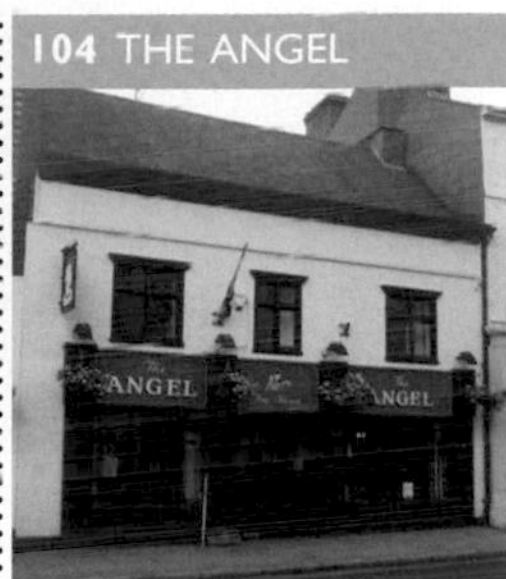

Welshpool

A popular, family-run, traditional Welsh pub serving great food and real ales

see page 293

105 TAN HOUSE INN

Llangyniew, nr Montgomery

Fantastic family run and family friendly pub serving fine home cooked favourites and real ale in an idyllic setting.

see page 293

106 THE TONTINE INN

Melverley

Serving fresh local produce The Tontine Inn is a real picture postcard country village on the borders of Wales and Shropshire.

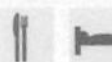 *see page 294*

107 THE BRADFORD ARMS HOTEL

Llanymynech

A top quality establishment on the Welsh border, serving fresh cuisine of the highest standard

 *see page 295*

108 THE LION HOTEL

Llansantffraid

A charming hotel dating back to the 19th century, it boasts the very best in cuisine and accommodation

 *see page 296*

show the clear influence of Italian and French styles of that time. Some striking original features still remain, including the lead statues and urns, an orangery and an aviary. The woodland, which was also landscaped in the 1700s, overlooks the Severn Valley.

A series of tragedies suffered by the Powis family, the last private owners, led to the castle being acquired by the National Trust in 1952. George, the 4th Earl of Powis, lost his elder son Percy at the Battle of the Somme in 1916, his wife died after a car crash in 1929, and his only surviving son Mervyn was killed in a plane crash in 1942. So, before his own death in 1952, the earl ensured that the castle, its treasures and its gardens should be looked after for the future by leaving Powis to the Trust.

Long Mountain stretches four miles along the Welsh side of the border east of Welshpool. It is crossed by Offa's Dyke and on its highest point is an ancient hill fort known as Beacon Ring. It was on Long Mountain that Henry Tudor camped in 1485 before crossing the border, defeating Richard III at Bosworth Field and ascending the throne of England as Henry VII.

AROUND WELSHPOOL

MIDDLETOWN

5½ miles NE of Welshpool on the A458

To the north of this border village lies **Breidden Hill**, which is thought to have been the venue for a fierce battle between the Welsh and the forces of Edward I in 1292. On the summit stands an obelisk, **Rodney's Pillar**, which commemorates Admiral Rodney's victory over the French off Domenica in 1782. A little way further along the A458 is the remote hamlet of Melverley whose church, perched above the River Vyrnwy, is one of the most delightful in the region, with a 'magpie' exterior, timber-framed walls and a tiny tower.

LLANGEDWYN

10½ miles N of Welshpool on the B4396

Just to the northeast of the village and close to the English border, lies one of Wales' most nationalistic shrines, **Sycharth Castle**. A grassy mound is all that remains of one of Owain Glyndwr's principal houses, which was immortalised in a poem by Iolo Goch, which speaks of its nine halls, many guest rooms and a church. The poem appears in a translation by Anthony Conran in the *Penguin Book of Welsh Verse*:

Here are gifts for everyone
No hunger, disgrace or dearth,
Or ever thirst at Sycharth!

MEIFOD

5½ miles NW of Welshpool on the A495

This picturesque village in the wooded valley of the River Vyrnwy is remembered in Welsh literature as being the location of the summer residence of the princes of Powys. The village **Church of St Tysilio and St Mary**, which was consecrated in

1155, is home to an interesting 9th century grave slab that bears old Celtic markings as well as a Latin cross and a Greek crucifix. According to legend, in AD 550, when St Gwyddfarch was asked where he would like to build his first church, he is said to have replied, in Welsh, "yma y mae i fod" ('here it is to be'). So the village got its name. The saint is thought to have been buried a short distance from the village. In the 9th century, while the princes of Powys had their main residence close by, Meifod became a religious centre and it is thought that the grave slab is a memorial to one of the princes.

LLANFIHANGEL-YNG-NGWYNFA

10½ miles NW of Welshpool on the B4382

In the small church of this tiny village are some interesting artefacts, a memorial to the Welsh writer, **Ann Griffith**, and some 15th century graves in the churchyard. Born in 1776 at a farm near Dolanog where she lived most of her short life, Ann only ever travelled as far as Bala, less than 50 miles distant, where she went to hear Thomas Charles preach. However, despite dying at the early age of 29 years, Ann wrote over 70 Welsh hymns, all dictated to a friend. In her home village of Dolanog, about 3 miles down the road, the Ann Griffiths Memorial Chapel was erected in 1903 and there is a 7-mile walk from Pontllogel to Pontrobert dedicated to her memory.

LLANWDDYN

14 miles NW of Welshpool on the B4393

The village lies at the southern end of **Lake Vyrnwy** (Llyn Efyrnwy), a four mile stretch of water that was created in the years following 1881 by the flooding of the entire Vyrnwy Valley to provide the people of Liverpool with an adequate water supply. Close to the dam, which is 390 yards long, 144 feet high and a splendid testament to Victorian engineering, is a monument that marks the beginning of the **Hirnant Tunnel** - the first stage of a 75-mile aqueduct that carries the water to Liverpool. Another striking building is the Gothic tower designed by George Frederick Deacon, engineer to the Liverpool Water Board. On higher ground is an obelisk that is a monument to the 44 men who died during the construction of the reservoir. To construct this, the first of several massive reservoirs in north and mid-Wales, the original village of Llanwddyn, home to some 400 people, was flooded along with the valley. On the hill south of the dam stands the 'new' village and the church, built by Liverpool Corporation in 1887. Photographs in the Lake Vyrnwy Hotel show the original village with its 37 houses, all now along with the church submerged under the Lake's 13,000 million gallons of water. The **Vyrnwy Visitor Centre** tells the story of the construction and is also home to an RSPB centre. There are four

109 THE KINGS HEAD

Meifod

A traditional style pub with oak beams and an open fire welcoming guests to stay, drink or dine with a succulent selection of home cooked treats to chose from.

see page 297

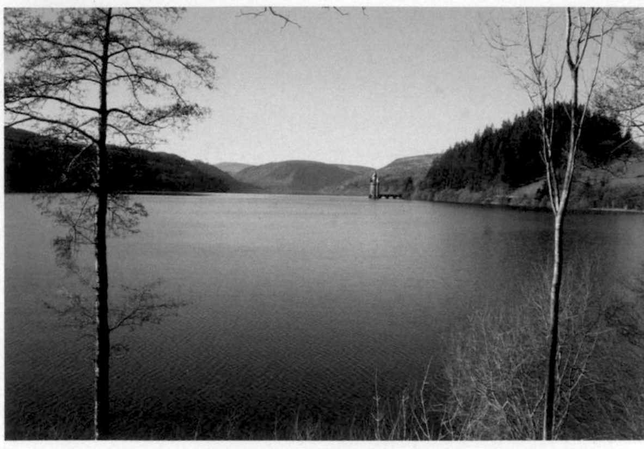

Lake Vyrnwy

RSPB hides at various points around the lake and guided tours can be arranged around the estate for schools and groups. A road circumnavigates the lake but walking around the lake or on any of the nature trails is an ideal way to observe the abundant wild and bird life that live around the shores. **Lake Vyrnwy's Sculpture Park** was started in 1997 and has evolved constantly ever since, using local timber and on-site materials. Local artists have worked in partnership with sculptors from Russia, Estonia, Lithuania and Australia. The local artists have been inspired by species found on the site, while the international artists have drawn inspiration from their homelands. The sculpture park is managed jointly by Severn Trent Water, the RSPB and Forest Enterprise Wales. **Bethania Adventure**, based at the Boat House, organises activities on and around the lake, including sailing, windsurfing, kayaking, canoeing, climbing and abseiling; the lake is also a favourite spot for anglers. With its lovely scenery and coniferous forests, the lake has doubled in films for Switzerland or Transylvania; it was also used for location shots in *The Dambusters.*

LLANRHAEADR-YM-MOCHNANT

13 miles NW of Welshpool on the B4580

Despite its relative isolation this village attracts many visitors who pass through on their way to **Pistyll Rhaeadr**, which lies up a narrow road to the northwest of the village. This is one of the Seven Wonders of Wales and, with a drop of 240 feet, is the highest waterfall in Britain south of the Scottish Highlands. The English translation of the name is Spout Waterfall, an obvious name as the water drops vertically for 100 feet before running into a cauldron, and on through a natural tunnel in the rock before reappearing.

It was while he was vicar at Llanrhaeadr-ym-Mochnant in the late 16th century that **Bishop William Morgan** made his famous translation of the Bible into Welsh. He was granted permission to carry out this work by Queen Elizabeth I, her father Henry VIII having banned any official use of the Welsh language. The villagers here maintain a tradition that was once common in the area - the Plygeiniau, a form of Christmas carol service, where groups of men wander from church to church giving unaccompanied performances of Welsh carols.

LLANFYLLIN

9 miles NW of Welshpool on the A490

This charming and peaceful hillside town lies in the valley of the River Cain where it joins the Abel. It was granted its charter as a borough in 1293 by Llewelyn ap Gruffydd ap Gwenwynwyn, Lord of Mechain; Welshpool is the only other Welsh borough to have been granted its charter from a native Welsh ruler. To celebrate the 700th anniversary in 1993 of the granting of the charter, a large tapestry of the town's historic buildings was created. It can be seen in the **Parish Church of St Myllin**, a delightful redbrick building dating from 1706. Overlooking the town is the beauty spot of **St Myllin's Well.** From the 6th century onwards water from the well has been thought to cure all manner of ailments. Certainly the view from the well over the town and to the Berwyn Mountains beyond, has restorative powers. St Myllin, a 7th century Celt, is traditionally alluded to as the first cleric to baptise by total immersion in his holy well. Opposite the church is the brick **Council House**, which has 13 wall paintings in an upstairs room. These were all done by a Napoleonic prisoner of war, one of several billeted in the town between 1812 and 1814. Ann Griffiths, the famous Welsh hymn writer, was baptised in Pendref Congregational Chapel, one of the oldest Non-Conformist places of worship in Wales, established in 1640; the present building dates from 1829.

Two miles southeast of Llanfyllin, off the A490, **Bryngwyn** is a handsome 18th century house by Robert Mylne, surrounded by 18th century and early 19th century parkland.

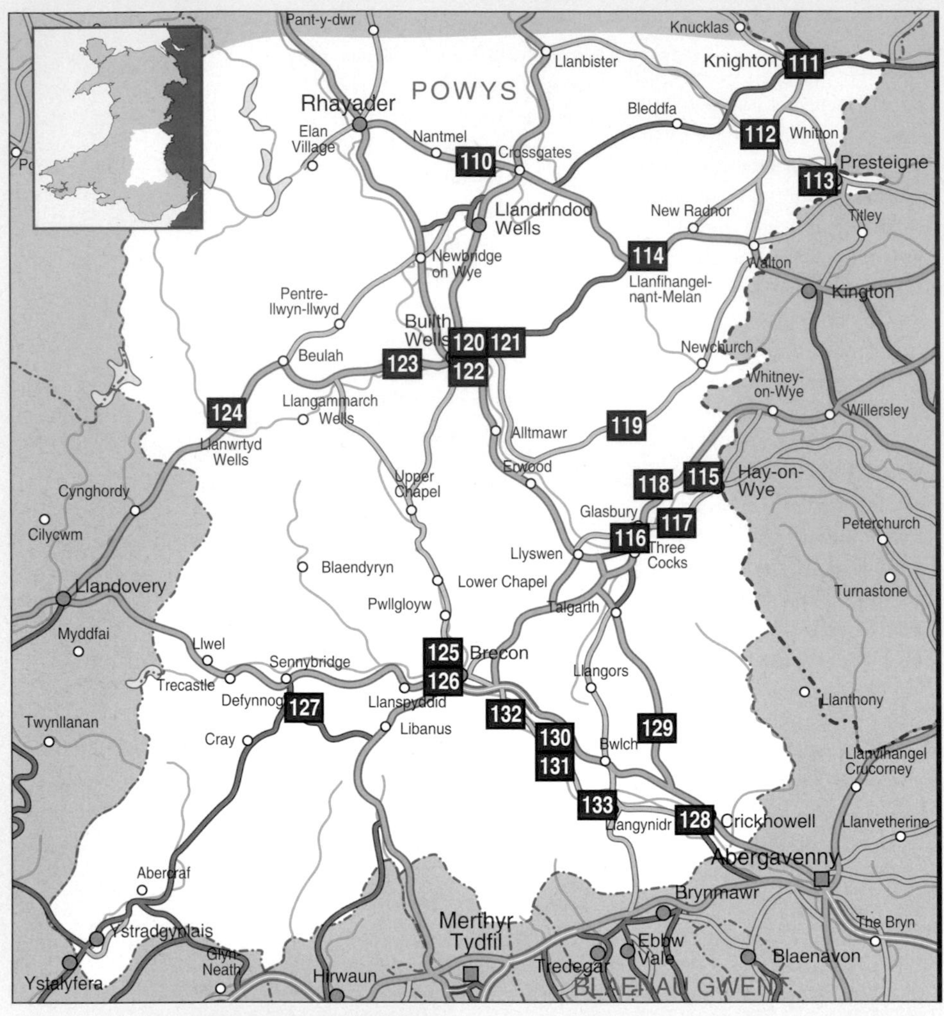

ACCOMMODATION

110	Gwystre Inn, Gwystre	pg 104, 298
112	Pilleth Oaks, Whitton, nr Knighton	pg 107, 299
114	The Red Lion Inn, Llanfihangel Nant Melan, nr New Radnor	pg 109, 301
115	The Start, Hay-on-Wye	pg 109, 302
116	The Harp Inn, Glasbury on Wye	pg 110, 302
117	The Hollybush Inn, Hay-on-Wye	pg 110, 303
119	Roast Ox Inn, Paincastle	pg 111, 304
120	Cedars Guest House & Restaurant, Builth Wells	pg 111, 305
122	The White Horse, Builth Wells	pg 112, 306
124	Stonecroft Inn, Llanwrtyd Wells	pg 113, 307
128	The Bridge End Inn, Crickhowell	pg 117, 310
129	The Farmers Arms, Cwmdu	pg 118, 311
130	Usk Inn, Talybont-on-Usk, nr Brecon	pg 118, 312
131	The Travellers Rest Inn, Talybont-on-Usk, nr Brecon	pg 118, 313
132	The White Swan, Llanfrynach	pg 119, 314
133	The Red Lion, Llangynidr	pg 119, 315

FOOD & DRINK

110	Gwystre Inn, Gwystre	pg 104, 298
111	George & Dragon Inn, Knighton	pg 107, 299

South Powys & Brecon Beacons

This southern region of the large county of Powys is steeped in history and there is evidence aplenty of turbulent times past, from the Romans onwards. The Celtic standing stones and burial chambers and the ruined castles are among the many notable buildings and memorials left by past inhabitants.

In the heart of the county (the northern part of this region) can be found the four spa towns of Llandrindod Wells, Builth Wells, Llangammarch Wells and Llanwrtyd Wells. Still popular tourist centres today, though no longer primarily spas, these places all grew and developed as a result of the arrival of the railways and the Victorians' interest in health. Although the architecture of these towns suggests that they date mainly from the 19th and early 20th centuries, there are the remains of a Roman fort (Castell Collen) close to Llandrindod Wells, and Builth Wells saw much fighting in medieval times. As well as the spa towns, the region also has the border settlements of Knighton and Presteigne, the second-hand book capital of the world Hay-on-Wye and the ancient cathedral city of Brecon, but it is perhaps for its varied countryside that south Powys is better known. Close to Rhayader, in the Cambrian Mountains, are the spectacular reservoirs and dams that make up the Elan Valley. Built at the end of the 19th century to supply water to the West Midlands, not only are these a great feat of Victorian engineering but the surrounding countryside is home to one of Britain's rarest and most beautiful birds - the Red Kite.

Further south lies the Brecon Beacons National Park which takes its name from the distinctively shaped sandstone mountains of the Brecon Beacons. To the east of the Brecon Beacons rise the interlocking peaks of the Black Mountains which stretch to the English border, while to the west is Black Mountain, which, though its name is singular, refers to an unpopulated range of barren, smooth-humped peaks.

PLACES OF INTEREST

110 GWYSTRE INN

Gwystre, nr Llandrindod Wells

Extremely popular for its home cooked food, the Gwystre Inn has a lot to offer.

see page 298

•

Wales is famous for its amazing little narrow-gauge railways, but it also has some full-size trains, too. One of the most popular tourist lines is the Heart of Wales Line that runs from Shrewsbury to Swansea, stopping at Llandrindod Wells en route. It promotes itself as 'one line that visits two viaducts, three castles, four spa towns, five counties, six tunnels and seven bridges'.

•

LLANDRINDOD WELLS

The most elegant of the spa towns of mid-Wales, Llandrindod Wells has retained much of its Victorian and Edwardian character and architecture. It was only a small hamlet until 1749 when the first hotel was built here. For a time, until that hotel closed in 1787, the town had a reputation as a haunt for gamblers and rakes. Despite its chiefly 19th and early 20th century architecture, Llandrindod Wells has ancient roots. To the northwest of the town lies **Castell Collen**, a Roman fort that was occupied from the 1st century through to the early 4th century and whose earthworks are clearly detectable today. The first castle was built of turf and timber in about AD 75, later versions were made of stone.

It was the Romans who first understood the possible healing powers of Wales' mineral rich waters, but it was with the coming of the railway in 1867 that Llandrindod Wells really developed into a spa town. At its peak, some 80,000 visitors a year would flock to the town to take the waters in an attempt to obtain relief from complaints and ailments ranging from gout, rheumatism and anaemia to diabetes, dyspepsia and liver trouble. Special baths and heat and massage treatments were also available. The most famous of the individual spas in Llandrindod during its heyday, **Rock Park**, is a typically well laid out Victorian park where visitors coming to the town would take a walk between their treatments. With particularly fine tree planting and shrubbery, the park is still a pleasant place today. Here and elsewhere in town, visitors can still take the waters or experience some of the more modern therapies.

Visitors can find out more about the spa's history at the **Radnorshire Museum** where there is a collection of Victorian artefacts along with relics excavated from Castell Collen. A splendid attraction in the Automobile Palace, a distinctive brick garage topped by rows of white lions, is the **National Cycle Collection**, an exhibition that covers more than 100 years of cycling history through an amazing collection of more than 250 bicycles and tricycles. Some date back as far as 1818. The collection displays every development from the hobby horse and bone-shaker to the high-tech carbon machines of today. Among the latter is Chris Boardman's

River Ithon - Llandrindod Wells

Lotus Sport Olympia Replica test machine from the 1992 Olympics. Also here are old photographs and posters, historic replicas, the Dunlop tyre story and displays on cycling stars. Tel: 01597 825531.

Just outside Llandrindod Wells, off the A44 Rhayader road, there is free access to **Abercamlo Bog**, 12 acres of wet pasture, which is home to water-loving plants, breeding birds such as the whinchat and reed bunting, and butterflies. Not far away, at Ithon gorge, is **Bailey Einion**, woodland home to lady fern, golden saxifrage, pied flycatchers, woodpeckers and cardinal beetles.

AROUND LLANDRINDOD WELLS

ABBEY-CWM-HIR

6 miles N of Llandrindod Wells off the A483

Standing rather forlornly in the lonely Clywedog Valley are the ruins of **Cwmhir Abbey.** It was founded in 1143 by the Cistercians who had grandiose plans to build one of the largest churches in Britain with a nave more than 242ft long - only the cathedrals of Durham, Winchester and York have a longer nave. Unfortunately, an attack by Henry III in 1231 forced them to abandon their plans. A slab on the altar commemorates Llywelyn ap Gruffydd, the last native prince of Wales, whose headless body is reputed to be buried here. His head had been despatched to London.

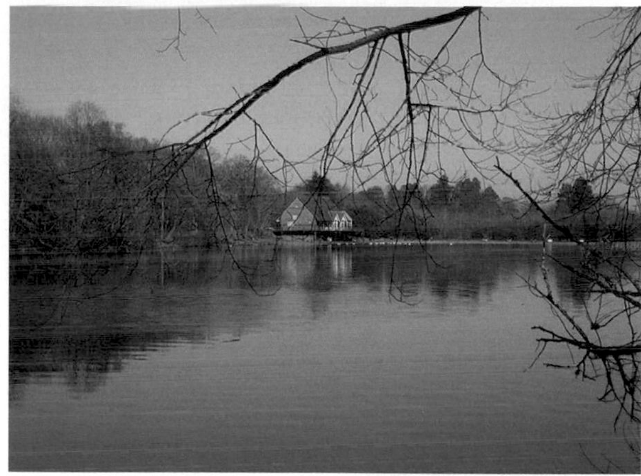

The Lake - Llandrindod Wells

RHAYADER

6½ miles NW of Llandrindod Wells on the A44

Often referred to as the Gateway to the Lakeland of Wales, Rhayader lies in a loop of the River Wye at the entrance to the magnificent Elan Valley with its impressive collection of dams and reservoirs. The town's name means 'Waterfall of the Wye' though the waterfall all but disappeared with the construction of a bridge over the river in 1780.

Little except some defensive ditches remains of Rhayader Castle, built here by Rhys ap Gruffyd in about 1177. Over the centuries, the town has been fortunate in avoiding major conflicts although there was some turbulence in the mid 1800s when the **Rebecca Riots** took place. These were protests against road tolls which were painfully expensive for local labourers and itinerant workers. The men dressed up as women to avoid being recognised, their female

•

Each year in the last full week of August, Llandrindod Wells hosts a Victorian Festival which swells the population of the town from its resident 5000 to more than 40,000. Horses and carriages, Victorian window displays, townspeople and visitors in appropriate garb all contribute to the jollity which culminates in a torchlight procession and fireworks display over the lake.

•

Welsh Royal Crystal, a manufacturer of hand-crafted lead crystal tableware, is located in the town of Rhayader and the factory takes visitors on a guided tour to watch the craftsmen at work. A century of skills is shown in the fine lead crystal tableware, stemware, giftware and trophies.

garb earned them the nickname 'Rebecca's Daughters', and they destroyed toll gates in protest at the high toll charges. The first gate to be destroyed was at Yr Efail Wen where 'Rebecca' proved to be a huge man called Thomas Rees. Many toll gates were demolished by the protesters until in 1844 the remainder were removed legally.

Rhayader is at one end of the beautiful **Wye Valley Walk**, which follows the river valley, criss-crossing the border, through Builth Wells and Hay-on-Wye to Hereford, Monmouth and Chepstow.

The area around Rhayader is still very rural and on the outskirts of the town lies **Gigrin Farm**, where visitors can see red kites at close quarters as they are feeding.

ELAN VILLAGE

8 miles W of Llandrindod Wells off the B4518

The village is close to the beautiful reservoirs of the **Elan Valley** - a string of five dammed lakes that together are around nine miles long and were constructed between 1892 and 1903. Built to supply millions of gallons of water to Birmingham and the West Midlands, the first of the dams was opened in 1904 by Edward VII and Queen Alexandra. The final dam, the Claerwen Dam, was finished in 1952. Dubbed the 'Lakeland of Wales', the five man-made lakes are surrounded by magnificent scenery and this is a popular area for walkers, cyclists and birdwatchers. The **Elan Valley Visitor Centre** incorporates a tourist information office and also has an exhibition telling the story of the building of the reservoirs together with lots of information about the red kite.

Percy Bysshe Shelley visited his cousin Thomas Grove at Cwm Elan after being expelled from Oxford for writing a treatise supporting atheism. Soon after this visit he eloped with the schoolgirl Harriet Westbrook and married her in Scotland. They returned to Wales and for a brief spell in 1812 stayed at a house in the area called Nant Gwyllt. Like Thomas Grove's house, it is now submerged under the waters of **Caben Coch** reservoir, but when the water level is low the walls of the garden can still be seen. In 1814 Shelley left Harriet for Mary Godwin, and soon after Harriet drowned herself in the Serpentine. Shelley married Mary, who was later to write *Frankenstein*. In 1822 Shelley himself drowned off the Italian coast.

ST HARMON

8 miles NW of Llandrindod Wells on the B4518

The diarist **Francis Kilvert** was vicar here in 1876 and 1877, after his time at Clyro. Kilvert was born near Chippenham in 1840 and was educated at Wadham College, Oxford. He was curate to his father in Wiltshire before taking up a post at Clyro in 1865, where he started his famous diaries which provide detailed, vivid and very personal accounts of life in the remote Welsh countryside in mid-Victorian times. To the southwest of St

Harmon lies **Gilfich Nature Reserve**, a Site of Special Scientific Interest at the mouth of the Marteg Valley. Oak woodland, meadows and upland moorland support a rich diversity of wildlife. In the ancient longhouse there are exhibitions on the history of the building and the surrounding wildlife.

KNIGHTON

Situated in the Teme Valley on the border of Powys and Shropshire, Knighton lies on the path of Offa's Dyke - the Welsh name for the town is Tref-y-Clawdd which means 'town of the dyke'. Appropriately, Knighton is home to the **Offa's Dyke Centre** where there is information about the long distance footpath that runs from Prestatyn to Chepstow. Here, too, visitors can find out more about the historic background to the 8th century dyke and the bloodshed of the battles that continued in the borderlands for hundreds of years.

Knighton and its near neighbour, the border town of Presteigne, saw many battles between the Anglo Saxons and the Celts. "It was customary for the English to cut off the ears of every Welshman who was found to the east of the Dyke (Offa's), and for the Welsh to hang every Englishman found to the west of it", wrote George Borrow in his 19th century book, *Wild Wales.*

Beginning in Knighton, **Glyndwr's Way** follows the route taken by Owain Glyndwr, one of Wales' favourite sons, as he fought the English for Welsh independence in the 1400s. This scenic and important route travels southwest to Abbey-cwm-hir, passing by the ancient abbey ruins, before heading northwards into the old county of Montgomeryshire and the market town of Llanidloes. The 128 miles of the path takes in some of the finest scenery in mid-Wales before reaching Machynlleth, from where it heads south-eastwards and finally ends at the border town of Welshpool.

High on a hill overlooking Knighton, the **Spaceguard Centre** occupies the former Powys Observatory. It was established in 2001 to develop and maintain world-class facilities for astronomical research and science education. One of its main activities is to observe and track comets and asteroids that might collide with Earth. Guided tours are available around the centre which has a planetarium, solar

111 GEORGE AND DRAGON INN

Knighton

A warm welcome is assured at this 19th century Welsh cottage pub serving fine wine and ale, great food with charming en suite guest accommodation.

see page 299

112 PILLETH OAKS

Whitton

Elegant 5 star bed and breakfast situated in 100 acres of scenic countryside with fishing and bird watching just seconds away.

see page 299

River Teme, Knighton

113 THE HAT SHOP RESTAURANT

Presteigne

Small, friendly and fully licensed restaurant serving high quality home-made food with organic ingredients.

see page 300

•

One of the Presteigne's most outstanding buildings is The Radnorshire Arms which dates from 1616. Originally built as a house for Sir Christopher Hatton, one of Elizabeth I's courtiers, this superb timber framed building became the property of the Bradshaw family before becoming an inn in 1792. The best known member of this family was John Bradshaw, who was Lord President of the Parliamentary Commission that brought Charles I to trial. He headed the list of signatories to the King's death warrant, refusing to let him speak in his defence.

•

telescope and camera obscura.

Beside the banks of the River Teme is **Pinners Hole**, a natural amphitheatre that is strengthened on one side by a superb section of Offa's Dyke where there is a stone that commemorates the opening of the footpath. Across the river lies **Kinsley Wood**, a sizeable area of native oak woodland. Sited on a hillside, trees of different species were planted to form the letters 'ER' to commemorate the Coronation of Her Majesty Queen Elizabeth II in 1953.

AROUND KNIGHTON

PRESTEIGNE

5 miles S of Knighton on the B4362

Once the county town of Radnorshire, tiny Presteigne remains a charming and unspoilt place on the southern bank of the River Lugg. In recent years it has seen an influx of escapees from urban stress and now has a smattering of craft shops, trendy cafés, antique and second-hand book shops.

A border town distinguished by its handsome black and white half-timbered buildings, Presteigne grew up around a Norman castle that has long since been destroyed; the site is now occupied by a pleasant park. Presteigne's history is as turbulent as that of most of the region: it was captured by the Mercians in the 8th century, besieged by Llywelyn in 1262 and pillaged by Owain Glyndwr in the early 15th century. By Tudor times the town had got its breath back and had become a peaceful market centre, but it was its position on a major mail coach route between London, Cheltenham and Gloucester and Aberystwyth that brought it prosperity and importance.

The town also claims the oldest inn in Radnorshire, the **Duke's Arms**, for which records show that an inn on the site was burnt to the ground by Owain Glyndwr in 1401. The rebuilt inn became a local headquarters for the Roundheads during the Civil War and in later centuries was an important coaching inn.

Although the **Judge's Lodging** only dates from 1829, it is another fascinating attraction in Presteigne. Designed by Edward Haycock and built on the site of the county gaol, this was the judicial centre for Radnorshire and the home of the Radnorshire Constabulary. Today, the house, with its adjoining court, has been furnished as it would have appeared in 1870 with many of the original furnishings and furniture. Visitors can explore the world of the judges, their servants and the felons. One of the trials conducted here concerned Mary Morgan who gave birth to an illegitimate child that her father urged her to murder. Her crime was detected and she was sentenced to death. Incredibly, her father was among the jury that found her guilty. In the churchyard of St Andrew there are two gravestones recalling the event; the first, erected at the time, is nauseatingly sanctimonious about "the victim of sin and shame"; the second, set up later by chastened townspeople, is inscribed "He that is without sin among you, let him cast the first stone at her".

OLD RADNOR

8½ miles S of Knighton off the A44

Situated on a hill, Old Radnor was once home to King Harold. The motte by the church was the site of his castle, while the church itself contains interesting examples of 14th century building design, as well as a huge font made from a glacial boulder.

NEW RADNOR

8½ miles SW of Knighton off the A44

Once the county town of Radnorshire, the village is overlooked by the remains of its 11th century motte and bailey **Castle**. Like many other strongholds in this border region, New Radnor Castle suffered at various hands: it was destroyed by King John, rebuilt by Henry III and destroyed again by Owain Glyndwr in 1401. New Radnor was the start point in 1187 of a tour of Wales by Archbishop Baldwin, who was accompanied by the scholar and churchman Giraldus Cambrensis. They preached the Third Crusade, and after the tour Baldwin, the first archbishop to visit Wales, made a pilgrimage to the Holy Land, where he died. Baldwin was the Bishop of Worcester before becoming Archbishop of Canterbury, in which capacity he crowned Richard I.

HAY-ON-WYE

This ancient town, tucked between the Black Mountains and the River Wye in the northernmost corner of the Brecon Beacon National Park, grew up around its Hay Motte which still survives across the river from the main town centre today. This castle was replaced by **Hay Castle**, a stone structure although this was all but destroyed in the early 1400s by Owain Glyndwr. A Jacobean manor house has since

Hay-on-Wye Castle

114 THE RED LION INN

Llanfihungel Nant Melan

Warm and friendly olde worlde inn serving great value traditional home cooking, fine wine and real ale with en suite accommodation.

see page 301

115 THE START

Hay-on-Wye

Beautiful 18th century bed and breakfast on the banks of the River Wye known for its tasty home cooked breakfasts.

see page 302

116 THE HARP INN

Glasbury on Wye

A traditional inn offering comfortable bed and breakfast accommodation and fine food

see page 302

117 THE HOLLYBUSH INN

Hay-on-Wye

Vibrant and quirky inn near the river Wye serving up great organic food and country ale alongside its own campsite and activity centre.

see page 303

118 THE RADNOR ARMS

Llowes

A beautiful stone built inn, which dates back more than 400 years

see page 303

been grafted on to part of the remaining walls and, close by, there are traces of a Roman fort.

Historic though this town may be, it is as the second-hand book capital of the world that Hay-on-Wye is best known. Among the town's many buildings can be found a plethora of book, antique, print and craft shops. The first second-hand bookshop was opened here in 1961 by Richard Booth, owner of Hay Castle, and since then they have sprung up all over the town - the old cinema, many houses, shops and even the old castle are now bookshops, at least 35 in all and with a stock of more than a million books. The annual **Festival of Art and Literature**, held every May, draws thousands of visitors to the town.

AROUND HAY-ON-WYE

CLYRO

2 miles NW of Hay on the A438

Although little remains of the Roman station that was here, the ruins of a motte and bailey castle built by the fiendish William de Braose can still be seen. The diarist **Francis Kilvert** was curate in the village between 1865 and 1872. In his journal, he describes both life in the village and the surrounding area. There are Kilvert memorabilia in his former home, now a modern art gallery.

A little way north of Clyro, **Cwm Byddog** is a 15-acre ancient woodland with pollarded oaks, bluebells in spring, the remains of a motte and bailey castle and a variety of birds, including the blackcap and the garden warbler.

PAINSCASTLE

5 miles NW of Hay on the B4594

Sometimes known as **Castell Paen**, the early motte built in 1130 by Payn FitzJohn was later rebuilt in stone and, by the late 12th century, was in the hands of the notorious William de Braose whose cruelty has earned him a place in Welsh folklore. He was given the nickname the "Ogre of Abergavenny" while his wife Maud is thought to have lived long after his death as a witch. Their names have also been given to several breeds of cattle in Wales including the de Braose Maud and the de Braose David.

In 1198, de Braose's stronghold of Painscastle was attacked by Gwenwynwyn, Prince of Powys, but William and his English army slaughtered more than 3000 of Gwenwynwyn's men and the prince's dreams of a united Wales died along with them. de Braose finally met his match for cruelty in King John who stripped him of his land; de Braose died a pauper. After her husband's death, Maud suggested that John had also killed his nephew Prince Arthur and for this accusation both she and her youngest son were imprisoned in Corfe Castle with little food to keep them alive. Legend has it that when, some 11 days later, the dungeon door was opened, both prisoners were dead. In an attempt to keep herself alive, Maud had half eaten the cheeks of her son.

Close to the castle remains is an altogether more pleasant place to visit, the **Tawny Owl Animal Park and Craft Centre**, which lies at Wernewydd in the shelter of beautiful hills. Opened in 1999, the park is named after the wild owls that live in the broad leaved woodlands surrounding the farm. As well as the owls (which are not caged), visitors can also see a whole range of farm animals at close quarters. Along with the animals and the farm trails, there are also traditional country crafts on display and for sale.

BUILTH WELLS

Another spa town , Builth Wells lies on the River Wye, which is spanned at this point by a six-arched bridge. The discovery of the saline springs in 1830 helped Builth Wells develop from a small market town into a fashionable spa that became even more popular with the arrival of the railways towards the end of the 19th century. As a result, many of the town's original narrow streets are dotted with Victorian and Edwardian buildings.

The town grew up around a Norman castle that changed hands many times during the struggles with the English. The inhabitants of Builth Wells earned the nickname 'traitors of Bu-allt' because of their refusal to shelter Llywelyn the Last from the English in 1282. Twenty years later Llywelyn took his revenge by partly destroying the Norman stronghold. At the **Castle Mound** only the earthworks remain of the town's 13th century castle that was built by Edward I on the site of the earlier motte and bailey structure. The earthworks can be reached by a footpath from the town centre.

River Wye, Builth Wells

119 ROAST OX INN

Paincastle

A traditional village inn well known for its excellent food, accommodation and conference facilities

see page 304

120 CEDARS GUEST HOUSE AND RESTAURANT

Builth Wells

Offering rooms with a view in scenic Builth Wells, this bed and breakfast has a popular restaurant attached serving great home cooked food each night.

see page 305

121 STRAND CAFE & RESTAURANT

Builth Wells

Popular family run cafe serving a large selection of homemade food and sweets throughout the day.

see page 305

122 THE WHITE HORSE

Builth Wells

A popular establishment offering the very best in food and accommodation

see page 306

123 PRINCE LLEWELYN INN

Cilmery, nr Builth Wells

An outstanding village inn serving the very best fresh Welsh produce.

see page 306

Since the 1963 opening of the **Royal Welsh Show Ground** at nearby Llanelwedd, the annual Royal Welsh Show, held in July, has gained a reputation as being the premier agricultural show in the country. Builth Wells is regarded as the centre for farming and agriculture in Wales and the show, visited by some 200,000 people, provides an opportunity for the farming communities to come together at what is considered to be one of the finest and most prestigious events of its kind. The dates for 2010 are 19-22 July, for 2011 18-21 July. The showground is also used for monthly flea markets and occasional collectors' fairs.

Although spa treatments are no longer available here, Builth Wells remains a popular touring centre and base. As well as the many shops and the weekly market on Mondays, visitors can also enjoy the wide variety of arts and cultural events held at the **Wayside Arts Centre**, housed in the town's Victorian Assembly rooms, or take a pleasant riverside stroll through **Groe Park**.

On the summit of the nearby mountain, Cefn Carn Cafall in Builth Wells, is a cairn that is said to have been built by King Arthur. The stone on top of the cairn bears the imprint of a dog's paw that, according to local legend, was left by King Arthur's dog, Cafall, while they were out hunting. Arthur built the cairn, placing the stone on top, and then named the peak. The story continues that if the stone is removed it will always return to this spot.

AROUND BUILTH WELLS

ERWOOD

7 miles SE of Builth Wells on the A470

Pronounced 'Errod', the village's name is actually a corruption of the Welsh Y Rhyd (the ford), a name that harks back to the days when the shallow crossing of the River Wye here was used by drovers. The station at Erwood, closed in 1962, has been turned into a centre for local art and craft and has a resident wood-turner.

CILMERY

3 miles W of Builth Wells on the A483

It was at this village on the banks of the River Irfon, in 1282, that Llywelyn the Last, while escaping after the abortive battle of Builth, was killed by the English. According to legend, the place where Llywelyn fell and died was once covered in broom which then ceased to grow on the site - in mourning for the loss of the last native Prince of Wales. Thirteen trees have been planted here to represent the 13 counties of Wales. The rough hewn stone **Memorial to Llywelyn the Last** describes him as "ein llyw olaf" (our last leader) while the English tablet beside the monument calls him 'our prince'. Following his death, Llywelyn's head was taken to London and paraded victoriously through the city's streets.

LLANWRTYD WELLS

13 miles W of Builth Wells on the A483

The appealing little town of Llanwrtyd Wells is surrounded by rugged mountains, rolling hills and the remote moorland of **Mynydd Epynt**. It was here, in 1792, that a scurvy sufferer discovered the healing properties of the town's sulphur and chalybeate spring waters. The town was soon welcoming a steady stream of afflicted visitors. Today, despite being listed as the smallest town in Britain in the *Guinness Book of Records*, Llanwrtyd Wells is still a popular holiday centre, particularly with those who enjoy bird watching, fishing and walking.

Anyone visiting Llanwrtyd Wells may well be surprised that somewhere so small could host so many events and festivals throughout the year. It is the home of the 'Man versus Horse' race in May, a Folk Weekend in spring and a late autumn Beer Festival. However the most unusual of all the events held here is undoubtedly the annual **World Bog Snorkelling Championship** that takes place each August. Competitors have to swim two lengths of a specially dug 180ft peat bog located a mile from the town. The swimmer's head must be submerged, and the use of the arms is forbidden. The latest variation of this extraordinary event, which came about after a drunken pub session and a wish to raise funds for charity, is bog-snorkelling on mountain bikes! The date for 2010 is 31 August.

Cambrian Woollen Mills, Llanwrtyd Wells

On the outskirts of the town lies the **Cambrian Woollen Mill**, which recalls the rich history of Wales' rural past. The first mill was founded in the 1820s, but its modern form dates from 1918, when it was opened by the Royal British Legion for the benefit of servicemen disabled in the Great War. A tour of the mill allows visitors to see traditional cloths being woven while, in the factory shop, there is a wide choice of beautifully finished items to buy.

On high ground to the northwest of the town is **Llyn Brianne**, the latest of Wales' man-made lakes, which was opened in 1973. The dam that holds the water is the highest of its type in the country - at 300 feet - and the grand scale of the lake has to be seen to be believed.

LLANGAMMARCH WELLS

8 miles W of Builth Wells off the A483

Situated where the Rivers Irfon and Cammarch meet, Llangammarch

124 STONECROFT INN

Llanwrtyd Wells

A traditional country pub well known for lovers of real ales and fine food.

see page 307

Wells was the smallest of the Welsh spas and was renowned for its barium chloride carrying waters that were thought to be useful in the treatment of heart and rheumatic complaints. Lloyd George was one of many notables who came to sample the waters. The old well and pump house are contained in the grounds of the Lake Country House Hotel.

ABERGWESYN

12 miles W of Builth Wells off the B4358

Situated in an isolated spot in the Irfon Valley, this riverside hamlet lies on an old drovers' route that twists and climbs through the **Abergwesyn Pass** which is known as the 'roof of Wales'. This is a beautiful pathway that centuries ago consisted of nothing more than dirt tracks along which the drovers would shepherd cattle and other livestock from one market town to the next. A number of drovers' routes can still be followed - some in part by car. Many of the roads are narrow and in the south one such route begins at Llandovery and travels across the Epynt mountain to the ford at Erwood.

River Usk, Brecon

BRECON

Famous for its ancient cathedral, Georgian architecture and annual Jazz Festival, Brecon lies on the banks of the River Usk at the confluence of the Rivers Honddu and Tarrell on the northern edge of the Brecon Beacons National Park. Established in 1957, the park's 520 square miles of scenic grandeur is dominated by a backbone of the highest mountains in southern Britain. Buzzards and ravens soar over the hills and in the west you can often see Red Kites, a magnificent bird of prey that was almost extinct in Britain a century ago.

The first evidence of a settlement in the area are the remains of the Roman fort **Y Gaer** which lie to the west of the town. First built in around AD 75, the fort was rebuilt twice before it was finally abandoned in about AD 290. A garrison for the 2nd Legion and the Vettonian Spanish cavalry, parts of the fort were excavated by Sir Mortimer Wheeler in 1924. Sections of the outer wall - in places 10 feet high - and traces of gates can be seen.

A walk along the promenade beside the River Usk leads to the remains of medieval **Brecon Castle** which can be found partly in the Bishop's Garden and partly at the

Castle Hotel. The town grew up around this castle which was built in the late 11th century by Bernard of Newmarch. It was besieged first by Llywelyn the Last and again during Owain Glyndwr's rebellion in the early 15th century. When the Civil War erupted, the people of Brecon were so determined to protect their thriving cloth-weaving trade that they dismantled the castle and the town walls to ensure that neither side would be interested in seizing Brecon.

Close by stands **Brecon Cathedral**, an impressive and magnificent building that originated from an 11th century cell of the Benedictine monastery at Battle in Sussex. The Priory Church of St John the Evangelist was elevated to the status of a cathedral in 1923. Inside there are many interesting examples of religious artefacts and of the chapels dedicated to craftsmen which once filled the aisle - only that to the corvisors (shoemakers) remains. Housed in a 16th century tithe barn is the cathedral's imaginative Heritage Centre.

Another of the town's old buildings, the elegant former Old Shire Hall, now houses the **Brecknock Museum** where visitors can see the old assize court as well as take in the extensive collection of artefacts and other items from past centuries, including the museum's large collection of Welsh love spoons. The town's second museum is equally fascinating. The **South Wales Borderers Museum** features memorabilia of the regiment's famous defence of Rorke's Drift. More than 300 years of military history are recorded here through various displays that include armoury, uniforms and medals. The regiment has taken part in every major campaign and war and has won 29 Victoria Crosses as well as more than 100 Battle Honours. Though its history is long and stirring, it is the regiment's participation in the Zulu wars that is best remembered and which was immortalised in the film *Zulu* starring Michael Caine. It recalls the heroic defence of Rorke's Drift in 1879, when 141 men from the regiment were attacked by 4000 Zulus; nine VCs were awarded here in a single day. The museum also has exhibits on the Old 24th Monmouthshire Regiment and the Royal Regiment of Wales (24th/41st Foot).

As well as having the River Usk flowing through the town, Brecon is also home to the **Monmouthshire and Brecon Canal**, a beautiful Welsh waterway which used to bring coal and limestone into the town. There are attractive walks along the canal towpath along with pleasure cruises on both motorised and horse-drawn barges. The canal basin in the town has been reconstructed and is now proving to be an attraction in its own right.

AROUND BRECON

LIBANUS

4 miles SW of Brecon on the A470

To the northwest of this attractive hamlet, on Mynydd Illtyd common,

125 BRECKNOCK WILDLIFE TRUST

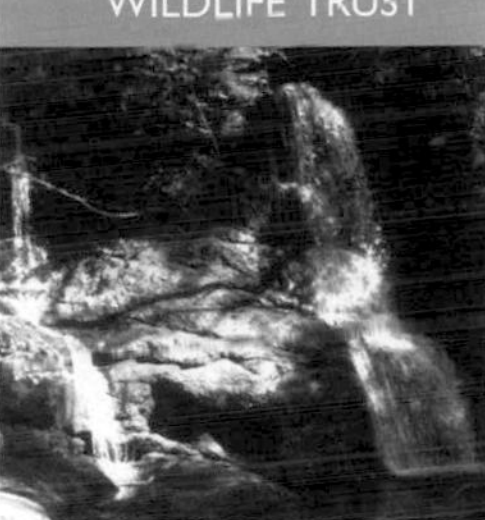

Brecon

The Trust is one of several based throughout the UK dedicated to preserving wildlife and the habitats it requires.

see page 308

126 PILGRIMS

Brecon

Charming licensed tea rooms set within the courtyard of the Cathedral serving fine organic traditional home-cooking.

see page 309

The Beacons, including the sandstone peaks of Pen y Fan and Corn Du, were given to the National Trust in 1965 and have become one of the most popular parts of the UK with walkers. (At 886 metres, Pen y Fan is the highest point in southern Britain.) The area is also important for sub-alpine plants and is designated a Site of Special Scientific Interest. But the very popularity of the Beacons with walkers has caused great problems, exacerbated by military manoeuvres and the sheep that have grazed here since Tudor times. Erosion is the biggest problem, and the National Trust has put in place an ambitious programme of footpath and erosion repair.

is the **Brecon Beacons Mountain Centre** where visitors can find out about the Brecon Beacons National Park from displays and presentations. There are also some interesting remains to be seen in the area - Twyn y Gaer, a Bronze Age burial chamber, and Bedd Illtyd, a more modest ancient monument said to be the grave of St Illtyd, the founder of the monastery at Llantwit Major. Brecon Beacons are a small part of the National Park.

YSTRADFELLTE

12 miles SW of Brecon off the A4059

This small village is a recognised hiking centre and the area of classic limestone countryside around it is one of the most impressive in the British Isles.

The narrow road heading north from the village climbs sharply and squeezes its way along a narrow valley between Fan Llia on the east side and Fan Nedd on the west. The **Maen Madog** is a nine-foot-high standing stone with a Latin inscription proclaiming that Dervacus, son of Justus, lies here.

To the south of Ystradfellte is Porth-yr-Ogof, a delightful area with a string of three dramatic waterfalls as the River Melte descends through woodland.

YSTRADGYNLAIS

18½ miles SW of Brecon on the B4599

The former mining community of Ystradgynlais is situated at the top end of the Tawe Valley, which stretches down to the city of Swansea, and close to the boundary of the Brecon Beacon National park. Iron was produced here as far back as the early 17th century and the legacy of this industrious past can still be seen, although the area surrounding Ystradgynlais is known as waterfall country and is popular with walkers, ramblers and cavers.

CRAIG-Y-NOS

15½ miles SW of Brecon on the A4067

The **Dan-yr-Ogof Showcaves**, the largest complex of caverns in northern Europe, lie to the north of this village. Discovered in 1912, the caverns have taken 315 million years to create and they include both the longest and the largest showcaves in Britain. Prehistoric tribes lived in these impressive caverns - more than 40 human skeletons have been found here. Exploring these underground caverns is only one aspect of this interesting attraction as there is also an award winning **Dinosaur Park**, where life size replicas of the creatures that roamed the earth during Jurassic times can be seen. The replica **Iron Age Farm** gives a convincing representation of how farmers lived so long ago.

To the east of the village lies **Craig-y-Nos Country Park** where visitors can enjoy the unspoilt countryside and the landscaped country parkland of the upper Tawe Valley. The mansion in the country park, known as **Craig-y-Nos Castle**, was once the home of the 19th century opera singer Madame Adelina Patti. She bought the estate in 1878 as a home for her and her second husband, the tenor Ernesto Nicolini, and lived here for 40 years. She installed an aviary, a little theatre modelled on Drury Lane and a winter garden that was subsequently moved to Swansea's Victoria Park. The castle is now a hotel.

SENNYBRIDGE

7½ miles W of Brecon on the A40

Situated along the southern edge of the Mynydd Epynt and on the northern border of the Brecon Beacons National Park, this village is very much a product of the industrial age. It only began to develop after the railways arrived here in 1872 and Sennybridge became a centre for livestock trading. However, the remains of **Castell Ddu**, just to the west of the village, provides evidence of life here from an earlier age. Dating from the 14th century and believed to stand on the site of an 11th century manor house, this was the home of Sir Reginald Aubrey, a friend of Bernard of Newmarch.

Two new waymarked walks have been opened on the Sennybridge army training area, beginning at **Disgwylfa Conservation Centre** on the B4519 Upper Chapel-Garth road. The centre has an interactive learning centre and military and conservation displays. One of the walks is accessible for disabled visitors.

CRICKHOWELL

Situated in the beautiful valley of the River Usk and in the shadow of the Black Mountains that lie to the north, Crickhowell is a charming little town with a long history. The town takes its name from the Iron Age fort, **Crug Hywell** (Howell's Fort) that lies on the flat-topped hill above the town that is aptly named Table Mountain. The remains of another stronghold, **Crickhowell Castle** - once one of the most important fortresses in this mountainous region of Wales - can be found in the town's large park. Built in the 11th century, only the motte and two shattered towers remain of the Norman fortress that was stormed by Owain Glyndwr and abandoned in the 15th century.

The picturesque and famous **Crickhowell Bridge**, which dates from the 16th century, spans the River Usk in the heart of the town. Still carrying traffic today, the bridge is unique in that it has 13 arches on one side and only 12 on the other! For the rest, this is a pleasant place, with some fine Georgian architecture which, due to its close proximity to the Black

127 THE TANNERS ARMS

Defynnog

In beautiful Brecon Beacon National Park this historic inn offers freshly prepared home cooking and Welsh ale and cider throughout the day.

see page 308

128 THE BRIDGE END INN

Crickhowell

A popular inn and restaurant located by the famed River Usk.

see page 310

Crickhowell

129 THE FARMERS ARMS

Cwmdu nr Crickhowell

Fantastic, friendly olde worlde inn serving up fresh home cooking every day, with en suite guest accommodation available.

 *see page 311*

130 USK INN

Talybont-on-Usk

Award winning food served bistro style in this 4 star hotel in the heart of a historic village.

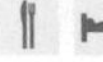 *see page 312*

131 THE TRAVELLERS REST INN

Talybont-on-Usk

Surrounded by beautiful scenery this inn serves some of the finest cuisine in the area.

 *see page 313*

Mountains and the National Park, is popular with those looking for outdoor activities including walking. Close by is Pwll-y-Wrach Nature Reserve in a steep-sided valley. Owned by the **Brecknock Wildlife Trust**, this woodland reserve has a waterfall and also a great variety of flora, for which it has been designated a Site of Special Scientific Interest.

AROUND CRICKHOWELL

TRETOWER

2½ miles NW of Crickhowell on the A479

This quiet village in the Usk Valley is the home of two impressive medieval buildings - **Tretower Court and Tretower Castle** (both in the hands of CADW). The elder of these historic sites is the castle where all that remains on the site of the original Norman motte is a stark keep that dates from the 13th century. The castle was built in this valley to discourage Welsh rebellion but, nonetheless, it was besieged by Llywelyn the Last and almost destroyed by Owain Glyndwr in 1403. Adjacent to the bleak castle remains stands the court, a magnificent 15th century fortified manor house that served as a very desirable domestic residence particularly during the less turbulent years following Glyndwr's rebellion. While the 15th century woodwork here and the wall walk, with its 17th century roof and windows, are outstanding, it is the court's **Gardens** that are particularly interesting. The original late 15th century layout of the gardens has been re-created in such a manner that the owner of the time, Sir Roger Vaughan, would have recognised them. Among the many delightful features is a tunnel arbour planted with white roses - Sir Roger was a Yorkist - and vines, an enclosed arbour and a chequerboard garden. Tretower Court's Gardens are best seen in the early summer.

TALYBONT-ON-USK

7 miles NW of Crickhowell on the B4558

Just beyond this attractive village, the Monmouthshire and Brecon Canal passes through the 375 yard long Ashford Tunnel while, further south still, lies the **Talybont Reservoir**. In this narrow wooded valley on the south-eastern slopes of the Brecons there are several forest trails starting from the car park at the far end of the reservoir.

LLANGORSE

8 miles NW of Crickhowell on the B4560

To the south of the village lies the largest natural lake in South Wales - **Llangorse Lake** (Llyn Syfaddan). Around four miles in circumference and following its way round a low contour in the Brecon Beacons, the waters of this lake were, in medieval times, thought to have miraculous properties. Today, the lake attracts numerous visitors looking to enjoy not only the setting but also the wide variety of sporting and leisure activities, such as fishing, horse riding and sailing, that can be found here. There is also a Rope Centre, with climbing,

Llangorse Lake

abseiling, potholing, log climbing and a high-level rope course.

TALGARTH

10½ miles N of Crickhowell on the A479

Lying in the foothills of the Black Mountains, Talgarth is an attractive market town with narrow streets that boasts many historic associations as well as some fine architecture. The 15th century parish **Church of St Gwendoline** has strong links with Hywell Harris (1714-73), an influential figure in the establishment of Welsh Methodism. Harris was also instrumental in establishing a religious community, The Connexion, which was organised on both religious and industrial lines.

Although this is now a quiet and charming place, Talgarth once stood against the Norman drive into Wales. Some of the defensive structures can still be seen today - the tower of the church and another tower that is now incorporated into a house. The latter tower has also served time as the jail.

On the outskirts of Talgarth stands Bronllys Castle a well-preserved centuries old keep built by the Norman baron Bernard of Newmarch. Originally a motte and bailey castle, it was later replaced with a stone edifice and now it is a lone circular tower standing on a steep mound that is in the hands of CADW - Welsh Historic Monuments.

LLANGYNIDR

4 miles W of Crickhowell on the B4558

Rising to the south of this riverside village on the open moorland of Mynydd Llangynidr, lies the **Chartists' Cave**, where members of the movement stored ammunition during their active years in the mid-19th century.

LLANGATTOCK

1 mile SW of Crickhowell off the A4077

The village church was founded sometime during the early 6th century and is dedicated to St Catwg, one of Wales' most honoured saints. He was born around AD 497 and by the end of his life, in around AD 577, Catwg, had become a Bishop and had taken the name Sophias.

To the southwest of the village, towards the boundary of the Brecon Beacons National Park lies the **Craig-y-Cilau Nature Reserve**. With over 250 plant species and more than 50 kinds of birds breeding within the reserve, this is one of the richest in the National Park.

132 THE WHITE SWAN

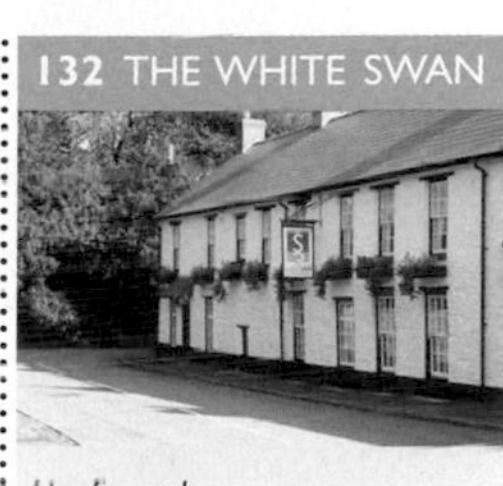

Llanfrynach

An elegant and rustic restaurant specialising in Mediterranean, French and traditional English cuisine.

see page 314

133 THE RED LION

Llangynidr

Great community pub with delicious food, ever changing ales, guest accommodation and entertainment for all.

see page 315

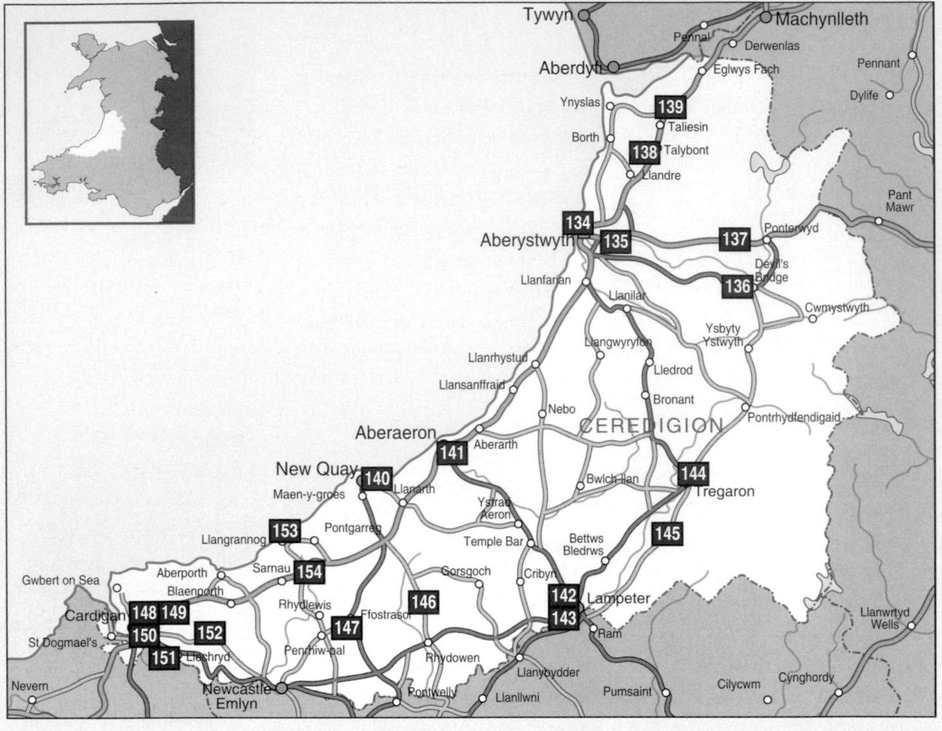

ACCOMMODATION

138 White Lion Hotel, Talybont, nr Aberyswyth — pg 126, 317
140 Penwig Hotel, New Quay, nr Llandysul — pg 127, 317
141 Feathers Royal Hotel, Aberaeron — pg 129, 318
142 Black Lion Hotel, Lampeter — pg 130, 319
143 Castle Hotel, Lampeter — pg 130, 319
144 Y Llew Coch, Tregaron — pg 132, 320
145 The New Inn, Llandewi Brefi, nr Tregaron — pg 133, 321
147 Tafarn Ffostrasol Arms, Ffostrasol, nr Llandysul — pg 134, 321
148 The Black Lion, Cardigan — pg 134, 323
150 Highbury Guest House & Restaurant, Pendre, nr Cardigan — pg 135, 324
151 Castell Malgwyn Hotel, Llechryd, nr Cardigan — pg 135, 325

FOOD & DRINK

134 The Carlton Restaurant, Aberystwyth — pg 122, 315
135 The Black Lion, Llanbadarn Fawr, nr Aberystwyth — pg 122, 315
138 White Lion Hotel, Talybont, nr Aberyswyth — pg 126, 317
139 Clettwr Cafe, Trerddol, nr Machynlleth — pg 126, 316
140 Penwig Hotel, New Quay, nr Llandysul — pg 127, 317
141 Feathers Royal Hotel, Aberaeron — pg 129, 318
142 Black Lion Hotel, Lampeter — pg 130, 319
143 Castle Hotel, Lampeter — pg 130, 319
144 Y Llew Coch, Tregaron — pg 132, 320
145 The New Inn, Llandewi Brefi, nr Tregaron — pg 133, 321
146 Tafarn Bach, Pontsian, nr Llandysul — pg 133, 320
147 Tafarn Ffostrasol Arms, Ffostrasol, nr Llandysul — pg 134, 321

Ceredigion

Ceredigion means the land of Ceredig, son of the Celtic chieftain Cunedda. The area is renowned for its unique brand of Welshness and ancient myths and legends are still vivid in the folk memory. The patron saint of Wales, St David, was born in Ceredigion and many famous Welsh princes are buried in the ruins of Strata Florida Abbey.

For visitors, though, this county is best known for its coastline on the great sweep of Cardigan Bay. Many of the one-time fishing villages have now become genteel resorts but few seem to have attained the great degree of brashness that is associated with other seaside holiday destinations. In the north of the county and close to the mouth of the River Dyfi is the great expanse of sand at Borth while, further south, the coastline gives way to cliffs and coves - once the haunt of smugglers.

Ceredigion's countryside features some of the most beautiful landscapes in Wales in which many rare species of birds, wildlife and plants abound. In particular, it is home to the graceful red kite. Keen birdwatchers are well served by nature reserves around the Teifi and Dyfi estuaries and at Llangranog, New Quay and Cors Caron.

The region is not as well endowed with castles as the counties further north, but Aberystwyth and Cardigan castles both saw fighting before they were left to ruins, and Cardigan is credited with being the venue for the first recorded Eisteddfod in 1176. This is also an important area of learning. St David's College at Lampeter, a world renowned ecclesiastical establishment, is now, as University College, part of the University of Wales, while Aberystwyth is home not only to the first university in Wales but also to the National Library of Wales.

Headland, New Quay

PLACES OF INTEREST

134 THE CARLTON RESTAURANT

Aberystwyth

Mother and son team offer lovely views across the bay with great homemade food all day every day.

see page 315

135 THE BLACK LION

Llanbadarn Fawr, Aberystwyth

A warm friendly pub serving the very best in real ales and fine food that has local produce at its heart

see page 315

ABERYSTWYTH

The largest town in Cardigan Bay, the seat of local government, the home of the University College of Wales and the National Library of Wales, Aberystwyth is not only the unofficial capital of mid-Wales but also a cosmopolitan coastal resort. Its Victorian and Edwardian heyday as a holiday centre has left a pleasing architectural legacy and its status as a university town means that there are plenty of pubs and they stay open later than in most of Wales.

Although there is evidence that the town is older, Aberystwyth as we know it, can certainly be traced back to the late 13th century when, in 1277, Edward I began building **Aberystwyth Castle.** He also granted a charter that made the settlement around the new fortification a free borough with a ditch and wall, a guild of merchants, a market and two fairs. In the early 1400s, Owain Glyndwr used the castle as his base for four years until it was recaptured by Prince Henry, later Henry V. There was more fighting here during the Civil War until it finally fell to Cromwell's soldiers in 1646 and was largely destroyed three years later. Today, the ruins, standing on the rocky headland, remain an impressive sight. Also on Castle Point can be found the town's **War Memorial**, a splendid monument that was commissioned the year after World War I ended; it is the work of the Italian sculptor Mario Rutelli.

In the years following the turmoil of the Civil War, and before the arrival of the railways, Aberystwyth remained essentially a fishing town, but with a growing shipbuilding industry. Although much of this industry has now ceased, **Aberystwyth Harbour and Marina** is still a bustling place that can accommodate more than 100 vessels. All manner of fish and seafood are still landed at the town quay

The arrival of the railways in the 1860s saw the town expand rapidly as first the Victorians and then the Edwardians made their way here to enjoy the sea air and the beauty of the great sweep of Cardigan Bay. The town's 700 feet long **Pier** was constructed in 1864 and the Pavilion at the end was added in 1896 to provide a capacious venue for light entertainment. Just to the north, along the coast from the town centre, lies the longest electric **Cliff Railway** in Britain - another product of the Victorian development which still carries passengers up the cliff face at a

Marina, Aberystwth

sedate four miles an hour. It was originally water-balanced but is now powered by electricity. From the summit there are panoramic views over the bay and inland to the Cambrian Mountains.

Opened nearly 100 years after the railway was constructed, and also on the cliff summit, is the **Great Aberystwyth Camera Obscura**, housed in an octagonal tower. A faithful reconstruction of a popular Victorian amusement, the huge 14 inch lens - the biggest in the world - gives visitors an even better view from this excellent vantage point.

While the town today certainly seems to cater to holidaymakers' every need, Aberystwyth is also a major seat of learning. The very first college of the University of Wales was established at Aberystwyth as was the very first Welsh medium primary school. The **Old College** was originally built in the 1870s to a design by JP Seddon and was intended to be a hotel designed to accommodate the influx of Victorian visitors. However the venture failed and in 1872 the high Gothic building was sold, becoming the first university in Wales and now home to the departments of Welsh, Education and Theatre, Film and Television. On the campus of the University of Wales is one the town's most striking buildings, the **Aberystwyth Arts Centre**, with a busy year-round programme of performances, exhibitions, cinema screenings, events, courses and workshops.

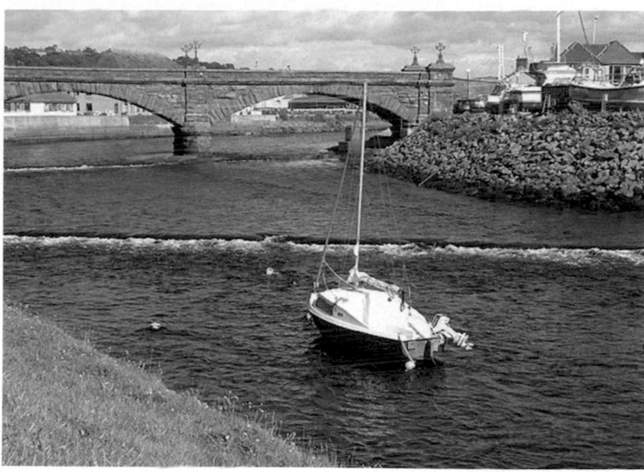

Afon Rheidol, Aberystwyth

The town is also the home of the **National Library of Wales**, one of only six copyright libraries in Great Britain and the keeper of the majority of materials that relate to the Welsh people and their culture. Founded in 1909 and eventually opened in 1937 by George VI, the library holds many early Welsh and Celtic manuscripts among which is the *Black Book of Carmarthen*, a 12th century manuscript that is the oldest in Welsh. Within the complex, the Drwm cinema and auditorium presents a wide range of screenings and performances.

AROUND ABERYSTWYTH

LLANBADARN FAWR

1 mile E of Aberystwyth on the A44

This village has now become a suburb of Aberystwyth but it was once a town in its own right and the seat of the oldest bishopric in Wales, established in the 6th

•

Housed in a beautifully restored Edwardian music hall, right in the centre of Aberystwth town, is the Ceredigion Museum (free). It boasts what has been described as "probably the most beautiful museum interior in Britain". The various exhibits tell the history of Cardiganshire through an interesting collection of materials: the history of seafaring, agriculture and silver and lead mining are all well chronicled.

•

136 DEVIL'S BRIDGE FALLS

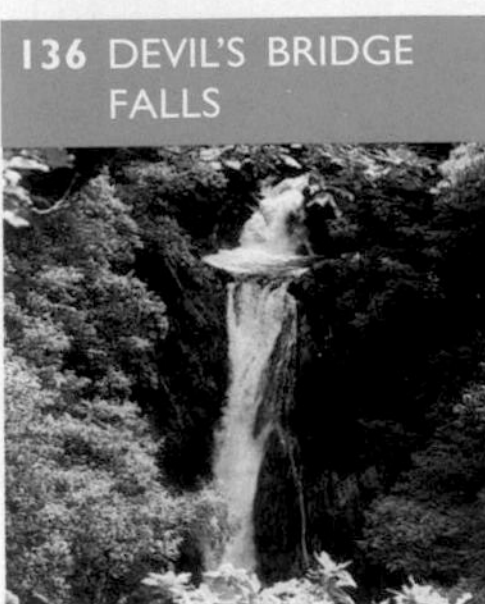

Devil's Bridge, Aberystwyth

The spectacular 300ft waterfalls can be seen in a breathtaking woodland setting.

see page 316

century. **St Padarn** established a small monastery here and the huge 13th century church is dedicated to him. It contains his tomb as well as two striking Celtic crosses from the 10th century that are associated with St Samson, Padarn's brother.

DEVIL'S BRIDGE

10 miles SE of Aberystwyth on the A4120

Devil's Bridge is the terminus of the **Vale of Rheidol Railway**, the narrow-gauge steam railway that runs for 12 miles from Aberystwyth through the Rheidol valley. It was built in 1902 for the valley's lead mines and continued as part of the British Rail network until the late 1980s when it was sold to the private company that now operates it from April to October. The attraction that draws even more visitors to Devil's Bridge is the sight of the splendid **waterfalls** that drop some 300 feet through a breathtaking gorge. While the scenery is marvellous, there are also three interesting bridges here - dating from the 11th, 18th and 20th centuries - which were built one on top of the other. An iron bridge built in 1901 straddles the top of the falls; just below it is a stone bridge of 1753 while, further down stream again, the original 11th century **Pont-y-gwr-Drwg** (Bridge of the Devil) spans the turbulent river. It was probably built by the monks of Strata Florida Abbey although local legend suggests that the bridge was built by the Devil and that he would claim the first soul to cross to the other side. However, an old woman, wanting to retrieve her stray cow, outwitted the Devil by throwing a crust across the bridge which her dog chased after. The Devil had to make do with the soul of the dog and the old lady safely retrieved her cow.

Along with the footpaths and nature trails that descend the 94 steps of Jacob's Ladder to view the falls, other paths lead to another vantage point - **The Hafod Arch**. It was erected in 1810 by Thomas Johnes, the squire of Hafod, to honour the Golden Jubilee of George III, the farmer king; Johnes also transformed the area with forestation, planting the surrounding countryside with more than four million trees as if in anticipation of the Forestry Commission who now own the land. The Arch, which marks the highest point on the former Hafod Estate of the old Aberystwyth-Rhayader road, is one of many points of interest on the **Pwllpeiran Trail**, a four-mile trail that affords exciting views over Hafod and the Upper Ystwyth Valley and provides information on the agriculture, forestry, wildlife and history to be seen along its route. One section of the walk joins the Cambrian Way Long Distance Path through Myherin Forest; on its way it passes through Gelmast farmyard, which was Thomas Johnes' original experimental farm.

YSBYTY CYNFYN

10½ miles E of Aberystwyth on the A4120

In the circular wall of the 19th

century village church dediated to St John are the remains of a Bronze Age **Stone Circle**. Two of the stones have been moved from their original positions to form the gate posts but many of the other ancient stones remain as they have for centuries.

PONTERWYD

10 miles E of Aberystwyth on the A44

An inn called the Borrow Arms recalls **George Borrow** who came here to dry out after falling into a peat bog. Norfolk born, Borrow was a noted philologist and linguist who travelled widely overseas, acting for a time as an agent for the British and Foreign Bible Society. Later, he tramped around England and Wales, sometimes with his step-daughter, and in 1862 published his best-known work *Wild Wales*.

Close to Ponterwyd is the **Nant yr Arian Visitor Centre**, a Forest Enterprise centre with forest walks and trails, a mountain bike trail, orienteering course, tea room, local crafts, and picnic and play areas. Here, too, is the **Kite Country Centre** and feeding station. Designated the Bird of the Century in 1999, the Red Kite was a fairly common bird in the Middle Ages, seen even in London scavenging in the streets. It was at that time considered useful and was even protected by the Crown, but with the passing of the Enclosures Act in the 16th century this impressive bird was among many species thought to be a threat to agriculture. Persecuted as vermin, they disappeared entirely from England and Scotland, although a few pairs remained in mid-Wales. With care from individuals and organisations, the numbers gradually increased, and now there are more than 300 breeding pairs in Wales. At 2 o'clock each afternoon the kites swoop down to be fed, joined by other species looking for an easy meal, including buzzards and ravens.

LLYWERNOG

9 miles E of Aberystwyth on the A44

Just to the north of the village lies the **Llywernog Silver-Lead Mine Museum and Caverns.** The museum covers the history of this major rural industry in mid-Wales. Llywernog opened in 1740 and enjoyed its most prosperous period between 1850 and 1879. In the slump that followed most of the mines closed for good, but Llywernog refused to die and was briefly reopened in 1903 as a zinc prospect. It was saved in 1973 by the present owners. Visitors are taken on a 30-minute underground tour exploring the miners' trail and, once outside again, can then pan for 'fool's gold' or try their dowsing skills by searching for veins of galena. Tel: 01970 890620.

TRE TALIESIN

7½ miles NE of Aberystwyth on the A487

This village was the home, in the 6th century, of one of the earliest recorded British poets, Taliesin. He is thought to have been buried here. The standing stone behind the village, **Bedd Taliesin** (Taliesin's Grave), actually dates

137 LLYWERNOG LEAD & SILVER MINE

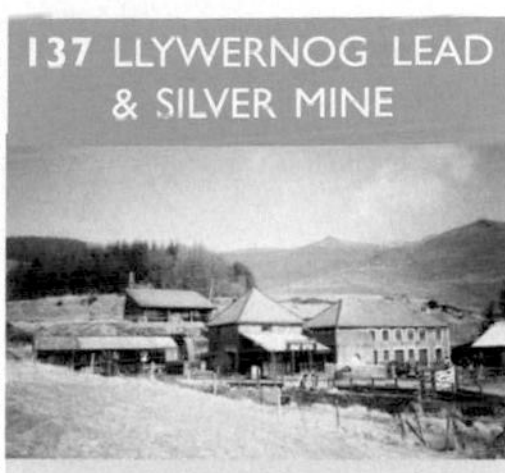

Ponterwyd, Aberystwyth

An opportunity to find out what life was like for the miners in the 18th century, with underground tours and interesting displays.

see page 316

138 WHITE LION HOTEL

Talybont

Much loved by the villagers of Talybont, this family run pub and B&B offers good wholesome food and ale in a friendly environment all day every day.

 see page 317

139 CLETTWR CAFÉ

Tre'r-Ddol

A family-run café, offering the very best in homemade cuisine

 see page 316

•

To the east of Borth lies Borth Bog (Cors Fochno), an important area of raised coastal peat mire (one of only two such areas in Europe) that supports an abundance of wildlife.

•

from the Bronze Age (around 15,000 BC) and while it marks a burial chamber it is unlikely to be that of the poet.

TRE'R-DDOL

8 miles NE of Aberystwyth on the A487

The former medieval deer park, **Lodge Park**, is now managed by Forest Enterprise who have restored this semi-natural woodland and have also preserved the northern boundary of the park that comprised a ditch and bank.

FURNACE

10½ miles NE of Aberystwyth on the A487

Dyfi Furnace (free) is an important early industrial site that has one of the country's best preserved charcoal burning blast furnaces. In the 18th century, this quaint old village was the site of an iron ore smelting foundry. The bellows that pumped the air into the furnace were powered by a huge waterwheel driven by the River Einion. The wheel has been restored to working order and visitors can browse around this industrial heritage site and museum.

The road opposite Dyfi Furnace leads up the **Cwm Einion** - Artists' Valley - which is so called because its lovely views made it a favourite haunt of 19th century water colourists. Walkers climbing up the valley will find pleasant woodland trails and picturesque picnic spots.

EGLWYS FACH

11 miles NE of Aberystwyth on the A487

Found in the sheltered waters of the Dovey estuary, the **Ynyshir RSPB Nature Reserve** provides sanctuary for a great many species of birds, in particular waders. It has an extensive network of walks, with bird watching hides, where visitors in winter can observe the unique flock of White-fronted Geese from Greenland and also the smaller flock of Barnacle Geese. This is also the most important breeding site in Wales for lapwings and redshanks. The Visitor Centre has copious information on the various species of birds found here and also arranges special interest guided walks on most weekends.

BORTH

5½ miles N of Aberystwyth on the B4353

The original settlement of this now popular seaside resort lies on the slopes of Rhiw Fawr and it is there that some of the older fishermen's and farmer's cottages can still be seen. The growth of the village began with the arrival of the railway linking it with Aberystwyth in the 1860s and its long, safe, sandy beach, along with the spectacular views out over Cardigan Bay and inland to the mountains, have ensured that it is still a popular holiday destination.

At very low tide it is possible to see the remains of a submerged forest that, according to local legend, once formed part of the dynasty of Cantre'r Gwaelod (the Lower Dynasty) which extended out into the bay and was protected by a huge sea wall. One night the gatekeeper is said to have had too much to drink and had forgotten to close the gates against the rising tide that, with the help of a storm, drowned the forest and the dynasty. A popular family attraction at Borth is **Animalarium**, an interesting collection of exotic animals including monkeys, crocodiles, large cats and reptiles.

YNYSLAS

7½ miles N of Aberystwyth off the B4353

Situated at the northern end of Borth beach, Ynyslas - the name means Green Island - extends to the Dovey estuary, where there are broad expanses of sand, particularly at low tide, although the swimming is unsafe. The **Ynyslas Sand Dunes and Visitor Centre** explains the natural beauty of the Dyfi in wildlife displays and slide shows. The Centre is home to an abundance of animals, birds, butterflies and moths. There is also a conservation shop selling books, stationery and 'green' pocket money gifts. From the centre there are glorious views over the river mouth to Aberdovey.

NEW QUAY

This small yet busy resort, whose harbour now boasts more yachts than fishing boats, built its economy on both shipbuilding and coastal trading. However, although these traditional ways of life declined in the 19th century as the rail links developed, New Quay has retained much of its maritime charm. The first vessel to be built here was a 36 ton sloop; the subsequent shipping boom brought a great deal of employment to the area and this caused the population to rise to 2000. Hand in hand with the shipbuilding and fishing industry, smuggling was also rife. In 1795 New Quay was described as a place of "infamous notoriety" and the headland was reputedly riddled with a network of caves where contraband was stored.

New Quay's natural surroundings as a port and harbour of refuge led to its being considered, at one time, as a suitable place from which direct

Fishing Boat, New Quay

140 PENWIG HOTEL

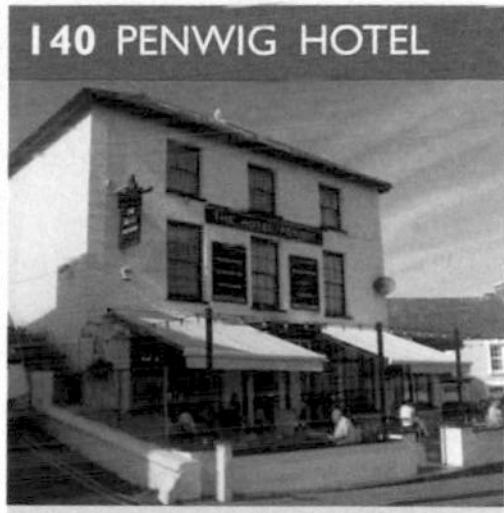

New Quay

Just minutes from the beach this fantastic hotel offers unrivalled views across the bay and delicious gastro-pub cuisine served in the popular restaurant below.

see page 317

•

To the south of New Quay there is a Heritage Coastal path that threads its way along the clifftops down through Cwmtudu to Llangranog and beyond. To the northwest of the town are the long sandy beaches of Treath Gwyn (White Beach) and Cei Bach (Little Quay) that were once a hive of shipbuilding activity and are now peaceful and secluded places.

•

communication could be made with Wicklow and Dublin. Today's visitors will find a variety of boat trips leaving from the main pier to cruise the waters of the Ceredigion Marine Heritage Coast. The cruises pass a rugged coastline whose cliffs support a myriad of sea bird colonies and there are regular sightings of bottlenose dolphins, porpoises and grey Atlantic seals. The **Lifeboat Station** at New Quay can be visited between 2 and 4.30 daily. One of the best-known figures in the area is the marine biologist Hanna Nuuttila, who earned the title RNLI Photographer of the Year 2008 for her photo of Pwllheli's Mersey Class boat aiding a yacht in trouble in a Force 8 storm. The **Heritage Centre** has displays on the town's history, including local characters, shipbuilding, smuggling and fishing. It also details what is being done to protect the area's bottlenose dolphins, grey seals and porpoises.

The sands and boating facilities at New Quay have long been an attraction for holidaymakers and the town's **Yacht Club** welcomes all visitors. The north beach leads to the rocky headland, New Quay Head, where an invigorating path follows the line of the sheer cliffs to Bird Rock, the home of many sea birds. Inland, the **Bird and Wildlife Hospital** treats and returns to the wild any birds or mammals needing veterinarian treatment, particularly birds involved in oil spillages.

Along with Laugharne in Carmarthenshire, New Quay lays claim to being the original Llareggub in Dylan Thomas' *Under Milk Wood.* Thomas and his family lived in New Quay for the last half of World War II and had an ambiguous relationship with the town: it is said that he was disliked in the town not least for his failure to pay his bills. On one occasion while drinking in his favourite watering hole, the Black Lion, Thomas had a row with an ex-commando officer just back from the front. The officer followed him home and shot at his rented bungalow with a machine gun. The officer was later tried for attempted murder but acquitted. Thomas's true opinion of New Quay may be inferred by spelling Llareggub backwards. In the spring of 2007, filming took place for a movie based on Thomas' life, *The Best Time of Our Lives*. Some scenes were shot on the beach at New Quay with Keira Knightley and Sienna Miller as the stars.

AROUND NEW QUAY

LLANINA

1 mile E of New Quay off the A486

This tiny village, with a long tradition of fishing, is also associated with the legend of King Ina of England. One day, in the early 8th century, a ship was wrecked on the rocks close to the village during a violent storm. A local fisherman, his wife and daughter, having seen the disaster, rowed out to rescue the stricken sailors. Once safe, the family, unable to understand the language spoken by the shipwrecked strangers, sent for a monk who told them that they had saved King Ina. In thanksgiving, the king built a church from which the present church, **Ina's Church**, takes its name. **Cerrig Ina**, Ina's Stones, can be seen offshore and mark the spot where the original church stood.

ABERAERON

4½ miles NE of New Quay on the A487

Situated at the mouth of the River Aeron, this is a delightful small town with charming Georgian houses, particularly around **Alban Square**. These are the result of astute town planning initiated in the early 19th century by the Reverend Alban Gwynne, who was happy to spend his wife's inheritance on dredging the Aeron estuary and creating this new port with its neat streets and elegant terraces. This was instrumental in turning the settlement from a small fishing hamlet into a bustling port that also became famous for its shipbuilding.

On the quayside, the former Sea Aquarium is where you can buy tickets for boat trips around the bay with a fair chance of spotting en route the dolphins who stay here all year round.

At the southern end of Aberaeron, Clôs Pengarreg is a craft centre housed in traditional stone buildings where visitors can see the beautiful products being hand-made and have the opportunity to buy a unique reminder of their time in the town.

Afon Aeron, Aberaeron

Just inland from the town is Aberaeron Wildlife Park, home to llamas, red deer, parrots, owls and an albino crow who starred in the TV series Gormenghast.

ABERARTH

6 miles NE of New Quay on the A487

Although often bypassed because of the charm of its more illustrious neighbour, Aberaeron, Aberarth is a picturesque village overlooked by **St David's Church**. Founded in the 6th century, and originally hidden from the sea, the church was rebuilt in 1860 but it still contains three early Christian inscribed stones from the 9th and 10th centuries.

PENNANT

8 miles E of New Quay on the B4577

In the 19th century, this village was the home of a recluse named **Mari Berllan Piter** (Mary of Peter's Orchard). Supposedly granted magical powers, her exploits were legendary: when a miller refused to

141 FEATHERS ROYAL HOTEL

Aberaeron

This impressive family run Georgian hotel is within walking distance of the shore, with a reputation for fantastic cuisine, luxurious accommodation and unbeatable service.

see page 318

142 BLACK LION HOTEL

Lampeter

Found right on the high street this relaxing and contemporary hotel also serves high quality food and drink for all.

see page 319

143 THE CASTLE HOTEL

Lampeter

Decked with a magnificent floral display this award winning hotel serves some of the finest home made food in the area.

see page 319

grind her corn she made his mill wheel turn the wrong way, a young girl who stole an apple from Mari's orchard was forced to walk home backwards and sometimes, it is said, that Mari turned herself into a hare. The ruins of Mari's cottage, known locally as The Witch's Cottage, can still be seen surrounded by her now overgrown orchard.

LLANARTH

3 miles SE of New Quay on the A487

A local story tells that one night the Devil tried to steal the bell from **Llanarth Church**. However, he made such a noise that he woke the vicar who, armed with a bell, a book and a candle, climbed up into the belfry to investigate. By solemnly repeating the name of Christ, the vicar managed to drive the Devil to the top of the tower and forced him to jump off. In the graveyard there is a strangely scarred stone that is said to bear the marks made by the Devil when he landed.

CROSS INN

2 miles S of New Quay on the A486

To the south of the village is **New Quay Honey Farm** which is the largest honey farm in Wales and is housed in an old chapel. The farm attracts more than 35,000 visitors a year and has a shop, tea room and the World of the Honey Bee exhibition. Travellers from all over the world have witnessed one of nature's most fascinating processes and sampled at first hand a wonderful range of natural hive products. In 1999 a meadery was added to produce some delicious honey wines which can be bought in the shop. The farm is also home to a tropical ant colony. Tel: 01545 560822

LAMPETER

Lampeter is best known as the home of University College. Founded in 1822 by Bishop Thomas Burgess of St David's, **St David's College**, as it was first known, is a world renowned ecclesiastical and predominantly Welsh speaking college that is the oldest institution in Wales. The main university buildings include CB Cockerell's original stuccoed quadrangle of buildings dating from 1827 which were designed to mimic an Oxbridge College. Underneath these buildings lies the town's old castle motte. Since 1971, the college has been integrated with the University of Wales - hence its new name **University College** - although the campus still retains its own unique atmosphere.

While the students add a certain bohemian flavour to Lampeter during term time, this is essentially a genteel and very Welsh town with a pleasant mixture of Georgian and Victorian buildings. Perhaps the most striking of these is the Black Lion on the High Street, an 18th century coaching inn complete with original stables and coach house. Also of architectural interest is Falcondale Hall which was built in the early 1800s for the local landowning family, the Hartfords. It is now a luxury hotel.

Back in the 1600s, on what is now Maesyfelin Street, stood the home of the **Lloyds of Maesyfelin**. When the only daughter of the family, Elen, became engaged to a certain Samuel Pritchard, her four brothers, fearing the loss of their inheritance, tied her lover underneath a horse and galloped him from Lampeter to Llandovery. Samuel died of his injuries and the brothers threw his body in nearby River Teifi. On hearing what had happened Elen was driven mad with sorrow and died soon afterwards. Samuel's father, Rhys, put a curse on the family and, just a short while later, their family house caught fire and burnt to the ground; the eldest brother, out of remorse or perhaps due to the curse, killed his brothers and then himself.

AROUND LAMPETER

CILIAU AERON

9 miles NW of Lampeter on the A482

Set in the beautiful Aeron Valley with extensive estate and parkland walks, **Llanerchaeron** (National Trust) is an 18th century Welsh gentry estate – a rare survival. Designed and built by John Nash, the house has many virtually unaltered features including a service courtyard with dairy, laundry, brewery and salting house. It gives a wonderful insight into how the Welsh gentry and their staff lived some 200 years ago. Also within the estate are two restored walled gardens and a working organic farm.

PONTRHYDFENDIGAID

15 miles NE of Lampeter on the B4343

Just a short distance from the village, and close to the ford of the Blessed Virgin, stands **Strata Florida Abbey** (CADW, free), a Cistercian house founded in 1164. This austere order was renowned for seeking out remote and isolated sites for its religious establishments and Strata Florida - the vale of Flowers - is one such site. Even though the abbey is in ruins today, it is still an evocative place for visitors. Just two years after its foundation the abbey's lands were overrun by Rhys ap Gryffyd but in 1184 he refounded the abbey; most of the buildings now seen in ruins date from this time. During the 12th and 13th centuries, Strata Florida became one of the most important religious centres in

Strata Florida Abbey

144 Y LLEW COCH

Tregaron

This bright red pub in the heart of Tregaron serves up real ale, old fashioned favourite dishes made with fresh Welsh produce with bed and breakfast or self catering accommodation available.

 see page 320

•

Housed in the Old National School in Tregaron, which opened in 1873, the Tregaron Red Kite Centre and Museum is an interesting and informative place which is dedicated to the red kite. It has the dual aim of providing people with a better understanding of these beautiful birds of prey and with ensuring their survival in this part of mid-Wales. Visitors to the centre can also see the kites being fed daily here during the winter months. Also on display at the museum are artefacts from Ceredigion Museum that relate specifically to Tregaron and the surrounding area.

•

Wales. Some of the last native princes and princesses of Wales were buried here, as was Dafydd ap Gwilym, probably the most famous of all Welsh medieval poets. In 1238, the Welsh princes swore their allegiance to Llywelyn the Great's son, Dafydd, at the abbey. This was also the time when the abbey flourished in terms of wealth, mainly through wool from the sheep that grazed on its vast lands.

After the Dissolution in the 16th century, the abbey and its lands passed through various hands and the ruins today consist mainly of the cloister, a monumental Norman west doorway, and the chapter house by the church that now serves as Pontrhydfendigaid's parish church. In the north transept stands a memorial to the poet Dafydd ap Gwilym. The yew tree that stands amidst the abbey's remains is thought to mark his grave. One legend associated with the abbey suggests that the Holy Grail, which was given to the monks at Glastonbury by Joseph of Aramathea, later ended up at Strata Florida. When the abbey, which formed part of the Nanteos estate, was left to fall into ruins, the cup, which had pieces bitten out of its sides by pilgrims convinced of its healing powers, was stored at Nanteos mansion.

TREGARON

9 miles NE of Lampeter on the A485

This small market town - a meeting place for 19th century drovers - still serves the remote farming communities in the Teifi valley. A stronghold of Welsh language and culture, it's an attractive place with a pleasantly old world atmosphere. Handsome Georgian and Victorian houses surround the market place, together with a fine old drover's inn, the Talbot Hotel. In the centre of the square stands a statue of **Henry Richard** (1812-1888), the Liberal MP and son of Tregaron, who was a vociferous supporter of disarmament and an advocate of arbitration in international disputes; he became known as the 'Apostle of Peace'.

In one corner of the square is the **Rhiannon Welsh Gold Centre** which stocks an up-market selection of jewellery based on Celtic designs and made partly from Welsh gold.

The land around Tregaron is sheep country and the town was to become famous for its woollen industry and, in particular, hand-knitted woollen socks. Most of the socks were transported to the mining communities of South Wales, but David Davies, an engineer from Llandinam, found another use for the wool - he used it to form a stable bed on which to lay the railway across Cors Caron bog. Lying to the north of the town, this ancient bog is home to rare flora and fauna. The land here was originally covered by a glacier which, at the end of the last Ice Age, melted to create a natural lake which filled with sediment and vegetation. The peat surface grew, creating three distinctive domes above the original lake bed level. The Old Railway Walk follows the trackbed of the old Manchester-Milford Haven railway, provides visitors with the chance to observe some of the 170 or so species of bird recorded here, including red kites, buzzards and sparrow hawks. The walk starts from the car park near Maesllyn Farm on the B4343, two miles north of Tregaron.

LLANDDEWI BREFI

7 miles NE of Lampeter on the B4343

The small community of Llanddewi Brefi (population 500) has become famous as the home of Daffyd - "the only gay in the village" in the TV comedy series *Little Britain.* Residents say the rather dubious fame has had little impact, although the village shop does sell T-shirts printed with the tag. But shop-keeper Neil Driver observed "I only sell the *Gay Times* to order, and one hasn't been placed with me yet!"

This traditional country village was host in AD 519, to a synod which was attended by St David. The meeting was called to debate the Pelagian heresy, a doctrine advocating freedom of thought rather than the biblical version of original sin that determined the morality of the time. **St David's Church**, in the village, stands on a mound said to have risen up as St David preached during the synod. The church itself dates from the 13th century and, inside, contains some old inscribed stones: one is known as St David's Staff and another has an inscription in the obscure Ogham language thought to commemorate a heretic of the type that St David was denouncing.

Close by are the sites of several hill forts including **Llanfair Clydogau**, where the Romans mined for silver. They sit beside the Sarn Helen - a military road. The road once connected a gold mine in the south, at Dolaucothi, with a fort at Bremia in the north.

CAPEL DEWI

8½ miles SW of Lampeter on the B4459

Close to the village is **Rock Mills Woollen Mill** which was established in 1890 by John Morgan whose descendants still weave here. The machinery is powered by a waterwheel – the only one of its kind surviving in Wales – that also drives a small alternator to provide lighting. The mill once provided power to the neighbouring church. From pure new wool, the mill produces all manner of woollen goods, including bedspreads, blankets and rugs, and it is one of the last traditional mills where the entire process, from fleece to fabric, may be viewed. Tel: 01559 362356

LLANDYSUL

11 miles SW of Lampeter on the A486

Set in the deep and picturesque valley of the River Teifi, this traditional little Welsh town was another centre of the woollen industry. Today, this tranquil little town is renowned for its outstanding scenic views, fishing and white water canoeing as well as for the delights of its Victorian

145 THE NEW INN

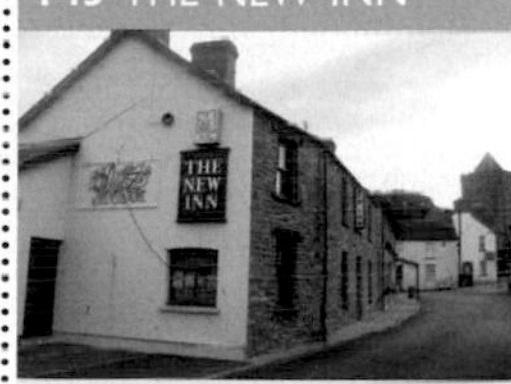

Llandewi Brefi

A charming and traditional inn located at the heart of one of the most famous villages in Wales.

see page 321

146 TAFARN BACH

Pontsian

The Davies family extend a warm welcome to their nineteenth century village inn which combines good food and real ale with traditional features and modern facilities.

see page 320

147 TAFARN FFOSTRASOL ARMS

Ffostrasol , nr Llandysul

A former coaching inn, which prides itself on good, locally sourced home cooked food.

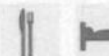
see page 321

148 THE BLACK LION

Cardigan

Restored to its former glory by the vibrant Phillips family, the Black Lion offers great food, drink and en suite accommodation in one of the oldest coaching houses in Wales.

see page 323

149 EAGLE INN

Cardigan

Traditional, home cooked food is the order of the day at the Eagle Inn, which dates back to the late 1700s.

see page 324

town centre. The agricultural nature of the area is reflected in the town's fortnightly livestock market.

Just outside the town, in the historic former Canbrian Mills, the **National Wool Museum** is a flagship museum in this part of Wales. It presents a comprehensive history of the Welsh woollen industry. A working mill on the site can be seen in operation and supports the production of fabrics in traditional Welsh patterns. The extensive displays here include the National Textile Collection.

A few miles up the A486, **Ffostrasol** is the setting for the annual **Cnapan Folk Festival**, the largest Celtic folk music event on the British mainland.

CARDIGAN

Once the busiest port in Wales, Cardigan is an ancient borough that received its first charter in 1199; it was at that time a power base of Lord Rhys, one of the last Welsh princes to rule an independent principality. The few remains of **Cardigan Castle**, which stand beside the river, conceal a turbulent history: built in the late 11th or early 12th century by Gryffydd ap Rhys, the fortifications were strengthened around 1170 before it passed into the hands of the Earl of Pembroke in 1240. Thought to be the site of the first Eisteddfod in 1176, the castle fell to Parliament in 1645 during the Civil War. Badly neglected over the years, the castle featured in BBC-TV's *Restoration* series but failed to win enough votes to get the funding it needed. However, a vigorous local campaign continues and the castle is now occasionally open to the public.

Rhys ap Gruffydd was said to have inaugurated the Welsh national eisteddfod at the castle in 1176. The **Gorsedd Stone Circle**

Gorsedd Circle - Cardigan

stone circle dates from 1976 when the eisteddfod was again held here to mark the 800th anniversary of the tradition. The central stone acts as the throne for the winning bard.

The River Teifi, which provides Cardigan with its Welsh name Aberteifi, continues to be fished for trout and some anglers still use the traditional coracle. Dating from pre-Christian times, coracles were once common on many of Britain's rivers and have changed little in design over the centuries. The silting up of the Teifi estuary, along with the arrival of the railway, were the main causes of Cardigan's decline as a major port which had, at one time, more than 300 ships registered here.

However, while the river is no longer at the centre of the town's economy it is still a place of charm enhanced by the six-arched **Teifi Bridge** an ancient structure which was rebuilt in 1726.

Housed in an 18th century warehouse on Teifi Wharf, the **Cardigan Heritage Centre** tells the story of this former county town, from prehistoric times through to the present day. From its origins in the medieval age to its heyday in the 18th and 19th centuries, the port, in particular, is explored through the eyes of those who lived here. In addition to the permanent exhibitions, there is a programme of temporary exhibitions covering a range of topics.

Those looking for performing arts and other cultural events will not be disappointed as the **Theatr Mwldan**, in the town, is one of Wales' leading theatrical venues.

Beside the river, just outside the town, is the **Welsh Wildlife Centre** (free), a nature reserve that provides a variety of habitats, including reed beds, woodland and meadow. As well as an extensive network of footpaths and being home to a surprisingly wide variety of flora and fauna, the reserve also has an excellent modern visitor centre.

AROUND CARDIGAN

ST DOGMAELS

1 mile W of Cardigan on the B4546

Situated on the western banks of the mouth of the River Teifi, it was here that the Lord of the Manor, Robert Martyn, founded **St Dogmael's Abbey** in the 12th century for the monks of the Benedictine order brought over from Tiron in France. An earlier Welsh abbey on the site was sacked by the Vikings. Adjacent to the abbey ruins is a church which features an inscribed Sagranus stone whose markings and Latin inscriptions provided the key to deciphering the ancient Goidelic language. Close to the abbey is **The Mill** (Y Felin), a water-powered flour mill.

GWBERT-ON-SEA

2½ miles N of Cardigan on the B4548

This small resort on the eastern banks of the River Teifi estuary is an excellent place for cliff walking and for looking out over the estuary and observing its wildlife.

150 HIGHBURY GUEST HOUSE & RESTAURANT

Pendre

Renowned for its fabulous home cooking and Sunday carvery, this Victorian guesthouse also offers homely en suite accommodation perfect for exploring the Cardigan coast.

see page 324

151 CASTELL MALGWYN HOTEL

Llechryd

Classic Georgian mansion in 8 acres of grounds offering first class cuisine, gracious surroundings and en suite rooms.

see page 325

152 PENLLWYNDU INN

Llangoedmor, nr Cardigan

A fairly new inn serving quality home made food

see page 326

A little way up the coast from Aberporth is the National Trust's beach at Penbryn, an SSSI, part of the Ceredigion Heritage Coast, and a good spot for insect, bird and dolphin spotting. The approach to this popular, sandy beach is by way of Hoffnant Valley from the Trust's car park at Llanborth Farm where a shop, café and WCs are open in season. The valley is known locally as Cwm Lladron, Robbers Valley, probably because of old-time smuggling connections.

Cardigan Island Coastal Farm Park is an ideal place from which to look out over Cardigan Island from the headland and also to observe the rare choughs that nest on the cliffs. In the caves below, a colony of seals breed and some lucky visitors may also spot Cardigan Bay's bottle-nosed dolphins. The farm is home, too, to friendly farm animals, including goats, sheep, pigs, ponies and ducks, as well as a llama, a wallaby and rare breed cows.

MWNT

3½ miles N of Cardigan off the A487

This beauty spot was on the Pilgrims' Route to Bardsey Island - the burial ground of over 20,000 Celtic saints - in the north. The tiny **Church of the Holy Cross** dates from around 1400 and stands on the site of a much earlier Celtic church, originally built in a hollow to hide it from view and to protect it from possible raiders coming by sea.

Much of the coastline here, including the cliffs, the rocky headland and the safe family beach, is owned by the National Trust. This area is a geological SSSI (Site of Special Scientific Interest) and is part of the Ceredigion Heritage Coast; it is especially rich in maritime flora. The bay was the site of a battle in 1155, when Fleming invaders were repelled by the local forces.

FELINWYNT

3½ miles NE of Cardigan off the A487

The village is home to the **Felinwynt Rainforest and Butterfly Centre** where, in a large tropical house, visitors are transported to the jungle to see the beautiful free-flying butterflies that live amidst the exotic plants. Sounds recorded in the Peruvian Amazon intensify the tropical atmosphere. There is also a rainforest exhibition, which explains the delicate ecology of this interesting habitat, a tea room and a gift shop. Tel: 01239 810882

ABERPORTH

6 miles NE of Cardigan on the B4333

The original village of Aberporth consisted of small, single storeyed cottages with thick mud walls and thatched roofs that reflected the simple and hard lives of those living in this fishing and farming community. Long ago Aberporth became famous for its herring industry as great shoals of the fish came to feed and spawn in the shallow waters of this sheltered part of the Cardigan Bay coast. Today, the village is a small yet thriving resort that is popular with yachtsmen.

TANYGROES

8 miles NE of Cardigan on the A487

Just north of the village, **The Internal Fire Museum of Power** explores the history of the stationary internal combustion engine in industry and agriculture. The collection covers early oil engines through to modern gas turbines, with an emphasis on diesel power from the 1920s to the 1960s. Exhibits are run daily, ranging from small farm engines through to 25-ton diesel engines. One of the oldest diesel engines in the world is on display here. Tel: 01239 811212

LLANGRANOG

9½ miles NE of Cardigan on the B4334

Lying in a narrow valley and rather reminiscent of a Cornish fishing village with its narrow streets dropping to the sea, Llangranog is one of the most attractive villages along the Ceredigion coast and its small beach can become crowded in summer. The headland and cliffs to the north of the village (now the property of the National Trust) offer excellent walks and dramatic scenery. The sheltered coves around Llangranog helped to sustain a thriving shipbuilding industry but they also proved perfect landing and hiding places for contraband and the area was rife with smuggling activity.

To the east of the village lies the **Walled Garden at Pigeonsford**, a Georgian walled garden which has been replanted with botanical collections of herbaceous plants and shrubs as well as vegetables and fruits. Maintained as a working garden, the walled garden is set in large and less formal grounds that include shrubbery, woodland and riverside walks.

HENLLAN

11½ miles SE of Cardigan on the B4334

This village is home to the **Teifi Valley Railway**, another of Wales' famous little trains. This narrow gauge railway, which originally served the slate quarries, was created from a section of the Great Western Railway (also known as God's Wonderful Railway) which served the rural areas of West Wales. Today's passengers can enjoy a 40-minute steam train journey through this delightful valley. At the Henllan terminus there are plenty of attractions to keep the whole family amused: woodland walks, crazy golf, the station tearooms and a gift and souvenir shop.

Also at Henllan are the remains of a World War II Italian prisoner of war camp. The church here was built by the Italians and was constructed of anything that was available and would normally be considered as rubbish - tin, hardwood, paper and so on. The results are amazing. The church can be visited by appointment.

153 THE SHIP (Y LLONG)

Llangrannog

Renowned for its creative menu, fresh fish dishes and unrivalled views across the sea, the Ship offers fantastic Welsh cuisine in a stylish and relaxed atmosphere.

see page 327

154 BRYNHOFFNANT INN

Llandysul

Just a short walk from the coast, this traditional inn offers great home cooked food and family entertainment.

see page 328

Teifi Valley Railway, Henllan

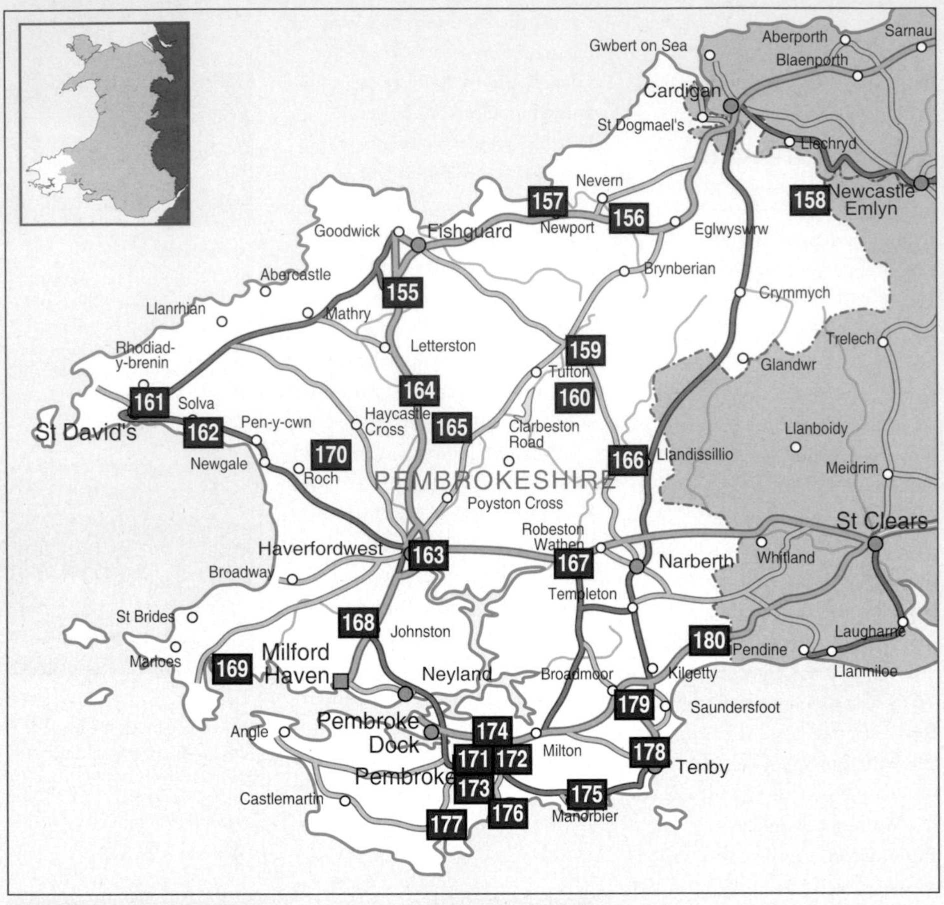

ACCOMMODATION

156 Salutation Inn, Felindre Farchog pg 141, 329
160 Twmpath Guest House, Maenclochog pg 144, 331
161 The City Inn, St Davids pg 145, 333
162 The Royal George, Solva pg 147, 334
164 The Wolfe Inn, Wolfcastle pg 148, 336
166 Nant-y-Ffin Hotel & Motel, Llandissilio, nr Clynderwen pg 149, 336
168 The Windsor Hotel, Johnston pg 150, 339
170 Nolton Haven Quality Cottages, Nolton Haven, nr Haverfordwest pg 152, 340
172 The Lion Hotel, Pembroke pg 153, 342
176 Stackpole Inn, Stackpole pg 154, 345
178 Tenby House, Tenby pg 156, 346
179 The Woodridge Inn Hotel, Saundersfoot pg 156, 347
180 Llanteglos Lodges & The Wanderer's Rest Inn, Llanteg, nr Amroth pg 157, 347

FOOD & DRINK

155 The Gate Inn, Scleddau, nr Fishguard pg 141, 328
156 Salutation Inn, Felindre Farchog pg 141, 329
157 Fronlas, Newport pg 141, 330
158 Nags Head Inn, Abercych pg 142, 331
159 Post Office Bistro & Bar, Rosebush, nr Clynderwen pg 143, 332
161 The City Inn, St Davids pg 145, 333
162 The Royal George, Solva pg 147, 334

Pembrokeshire

Pembrokeshire, which is known as Sir Benfro in Welsh, is home to Britain's only coastal national park - the Pembrokeshire Coast National Park. Running right around the ruggedly beautiful south western tip of Wales, around St Brides Bay and up along the north facing coast almost to Cardigan, the Park also includes quiet fishing villages, the huge cliffs at Castlemartin, sweeping golden beaches and small, often busy harbours. Although not strictly on the coast, the labyrinthine Cleddau river system also lies within the Park's boundaries and here there are delightful little villages such as Cresswell and Carew as well as the superb sheltered harbour of Milford Haven.

St David's Cathedral

Offshore there are various islands, including Grassholm, Ramsey, Skokholm and Skomer, which have changed little since they were named by Viking invaders. Many are now bird and wildlife sanctuaries of international importance. Grassholm is home to thousands of gannets, Skokholm has Manx shearwaters, Skomer has shearwaters and puffins. Ramsey harbours such species as choughs and the red-legged crow, and is also the resting place of many Welsh saints. One island, Caldey, has for more than 1500 years been the home of a religious community which continues today to live a quiet and austere life. Between their devotions, the monks of Caldey scrape a living from the land and are famous for their range of perfumes and toiletries inspired by the island's wild flowers. Pembrokeshire is the home of the corgi, which was brought to the notice of the Kennel Club by Captain Jack Howell. He presented Princess Elizabeth with her first corgi, and the rest, as they say, is history.

PLACES OF INTEREST

FISHGUARD

Situated at the mouth of the River Gwaun, from which the town takes its Welsh name Abergwaun, the geography of Fishguard can be somewhat confusing to visitors. The picturesque old harbour, a pretty little quayside lined with fishermen's cottages, is Lower Fishguard, which was the location for the fictional seaside town of Llareggub used in the filming in the 1970s of Dylan Thomas' play, *Under Milk Wood*, starring Richard Burton. The new harbour, built at the beginning of the 20th century, lies across the bay at Goodwick and it is from here that the ferries depart for Ireland. On the high ground between the two harbours lies the main town of Upper Fishguard, a bustling place packed with shops, restaurants and pubs.

It was here, in February 1797, that the last invasion of Britain took place when a poorly equipped band of Frenchman landed at Carregwastad Point. Under the command of an American officer, Colonel William Tate (who hoped to start a peasants' rebellion), the 1400 strong French expeditionary force - mostly ex-convicts - stole drinks and looted the local farms. Unchecked by the local militia, the unruly invaders set up headquarters at a nearby farm and, according to local tradition, several local women, dressed in red cloaks, advanced on the French soldiers. The women were led by Jemima Nicholas who carried a pitchfork, and the drunken invaders fled in terror mistaking the ladies for the British army. The French retreated to the beach below Goodwick, where they formally surrendered to Lord Cawdor just two days after landing. Jemima Nicholas, who is said to have captured 12 Frenchmen singlehanded, became famous as the 'General of the Red Army'. She died in 1832 and is buried in St Mary's Church.

A memorial stone was erected in 1897 as part of the centenary celebrations. It still stands near the entrance of Saint Mary's churchyard facing Main Street. In 1997, to mark the bicentenary of this bizarre event, Elizabeth Cramp RWS was commissioned to design **The Last Invasion Embroidered Tapestry**. Worked by more than 70 embroiderers, the 100-feet long tapestry is in the style of the famous Bayeux Tapestry and depicts scenes from the invasion. It now has its own gallery in Fishguard's recently renovated Town Hall.

French Stone, Fishguard

AROUND FISHGUARD

DINAS

3½ miles NE of Fishguard on the A487

The village is situated at the base of **Dinas Island (NT)** which is, in fact, a promontory that culminates in Dinas Head. At the end of the Ice Age it was indeed an island but over the millennia has gradually moved westward to join up with the mainland. The headland is an important nesting site for sea birds, and grey and Atlantic seals can often be seen swimming offshore.

NEWPORT

6½ miles E of Fishguard on the A487

Spread across a hillside that falls gently to the estuary of the Afon Nyfer river, Newport is an engaging place that is well geared up for tourists with a range of good accommodation, restaurants and pubs. As its name would suggest, Newport was once an important port; it had a brisk wool trade until the time of the great plague, when trade was diverted to Fishguard. Newport was also the capital of the Marcher Lordship of Cemmaes, which originated after the Norman Conquest - the only one not to have been abolished by Henry VIII. The people of Newport still elect their mayor annually and each August the mayor leads the ceremony of 'Beating of the Bounds' when he circles the town's boundaries on horseback. The Lords' Castle (private), which was built in the 13th century, has now been incorporated into a mansion house.

Newport's former school now houses the **West Wales Eco Centre** (free), founded in 1980 as the Newport & Nevern Energy Group. Its aim is the advancement of public education in all aspects of energy conservation and energy use. It hosts various exhibitions and offers advice on aspects of sustainable living.

Just north of Fishguard is **Carreg Coetan Arthur**, a burial chamber reputed (like a number of others!) to hold the remains of King Arthur.

Newport is an excellent base from which to explore the Preseli Hills to the south. It was from these mountains that the famous bluestones were taken to Stonehenge, an incredible feat of engineering involving transporting 8-tonne stones along rivers and over land to Salisbury Plain. In 1995, a ready-cut bluestone was discovered in the river near Milford haven. It is assumed that the mighty pillar had fallen off the barge during the long journey to Wiltshire some 4000 years ago.

NEVERN

8 miles E of Fishguard on the B4582

Nevern's **Church of St Brynach** is dedicated to the 5th century Irish saint whose cell was on nearby **Carn Ingli** - the Hill of Angels. Inside the church are two interesting carved stones. The Maglocunus Stone, dating from the 5th century, commemorates Maglocunus, the son of Clutor and it bears both Latin and Ogham inscriptions. The Cross Stone is

155 THE GATE INN

Scleddau

Traditional roadside inn known for serving classic home cooked pub favourites, well kept ales and a warm welcome.

see page 318

156 SALUTATION INN

Felindre Farchog

Outstanding hotel in beautiful riverside location offering excellent cuisine and 3 star en suite accommodation.

see page 329

157 FRONLAS

Newport

Friendly, family run licensed cafe serving homemade meals, snacks and crepes all day.

see page 330

158 NAG'S HEAD INN

Abercych

Fantastic olde worlde inn with an enchanting history serving great homemade food, drink and modern facilities.

see page 331

incised with a very early Celtic cross and dates from the 10th century. Outside in the churchyard with its ancient yews stands one of the finest Celtic crosses in Wales - **St Brynach's Cross**. Dating from the 10th or 11th century, the cross stands some 13 feet tall. According to tradition, the first cuckoo to be heard each year in Pembrokeshire sings from the top of the cross on St Brynach's Day (7th April). Another curiosity in the churchyard is the 'bleeding yew'. One of the trees exudes a browny-red sap from its bark. Local tradition asserts that it will continue 'bleeding' until a Welsh-born lord of the manor rules once again from Nevern Castle whose overgrown and tumbledown ruins stand high above the village to the northwest.

EGLWYSWRW

11½ miles E of Fishguard on the A487

To the west of the village lies **Castell Henllys**, an Iron Age fort that is still being excavated by archaeologists. While the dig is continuing throughout the summer months, visitors to this late prehistoric site can also see the thatched roundhouses and outbuildings created to give as true as possible an insight into the lives of Iron Age man. Events throughout the season help to portray the wide spectrum of Celtic culture, from story-telling and craft demonstrations to the celebration of ancient festivals. A sculpture trail through woodland and the river valley features works inspired by tales from The Mabinogion.

CILGERRAN

15 miles NE of Fishguard off the A478

The substantial remains of **Cilgerran Castle**, one the most picturesque in Wales, can be seen sitting on a rocky promontory overlooking the River Teifi. A tranquil site today, this land was once hotly disputed territory and the castle's defences reflect this - there are almost sheer drops on two sides of the building, while the 13th century twin round towers and curtain walls protect the flank away from the cliff. The building of the castle is thought to have begun around 1093 but it was strengthened by Gerald de Windsor, to whom it was granted by Henry I. Thereafter it changed hands many times, being partially sacked by Rhys ap Gryffydd in 1164, retaken by the Earl of Pembroke in 1204 and finally falling to Llywelyn the Great in 1233.

Cilgerran Castle

The castle is forever associated with the legend of Princess Nest, the Welsh Helen of Troy. In 1109 she was abducted by the besotted Owain, son of the Prince of Powys, who also imprisoned her husband, Gerald of Pembroke. Gerald escaped by slithering down a toilet waste chute inside the castle walls.

Cilgerran Castle was one of the earliest major tourist attractions in Wales - in the 18th and 19th centuries it was fashionable to take a river excursion to the ruins from Cardigan. The romantic ruins provided inspiration to artists as distinguished as JMW Turner and Richard Wilson.

The River Teifi is one of the few rivers in Britain where fishing from coracles can still be seen. In August, coracle races are held on the river at Cilgerran.

From the point where the A478, A484 and A487 meet, brown and white tourist signs lead to the **Welsh Wildlife Centre**, within the Teifi Marshes Nature Reserve on the banks of the Teifi. It's an excellent place for spotting birds and animals, wild flowers and butterflies. Wild footpaths pass through woodland, reed beds, meadows, marsh and riverside, providing the chance to see a vast variety of wildlife in different habitats, and the site commands stunning views. More than 130 species of birds have been recorded, and more than 20 mammals, including otter, red deer, voles, badgers and bats. Tel: 01239 621600

CROSSWELL

10 miles E of Fishguard on the B4329

This village, on the northern slopes of the Preseli Hills, is home to one of the grandest megalithic remains in Wales, **Pentre Ifan Burial Chamber** (CADW). An ancient chamber with a huge 16-feet capstone, the monument is made of the same Preseli bluestones that somehow found their way to Stonehenge on Salisbury Plain.

PONTFAEN

4½ miles SE of Fishguard off the B4313

The village lies on the western edge of the **Preseli Hills**, whose highest point, **Foel Cwmcerwyn** (1,759ft) lies to the southeast; the views stretch as far as Snowdonia to the north and the Gower Peninsula to the south. These hills have seen many inhabitants come and go and they are littered with prehistoric sites. There are Iron Age hill forts, Bronze Age burial cairns and standing stones scattered along the 'Golden Road', the ancient bridleway across the range.

LLANGOLMAN

11½ miles SE of Fishguard off the A4313

Housed in a renovated 18th century corn mill, **The Slate Workshop** is a place where the art of handcrafting quality Welsh slate items continues. A wide range of articles is made here, including high quality plaques, sundials, clocks and objets d'art. Many illustrate the great skill required to work and carve the slate.

To the south of the village

•

In the foothills of the Preselis is the Gwaun Valley, a truly hidden place that runs from the hills to Fishguard. Some of the locals in this area still celebrate New Year on 12 January, in keeping with the custom that predates the introduction of the Gregorian calendar in 1752.

•

159 POST OFFICE BISTRO AND BAR

Rosebush

Cosy village inn with a surprisingly lively atmosphere known for its great value bistro meals and live jamming sessions.

see page 332

160 TWMPATH GUEST HOUSE

Maenclochog

200 year old award winning guest house with the best breakfast and Welsh warm welcome around.

see page 331

•

The tales told by James Wade, one of Pembrokeshire's best known storytellers, are rather far fetched, but nonetheless delightful. On one occasion Wade, who died in 1887, recounted that, while he was fishing on Goodwick beach, a great carrion crow swooped out of the sky and carried him in its beak across the sea to Ireland. On reaching land, the crow dropped Wade and he landed in a cannon where he spent the night. As he was waking the next morning, the cannon was fired and Wade was rocketed across St George's Channel and he landed beside his fishing rod in the exact spot from which he had been plucked!

•

stands another interesting building, **Penrhos Cottage**, which is one of the few lasting examples of an 'overnight' house. If a man, with the help of his friends, could build a dwelling between sunset and sunrise, he was entitled to all the land that lay within, literally, a stone's throw from the door. This particular 'overnight' house dates from the 19th century and still contains the original furnishings.

GOODWICK

1 mile W of Fishguard off the A487

This once small fishing village is now effectively the base for Fishguard harbour which was built here between 1894 and 1906 by the Fishguard and Rosslare Railways and Harbours Company to provide a sea link between southwest Wales and Ireland. Still offering a busy ferry service today, Goodwick is older than it first appears. The settlement was known to ancient inhabitants as Gwlad hud a Lledrith - the Land of Mystery and Enchantment.

STRUMBLE HEAD

4 miles W of Fishguard off the A487

This huge headland, with its lighthouse warning ships off the cliffs on the approach to Fishguard harbour, offers some spectacular coastal scenery as well as an outlook over the great sweep of Cardigan Bay. Just to the east lies **Carregwastad Point**, a remote headland which was the landing place of the ill-fated French invasion of Britain in the 18th century. Also to the east is **Good Hope** (National Trust), a traditional farmed landscape with narrow fields, historical field boundaries, vernacular farm buildings and an unusually wide variety of plant life.

LLANGLOFFAN

6 miles SW of Fishguard off the A487

This village is home to the **Cheese Centre** where, in the heart of the Pembrokeshire countryside, traditional Welsh farmhouse cheese is made by the Downey family on their farm. The cheese-making process - from milk to the finished cheese - begins at 6am and visitors are welcome to view the process from 10am onwards. Llangloffan cheese is sold in specialist shops around the world but visitors to the centre have the chance to sample the cheese at the farm's tea rooms, as well as to look round the museum and meet the friendly farm animals.

PORTHGAIN

10 miles SW of Fishguard off the A487

As well as being a natural beauty spot, the sheltered harbour at Porthgain has added interest as the harbourside is dominated by the shell of a 19th century brickworks. This monument to the village's industrial heritage stands close to remnants from Porthgain's heyday as a slate and granite exporting port. Many buildings as far afield as London and Liverpool have Porthgain granite in their construction. Nowadays, it is difficult to imagine the hectic scenes of around a century ago when the harbour would have been packed with boats queuing for their cargoes of stone and brick needed for Britain's building boom. The harbour's almost unique personality has led it to being used as a location by film-makers.

ST DAVID'S

16 miles SW of Fishguard off the A487

Although it enjoys the status of a city because of its cathedral, St David's is actually an attractive large village. It was here, in the 6th century, that St David founded a religious order and on this site, in 1176, the magnificent **St David's Cathedral** was completed. It stands in a deep hollow below the streets so that not even its square 125ft high tower can be seen above the rooftops. The cathedral is approached by way of the medieval Tower Gate, the only one of the original four city gates to have survived. It contains an exhibition about the history of the city. From the Gate, a flight of steps, known as the 39 Steps after the Church of England's 39 Articles of belief, leads to the cathedral entrance. The undoubted highlight of the interior is the oak roof which displays wonderfully ornate carvings by 15th century craftsmen. Other treasures include an intricate 14th century rood screen, the exquisite 16th century fan tracery roof in Bishop Vaughan's Chapel, and some saintly bones which are believed to be those of St Caradoc. In 1120, Pope Calixtus II decreed that two pilgrimages to St David's were equivalent to one to Rome and successive British monarchs, from William the Conqueror to Queen Elizabeth II, have worshipped here. The Queen also has a special seat reserved for her in the cathedral and it was from here that Maundy Money was distributed for the first time in Wales.

Entrance to Porthgain

On the other side of the river, across from the cathedral and in the same grassy hollow, stand the ruins of **St David's Bishop's Palace**, a once imposing building. Even in its present ruined state, it still conveys the wealth and influence of the Church in medieval times. Most of the Palace's construction was overseen by Bishop Henry de Gower in the mid-1300s and he spared no expense on creating this lavish residence, which he felt befitted a leader of both the Church and State. There were two complete sets of state rooms at the Palace set around a courtyard; de Gower used one for his private business and the other for ceremonial

161 THE CITY INN

St David's

In the centre of historic St David in this great inn known for its home cooking, great hospitality and accommodation.

see page 333

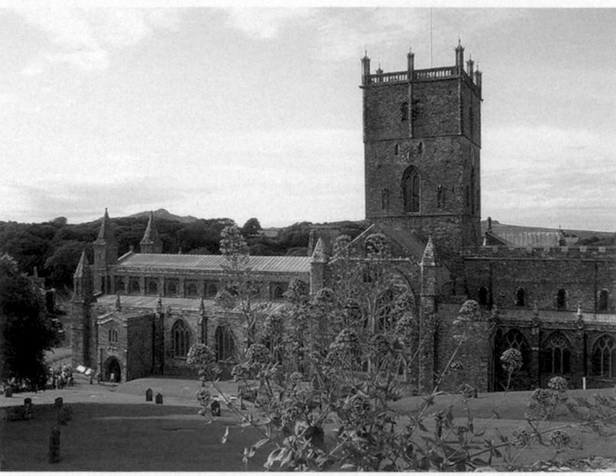

St David's Cathedral

entertaining. The palace fell into disrepair in the 16th century after the incumbent bishop stripped the roof of its lead in order to pay for his five daughters' dowries.

In August 2002, St David's hosted the National Eisteddfod, one of the highlights of which was the induction of the Archbishop-designate of Canterbury, Dr Rowan Williams, into the Gorsedd of Bards, a historic order of Druids. The ceremony was held in a circle of standing stones fashioned, like the stones at Stonehenge, from Pembrokeshire rock. The ceremony involved the singing of Welsh Christian hymns and the Welsh National Anthem, the reading of a citation by the Arch-Druid and the wielding of a giant ceremonial sword - a burdensome task entrusted to Druid Ray Gravell, a former Welsh rugby international. Dr Williams is the third Archbishop of Wales to be a member of the Gorsedd. Speaking Welsh is a prerequisite for consideration for nomination, with one exception - the Queen.

Just outside the city, in a stunningly beautiful spot overlooking the sea, are **St Non's Well** and the ruins of **St Non's Chapel**. The bay, too, is named after St David's mother - St Non - and legend has it that David was born here during a great storm in around AD 520. The waters of St Non's Well are said to have special powers for healing diseases of the eye and it was much visited during the Middle Ages by pilgrims to St David's. David's father was the chieftain Sant, his grandfather Ceredig, king of the region around Cardigan. Little is known about David, save that he received a formal education, gained great authority in the church and moved the seat of ecclesiastical government from Caerleon to Mynyw, now St David's. St David is a central figure in one of the many legends concerning how the leek came to be adopted as the national emblem of Wales. The legend states that just before a battle against the Saxons he advised the Britons to wear a leek in their caps to distinguish them from the enemy. St David's Day, March 1st, is the traditional national day of the Welsh, when Welsh people all over the world wear the national emblem, the leek, or the other national emblem, the daffodil. The Welsh words for leek and daffodil are the same (*cenhinen* means leek, *cenhinen pedr* means daffodil), which could explain why both are national emblems.

Another coastal beauty spot, which is also steeped in legend, is **St Justinian's**, a rock-bound harbour that is home to the St David's Lifeboat Station. The station can be visited daily between 10am and 4pm. Justinian was a 6th century hermit who retreated across to **Ramsey Island**, a short distance offshore, to devote himself to God. A strict disciplinarian, he must have been too severe with his followers as they eventually rebelled and cut off his head! Justinian is then said to have walked across the waters of Ramsey Sound, back to the mainland, with his head in his arms. Ramsey is a Norse name, a legacy of the Dark Ages when this part of the coast was terrorised by Viking invaders. Today, the island is an RSPB reserve that is home to an abundance of wildlife. Boat trips round the island offer visitors the chance to observe the numerous sea birds and the colonies of grey seals. Ramsey has the greatest concentration of grey seals among Pembrokeshire's estimated seal population of 5,000.

SOLVA

16 miles SW of Fishguard on the A487

Situated at the end of a long inlet and well protected from the sometimes stormy waters of St Bride's Bay, Solva harbour is one of the most sheltered in Wales. Green hills roll down to the quayside and this picturesque view was the last sight of Wales for many 19th century emigrants who sailed from Solva to America for 10 shillings - the price of a one way ticket. Now no longer such a busy port, Solva is a charming old seafaring village that boasts a good range of craft shops. **Solva Woollen Mill**, in the beautiful valley of the River Solfach, has been in continuous production since it opened in 1907. It now specialises in carpets and rugs, and visitors can usually see weaving in progress.

HAVERFORDWEST

This old county town, with its pleasant rural surrounding, stands on the banks of the labyrinthine Cleddau river system and is more or less in the centre of Pembrokeshire. Lining the steep streets of this hilly town are some fine Georgian buildings that date back to the days when Haverfordwest was a prosperous port trading largely with Bristol and Ireland.

However, the town predates this trading boom by several

162 THE ROYAL GEORGE

Solva

Children, dogs and muddy boots welcome at this fun and friendly pub specialising in fresh local seafood and fresh local music.

see page 334

Weir and Salmon Run, Haverfordwest

163 BRISTOL TRADER

Haverfordwest

A great friendly pub serving great food and real ales throughout the day in a scenic riverside location.

see page 335

164 THE WOLFE INN

Wolfecastle

Fantastic inn welcoming all the family for fine food, real ale and great accommodation all day every day.

see page 336

165 PUMP ON THE GREEN

Spittal

A popular village inn offering the very best in service and pub grub.

see page 337

centuries and its unusual name is a legacy of Viking raids. Set on a hill overlooking the River Cleddau is the striking landmark of **Haverfordwest Castle** which was built around 1120 by Gilbert de Clare. The town grew up around the fortress and throughout the 12th and 13th centuries it saw various noble residents including Gryffydd ap Rhys, Henry II and Edward I.

Haverfordwest also saw fluctuating fortunes during the Civil War as the town changed hands several times before it was finally taken by Parliament's General Laugharne in 1645. He ransacked the castle and the tumbledown remains offer little of interest apart from the former Governor's house which is now home to the town's **Museum and Art Gallery**.

The remains of a **Priory Church**, founded by Augustinian Canons in the early 13th century, can be found by the Western Cleddau river. Excavations of the priory land have revealed that there were gardens here in the cloister and also between the priory buildings and the river. The riverside gardens, which were laid out in the mid-15th century, provide a rare example of the sort of garden that is often seen in medieval manuscripts and the narrow raised beds have been replanted with plant species appropriate to the period.

Close by is a strange, ghostly border that cannot be seen. It is known locally as the **Landsker** (or land scar) it divides the English speaking 'little England beyond Wales' of south Pembrokeshire from the Welsh speaking north. This abrupt division of the county can be traced back to early medieval times when Norman invasions into these parts paved the way for Anglo Saxon and Flemish immigrants.

A line of castles was built from Amroth right across to Roch and, although the Landsker is an invisible border, its significance has been profound in the past. It was unthinkable that a marriage should take place between a man and a woman from different sides of the line even though they may have lived only a short distance apart.

AROUND HAVERFORDWEST

SCOLTON

4½ miles NE of Haverfordwest on the B4329

Scolton Manor House is a small country house dating from around 1840. Its interior provides interesting insights into the lifestyle of a fairly wealthy 19th century family. The house, stable block and exhibition hall form part of the **Pembrokeshire County Museum** and feature a number of displays that illustrate the history of this south-western region of Wales. Outside, there's a Carriage House displaying a collection of local artefacts, including traps. The surrounding **Country Park** has lovely landscaped grounds, nature trails, picnic areas and a play area. There's also an award-winning

Visitor Centre with an exhibition that looks to the future, highlighting in particular various green issues and the wildlife of the surrounding park.

LLYS-Y-FRAN

7½ miles NE of Haverfordwest off the B4329

The impressive dam built to form **Llys-y-fran Reservoir** in the 1960s has been constructed in sympathy with the surrounding countryside and, when it was officially opened in 1972 by Princess Margaret, the reservoir was able to meet the growing needs of the county's population and of the oil refineries at Milford Haven. Surrounded by the glorious **Country Park**, which lies in the shadow of the Preseli Hills to the north, there is a seven-mile perimeter path around the reservoir that provides an opportunity to possibly see some of the local inhabitants, including foxes, badgers, mink, squirrels and otters. The fishing on the reservoir is some of the best in Wales. It is regularly stocked with rainbow trout and has a steady population of brown trout.

CANASTON BRIDGE

7 miles E of Haverfordwest on the A40

To the south of the village can be found two very different attractions. **Blackpool Mill**, beside the Eastern Cleddau river, dates from the early 19th century and it is one of the finest examples of a water powered mill in Britain. Further south and hidden among trees is **Oakwood**,

Blackpool Mill, Canaston Bridge

Wales' premier theme park. It boasts Europe's longest watercoaster, biggest wooden rollercoaster and largest skycoaster. As well as the outdoor rides there is an all-weather complex with a multitude of games, puzzles and rides and also Playtown, which is aimed at younger children.

NARBERTH

9½ miles E of Haverfordwest on the A478

This agreeable little town set on a steep hill has become something of a magnet for shoppers because of its up-market shops and art galleries. According to The Mabinogion, Arberth (its Welsh name) was where Pwyll, Prince of Dyfed, held his court. **Wilson Castle**, in the southern part of the town, is a successor to the original fortification here. Only a few fragments still stand of the castle rebuilt in 1264 by Sir Andrew Perrot and dismantled following the Civil War.

166 NANT-Y-FFIN HOTEL AND MOTEL

Llandissilio

Fine family run hotel with spectacular restaurant, en suite accommodation and 200 seater licensed function room.

see page 336

167 THE BUSH INN

Robeston Wathen

A friendly team invite all guests to make the most of the great food on offer with deals throughout the week.

see page 338

168 THE WINDSOR HOTEL

Johnston

Great traditional pub welcoming visitors and their dogs, serving fine food, real ale alongside comfy en suite accommodation.

see page 339

•

East of the Cleddau toll bridge lies the tidal estuary formed by the confluence of the Western and Eastern Cleddau rivers, into which also flow the Rivers Cresswell and Carew. Winding a silvery ribbon through the rural landscape, it passes some of the Pembrokeshire Coast National Park's most beautiful scenery. Yet this area is so often overlooked by visitors that is has become known as the Secret Waterway.

•

MARLETWY

6 miles SE of Haverfordwest off the A4075

Cwm Deri Vineyard, to the south of Martletwy and set in the Valley of the Oaks, is the ideal place to see vines growing from spring through to the autumn harvest. At the vineyard shop visitors can purchase estate grown vintage wines, fruit wines and liqueurs. For younger members of the family, the vineyard is home to some rescued donkeys and there is also a teddy bears' hideaway.

THE RHOS

3½ miles SE of Haverfordwest off the A40

The Rhos, the only village in the ancient parish of Slebach, overlooks the Eastern Cleddau and here, close to the river, stands **Picton Castle**, the historic home of the Philipps family. It is still lived in by the direct descendants of Sir John Wogan, who had the castle built in the 13th century. Although the principal rooms were remodelled in the mid-18th century, some medieval features remain. In the 1790s, the 1st Lord Milford added the wing that now includes the superb dining room and drawing room.

The castle is also home to an **Art Gallery** with a permanent exhibition of paintings by Graham Sutherland. Outside, the gardens are equally impressive and include a walled garden with fish pond, rosebeds, culinary and medicinal herbs and herbaceous borders. In the extensive **Woodland Garden** there is a fine collection of woodland shrubs in among the ancient oaks, beeches, redwoods and other mature trees.

MILFORD HAVEN

6½ miles SW of Haverfordwest on the A40

As well as being the name of the town, Milford Haven is also the name of the huge natural harbour here. Described by Nelson as "the finest port in Christendom", the harbour offers some of the best shelter in the world to large ships as it is some 10 miles long by up to two miles broad. Norsemen used the harbour, as did both Henry II and King John who set sail from here to conquer Ireland, but it was Sir William Hamilton (husband of Lord Nelson's Lady Emma) who, having inherited two nearby manors, saw the potential of the Haven as a major harbour. Hamilton was away in Naples as an Envoy Extraordinary so he appointed his nephew RF Greville to establish the town around the harbour. Greville contracted a Frenchman, J-L Barrallier, to lay out the town and dockyard in a square pattern that can still be seen today. (The tomb of Sir William can be seen in the graveyard of St Katerine's Church, while inside the church are a bible and prayer book presented by Lord Nelson.) Although the docks, completed in 1888, failed to attract the hoped-for larger ships, the Neyland trawler fleet moved here and by the beginning of the 20th century, Milford Haven had become one of the country's leading fishing ports. During both

World Wars, the Haven was busy with Atlantic convoys but after 1945 there was a decline and trawling also began to disappear. However, since the 1960s Milford Haven has developed as a major oil port and is still used by the leading oil companies. New natural gas terminals and storage facilities have been built and work starts soon on a new power station on the north shore of the Milford Haven waterway.

Aptly housed in a former whale oil warehouse that dates from 1797, the **Milford Haven Museum** has a range of displays that follow the fortunes of the town and dockyard including hands-on exhibits tracing the town's history from a whaling port to a premier oil terminal.

SANDY HAVEN

8 miles SW of Haverfordwest off the B4327

The sheltered creek in this lovely village has been described as truly idyllic. Many birds can be seen feeding here, particularly at low tide in the spring and autumn. The picturesque banks of the creek are heavily clad with trees and a path from the village provides walkers with an excellent view of the entrance to Milford Haven harbour.

ST ISHMAEL'S

9 miles SW of Haverfordwest off the B4327

This small village on the Marloes and Dale Peninsula is named after a colleague of the 6th century St Teilo. Close by is evidence of even earlier inhabitants of the area. Just half a mile away stands the **Long Stone**, the tallest standing stone in the Pembrokeshire Coast National Park.

DALE

11 miles SW of Haverfordwest off the B4327

A delightful little sailing and watersports centre, Dale lays claim to being one of the windiest places in Britain - on average, it endures gale force winds on more than 30 days each year. However, on the other side of the climatic coin, Dale is also one of the sunniest places in the country with an annual average of 1800 hours a year - or five hours a day! To the south of the village, on the southern tip of the peninsula, is **St Ann's Head** where a lighthouse and coastguard station keep a close watch over the dangerous rocky shores at the entrance to Milford Haven.

MARLOES

11 miles SW of Haverfordwest off the B4327

This inland village, on the road to **Wooltrack Point**, has a sandy bay to the southwest with **Gateholm Island** at its western extremity. Only a true island at high tide, the name comes from the Norse for Goat Island and there are traces here of a possible monastic settlement.

Close by, at **Martin's Haven**, boats leave for Skomer and Skokholm Islands. Skomer Island National Nature Reserve and Skokholm and Grassholm provide some of the best and most spectacular birdwatching anywhere in Britain.

169 THE BROOK INN

St Ishmael's

Great village inn near the Pembrokeshire coast, specialising in traditional home cooking and great live entertainment.

see page 163398

Right up until the end of the 19th century the ancient custom of hunting the wren, which was supposed to embody the evils of winter, was followed throughout Wales. In Pembrokeshire, the hunting took place on Twelfth Night and the captured bird would be placed in a carved and beribboned 'wren house' and paraded around the village by men singing of the hunt. A particularly fine example of a wren house, from Marloes, can be found in the Welsh Folk Museum, at St Fagans, near Cardiff.

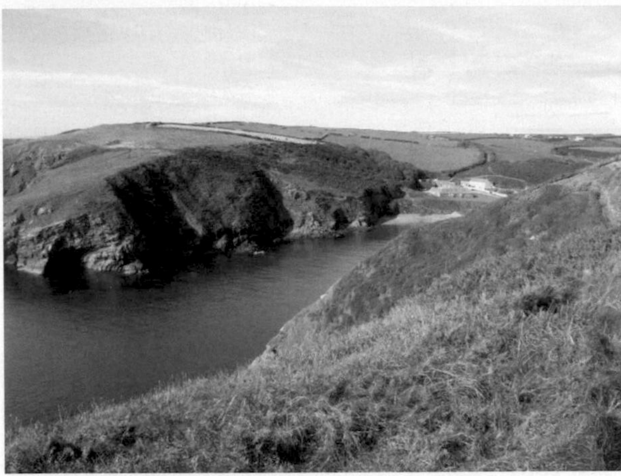

Nolton Haven

170 NOLTON HAVEN QUALITY COTTAGES

Nolton Haven

Holiday properties ranging from 5-star cottages to caravans, and from farmhouse B&Bs to the local hotel.

see page 340

171 PEMBROKE CASTLE

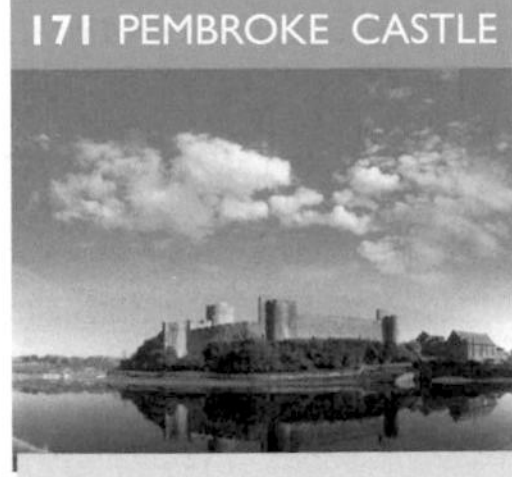

Pembroke

Dating back to the 12th century, this imposing structure is a magnet for lovers of history.

see page 341

NOLTON HAVEN

6½ miles W of Haverfordwest off the A487

The village sits at around the centre of St Brides Bay and the coastline here has steep, undulating cliffs and sandy beaches which have remained completely unspoilt despite being within easy reach of Haverfordwest and Milford Haven. As part of the Pembrokeshire Coast National Park, the coastline here is rich in outstanding natural beauty with a wide variety of natural amenities available to the holidaymaker including various short and longer distance footpaths from where an abundance of wildlife, sea birds and wild flowers can be seen. This area is a mecca for walkers, bird watchers, surfers, swimmers and sailors.

ROCH

5½ miles W of Haverfordwest off the A487

Found on a rocky outcrop overlooking the village and the surrounding plain, are the remains of **Roch Castle**, which was originally built in the 13th century by the feudal Lord of Roch, Adam de la Roche. A local story tells that de la Roche was told by a witch that he would be killed by a snake, but that if he could pass a year in safety, then he need never fear her prophecy. Accordingly, de la Roche had the castle built in such a way as to be out of reach of any snake and constructed on this particularly well defended site. His year free from snakes began and de la Roche moved into the top floor of the castle and remained there, in constant fear, for a year. The very last night of his self-enforced imprisonment was bitterly cold and someone sent a basket of firewood to the castle to help Adam pass the night in comfort. The basket was taken to his room and, as de la Roche was putting the logs on the fire, an adder crawled out from among the logs and bit him. The next morning, Adam de la Roche was found dead in front of his hearth.

PEMBROKE

This historic town on the southern side of the Pembroke River is notable for its long and unbroken line of well-preserved medieval town walls, dominated by the mighty fortress of **Pembroke Castle.** The castle was founded in the 11th century by the Montgomerys, who established the first timber castle on a rocky crag above the River Cleddau. The present structure was built between 1189 and 1245 and became the focal point for the control of "Little England Beyond Wales" as this area became known. The famous round keep is nearly 80ft tall with walls 19ft thick and the towers, turrets, oak-beamed halls, tunnels and battlements resound with history. In 1454, the castle and the accompanying earldom passed to Jasper Tudor, whose nephew, Henry Tudor, was born in the castle and later became Henry VII.

Just half a mile from the castle, across Monkton Pill, stood **Monkton Priory** which was founded in 1098 by Arnulf de Montgomery for Benedictine monks and was given to St Albans in 1473. The priory church, with its long narrow barrel-vaulted nave and monastic chancel, was rearranged in the 14th century and, after lying in ruins for many years, was restored again in the late 19th century.

AROUND PEMBROKE

UPTON

3 miles NE of Pembroke off the A477

Set in a secluded valley running down to the River Carew, **Upton Castle Gardens** has three raised formal terraces that drop down from the medieval castle. Along with the rose gardens and herbaceous borders, there are 40 acres of wooded grounds containing some 250 species of trees and shrubs. There's also a medieval chapel from which the walled garden can be seen.

CAREW

4 miles E of Pembroke on the A4075

Located on the shore of the tidal mill pond, **Carew Castle** is one of the few such buildings to display the development from Norman fortification (it was built between 1280 and 1310) to Elizabethan manor house. The site is much older, as archaeological excavations have found remains which go back some 2000 years. Various remarkable individuals have connections with the castle, but the castle displays also give insights into the lives of servants, craftsmen, priests and common soldiers of the time. A Great Tournament held at Carew in 1507 was attended by 600 nobles.

Here too can be seen one of only three restored tidal mills in Britain. **Carew Tidal Mill** still retains its original machinery. The Story of Milling exhibition traces the history of milling through the ages and the mill's role in the local community. While touring this lovely four-storey building, visitors are given explanations of each stage of the milling process. As well as the castle and the mill, the Carew site also incorporates a causeway, a medieval bridge and an 11th century **Celtic Cross** that is one of the best examples of its kind in Wales.

MANORBIER

5½ miles SE of Pembroke off the A4139

Manorbier is charmingly situated at the head of a valley that reaches down to the shore in a beautiful bay with a safe bathing beach. The

172 THE LION HOTEL

Pembroke

A historic and traditional hotel that moves with the times with great offers on its tasty homemade food and drink.

see page 342

173 BROWNS CAFÉ & RESTAURANT

Pembroke

A delightful café and restaurant owned by the same woman who opened it eight decades ago

see page 341

174 THE CASTLE INN

Manorbier, nr Tenby

A charming inn located in a beautiful village on the south Pembrokeshire heritage coast.

see page 343

175 FRESHWATER INN

Freshwater, nr Pembroke

A fine friendly inn serving outstanding food and real ale throughout the day whilst overlooking South Pembrokeshire's stunning coastline.

see page 344

176 THE STACKPOLE INN

Stackpole

Fine gastro-pub with en suite guest accommodation in a scenic location near the coast.

see page 345

village's name is thought to have been derived from Maenor Pyr (Manor of Pyr) and Pyr is believed to have been the first Celtic abbot of Caldey, living in the 5th century. Overlooking the bay of the same name, **Manorbier Castle** was conceived by Odo de Barri in 1095 when he built a wooden hall within a defensive structure but it was his son, William, who began construction of the stone fortification in the early 12th century. Famous for being the birthplace, in 1146, of Giraldus Cambrensis, Gerald of Wales, a monk and chronicler who wrote the first account of life in medieval Wales, the castle was described by him as being "the pleasantest spot in Wales".

Today, life size wax figures placed at various points, including the impressive great hall, the turrets and the chapel, bring the history of this ancient building to life as atmospheric music captures the castle's spirit. The castle gardens were laid out by JR Cobb in the late 19th century and there is also a late Victorian cottage with appropriate herbaceous borders lining the castle walls.

LAMPHEY

1½ miles SE of Pembroke on the A4139

Just northwest of the village, in the 13th century, the medieval bishops of St David's built the magnificent **Lamphey Bishop's Palace** as a retreat from the affairs of Church and State. Though improved over a period of 200 years, the major building work was undertaken by the dynamic Bishop Henry de Gower between 1328 and 1347 and he was responsible for the splendid great hall. Although now in ruins, this is a peaceful and tranquil site where successive bishops were able to live the life of country gentlemen among the estate's orchards, vegetable gardens and rolling parkland.

ST GOVAN'S HEAD

5 miles S of Pembroke off the B4319

The cliff scenery is at its most spectacular at St Govan's Head where the tiny religious site of the 13th century **St Govan's Chapel** huddles among the rocks almost at sea level. Accessible by climbing down 52 stone steps, this minute chapel was built on the site of a holy well that once attracted pilgrims who believed the well's waters to have miraculous healing powers.

Inside is a vertical cleft in the rock which, according to legend, first opened so that St Govan could hide inside and escape his enemies. Closing behind him, the rock did not reopen until the danger had passed. Accordingly, a wish made while standing in the cleft and facing the rock will come true provided the person making the wish does not change his or her mind before turning round. Although many miracles have been credited to St Govan he remains a mysterious and little known man. Some believe him to have been a disciple of St David while others claim that he was a thief who, having miraculously found the hiding place, became a convert. St Govan is also thought by some to have been a woman named Cofen - the wife of a 5th century chief - who became a recluse.

BOSHERSTON

4½ miles SW of Pembroke off the B4319

To the east of the village and occupying part of the former Stackpole estate of the Earls of Cawdor are **Stackpole Gardens**, which were landscaped in the 18th century. Romantic in style and containing some interesting and well-engineered water features, including an eight arched bridge, these are intriguing gardens to explore. The original manor house has gone but the 19th century terraces, woodland garden and summer house remain, along with a grotto, an ice house and three walled gardens.

Also within the Stackpole Estate are some beautiful woods, two miles of coastline and, at Stackpole Quay, what must be the smallest harbour in the country. It barely has space for two boats side by side.

PEMBROKE DOCK

1½ miles NW of Pembroke on the A477

Once an important naval dockyard, Pembroke Dock stands on the dividing line between the developed and the undeveloped shores of the Milford Haven. Downstream are the large petrochemical plants and oil terminals which take advantage of the Haven's deepwater channels while, upstream, are the enchanting waters of the Cleddau river system.

The town mushroomed in the 19th century when it was chosen as a site for the naval dockyard after Milford Haven, on the other side of the haven, refused to provide a site. The town was constructed on an American-style grid plan with wide streets which are lined with some sturdy Victorian houses. Today, its most visible activity is as the terminal for ferries sailing to Rosslare in Ireland.

TENBY

In Wales's National Tourism Awards, 2005, Tenby won top honours as the most popular tourist destination in the principality. The whole place is a real delight, prompting many eulogies such as this from the artist Augustus John: "You may travel the world over, but you will find nothing more beautiful: it is so restful, so colourful and so unspoilt." The artist was born in Tenby at **Belgrave House**, where a collection of his works, and those of his sister Gwen, can be found.

Tenby's Welsh name, Dinbych y Pysgod, means "Little Fort of the Fishes" and certainly its most photographed scene is the pretty harbour surrounded by pastel coloured Georgian houses. From the dockside arches, fishermen still sell the day's catch. The heart of the town still retains its charming medieval character together with the crooked lanes that are enclosed within its surprisingly well-preserved 13th century town walls. On one particular stretch, **South Parade**, the walls are still at their full height

•

Close to Bosherston harbour is the Gun Tower, reached by a footbridge off Front Street. It is one of several such towers built in 1851 to defend the Royal Naval Dockyard but this is the only one open to the public. Within the 3-storey building, visitors can see how soldiers lived in Victorian times, explore the magazine floor below sea level, go up to the roof where there is a genuine cannon, and browse around exhibits on topics such as the dockyard and the flying boats that operated out of Pembroke Dock for nearly 30 years. There are models of flying boats, of the Dockyard as it looked in 1855, and models and photographs of Royal Navy ships built at the Pembroke Dockyard.

•

177 THE POTTERY SHED AND CAFÉ

Tenby

Decorate ready made pottery and enjoy something to eat at this popular café

 *see page 345*

178 TENBY HOUSE

Tenby

A former medieval coaching-inn located at the heart of the seaside resort of Tenby.

 *see page 346*

179 THE WOODRIDGE INN HOTEL

Saundersfoot

Offering the very best in hospitality and comfort, the hotel is an ideal get-away

  *see page 347*

and the two tiers of arrow slits are very much visible; the **Five Arches**, a fortified gateway on the walls, is perhaps the most famous feature. Unfortunately, the same is not true for **Tenby Castle**, the scant remains of which can be found on a small headland. However, the ruins are well worth a visit for the spectacular views out across Carmarthen Bay and along the Pembrokeshire coast. A statue to Prince Albert can also be found on the headland along with **Tenby Museum**, which began life in 1878. As well as having archaeological and historical material relating to the area, the museum has a fascinating maritime section and an impressive art gallery.

The large and lavish **St Mary's Church** is another testament to the town's prosperous maritime past. The tower was built in the early 1300s and served as a place of sanctuary and as a lookout in times of trouble. The tower is topped by a small spire which is itself more than 500 years old. The whole structure stands 152ft high. The chancel is 13th century and its barrel roof has more than 75 bosses. A plaque commemorates the 16th century mathematician and alchemist, Richard Recorde (1510-1558), who invented the equals (=) sign. After a distinguished career in London, he died a pauper in King's Bench Prison, Southwark.

On the eastern side of the church, **Upper Frog Street** is notable for its varied craft shops and an arcaded indoor market with craft stalls and gift shops.

Tenby **Lifeboat Station**, which can be visited daily, was the first (in 2006) to receive the new Tamar Class slipway-launched lifeboat, the *Hadyn Miller*. A popular family attraction in Tenby is the **Silent World Aquariuam and Reptile Collection**, housed in a 19th century chapel.

Tenby Beach

AROUND TENBY

SAUNDERSFOOT

2½ miles NE of Tenby on the B4316

This picture postcard perfect fishing village is centred around its harbour, which during the summer months is packed with colourful sailing craft. The harbour was constructed in the 1820s primarily for the export of anthracite which was mined a short distance away and brought to the quay by tramway. Today, however, the industry has all but ceased and this resort, which has an attractive sandy beach, is probably one of the busiest watersports centres in South Wales.

AMROTH

4½ miles NE of Tenby off the A477

Lying at the most south-easterly point of the Pembrokeshire Coast National Park, this quiet village has a lovely beach overlooking Carmarthen Bay. As well as the delightful surroundings, the village is home to the enchanting **Colby Woodland Garden** (NT), an eight acre area of woodland set round a Nash-style house in a secluded valley. The garden contains one of the finest collections of rhododendrons and azaleas in Wales. The carpets of bluebells follow the displays of daffodils in the spring and there is a mass of colour during the summer when the hydrangeas flower, before the garden is taken over by the rich colours of autumn. The garden is part of the Colby Estate, which takes its name from John Colby, a 19th century industrialist.

Amroth is also the eastern terminus of the **Pembrokeshire Coast Path**, the 186-mile route that follows every inlet and rise and fall of the cliffs all the way to St Dogmael's near Cardigan.

STEPASIDE

4 miles N of Tenby off the A477

Between 1849 and 1877 this village, set in a wooded valley, had a thriving colliery and an iron works and, in 1877, the village school opened to provide education for the workers' children. Finally closing in 1992, the school has been reopened as the **Victorian School Museum** and provides today's visitors with the chance to experience a 19th century school day. Sitting at 100-year-old desks with slates and pencils, visitors can relive the austere school world of over a century ago. Outside, the playground has been re-created to match the environment where Victorian children would let off steam. Also at the museum is a display that brings the mining history of the village back to life. Along with the reconstructed mine shaft, visitors can see the hardships of the children as young as six who worked at the colliery until the school opened.

CALDEY ISLAND

2½ miles S of Tenby off the A4139

This peaceful and tranquil island, which along with its sister island of St Margaret's lies just a short distance off the coast from Tenby, has been the home of monks for some 1500 years. Currently, it is a working monastery with a community of 20 monks of the Reformed Cistercian Order. Today's monks live their lives according to the austere Rule of St Benedict which necessitates them attending seven services a day - the first beginning at 3.15am. Between their devotions, the monks of Caldey scrape a living from the land and are famous for their range of perfumes and toiletries inspired by the island's wild flowers. **St Illtud's Church**, along with the old 13th century priory ruins, can be visited, and a small museum tells the history of this beautiful island.

•

Close to the quay stands the Tudor Merchant's House (National Trust), a relic of Tenby's prosperous sea-faring days and a fine example of a comfortable townhouse of the 15th century. Narrow and built with three storeys, the house has been furnished to re-create the atmosphere and environment in which a wealthy Tudor family would have lived. The furniture is either genuine 17th or 18th century pieces, or reproduction items made in Tudor style without glue or nails. With a Flemish chimney, early floral frescoes on some of the interior walls and a small herb garden outside, there is plenty at the house to evoke the times of around 600 years ago.

•

180 LLANTEGOS LODGES & THE WANDERER'S REST INN

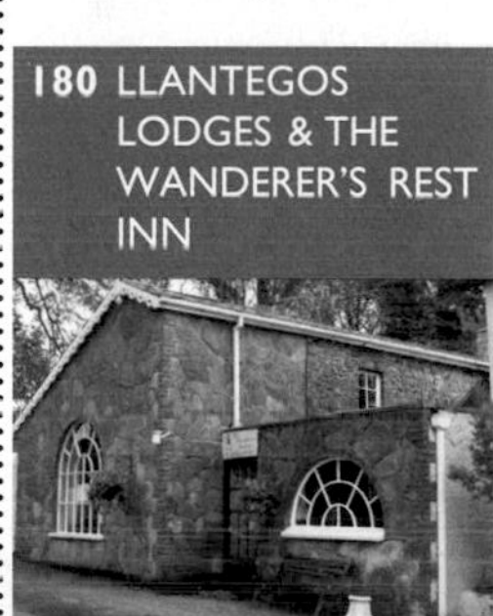

Llanteg, nr Amroth

Renowned for their rustic charm these self-catering lodges and B&B rooms are situated in ten acres of gardens.

see page 347

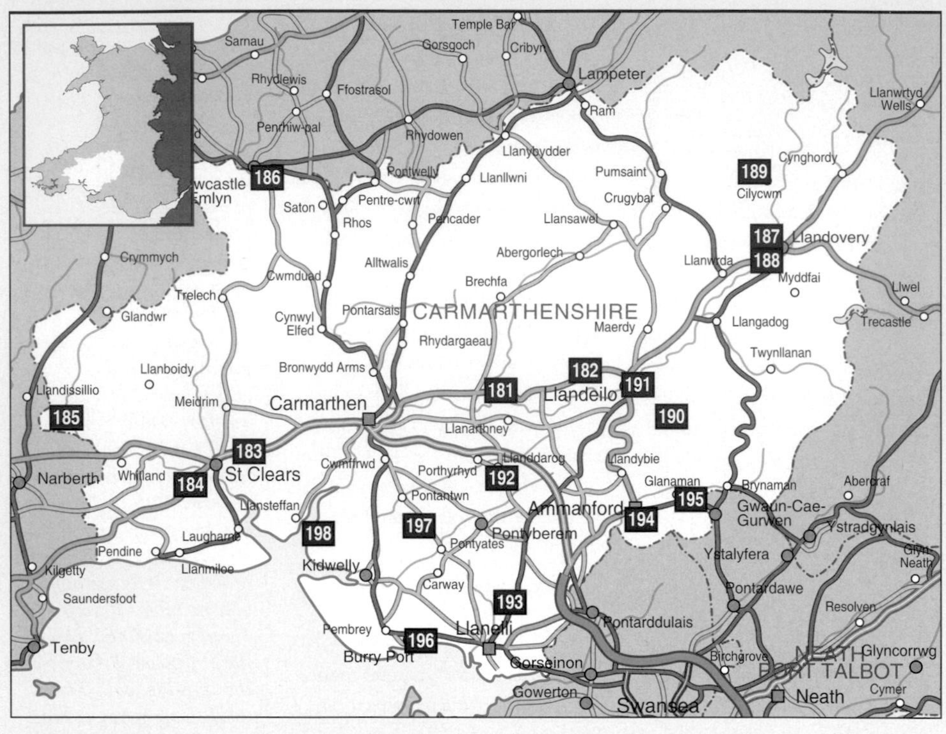

ACCOMMODATION

181 The Salutation Inn, Pontargothi pg 161, 348
183 The Forge Restaurant & Lodge, St Clears pg 164, 349
185 The Plash Inn, Llanfallteg pg 164, 351
187 The Drovers, Llandovery pg 166, 352
188 Penygawse Victorian Tea Rooms & Guest House, Llandovery pg 166, 352
189 Neuadd Fawr Arms, Cilycwm pg 167, 353
190 Cennen Arms, Trapp, nr Llandeilo pg 167, 354
192 The Abadam Arms, Porthyrhyd pg 168, 355
195 The Half Moon Inn, Garnant pg 170, 358

FOOD & DRINK

181 The Salutation Inn, Pontargothi pg 161, 348
183 The Forge Restaurant & Lodge, St Clears pg 164, 349
184 Mosaic @ The Old Rectory, Llanddowor, nr St Clears pg 164, 350
185 The Plash Inn, Llanfallteg pg 164, 351
186 Teifi Tea Rooms - Te Ar Y Teifi, Newcastle Emlyn pg 165, 351
188 Penygawse Victorian Tea Rooms & Guest House, Llandovery pg 166, 352
189 Neuadd Fawr Arms, Cilycwm pg 167, 353
190 Cennen Arms, Trapp, nr Llandeilo pg 167, 354
191 Caffi Salvador, Llandeilo pg 168, 355
192 The Abadam Arms, Porthyrhyd pg 168, 355
193 The Harry Watkins, Felinfoel pg 169, 356
194 The Square, Ammanford pg 170, 357
195 The Half Moon Inn, Garnant, pg 170, 358
196 Cornish Arms, Burry Port, nr Llanelli pg 170, 359
197 Tafarn Halfway Inn, Pontantwn pg 171, 358
198 The White Lion Hotel, Ferryside pg 171, 360

PLACES OF INTEREST

182 Aberglasney Gardens, Llangathen pg 162, 348

Carmarthenshire

A county of contrasts, Carmarthenshire has a wealth of interesting places and superb countryside to enchant the visitor. There are coastal strongholds at Laugharne and Kidwelly, abbey ruins at Talley and Whitland and the famous rugby and industrial centre of Llanelli. Covering some 1000 square miles, the county also has beautiful clean beaches, seaside towns and villages and rural idylls. A place of myths and legends, Carmarthenshire has remained essentially Welsh in most aspects.

The coastline, which is more than 50 miles long, includes the award-winning Pembrey Country Park and beach, once the site of a munitions factory, and Pendine, whose long stretch of sand saw many land speed world records established. Of the seaside villages, Laugharne is certainly the most famous, due mainly to the fact that it is the place where Dylan Thomas lived for the last years of his short life. But the village does not rely solely on its literary links as it also has one of the country's most handsome castles and offers wonderful views over the estuary of the River Taf.

Inland lies Carmarthen, the county town, whose origins lie back in the time of the Romans. The town is a centre for the agricultural communities of West Wales, and to the east is an area associated with the legends and mysteries of Merlin the magician. Also in this part of Carmarthenshire is one the country's most recent important projects - the National Botanic Garden of Wales.

River Towy, Llansteffan

Evidence of the Roman occupation of Carmarthenshire is most striking at the Dolaucothi Goldmines, to the northwest of Llandovery. At Cenarth, visitors can see salmon fishermen on the River Teifi still using the coracle, a tiny round boat whose origins are lost in the mists of time. A fascinating museum tells the story of these distinctive little craft.

•

Carmarthen has a thriving food market, where one of the local specialities on sale is Carmarthen ham, which is air-dried, sliced and eaten raw, like the Spanish Serrano ham. Legend has it that Carmarthen was Merlin's city, and according to one tradition the magician still lives in a cave on Merlin's Hill (Bryn Mtrddin), just outside Carmarthen, where he is kept in perpetual enchantment by Vivien, the lady to whom he taught all his spells.

•

CARMARTHEN

One of the oldest Roman towns in Wales, Carmarthen (or Caerfyrddin in Welsh) is now the county town of Carmarthenshire and lies at the centre of the West Wales agricultural community. The historic old part of Carmarthen grew up around **Carmarthen Castle** which was originally built in around 1109 by Henry I. Overlooking the River Tywi, little remains of the castle today except the early 15th century gatehouse. The **Guildhall**, which was built in 1767 to replace the hall of 1583, is in Nott Square - named after Major General Sir William Nott, victor of the First Afghan War in the 1840s and a native of Carmarthen - his father was landlord of the Ivy Bush pub. Now renamed the **Ivy Bush Royal Hotel**, it also has some notable literary connections. A stained glass window and stone circle commemorate the 1819 Eisteddfodd when Iolo Morganwg introduced the Gorsedd (Society of Bards) to the Eisteddfodd. The essayist and dramatist Sir Richard Steele stayed at the Ivy Bush in the later years of his life. Bad health and pressing debts had forced him to move to Wales, and he died in Carmarthen in 1729. A brass plaque on the wall of **St Peter's Church** commemorates him.

This church, which dates back to the 12th century, has many interesting features, including an organ thought to have been built in the reign of George III for Windsor Palace, and the impressive tomb of Sir Rhys ap Thomas, who led an army to fight for Henry Tudor at the Battle of Bosworth Field where Richard III was killed and Henry crowned King Henry VII on the battlefield.

The town's Victorian Old Art College has, since 1991, been the home of **Oriel Myrddin** (free), a contemporary craft gallery and regional art venue. Focusing on the present and the future, the work of some of the most innovative and interesting craftspeople in Wales is displayed here and, in the retail area, there is a wide range of crafts for purchase. By contrast, housed in a new development on the banks of the River Tywi is the **Carmarthen Heritage Centre** which, through displays, multi-media and video presentations, tells the story of the town from the time of the Roman occupation in AD 75 through to the present day. At the site of **Caer Maridunum**, the most westerly Roman fort in Britain, the remains of the **Roman Amphitheatre** can still be seen and the Roman town walls were known to have been visible in the 12th century.

Roman Amphitheatre, Carmarthen

AROUND CARMARTHEN

BRONWYDD ARMS

2 miles N of Carmarthen on the A484

From Bronwydd Arms Station (just off the A484 Carmarthen to Cardigan road) the **Gwili Railway** offers visitors the opportunity to step back in time and take a short steam train journey through the Gwili Valley on part of the old Great Western Railway line. This line originally opened in 1860 and, although it finally closed in 1973, since the late 1970s it has been run by volunteers. Trains run on timetabled days between April and October and in December. The station has a souvenir shop and sells hot and cold refreshments. Visitors can enjoy the train journey through a beautiful wooded valley, and the other end of the line, Llwyfan Cerrig, is the perfect place for a picnic by the river.

PONTARSAIS

5 miles N of Carmarthen on the A485

Pontarsais is best known as the home of the **Gwili Pottery** which has been producing fine hand-thrown and hand-decorated ceramics for more than 25 years. There's a wide variety of different pieces in more than 30 designs, both traditional and contemporary.

ABERGWILI

1½ miles E of Carmarthen off the A40

The **Carmarthen County Museum** occupies a lovely old house that was once a palace of the bishop of St David's and visitors to the museum can still see the bishop's peaceful private chapel. Concentrating on Carmarthenshire's past, the museum's displays range from Roman gold through to Welsh furniture and there is also a reconstruction of a school room. The palace's grounds, too, are open to the public, and the delightful parkland is ideal for a stroll and a picnic.

LLANARTHNE

7½ miles E of Carmarthen on the B4300

To the southwest of the village lies **Paxton's Tower**, designed by SP Cockerell and built in the early 19th century on the Middleton estate for William Paxton. It was dedicated to Lord Nelson. Constructed so that this Gothic eyecatcher could be seen from the main house, it affords panoramic views from the tower over the estate and Tywi valley.

To the south of Llanarthne, and set in the 18th century parkland of the former regency estate of Middleton Hall (which no longer exists), is the **National Botanic Garden of Wales** - a Millennium project that covers an amazing 568 acres on the edge of the beautiful Towy Valley. Dedicated to conservation, horticulture, science and education, this national botanic garden, the first to be constructed in Britain for more than 200 years, is centred around a great glasshouse designed by Norman Foster which is the largest single span house of its kind in the world. Among the many

181 THE SALUTATION INN

Pontargothi

Traditional and friendly village inn with accommodation serving great homemade food for all the family in front of a fine log fire.

see page 348

•

Llansteffan, along with Ferryside, its neighbour across the river mouth, is a paradise for walkers as well as sailors and the way-marked walks around the estuary take in some truly breathtaking coastal scenery. The promontory of Wharley Point, in particular, affords stunning views across the Taf and Tywi estuaries to Carmarthen Bay.

•

182 ABERGLASNEY GARDENS

Llangathen

One of the leading garden attractions in the UK, the site covers nine acres with different garden spaces.

see page 348

delights to be found within this old parkland are one of Europe's longest herbaceous borders, the recently restored Double Walled Garden, a Japanese garden, a bee garden with a million residents, lakeside walks and the Physicians of Myddfai, an exhibition that pays tribute to the legendary Welsh healers of the Middle Ages. Tribute is also paid to the Welsh botanist Alfred Russel Wallace, whose theories of natural selection paralleled those of Charles Darwin. This is also very much a garden of the future. In the Energy Zone, there is a biomass furnace using salvaged or coppiced wood for heating the site, and the Living Machine sewage treatment system. Another attraction is Millennium Square, a spacious venue for open air concerts and performances.

LLANGATHEN

11 miles E of Carmarthen off the A40

The village is home to **Aberglasney**, one of the oldest and most interesting gardens in the country. The first recorded description of Aberglasney house and gardens was made by the bard Lewis Glyn Cothi in 1477 when he wrote of "a white painted court, built of dressed stone, surrounded by nine gardens of orchards, vineyards and large oak trees." At the beginning of the 17th century the estate was sold to the Bishop of St David's and it was Bishop Anthony Rudd, whose grand tomb can be found in the village church, who improved both the house and gardens in a manner befitting a bishop's palace. At the heart of the 9 acres is a unique and fully restored Elizabethan/Jacobean cloister garden and a parapet walk, the only surviving example in the UK. Also remarkable is the Yew Tunnel, planted more than 300 years ago. The tunnel is created by training the 5 yew trees over the path and getting them to root on the other side.

GOLDEN GROVE

11 miles E of Carmarthen off the B4300

To the east of the village lies **Gelli Aur Country Park**, part of the estate of the ancestral home of the Vaughan family. It contains remnants of a 17th century deer park (where the deer still roam). The landscaped parkland was laid out in the 18th century and the country park also includes a Victorian arboretum planted by Lord Cawdor. Other attractions include nature trails, a new adventure playground and a cafeteria. The original mansion, now part of an agricultural college, was the work of the architect Joseph Wyatville.

LLANSTEFFAN

7 miles SW of Carmarthen on the B4312

This village, near the mouth of the River Tywi, is dominated by the ruins of **Llansteffan Castle** (free) on a headland above the estuary. The successor to an earlier defensive earthwork, the castle dates from the 12th century and its main remaining feature is the impressive gateway dating from 1280. To the southwest of the castle lies **St Anthony's Well**, the waters of which were thought to cure lovesickness.

LAUGHARNE

9 miles SW of Carmarthen on the A4066

Over the past few years this pretty rural town of Georgian houses on the estuary of the River Taf has become a shrine to the memory of its most famous resident, Dylan Thomas. The poet, together with his wife Caitlin and their three children, spent the last four years of his life living at **The Boathouse**, set on a cliff overlooking the Taf estuary. Discovering this small out-of-the-way place in 1949, Thomas famously "got off the bus and forgot to get on again". Approached by a narrow lane and now renamed the Dylan Thomas Boathouse, it's a remarkably evocative place, partly because of the many artefacts connected with the poet, partly because of the serene views of the estuary and its "heron-priested shore". In the family living room, a vintage wireless is tuned to the poet himself reading his own work. As well as the fascinating memorabilia on display here, there is also an interpretation centre, bookshop and tea room. It was while in Laugharne that Thomas wrote some of his best works, including the radio play *Under Milk Wood*, a day in the life of his imaginary village of Llareggub (read the name backwards to find why it has this odd name). Thomas, notoriously prone to destructive drinking sprees, died in The White Horse Bar in New York while on a lecture tour in 1953, at only 39 years of age. The parish church of St Martin, where he is buried, contains a replica of the plaque to his memory which can be seen in Poets' Corner, Westminster Abbey.

Lauhgarne is also home to one of the country's most handsome castles, "a castle brown as owls" according to Dylan Thomas. Originally an earth and timber fortress, **Laugharne Castle** (CADW) was rebuilt in stone around the 13th century and some of that fortification still remains, But it is the transformations undertaken by Sir John Perrot in the 16th century that make this a particularly special site. Granted Laugharne by Queen Elizabeth I, Perrot, an illegitimate son of Henry VIII, turned the castle into a comfortable Tudor mansion. In 1591 Perrot was found guilty of high treason and confined to the Tower of London where he died the following year. As soon as word reached Laugharne of his

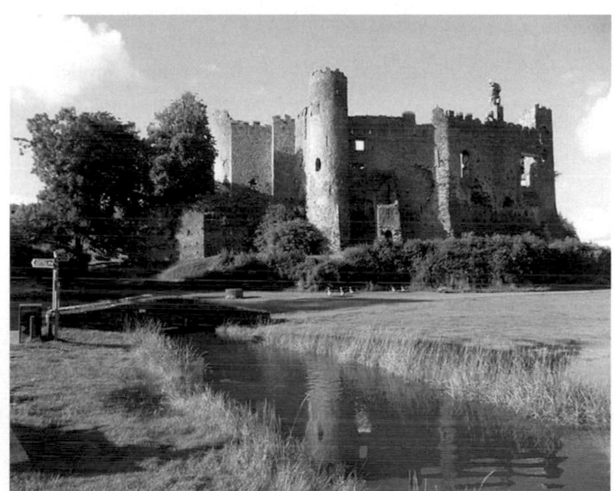

Laugharne Castle

183 THE FORGE RESTAURANT AND LODGE

St Clears

A charismatic converted blacksmiths provides a fine a la carte restaurant and en suite accommodation complete with its own swimming pool.

 *see page 349*

184 MOSAIC @ THE OLD RECTORY

Llanddowor

High class dining in the stylishly refurbished Old Rectory in the heart of Llanddowor village.

 *see page 350*

185 THE PLASH INN

Llanfallteg

Spectacular olde worlde pub with a vibrant atmosphere and quality home cooked food, real ale and pizza service.

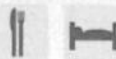 *see page 351*

conviction, looters stripped the castle of much of its finery. The devastation continued during the Civil War and an attack in 1644 left the romantic ruins seen today.

However, romantic though the castle ruins are, this is not all Laugharne Castle has to offer as the Victorian garden has been splendidly restored. Both the castle ruins and the superb surroundings have provided inspiration for artists over the centuries and, in particular, they are the subject of a dramatic watercolour by JMW Turner. Writers, too, have found this an inspiring place. Dylan Thomas wrote in a gazebo in the grounds, and Richard Hughes, author of A High Wind in Jamaica, stayed at the adjoining Castle House from 1934 to 1942.

PENDINE

13½ miles SW of Carmarthen on the A4066

The vast expanse of sand, six miles long, which makes Pendine a popular place with families for a day out by the sea was used in the 1920s by Sir Malcolm Campbell and others for attempting land speed records. In 1924, Sir Malcolm broke the World Motor Flying Kilometre Record here by averaging 146 miles per hour. He later raised that to 174 mph, and went on to achieve speeds in excess of 300 mph on the salt flats at Bonneville, Utah. In 1927, while attempting to beat Sir Malcolm's record, Welshman JG Parry Thomas was decapitated in an accident on the beach and his car, *Babs,* lay buried in the sand for some 44 years before being unearthed and restored. *Babs* can now be seen in all its gleaming glory at the **Museum of Speed**, which explores the history of this stretch of sand where so many records were broken. Not all the record attempts involved land vehicles as it was from these sands in 1933 that the intrepid aviatrix Amy Johnson set off on her solo flight across the Atlantic.

WHITLAND

13 miles W of Carmarthen on the B4328

This small market town and centre of the dairy industry is historically important as the meeting place of the assembly convened by **Hywel Dda** (Hywel the Good) in the 10th century. Born towards the end of the 9th century, Dda made a pilgrimage to Rome in AD 928 and, some 14 years later, he was ruler of most of Wales. Summoning representatives from each part of Wales to Whitland, Dda laid down a legal system that became known for its wisdom and justice. For its time, the code was remarkably democratic, including provisions such as the equal division of property between spouses on separation. The code remained in force in Wales up until the Act of Union with England in 1536. This system and its instigator are remembered at the Prince of Wales Design award winning building, the **Hywel Dda Centre**. Here, too, is a **Memorial** in the form of six gardens representing the six separate divisions of the Law: Society and Status, Crime and Tort,

Women, Contract, the King, and Property.

Just north of the town lie the remains of the once great **Whitland Abbey**, which was founded in 1140 by Bernard, the first Norman Bishop of St David's.

LLANBOIDY

12 miles NW of Carmarthen off the A40

In old stone farm buildings to the north of the village is a chocoholic's dream - the **Welsh Chocolate Farm**, where chocolates of all shapes, sizes and flavours are made. As well as watching chocolate-making demonstrations and touring the factory to see just how the chocolate is produced, visitors can buy gifts and treats for family and friends (and selves) at the farm shop which has the largest selection of chocolates in Wales. And as this is rich dairy country, there are also farmhouse cheeses and other dairy delights at the shop (don't even try to resist the homemade fudge!), along with a wide range of hand roasted coffee beans prepared daily.

CENARTH

16 miles NW of Carmarthen on the A484

This ancient village was first mentioned by Giraldus Cambrensis in the late 12th century when he passed through on his journey with Archbishop Baldwin. The village is situated on the banks of the River Teifi which at this point is famous for its rapids which are conveniently close to the road. This conservation village is also home to **Cenarth Mill**. Dating from the 18th century, the watermill has two pairs of stones (one for barley, the other for oats) and is powered by the river close to the rapids. Now restored and producing wholemeal flour, the mill complex also houses the **National Coracle Centre** where visitors can see a unique collection of these ancient boats from the UK, North America, Vietnam, India, Iraq, Tibet and elsewhere. Dating back to the Ice Age, these little round boats, once covered in skins, are still used for salmon fishing and at the Centre visitors can see demonstrations of coracles at work.

NEWCASTLE EMLYN

14 miles NW of Carmarthen on the A484

The first settlement here grew up around a loop of the River Teifi. At this strategic spot in 1240, Maredudd ap Rhys built **Newcastle Emlyn Castle**, which was to change hands many times over the years and was almost completely destroyed during the Glyndwr rebellion in the early 1400s. Having fallen into disrepair, the castle was granted to Sir Rhys ap Thomas by Henry VII in the late 15th century and became a country residence before being, once again, all but demolished during the Civil War for harbouring Royalist sympathisers. What remains is not particularly exciting but the setting, surrounded by the river on three sides, is pastoral and peaceful.

In medieval times, Newcastle Emlyn was an important farming and droving centre and it still has a cattle market every Friday.

186 TEIFI TEA ROOMS – TE AR Y TEIFI

Newcastle Emlyn

Susan and Jill showcase a delectable range of tasty home baked cakes, desserts and hearty hot dishes in the heart of Newcastle Emlyn.

see page 351

187 THE DROVERS

Llandovery

A beautiful 18th century town house offering the very best in comfort and cuisine

see page 352

188 PENYGAWSE VICTORIAN TEA ROOMS & GUEST HOUSE

Llandovery

Elegant Victorian tea room specialising in authentic blended teas, coffees and home cooked food.

 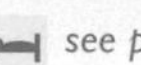 see page 352

The town has another small claim to fame since it was in Newcastle Emlyn that the first printing press in Wales was set up by Isaac Carter in 1718.

On the B4571 a mile north of Newcastle Emlyn are **Old Cilgwyn Gardens**. This is a 14-acre mixed garden set in 900 acres of parkland that includes a 53-acre Site of Special Scientific Interest.

LLANDOVERY

Visiting in the 19th century, the author George Borrow called Llandovery "the pleasantest little town in which I have halted". This appealing little market town stands at the confluence of the Rivers Bran, Gwennol and Tywi, so its Welsh name, Llanymddyfri (meaning the church amid the waters), seems particularly apt. The Romans came here and built a fort within whose ramparts a church was later built. The **Church of St Mary on the Hill** still has some Roman tiles within its walls; also of note here are the barrel-vaulted chancel and tie-beam roof.

The town boasts two famous sons: Rhys Pritchard, known as a preacher and as the author of the collection of verses *The Welshman's Candle*, was vicar here from about 1602; in the following century, the renowned Methodist poet and hymn writer William Williams was born in Llandovery. Amongst his many hymns, the best-known in English is *Guide Me, O Thou Great Redeemer*.

Llandovery Castle, the scant remains of which overlook the cattle market, (held every other Tuesday) was the most easterly Norman castle within Carmarthenshire. It was constructed in 1116 by Richard Fitzpons but was captured and destroyed some 42 years later. Although it was repaired in the late 12th century by Henry II, the castle was left to decay after 1403 and only the tumbledown remains are visible today. Henry IV stayed at the castle during his campaign against Owain Glyndwr. The king witnessed the hanging, drawing and quartering of Llywelyn ap Gruffyd Fychan, a Welsh patriot who is commemorated by an imposing monument on the castle mound.

The history of this town, which has pleased many before and since George Borrow, is told at the **Llandovery Heritage Centre** where the legends surrounding the hero Twm Sion Cati - the Welsh Robin Hood - and the local **Physicians of Myddfai** are also explored. The legend concerning

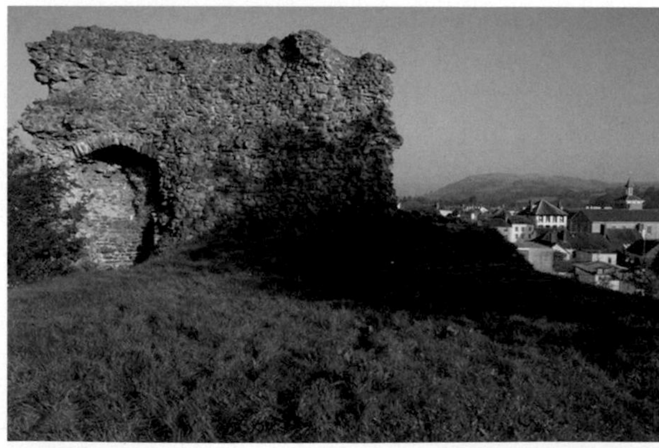

Llandovery Castle

the physicians is that a lady appeared one day from a lake in the Black Mountain. A local farmer's son fell in love with her and she agreed to marry him on condition that he did not hit her three times without cause. Over the years he had given her three light taps for what he thought was poor behaviour and sure enough she returned to the lake. But before disappearing she passed on her herbal healing secrets to her three sons, who became the first of the famous Physicians of Myddfai, a line of healers who practised from the 12th to the 18th centuries.

AROUND LLANDOVERY

CILYCWM

3½ miles N of Llandovery off the A483

The attractive **Dolauhirion Bridge**, spanning the River Tywi, was built in 1173 by William Edwards, and the village's chapel is said to have been the first meeting place of Methodists in Wales. Close by lies **Twm Sion Cati's Cave**, the hideout of the 16th century 'Robin Hood of Wales'. A poet whose youthful escapades earned him his title, Twm Sion (who died in 1620) curtailed his activities and settled down after marrying the heiress of Ystradffin; he even became a magistrate. He died in 1620.

LLANGADOG

5 miles SW of Llandovery on the A4069

This picturesque village set beneath the great bulk of Black Mountain in the Vale of Towy once boasted a castle, although all that remains today is a mound. The castle was destroyed by its owners in 1277 rather than letting it fall into the hands of the English.

BETHLEHEM

8 miles SW of Llandovery off the A4069

As Christmas approaches the village Post Office at Bethlehem experiences a remarkable upturn in business as people visit to have their mail franked with the evocative name.

To the southwest of Bethlehem lies **Garn Coch**, the largest hill fort in Wales, whose earthworks and stone ramparts cover some 15 acres.

TRAPP

12 miles SW of Llandovery off the A483

Situated on the top of a precipitous limestone crag on the Black Mountain and with a vertical 300ft drop to the River Cennen below, **Carreg Cennen Castle**, to the east of Trapp, enjoys one of the most spectacular locations of any Welsh castle. Although the present castle dates from 1248, some attribute a castle here to Urien, a knight of Arthur's Round Table. It remained a Welsh stronghold for less than 30 years, falling to Edward I during his first invasion in 1277. During the War of the Roses, the castle became a base for bandit Lancastrians. Taken on behalf of the Yorkists in 1462, the fortress was dismantled on the orders of Edward IV, leaving the romantic ruins seen

189 NEUADD FAWR ARMS

Cilycwm

Fine village inn in a scenic location with bed and breakfast accommodation and fantastic seasonal cuisine in its popular restaurant/bar.

see page 353

190 CENNEN ARMS

Trapp, nr Llandeilo

A fine traditional country inn serving fine food and great Welsh ales, with unspoilt views across the valley to the Black Mountain.

see page 354

191 CAFFI SALVADOR

Llandeilo

Highly recommended funky restaurant in the heart of Llandeilo serving the freshest local produce and fine fresh fish dishes in town.

see page 355

192 THE ABADAM ARMS

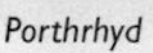

Porthrhyd

A real community hub pub offering a vast selection of fine home cooked cuisine all day every day.

 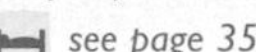

see page 355

today. A visit here is well worth the effort to enjoy the impressive views and to appreciate what a daunting task attacking the castle must have been. There is only one way up: a steep, grassy hill protected by a complicated system of defences.

In the converted barns of Llwyndewi Farm is the **Trapp Arts and Crafts Centre** which specialises in crafts from Wales. The shop stocks an interesting range of quality items including stained glass, lovespoons, pottery and jewellery, and the Art Gallery, on the first floor, is devoted to showing the work of local artists. Demonstrations and exhibitions run throughout the summer months and the centre has a coffee shop.

LLANDEILO

11½ miles SW of Llandovery on the A483

The former ancient capital of West Wales, Llandeilo's hilltop position shows off to best advantage this pretty little market town. Pastel coloured Georgian houses line the main road, which curves elegantly up from the **Tywi Bridge** whose central span is said to be the longest in Wales. The road continues to the Church of St Teilo, dedicated to the 6th century saint who gave the town its name.

In recent years the town has been upwardly mobile with an influx of smart shops and galleries, along with delis, cafés, restaurants and a stylishly revamped former coaching inn.

Llandeilo was one of the original founders of the Welsh Rugby Union, and the so-called Lichfield Gospels, the most perfect Welsh Christian manuscripts, were written here.

To the west of the town stands **Dinefwr Castle** (CADW), the former seat of the Princes of Deheubarth, one of the three ancient kingdoms of Wales. The fortress was built on the site of an Iron Age fort and legend has it that Merlin's grave is in the area. The castle ruins are surrounded by **Dinefwr Park**. Extensive areas of parkland were landscaped by Capability Brown in 1775 and incorporated the medieval castle, house, gardens and ancient deer park into one breathtaking panorama. Footpaths through the parkland lead to the castle, bog wood and beech clumps and offer outstanding views of the Tywi valley. The site is one of international importance for wintering birds, including white-fronted geese, shovelers, curlews and lapwings.

Also within the park is **Newton House**, originally built in 1660, provided with a new limestone façade in the 1860s, and restored by the National Trust in 2006. There is an exhibition on the first floor telling the story of the history and landscape of Dinefwr.

TALLEY

8½ miles W of Llandovery on the B4302

This village, with its backdrop of rolling hills, takes its name from Tal-y-llychau, meaning Head of the Lakes. Between two lakes lies

Talley Abbey, founded in the late 12th century by Rhys ap Gryffyd, and the only Welsh outpost of the austere Premonstratensian canons. One of the few remains to have survived is an immense tower which still overshadows the peaceful abbey lawns. The nearby 18th century **Church of St Michael** is something of an oddity: it was built with no aisle and its interior is entirely taken up with box pews.

PUMSAINT

8 miles NW of Llandovery on the A482

Near this hamlet, whose name means Five Saints, are the **Dolaucothi Goldmines** (National Trust), which date back some 2000 years to a time when the open-cast gold workings were secured by the Roman army. Once a likely source of gold bullion for the Imperial mints of Lyons and Rome, the mines are still in a remarkable state of preservation despite being abandoned by the Romans in AD 140; they were reopened for a short time between 1888 and the late 1930s. Visitors to this site in the beautiful Cothi Valley can see both the ancient and modern mine workings, including a number of the horizontal tunnels dug into the hillside for drainage and access. There is also the opportunity to try gold panning, see an exhibition of 1930s mining machinery and to tour the surrounding woodland on a waymarked trail. The site also has a shop selling Welsh Gold and a tearoom serving delicious home-cooked food. Fishing is available, and there's a 35-pitch site for touring caravans.

LLANELLI

Best known today for its enormous Felinfoel and Buckley breweries and perhaps even more famous as the home of the Scarlets, one of the most illustrious rugby teams in Wales; the saucepan tipped rugby posts at Stradey Park and the Scarlets' anthem, *Sospan Fach* ('little saucepan'), are both reminders of a time when Llanelli was a major industrial centre with thriving tinplating ('Tinopolis' was one of its names), steel, chemical and engineering works.

In Stepney Street, the Stepney Wheel was made in the early 20th century; this was an inflated spare tyre on a spokeless rim, to be fixed over a punctured wheel. In India, the term Stepney Wheel is still sometimes applied to any spare tyre.

Housed in a former mansion set in a large civic park with grand

193 THE HARRY WATKINS

Llanelli

Known for great hospitality and great pub cuisine, this friendly inn also offers a weekly quiz.

see page 356

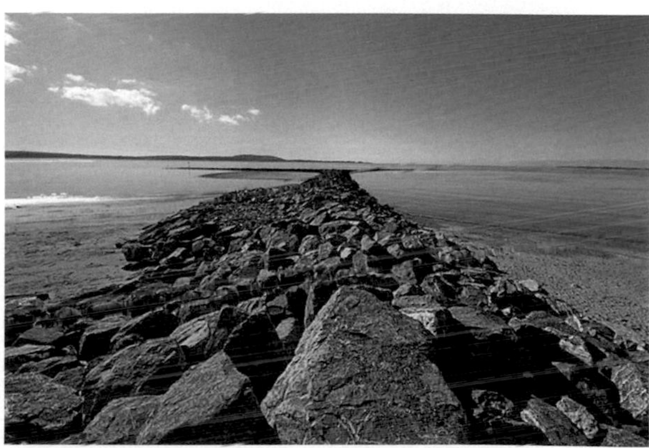

Breakwater at Llanelli

194 THE SQUARE

Ammanford

Chilled out, modern family pub serving great food and drink with live entertainment on the weekends.

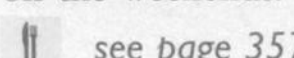

see page 357

195 HALF MOON INN

Garnant

Historic roadside inn with en suite guest accommodation, real ale and tasty traditional foods on request.

see page 358

196 CORNISH ARMS

Burry Port, nr Llanelli

Newly refurbished and stylish, this handsome inn offers great pub classics alongside chef's special fish dishes and real ale.

see page 359

sea views, **Parc Howard Museum and Art Gallery** (free) has a collection of local paintings and Llanelli pottery from 1839 to 1921 as well as displays on the history of the town and, curiously, a nightdress and chemise once owned by Queen Victoria.

One of the country's newer attractions, the **Millennium Coastal Park and Cycleway** (free) is located in Llanelli. Providing all manner of leisure activities and peaceful wildlife havens, the park incorporates wetlands, gardens, woodlands, a golf course and both sailing and watersports.

To the east of Llanelli lies the National Wetlands Centre of Wales which is one of the eight centres established by the Trust founded by Sir Peter Scott at Slimbridge in 1946. Also a haven for wild plant and animal life throughout the year, the centre's 200-acre salt marsh is home to flocks of curlew, lapwing and redshank which visitors can observe from secluded hides. The Discovery Centre has hands-on activities to help visitors find out about conservation.

AROUND LLANELLI

GORSLAS

9 miles NE of Llanelli on the A476

On **Mynydd Mawr**, a mountain to the north of the village, there was a well that, centuries ago, so legend says, was looked after by a man called Owain. After watering his horses one day, Owain forgot to replace the slab of stone which covered the well and a torrent of water poured down the mountainside. The great rush of water would have drowned the whole area if Owain had not galloped his horse around it and used magic to check the flood. The lake of water which was left is known as Llyn Llech Owain - the lake of Owain's stone slab.

Today, the lake forms part of **Llyn Llech Owain Country Park.** The lake and the peat bog that surrounds it have been designated a Site of Special Scientific Interest within which are a variety of rare plants such as Bogbean, Round Leafed Sundew and Royal Fern. The park's visitor centre has an exhibition that describes both the history and the natural history of the park.

PEMBREY

5 miles W of Llanelli on the A484

This village lies on the flat lands which border Carmarthen Bay and during World War II a Royal Ordnance Factory here produced munitions for the Allied Forces. At the factory's peak, in 1942, it covered some 500 acres and employed 3000 people; it ceased production in 1965. Since then the land has been landscaped, and as **Pembrey Country Park** it offers visitors an unusual mix of pine forests, sand dunes, beaches and such attractions as a dry ski slope, a toboggan run, a miniature railway and an adventure playground. **Pembrey Pines Trail** is a four-mile walk through dunes and woodland, with splendid views. There's also a visitor centre, and to the east lies **Pembrey Saltmarsh**, a local nature reserve and a Site of Special Scientific Interest. The park also includes **Cefn Sidan**, one of Europe's best and safest beaches, from which there are glorious views over the Gower coastline.

KIDWELLY

7½ miles NW of Llanelli on the B4308

This historic town, whose charter was granted by Henry I in the 12th century, boasts an ancient church and a 14th century bridge over the River Gwendreath. However, the most interesting and impressive building is undoubtedly the remarkably well preserved Norman **Kidwelly Castle** (CADW) which stands on a steep bluff overlooking the river. The castle spans four centuries but most of what remains today is attributed to a Bishop of Salisbury who endeavoured to build a home-from-home from Sherbourne Abbey in Dorset. One of Wales' best kept secrets, Kidwelly Castle gives a fascinating insight into the evolution of a medieval castle into a domestic dwelling of more settled times.

For hundreds of years, the ghost of Gwenllian, daughter of the King of Gwynedd and the wife of the Prince of South Wales, was said to haunt the countryside around the castle. During an attack on the Norman castle in 1136 which Gwenllian led, she was decapitated and legend has it that her headless ghost was unable to find rest until a man searched the battlefield and returned her skull to her. Princess Gwenllian was certainly a warrior, and she was perhaps also a writer. Some have attributed parts of *The Mabinogion* to her, and if the attribution is correct, she would be Britain's earliest known woman writer.

On the outskirts of the town, marked by its 164ft redbrick chimney, the **Kidwelly Industrial Museum** (free) is housed on the site of the oldest surviving tinplate works. Here visitors have a unique opportunity to see how the rolling mills produced the plate as well as learning something of the county's industrial past. The Museum contains Britain's sole surviving pack mill. June 18th 2009 saw the opening of the UK's newest racecourse, **Ffos Las**, which stages both flat and National Hunt races. It stands off the B4308 southeast of Kidwelly and is signposted from the A4138. Tel: 01554 811092

Kidwelly Castle

197 TAFARN HALFWAY INN

Pontantwn

Fine Welsh Inn offering great homemade food created with the best local produce.

see page 358

198 THE WHITE LION HOTEL

Ferryside

Great family run inn serving a good selection of British and French cuisine in a rural setting.

see page 360

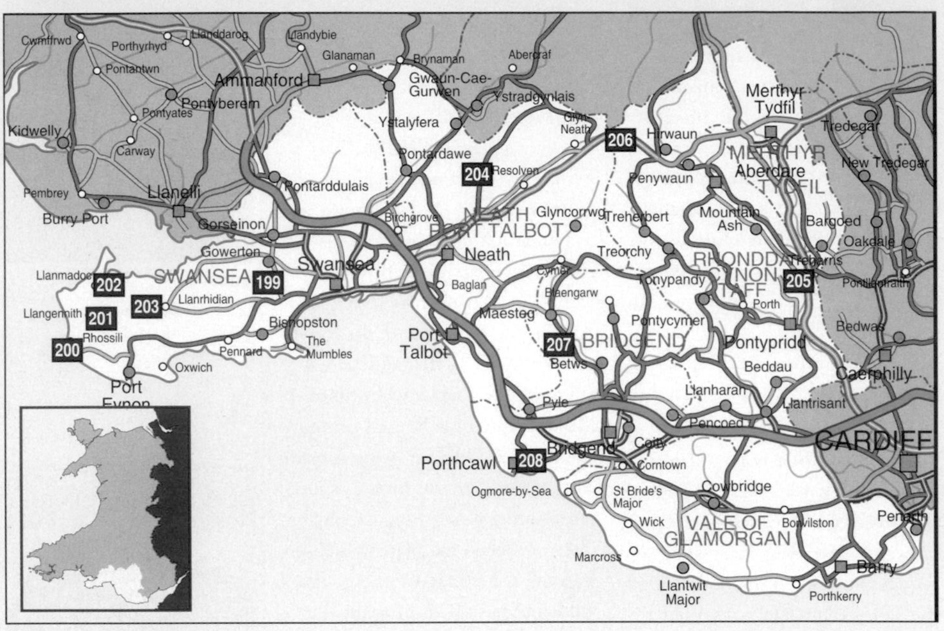

ACCOMMODATION

201	The Kings Head Inn, Llangennith	pg 178, 363
202	The Britannia Inn, Llanmadoc	pg 178, 364
208	The Globe Inn, Newton, nr Porthcawl	pg 186, 369

FOOD & DRINK

199	The Found Out Inn & Bistro, Dunvant	pg 175, 361
200	The Bay Bistro, Coffee House & Sam's Surf Shack, Rhossilli	pg 178, 362
201	The Kings Head Inn, Llangennith	pg 178, 363
202	The Britannia Inn, Llanmadoc	pg 178, 364
203	The Greyhound Inn, Llanrhidian	pg 179, 365
205	The Carne Park Hotel, Abercynon	pg 182, 366
206	The New Inn, Rhigos, nr Aberdare	pg 182, 367
207	The Old House Inn, Llangynwyd, nr Maesteg	pg 185, 368
208	The Globe Inn, Newton, nr Porthcawl	pg 186, 369

PLACES OF INTEREST

204	Cefn Coed Colliery Museum, Crynant	pg 180, 366

Gower Peninsula and the Heritage Coast

The delightful city of Swansea marks the gateway to the southernmost bulge of Wales, the lovely Gower Peninsula, a region designated an Area of Outstanding Natural Beauty. Much of it is owned by the National Trust. The Gower's southern coastline is made up of a succession of sandy, sheltered bays and along its whole coastline it is dotted with charming and relaxed seaside resorts.

This is also an area rich in natural beauty, with a long history that can be explored not only at the Gower Heritage Centre but also through its various castles, religious sites and ancient monuments. The area has many small family farms that yield some of the finest produce in south Wales; the Gower is known in particular for its cockles and its laverbread (edible seaweed). The peninsula was once the haunt of elephants, bears, rhinoceros and other large beasts whose bones have been found in the many caves on the shoreline.

The Vale of Glamorgan is characterised by gentle rolling hills, genteel towns, pretty villages and a splendid natural coastline. An area of rich farmland, the Vale stands at the foot of the spectacular valleys of south Wales and offers visitors an enticing heritage coastline. This is another area rich in history, where Norman warlords built their castles and where one of the oldest seats of learning was founded at Llantwit Major.

Behind the coastal region lie the valleys of southwest Wales which are known the world over for their coal mining and heavy industry heritage. The best known is the Rhondda Valley, where only one mine survives from the numerous collieries that once powered not just this country but many parts of the world. Though mining has all but gone from the valleys the heritage remains: the towns and villages with their rows of cottages where life revolved around the colliery, the chapel and the music, especially male voice choirs.

In many cases, nature has reclaimed the hills and vales once scarred by the mining industry and, while the legacy of pride in the industry remains, the various new country parks and nature reserves developed on the sites of the old mines are giving the area a new appeal.

Mumbles Head

If Dylan Thomas was Swansea's most famous son, its most famous dog was Jack, a retriever who lived in the city during the 1940s. He was reputed to have saved 27 humans and two dogs from drowning and was awarded the canine Victoria Cross.

SWANSEA

Swansea, Wales's city by the sea, is an attractive and welcoming place with an appealing blend of traditional and modern. It was founded in the late 10th century by Sweyne Forkbeard, King of Denmark - its English name means 'Sweyne's Ey' - ey being an inlet. **Swansea Castle**, which gained notoriety in the 18th century when the northern block became a debtors' prison, was first built by the Norman Henry de Newburgh in the late 11th century. However, it was all but destroyed by Owain Glyndwr in the early 1400s when he ransacked the town that had grown up around the fortification.

As early as the 14th century, shipbuilding and coalmining were important industries in the area and by 1700 Swansea was the largest port in Wales. Smelters from Cornwall arrived here, attracted by the plentiful supply of coal, and copper works also flourished; Nelson's ships were covered in Swansea copper. At one time 90% of the country's copper was smelted here and, in the heyday of the industry, other metals such as tin, lead, nickel and zinc were imported to the town for smelting and refining. In the 19th century, Swansea porcelain was another famous local product. Much of the traditional industry has disappeared and the old dock area has been transformed into a marina surrounded by stylish waterfront buildings. This **Maritime Quarter** is arguably the most impressive part of the town and is alive with cafés, pubs and restaurants. Here, too is the £33 million project that opened in late 2005, the **National Waterfront Museum.** Its 15 different zones are dedicated to topics such as coal, landscape, energy and genealogy. Inventive interactive technology allows visitors to fly over Swansea or go on a virtual shopping spree in the past. This impressive complex, generally regarded as the best museum in Wales, also contains several shops, a café and a waterfront balcony.

Also in this dockside quarter is the **Swansea Museum**, founded in 1835 and the oldest in Wales. Its displays combine bygone Swansea history and culture with new exhibitions and events. Among the displays are Swansea porcelain, a Cabinet of Curiosities, a Welsh kitchen and the Mummy of Tem-Hor. More artefacts from Egypt can be seen at the **Egyptian Centre** at Swansea University

Swansea Maritime Quarter

where more than 1000 objects, including impressive painted coffins and everyday household items dating back as far as 3500 BC can be seen. At the **Glynn Vivian Art Gallery** a broad spectrum of the visual arts is on display. Based on the bequest of Richard Glynn Vivian, the gallery houses an international collection of porcelain and Swansea china and various Old Masters as well as numerous paintings and sculptures by modern artists including Hepworth, Nicholas, Nash, Ceri Richards and Augustus John.

No coverage of Swansea would be complete without referring to the town's most famous son, Dylan Thomas, who described the town as viewed from his hillside home:

Ugly, lovely town crawling, sprawling, slummed, unplanned, jerry-villa'd, and smug-suburbed by the side of a long and splendid curving shore......

Dylan Thomas' former home on steep Cwmdonkin Drive in the Uplands displays a blue plaque with the simple inscription, "Dylan Thomas, Poet, 1914-53. Born in this house". The house can be viewed by appointment. Cwmdonkin Park, close to his home, was much loved by Thomas who featured the park in his poem *The Hunchback in the Park*. The **Dylan Thomas Centre** is dedicated to the poet's life and works, with exhibitions featuring some of his original manuscripts, letters to friends and family, and a moving American documentary about him. The Centre also contains a theatre space, two galleries, bookshops, craft shops and a restaurant. The poet is also honoured at the **Dylan Thomas Theatre** down in the Maritime Quarter which alternates productions of his work with others by local and visiting companies.

For real aficionados of the poet, there are **Dylan Thomas Trails** to follow - in the City Centre, Uplands, Mumbles and Gower - and the annual Dylan Thomas Celebration which attracts visitors from around the world.

The city was also the birthplace of other well-known people: Sir Harry Secombe, Catherine Zeta Jones, Michael Heseltine, Archbishop Rowan Williams and the singer Bonnie Tyler.

Swansea's **Botanical Garden** is located in the walled garden of Singleton Park, and at Planetasia visitors can wander round a glass pyramid with three climate zones. **Clyne Gardens**, at Blackpill off the A4067 Mumbles road, is famous for its marvellous rhododendrons, including national collections.

GOWER PENINSULA

MUMBLES

4½ miles SW of Swansea on the A4067

This charming Victorian resort grew up around the old fishing village of **Oystermouth**, which has its roots in Roman times and where the Normans built a castle to defend their land. Now in ruins, **Oystermouth Castle** was the home of the de Breos family and

199 THE FOUND OUT INN AND BISTRO

Dunvant

Family orientated, friendly pub in the heart of Dunvant offering real ale and great food all day every day.

see page 361

•

An unusual attraction in Mumbles is the Lovespoon Gallery, where visitors will find an amazing variety of these unique love tokens. Lovespoons were traditionally carved from wood by young men and presented to their sweethearts as a token of their devotion. The custom dates back many centuries, but in these less romantic days the spoons are often bought simply as souvenirs of Wales. The Gallery is open from 10am to 5.30pm Monday to Saturday.

•

the gatehouse, chapel and great hall all date from around the 13th to 14th centuries. Surrounded by small but beautiful grounds overlooking the bay, the ruins are now the scene of re-enactments which chart the history of the castle and, in particular, the siege of the fortress by Owain Glyndwr.

The churchyard of **All Saints Church** at Oystermouth contains the grave of Thomas Bowdler, the literary censor. In 1818 he published an expurgated edition of Shakespeare that omitted all words and expressions which he considered could not with propriety be read aloud by a father to his family. Although sexual references, however fleeting or obscure, were ruthlessly excised, cruelty and violence remained largely unexpurgated. Bowdler died at Rhydding, near Swansea, in 1825.

Mumbles is now a popular sailing centre, with numerous pubs - the Mumbles Mile is Wales' best known pub crawl - fine restaurants, a restored late-Victorian pier and, on the headland, a lighthouse guarding the entrance into Swansea harbour.

The **Mumbles Passenger Railway** was the world's first, and from 1807 to its closure in 1960 the five-mile line used in succession horse, sail, steam, battery, petrol, diesel and electricity. On Bank Holidays in the mid-Victorian period it was known to carry up to 40,000 passengers.

Beyond The Mumbles - the unusual name is derived from the French *mamelles* meaning 'breasts' and is a reference to the two islets of the promontory beyond Oystermouth - lies the lovely **Gower Peninsula**, designated an Area of Outstanding Natural Beauty. Gower's southern coast is made up of a succession of sandy, sheltered bays and the first of these, Langland Bay, is just around the headland from the village.

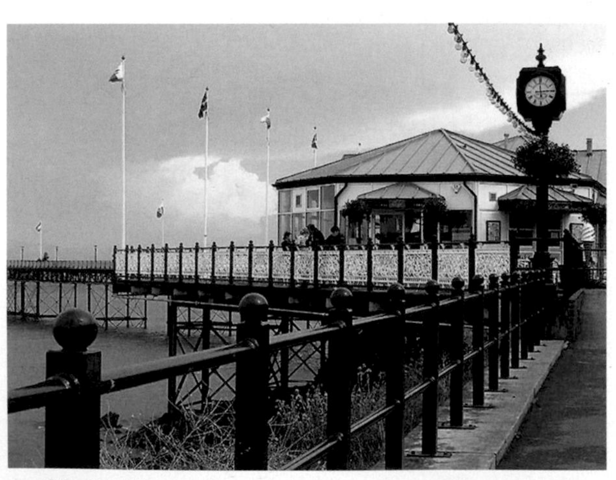

Mumbles Pier

PARKMILL

8 miles SW of Swansea on the A4118

This village is home to the **Gower Heritage Centre** which is itself centred around a historic water mill built in the 12th century by the powerful le Breos family, the Norman rulers of Gower. Originally constructed to supply flour for nearby Pennard Castle, this water mill is a rare survivor in Wales of a rural complex that would once have been found in most villages and hamlets. The Heritage Centre has displays on the history of this beautiful region along with a farming museum.

Visitors can also tour the mill, where the restored machinery grinds flour on most days. Younger visitors to the centre can make friends with the farm animals and everyone will enjoy wandering around the craft units and workshops where a wheelwright, a potter, a blacksmith and a mason can be seen plying their trades.

PENMAEN

7 miles SW of Swansea off the A4118

Tradition has it that a village is buried here beneath the sand dunes. The National Trust owns an area that includes High Pennard, topped by a prehistoric hill fort, and Three Cliffs Bay, where there are old lime kilns, an ancient burial chamber and a pillow mound - an artificial warren used to farm rabbits. Cut into the rocks is Minchin Hole, a geological Site of Scientific Interest where evidence has been found of mammals and early man.

OXWICH

11 miles SW of Swansea off the A4118

One of Gower's prettiest villages, Oxwich lies huddled along a lane at the western end of a superb three mile long beach. Once a small port exporting limestone and also a haven for smugglers, Oxwich is today a marvellous holiday area with safe bathing, clean beaches, wind surfing and water skiing. The village has some picturesque cottages of the traditional Gower style which include one that was once occupied by John Wesley. The village **Church of St Illtud**, half

Oxwich Castle

hidden by trees, is well worth seeking out as its ancient font is believed to have been brought here by St Illtud himself.

Just to the south of the village lies **Oxwich Castle**, which was once a grand Tudor manor house built around a courtyard. The splendid house was established by Sir Rice Mansel in the 1520s and added to by his son, Sir Edward Mansel, whose building work includes the Elizabethan long gallery. The Mansel family's time at this lavish mansion was short lived, and after they left in the 1630s the house fell into disrepair, although the southern wing was used as a farmhouse and the southeast tower still survives to its full height of six storeys.

For walkers there are plenty of footpaths to explore and the walk to **Oxwich Point**, in particular, provides some magnificent views of the Gower Peninsula. Close to the beach lies part of the **Oxwich Nature Reserve**, home to many rare species of orchid as well as

200 THE BAY BISTRO, COFFEE HOUSE AND SAM'S SURF SHACK

Rhossilli

Stunning licensed café bistro serving delicious food all day with unrivalled views across Rhossilli bay.

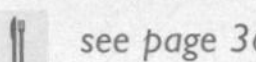

see page 362

201 THE KINGS HEAD INN

Llangennith

A fine family run inn offering olde worlde charm, an impressive variety of food and ale alongside 4 star accommodation.

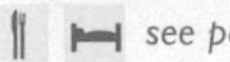

see page 363

202 THE BRITANNIA INN

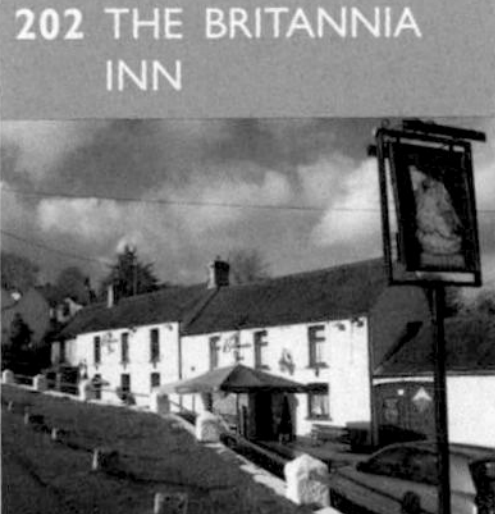

Llanmadoc

Picturesque village inn and restaurant with internationally experienced chefs and en suite accommodation.

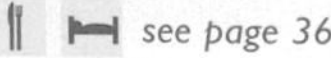

see page 364

other plant life and a variety of birds.

KNELSTON

12½ miles SW of Swansea on the A4118

To the north of this attractive village lies **Arthur's Stone**, a large burial chamber capstone. Traditionally, this is said to be the pebble which King Arthur removed from his shoe while on his way to the Battle of Camlann in the 6th century. According to legend, Arthur threw the stone over his shoulder and the stone lies exactly where it landed. Up until the 19th century, local girls would enact a ritual here to discover whether their lovers were true or not. At midnight and with a full moon, the girls would place a honey cake soaked in milk on the stone and then crawl under it three times. If their lovers were true, they would join them at this point.

RHOSSILI

16 miles SW of Swansea on the B4247

This village, on the westernmost area of the Gower Peninsula, is thought to have been named after St Fili, who is said to have been the son of St Cenydd. Inside the small church is a memorial plaque to a Gower man, Edgar Evans, who is perhaps better known as Petty Officer Evans, who died in the ill-fated expedition to the Antarctic led by Captain Scott in 1912.

To the west of Rhossili lies **Worm's Head**, an island which is a National Nature Reserve. Reached by a causeway at low tide, there is public access to the island, but those making the crossing should take great care not to be cut off by the tide. Worm's Head marks the southern edge of Rhossili Bay, whose beach can be reached by a steep downhill climb. At low tide, the remains of several wrecks can be seen, most notably the *Helvetia*, which was wrecked in 1887. The area is very popular with fishermen, surfers and bathers. Behind Rhossili Beach stretches **The Warren**, under the sands of which are the remains of old Rhossili village and church.

LLANGENNITH

15 miles W of Swansea off the B4271

This quiet village is home to St Cenydd's, the largest church on the Gower peninsula. It was built in the 12th century on the site of a priory founded six centuries earlier by St Cenydd and was destroyed some 400 years later by Viking raiders. Inside, there is a curious gravestone thought to mark the resting place of St Cenydd. To the west of the village and marking the northern edge of Rhossili Bay lies **Burry Holms**, another small island which can be reached via a causeway at low tide. On the island are the remains of an Iron Age earthwork and also a monastic chapel dating from the Middle Ages.

LLANRHIDIAN

10½ miles W of Swansea on the B4295

Close to the wild and lonely north coast of the Gower Peninsula, where some of the finest beaches in the country can be found, this village is also close to **Weobley Castle** (CADW). Dating from the early 14th century and built by the de Bere family, Weobley is more a fortified manor house than a castle and stands today as one of the few surviving such houses in Wales. On an isolated site overlooking the eerie expanse of Llanrhidian Marsh, this house has been remarkably well preserved and visitors can gain a real insight into the domestic arrangements of those days and, in particular, the owners' desire for comfort. In the late 15th century the house came into the hands of Sir Rhys ap Thomas, an ally of Henry VII, He made further improvements including the addition of a new porch and an upgrade of the accommodation in the private apartments. The castle also has an exhibition on the Gower Peninsula its history and other ancient monuments

LOUGHOR

6½ miles NW of Swansea on the A484

A strategic location on the mouth of the River Loughor gave this village prominence and importance down the centuries. The Romans built their station of Leucarum here in the 1st century, and in the early 12th century a Norman nobleman, Henry de Newburgh, built **Loughor Castle** on the edge of the Roman site. Unfortunately, all that is left of the stronghold, which protected the confluence of the Burry Inlet and the River Loughor, is the ruined 13th century square tower.

PORT TALBOT

Well known for its steel industry, Port Talbot was named after the Talbot family who were responsible for the development of the town's docks in the 19th century. Now called the Old Docks, this area saw significant expansion again in the 20th century when a new deep water harbour was opened by the Queen in 1970. Today Port Talbot is home to factories and processing plants, and also to the solar centre of **Baglan Bay Energy Park**, which explains the history of the area and its power generating potential and is the first stage of the regeneration of the Bay.

AROUND PORT TALBOT

NEATH

4 miles N of Port Talbot on the A465

While Neath's industrial history dates back to the late 16th century, when the first copper smelter in South Wales was built here by Cornishmen, the town has its origins in Roman times. Remains of Roman Nidum can still be seen close to the ruins of **Neath Abbey**, which was founded in the 13th century by Richard de Granville on land seized from the Welsh in around 1130. The abbey buildings were converted into a mansion for Sir John Herbert in the 16th century and it was later used to house copper smelters. It was also de Granville who built **Neath Castle**, in the mid 12th century, around

203 THE GREYHOUND INN

Llanrhidian

Handsome 19th century roadhouse noted for its appetising home-cooked food and real ales.

see page 365

•

Coal mining has taken place in the area around Port Talbot for centuries and during this time many superstitions have grown up. In 1890, the miners at Morfa Colliery reported seeing ghostly images in and around the colliery. They were said to be fierce hounds and became known as the 'Red Dogs of Morfa'. They would run through the streets with their appearance being accompanied by a sweet, rose-like scent which filled the mine shaft. Such were the number of eerie manifestations that on the morning of 10th March 1890, nearly half the morning shift failed to report for work. Later that same day, there was an explosion at the colliery - 87 miners died in the disaster.

•

Crynant

A fascinating museum telling the story of colliery life from Victorian times to th 1950s, aided by displays and artefacts.

 *see page 366*

which the town grew and whose scant remains can be found near a town centre car park.

Housed in the Old Mechanics Institute, the **Neath Museum and Art Gallery** has permanent displays on the history of the town, including finds from the time of the Roman occupation, as well as regularly changing art and photographic exhibitions. The museum has many hands-on activities, including grinding corn, using a Celtic loom and making a wattle fence.

Held each September, **Neath Fair** is the oldest such event in Wales, founded by Gilbert de Clare in 1280.

ABERDULAIS

6 miles N of Port Talbot off the A4109

From as early as 1584, when a copper-smelting furnace was established, the power generated by the magnificent **Aberdulais Falls** (National Trust) has been harnessed for a number of industries, including copper smelting and tin plating. Every day 160 million litres of dark green water cascade over the shelves and pools of the falls. Some of the environmentally friendly energy is still used via a waterwheel that is the largest in Europe. The Turbine House provides access to a unique fish pass and has interactive computer displays, display panels and observation windows.

CRYNANT

9 miles N of Port Talbot on the A4109

In the beautiful Dulais Valley, **Cefn Coed Colliery Museum** provides a wonderful opportunity for visitors to discover what life was like for the miners who worked underground in some of the most difficult conditions experienced anywhere in the world. Through photographs, maps and other exhibits, the tradition and legacy of mining are brought to life. The museum also has a well-stocked souvenir and gift shop, with one of the best selections of genuine and reproduction miner's lamps in the region. It is ideal for finding a special present from Wales. It is also home to the Neath Historical Model Railway Club. Tel: 01639 750556

PONT-RHYD-Y-FEN

3½ miles NE of Port Talbot on the B4287

This village was the birthplace of the actor Richard Burton.

CYNONVILLE

6 miles NE of Port Talbot on the A4107

Virtually surrounding the village (to the north, west and south) lies the **Afan Forest Park**, a large area of woodland where there are trails for cycling, walking and pony trekking. At the Park's **Countryside Centre** an exhibition explains, with the aid of hands-on displays, the landscape and history of the Afan Valley. The **South Wales Miners' Museum**, also at the centre, illustrates the social history of the valleys' mining communities.

MARGAM

3 miles SE of Port Talbot on the A48

To the southeast of the town lies **Margam Country Park**

surrounding a mansion built in the 1840s by the Talbot family. The land once belonged to **Margam Abbey**, a Cistercian house which was founded in 1147 by Robert, Earl of Gloucester. Following a violent revolt by the lay brothers, the abbey went on to become one of the wealthiest in Wales but, at the time of the Dissolution of the Monasteries, the estate passed on to Sir Rice Mansel, who built the first mansion on the estate in 1537.

The park today boasts several buildings left by previous owners including **Margam Abbey Church** (all that remains of the abbey), a classical 18th century orangery, recently restored monastic gardens, a unique fuchsia collection and a restored Japanese garden from the 1920s. This huge recreational area - the park covers some 800 acres - also includes various contemporary sculptures by artists as distinguished as Barbara Hepworth and Elizabeth Frink, a visitor centre, waymarked trails, a deer park, bird of prey centre and the **Margam Stones Museum**, where visitors can see a collection of early Christian memorials dating from Roman times through to the 10th and 11th centuries.

PONTYPRIDD

This friendly valley town is justly proud of its past which is revealed in the **Pontypridd Museum** housed in a splendidly ornate former chapel close to Pontypridd's historic stone bridge of 1776 over the River Taff. As well as its industrial heritage, the town has a long tradition of music. In Ynysangharad Park are two statues commemorating Evan James and his son, a song-writing team who were responsible in 1856 for composing the words and music of what was later adopted as the Welsh National Anthem, *Land of my Fathers* (*Hen Wlad fy Nhadau*). The museum also has exhibits on the opera stars Sir Geraint Evans and Stewart Burrows, who were born in the same street in nearby Clifynydd, and the durable warbler Tom Jones who was born in Pontypridd itself.

Just outside Pontypridd, at Fforest Uchaf Farm, is the **Pit Pony Sanctuary**, where visitors can meet some 25 horses and ponies, including several retired pit ponies.

AROUND PONTYPRIDD

LLANTRISANT

4 miles SW of Pontypridd on the B4595

This old town stands between two hills rising sharply from the valley of the rivers Ely and Clun. It takes its name, Three Saints, from Saints Illtud, Gwyno and Dyfod, to whom the parish church is dedicated. All that remains of 13th century **Llantrisant Castle** is part of a round tower known as the Raven Tower. It was probably to this castle, in 1326, that Edward II and Hugh Despenser were brought after falling into the hands of Queen Isabella.

One of several interesting features in Llantrisant parish church is the east window, which

•

A curiosity in the town of Pontypridd is John Hughes' Grogg Shop near the strikingly elegant railway station. On sale here is a bizarre collection of sculptural caricatures of Welsh rugby stars (and Johnny Wilkinson!) and other well-known Welsh personalities.

•

205 THE CARNE PARK HOTEL

Abercynon

The longest bar in Wales welcomes all for real ale, fine restaurant food and quality entertainment throughout the week.

see page 366

206 THE NEW INN

Rhigos

Great family inn known for its fine hospitality, high quality food made from fresh local produce and live weekly entertainment.

see page 367

was the work of Burne Jones and depicts an unbearded Christ, one of only three known such windows.

Though some of the traditional heavy industry still remains, Llantrisant is best known nowadays for being the home of the **Royal Mint**, which transferred here from Tower Hill, London in 1967. At the **Model House Craft and Design Centre** is a permanent Royal Mint display along with a shop, café, four rooms of studios and a programme of events and exhibitions.

Standing in the town centre is a statue of a figure dressed in a fox skin head-dress. This is the town's memorial to Dr William Price, an amazing and eccentric character who lived from 1800 to 1893. Espousing many causes, some of which scandalised straight-laced Victorian Britain, Price was a vegetarian who believed in free love, nudism and radical politics. His most famous deed, considered infamous at the time, was his cremation of his illegitimate son Iesu Grist (Jesus Christ) who had died in infancy. He burnt the small body in an oil drum on Llantrisant Common in January 1884. As a result of the controversy, and the ensuing court case, cremation became legal in Britain. The statue was donated by the Cremation Society. To commemorate his centenary, the Council constructed a heather garden which can be seen as one enters the town.

TREHAFOD

1½ miles NW of Pontypridd off the A4058

While this area was associated with heavy industry and, in particular, coal mining, the Rhondda and Cynon valleys of today are very different and the only working deep mine left in South Wales is **Tower Colliery**. In the Rhondda Valley alone there were once 53 working mines in just 16 square miles but, although they have now gone, the traditions of the colliery still live on.

When the Lewis Merthyr Colliery closed in 1983, it re-opened as the **Rhondda Heritage Park**, a fascinating place where former miners guide visitors around the restored mining buildings. As well as seeing the conditions in which the miners worked and hearing stories from miners whose families worked in the mines for generations, visitors can also see exhibitions on the role of the women in a mining village, the dramatic history of the 1920s strikes for a minimum wage and the tragedy of mining disasters. Between 1868 and 1919 in Rhondda one miner was killed every six hours and one injured every two minutes. The cultural and social history of a mining community, through brass bands, choirs and the chapel, is explored and visitors also have the opportunity to put on a hard hat and travel down the mine shaft in a cage.

ABERDARE

9 miles NW of Pontypridd on the A4233

Situated at the northern end of the Cynon valley, Aberdare, like other valley towns, is famous for its strong music tradition - particularly male voice choirs. In **Victoria Square** is a statue of the baton waving choir conductor, Griffith Rhys Jones (1834-1897).

The valley's other tradition, coal mining, is celebrated at the excellent **Cynon Valley Museum** which is housed in the town's former tram depot. Various exhibits portray the social and working conditions of the mid-19th century, along with displays of the 1926 General Strike and the Miners Strike of 1984-85. On a lighter note, there are also exhibits on teenage life through the centuries, miners' jazz bands and Victorian lantern slides.

Just a short distance from the busy town centre is the beautiful **Dare Valley Country Park** which was opened in 1973 on former colliery land and where trails tell of the natural and industrial history of the area.

MERTHYR TYDFIL

The main road in this area of Wales, the A645, acts as a dividing line: to the south are the historic valleys once dominated by coal mining and the iron and steel industries, while, to the north, lie the unspoilt southern uplands of the Brecon Beacons National Park. This rigidly observed divide is explained by geology, as the coal bearing rocks of the valleys end here and give way to the limestone and old red sandstone rocks of the Brecon Beacons. The close proximity of the two different types of rock also explains the nature and growth of industry in this particular area of South Wales as the iron smelting process required not just coal but also limestone. The iron ore was locally available too. These ingredients all came together in the most productive way at Merthyr Tydfil and this former iron and steel capital of the world was once the largest town in Wales. In 1831 its population of 60,000 exceeded that of Cardiff, Newport and Swansea combined. Merthyr was also home to the world's first steam engine to run successfully on rails. Made by **Richard Trevithick** the engine hauled 10 tons of iron, seventy passengers and five wagons from Penydarren to the Merthyr Cardiff canal.

The town took its name from the martyr St Tydfil, the daughter of the Welsh chieftain Brychan (after whom Brecon is named). She was martyred by the Irish for her

The landscape of Aberdare was once shaped by coal mines and heavy industry, but with the closure of the mines the countryside is, through ambitious land reclamation and environmental improvement schemes, returning to its pre-industrial green and lush natural state.

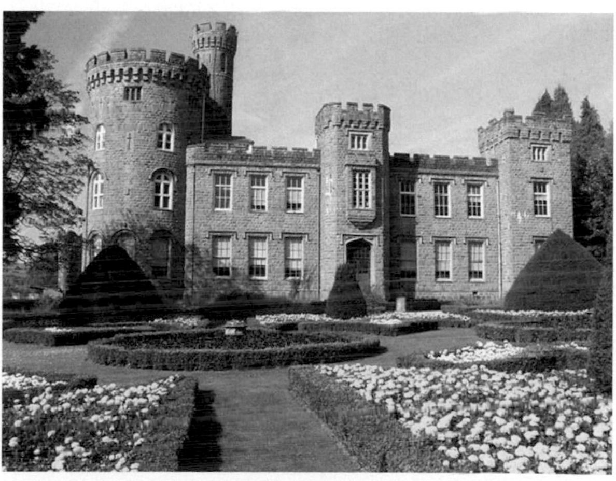

Cyfartha Castle, Merthyr Tydfil

Joseph Parry's Birthplace in Chapel Row provides a contrasting view of life in Merthyr Tydfil during its heyday. A superb example of a skilled ironworker's home, the cottage gives an interesting insight into the living conditions of those days. It was here that Joseph Parry, the 19th century composer famous for writing the haunting hymn Myfanwy, was born; on the first floor is an exhibition of his life and work.

Christian beliefs in AD 480.

Described as 'the most impressive monument of the Industrial Iron Age in Southern Wales', **Cyfarthfa Castle** is a grand mansion situated in beautiful and well laid out parkland. The castle was commissioned in the 1820s by the ironmaster William Crawshay, who constructed the grand house to overlook the family's ironworks, which at the time were the largest in the world. Today, this mansion is home to a **Museum and Art Gallery** which not only covers the social and industrial history of Merthyr Tydfil and the surrounding area but also has an extensive collection of fine and decorative art. The parkland, too, is well worth exploring, and the Visitor Centre has copious information on the park's amenities and natural history.

Another of the town's claims to fame lies in the political sphere: it was the first constituency in Britain to return a socialist Member of Parliament when Kier Hardie was elected to Westminster in 1900.

AROUND MERTHYR TYDFIL

PONTSTICILL

3 miles N of Merthyr Tydfil off the A465

From here the **Brecon Mountain Railway** travels a 2-mile scenic route up to Pontsticill Reservoir in the Brecon Beacons National Park. The charming vintage steam trains follow the tracks of the old Merthyr Tydfil to Brecon line, which has been re-opened by railway enthusiasts.

BRIDGEND

Known in Welsh as Pen-y-Bont Ar Ogwr (meaning 'the crossing of the River Ogmore'), this bustling market town lies at the confluence of the Rivers Ogmore, Garw and Llynfi and was once regarded as so vital a route that it had two castles, one on either side of the River Ogmore. The sparse remains of 12th century **Newcastle Castle** lie on the west riverside while the more extensive ruins of 14th century **Coity Castle** (CADW; free) stand guard on the other. Originally built by the Norman Payn de Turberville and strengthened over the following three centuries, Coity Castle was finally abandoned in the late-16th century. Its late-Norman decorated gateway is the only surviving feature of interest.

Bridgend's distinction as a market town dates back as far as the early 16th century and down the ages there have been tanneries, a woollen factory and local potteries in the area. Today, the Rhiw shopping centre, the new covered market and, on the northern outskirts, the giant McArthur Glen Designer Outlet with almost 100 stores, have made Bridgend something of a shopper's paradise.

AROUND BRIDGEND

TONDU

3½ miles N of Bridgend on the A4063

The nationally important Tondu Ironworks have now been incorporated into the **Tondu**

Heritage Park, while the site of an old colliery and open cast coal workings has been developed into the **Parc Slip Nature Reserve**. The reserve's network of paths leads visitors through the various different wildlife habitats, such as grassland, woodland and wetland, where a wide variety of plants, birds and animals have made their homes.

BETWS

5 miles N of Bridgend off the A4063

Just south of the village lies **Bryngarw Country Park**, which throughout the year presents a variety of enchanting landscapes including woodland, grassland, water features and formal gardens. A visitor centre provides information on the country park and on the many species of plants and birds to be found here. Perhaps the most interesting feature of the park is the exotic Japanese Garden, which was laid out in 1910 and where there are not only a series of interlinked ponds and an oriental tea garden pavilion, but also superb azaleas, rhododendrons, magnolias and cherry trees.

The house at the centre of the estate, **Bryngarw House**, was built in 1834 by Morgan Popkin Treherne as a 'small but elegant dwelling'; it has been restored and is now a bistro and conference centre.

MAESTEG

8 miles N of Bridgend on the A4063

This ancient market town with its broad main street, reputedly the widest in Wales, was the centre of iron making in the 1820s, but the last great furnace was 'blown out' in 1886; one of the ironworks is now a sports centre. Maesteg was once linked to the coast at Porthcawl by a tramway, traces of which can be seen at Porthcawl. The Tabor chapel in Maesteg was where *Land of My Fathers* was first sung in public in 1856. The Welsh words were written by Evan James, the music by his son James James. For 112 years, Talbot Street was the only alcohol-free high street in Britain, so covenanted in the will of the teetotal spinster after whom the street was named. In the summer of 2002, a restaurant owner challenged the covenant, and the magistrates ruled in his favour.

LLANGEINOR

5 miles N of Bridgend on the A4064

This pretty village has a handsome medieval church, **St Ceinwyr's Church**, on a mountainside which was built over the foundations of a religious site dating back to the 6th century. The church has a fine 15th century nave, a 16th century tower and a Norman font.

HOEL-Y-CYW

4 miles NE of Bridgend off the B4280

To the northeast of the village lies **Mynydd y Gaer**, a wonderful local landmark which, from its near 1000 foot high summit, provides spectacular views across the valleys to the north and the Bristol Channel to the south.

MERTHYR MAWR

2 miles SW of Bridgend off the A48

Situated down river from Bridgend,

207 THE OLD HOUSE INN

Llangynwyd

Thatched olde worlde inn with charisma and atmosphere to match, serving a vast menu created with the freshest local produce.

see page 368

208 THE GLOBE INN

Newton, nr Porthcawl

Vibrant village inn in historic Newton, serving a fine gastro-pub menu with specialty curries and real ale.

see page 369

this delightful village of thatched cottages bordered by meadows and woodland lies on the edge of **Merthyr Mawr Warren**, one of the largest areas of sand dunes in Europe. Parts of David Lean's *Lawrence of Arabia* were filmed in the dunes. Now a Site of Special Scientific Interest, the dunes offer the perfect habitat for a wide variety of plants and animals.

Surrounded by the dune system are the remains of **Candleston Castle**, a 15th century fortified manor house that was, until the 19th century, the home of the powerful Cantelupe family. Local children believe the house to be haunted but the biggest mystery of Candleston is the fate of the village of Treganllaw (meaning 'the town of a hundred hands') which is thought to have been engulfed by the dunes.

On the road approaching the village is the 15th century **New Inn Bridge** which has some interesting holes in its parapet through which in the old days sheep were pushed into the river for their annual dip!

NEWTON

4½ miles W of Bridgend off the A4106

Dating back to the 12th century, the village was founded as a 'new town' and by the 17th century was a thriving port from where grain and knitted stockings were exported. The imposing limestone **Church of St John the Baptist** was originally built for the Knights of the Order of St John of Jerusalem in the late 12th or early 13th century. On the nearby green is **St John's Well** where pilgrims would take refreshment from its supposedly healing waters.

PORTHCAWL

6 miles W of Bridgend on the A4229

Porthcawl is one of the region's most popular resorts, with clean sandy beaches at Sandy Bay, Trecco Bay and the quieter Rest Bay which boasts a European Blue Flag. **Coney Beach Pleasure Park** provides a wide variety of rides, from white knuckle roller coasters to more gentle carousels. This is also a haven for surfers, sailors and fishing enthusiasts, while the headlands above Rest Bay are the site of the famous Royal Porthcawl Golf Club.

The more dignified side of Porthcawl centres on the Edwardian promenade, a legacy of the prosperous days when this was a port exporting coal and iron. A good way of orienting yourself is to take a trip on the **Promenade Princess**, a road train that leaves from Coney Beach park. It passes the working harbour where, during the summer months, the veteran steamship *Balmoral* departs for cruises along the Bristol channel and across to Lundy Island. There is a **RNLI station** at the harbour (open daily for visits) and nearby there's a white-painted cast iron lighthouse built in 1866. In 2004 a Bronze medal was awarded to Porthcawl helmsman Aileen Jones, the first for a woman in 116 years. In the same rescue mission crewman Simon Emms was awarded the Thanks of the

Institution inscribed on vellum. In May 2009 the station took delivery of the first of the new Atlantic 85 Class boats, the *Rose of the Shires*. On the edge of the harbour is the **Jennings Building** of 1830, one of the oldest harbour buildings in Wales and now a Skating Centre. On its southeastern wall is a brass plug marking the highest recorded tide of 52ft. The road train continues along the promenade to Rest Bay, passing en route the **Grand Pavilion**, a wonderful Art Deco building of 1932 that plays host to all manner of live shows, cinema and private parties.

The history of the town can be discovered at **Porthcawl Museum**, where there is a fascinating collection of artefacts, costumes and memorabilia on display.

KENFIG

6½ miles W of Bridgend off the B4283

This village was originally founded in the 12th century by Robert, Earl of Gloucester, who also built **Kenfig Castle** here. However, some 400 years later the sands of Kenfig Burrows had swamped the settlement and the medieval town lies buried in the dunes although the remains of the castle keep are still visible. The legend of Kenfig Pool has it that on a quiet day when the water is clear, the houses of the buried town can be seen at the bottom of the lake and the bells of the old church can be heard ringing before a storm.

Today, this marvellous area of dunes to the northwest of the present village is the **Kenfig National Nature Reserve**. With more than 600 species of flowering plants, including orchids, a freshwater lake and numerous birds, this is a haven for all naturalists as well as ramblers.

PENARTH AND THE VALE OF GLAMORGAN

Often described as the 'garden by the sea', Penarth (the name means 'bear's head' in Welsh) is a popular and unspoilt seaside resort which developed in Victorian and Edwardian times. Built for the wealthy industrialists of Cardiff's shipyards, this once fashionable town has lost none of its late 19th and early 20th century elegance and style typified by the splendidly restored pier, the sweeping Esplanade, the abundant flower beds and the formal sea view gardens. Built in 1894, the **Pier** extends 685ft out into the channel and is a regular berthing point

Just up the road from the Nature Reserve in Kenfig is the Prince of Wales pub which was originally built in 1605 as a replacement for the Town Hall which had disappeared beneath the encroaching sands. The pub is notable for having experienced an unusual number of documented paranormal events.

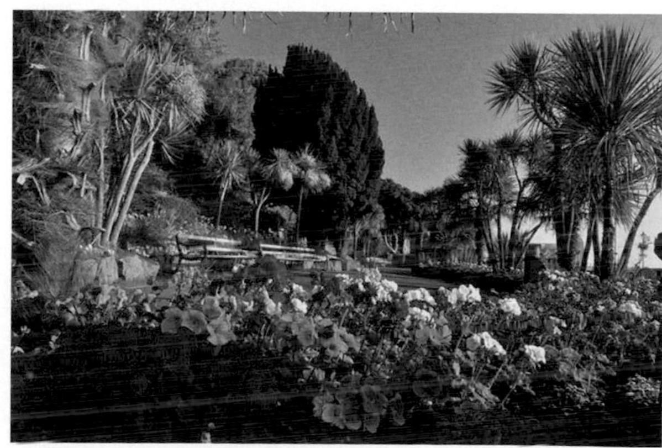

The Esplande, Penarth

To the south of Penarth lies Cosmeston, a Medieval Village that grew up around a manor house belonging to the Constantin family (some of the first Norman invaders in Wales) in the 12th century. However, in the mid-14th century the Black Death reached the village, killing around one third of the population. Following a period of decline it was left to decay. Today, several of the village's buildings have been reconstructed, allowing visitors, with the help of costumed characters, to gain a real insight into life in a medieval village.

during the summer for the cruise ships *Balmoral* and *Waverley* - the latter being the last sea-going paddle steamer in the world. From the Marina, a water bus sails across the freshwater lake to Cardiff's recently developed Bay area with its chic shops, restaurants, Welsh Assembly building and award-winning visitor centre.

Long before the town became popular as a resort, Penarth's picturesque setting had inspired many artists, amongst them JMW Turner who is commemorated in the **Turner House Gallery**, part of the National Museum of Wales, in the centre of the town.

If the town seems to have been lost in a time warp, a visit to the **Washington Gallery**, housed in a wonderful Art Deco cinema, will dispel this view through its exciting collection of modern and contemporary art.

From Penarth's Esplanade, a spectacular coastal path leads out to Lavernock Point. It was from here in 1897 that Guglielmo Marconi sent the very first radio transmission over water to the offshore island of **Flat Holm** some 3 miles distant. The transmission was brief - just the three words "Are you ready?" A tiny island with a wealth of wildlife, Flat Holm has a history that dates back to the Dark Ages, when it was used by monks as a retreat. Vikings, Anglo-Saxons, smugglers and cholera victims are known to have sought refuge on the island, which was also fortified twice, once by the Victorians and again in World War II. Today, it is a Site of Special Scientific Interest, with a local nature reserve that is home to the largest colony of gulls in Wales.

Cosmeston Country Park is an area of lakes, woodlands and meadows created from a disused limestone quarry. A peaceful and tranquil habitat for many birds and animals, with a wide range of plant life, the country park has a visitor centre, picnic areas and a café

AROUND PENARTH

BARRY ISLAND & BARRY

5 miles SW of Penarth on the A4055

Barry Island is not an island but a peninsula, facing Barry, whose natural, sheltered harbour has been used since Roman times; **Cold Knap Roman Buildings**, to the west of this seaside resort, are all that remains from those days. A popular place for holidaymakers for generations, Barry Island offers its visitors all the traditional seaside resort trappings, from sandy beaches to a funfair, as well as views across the Bristol Channel to the Somerset coast. Quieter souls will no doubt prefer either **The Knap** with its gardens and lake, or **Porthkerry Country Park** with some 220 acres of parkland, woods and meadows leading down to the sea.

The latest all-weather attraction is the **Barry Island Railway Heritage Centre**, which has a line from Barry Island into the neighbouring Waterfront Dock Development.

To the north of the resort is

the **Welsh Hawking Centre & Animal Park**, where 200 birds of prey – eagles, falcons, hawks, buzzards, owls – have their homes and provide regular flying demonstrations. The park is also home to rabbits, ducks and chickens.

Over recent years, Barry town's Waterfront development has inspired an ambitious multi-million pound regeneration programme, restoring key buildings and adding modern homes and commercial buildings. But perhaps the most impressive building in town is the 1899 **Dock Office Building**. Designed in neo-baroque Renaissance style, the building has a calendar theme: 365 windows, 52 marble fireplaces; 12 panels in the impressive porch; 7 lights in the window above the original doors, 4 floors for the seasons and 2 circular windows in the entrance hall representing the sun and moon.

Dock Office Building, Barry

LLANTWIT MAJOR

14 miles W of Penarth off the B4265

The centre of this delightful town with its narrow streets, quaint stone cottages, olde worlde shops and ancient inns is perhaps the Vale of Glamorgan's most historic settlement. It was here, in AD 500, that **St Illtud** founded a church and school. One of the great Celtic saints who travelled in Britain, Ireland and Brittany, St Illtud was the tutor of both St David and St Patrick. The latter was abducted from the monastery by Irish pirates and taken to Ireland where he later became the country's patron saint. Although little is known of St Illtud, he does feature in the book *The Life of St Samson of Dol* which was written around 100 years after his death. The church and school he founded here are believed to be the oldest learning centres in the country. The only remains of his original church to have survived are the dedication stones, but the imposing **Church of St Illtud** seen today is a combination of two buildings, one an early Norman structure and the other dating from the late 13th century. John Wesley, visiting in 1777, described the church as "the most beautiful as well as the most spacious church in Wales". Inside can be seen a fine collection of Celtic crosses which includes St Illtud's or St Samson's cross, which was found buried in the church grounds on top of two skeletons.

There are more ancient buildings in the town square. The **Old White Hart** public house was

The sands of Whitmore Bay are perfect for volleyball - there are volleyball courts on the beach throughout the summer and in August the island hosts the British Beach Volleyball Championship. For younger visitors, Triassic Towers offers the ultimate adventure experience with spiral climbs, hanging snakes, wavy stairs and crawl nets.

Sunset at Southerndown

built as a private dwelling for a Robert Raglan around 1440; twenty-five years later, he built another new house which has survived as the **Old School** and is used by community groups.

ST DONAT'S

15 miles W of Penarth off the B4265

Close to the village stands **St Donat's Castle** which dates from around 1300 and was once owned by the American newspaper magnate William Randolph Hearst. Hearst, whose life was fictionalised in the classic Orson Welles film *Citizen Kane*, spent huge sums of money restoring and furnishing this historic building in mock-Gothic style. Here he entertained film stars and other figures on the world's stage. The castle is now the international Atlantic College. Within its grounds is the **St Donat's Arts Centre**, the largest arts venue in the Vale of Glamorgan, which offers a full programme of exhibitions, cinema, dance, theatre and musical events. To the west of the village lies **Nash Point**, a headland with two lighthouses and the remnants of an Iron Age fort. This area of the coast is overlooked by limestone cliffs which through wind erosion have begun to resemble giant building blocks.

SOUTHERNDOWN

19 miles W of Penarth on the B4265

This popular holiday centre overlooking beautiful Dunraven Bay is home to the **Glamorgan Heritage Coast Centre** which has displays and information about the 14-mile long stretch of wild and beautiful coastline which begins in the west at Newton and was the first in Britain to be designated a Heritage Coast.

OGMORE

19 miles W of Penarth on the B4265

Lying at the mouth of the River Ogmore, this pretty village is also close to a ford across the River Ewenny where the impressive ruins of **Ogmore Castle** (private) can be seen. Built in the early 12th century by William de Londres, this was once the foremost stronghold in the area although all that can be seen today are the remains of a three storey keep and the dry moat. This is a great picnic spot with caves, rock pools and stepping stones across the river to Merthyr Mawr.

EWENNY

17½ miles W of Penarth on the B4265

This charming rural village is home to **Ewenny Priory**, which was founded in 1141 by Maurice de Londres, the son of William de Londres of Ogmore Castle. This is one of the finest fortified religious houses in Britain and, while its precinct walls, towers and gateways give the priory a military air, it is believed that they were built for reasons of prestige rather than defence.

Close by is 400-year-old **Ewenny Pottery**, still worked by the same family that founded it and said to be the oldest working pottery in Wales.

COWBRIDGE

12½ miles W of Penarth off the A48

This handsome and prosperous town, with the reputation of being the wealthiest in Wales, has been the principal market town of the Vale of Glamorgan since medieval times and is today noted for its quality shops, crafts and restaurants. The work of local artists and craftspeople can be seen at the **Old Wool Barn Craft Centre** which has studio workshops set around an attractive courtyard. The original Norman grid layout of the town is visible to this day, particularly in the mile-long main street. Parts of Cowbridge's 14th century town walls and one gatehouse, South Gate, still stand.

Across from the Grammar School, in the walled garden of Old Hall, is **Cowbridge Physic Garden.** Opened in 2006, the garden is designed to create awareness of the curative properties of plants.

The history of the town can be explored at **Cowbridge Museum** which is housed in two blocks of cells beneath a sturdy building that began as House of Correction before becoming the Town Hall in 1830. It's an elegant building with a clock tower, cupola and weathervane.

ST NICHOLAS

6 miles NW of Penarth on the A48

To the south of the village lie **Dyffryn Gardens** which, as part of the Dyffryn estate, were landscaped in the 19th century. One of the finest surviving Thomas Mawson gardens in Britain, Dyffryn offers a series of broad sweeping lawns, Italianate terraces, a paved court, a physick garden and a rose garden as well as a vine walk and arboretum. Perhaps the most impressive features are the Pompeian Garden and the Theatre Garden where open air plays and concerts are held.

•

Close to South Gate in Cowbridge is the Grammar School, founded in 1608 and rebuilt in the 1850s in Gothic style. Its most eminent alumnus is the actor Sir Anthony Hopkins. On the outskirts of the town is Llanerch Vineyard, the largest vineyard in Wales producing estate-bottled wines which are marketed under the Cariad label.

•

Cowbridge Physic Garden

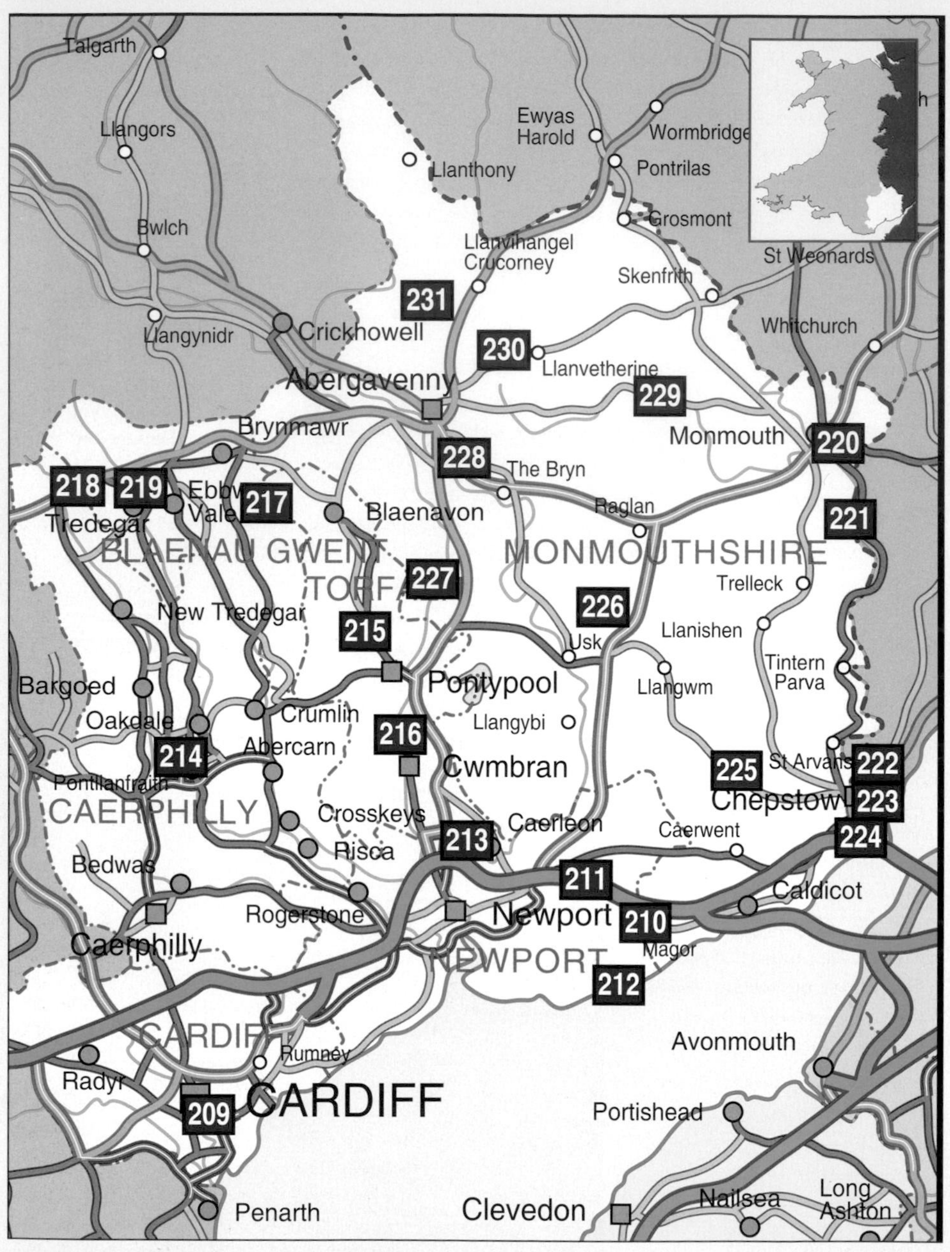

Talgarth
Llangors
Bwlch
Llangynidr
Crickhowell
Llanthony
Ewyas Harold
Wormbridge
Pontrilas
Grosmont
Llanvihangel Crucorney
Skenfrith
St Weonards
Whitchurch
231
230
Llanvetherine
229
Abergavenny
Brynmawr
Monmouth
220
228
The Bryn
218
219
Ebbw Vale
217
Tredegar
Blaenavon
Raglan
221
BLAENAU GWENT
MONMOUTHSHIRE
TORFAEN
227
Trelleck
226
New Tredegar
215
Llanishen
Usk
Tintern Parva
Llangwm
Bargoed
Pontypool
Oakdale
Crumlin
Llangybi
216
214
Abercarn
Cwmbran
225
St Arvans
222
Pontllanfraith
Chepstow
223
CAERPHILLY
Crosskeys
Caerleon
Caerwent
213
224
Risca
Bedwas
211
Caldicot
Rogerstone
Newport
210
Caerphilly
Magor
NEWPORT
212
CARDIFF
Rumney
Avonmouth
Radyr
CARDIFF
209
Portishead
Clevedon
Nailsea
Long Ashton
Penarth

Cardiff and Monmouthshire

History, ancient and modern, abounds in this region of South Wales, with the distinguished ruins of Norman fortifications and the remains of the industrial past of the valleys. The valleys of the Wye and Usk offer some truly glorious scenery as well as the equally breathtaking sight of Tintern Abbey. An inspiration for both poets and artists, this abbey was at one time one of the richest in the country and the magnificent ruins beside the River Wye are still a stirring sight.

This area, too, is one that saw much contest between the Welsh and the English, so not surprisingly there are numerous fortifications to be seen and explored.

Along this stretch of coastline lies Cardiff, the capital city of Wales and a place which is successfully blending the ancient with the modern. The Romans occupied various sites in this area, but it was heavy industry and the influence of the Bute family that made Cardiff such a powerful port. The home of Welsh rugby, with the superb Millennium Stadium and a recently rejuvenated waterfront, Cardiff is a city that vibrates with life, energy and enthusiasm.

To the north lie the valleys that provided so much wealth until the decline of coal mining and the iron industry. Much of the land that was once an industrial wasteland has been reclaimed by nature, with the help of sensitive human intervention, but there are still some monuments to the great industrial age remaining, chiefly at the Big Pit Mine and Blaenavon Ironworks.

ACCOMMODATION

FOOD & DRINK

PLACES OF INTEREST

209 CARDIFF CASTLE

Cardiff

Cardiff Castle is an unusual blend of Roman fort, medieval castle and fanciful Victorian gothic mansion.

see page 370

CARDIFF

The capital city of Wales is a fascinating place with an unexpected beauty, a long history, a sporting tradition and an exciting rejuvenated waterfront that is attracting visitors in their thousands. The Cardiff area was first settled by the Romans in the 1st century, but from their departure a few centuries later to the arrival of the Normans in the 11th century little was recorded of life around what is now Cardiff. In 1091, Robert FitzHamon built a primitive fortress on what remained of the Roman fortification and this was, over the years, upgraded to a stone castle around which the town began to develop. Overrun by Owain Glyndwr in the early 15th century, the town and its castle came into the hands first of the Tudors and then of the Herbert family and their descendants the Marquesses of Bute.

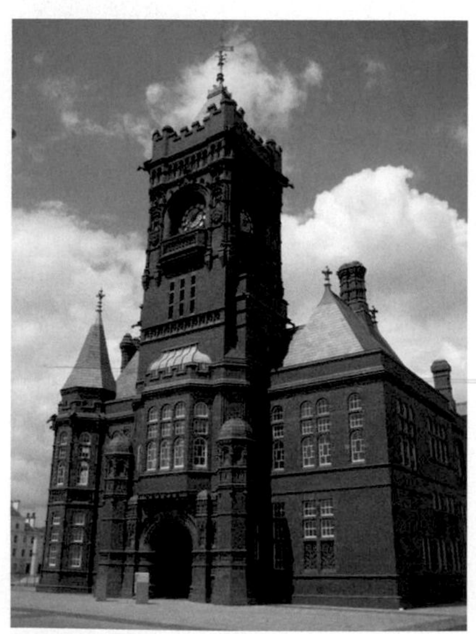

Pierhead Building, Cardiff

However, Cardiff is very much a product of the Industrial Revolution and its story is intertwined with that of the Marquesses of Bute. They controlled the docklands and, as the town began to thrive as a coal exporting port, the family made a vast fortune. Cardiff became the biggest coal-exporting port in the world, and at its peak in 1913 more than 13 million tons of coal were exported from the docks. Some of this wealth was poured back into the rebuilding of **Cardiff Castle**. A no-expense-spared project initiated by the 3rd Marquess, the castle is an extravagant and opulent Victorian version of a castle of the Middle Ages. It was designed by the eccentric architect William Burges who allowed his flamboyant imagination to run riot, Burges created magnificent rooms rich in murals, stained glass and marble which really do have to be seen to be believed. While this building is very much a flight of wealthy Victorian fancy, outside in the grounds can be seen the well preserved medieval castle keep and stonework dating from Roman times. Visitors to the castle today also have the opportunity to look around the **Welsh Regiment Museum** (41st/69th Foot) and look out over Cardiff from the top of the Norman keep.

The area once known as Tiger Bay - Cardiff's historic dockland and the birthplace of Dame Shirley Bassey - is one of the country's most exciting and imaginative regeneration developments. Now called **Cardiff Bay**, this revived waterfront is home to the new **National Assembly**, the impressive **Pierhead Building** which was built in 1896 for the Bute Docks Company and the **Cardiff Bay Visitor Centre**. At this award-winning tubular building, visitors can see a futuristic exhibition which lays out the full vision of the complete development which, among other aims, is reuniting the city with its dockland. The **Wales Millennium Centre** is an arts and cultural centre of world importance. Perhaps the single most important part in the revival of the Bay is the massive **Cardiff Bay Barrage**, a barrier that stretches for a kilometre across the mouth of the Bay. Of particular interest to children at Cardiff Bay is **Techniquest**, the country's leading science discovery centre, where visitors can explore many aspects of science and technology through a vast range of interactive exhibits. Tel: 029 2047 5475

The former church for Norwegian sailors, which is where the author Roald Dahl was baptised, is now the **Norwegian Church Arts Centre** which maintains the links which have grown up over the years between the two nations.

Although Cardiff's famous Arms Park, the home of rugby football for so many years, has gone, its replacement, the **Millennium Stadium**, has become an equally revered shrine to the Welsh national game and proved a highly successful replacement for Wembley as that new stadium was being built. The stadium's dazzling debut was to host the last great sporting event of the 20th century, the Rugby World Cup Final in November 1999, Visitors to the stadium can see the hallowed turf and learn how the pitch was laid, find out how the 8,000-ton roof opens and closes, and walk from the Welsh players' dressing room, through the tunnel and on to the pitch. A mile or so from Cardiff city centre stands **Llandaff Cathedral**, a beautiful building set in a grassy hollow beside the River Taff. The cathedral suffered severe bomb damage during World War II and part of its restoration programme included a controversial Epstein sculpture, *Christ in Majesty*, which dominates the interior. Inside, visitors will also find some delightful medieval masonry, a marvellous modern timber roof and some works of art by members of the Pre-Raphaelite movement.

Two miles north of the city centre, **Roath Park** is a 19th century urban park with handsome trees, formal flower beds, a wild area and a memorial to Scott of the Antarctic.

Friary Gardens, Cardiff

•

As might be expected in a capital city, Cardiff is home to many of the national treasures of Wales. At the superb National Museum and Gallery of Wales there is a vast collection of archaeology, natural history (including 55,000 live leaf-cutter ants!) and ceramics as well as permanent exhibitions on the Evolution of Wales, and Man and the Environment. The art gallery boasts a fine collection that includes the largest body of Impressionist paintings outside Paris and the best of Welsh art. The museum and gallery, along with the City Hall, are located in Cathays Park, where there are other civic buildings and also various departments of the University of Wales.

•

16th Century Cottage, St Fagans Museum

AROUND CARDIFF

ST FAGANS

4 miles W of Cardiff off the A48

On the outskirts of Cardiff, this picturesque village is home to the outstanding **St Fagans National History Museum** in the extensive grounds of St Fagans Castle, a splendid Elizabethan mansion. Founded in 1946, this is a museum unlike most others as it contains an assortment of buildings collected from all over Wales which have been re-erected in these glorious open-air surroundings. Within the 50-acre site you'll find a 17th century farmhouse from Gower, a tiny whitewashed chapel of 1777 from Dyfed, a Victorian schoolroom from Lampeter, a pre-war grocery, a terrace of iron-workers' cottages from Merthyr Tydfil, and a toll house of 1772 from Aberystwyth. There's also a pottery, tannery, bakery, smithy and three mills, most of them with workers demonstrating the original methods employed. Each of the 40 or so buildings has been furnished to reflect a period in its history. The museum also holds demonstrations on traditional craft skills and visitors can enjoy a delightful stroll round the formal gardens, the Italian Garden, the modern knot garden and the terraces that descend to a series of fishponds. There's a restaurant and coffee shop, a traditional bakehouse selling organic bread and cakes, a play area and a gift shop with products relating to the museum's collections.

TONGWYNLAIS

3 miles NW of Cardiff on the A470

Situated in the Taff Valley and hidden by trees, **Castell Coch** (CADW) appears to be a fairytale castle of the Middle Ages, yet it only dates from the 19th century. Built on the site of a 13th century castle, Castell Coch was designed by the eccentric architect William Burges for the 3rd Marquess of Bute as a companion piece to Cardiff Castle. As the Marquess was reputed to be the wealthiest man in the world - the family owned the thriving Cardiff docks - money was no object. While the medieval illusion of the place is maintained by the working portcullis and drawbridge, the interior decoration is perhaps even more astonishing. Perfectly preserved, each room is a masterpiece, with eye-catching details such as paintings of butterflies on the domed ceiling of the drawing room, scenes from Aesop's Fables and Greek mythology on the walls, and bird and animal mouldings around the doors.

The Marquess planted a vineyard in the castle grounds which, it is said, produced the only commercially made wine in Britain between 1875 and 1914. There are now more than a dozen commercial vineyards in Wales alone.

NEWPORT

With a population of about 120,000, Newport is the third largest city in Wales. It achieved city status in 2002 to mark the Queen's Golden Jubilee.

The town's **St Woolos Cathedral Church**, splendidly situated on the hilltop, is just the latest building on a site which has been a place of worship since the 6th century. The present structure is a medley of architectural styles that includes a magnificent Norman doorway and columns that are believed to have come from the Roman fort at Caerleon. The church was founded by St Gwynllyw (Woolos is the English version of his name), who before his conversion was a cruel and wicked man. He is said to have had a dream one night that he would go to a hill and find there a white ox with a black spot. This Gwynllyw did the next day and, finding the said ox, saw it as a sign from God and became a devout Christian. In the graveyard of St Woolos are the graves of some of the soldiers of the Welsh Regiment who were killed in the Battle of Rorke's Drift during the Zulu Wars of South Africa.

Just down the road from the cathedral, **Stow Hill** is notable for its Georgian and Victorian town houses, something of a rarity in Newport.

The city grew up around the docks at the mouth of the river Usk and from a population of 1000 in 1801 rocketed to 70,000 by the early 1900s.

The history of Newport's docks and the city itself is explored at the **Newport Museum and Art Gallery** with a range of displays on the city's origins, including a Roman mosaic floor which was excavated close by. Not to be missed here are the John Wait teapot display with some 300 weird and wonderful pieces, and the Fox collection of decorative art. Just to the north of the museum, on the

210 THE WHEATSHEAF INN

Magor

Dating back to the 14th century this popular inn offers the very best in accommodation, food and drink.

see page 371

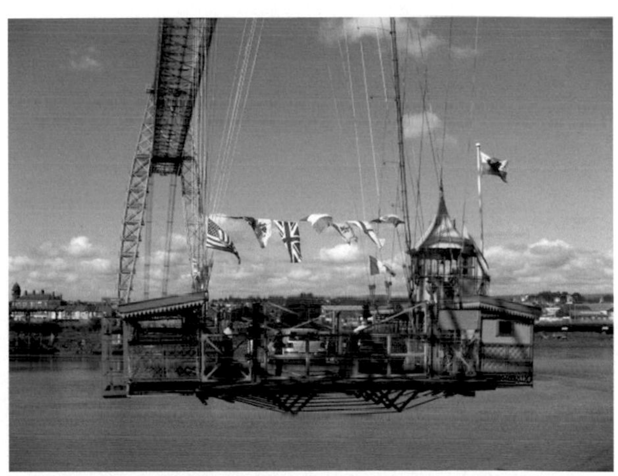

Transporter Bridge, Newport

211 THE OLD BARN INN

Llanmartin

Luxurious and chic en suite accommodation can be found in this rural inn, which serves phenomenal food throughout the day in its own restaurant.

 see page 372

212 THE ROSE INN

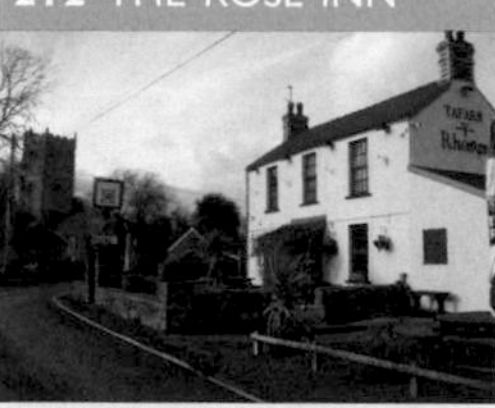

Redwick

Pretty 15th century inn serving fine food, wine and ale throughout the year, perfect for families with a children's play area in the garden.

 see page 373

213 ANGEL HOTEL

Caerleon

Real ales and traditional Welsh food served up daily in this welcoming inn with en suite accommodation.

 see page 137568

river bank, is another striking art work, Peter Fink's enormous red sculpture, **Steel Wave** of 1991, which represents steel and sea trades which have played such important roles in Newport's development. The sculpture is part of the city's Public Art Trail which also features an extraordinary **Kinetic Clock** which delivers a repertoire of shudders, spits and shakes on the hour, and a massive **Chartist Mural** depicting the Chartist uprising of 1839 when 22 protesters were killed by soldiers hiding in the Westgate Hotel. Both these works can be found in the pedestrianised John Frost Square. Westgate Hotel itself is a wonderfully ornate Victorian structure fronted by pillars from its predecessor which still bear the bullet pocks from the shooting.

Dominating the cityscape and an impressive reminder of Newport's more recent past is the massive **Transporter Bridge** across the River Usk. Specially designed in 1906 by Ferdinand Arnodin to allow traffic to cross the river without disrupting the movement of shipping, the bridge is one of very few of its kind: one is in Middlesbrough, two others are in France.

Newport was the home of the poet WH Davies, who penned the famous lines:

What is this life if, full of care,
We have no time to stand and stare...

To the west of the town is **Tredegar House and Park**, one of the finest examples of Restoration architecture in Wales and the home of the influential Morgan family for more than 500 years. Visitors can tour the rooms and discover just what life was like here, both above and below stairs, as well as finding out something about this great Welsh family. Its more colourful and famous members include Sir Henry Morgan, the notorious pirate, Godfrey, the 2nd Lord Tredegar, who survived the Charge of the Light Brigade and whose horse is buried in the grounds, and Viscount Evan, whose menagerie included a boxing kangaroo. The park that surrounds the house is equally impressive, with early 18th century walled formal gardens, an orangery with restored parterres, and craft workshops. Carriage drives through the parkland are available and children have their own adventure playground. There's a tea room and gift shop, and a suite of rooms is available for corporate events.

AROUND NEWPORT

CAERLEON

2½ miles NE of Newport on the B4236

Despite its close proximity to Newport, Caerleon has managed to maintain the air of a rural town, but its chief attraction is the remarkable Roman remains. Caerleon is one of the largest and most significant surviving Roman military sites in Europe. It was established in AD 75 by the 2nd Augustinian Legion and originally called Isca. A substantial Roman town grew up around the military base and among the remains to be seen at **Caerleon Roman Fortress and Baths** are a large amphitheatre where thousands watched the gladiators, the only surviving Roman barracks to be seen in Europe and a complex system of Roman baths which were the equivalent of today's sports and leisure centres. Finds excavated from the remains are on show at the **Legionary Museum**, where, along with the weapons, mosaics and models, visitors can see one of the largest collections of engraved gem stones.

Caerleon has more to offer than Roman remains - impressive though they are - and the town has some fine examples of timbered buildings. Also well worth a visit is the seemingly unpronounceable **Ffwrrwm Art & Craft Centre** (free) which is set inside an 18th century walled garden. The courtyard here contains several craft shops, a tea room, an art gallery and a sculpture garden. Sculpture is something of a Caerleon speciality. In midsummer it hosts a two week Arts Festival and International Sculpture Symposium which attracts sculptors from all over the world. The sculptors work in public so that visitors can see the works of art emerging from the raw materials, mostly wood.

PENHOW

7 miles E of Newport off the A48

This hamlet is home to Wales' oldest lived-in fortress, **Penhow Castle** which still has its stout Norman keep and an impressive 15th century Great Hall complete with minstrels' gallery. Visitors to the castle are invited to guide themselves through the various rooms using a recorded commentary on the 850-year history of the building. The castle was at one time owned by the family of Jane Seymour, Henry VIII's third wife, who died soon after giving birth to a son who became Edward VI.

CAERPHILLY

Despite being surrounded by shops, offices and houses, **Caerphilly Castle** completely dominates the town. A 'sleeping giant' of a castle, the fortress sprawls over some 30 acres making it the largest castle in Wales. In the whole of Britain it is only exceeded in size by Dover and Windsor.

It is also one of the finest surviving examples of medieval

•

Many people believe that Caerleon has links with King Arthur, asserting that the Roman amphitheatre was actually the site of the Round Table. Alfred, Lord Tennyson appears to have given this story some credit since he visited Caerleon, staying at the riverside Hanbury Arms, while seeking inspiration for his Arthurian epic, Idylls of the King.

•

Caerphilly Castle

214 PENLLWYN MANOR

Blackwood

An impressive and charming establishment dating back to the 16th century .

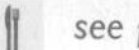
see page 374

military architecture in Europe. This great moated fortress was built largely in the late 13th century by the Norman Lord Gilbert de Clare. Along with the 'wall within walls' defence system, he also employed a mighty water defensive arrangement that included lakes and three artificial islands. The castle was restored in the 19th century by the Marquess of Bute, but nothing seems to be able to restore the castle's famous leaning tower which manages to out-lean even the better known Leaning Tower of Pisa. Today the castle is home to an intriguing display of full size working replica siege engines.

The town's **Visitor Centre**, as well as providing tourist information, has an exhibition on local history and culture, a display of Welsh crafts and a fine Welsh food shop. Caerphilly is famous for its distinctive white crumbly cheese, first made in 1831. It originated in the farms surrounding the town but during World War II and for a few years after, cheese-making was prohibited. It was only recently that production started up again and it is now possible to get locally made cheese once again.

AROUND CAERPHILLY

DERI

9 miles N of Caerphilly off the A469

To the north of Deri, in beautiful Darran Valley, lies **Parc Cwm Darran**, a glorious country park which, along with the adventure playground and informative Visitor Centre, also has a six-acre coarse fishery.

PONTLLANFRAITH

6 miles NE of Caerphilly on the A4048

Close to this town stands **Gelligroes Mill**, a 17th century water mill restored to full working order. In the early 20th century the mill was owned by Arthur Moore, a radio enthusiast, who on the night of 11th April 1912 claimed to have heard distress signals from the sinking *Titanic*. No one believed Arthur until two days later when confirmation of the disaster reached England

CWMFELINFACH

3½ miles NE of Caerphilly on the A4048

Covering some 1000 acres of both woodland and farmland, the **Sirhowy Valley Country Park** provides the ideal opportunity to walk, cycle or ride along the park's numerous trails. **The Full Moon Visitor Centre** has all the details of the park's natural history and of other activities here while in the heart of the country park is **Ynys Hywel Centre**, a converted 17th century farmhouse which has conference facilities and a weekend coffee shop.

CWMCARN

6 miles NE of Caerphilly on the B4591

Just to the west of the town lies **Cwmcarn Forest Drive**, a seven-mile stretch of high forest road that provides some of the most magnificent panoramic views of the South Wales countryside and the Bristol Channel beyond. Another attraction is the **Mabinogion Sculpture Trail**, which depicts characters from the Celtic folklore tales of the *Mabinogion*. The drive's visitor centre has details of the route and what can be seen at various points and also a coffee shop and a gift shop selling local handicrafts. Also here are a campsite and a mountain bike trail.

RISCA

5½ miles NE of Caerphilly on the B4591

To the south of Risca, at High Cross on the Monmouthshire Canal, is the **Fourteen Locks Canal Centre**. This complicated system of locks was constructed to raise and lower barges some 168 feet in just half a mile with only the minimal wastage of water. There are several guided walks from the centre which take in the locks, ponds, channels, tunnels and weirs, as well as the countryside in which the centre is sited. Open from Easter to September, the visitor centre has a display that follows the opening (in 1796), the growth and the heyday of the Monmouthshire Canal and the decline that started when the railways began to take trade off the water. The art gallery features three different artists each month.

NELSON

5½ miles NW of Caerphilly on the A472

As well as boasting an open air handball court dating from the 1860s (and still in use), this village is home to **Llancaiach Fawr Manor**, a handsome Elizabethan manor house which has been lovingly restored to the year 1645 and the time of the Civil War. During this turbulent time, the Pritchard family lived here and visitors to this living history museum can meet members of the family and their servants, all in authentic costumes, as they carry on with their daily lives. As well as preparing meals, gardening and exchanging gossip of the day, a number of events popular at that time, such as archery and falconry, are staged. This is a wonderfully entertaining and informative living history museum where visitors also get the chance to meet some of the eight resident ghosts on the special ghost tours.

PONTYPOOL

Known to have been in existence before the time of the Normans, Pontypool is credited with being the home of the Welsh iron industry. The first forge here is believed to have been in operation as early as 1425, and the first ironworks opened in 1577. It is said that the first iron working forge in America was started by emigrants from Pontypool in the mid-1600s. This valley also prides itself on being the earliest place in Britain to have successfully produced tin plate, in 1720. The town's industrial heritage can be explored at the **Pontypool Valley Inheritance Centre** where both the industrial and social history of the town and surrounding Torfaen valley is

215 THE LITTLE CROWN INN

Pontypool

Home cooking and local produce is the focus of the extensive menu at this delightful, hidden inn.

see page 376

•

The canals have played an important part in the development of Pontypool and this particular legacy is recalled at Junction Cottage, a tollkeeper's cottage of 1814 lying at the junction of the Monmouthshire and Brecon Canal and the River Lwyd.

•

216 THE CROSS KEYS INN

Cwmbran

A popular inn serving good quality food portions at reasonable prices.

see page 375

217 THE GOLDEN LION

Nantyglo

This lofty country inn with stunning views offers en suite guest accommodation and fantastic home cooking.

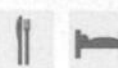
see page 377

detailed. The centre is located in the late-Georgian stables of Pontypool Park, once the home of the Hanbury family, who were, appropriately, owners of a local ironworks.

Pontypool Park is a 19th century landscaped park whose main attractions include a shell grotto and a unique double-chambered ice house. The formal Italian gardens have recently been restored with the help of Heritage Lottery funding.

Industry seems worlds away at **Llandegfedd Reservoir**, to the east of Pontypool, where the lake and surrounding countryside provide numerous opportunities for fishing, sailing, walking and bird watching.

AROUND PONTYPOOL

CWMBRAN

3 miles SW of Pontypool on the A4051

This new town in the old industrial valleys of South Wales was founded in 1949 and was once itself dominated by heavy industry. Today, the mines and large works have gone and major environmental improvement schemes, including planting forests, have taken away many of the old eyesores. Not far from the town are some interesting and historic places including the **Llanyrafon Mill and Farm Museum** and the **Llamtarnam Grange Arts Centre**.

Greenmeadow Community Farm, set within the town's planned green belt, is home to all manner of farm animals. Farm trails, a children's adventure playground and an unusual dragon sculpture are among the other attractions which go to provide a popular and entertaining day out.

If you'd rather go shopping, the **Cwmbran Shopping Centre** claims to be the largest undercover shopping complex in Wales.

BLAENAVON

6 miles NW of Pontypool on the B4246

Despite once having been associated with the heavy industries of coal mining and iron working, Blaenavon is set in surprisingly pleasant countryside which can be further explored by taking the **Pontypool and Blaenavon Railway**, the highest standard gauge track to have survived in Wales. Half the site lies within the Brecon Beacons National Park.

The oldest colliery in Wales, Big Pit Mine, closed in 1980, but has been reopened as the **Big Pit National Mining Museum.** This monument to the past employs former miners and engineers from the site to give guided tours accompanied by plenty of anecdotes. Visitors (children must be at least 5 years old and a metre tall), armed with helmet, lamp and battery pack, can travel down a 90-metre shaft in a pit cage and walk through the underground roadways, air doors, stables and engine houses. On the surface at this site, designated Britain's 18th World Heritage Site by UNESCO, there are more buildings to explore, including the winding engine-house, the blacksmith's workshop and the pithead baths.

The other side of the town's industry, iron working, can be discovered at the **Blaenavon Ironworks**, a marvellous site that not only represents an important aspect of the Industrial Revolution but is also one of Europe's best preserved 18th century ironworks. Built against a cliff-face in the 1780s and then at the cutting edge of technology, the steam-powered ironworks became the second largest in Wales. Visitors to the ironworks and the Cordell Museum can see the whole process of production, including the row of blast furnaces and ingenious water balance tower by which the material was transported. Here, too, the human element of the vast ironworks is covered, as a small terrace of workers' cottages, built between 1789 and 1792, has been preserved.

Other buildings of interest in Blaenavon include the wonderfully ornate **Working Men's Hall** in the town centre where miners paid a halfpenny (1.2p) a week to use the library, and the **Church of St Peter**, built to look like an engine house and with tomb covers, font and pillars all made of iron.

EBBW VALE

15 miles NW of Pontypool on the A4048

This old steelmaking town, whose member of Parliament was once the formidable orator and social reformer Aneurin Bevan, was transformed by the 1992 Garden Festival. Following the festival, the site was developed into **Festival Park** with houses, shops and a range of leisure activities. Within the 70 acres of parkland and woodland are ornamental gardens, a lake, owl sanctuary, woodland craft centre and, in summer, a Japanese Pavilion selling teas.

A monument to Aneurin Bevan stands on the outskirts of the town which still has a number of fine houses which were built by the wealthy steel and coal magnates of the area. The town itself lies in a crowded valley but just to the north stretch the moorlands of the lower Brecon Beacons and some spectacular country.

TREDEGAR

1½ miles W of Ebbw Vale on the B4256

This pretty town was the birthplace of **Aneurin Bevan**, founder of the National Health Service and Member of Parliament for Ebbw Vale. The ashes of Bevan, in 1960, and of his wife Jennie Lee, in 1988, were scattered in the hills above Tredegar.

It was in Tredegar that the novelist AJ Cronin worked as a doctor and where he collected information for his book, *The Citadel*, which was later made into a film starring Robert Donat and a television series with Ben Cross.

Brown and white tourist signs lead to the **Elliot Colliery Winding House**, now a museum of a colliery that once employed more than 2000 people.

Close by lies **Bryn Bach Country Park**, a 600-acre area of grass and woodland, with a 16-acre

218 PRINCE OF WALES INN

Princetown

Friendly family run inn known for its impressive home cooked menu and 3-star en suite accommodation.

see page 378

219 RAILWAY TAVERN

Dukestown

Fantastic inn serving great value for money food and ales alongside quality guest accommodation.

see page 378

Monnow Bridge, Monmouth

220 THE ROYAL OAK

Monmouth

Popular olde worlde inn serving up traditional pub fare and well kept ales, with camping and caravan facilities on site.

see page 379

man-made lake, an abundance of wildlife, a visitor centre and opportunities for walking, fishing, canoeing, climbing and abseiling.

MONMOUTH

This prosperous and charming old market town grew up at the confluence of three rivers - the Wye, Monnow and Trothy - which are all noted for their fishing. The River Wye is crossed by a five arched bridge built in 1617 but the Monnow boasts the most impressive of the town's bridges. **Monnow Bridge** is one of Monmouth's real gems, and its sturdy fortified gatehouse, dating from the 13th century, is the only one of its kind in Britain.

Long before the bridge was constructed, the Normans built **Monmouth Castle** here in around 1068. Later rebuilt by John of Gaunt in the late 1300s, the castle was the birthplace in 1387 of his grandson, later Henry V. It is believed he was born in the Great Tower, substantial parts of which still stand.

Much later, in the 17th century, **Great Castle House** was built by the 3rd Marquess of Worcester from the ruins of the castle and he lived here while his other homes, Badminton and Troy House, were being rebuilt. Today, the castle houses both the **Castle Museum** and the **Regimental Museum** where the histories of the castle and the Royal Monmouthshire Royal Engineers are explored. The **King's Garden** is a re-creation of a small medieval courtyard garden, planted with herbs that would have been common around the time of Henry V.

An earlier Monmouth man, **Geoffrey of Monmouth**, was the Prior at St Mary's before becoming Bishop of St Asaph in North Wales. It was probably in Monmouth that Geoffrey wrote his massive work, *A History of the Kings of Britain*, with its legends of King Arthur and Merlin.

Also in the town is the **Nelson Museum**, where a fascinating collection of material and artefacts about the great Admiral can be seen, including his sword and love letters to Lady Hamilton. This interesting collection of memorabilia was accumulated by Lady Llangattock, the mother of Charles Stuart Rolls, and generously donated to Monmouth. The history of the town is illustrated in displays in the same building as the Nelson Museum.

The exploits of the **Hon Charles Rolls** in cars, balloons and aeroplanes are also featured here. One of the most evocative pictures is of Rolls in the basket of his 'Midget' balloon at Monmouth Gasworks in about 1908. Some five miles from the town is the Rolls estate where Charles grew up and developed an early interest in engineering and motoring that led to his forming the Rolls-Royce company. Charles died in an air accident in 1910 and his statue, along with a monument to Henry V, can be seen in the town's main Agincourt Square. He is buried in the churchyard of St Cadoc's, at Llangattock-vibon-Avel, not far from Monmouth.

Another interesting building in Monmouth is the 14th century **St Mary's Church** whose eight bells are said to have been recast from a peal which Henry V brought back from France after his victory at Agincourt. The story goes that as Henry was leaving Calais, the ringing of bells was heard and he was told that the French were celebrating his departure. He immediately turned back and took the bells to give as a present to his native town.

One of the graves in the churchyard is that of an obscure house-painter called John Renie who died in 1832 at the age of 33. His headstone is an acrostic of 285 letters that reads "Here lies John Renie". This epitaph can be read over and over again, upwards, downwards, backwards and forwards, and if doglegs and zigzags are also included, it is apparently possible to read "Here lies John Renie" in 45,760 different ways. The memorial also records the deaths of his two sons, one at the age of one year and nine months, the other at the age of 83.

Just to the west of the town, and practically on the border with England, rises **The Kymin**, a National Trust owned hill overlooking the River Wye. From here there are spectacular views across the picturesque landscape. The **Round House**, also found here, was erected by the Kymin Club in 1794. The members of this club were local worthies who liked to hold open-air lunch parties on the Kymin. They decided to construct a building so that they could picnic inside in bad weather. The result is the Round House - round so that the views could be enjoyed from every part of the house. Offa's Dyke footpath runs through the land. Nearby is the **Naval Temple**, built to

221 THE BOAT INN

Penullt

Olde worlde riverside inn serving appetising food and real ales with regular live music sessions.

see page 380

Round House, Monmouth

commemorate the Battle of the Nile and opened in the early 19th century.

AROUND MONMOUTH

TRELLECK

4½ miles S of Monmouth on the B4293

This village's name means 'Three Stones' and these large prehistoric monoliths can be found to the southwest of Trelleck. For reasons unknown they are called **Harold's Stones**. They do not represent all the historical interest here as, close to the Church of St Nicholas, is a mound known as **The Tump**, which is all that remains of a Norman motte and bailey.

TINTERN PARVA

7½ miles S of Monmouth off the A466

This riverside village, which nestles among the wooded slopes of the lovely Wye Valley, is a most beautiful place and the whole of the valley, between Monmouth and Chepstow, is designated an Area of Outstanding Natural Beauty. Here are found the enchanting ruins of **Tintern Abbey** (CADW), which stand beside the river. The abbey was founded by Cistercian monks in 1131 and largely rebuilt in the 13th century by Roger Bigod, the Lord of Chepstow Castle. The monks farmed the rich agricultural land as well as remaining dedicated to their rigorous regime of religious devotions right up until the time of the Dissolution. A rich and powerful abbey in its day, Tintern is now a majestic ruin with much delicate tracery and great soaring archways still intact in a glorious setting that has inspired painters and poets such as Turner and Wordsworth.

A mile from the abbey, along the A466 Chepstow-Monmouth road, is the Victorian **Old Station** which now acts as a visitor centre for the Wye Valley. Here, too, are a countryside exhibition, a collection of signal boxes, a gift shop and a model railway.

Tintern Abbey

CHEPSTOW

12 miles S of Monmouth on the A48

This splendid old market town, which lies on the border with England, takes its name from the Old English 'chepe stow', meaning 'market place'. It occupies a strategic crossing on the River Wye - an important crossing between England and Wales. An elegant 5-arched cast iron bridge built in 1816 is still in full use. The Wye here is tidal and the difference between high and low tide is an extraordinary 49ft - only the Bay of Fundy on the Canadian/US border has an even higher difference.

Situated on a crag overlooking the river are the well-preserved ruins of **Chepstow Castle** which William Fitzosbern began building in 1067 as a base for the Norman conquest of south east Wales. Its importance can be judged from the fact that it was built of stone; most Norman fortresses of the time were in motte and bailey form, built of earth and wood. Chepstow Castle began life as a keep, and towers, walls, fortifications and gatehouses were added to prepare it for the Welsh wars, in which, as it happened, it played no part. The castle is open for visits throughout the year. A major exhibition ' A Castle at War' relates the history of the castle. A group of local people have come together to form the Chepstow Garrison; dressing up and re-enacting scenes from Chepstow's past, they have become a popular attraction for both local residents and tourists.

Built at the same time as the castle keep, and by the same William Fitzosbern, is the Parish and Priory **Church of St Mary**, which suffered considerable damage after the suppression of the Priory in 1536. The vast three-storey original nave gives some idea of the grand scale on which it was built The church contains some imposing and interesting monuments, including the Jacobean tomb of Margaret Cleyton with her two husbands and 12 children. This

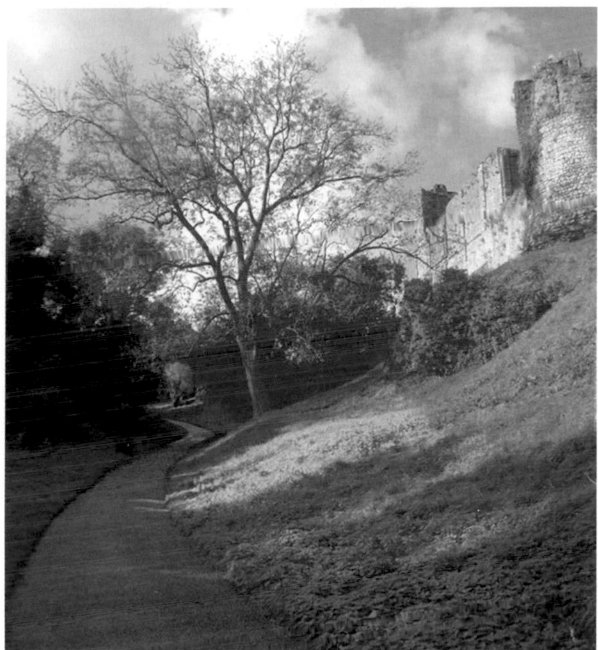

Castle Dell, Chepstow

lady paid for the town's gatehouse to be rebuilt in 1609. Also entombed here is Henry Marten, friend of Oliver Cromwell and signatory to the death warrant of Charles I. Marten spent many years imprisoned in Chepstow Castle in the tower that now bears his name. William Fitzosbern also founded the Abbey at Cormeilles in Normandy, with which Chepstow is twinned.

Opposite the castle is **Chepstow Museum** (free) where the rich and varied history of this border town is revealed. Housed in an elegant 18th century building that once belonged to a wealthy Chepstow merchant family, the museum has displays on the town's many industries, including

222 THE BOAT INN

Chepstow

Good food and service is the order of the day at this town inn overlooking the River Wye.

see page 381

223 LIVE AND LET LIVE

Tutshill

Quality homemade food served daily in this popular family run pub across the river from Cheptsow.

 see page 382

224 THE OLD FERRY INN

Beachley

Stunning riverside inn serving a vast and vibrant menu with beautiful views across to the Severn Bridge in its upstairs guest accommodation.

 see page 383

225 CARPENTERS ARMS

Shirenewton

Stunning country pub known for its picturesque location and award winning food

 see page 384

shipbuilding, fishing and the wine trade. Chepstow was at one time an important centre for shipbuilding, and one of the many photographs in the exhibition shows the closing stages in the building of *War Genius* in National Shipyard No1 in 1920. Ships were built here well into the 1920s, and the tradition was revived during World War II with the construction of tank landing craft.

Throughout the town itself, the medieval street pattern is still much in evidence, along with surviving sections of the town wall, called the Port Wall, and the impressive **Town Gate**. But Chepstow is also a thriving modern town, and its attractions include an excellent **Racecourse** offering both Flat and National Hunt racing - the highlight of the jumping season is the valuable and prestigious Welsh Grand National. The racecourse lies within the grounds of historic Piercefield Park. Piercefield Picturesque Walk was created in the 1750s by Valentine Morris the Younger and follows the Wye river cliff up to the Eagle's Nest.

Chepstow is at one end of **Offa's Dyke**, the 8th century defensive ditch and bank built by the King of Mercia. It is also the starting point for the long-distance Wye Valley and Gloucestershire Way walks.

CALDICOT

15 miles S of Monmouth on the B4245

Caldicot Castle dates from Norman times and was restored for use as a family house in the 1880s. Of particular note here is the sturdy round keep and the gatehouse dating from the 14th century. Inside, there's an interesting collection of furniture from the 17th to the 19th centuries. The castle, which is set within 55 acres of beautiful parkland, hosts occasional medieval banquets.

CAERWENT

14 miles SW of Monmouth off the A48

Close to the Wentwood Forest, this town - which is now more of a village - was the site of **Venta Silurum**, a walled Roman town built by the invaders for the local Celtic Silures tribe. Sections of the Roman defences still remain and are some of the best preserved in Britain, while inside the walls can be seen the remains of the forum basilica and the Romano-Celtic temple. Venta Silurum is thought to have been the largest centre of civilian population in Roman-occupied Wales.

Much of the present village is built of stone taken from the Roman site, including the Parish Church of St Stephen which was built in medieval times.

RAGLAN

6½ miles SW of Monmouth off the A40

To the north of this pretty village stands **Raglan Castle**, one of the finest late medieval fortresses in Britain. Built towards the end of the Middle Ages, and thus in relatively peaceful times, the castle was also constructed with comfort in mind and it represents wealth and social aspirations as much as military might. Started by Sir

William ap Thomas in 1435, the castle was continued in the same lavish manner by his son William Herbert who was responsible for the addition of the formal state apartments and the magnificent gatehouse. Despite being more a palace than a fortress, Raglan Castle withstood an 11 week siege by General Fairfax during the Civil War.

To the west lies **Clytha Castle**, a folly designed by John Nash for an owner of the Clytha Park estate in memory of his wife.

USK

11½ miles SW of Monmouth on the A472

This delightful small town, which takes its name from the river beside which it sits, was founded by the Romans in AD 75. Well known for its excellent local fishing - the River Usk is a fine salmon river - the town attracts fishermen from far and wide. The heart of the town is picturesque Twyn Square with its restored clock tower and 13th century gatehouse. Also noted for its floral displays and historic buildings, Usk is home to the **Gwent Rural Life Museum**, housed in an 18th century malt barn, which tells the story of life in this Welsh border region from Victorian times up until the end of World War II. Amassed over many decades by hundreds of local residents, the collection is huge and includes many vintage agricultural implements along with re-creations of a dairy, brewery, carpenter's, a laundry and a thatcher's. Adjacent barns contain collections of stage coaches and farm carts, and an exhibit on the Great Western Railway. Tel: 01291 673777

ABERGAVENNY

12½ miles W of Monmouth on the A465

A particularly pleasant and thriving market town, Abergavenny dates back to Roman times when the modest fort of Gobannium was established. Here, too, are the modest remains of the Norman **Abergavenny Castle** where in 1175 the fearsome Norman lord, William de Braose, invited the Welsh lords to dine and then murdered the lot while they were disarmed at his table. Not very much remains, as King Charles I ordered it to be destroyed. Today, the rebuilt keep and a Regency hunting lodge within the castle grounds are home to the **Abergavenny Museum** where exhibits from prehistoric times to the present day detail the history of the town and surrounding area. Displays include re-creations of a Victorian kitchen and a saddler's workshop.

Notable treasures in **St Mary's Church** include medieval choir stalls, fine altar tombs and an imposing double life-size wooden figure of Jesse, father of King David. There are also effigies of members of the de Braose family and of Sir William ap Thomas, founder of Raglan Castle.

A rather bizarre one-time resident of Abergavenny was Deputy Fuhrer Rudolf Hess who crash-landed his plane in Scotland in 1941and was detained in the

226 THE HALL INN

Gwehelog

Distinctive and traditional inn known best for its well kept ales and fine menu created with the best local produce.

see page 385

227 THE HORSESHOE INN

Mamhilad

A quality pub and restaurant nestled in an idyllic rural location

see page 386

228 THE HARDWICK

Abergavenny

Excellent family restaurant and inn serving up an exciting and innovative menu alongside en suite accommodation with views across the valley.

see page 387

229 WARWICKS COUNTRY PUB AND EATERY

Tal-Y-Coed

Handsome olde worlde country pub known for its lively atmosphere and high quality cuisine.

see page 386

230 THE WALNUT TREE

Llandewi Skirrid

Famous restaurant for fine dining at the foot of Skirrid Mountain, with cottage guest accommodation also available.

see page 388

231 THE CROWN AT PANTYGELLI

Pantygelli

Handsome 16th century inn with across the board fine dining and hospitality and spectacular views across the valley.

see page 389

town's mental asylum. He was permitted a weekly walk in the surrounding hills and was said to have conceived a love of the Welsh countryside.

One of the most accessible gateways to the Brecon Beacons National Park, Abergavenny is a popular place during the summer. Surrounded by glorious countryside, it is a place from where all manner of activities, including walking, pony trekking and canal cruising, can be enjoyed.

A popular walk from the town is to the summit of **Sugar Loaf** (1955ft), which rises to the northwest of the town and commands grand views across the Bristol Channel and to the Brecon Beacons, the Black Mountain foothills and Herefordshire. Important archaeological features include a boundary bank that encircles a former deer park linked to the Priory of Abergavenny, charcoal-burning sites and pollarded trees.

LLANTHONY

10 miles S of Hay off the B4423

In the beautiful Vale of Ewyas, also known as Llanthony Valley, **Llanthony Priory** was built on a spot which has links with the beginnings of Christianity in Wales, and in the 6th century was chosen by St David for a cell. Much less visited than Tintern Abbey, Llanthony has a more spiritual and evocative atmosphere and remains much as it has been for 800 years. The Priory was founded by the Norman William de Lacy in the 11th century when he established a hermitage that evolved into the priory whose wonderful ruins can be seen today.

The beauty and tranquillity of the location have inspired many: Eric Gill and Walter Savage Landor are among those who made their homes here. For many years the site was in a state of near decay, but the Welsh Office graded it as an Ancient Monument and so ensured its survival.

LLANVETHERINE

9 miles NW of Monmouth on the B4521

To the south of the village lies one of the Three Castles, **White Castle**, which is so called because when it was built the masonry was rendered with gleaming white plaster, patches of which can still be seen. Starting life as a simple earthwork not long after the Norman Conquest, White Castle was rebuilt in stone during the late 12th and 13th centuries to provide, along with Skenfrith and Grosmont castles, a triangle of fortresses to control this strategic entry point into Wales. Situated in a beautiful and isolated place, the ruins conjure up the romance of the Middle Ages. Much later, during World War II, Hitler's deputy, Rudolf Hess, fed the swans on the castle's moat while held at Abergavenny's mental hospital following his mysterious flight from Nazi Germany.

GROSMONT

9½ miles NW of Monmouth on the B4347

This village takes its name from the

French, 'gros mont', meaning 'big hill'; it is the site of **Grosmont Castle**, the most northerly of the Three Castles. Now in ruins, Grosmont started life as a steep earthen mound but, after having been replaced by a stone fortification, it was unsuccessfully besieged by both Llywelyn the Great and Owain Glyndwr. During exploration of the ruins, an Arabic 'faience jar' was found here - undoubtedly a relic from the Crusades.

Skenfrith Castle

SKENFRITH

5½ miles NW of Monmouth on the B4521

At this point the Monnow Valley forms something of a gap in the natural defences of the Welsh Marches and it was here that the Normans built **Skenfrith Castle** (National Trust), the last of the Three Castles - the others being White and Grosmont. Situated beside the river, Skenfrith Castle was built in the 13th century by Hubert de Burgh and is noted for its fine round tower keep and its well-preserved curtain wall. Once the troubled domain of medieval warlords, this border region is today peaceful and undisturbed.

Accommodation, Food & Drink and Places to Visit

The establishments featured in this section includes hotels, inns, guest houses, bed & breakfasts, restaurants, cafés, tea and coffee shops, tourist attractions and places to visit. Each establishment has an entry number which can be used to identify its location at the beginning of the relevant chapter.

In addition full details of all these establishments and many others can be found on the Travel Publishing website - **www.findsomewhere.co.uk**. This website has a comprehensive database covering the whole of Britain and Ireland.

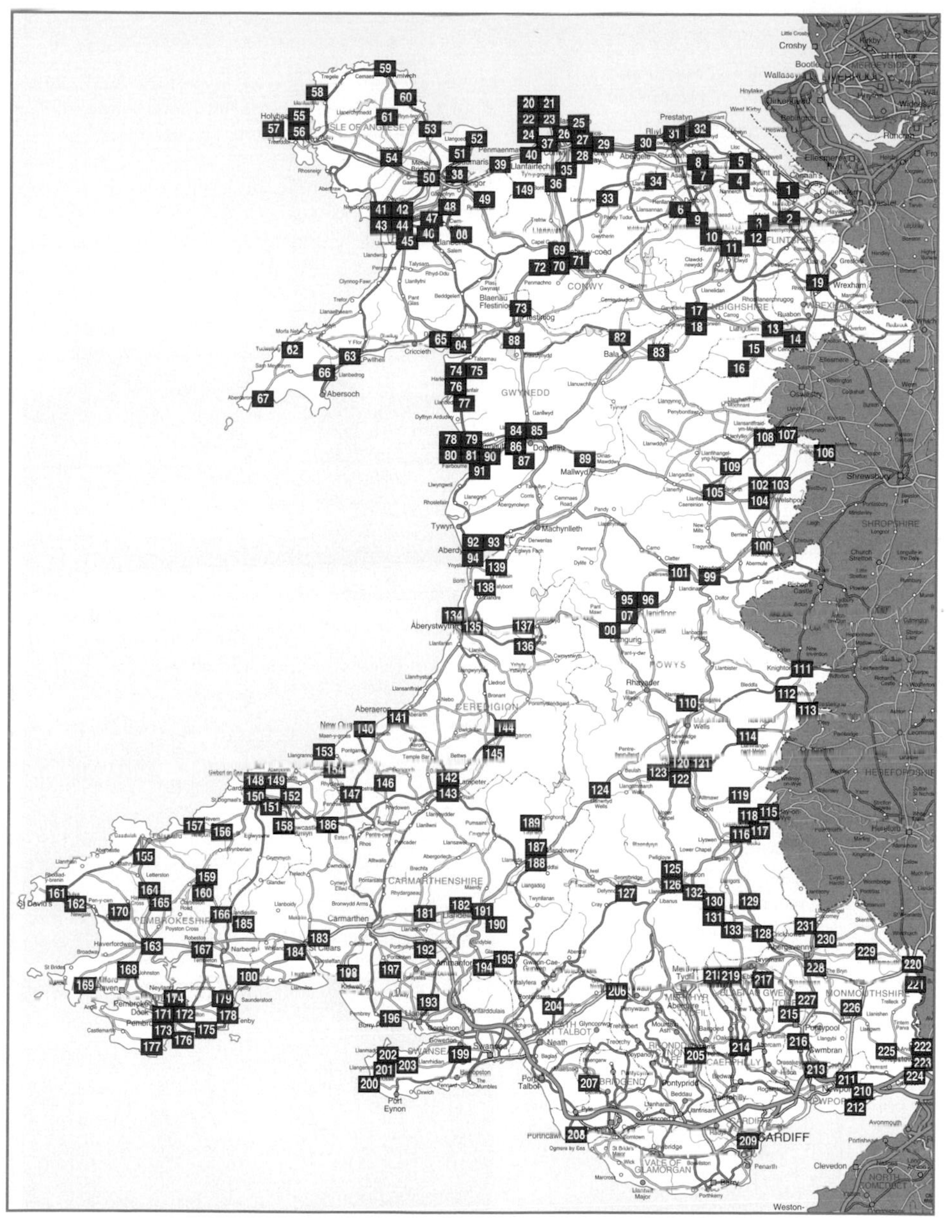
Crosby
Bootle
Wallasey
Birkenhead
Runcorn
Prestatyn
Holyhead
ISLE OF ANGLESEY
Penmaenmawr
Llanfairfechan
Bangor
Beaumaris
Abergele
Rhyl
Wrexham
Ruabon
FLINTSHIRE
DENBIGHSHIRE
CONWY
Blaenau Ffestiniog
Criccieth
Pwllheli
Abersoch
Bala
GWYNEDD
Dolgellau
Mallwyd
Machynlleth
Tywyn
Aberdyfi
Oswestry
Welshpool
Shrewsbury
SHROPSHIRE
Church Stretton
Aberystwyth
Llanidloes
Rhayader
POWYS
Knighton
CEREDIGION
Aberaeron
New Quay
Lampeter
Cardigan
Newcastle Emlyn
St Davids
PEMBROKESHIRE
Haverfordwest
Milford Haven
Pembroke
Pembroke Dock
Narberth
Tenby
Saundersfoot
St Clears
Carmarthen
CARMARTHENSHIRE
Llandovery
Ammanford
Llanelli
Swansea
The Mumbles
Port Eynon
Neath
Port Talbot
Bridgend
Pontypridd
Caerphilly
Merthyr Tydfil
Abergavenny
Brecon
Hay-on-Wye
HEREFORDSHIRE
MONMOUTHSHIRE
Pontypool
Cwmbran
Newport
Cardiff
Penarth
Barry
VALE OF GLAMORGAN
Porthcawl
Clevedon
Avonmouth
Weston-

1 THE BOOT INN

High Street, Northop,
Flintshire CH7 6BQ
Tel: 01352 840247

Offering a wide selection of homemade food, **The Boot Inn** is a quality village inn found in the delightful village of Northop, just off the A55, North Wales Expressway.

Leaseholder, Stephen Webster, has been at the inn for four months and is ably assisted by bar manager, Darren Cooper who has worked there for five years. Having been Stephen's local before he took over the lease, he has three years experience in the trade, and is extremely familiar with the needs of customers. Open all day, every day a lot of the dishes are made with local produce, adding to the quality of the food served. Among the dishes on the set menu are braised lamb chops in a minted gravy, pan fried chicken in a mushroom white wine sauce and sauté loin of pork in a creamy cider sauce. There is also a wide selection of homemade desserts, including pineapple syrup steamed pudding and baileys cheesecake. There are many changing ales for customers to enjoy too. On the a la carte menu main dishes include pan fried duck breast cooked in a cherry and port sauce and pan cooked prime sirloin steak and more traditional dishes, including steak and kidney pie. Vegetarians are well catered for and there is a special luncheon menu with all dishes freshly prepared. There is also an array of fish and pasta dishes as well as a special kids menu and snack and lite bite menu.

Food is served daily between 12pm-3pm and 6pm-9pm, except on Mondays. Due to its popularity weekends need to be booked.

Parts of The Boot Inn, which was called The Bell for a period of time, date back to the very early 18th century and this adds to the character of the place, which is popular with locals and visitors. Inside, the inn is welcoming and spacious and there is a fantastic outdoor, covered patio area for customers to enjoy on warmer days.

The outside area is a delightful find and there are many plants and flowers positioned, giving it a bright and cheery feel. The exterior is particularly charming and there is a small rear car park for customers to use.

The Boot Inn welcomes children and is well adapted for disabled customers. There is a quiz on a Monday from 8pm, and locals and visitors are invited to join in. All major credit cards are taken.

2 WHITE LION

Mold Road, Buckley, Flintshire CH7 2NH
Tel: 01244 548502
e-mail: whitelionbuckley@yahoo.co.uk

A family run public house with traditional home cooking at its heart, the **White Lion** is ever-growing in popularity. It has an outstanding beer garden for guests to enjoy on sunnier days as well as a stunning patio area. Standing on Mold Road, on the outskirts of Buckley, the establishment is run by Brian and Maureen Wall, who are the leaseholders, and their son and daughter, Adam and Jane. The family have run it for the past eight years and have a growing reputation in the area for the quality, home-cooked food they serve.

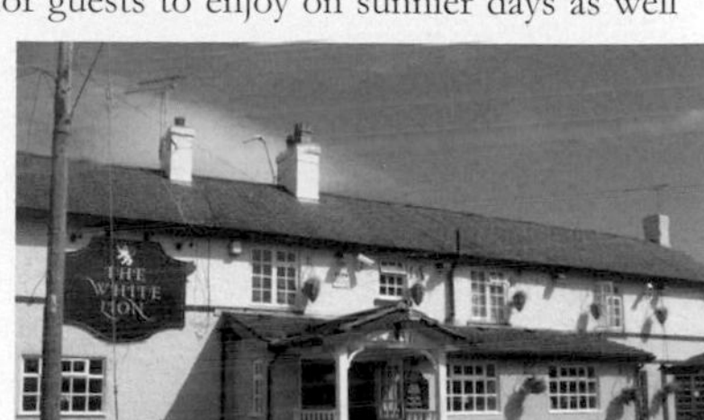

Dating back to the early 19th century, parts of the premises were once a Methodist meeting house. Formerly known as The Trooper, the White Lion is open all day every day and serves two real ales – the Old Speckled Hen is the regular one with a rotating guest ale too.

Most of food is created using fresh produce, which is a big plus for locals and the majority of the produce is sourced locally. Traditional roast dinners are the only dishes served on a Sunday and they are extremely popular, with many people coming back time and time again to indulge. Service on a Sunday is between 12pm and 5pm. During the week, from Monday-Thursday, food is served between 12pm-2pm and 5.30pm-8pm and on Friday-Saturday service is between 12pm-7.30pm. There is a wide selection of cuisine on offer, with an extensive menu that caters for vegetarians. Among the dishes on offer are minty lamb shank and Welsh cheese, leek and mushroom tart. All of the food is reasonably priced and there is a special 'under a fiver menu' as well as many snacks and lite bites on offer including a range of baguettes, paninis and sandwiches. Children are well catered for, with special children's meals as well as a range of home-made desserts. Although many of the dishes are traditional there are also plenty of other options to suit the most fussy of taste buds. Guests can enjoy their meals outside in the unbeatable beer garden or inside, which has a warm and traditional feel.

There is plenty of off-road parking and there are many entertainment evenings too. On Wednesday there is a quiz from 9.30pm, live entertainment from 9.30pm on a Saturday and on Sunday there is a poker league from 8pm. If it good, home-cooked food and plenty of family hospitality you are longing for, the White Lion is a must.

3 PLAS HAFOD COUNTRY HOUSE HOTEL

Gwernymyndd, Mold, Flintshire CH7 5JS
Tel: 01352 700177
e-mail: reception@plashafodhotel.com
website: www.plashafodhotel.com

Nestled in twelve acres of magnificent, landscaped gardens, with spectacular views, the renowned **Plas Hafod Country House Hotel** is an impressive establishment. One of the finest wedding venues and places to dine out in Wales, the hotel offers the very best in accommodation and cuisine. The family run hotel has been owned by Simon and Collete Buckley and Simon's parents, Janet and David for the past 20 years. It boasts eleven, individually decorated, en-suite bedrooms with period features. Three of the rooms are on the ground floor, making the hotel easily accessible for disabled customers. The Buckley's are extremely experienced and will do everything to make sure guests are well looked after.

Diners can enjoy meals in the restaurant or conservatory, both which are modern and tastefully decorated. The food served is extremely popular and there is an extensive menu, with a daily menu for lunch and evening as well as a set Sunday lunch menu. Simon is the head chef and second chef Dylan work together to create mouth-watering dishes. Among the dishes on offer are breast of Gressingham duck in a button mushroom, silver skin onion and garden peas and grilled peppered pork with a creamy peppercorn and brandy sauce. On a Sunday diners can enjoy a three course traditional Sunday lunch, served in the pavilion suite. Such is its popularity non-residents need to book at all times. Food is served from 12-2pm and 6.30-9.30pm every day. All major credit cards are taken.

4 THE CROWN INN

Village Road, Lixwm, Flintshire CH8 8NQ
Tel: 01352 781112 Mob: 07786 076526
e-mail: silverbullet56@msn.com

Offering the very best in hospitality, food and drink, **The Crown Inn**, which dates back to the 17th century, is extremely popular among locals and visitors. Owners, John and Judy Williams, have a wealth of experience in the hospitality trade, amounting to 50 years between them.

Visitors return again and again to eat at the inn, which is well-known in the area for the food it serves, cooked by chef, Judy. Dishes include wholetail scampi and steak and guiness pie and there is a daily specials board too. There is room for 62 diners, as well as seating in a spacious bar and outside area. Guests have a choice of two real ales, Robinsons Unicorn and rotating brewery guest ale.

The inn, which was formerly cottages, became an alehouse in the late 17th century. In later years it became an inn, where horses were stabled and in the late 19th century it was used as a mortuary. Located at the heart of the village of Lixwm it is found on the B5121, south of Holywell and close to the A541. The inn is open on Saturday and Sundays, and every weekday excluding Monday, except on bank holidays.

5 THE ROCK INN

St Asaph Road, Lloc, Holywell,
Flintshire CH8 8RD
Tel: 01352 710049

The Rock Inn, which has in some way existed here as an inn for over 300 years, is only a few convenient minutes away from the A55 North Wales expressway, in the welcoming village of Lloc. This delightful family-run Inn was recently taken over in January '09 and has been transformed into a fine bright and airy establishment which has proved popular with locals and visitors alike. Inside is a perfect mix of clean, minimal white washed walls, and traditional ceiling beams and wooden furnishings.

The intimate dining area, which can be adjusted to accommodate large groups at prior notice, is cosy and informal with a varied menu of home-cooked and largely locally-sourced produce, with vegetarian options available. Dishes such as traditional local gammon steak, with chips, onion rings and garden peas; home-made puff-pastry steak and Guinness pie with the option of chips or mashed potato; and the oh-so-tempting hot sugar Belgium waffle served with ice cream and a drizzle of golden syrup, are all already firm favourites. In addition to the regular menu is the specials board, which is always brimming with fresh seasonal dishes, and there is also a very popular Sunday roast with meat from a local butcher. To compliment, the Rock Inn has a large wine selection specially selected for flavour, and the bar has two rotating real ales, which can be either national or local brews.

Although all the food at the Rock Inn is very reasonably priced, it is worth noting that a meal special runs Monday to Saturday 12noon – 6pm where any two meals from the bar menu can be bought at an amazing set price. Also there is an open-to-all pub quiz which runs from 9pm on Sundays, and proves a fun and sociable way to end your week – particularly after one of their delicious roasts! The beer garden outside is a joy to relax in and take in some fresh Welsh air during the summer months, and in winter the bar and restaurant is warmed by a cosy fire. The Rock is open all day, with food being served between 12noon and 9pm, the bar is open until 11pm. Children are welcome, there is a large on-site car park which can accommodate coaches, and all major credit cards are taken. It is advised that you book prior to arriving for meals on Fridays and Saturdays as it does get quite busy.

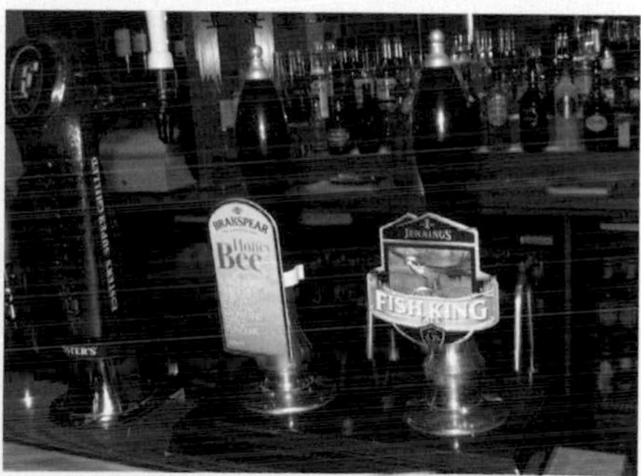

6 CASTLE HOUSE COUNTRY GUEST HOUSE

Plas Castell, Bull Lane, Denbigh LL16 3LY
Tel: 01745 816860
Fax: 01745 817214
e-mail: stay@CastleHouseBandB.co.uk
website: www.castlehousebandb.co.uk

Castle House Country Guest House boasts one of the finest locations in Wales, which comes complete with unrivalled quality facilities and comfort. Set in the ancient walled town of Denbigh in North Wales, overlooking the beautiful Clwyd valley sits this truly stunning guest house.

Owners Angie and Charlie Hobson have lived here since 2001 but only started providing these world class facilities this year. All that can be said is that it was truly worth the wait. The property is set within the tranquil grounds of the Plas Castell Estate with 2 acres of its own well kept gardens filled with shrubs, a fish pond, heather beds and a finely manicured croquet lawn that can be enjoyed all year round. The garden also holds a peaceful seating area that overlooks the valley where guests have the option of taking an alfresco breakfast, cream tea or a night cap before bed whilst drinking in the stunning view.

Take a short walk through the grounds and you will come across some of Denbigh's history right on your doorstep with both part of Denbigh's ancient town walls and the ruins of the Earl of Leicester's 16th century cathedral waiting to be discovered.

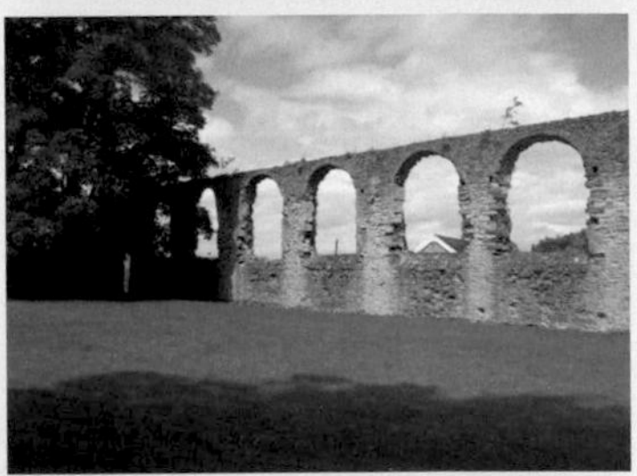

The guesthouse itself offers three bedrooms all reached by an impressive staircase. The large individually styled, sumptuously decorated bedrooms, have style, grace and oodles of space, the views are simply stunning.

There is also a romantic lounge in which to unwind and an elegant dining room which can provide specialty catering for small meetings and events, or simply afternoon snacks. Evening meals are available by prior arrangement from finely cooked two course meals for 2 to five course candlelit masterpieces for the entire family. Each morning a hearty breakfast is also on offer and like all the food here is locally sourced.

Nestled in the grounds are the secret gems of this business; two quality Cottage Suites each sleeping up to four people, from where Bed & Breakfast may be taken, with Breakfast being taken in the main house. Each is different in character but both with the unbeatable facilities that guests here have come to expect.

Angie and Charlie's aptly chosen slogan 'Indulgent, Luxurious, Different,' is devilishly accurate, this really is the place to take that luxury break away.

7 SALISBURY ARMS

Tremeirchion, St Asaph,
Clwyd LL17 0UN
Tel: 01745 710262

The Salisbury Arms started life as a 16th century coaching inn and fell into disrepair until it was recently taken over by experienced licensees Anna and Martin. The pair have painstakingly refurbished the place, adding a new kitchen and cellar with contemporary décor and furniture to all the public areas. This much needed facelift has transformed the Salisbury Arms back into the proud centre of Tremeirchion it once was.

The inn is now open every session and all day on Saturdays and Sundays. The inn is closed on Mondays, excluding bank holidays. Both Anna and Martin are qualified professional chefs, so it's easy to see why their customers rave about the food served here. The restaurant menu served Friday and Saturday evenings offers up a tempting range of freshly prepared starters that include smoked fish, cheeses, poultry and game to accompany a hearty selection of mains including slowly roasted lamb shank in red wine, venison casserole, oven roasted Gressingham duck, pork tenderloin and fish dishes such as fish pie, smoked haddock tagliatelle. The rest of the week a bar menu is available from 12-2:30pm and 5:30-9pm which encompasses a good range of light bites, filled sandwiches and jackets and other pub classics such as steak and Guinness pie, scampi, homemade lasagne, curry, BBQ ribs and burgers. On Sundays the inn serves up a traditional Sunday lunch from 12-4pm with all the trimmings. All dishes are cooked fresh to order, with the menus changing regularly to reflect the best in local produce that is used to create all dishes. Owing to popularity; it's best to book on weekends.

Although Martin is a chef first and foremost, he is also a true ale lover and prides himself on offering his guests a choice of four top condition ales at any one time. The bar stocks a brew specially made for the inn 'Tremeirchion Bitter,' with Burton Bitter as the other regular brew. Drinks can be enjoyed in the bars comfortable lounge area or outside in the large beer garden; ideal for those lazy summer afternoons. All major credit cards accepted.

8 THE SMITHY ARMS

Holywell Road, Rhuallt, St Asaph,
Denbighshire LL17 0TR
Tel: 01745 582298

Using local, seasonal produce **The Smithy Arms** is a hidden gem in the quiet village of Rhuallt. For people who love good quality home cooking the village inn draws them in like a magnet. Built in 1957 to replace premises of the same name, which stood nearby, the inn stands proud on the B5429, very close to junction 28 of the main A55, North Wales Expressway.

Carol and Steve have owned the child-friendly inn for eight years and have a growing reputation with locals and visitors. Open all day, every day, guests can enjoy one real ale, Marstano Burton Bitter and the fantastic food on offer, which is prepared and cooked by head chef, Em. Homemade lasagne and cajun chicken are among the wide selection of main courses on offer and there is an array of bar snacks, including fresh sandwiches and baguettes to choose from. Food is available every weekday between 12-2.30pm and 5.30-9pm and between 12-9pm on Saturday and Sundays.

The owners are very knowledgeable about the local area and can suggest local accommodation for visitors. The inn, which has a quality floral exterior and traditional, character-filled interior has plenty of off-road parking and accepts all major credit cards.

9 THE KINGS HEAD

Llanrhaeadr, nr Denbigh,
Wales LL16 4NL
Tel: 01745 890278

The Kings Head is situated in the small village of LLanrhaeadr, right next to the village church which is just a short drive south west of Denbigh. Tenant Rob Smyth has been here for 6 years and has a healthy following from locals and visitors alike who rave about the good atmosphere, fine cuisine and real ale. This early 18th century property is open all day every day, serving food from 12-2pm weekdays, 12-3:30pm weekends and 530-8:30pm Sun-Thurs and 5:30-9pm Fri/Sat. There is a good selection from the grill, light snacks and sandwiches, vegetarian dishes and speciality home cooked dishes like beef stroganoff or fruity chicken curry or popular fish dishes which include pan fried trout with almonds. A specials board also offers the best in seasonal produce and there is a good children's menu also.

The bar offers two real ales with Speckled Hen and Bass being making regular appearances, and a healthy selection of other drinks available. The traditional yet stylish décor that spreads the length of the Kings Head creates a perfect environment to relax and enjoy an evening in, with family friends or alone.

Accommodation is also available here all year round with two en suite rooms on offer at a very reasonable bed and breakfast rate. Children welcome, all major credit cards accepted apart from Amex and Diners.

10 DROVERS ARMS

Rhewl, Ruthin, Clywd LL15 2UD
Tel: 01824 703163

The **Drover Arms** is situated in the pleasant village of Rhewl alongside the A525 just a short drive north of Ruthin. Under the management of Robert and Michelle Strang the Drovers Arm is now a classy establishment with something for everyone, whilst retaining the olde worlde feel that has kept people coming here for years.

The building itself dates back to the 17th century is parts, but is brought right into the 21st century by the modern menus and newly introduced conservatory which looks over the well kept garden and patio area.

Food is available from 12-2pm and 6-9pm everyday apart from Tuesdays and it's recommended to book Sunday lunchtimes to avoid disappointment, when a carvery is on offer with both fish and vegetarian options available. Rob, a chef by trade with over 30 years experience has ensured a good choice for everyone with a children's menu, plenty of vegetarian options, an oriental selection for those fancying a taste of the exotic and a fabulous choice of locally sourced steaks to make your mouth water. Drovers specials include sautéed medallions of pork with a blue cheese cream sauce, beef bourguignon or fresh salmon fillet. The newly refurbished bar serves two real ales with a good selection of wines and spirits, and if you happen to visit on the second Friday of the month you will be serenaded by live welsh singing from 9pm!

11 CORPORATION ARMS

4 Castle Street, Ruthin, Clwyd LL15 1DP
Tel: 01824 704639

Located a mere stones' throw from the castle in the historic town of Ruthin is the **Corporation Arms**, known affectionately to locals as 'the Corpy.' It has been owned and run by Caroline and Phil for the past four years who offer the warmest of welcomes to both locals and visitors alike. They open all day every day serving a good selection of keg ales including Carling, San Miguel and Worthington with live entertainment on weekends when a lively disco or karaoke session takes the stage.

The Corpy really draws in the crowds however for its wide selection of excellent food at value for money prices. The menu is large and varied, encompassing dishes for every palette and appetite from starters and light bites, jackets, salads and sandwiches, to pizzas, burgers, succulent grills and mains which include steak and ale pie, Cajun chicken fajitas and lamb shank served in red currant and rosemary jus. Children are well catered for, as are vegetarians who can chose from dishes like Thai vegetable curry or broccoli and mushroom pasta bake. Food is served up from 12-3pm and 5-9pm Monday to Saturdays and from 12-3pm on Sundays and can be enjoyed either inside or outdoors in the charming courtyard or loft roof terrace on warmer days.

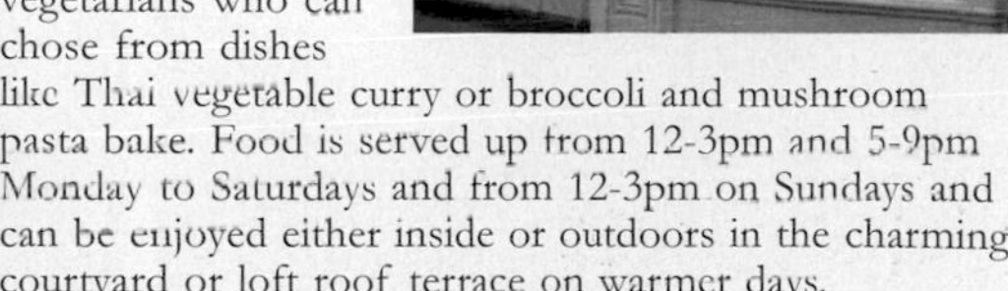

12 THE MINERS ARMS

Village Road, Maeshafn,
Denbighshire, CH7 5LR
Tel: 01352 810464

Renowned for the quality of its food and set in picturesque woodland, **The Miners Arms**, is a charming old inn dating from the early 1700s and located in an area of outstanding natural beauty. Managed by John and Gilly Walker, the former row of miners' cottages stands alongside an old drovers road. The inn, which is located in the delightful village of Maeshafn, once a mining and quarrying community, is just three miles away from Mold and one mile from the A494 and is accessed from either Llanferres or Gwernymynydd. The inn provides an ideal resting spot for visitors who want to explore the beautiful Clwydian range and the nearby Loggerheads Country Park. During the summer months visitors can enjoy meals or a drink in the outside beer garden, framed by trees. Alternatively the character-filled interior provides a cosy place to stop on colder days with a log fire to warm up any day. There is a choice of two bars and a dining room, which are tastefully decorated and serve fresh local produce. The extensive menu caters for children and vegetarians and there is a mouth-watering selection of daily desserts for diners to choose from. Dishes on offer include salmon with parsley sauce, steak and ale pie and Gary's authentic Indian chicken curry and there is a good range of desserts on the daily sweet board. For vegetarians there are plenty of dishes to choose from, including asparagus and lemon risotto, carrot and cashew nut roast and red onion and tomato tart. The child-friendly inn, which caters for groups and small private events, is extremely popular in the area and it is advisable to book in advance at weekends.

The bar sells three real ales, wines, spirits and soft drinks. Located in a peaceful village The Miners Arms is the perfect place for keen walkers to enjoy a meal or drink as it is in an area of outstanding natural beauty and close to many lovely walks and The Offa's Dyke Path – a long distance footpath that draws walkers from all over the world. For those wanting to enjoy a variety of entertainment, on the first Sunday in August the inn hosts a music festival and there are occasional folk nights held.

Food is served Tuesday 6-9pm, Wednesday – Saturday 12-2pm and 6-9pm. On Sunday dishes, including Sunday Roast are served between 12-4pm. All major credit cards are accepted and there is good disabled access throughout.

13 GALES OF LLANGOLLEN

18 Bridge Street, Llangollen LL20 8PF
Tel: 01978 860089
Fax: 01978 861313
e-mail: reception@galesofllangollen.co.uk
website: www.galesofllangollen.co.uk

Situated in the heart of the historic and charming town of Llangollen is a set of stunning facilities that offer a warm and amiable welcome all year round. Located on Bridge Street just off the main high street is **Gales Wine and Food Bar and Hotel** with conference rooms above, a shop and 400 year old cottages nearby to complete your stay.

The Gale family have been hard at work running this exquisite business since 1977. The business has been described by many as an extension of the family itself, springing from father Richard's own personal love of wine bars, wife Gillie's dedication to maintaining the hotel side of things (and Richard!) and kids Pip, Andrew and Holly who are now all fundamental parts of the business. Pip has firmly followed in his father's footsteps introducing new ideas whilst maintaining the traditional values acting as general manager, whilst Andrew who runs a photographic studio nearby has leant his talent to the design and publicity that draws in the crowds at Gales.

The wood panelled bar has scarcely changed since the seventies and is the real heart of the place, bursting with character. Naturally the wine list boasts flavours from across the globe at good value and is accompanied by a fine range of lagers and specialist spirits. Dining here is also unbeatable with an innovative daily changing menu which can include rustic tomato and chorizo soup, swordfish steak, Chinese noodles and the finest cuts of Welsh beef, served from 12-2pm and 6-9.30pm Mon-Sat.

Gales also offers 15 rooms for occupation; each individually decorated retaining many original features of the classic Georgian style in which they were built, all with en suite, tv and wifi facilities one room is ensuite with living room. A conference room is available for small conferences with all modern facilities included. But for those looking for a more secluded break there are two 400 year old 'forget-me-not' cottages to choose from that create a cosy and comfy environment from which to enjoy a bottle of wine purchased over the road at the Gale's shop.

This hardworking and eccentric family have really put Llangollen on the map, making a visit there truly worth it just to sample their fine wine, food and hospitality.

14 CHIRK CASTLE

Chirk, Wrexham LL14 5AF
Tel: 01691 777701
e-mail: gcwmsn@smtp.ntrust.org.uk

Chirk Castle, a magnificent Marcher fortress, was begun in the late 13th century on land granted by Edward I to Roger de Mortimer. Rectangular, with a massive drum tower at each corner, the Castle has been extensively rebuilt and altered from time to time down the centuries but remains a truly impressive sight. It was bought in 1595 by Sir Thomas Myddleton, Lord Mayor of London, and part of it is still lived in by the Myddleton family. Visitors can see the elegant state rooms, some fine Adam-style furniture, tapestries and portraits. By contrast, the dramatic dungeon is a reminder of the Castle's turbulent history, and that for some, life was not always so peaceful and genteel.

The estate is entered through a superb set of wrought-iron gates that were made by the famous Davis brothers of Bersham Ironworks. The Castle, whose walls are now partly covered in climbing plants, stands in an 18th century landscaped park whose layout is based on designs by William Emes. The grounds include six acres of trees and flowering shrubs, many of them planted by Lady Margaret Myddleton. There are handsome clipped yews in the formal garden, and a fine rose garden. Among other features are an avenue of lime trees, some 19th century topiary, a rockery and an old hawk house. One mile north of Chirk village and 9 miles south of Wrexham, the Castle is open to visitors from late March to early November, closed Monday and Tuesday except Bank Holidays.

15 THE GLYN VALLEY COUNTRY INN

Llanarmon Road, Glyn Ceiriog,
Llangollen LL20 7EU
Tel: 01691 718896
e-mail: info@glynvalleyhotel.co.uk
website: www.glynvalleyhotel.co.uk

Situated in the heart of Glyn Valley midway between Chirk Castle and Pystell Rhaeadr waterfalls is the **Glyn Valley Country Inn**, the perfect spot for a short break away in the countryside. With opportunities to arrange local activities from pony-trekking, to trout-fishing guest will not be short of things to do, and can relax each night in one of the inn's nine rooms which include family size, twins and doubles. Most of the rooms are en suite and come with a hearty breakfast in tow.

Guests can also come for dinner or drinks either in the elegant seventy-five seater restaurant where a regularly changing menu sports the best in fresh local produce including Ceiriog Trout. Known for its Swiss and seasonal dishes, the restaurant also serves up favourites like steamed salmon supreme and mature sirloin. Children and vegetarians are also well catered for. Owner and chef, Markus Imfeld, took over here in January 2009 but has put the place back on the map making it a beacon for good food in both mid Wales and Shropshire. All dishes come cooked fresh to order, and owing to popularity it's a good idea to book; especially at weekends.

The attractive wood panelled bar offers up to three real ales depending on season, alongside a range of other soft and alcoholic beverages with Sky Sports, a pool table and a darts board to entertain you. All major credit cards taken.

16 THE WEST ARMS

Llanarmon Dyffryn Ceirog, nr Llangollen,
Denbighshire LL20 7LD
Tel: 01691 600665
e-mail: gowestarms@aol.com
website: www.thewestarms.co.uk

Offering accommodation and cuisine of the highest standard **The West Arms** is an award winning inn located in the quiet village of Llanarmon Dyffryn Ceirog. Oozing warmth and character it is nestled at the foothills of the Berwyn mountains and has a fantastic reputation in the area for its features and facilities. There is a superb selection of spacious rooms and suites, many with exposed beams, all offering modern en-suite facilities you would expect from any quality inn.

Dating back to the 17th century The West Arms used to be a popular resting spot with cattle drivers coming down from the Welsh Hills en route to local markets. Now it is one of the finest places to dine out in Denbighshire and has accommodation to match. Owned and run by Sian and Lee Finch and head chef Grant Williams the team has a wealth of experience between them. Grant is an award winning chef who has cooked for HRH Prince Charles, and worked in kitchens around the world. He has been at The West Arms for 18 years. His cooking is outstanding and extremely popular with locals and visitors who return time and again to take advantage of the hotel's high standards and friendly, efficient service. The menu is fabulous with plenty of dishes, including medallions of Welsh beef on wilted spinach with pave potato laced in a port wine source. Honey roasted breast of gressingham duck resting on stir-fried pak choi finished in a burgundy sauce is another favourite. The desserts are a real temptation for sweet-toothed diners with an extensive list of tasty treats including coffee and vanilla panacotta with poached fruits. Due to its popularity diners are advised to book at all times to avoid disappointment - especially at weekends. The bar menu is available lunchtimes and evenings, providing substantial meals and there are additional choices on the specials board.

With an open log fire in winter the inn is extremely comforting and the hospitality is superb. Sian and Lee settled in the village in 2004 to manage The West Arms and moved from managing a country inn in Worcestershire. The charming inn is an ideal get away for those wanting a relaxing break and is set in a tranquil and picturesque village. It provides an idyllic and romantic setting and with a wedding license is an ideal location for a civil ceremony.

17 YUM YUMS

The Square, Corwen,
Denbighshire LL21 0DG
Tel: 01490 413725/412108/07950 979128

Located at the heart of the popular town of Corwen, **Yum Yums** is an extremely popular sandwich bar and takeaway business. Owned by Christine and Ed Stein for the past year, Yum Yums has a growing reputation and is soon to be extended and refurbished, with longer opening hours. Seating 12 inside and more than 20 in the outside courtyard area, the child-friendly establishment offers some fantastic homemade food, including sandwiches, jacket potatoes, paninis and salad bowls. Homemade breakfasts and cakes are also popular with customers. Yum Yums is a small, quality premises and its current opening hours are Monday-Saturday 9am-4.30pm.

18 OWAIN GLYNDWR HOTEL

The Square, Corwen,
Denbighshire LL21 0DL
Tel: 01490 412115
e-mail: ifor@btconnect.com
website: www.owainglyndwrhotel.com

Offering the very best in accommodation food and drink, the famous **Owain Glyndwr Hotel** stands in the centre of Conwen. The historic building dates back to 1329 and is named after Owain Glyndwr, the legendary Prince of Wales. The famous 2 star rated hotel is adjacent to the main A5 and stands proudly opposite the famous statue of Owain Glyndwr on his horse.

Combining heritage with the comforts and facilities of a modern hotel it has 13 character-filled en-suite rooms, which are individually and tastefully decorated. It has been owned, and personally run, by Ifor Sion for the past 12 years and is an ideal base for visitors wanting to explore North Wales.

Originally a monastery in the grounds of the church and later a coaching inn the hotel has a strong emphasis on good food. The produce is sourced and farmed locally and the changing menu takes full advantage of fresh, seasonal produce in the area.

Seating 20 diners the restaurant is popular in the area and the ideal venue for that special occasion. The hotel, which is open all year round also provides an excellent venue for business and boasts a restaurant, two bars, residents lounge, conference facilities and secure private parking. With spacious conference facilities the hotel provides an ideal 'away from the office' location for meetings and training events. Styled in a lecture theatre layout it seats 100 people and in a 'board room' style, 35 people, can work in comfort. Bursting with old world charm the hotel, which has oak beamed ceilings and panelled walls, has all the modern amenities of a first class hotel with free wi-fi internet access for residents.

The rooms all have baths and showers, except the single rooms, which just have showers and the excellent tariff includes breakfast

There is a log fire for guests to enjoy in the Saddle Bar with an extensive selection of beers, wines and spirits. Breakfast is served between 7.30am-9.30am, lunch from 12pm-2.30pm and evening meals between 7pm-9pm.

The child-friendly hotel is the ideal base for guests wanting to explore the Dee Valley and there are many attractions and activities in the surrounding area. Close by is the River Dee, Llangollen Railway and Churches of Saints Mael and Sulien.

No accommodation is available at Christmas and during the New Year period. Because of the hotel's popularity, it is advisable for larger parties to book. All major credit cards are taken.

19 TASTEBUDS

8 High Street, Wrexham LL13 8HP
Tel: 01978 290909

Drawing locals and visitors like a magnet, the widely acclaimed **Tastebuds** is the ideal place to eat for those who enjoy home-made food, warm hospitality and a smile. Located in the heart of Wrexham, the coffee shop is owned by business partners, Christine, Pam and Tracey, who had worked together previously, for someone else. The ladies took over the premises in May 2007 and have built up a strong reputation in the area for their quality home-made food. Inside, it is delightful with a fresh and modern feel to it and that aroma of home cooking, reminding you of your grandmother's house in days gone by.

There is seating for 32 people inside and eight outside and what it lacks in size, it certainly makes up for in quality.

The child friendly coffee shop is open seven days a week and serves a range of mouth-watering treats, including homemade cakes, pies, quiche and soups – even some of the bread is homemade. The English breakfasts, served daily are extremely popular and most of the dishes are made from local produce.

Tastebuds, which has been voted Best Independant Coffee shop in Wrexham, is open Monday-Saturday between 8.30am and 5pm and from 12pm-3pm for Sunday lunch and the full menu.

Disabled access is not a problem and only cash and cheque are accepted.

20 THE LILLY

West Parade, Llandudno,
Conwy LL30 2BD
Tel: 01492 876513
Fax: 01492 877916
e-mail: thelilly@live.co.uk

Newly refurbished and under the management of newlyweds Phil and Roxanne and daughter Lilly – **The Lilly** has it all, elegant rooms that overlook the sea and the Great Orme, quality dining and function rooms, breakfast buffets, afternoon tea and a fully licensed bar. Beautifully located within easy reach of many of North Wales' best castles, mountains and coast line.

Diners can enjoy the locally sourced menu from 6-9pm Tues-Sat prepared by award winning chefs. Dishes include asparagus truffle, Parma ham wrapped lamb shoulder and pan fried salmon with tomato vinaigrette. The bar serves a wide range of cask ales, wine, champagne, soft drinks, snacks, light bites and afternoon tea which can be enjoyed in the stylish yet relaxed atmosphere of the bar or the sun terrace outside.

Ideal for holidays with 12 en-suite rooms, tasteful and comfortably decorated the Lilly is the perfect spot for a fine dining experience and romantic weekend exploring the wilderness of the coast or a stylish afternoon bite, open daily from 12-9pm daily all year round.

21 EPPERSTONE HOTEL

15 Abbey Road, Llandudno,
Conwy LL30 2EE
Tel: 01492 878746
Visitors Tel: 01492 860681
Fax: 01492 871223
e-mail: epperstonehotel@btconnect.com
website: www.epperstone-hotel.co.uk

The Epperstone Hotel is located within the popular resort of Llandudno between the two shores, with stunning views across to the Great Orme. The hotel stands within ten minutes walk to the pier, shops, beaches and promenade making it ideally located for various kinds of holidays whether it's your main family holiday, or a short break away.

The hotel itself is over one hundred years old and its proprietor David Drew has gone to great lengths to preserve its elegant Edwardian charm. David has been running the hotel for the last 24 years and he has built up a regular clientele who enjoy the personal, yet non-intrusive style of service he provides. Guests can chose from eight en suite bedrooms with a range of twin and double options, each room being fully equipped with all modern amenities including tea and coffee making facilities, telephone, trouser press, hair dryer and electronic safe without losing the spacious, genteel feel of the rooms.

Guests at Epperstone can spend their time relaxing in the Victorian style conservatory which overlooks the hotel's award winning gardens, or perhaps the tranquillity of the Edwardian Blue lounge will appeal more with comfortable sofas, classic décor and stunning features that include original fire places and stained glass windows.

The hotel's own chef prepares guests breakfasts each morning in the sunlit dining room, where dinner can also be enjoyed by arrangement. Guests on a B&B and dinner rate can enjoy a variety of tasty dishes or indulge in the daily changing four course menu. Sample dishes include carrot and coriander soup; grilled salmon steak served with lime, lemon and hollandaise sauce; roast chicken with all the trimmings; goujons of plaice; or a vegetarian option prepared fresh to taste. Desserts include peach melba, ginger pudding, profiteroles, fresh fruit platter and a selection of cheese and biscuits. Coffee and after dinner mints are served in the conservatory, with other an extensive wine list also being available - as the hotel has its own license.

Senior citizens are advised to make themselves known in advance, as special discounts can be made for them, and other clients out of season. The hotel was awarded two stars by the AA at an 81% rating, proving that this hotel affords a graceful ambience at value for money prices.

22 GREAT ORME 'REST AND BE THANKFUL'

Marine Drive, Llandudno,
Conwy LL30 2XD
Tel: 01492 870004
website: www.restandbethankful.net

The well known Marine Drive that circles the Great Orme in North Wales is home to not only some of the best views in country, but to a rambler's haven; '**Rest and Be Thankful**.' Just past the lighthouse is this delightful café that started life some years ago as an ice cream parlour. Now opening daily from 10am-4pm, it has turned into quite the heritage spot detailing the area's history with a variety of publications and photo albums created by Llandudno's Heritage Trust that are available to browse whilst taking a well earned break from the 5 mile walk around Marine Drive.

A great selection of sandwiches, rolls, toasted sandwiches and Paninis are available alongside homemade soup of the day; perfect to warm you up after a windy walk! The cakes on offer here are also very popular with favourites including banana and walnut cake, carrot, coffee and Welsh classics like bara brith. A good selection of hot and cold drinks can be enjoyed inside or out; where the picnic benches overlook glorious sea views, perched atop 300ft of limestone cliff. Cash only.

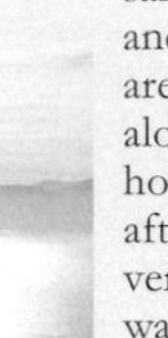

23 QUEEN VICTORIA

4 Church Walks, Llandudno LL30 2HD
Tel: 01492 860952
e-mail: tomlong3@hotmail.co.uk
website: www.queenvic-pub.co.uk

The Queen Victoria Pub and Restaurant is located just off the promenade in Llandudno, a stone's throw away from the shore at its stunning location on the Snowdonia coastline. The pub has a great reputation for being the area's finest traditional pub and restaurant with a rich atmosphere which keeps both locals and visitors coming back time after time.

Owners Tom and Carol took over the Queen Vic in June 2009, but have been in the trade for over 35 years, bringing all that experience with them. They have retained the pub's refined and traditional feel, with downstairs' striking scarlet walls adorned with a variety of antique trinkets, and upstairs light and fresh for the finest bistro dining the town has to offer. The menu is created to make the most of the great local produce in the area with an impressive selection that ranges from hearty grills such as the sirloin steak or a trio of lamb chop, to traditional family favourites like steak and ale pudding, hunters chicken and tikka massala with a fine choice of fresh fish dishes, salads and lighter bites also available. Vegetarians are also well catered for with a choice between classics like vegetarian lasagne and burgers to mouth-watering treats like Wild mushroom and asparagus risotto or mushroom and red pepper stroganoff. Those with a lighter appetite can chose from a range of filled sandwiches and Paninis, with a children's menu also available. Food is served from 12-9pm Monday to Saturday and 12-8pm on Sundays when a handsome Sunday roast is served up.

The Queen Vic isn't just for the hungry, it caters well for the thirsty; priding itself of offering a choice of four hand pulled cask ales which include Mastons Pedigree, Banks Bitter, Hobgoblin and a rotating guest ale. All major credit cards accepted.

Close to the start of the Great Orme tramway, the Queen Vic is ideally located for ramblers and walkers who have come to explore the area with the offer of a meal waiting for you when you return; perfect to warm you up after a blustery walk! Llandudno also holds many other attractions for visitors however with a golf course and theatre nearby, making the Queen Vic truly convenient for those pre-show dining experiences.

24 BELLE VUE HOTEL

25 North Parade, Llandudno,
Conwy LL30 2LP
Tel: 01492 879547
e-mail: enquiries@bellvue-hotel.co.uk
website: www.bellevue-hotel.co.uk

With spectacular views across Llandudno Bay the family-run **Bellevue Hotel** has facilities of the highest standards. With a warm and relaxing atmosphere the hotel is close to the town centre and is set in one of the best locations in Llandudno, offering stunning views from the front elevation. Inside it is elegant and modern, with a luxurious feel to it. One of the finest hotels in the area, the 15 bedrooms, spread over three floors, have recently been beautifully refurbished and are all en-suite, boasting colour televisions and coffee making facilities. Nine of the rooms have views across the bay and there is a selection of deluxe rooms, with enhanced facilities for guests to choose from, as well as double, twin and family rooms. The owner, Sandie, has run the hotel with her daughter and son-in-law, Nadene and Rafik and their daughter Layla for the past two years. The hotel is well-known in the area and has a growing reputation for its fantastic and luxurious home from home feel. The guest lounge is comfortable and tastefully decorated, providing the ideal space for visitors to relax and feel at home. After a day exploring the area guests are often found making the most of the top quality facilities and there is unlimited free access to Wi-Fi broadband. Popular with visitors are the hotel's freshly prepared cooked breakfasts, made with the finest ingredients, as well as the continental selection available from the hotel's buffet table.

The Bellevue Hotel is an impressive establishment, right on the sea front and outside, the terrace areas offer panoramic views across the bay and guests can enjoy breakfast there on sunnier days. The pretty patio area is particularly popular with guests, who often return time and time again to visit the hotel. The dining room is well presented and the restaurant is open all day for breakfast, lunch, and lite bites. Evening meals can be had by arrangement for residents only, with a daily, changing menu at a set price. Residents can also relax with a drink in the well-stocked bar lounge, which also boasts good views. The service is top quality and the family which owns it is welcoming and friendly. Although there are steps to get to the hotel, once inside there is a lift to all of the floors and various size rooms. Packed lunches can be provided on request and special rates can be arranged for groups.

25 PENRHYN OLD HALL

Penrhyn, Llandudno, Conwy LL30 3EE
Tel: 01492 549888

Set in a delightful, picturesque location, with a medieval manor house at its heart, **Penrhyn Old Hall** is a splendid cluster of buildings located just off the coast road (B5115) between Llandudno and Colwyn Bay. The hall is surrounded by woodland and provides the ideal place to dine for those wanting to enjoy a good quality meal in tranquil surroundings. Nestled in beautiful grounds the hall, which functions as a pub, restaurant and unique venue for parties and special occasions, is near to the town, country and coast and has plenty of off-road parking. From the outside the hall is an impressive establishment and inside it is warm and inviting with spacious rooms, full of character. With a fantastic ambience, the Tudor Bar and restaurant are open every day and with windows overlooking idilic backdrops it is the perfect venue for guests to enjoy a drink or meal. Serving, fresh, home-cooked food, made from local produce, Penrhyn Old Hall is popular with locals and visitors. There is an extensive selection of dishes to choose from on the daily changing menu, including daily lunches, a traditional Sunday lunch and a mouth-watering range of a la carte choice in the evenings from Wednesday-Saturday. Favourites include fresh salmon, Somerset lamb and roast beef. Seating is available for up to 40 diners and there are two real ales for guests to sample.

It is said by some that Roderick, grandson of the last King of the Britains,built a palace on this site in the 8th century. Nothing, of course of that building survives but a few parts of the medieval hall are still to be seen. Designated a Grade 1 listed building, the whole place is full of architectural and historic interest with some fascinating features including old fireplaces, remarkable frescoes, carvings and stained glass.

The Marsh family, Ann and George, acquired the property in 1963 and on their retirement in1988 left it to their children Kim and Guy, and Guy's wife Anne. One of the extensions houses the night club, which can be hired for functions, with room for up to 200 guests. Popular skittles nights are held in the Baronial Hall which is at other times available for private parties. The child-friendly restaurant is open from noon until 2.30pm, and in the evenings from 5.30pm to 11.30pm and are by booking only between 7pm and 9pm. Mastercard and Visa credit cards are accepted.

26 THE QUEENS HEAD

Glanwydden, Conwy LL31 9JP
Tel: 01492 546570
Fax: 01492 546487
e-mail: info@queensheadglanwydden.co.uk
website: www.queensheadglanwydden.co.uk

Voted AA Welsh Pub of the Year for 2009/2010 **The Queens Head** pub is one not to be missed. It is beautifully located in the idyllic country village of Glanwydden, just a short drive from the seaside town on Llandudno and the A55, within easy reach of many local amenities including Venue Cymru (theatre) and much more.

Locals claim the pub itself is the 'warmest and most wonderful place to eat and relax in peace' and a after just one visit you would have to agree. The dedication and charm exhibited by staff here is echoed in the property which houses a relaxed and friendly atmosphere for guests all year round. Owners Robert and Sally Cureton have been running the establishment for 28 years now and with the help of their head chef Barry Edwards who has worked his way up to the top since leaving college they have created a thriving business.Open for food from 12-2pm and 6-9pm Mon-Fri and 12-9pm on weekends, the Queens Head is renowned for its fine cuisine with chefs who are passionate about good food and local produce. The extensive menu is comprised of appetizers, hearty mains, seafood, pastas and vegetarian dishes, grills and steaks, light bites and Sunday roasts. Popular dishes include asparagus risotto, monkfish and king prawn curry, homemade steak and ale pie, char grilled welsh rump or warm brie and crispy pancetta ciabatta. Its best to book at all times to avoid disappointment.

The bar, complete with roaring log fire houses 3 real ales, a vast wine list and a good selection of spirits and soft drinks, is open from 11:30am-3pm and 6-10:30pm weekdays and from 11:30-10:30pm on weekends, the ideal place to unwind.

With no end to its facilities the Queens Head also has a 30 seater function room available for dinners and intimate Welsh weddings, complete with romantic and cosy accommodation just across the road at the lovingly restored Storehouse Cottage, sleeping two in decadent comfort with simply flawless facilities.

Whether you're in the area shopping, walking, cycling, or exploring the coast, The Queens Head extends a warm welcome to all, living up to its reputation as the finest pub in the area.

27 THE RENDEZVOUS CAFÉ

71 Abergele Road, Colwyn Bay,
Conwy LL29 7RU

Popular amongst locals and tourists, the café is located at the heart of the seaside resort of Colwyn Bay on the main Abergele Road. Having been a chef for 20 years, Ray, who has owned **The Rendezvous Café** with his wife Elizabeth for four years, serves some mouth-watering dishes. Seating 40 guests inside and eight outside the child-friendly café endeavours to use local produce where they can, adding to the quality of the food. Guests have an array of dishes to choose from the extensive menu or daily specials board. The breakfasts are extremely popular as well as pan fried liver and onions and homemade, steak and ale pie and homemade soups. Scampi, faggots, baked potatoes, lite bites and homemade desserts can also be ordered.

The delightful café is tastefully decorated and provides the ideal resting spot for visitors wanting to watch town life go by. Visitors to Colwyn Bay are in easy reach of the sea and the Pwllycrochan Woods and nearby attractions include the Welsh Mountain Zoo. Open six days a week the café is open 7.30am-3pm every week day and from 8am-3pm on Saturdays.

28 ST MARGARETS HOTEL

Princes Drive/Ellesmere Road,
Colwyn Bay, Conwy LL29 8RP
Tel: 01492 532718
e-mail: stmargarets@hotelcb.Fsnet.co.uk
website: www.st-margarets-hotel.co.uk

Standing in its own grounds, close to the centre of the seaside resort of Colwyn Bay, the **St Margarets Hotel** is a smart, impressive establishment dating back to the early 1900s. Monica Copley has owned the hotel for more than 20 years and offers guests an ideal place to relax and be pampered. Monica adds a personal touch to the 12 en-suite rooms and is well-known for the popular breakfasts she serves. Evening meals are available by arrangement and visitors often comment on Monica's superb cooking, with many describing the hotel as 'a particularly pleasing place to stay'.

29 THE MARINE HOTEL

Old Colwyn, Colwyn Bay,
Conwy LL29 9YH
Tel: 01492 515020
Fax: 01492 512710
e-mail: info@marinehoteloldcolwyn.co.uk

Dating back to the mid 1800s, **The Marine Hotel** is a delightful old coaching inn located in the small town of Old Colwyn, to the east of the seaside resort of Colwyn Bay. The owners Wendy and Brian have recently tastefully refurbished the nine guest rooms, eight of which are en-suite. Many of them boast original Welsh slate fireplaces and all have colour TV and complementary hot drink making facilities for guests to make the most of. With a friendly atmosphere and providing a great service the hotel is the ideal place to enjoy a three course meal with the family or a social drink in any of the well-decorated bars, which between them have a dartboard and new 50" plasma screen TV.

The traditional dining room can seat 36 guests and the menu caters for all tastes with traditional favourites, specials and vegetarians, mainly produced in-house using fresh local produce from the village butcher, baker and greengrocer. Although grills and steaks are what the hotel specialises in, there is a wide selection of different cuisine and plenty of home-made desserts. The child-friendly hotel boasts three friendly bars, which serve an extensive range of beers, wines, spirits and hot drinks and for those seeking entertainment there is often a quiz night on a Wednesday in the bar and karaoke at weekends. One real ale, Courage Best, is served which is popular among guests.

Under the personal supervision of Wendy and Brian, for the last 17 years the hotel has a fantastic reputation for the warm and friendly hospitality it offers and many guests are so impressed they visit time and again. The owners pride themselves on their good service and are more than happy to tailor events to clients' individual needs. There is a large function room that can be used for every occasion, including christenings, conferences, funerals, weddings and birthday parties, and Brian and Wendy have an excellent reputation for their hot and cold buffets.

Located just 400 metres from junction 22 of the A55 expressway the hotel is in the ideal location for guests wanting to explore the coast and mountains of North Wales. The Marine Hotel is within easy reach of historic castles, Snowdonia and Anglesey with stunning coastline, beaches, forests and lakes. There are also plenty of golf courses within a 5-10 mile radius as well as many other activities in the surrounding area. The hotel has plenty of off-road parking and accepts all major credit cards.

30 MORTON ARMS

Sandbank Rd, Towyn, Abergele,
Conwy LL22 9LB
Tel: 01745 330211
Fax: 01745 330211
e-mail: laverychris1@aol.com

Located in the centre of Towyn, on the dramatic welsh coast; **The Morton Arms** is an endearing family-run establishment which offers delicious food and comfortable accommodation, as well as plenty of the hospitality Wales is renowned for. The proud owners Chris and Lorraine have been here since 2002 and have transformed the Morton Arms, sat in its own lush 2 acres of land, into a popular destination for visitors and locals alike.

Many come to The Morton Arms for the delicious and extensive menu, available from both their relaxed, cosy bar area and their elegant main restaurant. The Morton grill and traditional English dishes, such as the local take on sausage and mash with Award winning Edwards of Conway sausages served alongside the choice of peas and chips or creamy mashed potatoes, and drizzled with rich onion gravy, are generously portioned and brimming with home-cooked flavours. The real treat however is in the very popular Chinese cuisine available here, which can be enjoyed in the restaurant or bought to you while you enjoy a drink in the bar - perhaps one of their Tetley or Worthington's keg draught ales. Food is served all week, 9am to late, with the Chinese menu being available from 4.30pm to 11pm.

Most weekends, The Morton Arms hosts excellent live entertainment with professional artists, also available some weekdays in the summer months.

A popular traditional Sunday lunch is served 12noon to 3pm and 5pm to 7pm on Sundays, which is advised to book in advance to avoid disappointment. This also applies to any visit to the restaurant, particularly on weekends and in season. Children are welcome, though they must leave by 8pm Friday, Saturday and Sunday.

Within the 2 acre grounds of the Inn, are comfortable chalet-style buildings which provide accommodation. The 20 chalets, which can be stayed in on a Bed & Breakfast or self-catering basis, come with their own off road parking and are available for 7½ months of the year.

31 THE IMPERIAL HOTEL

34 Bodfor Street, Rhyl LL18 1AU
Tel: 01745 338540
Mobile: 07867 657268

Norma and Ken offer you fantastic hospitality and service at **The Imperial Hotel**, located in the centre of the vibrant town of Rhyl. This impressive building dates back to the early 19th century and now operates as a 12 bedroom hotel with its own bar facilities. Each room is tastefully decorated with good facilities, one of which has its own en suite bathroom. All rooms come on a brilliant breakfast rate, and it's guaranteed that Norma's delectable breakfast will keep you filled up all day long.

The bar here which is open to both residents and non-residents sports a good selection of keg ales to choose from, with popular draughts such as Carling and John Smiths also available. Friday and Saturday nights here are not to be missed if you like karaoke which is on between 8:30pm until around midnight. Children welcome, cash payments only please.

32 PENDRE COFFEE SHOP

214 High Street, Prestatyn,
Wales LL19 9BP
Tel: 01745 853365
Fax: 01745 859071
e-mail: trixie@xln.co.uk

Pendre Coffee Shop is so much more than just a coffee shop, offering amazing food and great service for any occasion. You'll find it right on the high street in the heart of the busy town of Prestatyn. It was refurbished in 2006 to excellent standards and is the perfect spot for breakfast, lunch or afternoon tea before exploring this vibrant area of Wales.

Owners Janet and Bob have a phenomenal 50 years experience in the trade, taking over Pendre in 2005. Bob takes the helm in the kitchen offering a fantastic menu that includes a range of toasties and sandwiches, jacket potatoes, salads, vegetarian options, breakfasts and main meals. Locals and visitors alike flock here for Bob's breakfasts which are very reasonably priced but simply scrumptious with plenty of options for vegetarians and the chance to add extras if you fancy it, although the meals here are generously portioned so you may not need any! Bob also has his right hand lady Debra to help him in the kitchen who has won awards for her culinary skills. Popular dishes are the homemade soups and pies and the omelette selection.

Unlike many coffee shops, Pendre is licensed, serving a healthy range of spirits and bottled lagers. They also serve an impressive range of hot drinks that come with all the extras and choice of a specialist coffee shop with the option of vanilla, amaretto, coconut, hazelnut, Irish cream, caramel and many more. Soft drinks are also in plenty with fresh smoothies available made with fresh fruit, yoghurt and milk, and a choice of fruit juices, squashes, fizzy cans and milkshakes also available – perfect thirst quenchers.

Open from 9am-3pm daily for coffee trade, Pendre is also available for evening hire, making a popular venue for birthdays, anniversaries or other functions as its capacity is a staggering 60 people. Where you're coming here for just a light bite and break from exploring Prestatyn or celebrating something special Bob, Janet and their hardworking team guarantee that it will be an enjoyable experience, no request is too much trouble for them and ensuring you leave with a smile on your face.

33 THE OLD STAG

Llangernwyn, Conwy LL22 8PP
Tel: 01745 860213
e-mail: info@theoldstag.com
website: www.theoldstag.com

Located in a rural village in the North Welsh town of Conwy, **The Old Stag** is a quality village inn. Situated in the mostly Welsh-speaking village of Llangernyw, home to a 4,000 year old ancient yew tree, the inn dates back to the 17th century.

Popular with visitors, the tree, which some claim to be the oldest living tree in the country can be found in the nearby churchyard of St Digain's parish church. With real open fires, The Old Stag is overflowing with character and has beautiful low beams and hundreds of artifacts from bygone days. Serving freshly prepared food there is a good selection of dishes on the menu, with locally sourced ingredients at its heart. Having been a professional chef for 17 years Darryl Flynn is no stranger to serving mouth-watering dishes and owns The Old Stag with his wife Maria. Curries, pizzas and beer battered fish are among the most popular dishes and there are many homemade desserts for guests to enjoy, including warm apple pie with custard and cheesecake of the day with ice cream.

Open every day for lunch and dinner, food is served from 12-2.30pm and 5.30-9pm Monday-Saturday and 12-9pm every Sunday, when traditional Sunday roast dinners are served all day. Such is its popularity weekends need to be booked. Catering for everyone, there is an over 60s lunch club, allowing senior citizens to choose a main course and dessert from the special menu for £5.99. There is also a 'beat the clock' offer, meaning whatever time a customer orders from the menu between 5.30-7pm is what they pay for it. So if you order at 5.45pm you pay £5.45 for the meal. At The Old Stag there is always an offer to be had and other nightly specials include curry nights and fish supper nights amongst others. There is a wide choice of ales and lagers to enjoy, including one locally brewed ale and one nationally brewed.

Situated in the charming village of Llangernyw it is located on the A548 between Llanrwst and Llanfair Talhaiarn. The Old Stag really is a top quality olde Welsh pub. Before you even enter the inn there is charm written all over the impressive exterior and there is seating outside for those sunnier days. The inn has plenty of car parking facilities and welcomes families, including their pets. All credit cards, except Diners, are taken.

34 THE HAWK AND BUCKLE INN

Llannefydd, Denbigh,
Denbighshire, LL16 5ED
Tel: 01745 540249
e-mail: enquiries@hawkandbuckleinn.com
website: www.hawkandbuckle.co.uk

A magnificent hidden gem in the village of Llannefydd surrounded by hundreds of acres of rolling countryside, found sign-posted off of the A548 or B5381, **The Hawk and Buckle Inn** has been run by local couple Helen and Rod for two years. The inn dates in parts back to the 17th Century, though could be older, and has a delightful olde worlde feel with low ceiling and floor to ceiling beams and a roaring fire in winter. However, old as it is, the Hawk and Buckle has been very lovingly restored and comes with all the modern facilities to make your visit here a comfortable one.

The restaurant, which can be altered to accommodate individuals and groups, serves a delectable variety of home-cooked food, often from produce locally sourced, such as the *Hawk burger* made from 8oz of beef selected especially for the Inn by Daniel Jones Butchers of St Asaph, and topped with Welsh Cheddar and smoked bacon. For those less meat-inclined there are meals such as the delicious nut roast with homemade port and redcurrant sauce, served on a bed of steaming rice, as well as a variety of fish dishes. The cosy bar offers two real ales – The Rev. James and a rotating guest ale. Food is served 12noon – 3pm Wednesday to Friday and 6pm – 9pm all week, 12noon – late Saturday and Sunday. Monday and Tuesdays are closed for lunch except on bank holidays. Children are welcome and all credit cards taken (except Diner cards).

All of the eight rooms here include en-suites with Jacuzzis for that added touch of comfort, a hearty breakfast, and five are on the ground floor allowing easy access for visitors with mobility worries. The real feature however is the spectacular views over the countryside – ranging as far afield as Blackpool tower and the Cumbrian Hills!

35 BODNANT GARDEN

Tal-y-Cafn, nr Colwyn Bay,
Conwy LL28 5RE
Tel: 01492 650460
e-mail: office@bodnant-garden.co.uk
website: www.bodnantgarden.co.uk

Situated above the River Conwy, with spectacular views of the Snowdonia range, the National Trust's **Bodnant Garden** is one of the finest in the Britain.

The gardens were laid out by the 2nd Lord Aberconway in 1875 and were presented to the National Trust in 1949. The rhododendrons, camellias and magnolias are a truly magnificent sight in the spring, followed by herbaceous borders, roses and water lilies in the summer and glorious colours in the autumn.

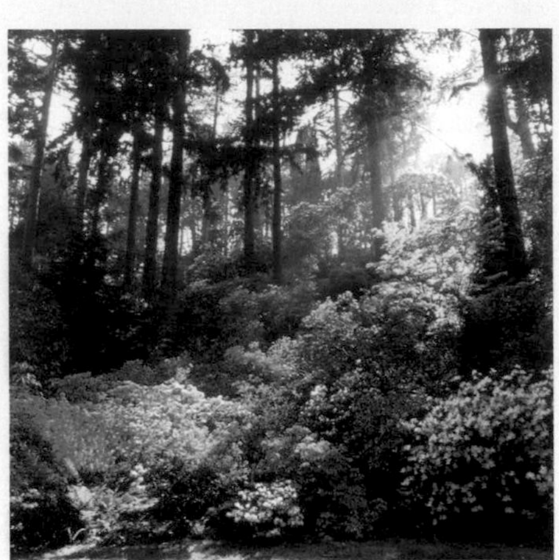

Bodnant has many other attractions, including a laburnum arch, a lily terrace and a stepped pergola; in the Dell, formed round a little tributary of the Conwy, is the tallest redwood in the country. The pretty Garden House was built in Gloucestershire in the 1730s and was later used as a Pin Mill before being brought to Bodnant in 1938. The garden has a shop (not National Trust) and a refreshment pavilion. Bodnant, which is open from mid-March to early November, is located off the A470 eight miles south of Colwyn Bay and Llandudno.

36 TAL-Y-CAFN HOTEL

Tal-Y-Cafn, Colwyn Bay, Conwy LL28 5RR
Tel: 01492 650203

Dating back to the early 18th century The **Tal-Y-Cafn Hotel** is a historic former coaching inn. Martin and Caroline Kinsley-Smith have owned the hotel, which boasts three stars, for a year and offer four quality en-suite bedrooms, which are all located upstairs. Martin has 24 years experience in the trade and the couple has a growing reputation among locals and visitors. The hotel has a fantastic, spacious beer garden, which is extremely popular in the summer months.

120 diners can enjoy meals in the spacious dining area at any one time and there is extra seating space on the patio overlooking the gardens. Open all day, every day, two real ales can be purchased from the bar and quality dishes, made from local produce, are available daily between, 12-9pm. Dishes include steak and Tal-Y-Cafn bbq ribs and grilled salmon, served with seasonal salad and new potatoes. Due to the popularity of the hotel weekend meal bookings have to be booked in advanced.

The child friendly hotel has accommodation available all year round and is adjacent to the A470 at the junction with the bridge over the River Conwy towards the B5106. Parking is not a problem with a good sized off-road car park and breakfast is available by arrangement.

37 FISHERMAN'S CHIP SHOP

3 Castle Street, Conwy, LL32 8AY
Tel: 01492 593792

If you want to sample Britain's national dish at its very best, a visit to **The Fisherman's Chip Shop** is highly recommended. Located in the town centre of Conwy, it has been owned by Peter and Tracy Nolan and their son Chris for 27 years and has a great reputation in the area. Popular with locals and visitors they are kept extremely busy all year round. Offering a takeaway service, as well as being a sit-down restaurant, there are plenty of dishes for customers to choose from, including a wide selection of fish dishes, burgers (including a veggie burger), chicken dishes and many daily specials, all at value-for-money prices. In season, mussels are also added to the menu, which includes some local produce.

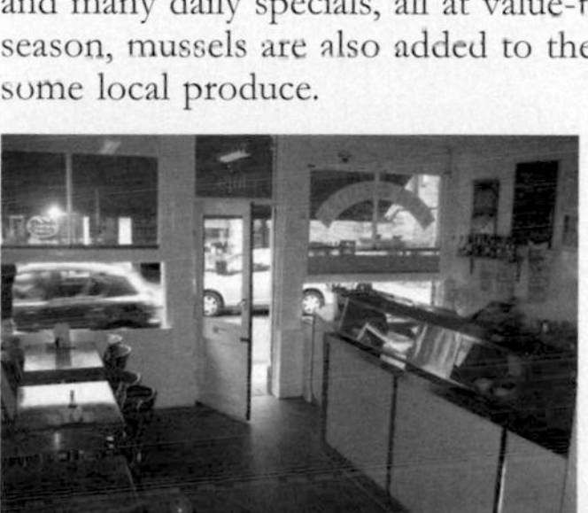

Spread over three floors and easily accessible for disabled customers, there's seating for more than 50 diners. Inside it is clean and modern allowing customers to enjoy a quality meal out.

Ever-growing in popularity the Fisherman's Chip Shop is open every day during the summer season from 11.30am to 9pm. In winter, it is open 11.30am-2.30pm and 5.30pm-8pm. Payment is by cash or cheque only. No bookings are taken.

39 MIN-Y-DON

Promenade, Llanfairfechan,
Conwy LL33 0BY
Tel: 01248 680742
e-mail: sharoncraven44@aol.com
website: www.min-y-don.co.uk

With beautiful sea views the **Min-y-don** is a superb bed and breakfast, which boasts some of the finest rooms in the area. Overlooking the sea at Llanfairfechan, Min-y don is a child friendly B&B owned by Sharon and having lived there for 26 years she is the perfect host. Sharon transformed the 19th century building into a fantastic B&B in April 2009 and is already building a positive reputation in the area.

There are three luxurious rooms to choose from upstairs (one en-suite), all of which are elegant and tastefully decorated. Sharon's hospitality is great and the breakfasts are outstanding. Guests can wake up knowing they are in an ideal location for exploring the area, being just 200 yards from the fantastic sandy beach and small children's play area. The B&B has a spectacular raised terraced area where guests can relax after a day out and watch the sun go down over Anglesey.

If it is a higher viewing point you are after then a walk in the Snowdonia mountains is a must, offering breathtaking views of the Irish Sea and The Menai Strait. The village has a lot to offer, with a boating lake, which has swans nesting on it, a bowling and croquet green.

38 THE WHITE LION INN

289 High Street, Bangor LL57 1UL
Tel: 01248 361999
e-mail: admin@he-whitelion.co.uk
website: www.the-whitelion.co.uk

Offering the very best hospitality a city public house can **The White Lion Inn** is located in the centre of the historic city of Bangor. Thriving on local customers the inn is extremely popular for its 'pub' atmosphere, fantastic cooking and well kept ales. Owned by Jane and Martin Shaw since December 2007 it now welcomes visitors from all over the world. It is the Shaw's first business venture and they have totally transformed the place. Their hard work has been well worth it and the place is constantly bustling with people soaking up the hospitality and ambience. Situated in one of the smallest cities in Britain, which is also a popular university city, there is plenty going on in the area, making The White Lion Inn the perfect resting spot.

Open all day every day the draught keg ales are kept in top condition and favourites with regulars include Carling and John Smiths Smooth. In the kitchen you will find Jane, who is a master cook. Her food is absolutely delicious and the dishes are made with the finest local produce, wherever possible. There is an extensive menu boasting the very best cuisine that is all freshly prepared and cooked to order. Main courses include many traditional favourites, including chilli con carne and homemade steak and ale pie. There are also plenty of curries, beef, chicken and fish dishes to choose from. For vegetarians options include vegetable lasagne and cheese and broccoli bake. Catering for everyone there is also a special 'kiddies corner meal deal' for families to take advantage of and for sweet toothed customers there is a selection of tasty desserts on offer, including Alabama chocolate fudge cake and hot apple pie. If you can't decide from the main menu there is also a daily specials board.

Food is served Monday – Saturday from 10am-3pm and between 12-4pm on a Sunday when a traditional Sunday roast dinner can be enjoyed. With a choice of pork, turkey, beef or lamb, as well as a vegetarian option, it is extremely popular. Inside the child-friendly inn it is tastefully decorated and there is plenty of room in the dining area for guests to relax. There is no problem with disabled access.

On Wednesday and Thursday locals and visitors are encouraged to provide the entertainment with Karaoke from 9pm and on Tuesdays a quiz is held. There are also various charity events throughout the year.

40 THE GLADSTONE

Ysguborwen Road, Dwygyfylchi,
Conwy LL34 6PS
Tel: 01492 623231
e-mail: thegladstonepub@hotmail.co.uk
website: www.thegladstone.co.uk

An award winning, four star, free house on the spectacular North Wales coast, **The Gladstone** is a popular, family run establishment. Serving the very best in homemade meals, with all produce sourced locally, wines and real ales. The inside is as impressive as the outside, boasting six individually designed en-suite rooms. Open all day every day the beautiful coastal pub has a fantastic reputation in the area, winning numerous awards for their real ales and their food. Along side The Gladstone is their holiday cottage which is available to rent with breath taking views of the coast and the mountains!

42 MENAI BANK HOTEL

North Road, Caernarfon,
Gwynedd LL55 1BD
Tel: 01286 673297
e-mail: info@menaibankhotel.co.uk
website: www.menaibankhotel.co.uk

With outstanding views overlooking the Menai Straits the owners of the **Menai Bank Hotel** offer the very best in hospitality and accommodation.
With 15 superb en-suite rooms it is owned and personally run by Patrick and Rachel Coyne who really go out of their way to create a friendly and homely atmosphere for guests. The mouth-watering breakfasts, made from the finest locally sourced produce, have been rated among the best in North Wales. Close to Snowdonia, the impressive establishment has a fantastic garden patio with incredible sea views as well as a lounge area and games rooms that has guests visiting and revisiting.

41 CAERNARFON CASTLE

Caernarfon, Gwynedd LL55 2AY
Tel: 01286 677617

Mighty **Caernarfon** is possibly the most famous of Wales' many castles. Its sheer scale and commanding presence easily set it apart from the rest and, to this day, still trumpet in no uncertain terms the intentions of its builder, Edward 1. Begun in 1283 as the definitive chapter in his conquest of Wales, Caernarfon was constructed not only as a military stronghold but also as a seat of government and royal palace.

The castle's majestic persona is no architectural accident: it was designed to echo the walls of Constantinople, the imperial power of Rome and the dream castle, "the fairest that ever man saw", of Welsh myth and legend. After all these years, Caernarfon's immense strength remains undimmed. Standing at the mouth of the Seiont river, the fortress (with its unique polygonal towers, intimidating battlements and colour banded masonry) dominates the walled town also founded by Edward. Caernarfon's symbolic status was emphasised when Edward made sure that his son, the first English Prince of Wales, was born here in 1284. In 1969, the castle gained worldwide fame as the setting for the investiture of Prince Charles as Prince of Wales.

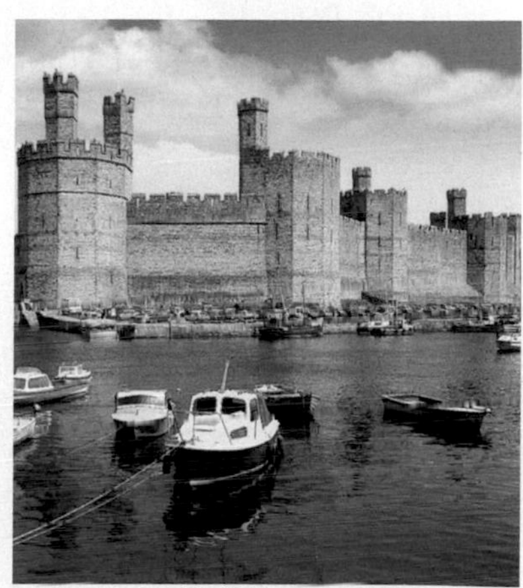

History comes alive at Caernarfon in so many ways - along the lofty wall walks, beneath the towered gatehouse and with imaginative exhibitions located within the towers.

43 BLACK BOY INN

Northgate Street, Stryd Pedwar a Chwech,
Caenarfon, Gwynedd LL55 1RW
Tel: 01286 673604
e-mail: office@black-boy-inn.com

The **Black Boy Inn** has been providing guests with a comfy place to stay and recharge their batteries with a glass of ale or some fine home cooked food for over 6 centuries now and is one of the oldest pubs in Wales. Situated within the medieval town walls of the historic Caenarfon, the Black Boy is ideally located for exploring North Wales, just a short drive from the outstanding beauty of Snowdonia National Park, some of the country's finest archaeological sites and many other local attractions.

John and Chris Evans have been running the Black Boy for over 6 years now, but have plenty of experience between them having been in the trade for over 30 years. They offer the warmest hospitality and are dedicated to keeping the both the history and the atmosphere of the Black Boy alive, maintaining high standards in all facilities whilst retaining the buildings original oak beams and keeping the open log fire roaring in the winter months. Guests can also enjoy the benefit of outdoor seating in the sunshine.

Open all day every day the black boy serves four well kept real ales including Hancock's and Purple Moose, taking you back to days when local salmon used to stop for a drink after a long days work. Excellent food is served daily from 12-9pm and keeps the place bustling with guests all day, making it advisable to book at all times. Guests can chose from the specials board or the main menu which is created from mostly local produce and cooked to order. Dishes include cassoulet of duck leg and smoked sausage, grilled belly pork, fajitas, butterflied mackerel and the traditional Caernarfon Lob Scouse.

Currently there are 15 top quality en suite rooms to choose from (2 of which are on the ground floor), but by 2010 there will be a further 10 each individually decorated in keeping with the buildings glorious history. Rooms come on a very reasonable bed and breakfast tariff offering a hearty welsh breakfast to start each day exploring this fine area. The Black Boy is the perfect place to stay or dine and soak up some fine Welsh culture.

44 GWESTY BRON MENAI

North Road, Caernarfon,
Gwynedd LL55 1BA
Tel: 01286 675589
e-mail: enquiries@bronmenai.co.uk
website: www.bronmenai.co.uk

Having run guest houses in the area for more than 20 years, owners, Alan and Val Ashcroft, offer a first class service to guests. They personally run the **Gwesty Bron Menai** with their daughters Nicci and Jackie, and son Anthony. The entrance is extremely attractive and the path to the front door has fantastic floral decor. Located in the historic town of Caernarfon and dating back to the early 1840s the guest house can be found off the A487 towards the town centre. It has been tastefully restored and offers 10 en-suite rooms of the highest quality. They are all beautifully furnished and there is a twin room on the ground floor with a large bathroom, which is easily accessible for disabled guests, as is the dining room.

Close to the Menai Straits the family-run guest house has a relaxing ambiance to offer and there is a fully licensed restaurant and bar for guests to make the most of. For those wanting to explore the area the town's historic castle is just a short walk away and the Welsh Highland Railway is an attraction popular with many visitors. The tariff includes a hearty breakfast and there is a separate evening menu. No children under the age of 10.

46 TY'N YR ONNEN

Waunfawr, Caernarfon,
Gwynedd LL55 4AX
Tel: 01286 650281 Fax: 01286 650043
e-mail: tom.griffith1@btopenworld.com
website: www.tyn-yr-onnen.co.uk

Set on a the hillside of a traditional working Welsh farm, **Ty'yr Onnen** is the perfect spot for families to take a slice of the outdoors off the beaten track and enjoy this secluded caravan and camping park.

The farm has been in the Griffiths family for over 300 years and offers over 400 acres of heath and heather land, rugged walks and the challenge of climbing Moel Eilio, on top of a range of activities that include a children's play area complete with swings, basketball and animal park with plenty of donkeys, lambs, chickens, ducks, lammas and peacocks to feed and pet. The campsite has its own games arcade with a pool table, video machines, darts and more, with more than enough room for all the outdoor sports and BBQs you could want. The site has first rate facilities with hot showers, laundrette, mother and baby and disabled bathrooms and there is a licensed restaurant within walking distance for those nights when cooking on gas stoves with your own ingredients from the farms own produce shop isn't enough.

Well sheltered pitches with convenient hook ups and the most glorious views Wales has to offer are all available at Ty'n Yr Onnen; why not start your family tradition here. Weekly stays only from Easter to the end of October.

45 THE NEWBOROUGH ARMS

Bontnewydd, Caernarfon,
Gwynedd LL55 2UG
Tel: 01286 673126
e-mail: jamestrew@btconnect.com

Known by locals as one of the best inns in Gwynedd, **The Newborough Arms** is a people magnet, drawing in the crowds from far and near to sample the culinary delights on offer alongside unbeatable hospitality. It's located in the pretty village of Bontnewydd which is just a short drive from the historic Welsh town of Caernarfon off the A487.

Current leaseholders Gill and James have been running it for 18 months and have made a fantastic start. Gill has much experience in the trade but it is James' first venture giving them both the experience and fresh outlook that makes this place so unique. The pair and their hardworking team are dedicated to delivering a high quality service to all their guests, priding themselves on making good honest home cooked food, made with the freshest local ingredients. In turn their dedication repays them as the Newborough Arms is always busy, making it advisable to book most nights.

Food is served daily from 12-9pm and guests can chose from a variety of menus that sample light bites and lunches, combos, grills, fish dishes, pies, curries, pastas and other pub favourites. Popular dishes include the rump steak and ribs, grilled trout, seafood pasta and the homemade steak and ale puff pastry pie. Most dishes come served with freshly prepared home cut chips and garnish. Pensioners and children can also benefit from their own special menus, although the mouth watering Sunday lunch carvery usually makes first choice every time.

The bar area itself is fresh yet in keeping with the inn's history and beautiful architecture and garden. It is open all day every day and serves a handsome selection of real ales including Theakston's Mild, Marstons Pedigree, Old Speckled Hen and a local favourite brew straight from the nearby Snowdonia brewery. But whatever you're drinking you're sure to feel right at home as Gill and James go out of their way to ensure your visit is an enjoyable one. They provide live entertainment at least once a month and run a folk singing club every other Thursday night which always creates a great atmosphere.

Although there is currently no guest accommodation, plans are in place to create some so please ring for details.

47 PLAS TIRION FARM

Llanrug, Caenarfon, Gwynedd LL55 4PY
Tel: 01286 673190
e-mail: cerid@plastirion.plas.com
website: www.plas-tirion.co.uk

Stay at **Plas Tirion** on a scrumptious bed and breakfast rate that offers first rate country comfort from its welsh speaking hosts and a locally sourced home cooked breakfast in true rustic farmhouse style.

Open Easter to October, this 19th century family run working farm sits on 300 acres of beautiful land. It's located just a short drive from Caernarfon castle and Snowdonia mountain railway. Guests can relax in the cosy lounge or stroll the farmland paths whilst watching the sun set towards the Menai Straits. Those who want a more active break have plenty of golfing, fishing, sailing and pony trekking nearby.

48 TY MAWR TEAROOMS, RESTAURANT AND B&B

Groelslon Ty Mawr, LLanddeiniolen,
nr Caernarfon, Gwynedd LL55 3AW
Tel: 01248 352791
e-mail: ruth@tymawrbb.wanadoo.co.uk
website: www.tymawr-bandb.co.uk

Situated in the heart of Snowdonia with stunning views across the country, you'll find **Ty Mawr Tearooms and Restaurant** just off the A55 near junction 11. A warm welcome will greet you from owners Ruth and Mark Higgin who have been running this charming establishment for 4 years now. Renowned for its unbeatable hospitality and fine home cooking, Ty Mawr attracts a healthy clientele from both locals and those looking for a cosy place to refill their tanks after exploring the striking countryside around.

On offer is a licensed restaurant serving up a traditionally home cooked menu created with local welsh produce. Open between 12-8pm from March-November for both main meals and as a tea room serving tasty treats and a wide range of teas and fresh coffees. Ty Mawr can also be hired out for private parties and functions including the well kept beer garden which has beautiful views across the land.

Above this delightful venue is a homely bed and breakfast with 5 spacious and homely rooms all equipped with tea and coffee facilities, colour TV and 4 have en suite bathrooms. Residents can enjoy the benefits of the comfy residents lounge and a hearty breakfast in the morning sure to set you up for a day's exploring. B&B open all year round.

49 THE JOYS OF LIFE COUNTRY PARK

Coed Y Parc, Bethesda,
Gwynedd LL57 4YW
Tel: 01248 602122
e-mail: enquiries@thejoysoflife.co.uk
website: www.thejoysoflife.co.uk

Drs Wendy and Ieuan welcome families, walkers and ramblers, work parties and conferences, bird watchers, reunions and courses to **The Joys of Life**; their very own country park located in a secluded part of the magnificent Snowdonia National Park. The grounds cover ten acres of nature reserve, and sports its own small lake with glorious views across the surrounding mountains.

The park holds two self catering cottages; 'Bryn Llys' which sleeps up to fourteen people in a variety of twinned and family rooms; which have a double bed and twins on a balcony styled gallery above. Bryn Lys is four star rated cottage, with high class modern facilities and décor that compliment the buildings one hundred year old status. Perfect for family reunions or courses, the building holds a games room/lecture room, large lounge and large fully fitted kitchen and dining area. The second cottage 'Hafan' sleeps up to four guests with one twin room and one double room. This cottage has been fully fitted for disabled customers with wheelchair access and a disabled toilet and shower room. Rated five star; this cottage also has a spacious, modern kitchen/dining room and stylish lounge with comfortable leather armchairs and original stone walling. All rooms have en suite bathrooms. Both properties also have attractive outdoor seating areas where the sunshine and the sounds of nature can be gently soaked up.

At the main house, a range of bed and breakfast accommodation is also available in either family, twin or double rooms all of which are en suite. Each room also has colour TV, tea and coffee making facilities, and hairdryer. A hearty breakfast is served up for all guests in the main house which has beautiful views across the park's grounds. Guests staying at the bed and breakfast are ideally placed to take advantage of the large range of activities that can be arranged via the park in the local area, which includes mountaineering, cycling, walking, fishing, bird watching, photography and painting. Within just a few miles of the coastline, the park is in easy reach of several sandy beaches and medieval castles for a more tranquil itinerary. Regardless of what kind of perfect day you fancy, you are sure to find it here.

50 BULKELEY ARMS HOTEL

Uxbridge Square, Menai Bridge,
Anglesey LL59 5DF
Tel: 01248 712715
e-mail: info@bulkeleyarms.co.uk
website: www.bulkeleyarms.co.uk

A very warm Welsh welcome greets you on entering the **Bulkeley Arms Hotel** where proud tenant Maldwyn Jones now resides. Maldwyn has been here for over a year now, bringing this traditional pub on in leaps and bounds with his big heart and traditional approach. Traditionally decorated with a homely feel there is a large bar offering 2 real ales, Robinson's Unicorn and a seasonal rotating brew, with a good selection of keg ales including a draught German bitter. A small but tasty menu offers 'bridge the gap' dishes, all cooked fresh to order from opening until around 9pm each night.

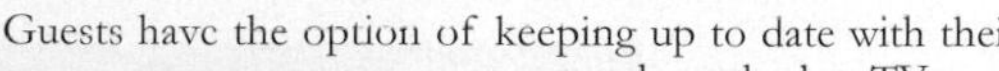

Guests have the option of keeping up to date with their sports where the bar TV shows sky sports rugby and the lounge TV shows the football. Other entertainment on offer included live acts on Saturdays from 9pm and a popular karaoke night on Fridays from 8:30pm until midnight. Families are more than welcome here and can book to stay in one of three upstairs en suite rooms; one single, one twin and one family room. The Bukeley has also proved a popular place for ramblers getting a good night's kip before the next day and motorcyclists who are provided with covered and secure parking for their vehicles. Within sight of the famous bridge and mainland Wales the Bukeley is ideally located for a break away.

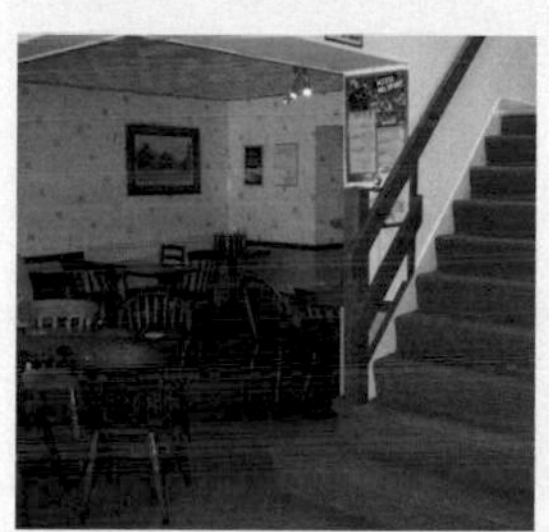

51 THE LIVERPOOL ARMS HOTEL

Beaumaris, Isle of Anglesey LL58 8BA
Tel: 01248 810362
Fax: 01248 811135
e-mail: enquiries@liverpoolarms.co.uk
website: www.liverpoolarms.co.uk

The famous **Liverpool Arms Hotel** stands within historic Beaumis, looking towards the scenic Menai Straits. Dating back to 1706 this building has real character and charm, its handsome Georgian front inviting you in to a friendly and welcoming bar with true atmosphere. Tenants for over 8 years now Matthew and Sarah Ormond have created a popular destination for visitors to Beaumis whether it is for a short break away or business trip.

The main attraction – the Admirals Tavern houses 3 well kept ales, filled with nautical memorabilia to keep you interested all evening. A tempting and varied menu is available daily from 12-9pm in season and from 12-2pm and 6-9pm in low season. The pair prides themselves on serving great food made with local produce with the assistance of two fantastic chefs. Favourite dishes include a mighty mixed grill, baked salmon supreme and mushroom and spinach lasagne. Guests can choose from a variety of menus and a daily changing specials board.

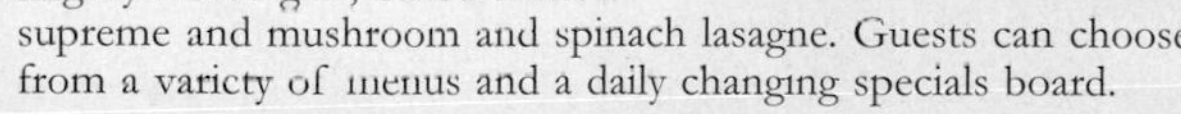

The hotel also boasts 14 grand en suite guest rooms, with stunning décor in keeping with the buildings grade II listed status and a choice of family or four poster rooms. All rooms come with TV and coffee making facilities, with most also accessing free wifi. On a hearty breakfast rate this is truly first class, a must visit gem in Anglesey's crown.

52 TAFARN Y RHYD

LLangoed, Anglesey LL58 8NT
Tel: 01248 490567

Set in one of the most beautiful locations in Anglesey in the historic coastal town of Llangoed is **Tafran Y Rhyd**, one of the area's best pubs with bed and breakfast attached. An ideal place to holiday with reasonable rates and close to many local tourist attractions including castles, golf courses and coastal paths.

Leaseholders Prydwen and Nick have been running the establishment for 12 months along with daughters Sarah and Chantelle, but have plenty of experience in the pub trade and have made an excellent start to their time here. The family have created a vibrant and friendly atmosphere for guests and their dogs all year round. In the winter months the pub is open from 5pm onwards Mon-Fri, but open all day every day in the summer months when drinks can be enjoyed in the beer garden outside.

The bar serves a good selection of soft and alcoholic drinks, but favourites here are Fosters and John Smith's Smooth draughts. Guests can dine either in the bar or a separate eating area from 12-9:30pm in summer and on evenings and weekends in the winter months. Prydwen's delicious menu serves up a handsome selection of starters, mains, grills, veggie options and desserts served with a choice of custard or ice cream. Dishes include a full rack of bbq ribs, lamb shank and grilled salmon but the local favourites are prime Welsh sirloin steak, whole tail scampi and pie of the day. All meats are locally reared and as much local produce is used as possible, cooked to order, guaranteeing an authentic welsh taste – Prydwen also speaks Welsh to add to the equation! A light bite menu is also available for smaller appetites serving Paninis, jacket potatoes and sandwiches.

More than just a quiet coastal pub, Tafarn also puts on live entertainments some weekends and a very well attended bingo night every other Friday so make sure you get there early!

Guests also have a choice of 3 upstairs rooms, one of which is en suite and come on a room or B&B rate. All are more than comfortable and tastefully decorated, giving guests a peaceful night's sleep after a satisfying meal downstairs.

53 THE BREEZE HILL HOTEL

Benllech Bay, Isle of Anglesey LL74 8TN
Tel: 01248 852305
e-mail: contact@breezehill.co.uk
website: www.breezehill.co.uk

The Breeze Hill Hotel has gone from strength to strength since local couple David and Cheryl Jones took over the running of the place three years ago. Standing in its own grounds, set back off the main A5025, the hotel boasts beautiful views of the sea. With miles of coastline to explore and many water sports to try your hand, in an area of outstanding natural beauty, visitors will be in need of somewhere to relax after a busy day.

The hotel has a charming and comfortable lounge bar for guests to make the most of and with four upstairs, spacious en-suite rooms (two with sea views) guests can wind down in private. Open all day every day meals are served in the bar lounge. David does most of the cooking, using as much local produce as he can - creating plenty of good quality dishes. Pan fried duck breast with orange and thyme sauce; and braised lamb shank with tomato and rosemary gravy are among the choices on offer. Food is served between 12-2pm and 6-9pm each day.

The hotel has a function room that seats 100 people and there is a large off road car park.

55 JWMPIN JAC'S CAFÉ BAR

20 Marine Square, Holyhead,
Isle of Anglesey LL65 1DE
Tel: 01407 765003
e-mail: jwmpinjacs@msn.com
website: www.jwmpinjacs.com

Priding itself on high quality food, drinks and service **Jwmpin Jac's Café Bar** is extremely popular in Holyhead. The owners, Nicola and Simon, have been there for three years and having been recently completely re-decorated it offers a comfortable environment for customers to relax.

All of the food is freshly prepared and freshly ground Lavazza Italian Coffee is served along with a range of other hot and cold drinks, including milkshakes and frascatos. Customer's needs are of the utmost importance at Jwmpin Jac's Café Bar and this lends itself to the friendly atmosphere the place has. There are a range of delicious fresh pizzas to choose from - all prepared fresh to order. Freshly baked jacket potatoes, nachos, salads and paninis are also offered and vegetarians are well catered for. Open 10am 10pm every day 30 people can be seated upstairs in the Harbour Terrace Lounge, which has fantastic panoramic views of Holyhead Bay, and 24 people downstairs.

Nicola and Simon are always pleased to welcome children and daily newspapers and wireless internet access is available. There are disabled and baby changing facilities available on the ground floor. All major credit cards are taken. The premises are also available for business, private and club functions.

54 MONA HOUSE COFFEE SHOP

Buckley Square, Llangefni,
Isle of Anglesey LL77 7PH
Tel: 01248 724070

Easily accessible and centrally located on the corner of Buckley Square in the historic market town of Llangefni is Mona House Coffee House. It has been described by locals as the best place to dine in Llangefni during the day time, proving that this lovely business is much more than a small town coffee shop.

Mona House is owned and run by Ian and Caren Ault who have been running the show for over two years now. Over this period they have built up a loyal following from the townspeople and visitors are noted to return again and again whenever they visit the area to sample the delights cooked up inside and enjoy the excellent hospitality offered by staff.

The coffee house itself is a bright and breezy affair with relaxed yet stylish interior, lined with large windows overlooking the square – the perfect spot to people watch! Open 6 days a week from 8:30am-4pm (only closed on Sundays) Mona House is busy, particularly on market days (Thursday and Saturday) when it is advisable to book.

Guests can choose off the daily specials board, or the printed menu which changes regularly to keep things fresh. Customers have the option of choosing from a hearty selection of breakfasts, salads, jacket potatoes, toasted sandwiches, regular sandwiches, main meals or a selection of homemade cakes and desert. The choice is more than adequate for every taste and appetite with sandwich fillings ranging from brie, bacon and cranberry to good old cheese and pickle! Popular main meals include Welsh rarebit, grilled plaice, cauliflower cheese or the soup and sandwich combo. Everything is very reasonably priced and comes made to preference with local produce ensuring satisfaction across all boards.

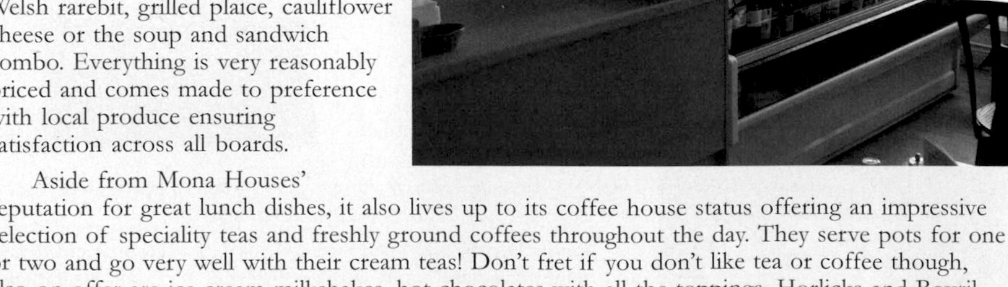

Aside from Mona Houses' reputation for great lunch dishes, it also lives up to its coffee house status offering an impressive selection of speciality teas and freshly ground coffees throughout the day. They serve pots for one or two and go very well with their cream teas! Don't fret if you don't like tea or coffee though, also on offer are ice cream milkshakes, hot chocolates with all the toppings, Horlicks and Bovril, along with a selection of other soft or alcoholic chilled drinks.

All major cards accepted, disabled toilet.

56 BAR2TWO

5 Victoria Terrace, Holyhead,
Isle of Anglesey LL65 1UT
Tel: 01407 762971
e-mail: bar2two@btconnect.com
website: www.bar2two.com

Oozing with class and with facilities and hospitality second to none **Bar2two** is a great place to visit. Offering the very best cuisine, and a selection of well kept ales, a warm welcome is given to customers all year round. Allan and Sarah have owned the bar for three years and Allan has more than 30 years experience in the trade. Formerly the Eagle and Child the new business is a real success and has a growing reputation in the area.

The restaurant, located upstairs, seats 28 diners and all of the dishes are cooked fresh to order, using local produce. There is a wide selection on all of the menus and starters include chef's homemade soup and Bar2two house pate. Steak and ale pie, sirloin steak, Holyhead lamb and lasagne are just some of the dishes on the main menu and vegetarian dishes change daily. There is also a fantastic selection of mouth-watering salads. The desserts are extremely tempting and homemade bakewell tart, caramel meringue glace and apple pie and custard are among the choices for sweet-toothed customers. Open all day every day, food is available from 12-5pm daily and the restaurant is open from 5pm close.

Bar2two is a fine establishment, boasting excellent facilities. Located in the largest town on the island of Anglesey – the busy ferry port of Holyhead – Bar2two provides the perfect place for visitors to the area to dine out. There are plenty of attractions nearby, including fishing and golf; and there are many beaches and walks to enjoy. The premise is tastefully decorated throughout with modern décor and furnishings.

The dining area is absolutely stunning. It is spacious and with a red and black theme it has a warm and friendly atmosphere. Children are welcome and are well catered for with a special 'Kid's Corner' menu, with fish fingers, chips and beans as well as pasta and meatballs on offer. A carvery can be enjoyed on a Sunday between 12-6pm and during peak periods bookings need to be made. There is a wide variety of drinks on offer with Carling and John Smiths Smooth being popular choices.

On a Friday, Saturday and Sunday customers get the chance to provide the entertainment with karaoke and the bar has a late licence until 2am. Allan and Sarah cater for all types of private functions and outside catering is available. Disabled access is not a problem. All major credit cards are taken.

57 SOUTH STACK KITCHEN

South Stack, Holyhead,
Isle of Anglesey LL65 1YH
Tel: 01407 762 181

Located on a cliff top, with spectacular views of the coastline, the famous **South Stack Kitchen** is a place all visitors to this scenic island go. It is a stones throw away from the steps that lead down to the historic South Stack Lighthouse. Owner David Edwards has been running this quality establishment since July 1985. A lot of the produce is sourced locally and favourites include homemade soups, scones, quiches and the quality breakfasts on offer. Seating 90 inside and many more outside, during its seasonal opening from Easter to mid-October the South Stack Kitchen is open from 9.30am-5.30pm. Cash only.

59 THE LIVERPOOL ARMS

Machine Street, Almwich Port,
Isle of Anglesey LL68 9HA
Tel: 01407 839396

The historic **Liverpool Arms** stand in Almwich port, just a short drive or walk from the main A5025 Anglesey coast road. The premises dates back to 1860 and is run by Welsh speaking Antony and Mary Williams for over two years now, they attract both locals (and their dogs) and visitors alike who mix freely whilst enjoying their fine brand of Welsh hospitality.

Open all day every day they stock a fine selection of keg draught ales. Drinks can be enjoyed within the atmospheric bar area or in the spacious beer garden at the rear. Guests have the option of sampling Antony and Mary's generous cooking between 12-8pm daily. They serve a small selection of starters, children's dishes, bar snacks, and mains. Dishes include cream cheese and broccoli bake, Welsh black beef pie and chilli con carne. The real attraction here though is the pairs' meal deal where they serve large portioned chips and peas with either scampi, cod, sausages, roast chicken or a burger for just £2.99 – amazingly the price is low but the quality isn't and it keeps the Liverpool Arms busy most nights!

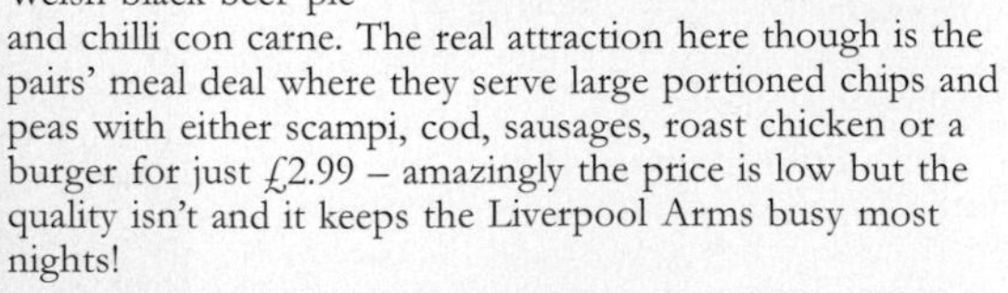

There are also 4 upstairs guest rooms that come on a room only or B&B rate, available all year round. Each room is well furnished and traditionally decorated, chose from a double or single room.

58 THE LOBSTER POT

Church Bay, Isle of Anglesey LL65 4EU
Tel: 01407 730241 / 730398
e-mail: mail@lobster-pot.net
website: www.lobster-pot.net

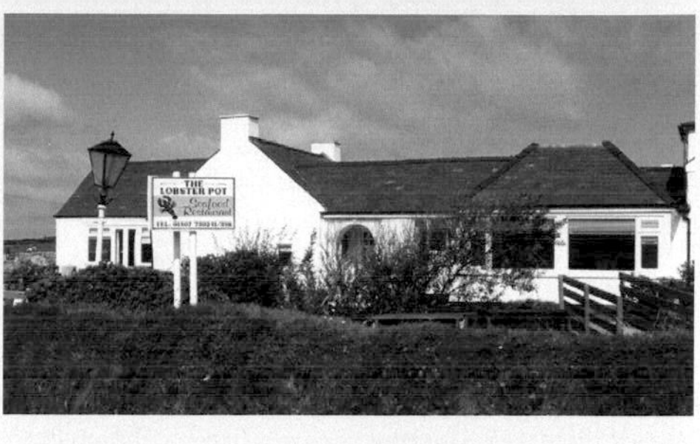

Situated in one of the most beautiful locations on this holiday paradise **The Lobster Pot** is a renowned seafood restaurant offering the very best in seafood cuisine. The menu is composed almost entirely of seafood and specialties include lobster. The fish is locally caught and fresh daily adding to the quality of the place, which is one of the finest places to dine on the Isle of Anglesey. The lobster dishes are to be highly recommended with options including the lobster pot paella, grilled lobster and the lobster pot surf and turf. Fisherman's pie and grilled king scallops are just some of the many more delights on offer.

The Lobster Pot has been personally run by Steffan and Wendy Coupe for the past five years. They have plenty of experience between then having both started life here in the kitchen more than 15 years ago. Located in the picturesque Church Bay, the candlelit restaurant has spectacular views overlooking the sea. It recently had an extension built and the interior and exterior are magnificent. Inside, the oak-beamed restaurant seats 90 diners and on brighter days meals can be enjoyed in the restaurant's own garden, which has its own stream running through it.

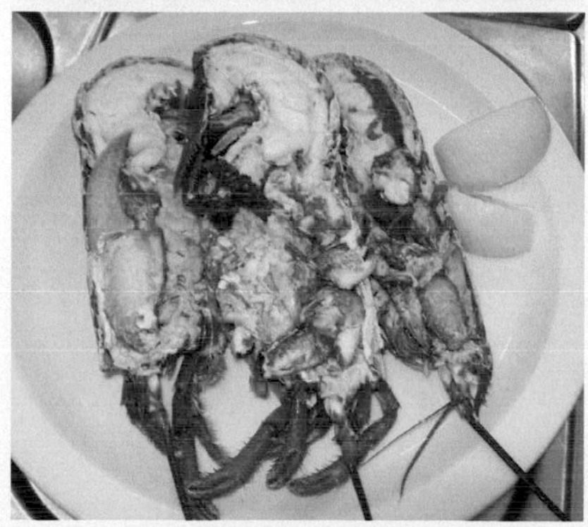

The emphasis is very much on local produce and a friendly, informal family atmosphere. The oysters and mussels served are from the Menai Straits and scallops and prawns are delivered almost daily from a local supplier. Winkles are picked at low tide from the bay and are freshly boiled and served in the bar as a complimentary appetiser. If fish doesn't take your fancy there is a good selection of quality beef steaks, lamb, chicken and pork all supplied from an award winning local butchers. During the summer the restaurant is open Tuesday-Saturday 12-1.30pm and 6pm onwards. In the winter it is open Thursday-Saturday from 6pm onwards. On a Sunday diners have a choice of roast dinners with a variety of succulent local meats on offer. There are also seafood choices. Sunday lunch is served between 12-2pm. The restaurant is also open every Bank Holiday Sunday and Monday. Such is the popularity of this delightful seafood restaurant booking is advisable.

Private parties can be catered for and there is self-catering accommodation available. The Lobster Pot Cottage sleeps four and The Anchorage sleeps eight. To find it follow the signs off the main A5025. All credit cards taken, except Diners.

60 MINFFORDD SELF CATERING AND CARAVAN PARK

Minffordd, Dulas,
Isle of Anglesey LL70 9HU
Tel: 01248 410678
Fax: 01248 410378
e-mail: enq@minffordd-holidays.com
website: www.minffordd-holidays.com

Minffordd has been owned by the Hughes-Roberts family for many years, the campsite opening 54 years ago and the self catering has been running since 1985. They have won many awards for their hospitality, providing luxury self catering holidays in their 4 and 5 star cottages all year round and caravans on a small 5 star garden park March - October.

Situated on the North East coast of Anglesey just two miles from the picturesque village of Moeflfre, the caravan park is a small but beautifully kept affair with 10 quality caravans complete with garden furniture to entertain an al fresco lifestyle in the summer months. There are a range of caravans to choose from in style and price but all come with a fully fitted kitchen, gas fires, hot water, heating and TV/DVD player so every need is catered for. There is a small and safe play area for small children and a larger paddock for those family ball games.

The self catering cottages also come fully equipped with the above and more to enable guests to fully relax and unwind in these charming properties which are completely separate from the caravan site. Each property is spacious and stylishly decorated to create that home from home feeling. Guests can chose from larger houses sleeping up to 9 people complete with conservatories and decking or smaller luxury affairs for 4 people.

61 DRWS Y COED

Llannerch-y-Medd, Anglesey, LL71 8AD
Tel: 01248 470473
e-mail: drwsycoed2@hotmail.com
website: www.smoothhound.co.uk/hotels/drwsycoed.html

Welcome to **Drws y Coed**, a wonderful retreat situated off the beaten track in the heartland of Anglesey. A perfect place to enjoy peace, tranquility and wonderful panoramic views of the countryside and Snowdonia mountain range.

The farmhouse is nestled within a large working beef, sheep and arable farm and the interesting traditional farm buildings are grade II listed. Lovely walks where wildlife can be seen. The quality farmhouse has a four star rating by Visit Wales and Welsh speaking Jane Bown is a perfect host. She has been at Drws y Coed for many years and visitors return time and time again to enjoy the wonderful service and setting.

Open all year round there are four quality en-suite bedrooms. They are decorated and furnished with all facilities and attention to detail. Guests can relax in the inviting spacious lounge with antiques and log fire. A delicious farmhouse breakfast is served in the cosy dining room.

Drws y Coed is centrally situated to explore the island's coastline and attractions, 10 minutes to beaches and 25 minutes to Holyhead Port. Credit cards taken.

62 THE LION HOTEL

Tudweiliog, Pwllheli, Gwynedd LL53 8ND
Tel: 01758 770244

The lovely Lee family welcome you to their fine village inn, the true heart of this rural community and a long standing favourite for both locals and tourists alike. The Lee family have been here for over 40 years now and provide a stellar service to all who walk through the door, offering quality accommodation, food and drink all year round.

There are 4 en suite rooms available to let all with high quality facilities, tasteful décor and more than comfortable furnishings. Guests staying here can benefit from not only the area's history but the history of the building itself which has long played a part in the village's life. The rooms here simply ooze character, creating a dynamic yet cosy haven for guests who return from a day exploring the area.

Open every session and all day on Saturday and Sunday **The Lion Hotel** is a busy place most of the time, although the family don't take table bookings, preferring to work on a more casual first come first served basis. The majority of the food served here is made with locally sourced produce and is freshly prepared by the family on the premises each day. Food is available each day from 12 to 2pm and from 6-8:30pm and in the summer months is available between 12-2:30pm and 5:30-9pm each day allowing guests to take advantage of al fresco dining in the spacious beer garden on site, complete with a small play area for children. The menu here might be small but is ever changing reflecting the area's best seasonal produce and can include dishes like homemade crab and artichoke soup, Welsh rib eye steak, lamb Thai curry, vegetable enchiladas and baked haddock fillet. Diners here strongly recommend the dessert creations on offer, changing daily – the clear favourite being the classic 'toffee lumpy bumpy!'

The Lion Inn however is equally pleasant for a quiet drink with friends, priding itself on offering 3 real ales in season, one of which comes from the nearby famous Welsh Purple Moose Brewery and the others on rotation. A good selection of other soft drinks, lagers and wines is also available, not counting the fine selection of malt whiskeys on offer to warm you in the winter months.

63 BAY VIEW GUEST HOUSE

Bay View Terrace, Pwllheli,
Gwynedd LL53 5HN
Tel: 01758 613808 Mob: 07968700975
e-mail: Bayview@toucansurf.com

Situated in the heart of Pwllheli, just yards from the main railway station and within easy reach for all the local amenities – **Bay View Guest House** is an ideal base to explore this particularly charming area of Wales. This place does exactly what it says on the tin, offering beautiful views of the nearby bay and harbour whilst offering some of the best Welsh hospitality around.

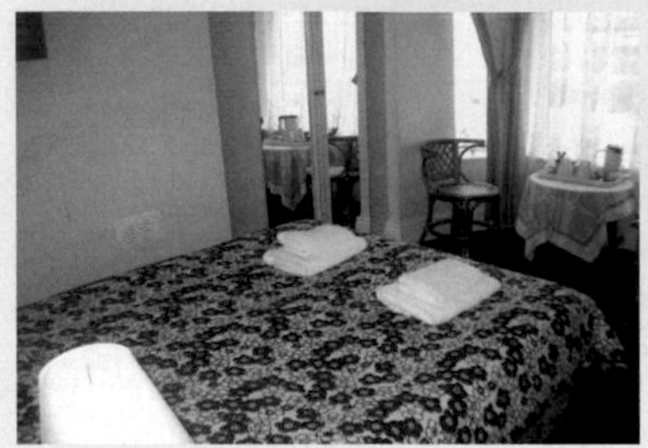

Owners Helmut and Jacky have been providing an excellent service for over five years now, building themselves quite the following with visitors to the area. Offering 6 guest rooms in varying sizes from singles to family rooms there is something for everyone. All rooms have a clean and homely quality to them and come on a fantastic value for money bed and breakfast rate. The breakfast is served from 7am-9am daily and is of a fine Welsh variety and is sure to set you up for the day with portions as generous as they are tasty.

64 PORTMEIRION VILLAGE & GARDENS

Portmeirion, Gwynedd LL48 6ET
Tel: 01766 770000 Fax: 01766 771331
website: www.portmeirion-village.com

Few places in Wales, or indeed anywhere else, are as fascinating as **Portmeirion**, the brainchild of the inspired Welsh architect, conservationist and tireless campaigner for the environment Sir Clough Williams-Ellis. On his own private peninsula on the coast of Snowdonia, he designed Portmeirion to show how a beautiful place could be developed without spoiling it. He transformed the site into a largely Italian-inspired fantasy, building some properties and rescuing others from elsewhere and rebuilding them here. Nothing is ordinary, and visitors will find a surprise at every turn - a castle, a lighthouse, a bell tower, a town hall, a triumphal arch, a tollgate, grottoes, statues and colonnades.

Clough Williams-Ellis opened the main house as a hotel, and from the start Portmeirion attracted the famous; Noël Coward wrote *Blithe Spirit* while staying here in 1941. The hotel has 14 guest rooms, and 26 more are spread among the houses and 11 in Castell Deudraeth, a superbly modernised Victorian mansion. There are restaurants and several shops, two of them selling the famous Portmeirion pottery and one selling memorabilia of the cult TV series *The Prisoner*, which was filmed here. The woodland gardens are an attraction in their own right, and beautiful gardens also surround the Clough Williams-Ellis ancestral home at nearby Plas Brondanw.

66 GLYN Y WEDDW ARMS

Abersoch Road, Llanbedrog, nr Abersoch,
Gwynedd LL53 7TH
Tel: 01758 740212 Fax: 01758 740257
e-mail: info@glynyweddw.co.uk
website: www.glynyweddw.co.uk

Located happily in the heart of the village of Llanbedrog near Abersoch is **Glyn Y Weddw Arms**. It is a fine establishment, known to both locals and visitors to the area alike for its great food, fine facilities and inviting atmosphere. The Inn has a homely country feel about it with wooden beams and stone flooring, chequered curtains and light décor – the perfect environment for a family meal or a good catch up with friends.

Martin has been here for 22 years now, starting life here as an enthusiastic manager and eventually falling in love with the place as so many others have and becoming owner 11 years ago. He prides himself on providing his customers with a quality service that is great value for money which in itself creates the buzzing atmosphere people love so much.

The bar area serves a great selection of soft, alcoholic, hot and cold beverages with a rotating choice of real ales which often includes the classic Robinsons Unicorn. Food is served from 12-9:30pm daily in season and from 12-2:30pm and 5:30-9pm Mon-Fri and 12-9pm weekends out of season. Being the main attraction here, there are several different menus to suit all tastes and appetites reflecting the great seasonal Welsh produce used here. The lunch time menu includes sandwiches, toasties, jacket potatoes, baguettes and hearty brunches, whilst the main menu includes a massive array of dishes from grills, to curries, to pasta dishes, fish, burgers, pizzas, vegetarian dishes and classic pub grub; there is even a section especially for the gravy lovers amongst us who can chose from steak and ale pie, steak and kidney pudding and a delicious welsh lamb and leek casserole. Other favourite dishes include the chicken Korma, the Sicilian pizza and the sirloin. Children can chose from their own menu which includes Bolognese, salad, pizza, burgers and fish cakes, and on Thursday nights and all day Sunday the whole family wins when an impressive carvery is put on! Saturday nights are special here too though as its special mixed grill hot buffet night where guests can take a look at the best meats around or sample from the home cooked specials board which changes daily. A truly great family affair, this place is not to be missed in your welsh holiday this year.

67 GWESTY TY NEWYDD

Aberdaron, Pwllheli, Gwynedd LL53 8BE
Tel: 01758 760207
website: www.gwestytynewydd.co.uk

Gwesty Ty Newydd is a family run hotel. It is situated in an unique position on the sea shore of Aberdaron on the Lleyn Peninsula. Gwesty Ty Newydd has been fully refurbished to a very high standard. All the guest bedrooms are en-suite, plus all the first floor sea facing bedrooms have Balconettes, with breathtaking views of the bay.

The décor is contemporary in style with solid pine furniture. All the rooms have Flat screen remote colour TV, tea & coffee making facilities, hairdryer and free internet connection.

Disabled guests are welcome at Gwesty Ty Newydd, where 2 bedrooms have been specially adapted for wheelchair use in accordance with National Accessible Scheme Category 2 guidelines. There is easy access to the hotel and once inside there is level access to reception, the bar and the dining room and a lift to the bedrooms.

Aberdaron is the last stop on the pilgrims' route to Ynys Enlli (Bardsey Island), which is said to be the resting place of 20,000 saints! Visit Aberdaron and enjoy faboulous coastal walks, fishing trips, sightseeing, boat trips and fun for all the family on the beach. End your day with some tasty homemade food served in our dining area overlooking the sea. Come and visit us for a truly relaxing break!

68 THE PEAK RESTAURANT

84-86 High Street, Llanberis, Gwynedd, North Wales LL55 4SU
Tel: 01286 872777
website: www.peakrestaurant.co.uk

Situated in the heart of glorious Snowdonia National Park is one of Wales' best kept secrets; **The Peak Restaurant**. Found in the popular village of Llanberis, this restaurant is host to Chef Angela Dwyer who has a fine reputation for inspirational cooking; having working as head chef in many coveted restaurants across the globe including LA's Chez Panisse, London's 192 and the Groucho Club. With over 30 years of experience her menus draw in the crowds like magnets making booking essential.

The menu itself changes monthly with dishes such as signature Peak Bouiibaise, Welsh local Rib Eye Steak and Sauteed fillet or Salmon and Seabass with potato cake and lemon butter often gracing the tables. A fantastic range of vegetarian and gluten free dishes are also available alongside a gluttonous selection of homemade puddings that includes chocolate pot with fresh cream, baked lemon cheesecake with raspberry compot, and warm poached winter fruit with vanilla ice cream. Guests describe the food as 'gourmet food in portions that fill you up without pretention from a renowned chef' – who could ask for more?

Open from 7pm each evening, earlier in the summer months and closed on Mondays and Tuesdays in the winter months. Children welcome, all major credit cards accepted.

69 THE GWYDYR HOTEL

Betws-y-coed, North Wales, LL24 0AB
Tel: 01690 710777
e-mail: gwydyrhotel@btconnect.com
website: www.gwydyrhotel.co.uk

Nestled in Betws-y-coed, the principal village of the spectacular Snodonia national park and the most popular inland holiday resort in Northern Wales, is the beautiful **Gwydyr Hotel**. Run by experienced hoteliers' and brothers David & Owen for some years now, this hotel is full of character and is a popular holidaying destination, particularly with fishermen. The scenic Gwydyr Hotel fishery, which has been renowned for over 150 years for its fine salmon and sea trout fishing, offers over tranquil12 miles of fishing on spate rivers – namely the Conwy and Lledr. The best time to catch both of these beautiful fish starts in May, and runs throughout the summer months – there is potential to catch one up to 20lb in high season! Fly fishing is the encouraged however spinning, worm and shrimp may be used in suitable conditions, other tips and regulations are available from the hotel, as well as fly fishing tuition for those beginning or just brushing up on their technique. And there is peace of mind knowing on your return you are guaranteed a warm welcome, good food, fine ale and wines to complete your enjoyment, (or drown your sorrows!).

The hotel itself provides light and spacious accommodation, all of which come with en-suite (with bath and shower), telephone, television, radio and hot beverage facilities.

The beautifully tasteful decor and furnishing runs throughout the hotel, all the way to the large, comfortable Victorian style drawing room, which is a well-liked area for guests to relax or play games after a day exploring the all the area has to offer. There is also the smaller and more intimate sitting room, with comfy sofas and fireplace in the colder months.

There are a variety of tariffs available – from just bed & breakfast, to bed, breakfast and a delicious evening meal. There are some shockingly reasonable prices for two or three day mini-breaks to this fine-looking hotel, as well as specific fishing breaks.

Delectable home-cooked breakfast, luncheon and dinner can be enjoyed either from the spacious dining area, or there is also an informal bar menu available from the bistro daily between 12noon and 9pm. Also, indications of the relaxed pace of life here, the perfect treat after an active day is the cream teas which are also served daily.

70 PLAS DERWEN

Holyhead Road, Betws-y-Coed,
Gwynedd LL24 0AY
Tel: 01690 710388
e-mail:
davehalewood@mobileemail.vodaphone.net
website: www.plasderwen.com

With a great restaurant and six beautifully decorated rooms, of the highest standard, **The Plas Derwen** is the ideal place for visitors to stay. Located in the heart of the popular town of Betws-y-Coed, which attracts visitors from across the world it is one of North Wales' most popular inland resorts.

The Plas Derwen, which is a café and restaurant, is extremely popular during the day and evening. There is a wide selection of freshly cooked dishes to choose from and there are always one or two Welsh specials to enjoy. Visitors come on a B&B basis enjoy a full cooked breakfast that includes a fresh fruit platter and cereal, served each day between 8.30 and 9.30am and can be enjoyed relaxing in the breakfast room located on the ground floor overlooking the river Llugwy. The finest Welsh produce is used in all of the dishes and there is a coffee shop menu, extensive a la carte menu as well as a specials board. Welsh lamb casserole topped with herbed cheesy scone is among the delicacies on offer, as well as ham and leek pie topped with Caerphilly mash. The cosy restaurant is open daily from mid day until 8.30pm weekdays and 9.00pm weekends, during the summer months. And winter 12.00 until 6pm weekdays and 12.00 until 8.30pm weekends. During the day there is a wide selection of sandwiches, jacket potatoes, ploughman platters and salads to choose from. Afternoon Welsh cream teas are also served alongside a wide range of homemade cakes.

The Plas Derwen is personally run by David and Pam Halewood. Individually and tastefully decorated throughout the bedrooms and dining area are extremely elegant and modern. There are three double en suite bedrooms on the first floor and two standard rooms on the second floor. A family room is located on the top floor with a double bed and a single day bed. All of the rooms are extremely comfortable ensuring a great nights sleep after exploring the local museums and general area, which offers mountain bike hire as well as numerous activities at a number of outdoor centres.

Situated in a spectacular valley in the Snowdonia Forest Park there are some stunning views to be enjoyed, whether it be mountains or dense woodland. There are also plenty of walks to be enjoyed and a visit to the world famous Swallow Falls is highly recommended. The Plas Derwen is closed during December and January. Cash and cheque only.

71 THE WHITE HORSE INN

Capel Garmon, Llanrwst,
Conwy LL26 0RW
Tel: 01690 710271
e-mail: ralton@btconnect.com
website:
www.whitehorseinnsnowdonia.co.uk

A friendly and hardworking team welcome you to **The White Horse Inn**, located centrally in the pleasant village of LLanrwst in the heart of Snowdonia. Mother and daughter team Margaret and Karen keep this 18th century inn busy every night with their fine hospitality and dedication to serving the best dishes in town.

The traditional interior with original oak beams and stone walling exudes character making it a truly lovely spot to stay the night or dine with family whilst exploring the beauty of the surrounding national park. Open daily from 6-11pm, the cosy bar serves two real ales, the reverend James and a guest rotating ale from a local brewery. On Sundays a generous Sunday lunch is served up cooked with as much local produce as possible for an authentic taste. Other traditional dishes grace the well tested menu, making it necessary to book on weekends.

© Copyright Phil Champion
licensed for reuse under the Creative Commons Licence.

There are 5 country cottage styled en suite bedrooms to choose from on a bed and breakfast rate with plenty of space and large windows overlooking the village. Just a short drive from the popular Behws-y-Coed and other local attractions the White Horse is ideally situated, adding further charm to its rural location.

72 PLAS HALL MANOR

Pont-Y-Pant, Dolwyddellan,
Conwy LL25 0PJ
Tel: 01690 750206
e-mail: plashallhotel@aol.com
website: www.plashall.co.uk

A perfect country escape, the **Plas Hall Manor** is an impressive establishment in a delightful location. Set in four acres of grounds, alongside the River Lledyr, it boasts 13 en-suite bedrooms, a self contained holiday flat, bar, lounge and restaurant. Originally built in 1829 by a local mine owner it was converted to a hotel in the early 1980s. Owner John Ross has totally transformed the place since he bought it, boarded up, in 2002 - giving it a fantastic new lease of life.

Situated just off the A470, three miles south of the popular inland resort of Betws-y-Coed, which lies in a splendid valley in the Snowdonia Forest Park, the child-friendly manor is the ideal get-away. The majority of the rooms have great views overlooking the valley and river and some have balconies looking out over the stunning grounds. Popular among those who like fishing, guests can take advantage of the hotel's fishing rights on the River Lledyr where salmon and trout can be caught in season. There are also many beautiful lakes, mountains and famous walks to enjoy in the area.

Plas Hall Manor is open every day from 8am until midnight and can be booked for parties, weddings and any other tailored event. Children and dogs are welcome.

73 QUEENS HOTEL

High Street, Blaenau Ffestiniog,
Gwynedd LL41 3ES
Tel: 01766 830055 Fax: 01766 830046
e-mail: queens_hotel@hotmail.co.uk

The impressive **Queens Hotel** stands in the historic town of Blaenau Ffestiniog, now restored to its once former glory by its hard working leaseholders who took over in August 2008. The Queens Hotel was previously known for its great facilities and casual atmosphere, yet fell into disrepair for a sad few years. After much TLC and dedication the Queens Hotel now stands better than before, newly redecorated and refurbished and ever popular with all those who cross its threshold.

Open all year round as a pub and restaurant, there are also 12 fine en suite rooms to choose from. There are a variety of different sized rooms, from singles right the way to family sized. Guests can stay on a B&B or a B&B and dinner rate which comes highly recommended, as both the breakfast and dinner portions here are both generous and tasty. The pub offers food all day long from 11am until close with a great selection of light bites and main meals all for excellent value. The chef is heralded by locals as being a truly fantastic cook and is responsible for the creation of most dishes here. You choose off the printed menu, but if you fancy something not on the menu and Debra has the stock she'll do her best and cook up whatever you fancy! A fine selection of soft and alcoholic drinks is also available throughout the day to be enjoyed in the lofty ceilinged bar area along with two rotating real ales. Overnight guests have the benefit of having drinks available to them 24 hours a day, perfect for that night-cap.

Apart from the welcoming atmosphere and fine hospitality offered by the team here, the Queens Hotel makes an ideal spot to stay for other reasons, located nearby to the beautiful Snowdonia National Park and mountain railway it's perfect for railway enthusiasts or ramblers. Close by there are also numerous lakes to entertain anglers of all abilities and the owners have recently opened a fishing tackle shop at the rear for the convenience of their guests and day visitors alike.

74 THE CASTLE RESTAURANT AND ARMOURY BAR

Castle Square, Harlech,
Gwynedd LL46 2YH
Tel: 01766 780416

The warm and historic **Castle Restaurant and Armoury Bar** sits right across from the beautifully ancient Harlech Castle, one of Wales' best known castles and indeed area for tourists who enjoy enveloping themselves in Harlech's history whilst rambling around both the town and castles ramparts which look across the rolling Welsh countryside.

New owners Kath and Wayne Sampson have only just taken over this atmospheric establishment but are set to succeed and bring a taste of the exotic to this traditional restaurant, having previously had plentiful experience running a popular restaurant in the Caribbean. The pair's lively and light hearted attitude combines with their restaurants classic Welsh feel to create a vibrant and interesting atmosphere in which to enjoy a fine meal with family friends or partners.

The restaurant & bar will be open every day in season, serving light lunches and evening meals - the majority of which are created with Welsh local produce. Lunchtime menu's will have a more traditional taste, whilst evening meals are contemporary Caribbean cuisine; the upstairs cocktail bar serves light bites, cocktails, wines, beers and main line drinks.

75 THE LION HOTEL

Pen Dref, Harlech, Gwynedd LL46 2SG
Tel: 01766 780731
e-mail: lionhotel@unicombox.com

Local couple Rhian and Ieu and their family took over **The Lion Hotel** in May this year and have made a fantastic start to running the place. Restored to its former glory as the hub of its community, the Lion now draws in customers both local and holiday makers to enjoy the particularly fine brand of Welsh hospitality served up here.

Open all day every day, the Lion is a popular pub serving a range of well kept ales including Spitfire, Tiger and Flowers IPA. The bar area is cosy and filled with character, retaining original interior stone walling and large sash windows amongst warm colours and traditional furniture. It makes a lovely spot to enjoy a game of darts or cards with friends or family or even a few light games of pool. Great pub grub is served here too by Chef Katy and Rhian from 12-2:30pm and 6-9pm Mon-Fri and from 12-9pm on weekends, when Giant Yorkshire puddings filled with beef, lamb or sausages with veg, mash and gravy are also served. Dishes include 8oz Welsh black beefburger, a full rack of ribs, welsh black beef curry, salmon in white wine sauce and steak and kidney pie.

There are also five upstairs en suite rooms to chose from all year round. Children and dogs welcome.

76 CEMLYN TEA SHOP

High Street, Harlech, Gwynedd LL46 2YA
Tel: 01766 780425
e-mail: tea@cemlyntea.co.uk
websites: www.cemlyntea.co.uk or
www.cemlynrestaurant.co.uk

Cemlyn Tea Shop is located centrally on the main high street in Harlech and the perfect spot to stop for your afternoon tea or light lunch whilst enjoying an afternoon in this pleasant and historical town. Owned and run by Geoff and Jan Cole for many years now, Cemlyn is a place with heart and vision. It's owners pride themselves on not only providing high quality, honest welsh food and drink for their clients but also on doing their bit for the planet too by supporting their local farmers and suppliers and organisations that base their products on sustainability such as the Rain Forest Alliance. This friendly couple endeavour to ensure that you and your stomach enjoy your visit by offering one of the warmest welcomes to their light and fresh tea shop.

Although Cemlyn goes much further than being just a tea shop it certainly does its name justice by providing twenty-eight varieties of tea, all of which come 'loose leafed' with a choice of lemon, milk or soya milk. They serve the usual choice of traditional and well known teas as well as a range of in-house mixes and more exotic flavours including kiwi and strawberry, South African Rooibos and Gunpowder Temple of Heaven. There is an equally good range of coffees to hand along with other soft and alcoholic drinks most of which are sourced from within Wales.

On offer to eat is an impressive selection of traditional and special cakes freshly made on the premises. There is also a special chocolate selection including chewy chocolate brownies, rich chocolate cake and chocolate chip and walnut cookies – irresistible!

Served from noon until 4pm is a great range of sandwiches made with homemade bread, including red salmon and cucumber, mature welsh cheese and smoked chicken and brie, baked potatoes and homemade special recipe soup, not forgetting the real deal Welsh rarebit. The secret to the good taste here being knowing where the produce comes from – Geoff and Jan can tell you where each and every ingredient originated from the chicken right down to the buttermilk. This place is a must stop for good honest food and a lesson on how to be green the right way – with food and drink this good you'll never want to eat food sourced outside Wales again.

77 THE VICTORIA INN

LLanbedr, Gwynedd LL45 2LD
Tel: 01341 241213
Fax: 01341 241644
e-mail: junevicinn@aol.com
website: www.victoriainnllanbedr.co.uk

The Victoria Inn is found in the charming village of Llanbedr, adjacent to the A496 coastal road, just a few minutes drive from the historic Harlech. The building itself holds much history as remains today the heart of LLanbedr as it did many, many years ago; providing good quality food and drink for the locals and weary travellers of years gone by. The inn is currently run by Gemma Barry whose parents previously ran the inn for over 20 years. Very much a family affair, mum June still pitches in to help Gemma along with a hard working team of staff including Gemma's right hand Jean. The team endeavour to provide high quality in this lovely inn offering top standards at reasonable prices throughout the year.

Open all day every day, the inviting bar area offers three real ales straight from the popular Robinson's Brewery Range amongst a good range of other soft and alcoholic beverages. Guests also have the option of dining here and choosing off the large bar menu which comprises a good range of light bites and snacks, starters, mains and grills, available from 12-9pm every day. Popular main dishes include homemade steak pie, lamb henry and the Vic filler burger topped with bacon and cheese. Guests can also chose of the ever changing specials board displaying dishes such as pork escalope and stilton, piri piri chicken and a fish platter, or sample the Victoria's popular Sunday lunch when it is advised to book to avoid disappointment. Most of the food here is made using fresh local produce where possible, but much of the food served on your plate comes from the Victoria's very own market garden.

Gemma and her team also offer high class quality accommodation throughout the year, ranging from single rooms to standard to grander 'superior rooms.' All rooms are en suite, with only one of the rooms being shower only – the others having both bath and shower facilities. The tariff includes a hearty breakfast served daily from 8:30-11am so if you want a bit of a lie in you don't have to worry about missing breakfast for it!

The Victoria Inn really is an ideal base for exploring Snowdonia's beautiful countryside and the surrounding towns at leisure with mountains, lakes and beaches all within your reach.

78 BRYN MELYN GUEST HOUSE

Panorama Road, Barmouth,
Gwynedd LL42 1DQ
Tel: 01341 280556
e-mail: info@brynmelyn.co.uk
website; www.brynmelyn.co.uk

Located high up on the cliff side, looking down over Barmouth Bay, **Bryn Melyn Guest House** has eight superb en-suite guest rooms. The rooms (six doubles and two twins) are all situated upstairs and are spacious and tastefully decorated, with several boasting some of the finest views in the area. Bryn Melyn Guest House is just a ten minute walk from the scenic harbour of Barmouth. The classic Welsh seaside town is popular among visitors and there are some great walks and cycles to be had as well as other outdoor activities.

Set on a south facing hillside the guest house provides an ideal get-away, with stunning views overlooking the Mawddach Estuary, the Cadair Range and Cardigan Bay. There is a fantastic panoramic outdoor terrace for guests to make the most of on brighter days and also a comfortable lounge bar for guests to relax in after a busy day exploring the area. (The premises are licensed for residents). The tariff includes a hearty breakfast, which is available from 8am-9am and those guests wanting it earlier can, on request. Evening meals are also available by arrangement between 6pm and 8pm. All major credit cards taken. Free wi-fi access. Off road parking.

79 CRYSTAL HOUSE HOTEL

19 Marine Parade, Barmouth,
Gwynedd LL42 1NA
Tel: 01341 280603
e-mail: info@crystalhouse-barmouth.co.uk
website: www.crystalhouse-barmouth.co.uk

Crystal House Hotel is a beautiful and impressive Victorian building that overlooks the scenic beach at the popular seaside town of Barmouth. This lovely B&B has been owned and run by Stephen and Katie since December 2008 and has already received rave reviews from its guests. There are nine spacious and comfortable rooms available, six of which are en suite and all able to accommodate families. Stephen and Katie themselves have a young family, adding to the homely feel and relaxed atmosphere of the place. A generous breakfast is included in the tariff, cooked by Stephen's well experienced hand and is guaranteed to last all day. Out of season there may be special offers so please ring for details.

80 GOODIES

33 High Street, Barmouth LL42 1DW
Tel: 01341 281162
e-mail: kimcartledge@hotmail.co.uk

Goodies is located on Barmouth's main high street and is popular amongst locals who recommend it for its homemade food and friendly service. Goodies is owned and run by Kim Cartledge and has been since 1986 when she originally opened it as a deli. Today it stands a successful cafe with a cosy and traditional decor inside and tables to people watch from outside.

Kim's hard working team of staff Denise, Eira and Lynn serve up a range of teas, coffees and soft drinks alongside a wealth of homemade cakes, pies, scones and main dishes, most of which are on display as you enter the cafe. Each dish is freshly prepared each day using the best local produce around. Open seven days a week from May to October, and closed on Sundays in the other months, Goodies welcomes families and children also; making it an ideal spot to take an afternoon break from a day's shopping in Barmouth's centre. Cash and cheque only please.

81 THE ANCHOR RESTAURANT & KNICKERBOCKERS ICE CREAM PARLOUR

The Quay, Barmouth,
Gwynedd LL42 1ET
Tel: 01341 281126 Fax: 01341 281444
e-mail: davinalynch@aol.com
website:
www.pembrokehousebarmouth.co.uk

The splendid **Anchor Restaurant** runs hand in hand with **Knickerbockers Ice Cream Parlour** in the popular seaside town of Barmouth. Located ideally for day visitors and tourists, both are set on the lively quay on Barmouth's sea front, surrounded by many charming shops in which to browse. Both are run and owned by Davina and Warren Lynch, who provide great traditional food, drink and delicious ice cream for the locals and holiday makers of Barmouth year in year out.

The Anchor is a traditional restaurant with modern styling, serving a handsome array of freshly cooked food. Perfect for families and couples visiting the area there is outdoor seating from which the view can be appreciated. Open from 9am-9pm daily in summer and 9am-6pm in winter, each day from noon it serves up a large menu comprising many meat, fish, pasta, steak and starter dishes. Favourite dishes include lamb shank; special paella with fish, ham, chicken, chorizo and prawns; fish pie, the Anchor's famous freshly battered cod, chunky chips & mushy peas, Welsh black steaks, combos and seafood dishes.

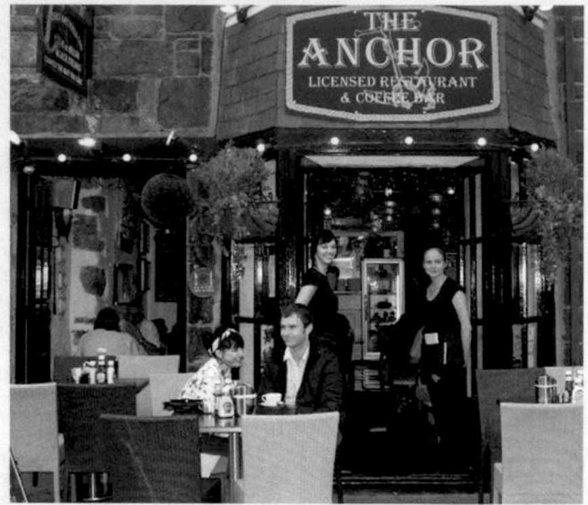

Although the Anchor serves up some tasty desserts to finish off your meal, next doors Knickerbocker Ice Cream Parlour really takes the crown when it comes to catering for a sweet tooth. Again with outdoor and indoor seating, guests can enjoy staggering range of 50 traditional and specialty flavours of ice cream along with other classic desserts such as banana splits, knickerbocker mess and of course the classic knickerbocker glory. Open from 9am-9pm in summer and 9am-6pm in winter.

On top of this Davina and Warren also rent out two luxury self catering apartments with top notch high quality facilities and stylish décor for the convenience and comfort that makes the perfect seaside holiday. But of course if you're feeling lazy you can simple pop to the quay for what you can guarantee will be a fantastic slap up meal.

82 HEN SIOP FRONGOCH

Frongoch, Bala, Gwynedd, LL23 7NT
Tel: 01678 520285
e-mail: merfyn@hensiopfg.plus.com

Hen Siop Frongoch, located in the pretty village of Frongoch, north of Bala where the A4212 meets the B4501, is the epitome of fine Welsh cooking and that famous Welsh hospitality. As popular with locals as it is with visitors - and both English and Welsh speaking - it is hard to believe only a few years previously this fine dining establishment had been the village shop and post office! Following a conversion and refurbishment, it has become a delightful light restaurant, with beautiful views of the hills and the smell of fine home-cooked food wafting out into the village – making this a popular spot all year round.

The menu is all home-cooked and made from locally sourced produce, so everything is always fresh and seasonal. The hearty breakfasts are very popular with customers, as are the tender Welsh lamb shank with mint gravy, home-made pie and chips, and the pan fried fresh salmon fillet with tarragon sauce. There are also a lovely variety of home-made own chutneys, jams, pies and cakes (as I'm sure everyone wants to take a little of Hen Siop Frongoch home with them!) and they make and deliver 'meals on wheels' to the local community.

82 HEN SIOP FRONGOCH

Frongoch, Bala, Gwynedd, LL23 7NT
Tel: 01678 520285
e-mail: merfyn@hensiopfg.plus.com

Mae **Hen Siop Frongoch**,a leolir ym mhentref tlws Frongoch,i'r gogledd o Bala lle mae'r A4212 yn cyfarfod a'r B4501, yn ymgorfforiad o goginio Cymreig graenus a'r Croeso Cymreig enwog. Mor boblogaidd gyda'r ardalwyr a'r ymwelwyr-yn siaradwyr Cymraeg a Sasneg- mae'n anodd credu mai siop leol a swyddfa bost oedd y sefydliad ciniawa ardderchog hwn ychydig flynyddoedd yn ol.Yn dilyn trawsnewid ac adnewyddu mae nawr yn fwyty golau a dymunol gyda golygfeydd hardd o'r bryniau a chwa o arogl bwyd cartref gwych yn ymledu allan i'r pentref gan wneud hwn yn leoliad poblogaidd trwy'r flwyddyn.

Mae'r fwydlen yn fwyd cartref ac yn defnyddio cynyrch lleol lle bo modd gan sicrhau fod popeth o hyd yn ffres a thymhorol.Mae'r brecwast sylweddol yn boblogaidd iawn gyda'r cwsmeriaid fel mae'r coes las cig oen Cymru gyda grefi mintys, pastai cartref gyda sglodion cartref a'r eog wedi ffrio gyda saws taragon. Mae yma hefyd amrywaieth wych o jamiau, shwtni, peis a chacennau(gan fod pawb dwi'n siwr am fynd a darn bach o Hen Siop Frongoch adref gyda hwy!) ac maent hefyd yn cyflenwi prydau poeth i'r cartref yn y gymuned leol.

83 THE BRYNTIRION INN

Llandderfel, Bala, Gwynedd LL23 7RA
Tel: 01678 530205 Fax: 01678 530723
e-mail: thebryntirioninn@aol.com
website: www.bryntirion.co.uk

The popular **Bryntirion Inn** sits in the charming village of LLandderfel in North Wales. Known best for its excellent cuisine and facilities, the Bryntirion draws in a good crowd ranging from locals to holiday makers and couples who take advantage of the pleasant bed and breakfast attached, ideally located in a rural location within reach distance of most of the north's best attractions.

Owned and run by Martin and Linda, the Bryntirion is open all day every day; the pair pride themselves on providing a relaxing and homely environment for their offering fine cuisine and real ale all day every day. Guests can enjoy food and drink either in the oak beamed traditional bar or in the newly created modern outdoor seating area choosing from a variety of soft or alcoholic beverages including two real ales; one from the famous Purple Moose brewery and another guest rotating ale with 4-5 different ones to sample throughout the month. Fairtrade teas and coffees are also available.

Delicious food is available from 12-3pm and 6-9pm Mon-Sat and from 12-8pm on Sundays prepared by Martin's experienced hand, having spent much of his career as a head chef. Locals rave about the food served here where the menu changes regularly to reflect the best seasonal and local produce around. Always on offer though is the popular Sunday Lunch served between 12-6pm and the world famous Welsh Black beef, mushroom and ale casserole served in a Bryn bara which has found its way across the seas to Australian menus – it is something not to be missed. Other popular dishes include lambs liver and onions, and the fresh fish dishes such as four fish stew, hot smoked salmon salad and oven baked sea bass. With a tasty and varied choice there is something for everyone including the kiddies, who can choose of their own menu or have half portions from the main menu.

Martin and Linda also provide two double en suite rooms all year round on a great bed and breakfast rate with free wifi thrown in too. Guests with camper vans however are also welcome to park in the inn's own rear car park overnight.

84 UNICORN INN

Smithfield Square, Dolgellau,
Gwynedd LL40 1ES
Tel: 01341 422742

The Unicorn Inn sits in the charming Smithfield Square in the popular Welsh town of Dolgellau. This olde worlde inn offers a quiet but welcoming place to relax and dine in with beautiful period features including an open log fire and oak beams. Like any good old inn the Unicorn is filled with relics of its past showing its history if you care to look. Barry and Shirley Jones have been here for 11 years now and continue to offer a great traditional service throughout the week, open from 11am-4pm and 6pm-close Mon-Thurs and all day Fri/Sat/Sun.

On offer in the atmospheric bar are two real ales, Bass and Green King IPA along with a good selection of other soft and alcoholic drinks. In keeping with the old fashioned theme the menu is on the chalkboard serving up great home cooked pub favourites with the steak and kidney pie and the liver and onions being the local choice. Local produce is used where possible. Though homely inside there is also a small outdoor seating area for the warmer months. Cash only please.

85 THE STAG INN

Bridge Street, Dolgellau,
Gwynedd LL40 1AU
Tel: 01341 422533
e-mail: jocheckley@hotmail.co.uk
website: www.myspace.com/thestaginn

The Stag Inn is a true pub's pub, located centrally in the popular town of Dolgellau on Bridge Street. The premises was previously an old coaching Inn built before 1771, a date that is inscribed on the old wooden beam above the pub's cosy fireplace. The building now retains much of its old charm and character and is full of signs that indicate its fascinating history if you dare to ask.

Jo has been leaseholder here since April 2002 and with Geraint (the bar manager) they have built a thriving trade to the townspeople and tourists alike. They share the building with the ghost of an old landlord who appears at 2am each morning near the pubs popular poolroom and old tidemarks on the wall which show the depth of the water when the pub was previously flooded, but this does not detract from the cosy, traditional pub feel that the Stag exudes.

Open all day every day, the Stagg offers a minimum of two real ales with Banks Original being the regular brew. A good selection of wines, spirits, beers and soft drinks is also available. Food is served here daily from 12pm onwards with a menu that any traditional Welsh pub would be proud of. Dishes on offer include steak and Guinness pie, chicken and leek pie, vegetarian crispy bakes, and toasted or regular sandwiches with a wide range of fillings. The specialty here is the large filled Yorkshire pudding dish with a choice of various fine welsh meats, homemade stuffing and gravy. Locals recommend the 'basket meals' which comprise pub favourites and chips served at reasonable prices in handy baskets. It is recommended to book for parties of 6 or more. The Stag also caters for afternoon tea, serving homemade Welsh bara brith(fruit cake) with a pot of tea or coffee.

The Stag is a popular place to dine and visit with the warm welcome, good pub grub and Welsh speaking staff making a very entertaining evening – and with ferrets recently being added to the large list of pets welcome in their pet corner there really is no end to the welcome they extend your way. Cash only please.

86 ROYAL SHIP HOTEL

Queens Square, Dollgellau,
Gwynedd LL40 1AR
Tel: 01341 422209 Fax: 01341 424693
e-mail: royal.ship.hotel@btconnect.com
website: www.royalshiphotel.co.uk

The Royal Ship Hotel is a fine early 19th century coaching inn located in the heart of the old market town of Dolgellau. An impressive and historical building, the Royal Ship has been extended and modernised over the years giving it the space and style to house a fully fledged hotel with bar and restaurant behind its attractive ivy-clad façade. An ideal base for exploring north and mid Wales, the Royal Ship is in prime location in Snowdonia's National Park, just two hours away from major international airports and surrounded by countless mountains, rivers, fishing lakes and is also within just a few minutes' drive from the coast of the Irish Sea.

Run by Angela and Bernhard for the past 8 years, the hotel offers 23 well furnished bedrooms with both TV and tea and coffee making facilities, 17 of which are en suite with the other 6 rooms having their own privately allocated bathrooms. Guests can chose between single, double, twin, triple and family rooms most of which have stunning views across the Cader Idris Mountain Range, with some having quainter views across Dolgellau's Town Square. Rooms can come on a bed and breakfast rate, but for groups of more than 10 tariffs can include dinner also. Dogs welcome. Breakfast here is generous and served between 8-9:30am each day.

The atmospheric bar and restaurant areas are well worth a visit serving up vast and varied award winning menus throughout the day. Lunch is served between 12-3pm, and dinner is served between 6-9pm however a smaller menu comprising light bites and snacks is available between 3-6pm to make sure no-one goes hungry. A popular place to dine, it is recommended to book, particularly at weekends. Guests can choose from a senior citizens menu, a healthy eating children's menu, the main al la carte menu, the bar menu or the daily specials board and when the national seafood fortnight is running, guests can choose from their fresh fish menu, or on Sundays can select something tasty from the popular Sunday lunch menu. Popular dishes include venison sausage and mash, steak and ale pie, pan seared monkfish, Welsh black rump steak, grilled red snapper fillet and Mediterranean vegetable bake.

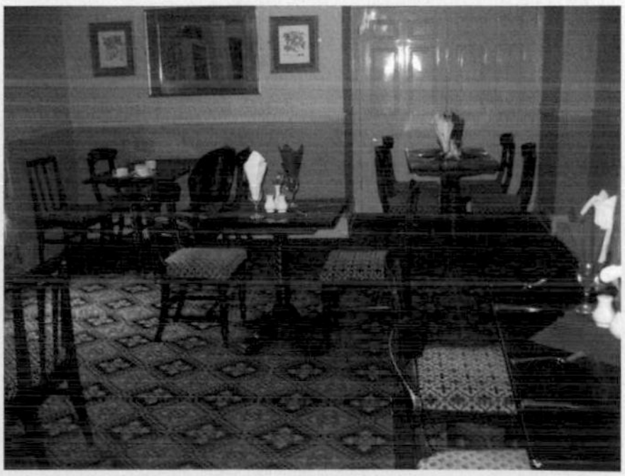

87 GWESTY GWERNAN HOTEL

Islawrdref, Dollgellau,
Gwynedd LL40 1TL
Tel: 01341 422488
e-mail: gwernanhotel@btconnect.com
website: www.gwernan.co.uk

Situated in the idyllic hamlet of Islawrdref, just a mile or so from the popular town centre of Dollgellau is **Gwesty Gwernan Hotel**. This place has an impressive reputation that is second to none and prides itself on delivering a quality experience across all aspects. Set in twenty-four acres of its own stunning grounds complete with its own twelve acre well stocked fishing lake, Gwesty Gwernan makes a fine spot for a rural break away in which the beauty and remoteness of the Welsh countryside can be truly appreciated.

Run by local family Eleri and Geraint Roberts and their chef daughter Ruth for the past two years, this place holds a classy yet inviting atmosphere for its guests as the elegant décor combines with homely finishing touches to create a true home from home feel.

There are six well furnished en suite bedrooms to choose from in variety of sizes, all with the best modern fixtures and facilities. The main attraction for these rooms though is the stunning views offered from each window, many stretching across the lake. A hearty breakfast is included in the tariff; a perfect start to a day's fishing. Guests also have the benefit of using the hotels fantastic lounge bar and restaurant which are open to non-residents also.

The handsome wood panelled lounge bar seats ten before a roaring log fire, offering an extensive wine list, fine real ales and a good selection of other beers and spirits. The 24 seater restaurant serves food from 12-3pm and 6-8:30pm each day, but in winter is only open from Thursday-Sunday. Ruth's fine home cooked menu uses as much local produce as possible and is guaranteed to please serving a good choice of starters, mains and daily specials which include sweet chilli fishcakes, Welsh black sirloin steak and aubergine and walnut bake. Due to its popularity it's advised to book in advance, particularly evenings and weekends.

Guests have adequate safe and secure parking for both bikes and cars so they are free to leave their transport at the hotel and explore the grounds and lake at their own pace.

88 BRYN ARMS

Gellilydan, Bleanau Ffestiniog,
Gwynedd LL41 4EN
Tel: 01766 590379
e-mail: brynarms@googlemail.co.uk

The Bryn Arms is situated in the idyllic hamlet of Gellilydan off the A487, just a short drive from the popular destinations of Bleanau Ffestiniog and Porthmadog. Owned and run by Bob, Ann and Sarah for the past 3 years now, this family have much experience in the trade and it shows as the Bryn Arms offers a tasty and varied menu to suit everyone's taste alongside the traditional real ales rotating throughout the year and occasional entertainment on Saturday nights.

Open all day everyday in the summer months and evenings and weekends in the winter months, the bar serves locally brewed ale from the famous Purple Moose Brewery and another rotating guest ale too, with a pool table inside and large beer garden and children's play area it's the ideal spot for families to relax with a meal or drink. The restaurant is open from 5-9pm in winter and all day in the summer serving Bob and Sarah's handiwork which includes spinach and red pepper lasagne, welsh black beef pie, surf and turf and special marinade ribs, not to mention the choice of fish dishes, kids dishes and spicy dishes available. Due to popularity of both takeaway and restaurant it's best to book to avoid disappointment.

89 Y LLEW COCH – THE RED LION

Dinas Mawddwy, Gwynedd SY20 9JA
Tel: 01650 531247
e-mail: berwynhughes@yahoo.co.uk
website: www.llewcoch.co.uk

The Red Lion is the heart of Dinas Mawddwy with a fine, traditional yet lively atmosphere where this inn's history envelopes you from the second you walk in. An impressive fire place greets you, adorned like much is the building in relics of its fascinating past. Owned and run by mother and son team Beryl and Berwyn Hughes, there is great food, real ale and accommodation available all year round.

There are six rooms to choose from, four of which are en suite and ideally located for exploring the charming local area or simply toddling off to bed after sampling the fine ale of offer below. On offer are a range of locally welsh brewed and nationally brewed ales, along with tasty food from 12-2pm and 6-9pm each day.

The food is what people really come for here, all made using local produce, prepared fresh each day. Local favourites are the variety of hearty homemade pies and the succulent Sunday lunch carvery which fills the place each weekends so it's advised to book to avoid disappointment.

90 GRAIG WEN GUESTHOUSE

Arthog, Dollgellau, Wales LL39 1BQ
Tel: 01341 250482
e-mail: hello@graigwen.co.uk
website: www.graigwen.co.uk

Sarah and John escaped their 9-5 desk jobs for 45 acres of beautiful, rugged land that nestles itself in the magnificent Snowdonia National Park. They now run **Graig Wen**, a stylish B&B with stunning views across the Mawddach Estuary. It is a refurbished Victorian slate cutting mill with slate floors, furniture custom-made with Welsh materials mixed with modern design for a refined, contemporary feel.

There are 5 en suite rooms to choose from, which feature artwork by Welsh language bands from the 60s and 70s alongside stylish modern bathrooms and decadently comfortable beds. A fantastic big breakfast is included in the tariff and is made using the best local produce.

Sarah and John also offer self catering cottages and yurts for hire, and a campsite for touring tents, caravans and motorhomes – which is a popular stop off for guests who want to enjoy the pleasant Mawddach Trail from Barmouth to Dollgelau, or simply enjoy the masses of wildlife that inhabit the area which includes woodpeckers, herons, buzzards and badgers.

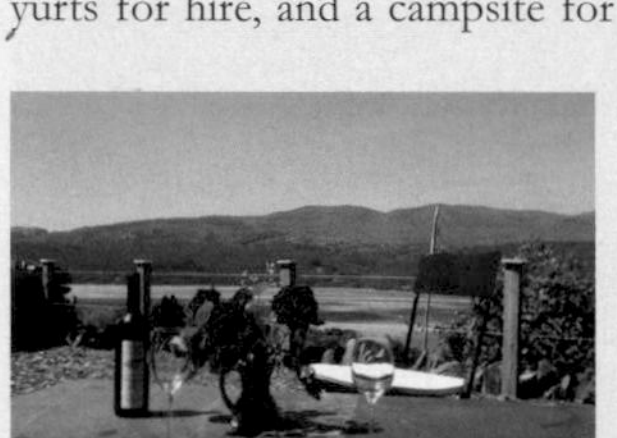

Children over 10 are welcome in the B & B, as are dogs on leads. Good disabled facilities in the B&B; ring for details. B&B open Jan-Nov, Cottages open all year apart from Nov, Yurts – April-Oct, Campsite – March-Dec. During high season guests can enjoy exciting bushcraft workshops.

91 SPRINGFIELD HOTEL

Beach Road, Fairbourne LL38 2PX
Tel: 01341 250414
e-mail: springfield.hotel@btconnect.com

Tenants Wayne and Jules offer a warm welcome to their fine family run hotel situated on the edge of Snowdonia National Park, just minutes from the mountains and seconds from the sea. Located in the unspoilt village of Fairbourne beneath the Cader Iris mountain range this hotel is ideally located with fantastic facilities for all.

Offering 14 stylish and chic guest rooms - some with en suite ranging from single to family sized rooms – **Springfield** is a great place to stay with views from each room. Guests and non-residents can enjoy the fine cuisine, drink and entertainment available downstairs in the bar or al a carte restaurant '52° West,' with views across Springfield's spacious gardens and sun terrace.

Open every session and all day from Fri-Sun, the bar serves a good range of real and local ales. Guests can chose off the bar or light lunch menu or the handsome restaurant menu which includes T-bone steaks, BBQ ribs, poached salmon and farmhouse chicken. A children's menu is also available – this place is very much family orientated with a Quiz on Mondays, karaoke on Thursdays and Sundays and live entertainment on Saturday night, what more could you ask for?

92 CARTREF GUEST HOUSE

Aberdovey, Gwynedd LL35 0NR
Tel: 01654 767273
e-mail: stay@cartref-aberdovey.co.uk
website: www.cartref-aberdovey.co.uk

Cartref Guest House is a stunning 100 year old building sat in its own well kept gardens, in prime location for exploring the thriving seaside town of Aberdovey. It is owned and run by William and Jules Moeran who have been here for over 10 years now, and they continue to provide outstanding accommodation and the warmest of welcomes to all who stay here.

The building itself was sympathetically refurbished in 2008 to combine the place's beautiful period features with the contemporary styling of the 21st century. William and Jule's aim is to provide four star quality for visitors who want comfortable and stylish interiors without the formality and expense of a top hotel – and according to the many repeat guests they attract they achieve this aim well. There are five en suite rooms to choose from all with flat screen digital TV, free wifi, complimentary refreshments, plush furnishings and a superb choice of breakfast in the mornings served between 8:30-9am each day.

93 MEDINA COFFEE HOUSE

Medical Hall Annex, Aberdovey,
Gwynedd LL35 0EB
Tel: 01654 767159

The name **Medina Coffee House** simply does not do this charming establishment justice. Serving so much more than just coffee, Medina is accessed via a small entrance on the main road in the thriving town of Aberdovey. This long narrow entrance then reveals one of Aberdovey's most popular venues for afternoon relaxing serving a surprising range of light lunches and tasty snacks.

Created and owned by Liz and Peter in July 2007, the pair have truly made a success of their first venture together. Their combined experience in the trade works well and has created a lively yet casual atmosphere for guests to enjoy the quality in both service and produce they serve day in, day out. Medina is open seven days a week from 10am-5pm in the summer and 10am-4pm in the winter. Guests can sit inside, upstairs or downstairs amid the light and homely décor or can enjoy al fresco dining in the stylish courtyard that backs onto a stunning cliff face for a wall. A real sun trap in the summer, it's easier than you would think to while away an afternoon here catching up with friends or sharing a cream tea with a loved one in front of this pleasant backdrop.

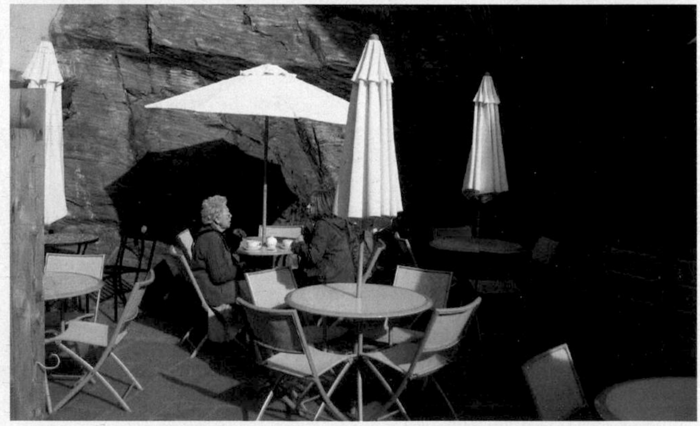

Drinks on offer include a large and flexible range of teas and coffees, including iced teas and coffees, traditional blends and chai, hot chocolates, milkshakes and other soft drinks. Food is available throughout the day, all freshly cooked by Liz. On offer are a range of breakfasts available from 10am-12pm, a large choice of filled sandwiches, Paninis and ciabattas that include the traditional fillings as well as more exotic choices such as chicken, apricots and walnuts or duck in hoi sin sauce. There are also an equally good range of jacket potatoes to choose from all served with a fresh salad, but the popular choice is Liz's small selection of tapas including humous, sundried tomatoes, chorizo, stuffed peppers, olives and ciabatta – coming in two sizes so you can chose how many lucky friends you want to share with! Regular guests here rave about the range of desserts and cakes baked here on the premises – those with a sweet tooth will not be disappointed.

With so much of offer in such a pretty location, this place should not be missed as it also comes highly recommended by local bed and breakfast owners whose guests frequent Medina. Closed on Wednesday during Winter.

94 MONTY'S CARVERY

1 Chapel Street, Aberdyfi,
Gwynedd LL35 0EL
Tel: 01654 767080
Fax: 01654 767993

A rare gem in today's fast food and international diet, **Monty's Carvery** sets itself apart as a fine example of honest Welsh cooking. Guests come from far and wide to sample the tastes of old fashioned home dishes in a friendly and inviting dining atmosphere. Located just a minute's walk from the popular town of Aberdovey/Aberdyfi's main coastal road and just a stone's throw from the seashore, Monty's makes the perfect place to stay or dine as it also has convenient guest accommodation.

Owners Paul and Clare only took over this business in May 2009 but their hard work and expertise in the kitchen has really paid off, as they have created quite a name for themselves in the real food lover's books, drawing guests like a magnet.

Open seven days a week each evening from 6pm until closing, diners are required to book at all times to avoid disappointment. Last orders are usually taken at 8:30pm to reflect the time and care it takes to prepare each dish to the finest standards. Each evening there is a carvery on offer with a choice of two succulent meats which is the main attraction – it's all in the name. However the couple also serve up a small menu of other wholesome dishes that appear on their regularly changing blackboard menu. Favourite dishes include Turkey and Gammon Pie, stew and dumplings, and liver and onions. All dishes are homemade on the premises with fresh local produce. Children can chose from the healthy menu 'Mini Monty's' also so parents can rest assured their kids will be eating good honest food along with them. A truly great place for families to dine together, Monty's is only licensed for diners.

The guest accommodation here comes in the form of a two bed-roomed flat complete with self contained kitchen, living room and bathroom all located just above the restaurant for convenience. Unusually the tariff here is not bed and breakfast but bed and dinner as guests are able to choose an evening meal of their choice to take below in the restaurant. Please ring for details. All major credit cards accepted apart from American express and Diners.

95 THE RED LION HOTEL

Longbridge Street, Llanidloes,
Powys SY18 6EE
Tel: 01686 412270
Fax: 0186 412681
e-mail: geoffhawkins@btconnect.com

Located in the heart of the small market town of Llanidloes, **The Red Lion Hotel** is easy to find with its large, brilliantly red lion standing guard over the portico entrance. Owned and run since 2004 by the Hawkins family; Geoff and Eileen and their son Steven – this traditional style hotel has a relaxing atmosphere for all the family with restaurant, bar area and games room complete with its own pool table and other more traditional pub games.

The food served here is honest-to-goodness pub grub at value for money prices. Chose from either the printed menu or from the specials board where there is a great range of food from light bites, jackets, sandwiches, fish dishes, grills and mains. Served from noon until 9pm Monday to Saturday; favourites include the fisherman's platter, minted lamb shank and the basket meals. With all the dishes, fresh local produce is used wherever possible. For local diners, the Red Lion's Sunday carvery is the first choice served from noon until 2pm – where booking is essential to avoid disappointment.

The bar is open from 11am until midnight from Monday to Friday and from 11am-1am on weekends. Ale lovers will not be disappointed with regular brew Timothy Taylor Landlord on tap, alongside three other rotating guest ales to sample. With comfortable seating, leather couches and fantastic hospitality the family have created a brilliant environment to dine or drink in. Larger parties are welcomed here but booking ahead is a necessity so that the team can ensure all your needs can be met. There is also a small outdoor area that can be enjoyed in the summer months.

The hotel also makes a perfect place to stay to explore any part of Wales as Llanidloes is located in its exact centre. There are nine well equipped en suite bedrooms that come on a hearty bed and breakfast tariff. The pub downstairs has good disabled access and is wheelchair friendly, but please ring for details on the rooms. All major credit cards are accepted..

96 THE ROYAL HEAD

Shortbridge Street, Llanidloes,
Powys SY18 6AD
Tel: 01686 412583

Situated in the heart of the historic market town of Llanidloes, just off the main A470 is the Royal Head. A stunning building whose exterior stretches black and white timbered along the main street; it offers a great pub dining and drinking experience alongside quality bed and breakfast accommodation all year round.

Local family John and Sandra Stephens and their children Garth and Leah have owned and run **The Royal Head** for the past 4 years, creating a lively and stylish atmosphere for their clientele by contrasting the building's period features with sleek leather furniture. The bar features a wealth of gnarled black beams, comfy sofas and tub chairs where three real ales can be enjoyed all day everyday; Brians SA, Worthington and Abbot Ale.

Food is available each day between 12-2pm and 6:30-9pm and is all prepared fresh in the kitchen by Sandra herself. Her menu has everything a good pub menu should have with a choice from homemade steak and ale pie, broccoli pasta bake, beef lasagne, battered cod, a variety of curries, Japanese breaded king prawn salad, jacket potatoes and sandwiches with a variety of fillings and a hearty 8oz steak. Guests can also choose from the daily specials board. All dishes are homemade and created using as much local produce as possible. Children can chose from their own menu or take half portions of the above. Most popular with local families however is the succulent roast which is added to the menu every Sunday lunchtime. In the summer months guests also have the option of dining al fresco in the spacious beer garden to the rear of the building.

Great guest accommodation is available throughout the year too on a hearty bed and breakfast tariff, making the Royal Head an ideal spot to stop for a long weekend exploring this scenic area of Wales. There are three upstairs rooms to choose from, one of which is a double en suite, with the other two twin rooms having access to their own private bathrooms. Each is freshly decorated with its own unique style with plenty of storage space.

97 THE GREAT OAK CAFÉ

12 Great Oak Street, Llanidloes,
Powys SY18 6BU
Tel: 01686 413 211

Ms Gerry Collins took over the **Great Oak Cafe** in Autumn of 2006 and carried out a refurbishment in Spring 2007, around the same time the café achieved Fairtrade status. The cafe is well known throughout the area and beyond and is highly regarded for the wholesome and appetizing fare on offer, cooked fresh everyday using fresh ingredients and uses 17 mainly local suppliers. The café serves organic fairtrade coffee and hot chocolates made to order, fairtrade speciality teas, soya milk shakes, fruit juice, organic sparkling cans, ciders and ales.

The dedicated staff of Rosie, Mandy, Isla, Orla and Bryony are friendly, charming and efficient. The menu of vegetarian wholefood changes daily and caters for special dietary needs such as vegan, wheat and dairy free, and serves a tasty Soup of the Day and includes dishes such as lasagna, quiche, Thai or Indian curry or root vegetable hot pot and has an extensive freshly made salad bar.

Then there are the wonderful homemade cakes such as apricot and date flap jacks, coffee and walnut, chocolate and a variety of fruit cakes. Food can be eaten in or for take out. The licensed cafe provides a venue for local musicians and displays art by local artists and is available for private functions and buffets.

Open 9am-5pm Mon-Sat and also open in season on Sundays too 9.30am-2.30pm. On the first Friday of the month there are 4 or 5 course themed food evenings from 7.30pm. There is a charming courtyard and pavement tables. The café has good disabled access, children and nursing mothers welcome with high chairs and changing facilities available.

99 ROBERT OWEN MUSEUM

The Cross, Broad Street, Newtown,
Powys SY16 2BB
Tel: 01686 626345
website: www.robert-owen.midwales.com

Robert Owen was born in 1771 in Newtown, son of a local saddler and ironmonger. His working life began as a drapers assistant but he went on to become one of the most successful mill owners of the Industrial Revolution and a pioneer for social reform. The **Robert Owen Museum** is intriguingly laid out and includes fascinating items on display, such as a 'Silent Monitor'. A film can be viewed, telling the story of his early life and achievements. The museum is open all year except Christmas week and Good Friday, Monday to Friday 9.30am-12 and 2pm-3.30pm, Saturday 9.30am-11.30am. A range of souvenirs and postcards is available for purchase and entry is free.

100 MONTGOMERYSHIRE WILDLIFE TRUST

Collot House, 20 Severn Street,
Welshpool, Powys SY21 7AD
Tel: 01938 555654
e-mail: montwt@cix.co.uk
website: www.montwt.co.uk

Montgomeryshire is home to some very special wildlife, including the red kite, otter and dormouse. It is also a landscape clothed with important habitats such as woodland, unimproved grassland and moorland. The **Montgomeryshire Wildlife Trust** is dedicated to conserving and enhancing wildlife habitats and protecting threatened species for the enjoyment of this and future generations. Why not enjoy the wildlife at any one of 13 fantastic nature reserves? Better still, become a member! Contact the Trust for further details.

98 THE BLUE BELL INN

Llangurig, Llanidbes, Powys SY18 6SG
Tel: 01686 440254
e-mail: lizanddewi@hotmail.co.uk
website: www.bluebell-inn.co.uk

The Blue Bell Inn is a delightful village inn, which whole-heartedly welcomes locals and visitors to enjoy fine real ales and delicious home cooked food. Liz and Dewi Jones are perfect hosts and lived locally before taking over the inn, which is traditionally furnished with an original fireplace in the bar area. Located in Llangurig - the highest village in Mid Wales – The Blue Bell Inn is a Grade II listed building, dating back to the 16th century.

Retaining many of its original features the child-friendly inn offers nine comfortable bedrooms - most with en-suite facilities (the single rooms have a communal bathroom). All of them have colour TV and tea and coffee making facilities (one room located on the ground floor).

There is a good selection of beers, wines and spirits to enjoy as well as seasonal real ales - some brewed in Wales (Rev James and Butty Bach). A good variety of bar meals are offered all day and there are some great home cooked dishes to choose from listed on the daily specials board. Among the most popular dishes are Liz's homemade steak and ale pie, liver and onions and her Sunday lunches. Vegetarians are well catered for with dishes including broccoli & cheese bake and Thai vegetable curry. There are some fantastic grilled dishes too that are popular with diners and a range of meat and fish dishes to satisfy the fussiest of eaters. The Blue Bell Inn has a tastefully decorated restaurant seating up to 22 diners. It has an extensive menu, which contains good home cooked food at reasonable prices and a good selection of fine wines. Food is available daily between 12pm-9pm.

Situated on the junction of the thoroughfares of the A470 and the A44, the Welsh Coast of Aberystwyth and Cardigan Bay are only a short drive away. The inn is in an ideal location for visitors to the area to stay or those travelling around Wales. Llangurig is in the heart of the country and is popular for B&B with ramblers, cyclists, fishermen, motorbike and rally enthusiasts. The surrounding area has a lot to offer with the Hafren Forest, Wye Valley walk, Sweet Lamb Rally Complex, Elan Valley and Clywedog Dam all within easy traveling distance. Inside there is a games room with a pool table, dart boards, dominoes, cards and a fruit machine for customers to use. All major credit cards taken.

101 THE RED LION

3-4 Main Street, Caersws,
Powys SY17 5EL
Tel: 01686 688023
e-mail: thelioncaersws@tiscali.co.uk

The Red Lion is an excellent base for exploring the beautiful area of Powys, located centrally in Caersws main street. It is run and owned by Jayne and David who are ably assisted by their daughter Mandy and her husband Jim. This charming family work tirelessly to create a relaxing and friendly environment that is as inviting to locals as it is to tourists. They offer three upstairs rooms that vary in size, each of which has en suite facilities. Rooms also come on a generous bed and breakfast tariff.

The inn, much like the rooms, retains a traditional feel with roaring log fires and wooden beamed ceilings; which showcase the inn's history. Open from 3pm-close Mon-Thurs and from 12pm-close from Fri-Sun in the winter months and everyday from 12pm-close in the summer months. The Red Lion is an ale lover's paradise; with over twenty real ales to sample over one month rotating from local breweries. Guests can enjoy fine drink and hospitality throughout the day with a small rear patio and plenty of off road parking also.

102 RAVEN INN

Raven Square, Welshpool,
Powys SY21 7LT
Tel: 01938 553070
e-mail: steve.raveninn@btconnect.com
website: www.theraven-inn.co.uk

Located next door to the Llanfair light railway, one of Welshpool's most popular local attractions, the fantastic **Raven Inn** prides itself on serving pub food of the highest standard. Stephen Griffiths and Lee Bocking are the tenants of the inn and Stephen is also the head chef. Working alongside him in the kitchen is second chef John McIntyre and together they have created a delicious menu bursting with a new range of seasonal dishes, which are all freshly prepared to order. All of the dishes are made with high quality, locally sourced Welsh produce and there is plenty on the menu to choose from.

There is a good selection of bar meals, light lunches, soups and freshly cut sandwiches to enjoy and in the evening visitors can dine in the restaurant. Chef's homemade Celtic pride Welsh lasagne is a popular choice and there are a number of dishes suitable for vegetarians, including chefs homemade mushroom, leek and spinach lasagne topped with mozzarella cheese. The extensive and appetising dessert menu boasts a range of locally homemade desserts, including lemon cheesecake with a fruit compote, sticky toffee roulade and cherry bakewell tart. There is also a new takeaway menu, specials board and a wide range of lite bites including filled baked potatoes, filled toasted folded naan bread and a range of mouth-watering omelettes.

The exterior of the pub is particularly impressive and welcoming and inside it is full of character and olde world charm. Raven Inn is child-friendly and there is an exciting play area for youngsters to enjoy before or after their meals. Outside there is a superb beer garden and with a large car park to the rear of the pub, parking is not an issue. The inn has its own private function room, which is an ideal venue for those wanting to host a special occasion. Function room buffets range from £5.95 per person to £10.95 for a hog roast. With room for up to 100 people, or 60 seated, the function room can be tailored to individual needs and weddings, funeral teas, corporate meetings and christenings can all be catered for, along with other events.

Well known for its entertainment evenings there is something for everyone. Jazz can be heard one a month during the afternoon and the inn also hosts themed food evenings, curry nights, steak nights, senior citizen's lunches and live bands throughout the year. If it is top quality fresh food, made with the best local Welsh produce, you are longing for the Raven Inn is highly recommended.

103 REVELLS

Berriew Street, Welshpool,
Powys SY21 7SQ
Tel: 01938 559000
e-mail: craig@revellsbistro.co.uk
website: www.revellsbistro.co.uk

Occupying a beautifully restored art deco cinema, **Revells Bistro & Restaurant** is one of the best places in the area to enjoy good food and company. Owners, Craig and Rhian Humphreys have run Revells since 1991 and put the bistro firmly on the map. With its warm and relaxing atmosphere, the former cinema, opened in 1938, is extremely popular with locals and visitors.

The well-established, child-friendly, bistro offers a wide choice of homemade dishes, including lasagne, quiche, soup and a good choice of pasta dishes on its lunchtime menu. Char-grilled steaks, roasts, vegetarian options, paninis, baguettes and filled croissants are also available along with light snacks, freshly baked cakes and specialty coffees. Seating up to 50 people, the café/bar, by day, is open Monday-Saturday between 10am and 4pm. The exceptional quality of locally sourced produce and service runs into the varied evening menu, with plenty of mouth-watering dishes to choose from, including Welsh rack of lamb, pan seared Queen scallops and homemade Gnocchi. On a Thursday food is served from 5pm-8.30pm and Friday and Saturday evening service is between 6pm-9.30pm. On a Sunday diners can relax and enjoy the finest of Sunday traditional lunches, choosing from a selection of succulent cuts of meats, all served with home roasted and seasonal vegetables. Inside, the establishment is full of olde-world charm and offers a delightful environment in which to enjoy some of the finest food in Wales. It is bursting with character and there is a lot of antique furniture and vintage photographs of old Welshpool on the walls, giving it that homely feel. There are newspapers for adults to ponder over as well as toys to keep the children occupied.

Located in the bustling market town of Welshpool, in the picturesque upper reaches of the Severn Valley, Revells is the ideal place for visitors to stop. Close to the border between Wales and England, the area has plenty of attractions and activities at its fingertips. Every other weekend Revells hosts either a food themed evening - Italian, Spanish, French and fresh fish, for example - or live music by groups from around the world. The establishment also boasts a delicatessen, with a wide selection of Shropshire cured meats, Welsh cheeses, local olives, specialty jams, chutneys, fair trade chocolate, herbs and spices, and breads. It is open Monday Saturday 10am-4pm. Disabled access is not a problem and there is a disabled toilet for customers to use.

104 THE ANGEL

Berriew Street, Welshpool,
Powys SY21 7SQ
Tel: 01938 553473
e-mail: theangel.welshpool@tiscali.co.uk
website: www.theangelwelshpool.co.uk

The Angel is a family-run pub in the popular market town of Welshpool, located on the border of England and Wales. Owned by Craig and Rhian Humphreys since 1995 the pub has a great reputation with locals and visitors. The pair is extremely experienced in the industry and has owned the beautifully restored art deco cinema, Revells Bistro & Restaurant on the same street since 1991.

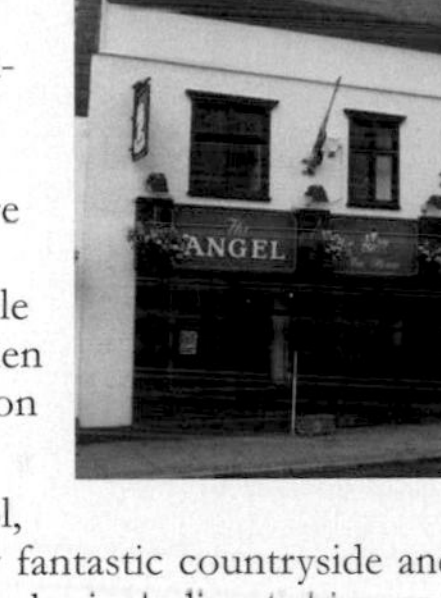

The Angel is a place where young and old, tourists and locals mix freely and this adds to the superb atmosphere it has. If it is great pub grub in a traditional Welsh pub you are after this child-friendly establishment is definitely the right place to go. There is an extensive menu of great food for customers to choose from and a daily specials board will make sure the fussiest of eaters are catered for. With two rotating real ales to sample the hidden rear beer garden is a superb spot to relax on sunnier days.

Located in Welshpool, the pub is surrounded by fantastic countryside and there are many things to do nearby including fishing and golf. The Angel is open from Sunday-Thursday from 12pm-12am and on Friday and Saturday from 12pm-1am.

105 TAN HOUSE INN

Llangyniew, Powys SY21 0JR
Tel: 01938 810056

Found just south-west of Meifod in the beautiful Welsh countryside adjacent to the A495 sits the family run **Tan House Inn**, a superb spot to relax with a few cold drinks or dine in style with all the family. The premises itself dates back to the early 19th century, but current owners Roger, Jenny and Emlyn have been running the show for a year now.

Open from 5pm until close daily and open from 12-2pm on Wednesdays and weekends. They serve two real ales; Brains S.A and a rotating guest ale along with a large selection of soft drinks, spirits and wines. The food here is fantastic and authentically homemade which means that it is advisable to book, particularly on weekends. Jenny's daughter Sarah is the chef here cooking up a delicious menu created completely from local produce which includes puff pastry fish pie, spinach and potato bake, creamy pesto pasta or succulent steaks served with all the trimmings. On Sun/Tues/Wed evenings however Jenny and Emlyn step up to the plate offering a smaller menu that includes all the locals' pub favourites.Also available are the mid week & Sunday carverys from 12 - 2pm.

There is also a 100 seater function room available to hire, complete with a quality patio area and large off road car park.

106 THE TONTINE INN

Melverley, Oswestry SY10 8PJ
Tel: 01691 682258
website: www.thetontineinn.co.uk

A real picture postcard country village Inn, **The Tontine Inn** is located in a superb setting, close to an historic church and the River Vyrnwy in the picturesque village of Melverley. Popular among visitors and locals the Inn is found off the B4393 on the borders of Powys and Shropshire. The original Inn dates back to 1878 and was recently refurbished and re-opened in August 2008 under the personal care of the owners, Roy and Anne Poole and their daughter Jen.

The Inn has two comfortable en-suite rooms, which are available all year round. Located upstairs, they include one double/family room and a twin/super king room. Single occupancy is available. Each room is reasonably priced and the tariff includes a hearty breakfast to set visitors up for the day exploring the area.

Open all day, every day for drinks, two real ales are served, one being locally brewed at the Stonehouse Brewery called Station bitter. With seating for 40 people the dining area is well laid out, with a relaxed and friendly ambience, ideal for enjoying something to eat. There is also a lounge area with comfy sofas and a separate bar and games room including a pool table and sky T.V. The Inn boasts a fantastic patio area and beer garden, which is spacious and welcoming and the ideal spot to enjoy a cold drink or bite to eat on a summer's day. The outside of the Inn is well presented and inside is modern, clean and tastefully decorated.

Starters, Tontine favourites, specials, desserts, side orders and a good choice of bar snacks are available with all dishes being freshly cooked to order, adding to the quality of the food served. The majority of produce is sourced locally and among the favourites on the extensive menu is chef's cut of Herefordshire steak, shoulder of lamb, braised Shropshire beef and lemon battered cod with vegetarian options always available, there is a good range of sweets too. Traditional roast dinners are served on a Sunday from 12noon-4pm and food from the main menu is served from 4pm-8pm. From Monday – Thursday food is served between 12noon-2:30pm and 5:30pm – 9pm. Such is the popularity of the Tontine inn; bookings need to be made Friday – Sunday. Friday food is served 12noon-2:30pm and 5:30pm – 9:30pm and on Saturdays meals can be enjoyed from 12noon-9:30pm. The Tontines pensioners menu is available Monday – Friday 12noon-2:30pm. With an off-road car park, parking is not a problem. All major credit cards are taken.

107 THE BRADFORD ARMS HOTEL

Llanymynech, Powys SY22 6EJ
Tel: 01691 830582
e-mail: catelow@tesco.net
website: www.bradfordarmshotel.com

An impressive, family run establishment, **The Bradford Arms Hotel** dates back to the late 17th century and can be found in the idyllic village of Llanymynech. With a four star AA rating, the hotel boasts five superb en-suite rooms, finished to the highest of standards, and all have tea and coffee making facilities, a shower, hair dryer, direct dial telephone and colour television. Owned by award-winning catering team, Bob and Cath Hedley, the cuisine served is of the best quality and meals can be enjoyed in the relaxing and spacious conservatory or the more formal dining space in the restaurant, which is ideal for private parties.

The finest local produce is used, making the food extremely popular with guests. Whether it is a light lunch, three course meal or traditional Sunday lunch you are after the hotel serves exceptional meals. Guests are spoilt for choice with an extensive menu boasting top quality meats, fish and vegetables. Pork a la Mutarde, steak 'n' kidney pudding, lasagne al forno and gammon steak garnis are among the dishes on offer and starters include pan fried garlic mushrooms and smoked salmon coronets. Vegetarians are well catered for with dishes including chick pea enchiladas and mushroom stroganoff. The mouth watering desserts, which are all made fresh on the premises, are extremely popular with diners. Dark chocolate and mint terrine, raspberry and white chocolate crème brulee and homemade bread and butter pudding are just some of the choices on offer. Food is served 11.30am-2pm and 6.30-9pm every day and such is its popularity booking are required for Friday and Saturday.

Accommodation is available all year round and there are two ground floor rooms, one of which is adapted for disabled customers. The tariff includes breakfast. Located on the Welsh border with Shropshire the hotel was originally a coaching inn, which in the early 1900s formed part of the Earl of Bradford's Estate. From the outside The Bradford Arms Hotel is an impressive establishment and inside, the hotel is tastefully decorated and the dining room is spacious and well laid out, providing the ideal setting to enjoy a top quality meal. Being close to the Ofas Dyke path, which is in an area of outstanding beauty and historic interest, the hotel is in the perfect location for guests who want to explore the Welsh border. The child-friendly hotel has plenty of off road parking for guests to use. All major credit cards are taken.

108 THE LION HOTEL

Llansantffraid, Powys SY22 6AQ
Tel: 01691 828207
e-mail:
lionhotel.llansantffraid@btconnect.com
website: www.thelionhotel-llansantffraid.co.uk

Dating back to the 19th century **The Lion Hotel** is a charming establishment that boasts cuisine and accommodation of the highest standard. A former county court house and a current listed building the elegant hotel has six tastefully decorated en-suite rooms and is owned by Oliver Parry and Mick Snelling. Situated in Llansantffraid it can be found on the A495 at its junction with the B4393 and has been much improved since the arrival of the experienced licensees.

A historic inn for around 150 years it is open each session, every day during the summer months and all day Saturday and Sunday. In the winter months it is closed on Monday and Tuesday lunchtimes. Priding itself on real ales, which often have visitors returning again, the hotel has at least two to choose from, with a regular real ale brewed locally. Such is the popularity of the restaurant, which has a daily changing menu, boasting the finest local produce, weekends need to be booked. The delicious food on offer is extremely fresh and diners return time and again to sample dishes from the hotel's traditional and modern menus. The a la carte menu is certainly one to spoil you for choice and there is even a daily specials menu to suit the most discerning diners. Cuisine on offer includes smoked haddock and salmon pie with mixed seafood as well as lamb shank braised in rosemary and red wine gravy and locally sourced wild game features throughout the Winter months whilst in season. Sweet-toothed customers will no doubt be satisfied with the extensive list of tempting, luxurious desserts, including Irish cream brulee with almond crisp biscuits and strawberry and white chocolate truffle torte with wild berry coulis. Food is served Monday-Friday 12-3pm and 6-9pm and on the weekend between 12-9pm. The child-friendly restaurant seats 40 and the lounge bar seats 30.

Upstairs the comfortable en-suite rooms are available all year round for bed and breakfast or half-board. The Lion Hotel really is an atmospheric, friendly country inn and its location in the tranquil area of Llansantffraid provides the ideal resting spot for holiday-makers or business travellers. Surrounded by beautiful countryside there is plenty to see and do, including pheasant shooting, fishing, golf and visits to places of historic interest. Walkers and those who like the outdoors will be in their element as the hotel is close to the Llanrhaeadr Waterfalls, Lake Vyrnwy, Offa's Dyke and Snowdonia National Park. There is plenty of off-road parking and all major credit cards are taken.

109 THE KINGS HEAD

Meifod, Powys SY22 6BY
Tel: 01938 500171
Fax: 01938 500171
e-mail: kings-headhotel@btinternet.com

The Kings Head is situated centrally in the vibrant town of Meifod, situated in the heart of the Welsh countryside just off the A495. You can be assured of a warm welcome and friendly atmosphere from leaseholders Rob and wife Rachael who have been running this establishment for over 14 years now. Dating back to 1748 with oak beams, original fireplace and a beautiful ivy covered façade with large sash windows this place is hard to miss.

The premises has been completely refurbished over the last few years to ensure that any visit here is a refreshing and comfortable one. There is now new furniture, new décor and new menus to boot, giving the place the injection of life it really needed. Now thriving and popular with Meifod's residents the Kings Head Hotel is open for business every day all year round.

There are 5 upstairs en suite rooms to choose from, with a four poster bed on offer for those romantic weekends away. Each room provides a fresh yet cosy environment for guests with comfortable beds and plenty of storage. Rooms are on a bed and breakfast tariff that includes a hearty full English breakfast to prepare you for the day ahead.Both residents and non-residents can also enjoy the inviting atmosphere of the hotels bar. They currently serve Green King ale but promise to bring in more local brews soon. A good selection of other draught lagers, bitters, spirits, wines and soft drinks is also available. Food is served daily from 12-9:30pm, guests can chose from various menus or the specials board which changes fortnightly. Rob's skills extend to the kitchen producing a tantalising selection of treats from jacket potatoes, baguettes, soups and light bites to full evening meals. Favourites include mussels and chorizo sausages in a Mediterranean tomato sauce, butternut squash and cashew nut roast, slow cooked pork hock and duck breast not to mention the large choice of steaks on offer including rib eye and salmon. Sunday lunches are also very popular here and it is advised to book on weekends. The couple also make their own cakes and preserves which are on sale to the general public.

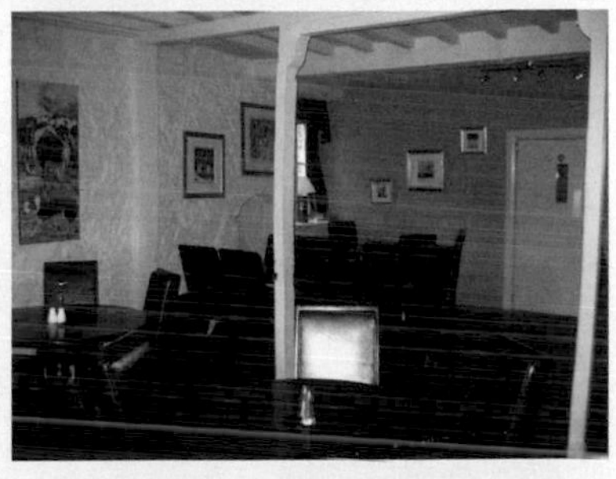

Guests also have the option of camping or parking their caravan in the land behind the Kings Head which also has an ample beer garden, football pitch and play area for children.

110 GWYSTRE INN

Gwystre, Llandrindod Wells,
Powys LD1 6RN
Tel: 01597 851650

The Gwystre Inn is an extremely popular place for locals and visitors to eat, drink and stay. Good food is a major attraction here with extensive a la carte and bar menus offering dishes based on locally produced ingredients. Home cooked food is extremely popular at the Gwystre Inn with traditional favourites, including home made steak and ale pie and cottage pie among the most favoured dishes. Char grilled steak is one of the most popular dishes with guests. The extensive menu, which is created using as much local produce as possible, has something for everyone and the desserts menu is also very comprehensive with some mouth-watering choices. Roast dinners are a speciality on Sundays with a choice of four different joints and there is a special children's menu to suit younger guests. Portions are generous and very reasonably priced. To avoid disappointment it is wise to book ahead for Friday and Saturday evenings and for Sunday lunch. If you are lucky with the weather, you can enjoy your refreshments in the pleasant beer garden with its attractive stream. Food is served every day from noon until 2.30pm and from 6pm to 9.30pm.

To accompany your meal, there's an extensive choice of beers, wines and spirits, including one real ale – Rev James. The Gwystre Inn has just got pear cider on draught. Located on the main A44 between Rhayader and Cross Gates, the Gwystre Inn, which has a history that stretches back to the 1700s when it stood on a drover's road, is in an ideal location for exploring Powys and the surrounding area.

The inn offers comfortable B&B accommodation with four en-suite bedrooms (two doubles, one twin and one family room). All of the rooms are located upstairs and have a TV and hospitality tray. The tariff is very reasonable and includes a hearty home-cooked breakfast. The tenants, Peter and Linda Ramplee, are a warm and friendly couple and really do ensure guests are happy.

Inside, the inn is tastefully decorated and the tables in the dining area are suitably spaced. The inn is full of character, with dark wood and a red theme evident throughout. There is a range of pub games to enjoy over a drink, including darts and coits. Superb food is why customers return time and time again to the Gwystre Inn. All major credit cards are accepted and there is ample off road parking.

111 GEORGE AND DRAGON INN

4 Broad Street, Knighton,
Powys LD7 1DL
Tel: 01547 528532
e-mail: justinrees@tiscali.co.uk
website: www.thegeorgeknighton.co.uk

The George and Dragon Inn dates back to the early 19th century and retains many of its beautiful original features such as stone walling, low beamed ceilings and a wood burning stove. The inn's Welsh cottage character combined with the warm welcome owners the Rees family give keeps customers coming back again and again.

The bar is always well stocked with wines from the inn's own wine cellar, real ales and more with fine food being served up each day from 12-2pm and 6:30-9pm except on Monday lunchtimes. Chef Steve assists the family in creating a range of dishes to suit every taste including classics like steak and ale pie, lasagne and succulent sirloin steaks with other favourites like homemade fish pie, braised lamb shank and homemade chicken korma. Vegetarians are also well catered for dishes like delicious brie, courgette, potato and almond crumble. A good selection of lighter bites is also available throughout the day with a choice of filled sandwiches, rolls, baguettes and jackets with plenty of children's options.

The inn also offers fine accommodation in converted stables to the rear, each with immense character and comfort. There are two doubles and three twins to choose from; each fitted with en suite shower room, TV and refreshment tray. Compliments include a hearty breakfast and all the advice on the area's best walks and activities with hampers available on request. All major credit cards accepted.

112 PILLETH OAKS

Whitton, Knighton, Powys LD7 1NP
Tel: 01547 560272
e-mail: hoods@pillethoaks.co.uk
website: www.pillethoaks.co.uk

Located in one hundred acres of scenic countryside is one of Wales' finest bed and breakfasts. Built in 2000, this magnificent property has three stunning en suite rooms, each of which sports glorious views across the Lugg Valley. The rooms are well furnished and decorated in an elegant country cottage style, befitting the house's stately feel.

Owners Heather and Peter Hodd offer their guests a warm welcome throughout the year serving up a fine breakfast each morning in the downstairs of their luxury home which also holds a large lounge and terrace for guests to use. Evening meals are available by prior arrangement, making a stay at this 5 star property convenient as well as classy.

Ideal for couples or families (children over 12 only please) who want a rural break away, the bed and breakfast is within easy walking distance to a bird-watching hide and fishing site, with endless hours of glorious countryside walks in the area which circle the grounds lakes which cover over 4½ acres of land.

113 THE HAT SHOP RESTAURANT

7 High Street, Presteigne LD8 2BA
Tel: 01544 260017
e-mail:
thehatshoprestaurant@googlemail.com

The Hat Shop Restaurant located on the main high street in Presteigne is a small, friendly, fully licensed restaurant that prides itself on serving high quality home-made food including its own organic homemade bread. It is owned by business partners Pam, Nicola and Ruth who collectively have over 30 years of experience running the place. They have created a popular environment for locals and guests to the area who come to enjoy the fine cuisine of offer. Some of the produce used here is grown by the team themselves and they buy the rest from local independent suppliers.

The menu is constantly changing with a range of hot and cold meals, vegetarian options, fish and meat dishes with a range of puddings, cheese, kebabs and tapas available. Why not try the salmon, sea bass and grilled scallops medley with Champagne sauce or the hearty venison casserole with chestnuts or the veg and nut crumble for the vegetarians. The bar is stocked with an interesting range of beers, carefully selected wines and homemade soft drinks.

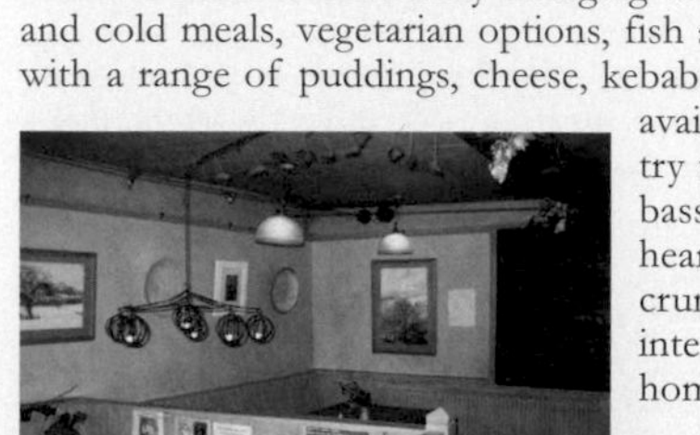

Open Mon-Sat 12-2pm and 6-9pm, booking advised at all times but essential on weekends. Children welcome, all major credit cards accepted.

114 THE RED LION INN

Llanflhangel Nant Melan
near New Radnor, Powys LD8 2TN
Tel: 01544 350220
e-mail: theredlion@yahoo.co.uk
website: www.redlionmidwales.co.uk

Just three miles from New Radnor on the A44 is **The Red Lion Inn** in the heart of the picturesque village of Llanfihangel Nant Melan. The inn itself was built in 1592 as an ancient Drover's Inn but today stands the hub of its small community, welcoming visitors from near and far to enjoy the jovial atmosphere and the rolling countryside that surrounds it.

The inn is owned and run by Sandra and John Rathbone, who have maintained the inn's historic status by preserving many of its original features such as the wooden beamed ceilings and the large wood burning stove. Meals can be eaten throughout the inn or in warmer weather can be taken outside to be enjoyed in the inn's lovely beer garden which sport wonderful views across the valley. Food is served Monday to Saturday from 12-2pm and 6-9pm and from 12-8pm on Sundays when a traditional Sunday lunch is served and booking is advised. The main menu changes four times a year to reflect the best seasonal produce around at the time, but specialises in fine traditional and modern home cooking. The most popular dishes are Welsh Black Beef sirloin steaks, Welsh lamb steaks and the organic Salmon dish. Vegetarians are well catered for as are children who can choose from their own menu. Throughout the week, a range of special food nights are offered to get the best value for money; with homemade pies being the speciality on Mondays, Wednesday night is steak night, Thursday night is curry night - with a pensioners special on from 12-2pm, Fridays are good old fish and chips night, and on Saturdays a two course special deal is available.

The bar is well stocked to provide the perfect accompaniment to your meal, regardless of taste or budget with a well balanced selection of wines and real ales to choose from.

Sandra and John also offer seven warm and comfortable en suite rooms, all of which have colour television, radio/alarm clock and complimentary tea and coffee trays. Guests can choose from three double rooms, one twin, and motel styled rooms which also include family/double rooms and a twin. Well behaved pets are welcome to accompany their owners who can take advantage of not only the local beauty spots but the inn's very own private garden.

115 THE START

Hay-on-Wye, Herefordshire HR3 5RS
Tel: 01497 821391
e-mail: dawn@the-start.net
website: www.the-start.net

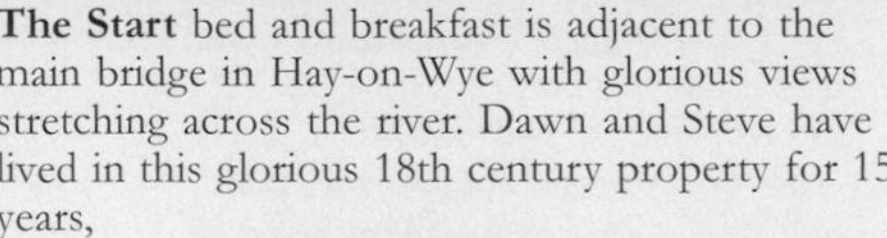

The Start bed and breakfast is adjacent to the main bridge in Hay-on-Wye with glorious views stretching across the river. Dawn and Steve have lived in this glorious 18th century property for 15 years, converting their home into a bed and breakfast 7 years ago. They provide award winning facilities for their guests who can choose from three well furnished bedrooms. Guests can either stay in one of two double bedrooms or a twin bedroom; all of which have en suite facilities. All rooms also come with TV, wi-fi and tea and coffee making facilities.

Patrons staying at the bed and breakfast comment on not just the tranquil and friendly environment that their hosts have created for them, but the quality of the breakfast served up each morning as part of the tariff. Breakfasts come in variety of shapes and sizes depending on what you fancy, but all are cooked using the best fresh local produce and are sure to last you throughout the day – a perfect start to your day. With stunning surroundings and plenty of scope for walkers and hikers the Start makes an ideal base, with packed lunches also available on request.

116 THE HARP INN

Glasbury on Wye, Powys HR3 5NR
Tel: 01497 847373 / 07982130161
e-mail: info@theharpinn.co.uk
website: www.theharpinn.co.uk

Dating back to the early 18th century, **The Harp Inn** is a traditional country inn offering comfortable bed and breakfast accommodation. There are some spectacular views overlooking the River Wye to be enjoyed. The free house has been owned and personally run by Grahame and Jayne Day for the past three years.

Popular with walkers, canoeists, cyclist, climbers, fishermen and those just simply wanting to relax, the inn has five rooms (three en-suite), all overlooking the River Wye and located upstairs. The tariff included a hearty Welsh breakfast, which is sure to set up any visitor for a day of exploring the area. A part from Monday lunch times, food is served between 12pm-2pm and 6.30pm-8.15pm and on Sundays between 12pm-2pm and 7pm-8.15pm. Such is the popularity of the Sunday lunches it is advisable to book, and the same goes for Friday evenings.

The inn offers a range of traditional cask ales from Herefordshire and Wales, with a variety of guest ales from further afield. A quiz is held on a Thursday evening from

117 THE HOLLYBUSH INN

Hay-on-Wye, Herefordshire HR3 5PS
Tel: 01497 847371
e-mail: hollybushcamping@btconnect.com
website: www.hollybushcamping.co.uk

The vibrant and quirky **Hollybush Inn** offers 5 beautifully furnished rooms throughout the year with a choice between 3 en suite double rooms; some complete with own fireplace, or a family room and 2 twin rooms with a shared bathroom. Guests at the inn and non-residents can enjoy the lively atmosphere below in the inn's bar and restaurant which prides itself on catering for special dietary requirements such as vegans, vegetarians and more. All meals are cooked fresh to order with local organic produce so you can really taste the difference. The bar offers a fine choice of country wines, real ales and ciders that can be enjoyed within the cosy inn, or outside in the inn's spacious beer garden which has access to the glorious River Wye. Alternately, live music is provided most weekends from a variety of local performing artists.

The inn also sports its own campsite with options for camping in fields or wooded areas in either tents, caravans or a range of fantastic tipis that are available to hire. Guests can enjoy the great range of outdoor activities the team arrange also which includes kayaking, canoeing, cycling and hiking, please ring for details.

118 THE RADNOR ARMS

Llowes, Radnorshire HR3 5JA
Tel: 01497 847460

The Radnor Arms, situated in Llowes, was originally a Drovers Inn and dates back more than 400 years. The handsome, stone built inn is set against a stunning backdrop of the Black Mountains, with magnificent scenery in all directions, including the Begwins, the Brecon Beacons and the Wye Valley. Owner, Colin Thomson, is an experienced hotelier and took over the running of the establishment in May 2009.

The pub is very popular with locals and visitors and is well known for its fine food and good ale. The dishes available are listed on an ever changing blackboard with something for everyone. Local produce is at the heart of the menu. One real ale is served. During the winter months the pub is open Wednesday Saturday for food between 6.30pm-9.15pm and for Sunday lunch.

The Radnor Arms is child friendly and from Easter 2010 a camp site to the rear of the property, overlooking some spectacular views, will be complete. The camp site might keep a couple of its own tents on site, which will be available to hire. (Phone The Radnor Arms for more details.) All major credit cards taken. Disabled access not a problem.

119 ROAST OX INN

Paincastle, Powys LD2 3JL
Tel: 01497 851398
e-mail: info@roastoxinn.co.uk
website: www.roastoxinn.co.uk

Located in the picturesque village of Painscastle, the **Roast Ox Inn** is a traditional public house well known for its excellent food. The village is sometimes known as Castell Paen and is five miles north west of Hay on the B4594. Boasting views over some spectacular countryside the inn is in easy reach of several sleepy market towns including, Hay-on-Wye, Builth Wells, Kington and the city of Hereford. Offering the very best in finest local produce the inn has a restaurant seating 60 people.

The extensive and reasonably priced menu has some really fine dishes listed including roast duck with cointreau & orange sauce as well as trio of grilled lamb chops with redcurrant and minted gravy. More traditional choices include chilli con carne and classic spaghetti bolognaise. Customers can also choose from the daily specials board. Food is served daily between 12pm-2pm and 7pm-9pm and a carvery is available Sunday lunchtimes. Such is its popularity weekends need to be booked to avoid disappointment. The inn offers between three and six real ales (Hook Norton is the regular) as well as up to four draught ciders and a good selection of wines and malt whiskies. With fantastic views in every direction, on brighter days guests enjoy making the most of the outside seating area.

Although there has been an inn on this site for at least 500 years, the Roast Ox is comparatively recent – an earlier inn was completely destroyed by fire in 1991. The inn retains a number of its original features whilst benefiting from 21st century facilities. Upstairs there are ten fully en-suite letting rooms and superb conference facilities with full audio-visual equipment. The Roast Ox Inn can cater conferences for up to 30 people and there is wireless broadband available if internet access is required. Meals and accommodation can be arranged with self-tailored conference packages to suit the customer.

The Roast Ox Inn provides an ideal base for those planning on visiting the many shows held in the area throughout the year including the popular Royal Welsh Show, the Brecon Jazz Festival, the Haye on Wye Music Festival and its world famous Festival of Literature. Canoeing, horse-riding and pony-trekking are just some of the activities on offer in the area and the Tawny Owl Animal Park and Craft Centre is popular with visitors. There is ample parking. All major credit cards taken.

120 CEDARS GUEST HOUSE AND RESTAURANT

Hay Road, Builth Wells, Powys LD2 3BP
Tel: 01982 553356
Fax: 01982 553193
e-mail: cedarsguesthouse@yahoo.co.uk
website: www.cedars.co.uk

Val and Heulwen Morris welcome guests to their brilliant bed and breakfast with restaurant attached; located in the heart of the scenic Builth Wells. They have been running this popular establishment since 1990 and have created quite a following for both the accommodation and the restaurant which prides itself on offering great home cooked food throughout the year.

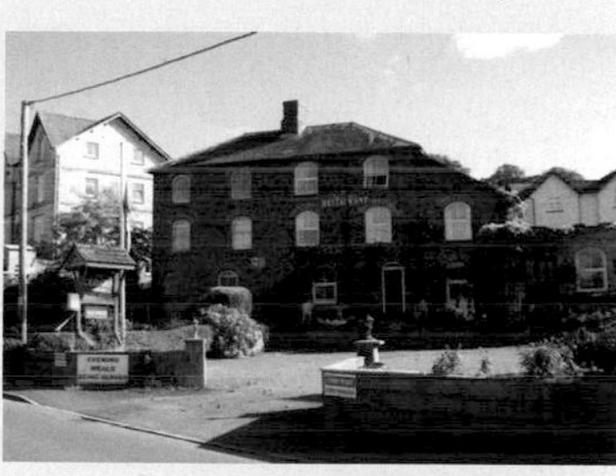

Open to both residents and non residents, the restaurant is open from 6pm onwards serving a larger variety of home cooked dishes – all created with the best seasonal local produce around. The restaurant itself has a homely country feel, looking out over the **Cedar's** own beautifully kept gardens. On Thursday nights, the restaurant fills in anticipation of its popular curry night, when it is advisable to book.

Guests staying at Cedars have a choice of coming on a bed and breakfast or bed and breakfast and dinner tariff. There are seven upstairs rooms, two of which are single and share a bathroom, whilst the others have en suite facilities.

121 STRAND CAFE & RESTAURANT

2 Groe Street, Builth Wells,
Powys LD2 3DW
Tel: 01982 552652

Located in the heart of the well known Builth Wells is the refined **Strand Cafe and Restaurant**. Run by local family Anne, John and daughter Mairwen, it specialises in homemade Welsh cuisine. All of the produce used in dishes here is sourced from local suppliers. Anne and Mairwen cook up a selection of light bites, salads, jackets and cakes along with a main menu that comprises all day breakfasts, omelettes, fish and vegetarian dishes and other homemade favourites like cottage pie and chicken curry. Specials include soup, faggots and Welsh beef stew. The cafe is also popular for its tasty selection of cakes and pastries. Open 9am-5pm Mon-Sat and Sundays in summer and school holidays.

122 THE WHITE HORSE

13 High Street, Builth Wells LD2 3DN
Tel: 01982 553171

Offering the very best in food and accommodation, **The White Horse** has a strong reputation in Builth Wells. Leaseholders, Tavis and Becky, have run the establishment for two years. Locals and visitors mix freely and enjoy the live music events, which are held once a week, either on a Friday or Saturday.

Accommodation is available all year round, with four comfortable en-suite rooms (all located upstairs). The tariff includes breakfast. The majority of the produce used at The White Horse is sourced locally and the extensive menu has something for everyone. The dishes are very traditional and include homemade steak and ale pie; gammon egg and chips; and homemade lasagne. If you are after something lighter, there are a range of tasty filled sandwiches, baguettes and jacket potatoes to choose from. Food is served weekdays between 11am and 3pm and on the weekends between 10am and 4pm. It is advisable to book for Sunday lunch. Although no real ales are served, there is a good selection of draught keg ales to choose from, with Carling and Strongbow among the most popular.

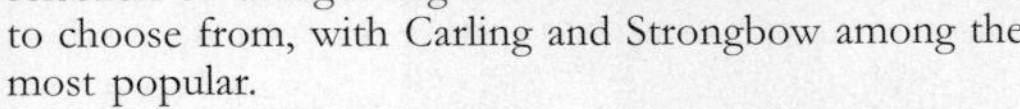

Children are welcomed at The White Horse and as well as serving ½ portions of any of the main meals there is a special children's menu too.

123 PRINCE LLEWELYN INN

Climery, Builth Wells, Powys LD2 3NU
Tel: 01982 552694

The Prince Llewelyn Inn is an outstanding village inn situated in Climery. Located three miles west of Builth Wells, on the A483, local couple Phil and Mair Hughes has owned the inn for the past two years. With a growing reputation for well kept ales and fine foods the Prince Llewelyn Inn is extremely popular in the area.

All of the meals served are freshly prepared and cooked to order and main courses include a range of steaks, lasagne and honey roasted half duck with orange sauce. The inn is family friendly and there is a special children's menu with all meals including a complimentary scoop of ice-cream to follow. Phil cooks all of the food and he uses Welsh produce wherever possible. Food is available every day between 12-2.30pm and 6-9pm. Such is the popularity of the premise it is advisable to book at weekends.

Inside, the inn is tastefully decorated combining olde worlde with the modern and outside there is a pleasant beer garden and safe children's play area for younger customers to enjoy. For disabled customers there is a ramp from the car park to the disabled-friendly and impressive building. Off road parking is available.

124 STONECROFT INN

Dolecoed Road, Llanwrtyd Wells,
Powys LD5 4RA
Tel: 01591 610332 / 610327
e-mail: party@stonecroft.co.uk
website: www.stonecroft.co.uk

A well known premise for lovers of real ales and fine food the **Stonecroft Inn** is a traditional warm and friendly country pub. The family friendly inn has a large riverside garden, which is popular on sunnier days. There is an extensive menu, boasting the finest local produce, and meals can be enjoyed in the bar, dining area or garden. There is a menu specially adapted for children and the aviaries and play fort keep younger guests entertained.

The inn has an ever growing reputation for its delicious meals and bar snacks with hot food and hot drinks available throughout opening hours. The lamb shank is one of the inn's tasty specialities and roast dinners are available every day. The inn features in CAMRA's Good Beer Guide and has always had a minimum of four real ales on tap plus a rotating real cider. The inn's owners Peter and Jane Brown, who both cook, say they provide their customers with more than 200 real ales each year. Inside you will find a games area with pool and darts and the inn regularly hosts quality live music. In November it hosts a Beer Festival at which more than 70 real ales are available to sample.

Located on the Sustrans route the inn is popular with cyclists, bikers and walkers. There are hundreds of miles of published routes for mountain biking and on and off road cycling in some of the most spectacular countryside in Wales.

The inn offers comfortable accommodation with six en-suite guest bedrooms – all tastefully decorated. More rooms are available in the adjacent Stonecroft Lodge where self catering accommodation is available in either private or shared rooms, perfect for backpackers, motor and mountain bikers, families, youth groups and so on. The kitchen is fully equipped and the property is centrally heated and has an open fire, satellite TV, DVD and video in the large L-shaped lounge and dining room. There is also a washing machine and tumble. The inn is just a seven minute walk from Llanwrtyd Wells Railway Station and many visitors use the inn as a base to explore the surrounding area, which boasts gold mines, crystal factories and caves. The railway station is on the Swansea to Shrewsbury Heart of Wales Line.

The inn is open from 5pm Monday-Thursday and from midday on Friday, Saturday and Sunday. Food is served between 12-3pm and 6-9pm. All major credit cards taken.

125 BRECKNOCK WILDLIFE TRUST

Lion House, Bethel Square, Brecon,
Powys LD3 7AY
Tel: 01874 625708. Fax: 01874 610552
e-mail: brecknockwtgcix.co.uk
website: www.wildlifetrust.org.uk

The Brecknock Wildlife Trust is part of the UK wide movement of county based Wildlife trusts. It is a registered charity operating in the county of old Breconshire, now the southern portion of Powys. To achieve its objectives of protecting wildlife and the habitats required for wildlife to thrive, the Trust owns and manages 18 nature reserves, provides advice to planners, landowners and farmers, operates species projects and promotes a greater understanding of wildlife and the environment through lifelong learning opportunities for adults and children.

The Brecknock Wildlife Trust is a membership organisation and its members play a significant role in carrying out the work of the Trust. In a voluntary capacity, members work with local schools, undertake practical projects on nature reserves and in the local community, carry out surveys, adopt local roadside verges and campaign for wildlife.

127 THE TANNERS ARMS

Defynnog, Brecon Beacons National Park,
Powys LD3 8SF
Tel: 01874 638032
e-mail: info@tannersarmspub.com
website: www.tannersarmspub.com

The Tanners Arms is located within the beautiful Brecon Beacons National Park in Defynnog and is a popular place for locals and visitors alike who enjoy the selection of well kept ales and food on offer. The inn itself dates to the early 1870's with a long and interesting history that includes a life as a workers cottage for the nearby Tannery. The bar stocks two real ales and two real ciders from Welsh breweries alongside a restaurant that offers an exciting range of home-cooked freshly prepared dishes. The majority of ingredients are locally sourced and combined to form dishes such as the delicious Steak, Port and Ale Pie , the Pen y Fan Mixed Grill and the Tanners Chicken , a succulent oven roasted breast wrapped in bacon and cheese in a fine cider sauce. There is a good choice for vegetarians, children and those on a gluten free diet – all served daily from 6-9pm and on weekends from 12-2pm. Owing to popularity booking is recommended on weekends.

Owners Alun and Brenda also offer a great function room for hire, a traditional Sunday lunch and in the future will be providing guest accommodation so please ring for details. Open throughout the year from 5pm-close Mon-Thurs and from 4pm-close on Fridays and from 12pm on weekends the inn is a hive of activity with themed food nights and a range of special deals on offer.

126 PILGRIMS

Brecon Cathedral Close, Brecon,
Powys LD3 9DP
Tel: 01874 610610
Mobile: 07970997904
e-mail: pilgrimstearooms@btconect.com
website: www.pilgrims-tearooms.co.uk

Pilgrims award winning tea rooms are situated in the tranquil Brecon Cathedral Close. The tearooms retain much of the style of the adjacent sixteenth century tithe barn, which houses the Cathedral shop and Heritage Centre Museum (free entry).

The tea rooms are run by Janet Williams who has gained an impressive reputation for Pilgrims by cooking delicious fresh meals daily, using local and organic produce whenever possible and serving it in a warm, friendly atmosphere. The tea rooms are fully licensed serving a selection of wines, local ales and cider and a range of hot and cold soft drinks and there is seating in the tearooms, the Heritage Centre or alfresco around the tearooms herb garden.

- Open every day for morning coffee, lunch and afternoon tea. Traditional Welsh home-cooking
- A unique setting in the grounds of Brecon Cathedral Outside functions catered for.
- Available day and evening for private functions. Booked groups welcome. Open some evenings in conjunction with musical events in Brecon Cathedral.

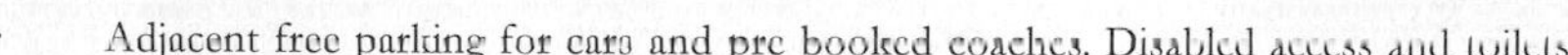

- Adjacent free parking for cars and pre booked coaches. Disabled access and toilets

A main menu is available from 12 until 2.30 which include a selection of home-made soup and bread, quiches, salads, sandwiches, jacket potatoes, casseroles, pies and delicious desserts. Traditional Sunday roasts are extremely popular and advanced booking is advisable. The tea rooms open daily throughout the year from 10 until 5pm. but close a little earlier during the winter months. Janet also provides outside catering for family, private and corporate functions. Particularly popular is Pilgrims food which can be delivered to, or collected by, self caterers at bunk houses and cottages in the Brecon Beacons area. Janet also takes her fresh welsh cakes, bread and specialities to Farmers Market in Brecon Market Hall.

Why not stop by and sample some of her traditional delights whilst taking full advantage of all that Brecon has to offer.

128 THE BRIDGE END INN

Bridge Street, Crickhowell,
Powys, NP8 1AR
Tel: 01873 810338
e-mail: info@thebridgeendinn.com
website: www.thebridgeendinn.com

Located in the thriving market town of Crickhowell, **The Bridge End Inn** is nestled between the Black Mountains and the Brecon Beacons. It is an exceptional public house, located at the edge of the Brecon National Park. The community of Crickhowell is extremely friendly and there are plenty of individual shops and popular restaurants for visitors to explore. The inn is next to the River Usk, which is a popular fishing river, attracting many people to the area.

The Bridge End Inn offers bed and breakfast in an out cottage attached to the pub. The cottage has three rooms comprising of one double en-suite, one double and a single. Although they are small and compact, the cottage really has a warm home from home feel about it and is very comfortable. Dating back to the 16th century, the former coaching inn looks delightful from the outside with its white and black theme and inside it doesn't disappoint. Inside the inn, it is brimming with character. The dark wooden furniture and stone walls really add to the atmosphere of the place. There are plenty of ornaments and pictures decorating the inn, and if you are interested in the history of the area then you will be in for a treat.

The restaurant is extremely popular, and has a fantastic reputation in the area. The chefs are local and produce outstanding food, using produce from local suppliers. The bar has a wide selection of real ale beers and good wines to sample. The atmosphere is wonderful and there are some wonderful local friendly characters. On warmer days the beer garden is definitely worth a look. Overlooking the Usk, the owners claim it to be one of the best views in Wales. Trout and salmon can be seen leaping up the stream.

There are plenty of activities to enjoy in the area. Beautiful scenery makes it an ideal place to enjoy walking and cycling and many visitors like to have a go at trout and salmon fishing on the famed River Usk. A lot of people visiting Crickhowell like to relax and retire to the restaurant or bar at The Bridge End Inn for the evening. Surrounded by the beautiful Welsh countryside, Crickhowell is still within easy reaching distance of Cardiff, which is just 40 minutes away.

129 THE FARMERS ARMS

Cwmdu, nr Crickhowell,
Powys NP8 1RU
Tel: 01874 730464
e-mail: ursellathome@aol.com
website: www.the-farmers-arms.com

The Farmers Arms is situated in Cwmdu, just North West of Crickenhowell on the A479. It is owned by Chris and Lyndsey Ursell who pride themselves on running a warm and friendly pub that serves great, honest home cooking. Food is served from 12-2pm and 6-9:30pm Tuesday to Saturday and on Sundays from 12-8pm. Lyndsey's menu is across the board and includes dishes such as a succulent 12oz Welsh sirloin; a seafood platter which is comprised of scampi tails, queen scallops and strips of haddock and plaice; and a creamy vegetable and stilton crumble. All dishes are cooked fresh to order and created using the best local produce for that authentic farmhouse taste.

Guests can dine throughout the inn; with its rustic farm house feel and well stocked bar it is an easy place to relax. There are also two real ales to enjoy with a guest ale occasionally making an appearance. Chris and Lyndsey also offer fine en suite accommodation for guests with a choice between a double room and a family room. The tariff includes a hearty breakfast.

Children are welcome. All major credit cards accepted.

130 USK INN

Station Road, Talybont-on-Usk, Brecon,
Powys LD3 7JE
Tel: 01874 676251
Fax: 01874 676392
e-mail: stay@uskinn.co.uk
website: www.uskinn.co.uk

The **Usk Inn** was established in the 1840s when the Brecon to Methyr Railway was being constructed. It stands opposite the former railway station and yard on the edge of the village which itself lies within the Brecon Beacons National park. Back in 1878, the inn's patrons must have felt in need of another drink when the 'wild run' of that year spilled the locomotive Hercules onto the station road!

Owners of the Usk Inn, Andrew and Jill Felix, took over here in February 2006 having previously owned the Aberthaw Hotel in Barry. They were dedicated to finding suitable premises in the area to realise their ambition of owning a quality hotel. The Usk currently has a 4 star rating and they are both determined to retain this prestigious award.

They aim to exceed their guests' expectations, whether in the cosy bar with its armchairs, sofas and games stack or in the bistro-styled restaurant, which has earned a rosette for its food. The menu changes regularly according to the availability of fresh local produce, whilst the specials board reflects some classics that never change such as steak and ale pie or succulent sirloin steak. Andrew is the chef here and specialises in fish dishes such as sautéed garlic and lime Crevettes, and scallops with black pudding salad. The menu also offers a good choice of poultry, meat and seasonal game dishes such as Guinea Fowl, roast duck and venison sausage. To compliment your meal there is an extensive choice of wines, or if you prefer a choice of two real ales on tap. Food is served between 12-2:30pm and 6:30-9:30pm each night. Children can dine from their own menu or take half portions from the main menu.

The bar along with its log fire provides respite for weary walkers and cyclists and remains open throughout the day. In warmer months there is plenty of outdoor seating in the charming tree fringed beer garden.

The inn also offers quality guest accommodation in ten upstairs en suite rooms which have been awarded 4 stars from both the Welsh tourist board and the AA.

131 THE TRAVELLERS REST INN

Talybont-on-Usk, nr Brecon,
Powys LD3 7YP
Tel: 01874 676233
e-mail: travellers.rest@hotmail.co.uk
website: www.travellersrestinn.com

The Travellers Rest Inn is located within the Brecon Beacons National Park offering some of the most spectacular scenery in Wales. A paradise for walkers, mountain bikers, horse riders, and all lovers of the outdoors. Situated on the banks of the tranquil Monmouthshire and Brecon Canal the Travellers Rest provides a superb base from which to explore the area. You could park the car and forget it. Alternatively the market towns of Brecon and Abergavenny, with their annual jazz and food festivals are a short drive away. The Travellers Rest is a perfect location for the literature festival, and the world famous book shops in Hay on Wye and the Royal Welsh Show in Builth Wells.

The Travellers Rest - originally bought as a cottage by Mr. William Jones, a local maltster in 1829 became the embryo of the Travellers Rest Inn. It has been altered and extended over time and the garden room restaurant is planned for summer 2010. The accommodation in 4 spacious en suite rooms furnished in an eclectic style from antique, restored collectables to modern contribute to the uniqueness of the Travellers. They have their exclusive entrance enabling guests to come and go as they please.

Breakfasts are bountiful, designed to sustain until returning for dinner in the evening. However packed lunches are provided on request.

Joy and Doug Browning , hosts for the past 20 years, have a well established reputation for fine food prepared from the choicest ingredients , many of which are grown and reared within 4 miles. Fresh fish is delivered 3 times a week from Devon. Signature dishes such as - Abergavenny Chicken- succulent chicken supreme, shallots, Herefordshire cider, honey and cream. Prime Welsh Beef fillet with a rich Port and Peppercorn sauce. Locally farmed Venison in red wine, wholegrain mustard cream. Joy's Nut and Vegetable Roast has no fewer than 23 ingredients served with mushrooms sautéed with Madeira have diners returning from far and wide.

There is a small well stocked bar and a comprehensive wine list to suit all tastes.

Special Dinner Bed and Breakfast breaks are available for Wednesday and Thursday all year round.

Just 3 hours from London, 75 minutes from Cardiff, Bristol or Hereford, this gem is a peaceful haven in which to unwind from the stresses of modern life, The Travellers Rest is highly recommended.

132 THE WHITE SWAN

Llanfrynach, Brecon, Powys LD3 7BZ
Tel: 01874 665276
e-mail: lee.havard@hotmail.co.uk
website: www.the-white-swan.com

Situated in the picturesque village of Llanfrynach found just three miles east of Brecon on the A40 is the spectacular **White Swan**. Outstanding in all departments, this stunning restaurant is guaranteed to make any evening a special one with a carefully created yet relaxing atmosphere, fantastic food, and un-intrusive, efficient hospitality.

The White Swan is easy to spot with its long, brilliant white front and large sash windows. The interior has a definite rustic feel with large comfortable dining chairs, stone walling, open log fires and low beamed ceilings. It is run by Lee and Debbie who have been here for the past 18 months. The pair make a great team; Lee with over 20 years experience as a professional head Chef and Debbie as manager; making sure things run smoothly. They are open every session serving a variety of drinks including a choice of three Welsh brewed ales. Food is served between 12-2pm and 7-9pm; booking is advised to avoid disappointment as the White Swan is a very popular place to dine. Closed on Monday (except bank holidays).

Lee's specialties are Mediterranean, French and traditional English dishes, and he has created a fine menu to reflect this. Dishes include slow roast lamb shoulder, Gressingham duck, venison wrapped in pancetta, cherry tomato, chorizo and basil risotto, potato cannelloni, and ox with parsnip mash. Guests can choose from the a la carte menu which changes monthly to showcase the best in local produce and game, or the specials board which changes daily and includes fresh fish dishes. The sweet menu also impresses with a fine selection of intricate creations such as chocolate and hazelnut tart with fruit and nut cluster and cream and raspberry sorbet, as well as having classics such as sticky toffee pudding and apple crumble. On Sundays Lee serves up a succulent roast with a variety of options. Children are welcome to dine throughout the week, but on Saturday evenings it is adults only. The restaurant seats up to 80 guests, but there is room for more outside in the well kept patio garden. All major credit cards accepted, large off road car park.

Lee and Debbie also offer fully fitted self catering accommodation in the next village along. Please ring for details.

133 THE RED LION

Duffryn Road, Llangynidr,
Crickhowell NP8 1NT
Tel: 01874 730223
e-mail: sarah_farr@btinternet.com
website: www.redlionpowys.com

Set in the heart of Llangynidr village found on the B4558 West of Crickhowell is **The Red Lion**. It has been owned and run by Sarah and Adrian Farr for the past two years and they have created an inn that is as popular with visitors to the area as it is with locals.

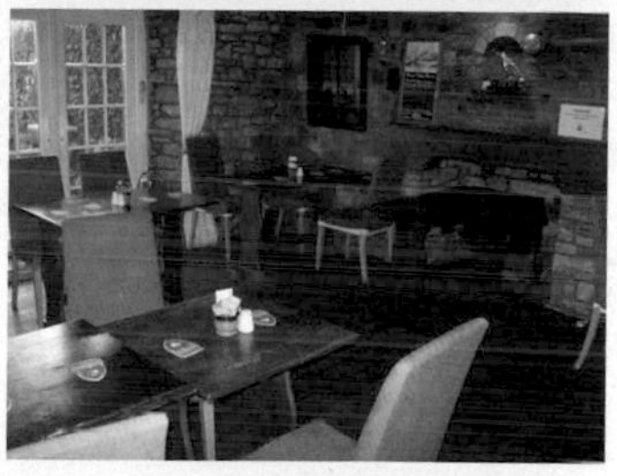

Open all day every day they serve up food daily from 12-2:30pm and 6-9pm from a great menu that comprises traditional favourites such as rump steak, ham egg and chips and a traditional Welsh lamb stew, to speciality dishes such as root vegetable pie, sizzling Cajun chicken, crab cakes and homemade beef enchiladas. There are plenty of lighter bites available for those with a smaller appetite including soup, and a selection of filled rolls and jacket potatoes. Wednesday lunchtimes are bargains for the over 60's with special discounted foods and a themed food night runs once a month.

The well stocked bar offers a vast choice which includes three rotating ales so there is always a new brew to sample and plenty of entertainment with a quiz every Thursday fortnight from 8pm and a great garden play area for the kids.

Sarah and Adrian also provide guest accommodation; offering a double room with en suite facilities and a twin with its own private bathroom, both of which come on a hearty breakfast rate.

134 THE CARLTON RESTAURANT

32-34 Greatdarkgate Street, Aberystwyth,
Ceredigion SY23 1DE
Tel: 01970 612314
e-mail: enquiries@thecarlton.info
website: www.thecarlton.info

Located on Aberystwyth's main street, is **The Carlton Restaurant**. Run by Martin Samuel and his mother Maria for over seven years, the Cartlon has a wealth of experience in providing their guests with great food every day. Open from 9am-5pm Mon - Sat and 10am-2pm on Sundays guests can chose from a selection of all day breakfasts, lunches, main meals, jacket potatoes and sandwiches. The food here is all about home cooking with great locally sourced ingredients. Popular dishes include the farmhouse gammon steak and the homemade steak and ale pie. The team also serve up a range of homemade desserts and snacks.

135 THE BLACK LION

Llanbadarn Fawr, Llanbardan, Aberystwyth,
Ceredigion SY23 3RA
Tel: 01970 623448

Situated in the hamlet of Llanbadarn Fawr, **The Black Lion** is just a short walk from the centre of Aberystwyth. It was built in 1720 and its current tenant, Kara Bland, manageress, Rebecca, and chef, Rachel, offer a very warm welcome to locals and visitors. Kara took over the child friendly pub with her team in April 2009 and it has a growing reputation, serving the very best in real ales and fine, freshly cooked food. Homemade Welsh beef lasagne is just one of the options from the extensive menu that has local produce at its heart. Such is the popularity of Sunday lunch it is advisable to book. Worthy of a visit is The Nags Head also run by Kara, in central Aberystwth.

136 DEVIL'S BRIDGE FALLS

Devil's Bridge, Aberystwyth,
Ceredigion SY23 3JW
Tel: 01970 890233

Take a walk along the Nature Trail and see the spectacular 300ft waterfalls and the view of the three bridges which span the breathtaking woodland gorge. The first bridge is reputed to have been built by the Devil but in reality it was built in the 11th century by the monks; the middle bridge was built in 1708, wider than the lower bridge, to take horse drawn vehicles; the top bridge was built in 1901 to cope with modern traffic.

Cross the humped bridge spanning over the Mynach river at the bottom of the waterfalls and begin to ascend the other side of the gorge. Go into Robbers Cave, an old hide-out place next to the waterfall. Alternatively, chose the easier, short walk to view the three bridges and the Devil's Punchbowl. Discover the legend, of how an old lady and her dog outwitted the Devil.

Allow at least half hour for the long walk, (but you can stay longer), 10 mins for the short walk and wear sensible shoes. Not suitable for elderly or disabled due to steps. Open all year.

137 LLYWERNOG LEAD & SILVER MINE

Ponterwyd, Aberystwyth,
Ceredigion SY23 3AB
Tel: 01970 890620 Fax: 01545 570823
e-mail: enquiries@silverminetours.co.uk
website: www.silverminetours.co.uk

The mining of silver-rich lead ore was an important industry in the Plynlimon Mountains of mid-Wales in the 1860s. Most of the mines were later abandoned but **Llywernog Lead & Silver Mine** survived and was saved from dereliction by the late Dr Stephen Harvey and his son Peter, who now run this seven-acre heritage site. Visitors can follow the Miners Trail, take the underground tour to the Great Chasm and see the working water wheels, mining machinery and mineral displays. The site, which has a souvenir shop and tea room, is open from April to October; closed Saturdays except at Easter and in August.

139 CLETTWR CAFÉ

Trerddol, Machynlleth, Powys SY20 8PN
Tel: 07792520306
e-mail: sbradley88@aol.com

The family run **Clettwr Café** has a good local following and has a fantastic reputation with visitors. Owned by Heledd Bradley and her daughters, Tara and Louise, for the past seven months there is some excellent cuisine on the menu. All of the food is cooked to order and Heledd's homemade dishes are very popular with customers. Homemade lasagne and leek and potato bake are among the favourites and there are plenty of sandwiches, jacket potatoes, salads and snacks to choose from. Seating up to 50 people the café is open Monday-Saturday 8am-5pm and Sunday 9am-5pm in winter months and for an extra hour each evening in the summer.

138 WHITE LION HOTEL

Talybont, Aberyswyth,
Ceredigion SY24 5ER
Tel: 01970 8322245
e-mail: nicolabyrne647@btinternet.com

The White Lion Hotel in Talybont has recently been taken over by local family Nicky and Shaun Burne and their daughter Teri who have continued to create a warm and happy environment for Talybont residents and visitors since their arrival. Nicky previously worked at the White Lion for 21 years before taking ownership and her wealth of experience at this venue really shines through. The family are much loved by the village, who enjoy the quality service they bring day in, day out.

Open all day every day serving a wide variety of soft and alcoholic drinks, the bar also offers a choice of three real ales including a guest rotation, Banks Original and Banks Bitter. Food is served from 12-3pm and 6-9pm daily – it's best to book, especially on Sundays as a fantastic Sunday lunch is served and has quickly become the areas favourite. The ethos of dining at the White Lion relies on good wholesome food; all dishes come freshly prepared on the premises, cooked to order and are made from local produce. Portions are generous and very reasonably priced, ensuring that the feeling of well being and homeliness extends to your stomach too!

Four quality en suite rooms are also available throughout the year on a great bed and breakfast rate.

140 PENWIG HOTEL

South John Street, New Quay, Llandysul,
Ceredigion SA45 9NN
Tel: 01545 560910
e-mail: penwig@sabrain.com

Penwig Hotel sits in an unbeatable location overlooking the New Quay Bay. Run by father and daughter team Michael and Sam for twelve years now, it is a very popular place for visitors to the area who enjoy the unrivalled views, fine ale, delicious food and high quality rooms on offer.

There are seven en suite rooms to chose from; one of which is located in a charming cottage to the rear which sleeps up to four guests. All rooms come on a bed and breakfast rate and have the option of dining in Penwig's great restaurant and pub.

Whether dining inside or al fresco to admire the sunny bay, guests will not be disappointed. Head Chef Jason offers an impressive menu of delicious gastro-pub cuisine. From starters, light bites, sandwiches, sweets and mains there is plenty to choose from. Dishes include 'the sausage pot,' Celtic pride sirloin and a melt in your mouth chocolate fondant. A fine selection of soft and alcoholic drinks is available to relax with, including three real ales direct from the Brains Brewery.

141 FEATHERS ROYAL HOTEL

Aberaeron, Ceredigion SA46 0AQ
Tel: 01545 571750
Fax: 01545 571760
e-mail: enquiries@feathersroyal.co.uk
website: www.feathersroyalhotel.co.uk

The **Feathers Royal Hotel** continues a strong tradition of hospitality, dating back to 1815 when it was originally built as a coaching inn for weary travellers. Today it stands one of Ceredigion's finest hotels with a reputation for comfort and class. It is set within the picturesque Georgian seaside harbour town of Aberaeon, just off the A487; ideally located for exploring this area of the coastline.

The Feathers is run by the Collier family made up of Lesley and Richard and their daughters Rebecca, Rachel and Ruth. They have spent their last few years at the Feathers building a reputation for high standards across all boards. The family helped to restore the Feathers to its former glory after a total refurbishment which has left the hotel handsomely decorated and decadently comfortable for guests staying for both business and pleasure.

There are thirteen bedrooms available each with luxury en suite bathroom, tea and coffee facilities, hairdryers, phones, broadband, flat screen TV and Sky. There is a choice of single, twin, double and family rooms; all of which are available on a fantastic bed and breakfast tariff with a choice of continental or a full Welsh cooked breakfast. One room is fully fitted for disabled customers.

The hotel also sports a fine restaurant which serves food from 12-2:30pm and 6-9pm each day. The head chef here and his team offer a remarkable dining experience that showcases the best, fresh Welsh produce in the area in a variety of succulent dishes. Favourites include the trio of Welsh lamb, wrapped pork loin and peppered monkfish. The restaurant also puts on entertaining speciality nights such as 'Italian night' where guests can chose from a selection of authentic Italian dishes and wine for a fantastic inclusive price.

The Welsh Cob bar and lounge is also available to guests serving a good variety of teas, coffees, snacks and light meals throughout the day and a carvery roast each Sunday. It stocks a fine selection of beers, malt whiskies, spirits and wines also.

Owing to the hotels fine décor and flawless service it is a popular place for functions with a marquee style room for hire seating up to 400 guests.

142 BLACK LION HOTEL

High Street, Lampeter,
Cereidigon SA48 7BG
Tel: 01570 422172
Fax: 01570 421172
e-mail: blacklion2@sabrain.com

The **Black Lion Hotel** is located on the main high street in the bustling town of Lampeter. It is a popular destination for visitors to the area who are looking for clean, stylish and comfortable accommodation with great amenities right on their doorstep.

The hotel itself has eighteen well equipped en suite rooms, designed for comfort and convenience on either a room only or bed and breakfast tariff. Guests can benefit from the hotel's own restaurant and bar; both of which are favourites for non-residents also.

The relaxing and contemporary style of the bar and restaurant are complimented by the hotel's smooth service which provides great food and real ale from 12-9pm Mon-Sat and 12-8pm on Sundays. The food here comes highly recommended, making it a necessity to book from Wed-Sat to avoid disappointment. The menu offers a plentiful selection of light bites, sharers, mains, grills, pub classics and a Sunday lunch; all created using mostly local produce. The fish dishes here are particularly popular, including the swordfish steak, although other favourites include fajitas, ribs and homemade steak and ale pie.

143 CASTLE HOTEL

High Street, Lampeter,
Ceredigion SA48 7BG
Tel: 01570 422554

Extremely popular with locals and visitors the award winning **Castle Hotel** is decked with a magnificent floral display. Located in the heart of Lampeter there is always a buzz around the child friendly hotel no matter what time of year it is. Since 2004 the hotel has won the Lampeter in Bloom contest three years running and has also won a number of other awards for its floral exterior. The owners John and Wendy Nicholas are very experienced in the business and it shows in the expert service and hospitality they and their staff offer.

The hotel is as attractive inside as it is outside and the smell of Wendy's home cooked food is enough to draw anyone into the separate restaurant. The menu is based around fresh, locally sourced ingredients and includes a wonderful steak and ale pie, along with seafood dishes, grills, curries, vegetarian dishes and some chef's specials. There is a selection of well-kept real ales with Brains and Buckley's as the regular brews.

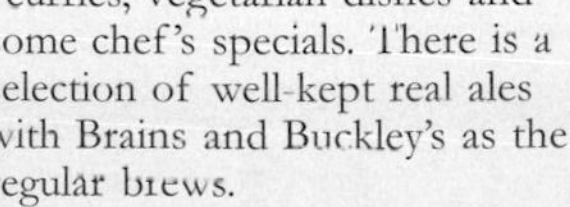

If you are staying in the area the hotel has nine comfortable guest bedrooms, all with en-suite facilities and attractively furnished and decorated. There is an off road car park for visitors and guests. All major credit cards accepted, except American Express.

144 Y LLEW COCH

Pontrhydfendigaud Road, Tregaron,
Ceredigion SY25 6HH
Tel: 01974 298266
e-mail: yllewcoch@hotmail.com

Hard to miss, this bright red pub sits in the heart of the historic market town Tregaron in the middle of the scenic Ceredigion. It's new owners Kat Sinnott has only been here a few months but is already raising standards and bringing Y Llew Coch back to its former glory, owing no doubt to her wealth of experience as a hotelier and licensee.

Open all day every day she serves a range of fine real ales and a good choice of fantastic pub grub which includes many traditional and old fashioned Welsh dishes. Only the finest and freshest local Welsh produce is used, making it easy to see why this place is a popular stop for a good old afternoon pub lunch. The all day breakfast is fast becoming a local favourite and is sure to do what it says on the tin.

Quality accommodation is also available here throughout the year, with a choice of four en suite upstairs rooms on a bed and breakfast rate or the rent of a charming self contained self catering flat to the rear of the premises that sleeps two people – but if guests are feeling lazy the breakfast tariff can happily apply.

145 THE NEW INN

Llandewi Brefi, Tregaron,
Ceredigion SY25 6RS
Tel: 01974 298452
e-mail: newinn1@hotmail.com

Located in the welsh speaking village of Llandewi Brefi, which acquired national fame as the home of Daffyd - "the only gay in the village" - in the TV comedy series Little Britain, **The New Inn** is a charming traditional inn dating back to the late 1890s. At the heart of the village the olde worlde inn is a delightful and welcoming hostelry popular with locals and visitors alike. Yvonne Edwards has owned The New Inn for almost 20 years and it is the outstanding home cooking on offer that has people returning for more.

Food is served throughout the day until 9pm and 95% of the ingredients used here are sourced locally. Among the favourites are home-made faggots and curries. On Sundays between noon and 2pm a traditional roast is served – this is very popular so it is advisable to book ahead. The well-stocked bar provides a wide choice of beverages including two real ales – Timothy Taylor Landlord and Cambrian Bitter. The child-friendly inn also offers accommodation all year round with a choice of two doubles and two singles. The inn is open all day every day except on Mondays unless it is a Bank Holiday. There's good disabled access and the pub has its own off road parking.

147 TAFARN FFOSTRASOL ARMS

Ffostrasol, Llandysul,
Ceredigion, SA44 4SY
Tel: 01239 851348
e-mail: ffostrasolarms@btinternet.com

Diners rarely leave disappointed from the former coaching inn, which is owned and run by the brother and sister team of Arthur and Betty Davies. Arthur, a local farmer has had the property for more than ten years and gave it a major makeover recently, keeping the old hostelry's charm and character.

Good food is a priority at the **Tafarn Ffostrasol Arms** with traditional favourites scattering the main menu. Old favourites include beef lasagne and home made beef and ale pie. There is also a range of steak, fish and vegetarian dishes on the extensive menu, which uses local produce wherever possible (A children's menu is available). On Sunday lunch time Betty takes over the kitchen and her roast dinners are so popular that booking is essential. Food is served from 12pm-2.30pm and from 5.30pm-9pm every day. The well stocked bar offers a wide choice of bevereges including two real ales – Hancocks HB and Brains SA, which can be enjoyed in the beer garden, which has a retractable awning. There are two self-contained flats located above the main premises, which are available all year round. The inn also caters for functions, from day trips, to weddings.

146 TAFARN BACH

Pontsian, Llandysul,
Ceredigion SA 44 4TZ
Tel: 01545 590269
e-mail: cadilois@btinternet.com

Found on the outskirts of Pontsian village, just north of Rhydowen adjacent to the B4459 is the charming country inn of **Tafarn Bach**. It dates back to the early 19th century, combining many beautiful original features with modern facilities. Set in a scenic location full of history and charm it's a lovely place to stop off after a day's exploring.

It has been run by Julia, Dorian and the rest of the Davies family for the past six years, in which time they have created a friendly, family environment to dine, drink or and relax in. Open from 5pm on weekdays and from 11am on weekends, it is a popular place to be.

The bar offers two real ales which include the regular Buckley's Bitter and a guest ale on rotation from local breweries. The traditional décor is complimented some evenings by live entertainment, please ring for details.

A fantastic selection of great food is also available here from 6pm onwards during the week, and from 11am on Saturdays and from 12:30pm on Sundays. Guests can choose from the printed menu or the daily changing specials board. Both menus are artfully created using only fresh local produce, some of which even comes from the family's very own vegetable plot. The style centres on traditional homemade pub food which includes a variety of hearty grills, homemade pies, fish and vegetarian dishes, curries and salads; something for everyone. According to those that dine here the most popular dishes are the steak and kidney pie and the spiced lamb meatballs. The family are keen to cater for all dietary requirements and a children's menu is also available. On Sundays there is a treat for all the family with a hearty Sunday lunch with a choice of 3 meats and fresh home grown vegetables.

Tafran Bach also caters for larger events such as birthdays or anniversaries with a large, well equipped function room available for hire with up to eighty seats.

Whatever the occasion, the Davies family ensure good service, a warm welcome and high quality food and drink throughout the year in a truly charming venue.

148 THE BLACK LION

High Street, Cardigan,
Ceredigion SA43 1HU
Tel: 01239 612532
Fax: 01239 621509
website: www.theblacklion-hotel.co.uk

Situated in the heart of the vibrant town of Cardigan right on the high street is **The Black Lion**. The property dates back to the early 12th century in parts and is believed to be the oldest coaching house in Wales. Sadly the inn had been closed for some time but re-opened recently after the arrival of its new owners in June this year.

The Phillips family include parents and owners Peter and Anne, daughter and manager Olivia and other daughters Michelle, Louisa and Nicola. Every individual in this charming family have put endless hours of hard work and dedication into renovating the Black Lion and have truly given it a new lease of life. They have restored the inn to its former glory as one of the most popular places to go drink and dine Cardigan, being careful to retain its olde worlde charisma whilst installing modern facilities throughout.

Open all day every day, food is served between 12-2:30pm and 6-9pm Monday to Saturday and from 12-2:30pm on Sundays. The menu here might be small, but it is well thought through. There is a small selection of light bites, sandwiches and main meals available, all made with local produce where possible. Popular dishes include steak and ale pie and spicy chicken Goujon. On Sundays an impressive Sunday roast with all the trimmings is added to the menu. The family also provide a daily specials board with a small but delicious selection of desserts that are not to be missed.

A good selection of soft drinks, wines and spirits is served throughout the day along with a choice of two real ales; London Pride and Bombardier.

The renovations here also included creating fourteen beautiful upstairs en suite rooms, which range from single to family in size. Each room is uniquely decorated and stays true to the property's period style whilst also offering modern facilities and comfort. They are available throughout the year on a hearty bed and breakfast tariff, making them an ideal option for short breaks away exploring this inviting area.

149 EAGLE INN

Castle Street, Cardigan,
Ceredigion SA43 3AA
Tel: 01239 612046

Dating back to the late 1700s the child-friendly **Eagle Inn** offers good quality, wholesome food and real ales every day. Owners Marianne and Peter Warren have owned the inn for three years and it has recently been refurbished to a very high standard. With a new lease of life it is extremely popular with locals and visitors – many who come to enjoy the two real ales on offer. Quality, traditional, home cooked food is the order of the day here and all produce is sourced from within Wales. Marianne is a superb cook and her dishes have people visiting and revisiting.

150 HIGHBURY GUEST HOUSE & RESTAURANT

Pendre, Cardigan, Ceredigion SA43 1JU
Tel: 01239 613403
Fax: 01239 613403
e-mail: highburyguesthouse@live.co.uk

The Highbury Guest House and Restaurant is owned and run by local famers Angela and Jimmy Wilson, a charming pair who are dedicated to satisfying their guests. Located in Pendre along the beautiful Cardigan coast, this late Victorian Villa makes a pleasant place to take a short break away.

They have seven en suite rooms available and three more rooms with their own private bathrooms. All are well maintained and homely, each available on a bed and breakfast rate or bed and breakfast and dinner rate which includes a meal in the downstairs restaurant.

The restaurant is open each evening from 6:30-8:30pm and serves a great selection of handsomely cooked homemade meals prepared. Only fresh local produce is used in the food here, giving an authentic Welsh taste that is truly brought to life by Angela's culinary skills. Popular to locals and guests alike, the restaurant seats fifty people and also offers a succulent carvery between 12-2pm each Sunday lunch time.

151 CASTELL MALGWYN HOTEL

Llechryd, Cardigan,
Ceredigion SA43 2QA
Tel: 01239 682382
e-mail: reception@malgwyn.co.uk
website: www.castellmalgwyn.co.uk

Dating back to 1795, the **Castell Malgwyn Hotel** is a classic Georgian mansion which was built by Sir Benjamin Hammet as his private residence. He loved it so much he declined the honour of becoming Lord Mayor of London so that he could remain at his beloved mansion house. He was fined £1000 for avoiding his duties!

Located in the beautiful Teifi valley, the hotel stands in an 8 acre estate that includes a beautiful driveway, glorious woodland and a stretch of private fishing on the Teifi, which is renowned for its sea trout and salmon. Guests can play on the croquet lawn made for Lily Gower (English Champion) or walk along the river bank through the gorge to Cilgerran Castle.

The hotel itself still retains much of its original Georgian charm and architectural features.

Guests can dine in "Lily's", the hotel's renowned restaurant, and savour the local and international first class cuisine prepared by the chef from fresh local produce. And, perhaps, enjoy a fine wine from the carefully selected wine list. Afterwards, relax in the Lounge or Library Bar and enjoy the ambience before mounting the original Georgian staircase to one of the bedrooms each tastefully decorated in an individual style and all with a refurbished bathroom.

152 PENLLWYNDU INN

Llangoedmor, nr Cardigan SA43 2LY
Tel: 01239 682533

Quality home made food is what draws people back time and again to the **Penllwyndu Inn**. Located near Cardigan it was established as an inn in 1985 and the leaseholders, Ryan and Pat Williams, are extremely familiar with the premises as it was their first home together.

Now well-established the inn serves a selection of real ales – Buckleys Best, Speckled Hen, Directors and excellent food is available daily with local produce at the heart of the menu. Home made dishes are the speciality at the Penllwyndu Inn and among the most popular dishes is duck breast in a black cherry sauce with kirsch. Food is served during opening hours until 9.30pm and traditional favourites include lasagne, cottage pie, chilli, soups and so on. The restaurant seats 30 diners and customers can also eat in the bar area and in the secluded beer garden on brighter days. Such is the popularity of the place booking is strongly recommended for Friday and Saturday evenings. Children are welcome and for the younger guests there is a special children's menu. If you don't fancy eating out takeaways are available. The Penllwyndu Inn has good disabled access and all major credit cards are accepted.

153 THE SHIP – Y LLONG

Llangrannog, Ceredigion SA44 6SL
Tel: 01239 654510

The Ship – Y Llong sits in an eye catching location on the coast of beautiful Llangrannog. Owned and personally run for the past year and a half by Sara Beechly and her father Mansel along with the expert help of Chef Gareth, the Ship has become a popular place to dine. It is renowned for its creative menu and unbeatable location, offering unrivalled food and views across to the sea simultaneously.

Guests dining here can also benefit from the themed evenings the team offer; held twice a month throughout the winter. Aimed at celebrating both Welsh food and culture these evenings are a must try for new comers to Wales who can enjoy true Welsh hospitality in a relaxing, yet stylish environment. Please ring for details.The Ship is open all day everyday and serves food between 12-2:30pm and 6-9pm daily. The bar offers between two and four real ales, all of which are brewed within Wales and usually from the Purple Moose or Thomas Watkin Breweries. A good selection of other fine wines, spirits and soft drinks is also available.

There are a choice of menus available including a full lunch menu, evening, bar and children's menu. All menus come in both English and Welsh languages for guests convenience. Each offers truly exquisite cuisine, the majority of which is made from locally sourced produce. The most popular dishes here are the seafood dishes which include Llangrannog crab cakes, pan fried salmon and fish of the day. All fish served here are caught in the bay by Mansel himself, so freshness is guaranteed. The menu also includes a large range of other dishes to such as butternut squash risotto, chicken with chorizo ratatouille, braised lamb and stuffed mushrooms so there is something for everyone. On Sundays there is a separate lunchtime menu which reflects both Gareth's wealth of experience but also the best seasonal produce in the area. Diners have the option of eating within the Ships stylish interior or taking their meal al fresco on the patio area where there is room for a further thirty guests in the summer months.

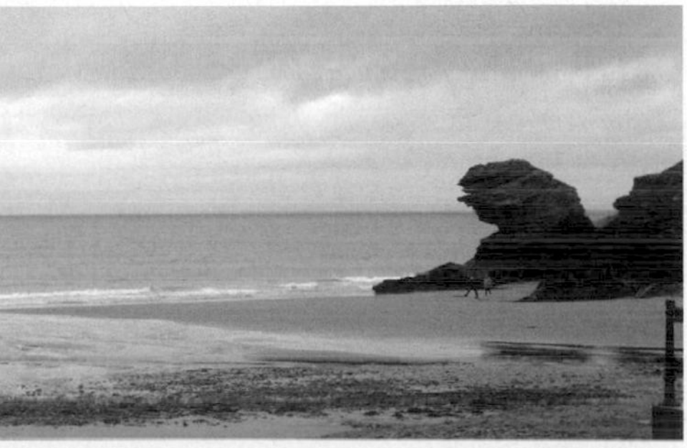

154 BRYNHOFFNANT INN

Brynhoffnant, nr Llandysul,
Ceredigion SA44 6DU
Tel: 01239 654961

The **Brynhoffnant Inn** stands aside the main A487 coastal road between Aberaenon and Cardigan. It is an impressive building that dates back in parts to 1860 when it was once a fine coaching inn. Today it still sports many beautiful period features such as low beamed ceilings and exposed original stone walling giving it a traditional feel. Run by John and Michelle for the past two years it attracts many visitors for its great collection of homemade food.

Open all day everyday there is a real ale on offer with guest ales also appearing in the summer months when the inn's large beer garden is at its best. Food is available daily from 12-9pm Mon-Sat and from 12-3:30pm on Sundays when a succulent 3 meat roast is on offer. All other main dishes are created by Michelle using Welsh produce only. Particularly popular are the steaks, steak and ale pie and the vegetarian choices such as the broccoli and brie rosti or the lasagne. On Thursday nights a popular 'curry and a pint' deal is also on offer. Children are welcome and can choose from their own menu. John and Michelle also offer great family entertainment with a Bingo night every Wednesday from 9pm and live music once a month.

155 THE GATE INN

Scleddau, Dwybach, Fishguard,
Pembrokeshire SA65 9QY
Tel: 01348 873739

Impossible to miss this bright green roadside inn sits adjacent to the A40, just south of Fishguard in the charming hamlet of Scleddau. **The Gate Inn** has a long and interesting history which you can find out from owner Lesley Llewellyn who has been running the inn for the past 10 years. A warm welcome is extended to all who come to enjoy the good home cooked food and well kept ales served all day every day.

The bar offers a choice of two rotating real ales from local breweries for ale lovers alongside a good choice of wines, spirits and lagers. Food is available daily from 12-2pm and 7-9pm and is cooked up by Lesley herself using only local produce sourced from within Wales. The menu offers good old pub classics such as lasagne, burgers, scampi and battered cod. Other favourites include homemade chicken or vegetarian curry, pasta bake and a mighty mixed grill. Children's options are available. On Sundays Lesley serves up a popular Sunday lunch, so it's best to get there early to avoid disappointment. Cash and cheque only please.

156 SALUTATION INN

Felindre Farchog, nr Newport, Crymych,
Pembrokeshire SA41 3UY
Tel: 01239 820564
Fax: 01239 820355
e-mail: johndenley@aol.com
website: saltuationcountryhotel.co.uk

The village of Felindre Farchog lies within the Pembrokeshire Coast National Park and is well worth seeking out in order to visit a charming old hotel; the **Salutation Inn**. This ancient 16th century coaching inn is set right on the bank of the river Nevern whose beautiful valley provides guests with a peaceful and relaxing haven away from the pressures of life.

Hosts at the Salutation Inn are John and Gwawr Denley who in April 2006 opened their stylish new restaurant called 'Denleys' which is set in beautiful surroundings overlooking the river. It serves delicious food, prepared using fresh local produce such as Welsh beef and Preseli lamb. A typical menu might also offer as a starter chicken liver parfait with homemade date chutney and toast. For the main course, how about tasty deep fried salmon, pepper and mozzarella fishcakes with a lemon cream sauce. To round off a meal here there are some glorious deserts, locally made ice creams or a selection of fine Welsh cheeses. For lighter appetites, the bar serves a good selection of tasty snacks. Food is available every lunchtime from 12:30-2:30pm and every evening from 6:30-9:30pm.

In addition to the restaurant there's a lounge bar and a local's bar with its own pool table. Amongst the comprehensive range of beverages there are between two and four real ales on tap with Double Dragon being the regular brew.

Accommodation at the Salutation boasts a fantastic three star rating from the Welsh Tourist board. There are eight well appointed guest bedrooms; all located on the ground floor and all with en suite facilities, television and hospitality trays. Guests can choose between a twin, double or family room.

The hotel provides an ideal base for country leisure activities – including bird watching, fishing and horse riding. The area is also a great location for water sports. Close by is one of the most spectacular sections of the Pembrokeshire Coast Path and there is also excellent walking in the hills around Carn Ingli mountain. Special arrangements can be made for Salutation Inn guests to enjoy a round of golf at the links course near Newport which commands stunning sea views.

157 FRONLAS

Market Street, Newport,
Pembrokeshire SA42 0PH
Tel: 01239 820351
e-mail: joy.solov@btinternet.com

Situated in the heart of the lively seaside town of Newport, opposite the Spar shop is **Fronlas**. It is a great family run cafe in an ideal location for exploring the rugged coastline with both Fishguard and Cardigan Bay only a short drive away. It's appealing stone walled front and striped awning provide a friendly welcome to guests who can enjoy their choices either outside to people-watch or in the light, homely atmosphere within, where the tempting aroma of good old home baking wafts through.

Fronlas is run by the charming Solov family, made up of Joy and Samm and their daughter and son Kate and Russell. All the family take a hand in cooking some of the delights on offer here and are never without a smile on their face. Their priorities are customer satisfaction, made obvious by the friendly and efficient service offered at all times.

Open from 9am-9pm throughout the Summer and from 10am-4pm from September to March, the cafe is a popular place to dine or drink as it serves a wide variety of hot and cold drinks and is licensed to sell beer, wine and cider. Particularly popular are the range of cooked breakfasts here which range from simply tea and toast to a gargantuan full English, also available as a vegetarian option. There is also a good range of light bites which include a selection of baguettes, paninis, jacket potatoes, sandwiches, toasties and soups. Main meals include chilli con carne, sausage and mash, bean goulash and bolognaise. A good choice of homemade cakes which are made on the premises are also available. Fronlas secret weapon however is its status as the only creperie in North Pembrokeshire, serving a tantalising range of sweet crepes, Belgian waffles and savoury galettes. Each comes with a variety of fillings from sugar and lemon, maple syprup, honey or ice cream for the sweet ones or a choice of med veg & goat's cheese, tuna mayo & sweetcorn, ham, leek & cheddar or cheddar & tomato for the galettes. They really are worth a try – and might even be converted to your favourite. For some guests, it's what keeps them coming back to Fronlas time and time again.

Whatever your choice here, the Solov's will endeavour to meet any dietary requirements including vegan, vegetarian and gluten free. A children's menu is also available. Well behaved dogs are welcome inside and outside.

158 NAG'S HEAD INN

Abercych, Boncath,
Pembrokeshire SA37 0HJ
Tel: 01239 841200

Located on the banks of the river Teifi, exactly at the border between Pembrokeshire and Carmarthenshire is the **Nags Head Inn**. A fine olde worlde inn that sits alongside the entrance to the enchanted valley that features in the famous Welsh folk tales of the Mobinogion; it retains many period features such as brick fireplaces and beamed ceilings. Owned by Sam Jamieson who has been running the inn for the past 14 years; it provides great food, drink and modern facilities for all, with a large undercover outdoor seating area and fabulous children's play area. Open every session from Tues-Sat and all day on Sundays, the bar offers a wealth of ales and beer, showcasing hundreds of bottles as an interesting display throughout the pub. Three ales are available including the Nag's own brew. Food is served from 12-2pm and 6-9pm daily. Owing to popularity, booking is recommended on weekends. Dishes include Smugglers chicken, Pembrokeshire hot and spicy sausage and potato pie, goat's cheese cannelloni, steak and ale pie and a range of handsome grills. Where possible local produce is used. Children have their own menu.

160 TWMPATH GUEST HOUSE

Maenclochog, Pembrokeshire SA66 7RL
Tel: 01437 532990
Mobile: 07917 223252
e-mail: enquire@twmpath.co.uk
website: www.twmpathguesthouse.co.uk

Diane Davies is the proud owner of **Twmpath Guest House** adjacent to the B4313 in pretty Maenclochog. Affectionately known to those who have seen an aerial photo of the property as 'Little Island in Pembrokeshire,' this bed and breakfast is a home from home for all who visit as its thoughtful and dynamic décor, rustic feel and unbeatable hospitality ensure each stay is a great one.

There are three rooms to choose from, all of which have en suite facilities and a 4 star rating from the Welsh Tourist Board. One room is fully adapted for disabled customers, families welcome and dogs by prior arrangement. Guests can enjoy the property's cosy dining area and lounge where you can sink into a comfy arm chair before a roaring fire beneath gnarled 200 year old beamed ceilings.

Diane has won numerous awards for her guest house which highlights how thoroughly pleasant a stay here is. Amongst them are the Cyclists and Walkers Welcome award, the Warm Welsh Welcome award and the Pembrokeshire Produce award, Diane is renowned for her hearty breakfast.

Cash and cheque only please.

159 POST OFFICE BISTRO AND BAR

The Old Post Office, Rosebush,
Clynderwen, Pembrokeshire SA66 7QU
Tel: 01437 532205

The Post Office Bistro and Bar is located in the pretty village of Rosebush, just a short drive from the stunning Pembrokeshire coast line between Fishguard and Maenclochog. The village itself is a popular place to visit, surrounded by many beauty spots and historical sites of interest including Duffryn Syfynwy; a set of 18 large ancient stones surrounding a Cairn. The bistro and bar are therefore ideally located for couples, families and singles of all ages and abilities to stop off for a delicious bite to eat or cosy drink by the fire after rambling around the area.

The inn has been run by Ruth and Derrek for the past 4 years, in which time they have established a lively and dynamic atmosphere for their guests who come from near and far to enjoy the spread of quality food served in the bistro and live music from the various jamming sessions put on each week. On the second Friday of every month the session invites acoustic folk players, whereas the last Friday invites bluegrass pick and Sundays mean electric golden oldies rock and roll and country music. The team always welcome newcomers and ensure that any night had here is a memorable one with some good names appearing on the circuit too. Contrasting the animated atmosphere, the inn itself has a traditional olde worlde décor, with its past life as a post office well documented upon its walls. The bar is on the cosy side but is amply stocked with a good selection of well kept real ales, wines and spirits.

The bistro prides itself on serving up an exciting home cooked menu, without forsaking all the usually favourites. The team are happy to cater for special dietary requirements and specialise in creating tasty dishes for vegans and vegetarians alike. The menu changes daily to reflect the ingredients available that day as the team only cook with the best fresh local produce in the area. Food is served from 6pm-close Tuesdays to Saturdays and 12pm-close on Sundays in the Winter months and every day in the summer months from 12pm-close apart from Mondays when the inn is closed all year round. Children are welcome and can dine throughout, although booking is recommended at all times to avoid disappointment. All major credit cards accepted.

161 THE CITY INN

New Street, St Davids,
Pembrokeshire SA62 6SU
Tel: 01437 720829
e-mail: howardnush1967@tiscali.co.uk

Just a short walk from the centre of historic St David's is **The City Inn**. This charming town is best known for being the smallest cathedral town in the country and making the inn the ideal place for a relaxing drink or a bite to eat after exploring the town's stunning and unusual cathedral, best shops and sights. It has been owned and run by mother and son team Howard and Pauline Bush since 1995.Their priority is customer satisfaction, creating a chilled out, friendly environment for all. Their hard work over the years has built them up an impressive following from the town inhabitants and visitors to St David's alike who come to sample the great home cooking.

Guests here can choose from 11 attractive and well furnished rooms, 9 of which have excellent en suite facilities. There is a range of rooms available from twins and doubles to family rooms, all of which have been given a 3-star rating by the Welsh Tourist Board. Children are very welcome. A hearty breakfast is included in the tariff which is guaranteed to set you up for the day, making the inn the perfect place to take a short break or long weekend away getting to know this charming town.

The bar is open from noon to midnight throughout the week and open until 1am on Friday and Saturday nights. A great selection of soft and alcoholic beverages is on offer behind the well stocked bar which includes a real ale; Double Dragon from the now famous Felin Foel Brewery.

Food is on offer every day in the summer months from 6pm onwards where guests can choose from the main menu or specials board, both of which specialise in wholesome home cooking. All dishes served here are created using as much local produce as possible and change regularly. Dishes include a succulent sirloin steak, beef lasagne, chicken, plaice, scampi, a choice of curries, and vegetarian options which include mushroom stroganoff and a leek and red Leicester quiche, alongside pub classics like ham egg and chips.

There is a large off road car park for guests' convenience; all credit cards are accepted apart from American Express and Diners.

162 THE ROYAL GEORGE

13 High Street, Solva,
Haverfordwest SA62 6TF
Tel: 01437 720002
e-mail:
enquiries@theroyalgeorgesolva.co.uk
website: www.theroyalgeorgesolva.co.uk

The Royal George is a fantastic, fun and friendly pub run by a leaseholder Barry, manager Sophie and their hardworking team of staff. Barry has been here since March 2008 and has endeavoured to provide the locals and visitors to Solva a lively place to unwind after exploring the area, which offers a range of breathtaking walks along the coast and quirky shops within the town.

The pub is known best for its lofty position on the high street, providing panoramic views out to sea from its rear patio, but you'll be missing out if you don't sample some of the fine food on offer. The Royal George specialises in local seafood in its restaurant, which is caught fresh daily in the bay. In season, food is available from 12-9pm and most sessions out of season. The menu includes a fantastic range of classic pub cuisine, all homemade and cooked to order by our local chef Dom Brodie. Local produce is used wherever possible and the team pride themselves on offering some of their very own produce which they smoke on the premises. This includes smoked fish, chicken and prawns. Throughout the day the George runs a great light bites menu sampling a selection of filled sandwiches, jacket potatoes and smaller meals. Hidden away upstairs above the main pub and restaurant is another gem, the George's own Chinese restaurant and takeaway for when you fancy something a bit different; ideally placed – you can take a stool at the well stocked bar for a glass of wine or pint while you wait for your order to be ready! The bar also offers three well kept real ales which include Celtic Pride, Worthington and a guest ale which rotates from local breweries.

The bright and cosy atmosphere in the George is further enhanced by the great entertainment it puts on week in, week out for all the family. Thursday night is quiz and music night with a daunting gallon of beer for the lucky winners and a raffle with some fantastic prizes up for grabs. On selected weekends the team invite in local bands and musicians to play live which includes artists like 'Honey Fungus,' 'Neptune's Retreat' and 'Slung Together,' making for a really fun and vibrant night out to give your support to local up and coming bands.

Accommodation is available here throughout the year with a choice of three rooms, one of which is family sized. Two rooms have stunning sea views and en suite facilities. All major credit cards accepted except Diners, children, muddy boots and dogs welcome!

163 BRISTOL TRADER

Quay Street, Haverfordwest,
Pembrokeshire SA61 1BE
Tel: 01437 762122
Fax: 01437 776724
e-mail: bartrader@tiscali.co.uk
website: www.bristoltrader.com

Situated in a fine location alongside the Western Cleddau river system is the **Bristol Trader**. It serves great food and drink throughout the day and is best known for its friendly atmosphere. Found right on Quay Street in the bustling town of Haverfordwest, the pub is easy to spot with its large bay dining area.

It is owned and run by Margaret and Brian Harries, a local couple who have put their heart and soul into creating a truly relaxing environment over the past six years for both locals and visitors to the area alike. Their priority is customer satisfaction and they are always keen to hear comments from customers which are invaluable as they strive always to maintain their high standards.

Food is served daily from Monday to Thursday from 12-8:30pm and on Fridays and Saturdays from 12-7pm and 12-3pm on Sundays when a spectacular carvery is dished up. The focus with food here is on using fresh local produce whenever possible to create great tasting food. Owing to popularity, it's an advantage to book. Guests can choose from the main menu or the specials board. The main menu includes a range of jackets, Paninis, main dishes and pub classics like ploughman's, chicken curry or chilli con carne. Popular main dishes include grilled haddock in herbs and butter, a Cajun rib-eye steak and the beef lasagne, but locals rave about the pub's deep fried 'sexy' wedges either served with bacon or mushrooms for vegetarians, drizzled in onion, garlic and sweet chilli sauce, melted cheese, salad and coleslaw. The inn also offers a small buffet menu for events and other functions that can be held at the Trader throughout the year, please ring for details.

A great selection of speciality teas and coffees, hot chocolates and beers is available with a fine wine list to accompany your meal. There are three real ales on offer throughout the day, with Worthington being the regular alongside other rotating guest ales from local breweries. The pub features in the 2010 Good Beer Guide. Guests can dine and drink throughout, ordering at the bar each day from 11am until close. Children and well behaved dogs are welcome, so the Trader is a popular place with families and walkers alike who can enjoy a well earned rest inside or outside on the great patio area which overlooks the river itself.

164 THE WOLFE INN

Wolfcastle, Haverfordwest,
Pembrokeshire SA62 5LS
Tel: 01437 741662

Thie spectacular **Wolfe Inn** is named after the famous Admiral Wolfe and dates back hundreds of years to that era. Situated alongside the main A40 at Wolfe's Castle between Haverfordwest and Fishguard the inn is easily located and draws visitors from miles around to sample the fine cuisine on offer.

Chef Martin and his wife Alison have many years experience in the trade and offer 2-3 real ales each session alongside food served between 12-2:30pm and 6-9pm each day. The inn seats up to 80 guests over three cosy dining areas, with a choice from the main menu and the specials board. Favourite dishes include salmon, cod and spring onion fishcakes; crepes 'Fruits de Mer;' Texan barbeque chicken; rabbit casserole; and venison and cranberry pie. A good range of vegetarian options, children's meals and grills are also available which go well with Martin's range of speciality sauces. All dishes are created using local Welsh produce. Booking is recommended Fri and Sat evenings, Sunday lunch and throughout the summer holidays when food is available all day on Sunday.

Martin and Alison also offer three upstairs en suite rooms, with one twin, one double and one family room to choose from. Tariff includes a hearty breakfast, all major credit cards accepted apart from American Express and Diners.

166 NANT-Y-FFIN HOTEL AND MOTEL

Llandissilio, Clynderwen,
Pembrokeshire SA66 7SU
Tel: 01437 563423
Fax: 01437 563329
e-mail: info@nantyffin.co.uk
website: www.nantyffin.co.uk

Situated in between the popular seaside resorts of the Pembrokeshire coastline and the Preseli Mountains the **Nant-Y-Ffin Hotel and Motel** is ideally located for exploring the area. Owned and run by Emrys and Anne Murrows and their children Rhian and Brian, this family hotel offers 24 en suite guest rooms on a hearty B&B or B&B and dinner rate. One room is fully adapted for disabled customers, with 14 rooms also easily accessible on the ground floor.

Food is available from 9am-9pm daily in the hotel's spectacular restaurant where guests can choose from the main menu or the daily specials board which samples great winter warmers such as soft braised Welsh beef pot roast, rack of local lamb and potato lattice, and beef wellington with mushroom pate. Other dishes include noodle stir fry, sweet and sour chicken, rigatoni pasta with tomato vodka cream sauce and good old fish and chips. On Sundays a handsome Sunday lunch is served with 3 courses and options of turkey, beef, lamb, salmon and vegetarian. The restaurant is fully licensed and holds a great selection of draught keg ales and bottled real ales.

A magnificent and recently re-modelled function room is also available to hire which seats up to 200 guests and is perfect for conferences, exhibitions special occasions as it is licensed for marriages and civil partnerships.

165 PUMP ON THE GREEN

Spittal, Haverfordwest,
Pembrokeshire SA62 5QT
Tel: 01437 741749
e-mail: lizblackburn2000@btinternet.com

The **Pump on the Green** is an outstanding village inn offering the very best in service and pub grub. Liz and Ade took over the running of the inn this year (2009) and, with a lot of previous experience, are already putting the place back on the map. Dating back to the early 19th century the inn is located in the picturesque village of Spittal and is found east off the A40 and west off the B4329.

The inn offers three popular real ales, with Speckled Hen the regular as well as two rotating guest ales. Ade prepares and cooks all of the meals on the menu, which although limited at the moment, is soon to be extended. Home cooking is the order of the day at the Pump on the Green. Traditional meals, including faggots, peas and chips; a wide range of steaks and fish dishes are available. Among the most popular dishes are mixed grill and gammon – both are served with chips, jacket or boiled potatoes. On brighter days meals and drinks can be enjoyed in the beer garden, located to the rear of the child-friendly inn. Food is served between 6pm and 10pm every evening and Sunday lunch times. Such is the inn's popularity it is advisable to book on Sundays.

The Pump on the Green is at the heart of village life and is extremely popular with the local community and visitors. Spittal lies between Haverfordwest and Fishguard and is located in Pembrokeshire, close to the towns of Tregggarne, Rudbaxton and Walton East. The county, which lies in the west of Wales has plenty to offer visitors, many who return time and time again to take in the beautiful scenery. Bordered by the sea on three sides, it is a maritime county, which has a strong focus on tourism. Places to see in the area include Scolton Museum and Visitor Centre, Oakwood Theme Park and Folly Farm.

The Pump on the Green is open from 4.30pm from Monday through to Thursday and all day on Fridays, Saturdays and Sundays. It is closed lunch times Monday – Thursdays. All major credit cards taken. Disabled access is not a problem.

167 THE BUSH INN

Robeston Wathen, Narbeth,
Pembrokeshire SA67 8EP
Tel: 01834 860778
e-mail: kezffc@yahoo.co.uk
bushinn@rocketmail.com
website: www.thebush-inn.co.uk

Conveniently located beside the A40 on the edge of the pleasant village of Robeston Wathen is the **Bush Inn**. The inn has earned a glowing reputation from both locals and visitors to the area who praise the fine selection of honestly priced, quality cuisine served here each day. Pivotal to the inn's success are three of owners Kerry, Tammy and Ann who have made the Bush the thriving community base it is today. Their priority is meeting their customers' needs and they showcase a variety of 'value for money' deals to highlight this.

Food is served daily from12-9pm Monday to Saturday and a succulent carvery is also available between 12-4pm every Sunday. Owing to the popularity of the food here, it is advised to book on weekends. The menu is created using fresh local produce where possible and provides a range of starters, salads, fish, vegetarian dishes, steaks and grills, main courses and lighter bites for lunchtimes. Popular dishes are the locally produced beef steaks, the homemade pie of the day, the rack of ribs and the fresh local trout. The local favourites though are Kerry's curry of the day, which can also be taken advantage of each Tuesday night when from 5-9pm guests can choose their freshly prepared curry of choice and a drink for under £10. Senior citizens are also well catered for here with an senior citizens menu served daily from 12-4pm Monday through to Thursday with a choice that includes battered cod, pie of the day, lasagne, ham egg and chips and a choice of tasty desserts. Children are welcome at all times and can dine from their own separate menu.

But if food is not on the agenda, the Bush also provides a relaxing place to have a drink or two. The bar is open all day every day; its pleasant brick and wrought iron interior provide a friendly backdrop to enjoy the choice of two real ales that are on offer; rotating from local breweries. There is good disabled access throughout, all major credit cards accepted apart from American Express and Diners.

168 THE WINDSOR HOTEL

Church Road, Johnston,
Pembrokeshire SA62 3HE
Tel: 01437 890080
e-mail: sprkatheri@aol.com

Situated halfway between Haverford West and Milford Haven in the village of Johnston you will find **The Windsor Hotel**, a striking building with a large bay frontage. The hotel is owned and run by Katherine and Fred, originally from Berkshire, who extend a warm welcome to locals and visitors alike (and their dogs!). The hotel's bar area is furnished in a traditional style and is stocked with a wide selection of beverages, including two rotating real ales.

In the separate restaurant which seats up to 65, food is served daily between 12-2pm and 6:30-9pm, apart from Sunday nights. A fine choice of grills, starters, mains, light bites and vegetarian options are available with Welsh lamb steak in red wine and garlic sauce, tuna steak, and Moules Marinere being popular choices. Other favourites include salmon, pork, vegetable stir fry and homemade lasagne. On Sundays a handsome lunch is served, when booking is recommended. Local produce is used where possible.

Guest accommodation at the Windsor includes five well appointed and comfy rooms, two of which have en suite facilities. Children are welcome and all major credit

169 THE BROOK INN

Trewarren Road
St Ishmael's, Pembrokeshire SA62 3TE
Tel: 01646 636277
e-mail: coepeter@aol.com

Peter and Angie Coe have been in the trade for the past 30 years and previously owned the **Brook Inn** for 5 years before leaving in October 2003. They returned here in March 2009 and their wealth of experience and knowledge of the local area makes them both superb hosts and fonts of knowledge for visitors to the pleasant village of St Ishmael's, which is just a stones' throw from the stunning Pembrokeshire Coastline.

Angie is the chef here and serves up delicious food from 4-9pm Monday to Saturday and 12-9pm on Sundays in the winter time, and all day in the summer months from 12-9pm when guests can also take advantage of the spacious rear beer garden. She specialises in traditional home cooking, created with fresh local produce. Specials include large Yorkshire puddings filled with sausage, mash, peas and onion gravy, homemade fish pie with chunks of cod, wild salmon and prawns, and Welsh Lamb stew. Angie also cooks up speciality deep base pizzas which are particularly popular. The bar opens from 4pm-close Mon-Thurs and from 12-close Fri/Sat/Sun in winter, and from 12-close in the summer months with two real ales on offer.

Why not come along on Thursday nights for the weekly poker game from 8pm or the live music and karaoke night on Saturdays, a real fun night out for all the family. Children and dogs welcome, all major credit cards taken.

170 NOLTON HAVEN QUALITY COTTAGES

Nolton Haven Farmhouse,
Nolton Haven, Haverfordwest,
Pembrokeshire SA62 2NH
Tel: 01437 710263
Mobile: 07780 697018
e-mail: qualitycottages@noltonhaven.com
website: www.noltonhaven.com or
www.noltonhavenqualitycottages.com

Nolton Haven is a quiet hamlet that lies at the centre of the beautiful St Brides Bay coastline with its steep, undulating cliffs and sandy beaches. Lying within the Pembrokeshire National park and completely unspoilt, it's the perfect place for a peaceful rural holiday. **Nolton Haven Quality Cottages** has been set up by Jim and Joyce Canton as a joint marketing scheme with cottage owners in and around Nolton Haven to provide prospective holiday makers with a one stop shop to provide all the relevant information for arranging an excellent holiday.

Properties range from 5 star cottages to caravans, from farmhouse B&Bs to the local hotel. Sample properties include Brooklyn and Beach Cottages with 3 bedrooms sleeping up to 8 people within 30 yards of the beach and just 60 yards to the pub – perfect for a family get together. Kate's Flat sleeps 2 people just 50 yards from the beach and has its own external stairway, or for a larger party Camrose House is a 5 bed roomed Georgian Country House set in its own extensive, yet secluded grounds which can accommodate up to 14 people. Bed and breakfast establishments include the Mariners inn beside the beach at Nolton Haven, and Glebe House, the former vicarage at Nolton Haven.

Jim and Joyce let all the Welsh Tourist Board 3,4 and 5 star holiday cottages in Nolton Haven that have a sea view. They and their family live in Nolton Haven, and have recently converted part of their own home into tremendous bed and breakfast/self catering accommodation to add to their books.

The whole of the coastline here is part of the National Park, an area of outstanding natural beauty with a variety of natural amenities to the holiday maker, including the coastal path which extends more than 160 miles and passes through the haven. There is an abundance of wildlife, sea birds, wild flowers and beaches safe for swimming, surfing, boating and fishing. Within a short distance is Newgale, well known for its surf along 3 miles of golden sands; St David's – the smallest cathedral city in Britain; and nearby are the coastal villages of Little Haven and Solva which has a particularly beautiful natural harbour. Interesting places to visit include Preseli Hills and the Cleddau estuary, woollen mills, craft shops, potteries and boat trips to Pembrokeshire's island and bird sanctuary.

171 PEMBROKE CASTLE TRUST

Main Street, Pembroke,
Pembrokeshire SA71 4LA
Tel: 01646 681510 Fax: 01646 622260
e-mail: pembroke.castle@talk21.com
website: www.pembrokecastle.co.uk

Looming magnificently above the main street of the town, **Pembroke Castle** is one of Britain's most impressive medieval monuments. It was founded in the 11th century by the Montgomerys, who established the first timber castle on a rocky crag above the River Cleddau.

The stone building which stands today is one of the foremost examples of Norman architecture in the country. It was commenced in the 12th century by Earl William Marshal, and his famous round keep is nearly 80 feet tall with walls 19 feet thick. In 1454 the mighty fortress was held by Earl Jasper Tudor, and the castle is renowned as the birthplace of Jasper's nephew, Henry Tudor, who was to become Henry VII after defeating Richard III at the Battle of Bosworth - thus founding the Tudor dynasty. During the Civil War the castle was held by both the Parliamentarians and the Royalists, and Cromwell travelled there to begin the siege that led to it finally falling under his control. Restoration work in the late 19th century and again in the 1930s has preserved many of the features of the castle that might otherwise have fallen into ruin. The walls, the towers, the turrets, the tunnels and the battlements resound with the history of the centuries, and are an irresistible attraction for lovers of history and for children.

173 BROWNS CAFÉ AND RESTAURANT

51 Main Street, Pembroke,
Pembrokeshire SA71 4DA
Tel: 01646 682419

Opened by the Brown family in 1928 this delightful café and restaurant remains in the same hands to this day … quite literally. Constance Brown is 102 and still works at the premise she opened more than eight decades ago. She is helped by her son and daughter, Hilton and Glenys, and her grandson, Steve.

Constance certainly makes **Browns Café and Restaurant** unique and perhaps this is one reason the place is so popular with locals and visitors of Pembroke. Located in the beautiful county of Pembrokeshire in west Wales, it has a warm and friendly atmosphere and serves traditional favourites, including cooked breakfasts, fish and chips and a wide range of home made dishes.

If it is just a quick drink and cake you are after, don't worry, Browns Café and Restaurant is definitely a good choice for that too. All of the produce on the menu is sourced from within Wales and there is a special children's menu to keep younger guests happy. The highly recommended Browns Café and Restaurant seats up to 76 people and is open every day between 9am-5pm, apart from on Sundays when it is closed. Cash and cheque only.

172 THE LION HOTEL

High Street, Pembroke,
Pembrokeshire SA71 4JS
Tel: 01646 684501
Fax: 01646 686930
e-mail: info@pembrokehotels.co.uk

Situated right on the main high street of the historic and beautiful town of Pembroke is **The Lion Hotel**. It is set between the grand north and west gates of the town walls and just a stone's throw from Pembroke's castle itself. It is believed that the hotel dates back in parts to 1669, and much of its impressive history is showcased throughout via original paintings and relics. Hard to miss, its purple walls and large sash windows invite guests in to an equally appealing interior that is in keeping with the buildings history, without forgoing any comfort.

The hotel is run and owned by the friendly Jones family and their small team of dedicated and hard working staff. It is a firm favourite with both locals and visitors alike who enjoy its convenient central location and fantastic facilities. Each room here comes on a generous bed and breakfast tariff and are fully fitted with en suite facilities, Freeview TV, wireless internet and a tea and coffee station. Guests can choose from single, double or family sized rooms, many of which have glorious views across the town.

The team here also serve up a fine array of food for non-residents and guests alike, available daily from 12-3:30pm, 6-9pm Monday to Saturday and from 12-3:30pm on Sundays when an impressive Sunday lunch is served. Guests can choose from 1, 2 or 3 courses for their Sunday lunches with a range of meats to decide between. Booking is strongly recommended. The menu comprises a great selection of light bites and homemade main meals, which are all created using the best local produce where possible. Favourite dishes include the homemade curries, the beef lasagne, and chilli con carne and the fantastic Steak Sizzler special. The hotel may be a traditional one, but is moving with the times in terms of prices, offering a 'Munch the Crunch' deal from Tuesday to Thursday where guests can get a main meal and a pint for just £5.

A great choice of rotating real ales are available on tap here too with Reverend James being the regular. A good selection of soft and other alcoholic drinks are also available. Children welcome.

174 THE CASTLE INN

Manorbier, nr Tenby,
Pembrokeshire SA70 7TE
Tel: 01834 871268
e-mail: bracecatherine1@yahoo.co.uk

Located in the beautiful village of Manorbier on the south Pembrokeshire heritage coast is the charming **Castle Inn**. Personally run by Irene Brace for the past 4½ years, it dates back, in parts, to the 18th century and once housed a cobblers shop, before it was knocked into one.

Food is served in winter 6-9pm on Friday and Saturdays and from 12pm-2.30pm for Sunday lunch. In summer months food is served from 12pm-3pm and 6pm-9.30pm. The most popular dishes are steaks and lamb shanks and the majority of produce is sourced locally. There is an extensive menu to choose from and additional choices on the specials board. The food Irene cooks is extremely popular with locals and visitors and such is the popularity of the dishes served it is advisable to book at weekends. The rotating real ales are popular and many of them are from Welsh breweries. During summer months the inn is open all day every day and in winter months (end of October-Easter) it is open from 5pm on week days and from 12pm-close on the weekends. The child friendly inn likes to entertain and there is normally live music on a Saturday evening. There is a take away pizza service too.

175 FRESHWATER INN

Freshwater East, Pembroke,
Pembrokeshire SA71 5LE
Tel: 01646 672828
Mobile: 07780 697018
e-mail: richardashley@btinternet.com
website: www.freshwaterinn.co.uk

Built in 1912 at the Grotto Country Club, **The Freshwater Inn** is set in lovely gardens and enjoys spectacular views along the South Pembrokeshire Heritage Coast. Since 2004, the inn has been owned and run by Richard and Carol, a really friendly and welcoming couple. Their speciality is great food and great hospitality making their inn a fast favourite with all who pass by.

Devotees of real ales will be happy here as at any one time there are four ales on tap with Double Dragon and Celtic Pride as the regulars along with two rotating guest ales. Over the course of one year, Richard hopes to have offered his customers over 30 different real ales.

A fine menu is served up each day from 12-2pm and 7-9pm Monday to Saturday and from 6-9pm on Sundays. Richard is the chef here with many years of experience and is often ably assisted by Carol. The menu focuses on showcasing local produce, and changes regularly to reflect this. Guests can choose from the main menu or the daily specials board. Dishes include a great range of starters, steaks and griddles, chicken, fish and homemade specials. Favourites include a gargantuan 16oz rump steak, peppered pork cooked in cider, steak ale and stilton pie and Richard's specialty salmon supreme or Moules Marinere. A good range of lighter bites and bar snacks is also available throughout the day ranging from sandwiches, burgers, hot baguettes, jackets, ploughman's, fresh salads and brunches. Owing to the quality of the food combined with its very reasonable pricing booking is essential at weekends and at all times during the summer season.

In good weather, guests can enjoy their dinner or drinks in the inn's lovely rear beer garden which commands wonderful countryside views across to the bay. The inn accepts all major credit cards except Diners, and there is ample off road parking. Children and well behaved dogs are welcome, making the inn a great place to stop off after a family walk along the coast.

176 THE STACKPOLE INN

Jason's Corner, Stackpole,
Pembrokeshire SA71 5DF
Tel: 01646 672524
Fax: 01646 672716
e-mail: info@stackpoleinn.co.uk
website: www.stackpoleinn.co.uk

Set in a beautiful location just south of Pembrokeshire amid scenic countryside and close to the coast, is **The Stackpole Inn** with its charming ivy covered walls and well maintained front garden. Inside it is warm and cosy with many fine original features such as exposed stone walling, open fireplaces and low beamed ceilings.

It is run by local couple Gary and Becky Evans who have been here since spring 2007. They have created one of the area's premier gastro pubs serving up a menu created by professional chefs and made using local produce only. Food is available from 12-2pm Mon-Sat, from 12-2:30pm on Sundays, and every evening from 6:30-9pm. Particularly popular are the Sunday lunches and the fish specials which include oak smoked salmon and steamed mussels along with other popular dishes such as pan seared Welsh sirloin, ravioli of char grilled vegetables and organic chicken filled with gremolata. Owing to popularity it is best to book on weekends.

Gary and Becky also offer outstanding accommodation in four guest rooms with en suite facilities. Two rooms are on the ground floor, and there is good disabled access throughout the inn. Children welcome, all major credit cards accepted.

177 THE POTTERY SHED AND CAFÉ

Tudor Square, Tenby, Pembroke SA70 7AD
Tel: 01834 844894
website: www.potteryshed.co.uk

The Pottery Shed in Tenby, opened in July 2009 after a complete refurbishment of the old offlicense and offers a selection of exciting new products and parties. The shop boasts the widest selection of ready to paint pottery ready for you to paint. Absolutely no artistic skill is required and with fully trained staff on hand, your individual creation will be a joy to make. From princesses to rugby players, Disney characters to moneyboxes, plates to cups, the list is endless. If your stuck for ideas, they have hundreds of books, stencils and ideas to help you get creative. The cafe serves home made cakes and light lunches and is the perfect place to relax and get creative!

At the Pottery Shed, they also offer some very special parties:

Children's Birthday Parties - With three party types to choose from, why not treat your children to something creative and fun for a few hours, with their own handmade gift at the end.

Jewellery-making Parties Children get to make two items of sculptured jewellery using beads, leather and wire. They get to decorate their own party bags and take their new designer jewellery home with them at the end of the party.

Soap-making Parties - Children can make their own bath-time creations/treats from a range of products from shimmering body glitters, fizzing bombs, funky gloss, the list is endless. All soaps and bombs are safe and 100 per cent child/adult friendly; this is a messy fun way to get your little ones clean!

Open 9am - 8pm (summer months)
10am - 5pm (winter months)

178 TENBY HOUSE

Tudor Square, Tenby,
Pembrokeshire SA70 7AJ
Tel: 01834 842000 Fax: 01834 844647
e-mail: tenby.house@btconnect.com
website: www.tenbyhousehotel.com

Originally a medieval coaching-inn, **Tenby House Inn** is a character-filled hotel located at the heart of the beautiful seaside town of Tenby. Located on the south side of Tudor Square, Tenby House has the proud history of being the home of Sir William Paxton, who made it into the fine bathing spa of regency times, creating many of the attractive and picturesque buildings that give the resort its unique character. Formerly known as "The Globe Inn", the site was developed by Sir William Paxton in 1802 and many of the features he added have been preserved.

There are 18 en-suite rooms, all of a high standard, and decorated to echo the grandeur and style of the Regency building. Some of our rooms adjoin a grand balcony, which overlook Tudor Square. Not only is Tenby a medieval walled town, but one of Wales' favourite seaside resorts, in the only coastal National Park in Britain, too. Its ancient harbour is extremely popular with artists and photographers and its four sheltered beaches and safe bathing waters attract many a family. Tenby House is in the ideal location for those wanting to explore the rugged coastline, valleys and hills of Pembrokeshire. There is plenty to do in the area with several golf courses, a world famous sea bird sanctuary, Stone Age caves and tombs, Iron Age forts, Norman Castles and other ancient monuments.

Owner, Lesley Fisher and her family are friendly hosts and many guests visit and revisit. The bars are popular with residents and local people and children are made welcome. The inn's tastefully decorated restaurant is renowned for its locally caught seafood and prime welsh steaks. The home-made dishes are popular with diners and Welsh Black Beef Curry and Lasagne are among the favourites. There is a range of filled sandwiches, jacket potatoes, salads and lite bites available at lunch times. Paxton's Bistro, which is also available for weddings, buffet receptions, private parties and small conferences, offers a wide range of cuisine, using Pembrokeshire produce where possible.

On a sunnier day the courtyard provides a suntrap and a pleasant meeting area for cool drinks with friends and family and makes for a relaxing end to a busy day. Two real ales are served – Brains Bitter and Coors Bitter. In season food is served everyday between 12-3pm and 5.30-9pm. During winter months food is served between 12-2.30pm and 8.30pm. The tariff is very reasonable and includes a hearty breakfast.

179 THE WOODRIDGE INN HOTEL

Wooden, Saundersfoot,
Pembrokeshire SA69 9DY
Tel: 01854 812259
e-mail: info@thewoodridgeinnhotel.com
website: www.thewoodridgeinnhotel.com

Offering the very best in hospitality and comfort, **The Woodridge Inn Hotel** is an ideal get-away for those wanting to enjoy a peaceful break away from the hustle and bustle of a seaside resort. The hotel is within easy reach of the beautiful Pembrokeshire coastline and countryside and is extremely popular with walkers, cyclists, golfers and bird watchers.

Boasting 17 large en-suite bedrooms, all with well appointed fixtures, fittings and furniture, the modern hotel opened in 2007. The rooms (double, twin, family, executive and disabled) are spread out over three floors. Surrounded by beautiful National Trust countryside the Woodridge Inn Hotel, which is open all year round, boasts a panoramic view of the sea and countryside from appointed second floor rooms. There is a public bar next door serving meals and bar snacks from 12pm onwards with a separate dining room and outdoor seating/eating areas.

There is an array of 18-hole golf courses between a 4 and 22 mile radius of the hotel and local bus services run hourly to Tenby, Saundersfoot, Narberth and Haverfordwest. Part of The Landsker Walk is adjacent to the hotel's spacious car park and the Pembrokeshire coastal walk is a short distance from the hotel.

180 LLANTEGLOS LODGES & THE WANDERER'S REST INN

Llanteg, nr Amroth, Pembrokeshire SA67 8PU
Tel: 01834 831677/831371
e-mail: llanteglosestate@supanet.com
website: www.llanteglos-estate.com

Tucked away in beautiful rural Pembrokeshire, **Llanteglos Estate** is a 10-acre site just 1½ miles above the beach at Amroth, with self-catering lodges, bed and breakfast rooms and its own traditional pub.

The well-appointed self-catering lodges (Visit Wales 3 & 4 Star) are situated in the leafy seclusion of the original orchard and gardens of the main residence on the site. Close by is a children's play area, tennis court and field for exercising dogs. For those preferring bed and breakfast, there are 5 modern en-suite guest rooms boasting views over the gardens. After a peaceful night's sleep, be prepared for a hearty breakfast to start your day!

The site's licensed clubhouse, "The Wanderer's Rest Inn", is renowned for its rustic charm and family-friendly atmosphere and is open nightly in peak periods and part-weeks at other times. In addition to a well-stocked bar, evening meals are available, with steak platters a speciality of the house.

Although enjoying rural seclusion, Llanteglos is easily accessible by road (40 mins from the end of the M4) and the many and varied visitor attractions of South-West Wales. The site is open year round and wonderful in all seasons!

181 THE SALUTATION INN

Pontargothi,
Carmarthenshire SA32 7NH
Tel: 01267 290336
e-mail: salutation_inn@yahoo.co.uk
website: www.salutation-inn.co.uk

The Salutation Arms sits in the centre of the charming village of Pontargothi, offering a warm welcome to tourists and locals alike who come to enjoy the traditional, friendly village inn atmosphere amid beautiful period features such as beamed ceilings, timbered walls and roaring log fires. It is owned and run by Sue and Kel who pride themselves on serving up great food alongside great hospitality.

Food is served seven days a week from 12-9pm. All dishes are cooked fresh to order by Sue herself, who has created a special menu with something for everyone comprising starters, hearty grills, homemade specials, fish dishes straight from the river Cothi, and a choice of vegetarian dishes. Popular choices are the sirloin steak, homemade steak and Guinness pie, pan fried sea bass and the mushroom stroganoff. On Sundays a popular 1, 2, or 3 course lunch is served with all the trimmings. Children can choose from their own menu. Booking is advised on Saturday nights to avoid disappointment.

Sue and Kel now also provide an upstairs en suite apartment for rent all year round on either a bed and breakfast or self catering tariff. All major credit cards accepted.

182 ABERGLASNEY GARDENS

Llangathen, Carmarthenshire SA32 8QH
Tel: 01558 668998
e-mail: info@aberglasney.org.uk
website: www.aberglasney.org.uk

Aberglasney is one of the country's most exciting garden restoration projects, and the gardens are well on the way to becoming one of the leading garden attractions in the UK. The recovery and restoration are taking place under the aegis of the Aberglasney Restoration Trust, set up in 1995, and the nine acres contain six different garden spaces including three walled gardens. At the heart is a unique, fully-restored Elizabethan/Jacobean cloister and parapet walk giving wonderful views over the site. The gardens have already won many awards from the Wales Tourist Board and other prestigious bodies. There's a café in the gardens.

As well as the magnificent gardens, the house is also undergoing restoration. Its history dates back over many centuries and, through scant recorded deatils, is thought to have been originally owned by the Lords of Llangathen, before passing into Tudor hands.

183 THE FORGE RESTAURANT AND LODGE

St Clears, Carmarthenshire SA33 4NA
Tel: 01994 230300
Fax: 01994 231577
e-mail: BRIDGET@theforgelodge.co.uk
website: www.theforgelodge.co.uk

Jeffrey Hill and his family created this fine establishment over 50 years ago converting it from the village blacksmiths to the great lodge it is today, providing high quality guest accommodation and facilities throughout the year.

There are 18 guest rooms available all of which have en suite facilities and a 3 star rating by the Welsh Tourist Board. Guests can choose from a range of singles, twins or family rooms and have exclusive access to the lodge's private indoor heated swimming pool, steam room and sauna; perfect for pampering yourself after a long walk in the surrounding countryside.

The lodge also sports a fine 96 seater a la carte restaurant which serves food daily from 8:30am-9:30pm. An efficient and friendly waitress service brings you a range of grills, poultry, fish, salads and traditional pub meals which include home cooked ham, chicken and mushroom pie, curry and burgers. Popular dishes from the a la carte menu include a 10oz fillet steak, Welsh lamb chops, fresh local trout and roasted duck. Sunday lunch here is also very popular, so it's best to book. A function room seating 100 guests is also available to hire for small functions and parties with ever popular home cooked catering available, please ring for details.

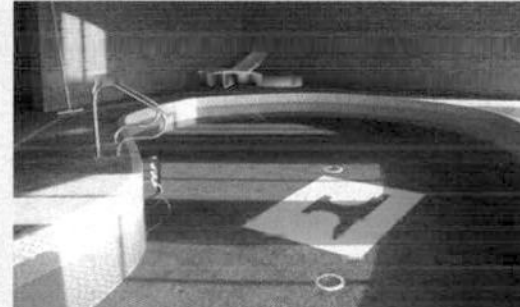

184 MOSAIC @ THE OLD RECTORY

Llanddowor, St Clears,
Carmarthenshire SA33 4HH
Tel: 01994 230030 Fax: 07595 320180
e-mail: info@mosaicdelibistro.co.uk
mosaicattheoldrectory@googlemail.com
website: www.mosaicdelibistro.co.uk

Fans of the spectacular **Mosaic Restaurant** in the centre of Carmarthen will be pleased to know that the high class dining experience has expanded further to the charming village of Llanddowor in Carmarthenshire. Just a short drive from the A477 west of St. Clears is the new establishment; Mosaic @ The Old Rectory. Owned and run by the talented team behind Mosaic in Carmarthen, the Rectory is helmed by Andrew John and Brennan Street. Both men are talented and experienced chefs whose skill is reflected in the innovative menu they present.

The Rectory itself dates back to 1823 and a thorough refurbishment has turned it into a stylish and classy establishment, filled with original features that complement the chic styling well. Opening in July this year, the Rectory has built up an impressive following, making it necessary to book at all times to avoid disappointment. Open from Wed-Sat 12-4pm and 6:30pm-close and 12-4pm on Sundays, guests have the option of enjoying full a la carte dining in the main restaurant, or in the smaller, shockingly red bar area. The team hope to open a more intimate private dining room upstairs for up to ten guests in the near future. Meeting rooms can also be hired here.

The main menu here serves a range of exciting international cuisine that is all created using only the best locally sourced produce from within a 20 mile radius. The menu changes every two months, however some favourite dishes include 24 hour marinated beef fillet, smoked fillet of fish, and an organic hand-reared lamb loin steak. A delectable selection of starters and desserts are also available to include seafood chowder, goat's cheese and cranberry crostini salad, gooseberry and treacle crunch, chocolate truffon and a zingy citrus posset. An extensive wine list provides the perfect accompaniment to any dish here, but a good range of other soft and alcoholic drinks is also available. Children are welcome and can dine from half portions or something made to order if possible.

Diners will also soon be able to benefit from an atmospheric coffee/liqueur lounge in which to enjoy pre or post dinner drinks. All major credit cards accepted.

185 THE PLASH INN

Llanfallteg, Whitland,
Carmarthenshire SA34 0UN
Tel: 01437 563472
e-mail: plash@btconnect.com
website: www.winapubinwales.co.uk

Found in the tiny village of Llanfallteg just east off the A478 or north off the A40 is the spectacular **Plash Inn**. Offering the very best in hospitality, real ale, food and accommodation this olde worlde inn is popular with all those who come across it, always returning for more.

Dating back to the early 19th century in parts, this lively pub was once the railway inn between the now closed Cardigan and Whitland line. It is now run and owned by experienced licensees and caterers Christie and Steve Goymer who have put the Plash back on the map over the past 5 years. A great stop off for walkers or those fancying a rural break away in the fully fitted self catering cottage also on hand here; there is a great range of home cooked dishes served until 10pm daily. Popular choices here are the homemade curries and Welsh beef steak specials, along with the renowned eat in or take away pizzas. Children are welcome to join in this vibrant environment with quiz night on Tuesday from 8pm and acoustic open mike night also on offer.

186 TEIFI TEA ROOMS – TE AR Y TEIFI

Sycamore Street, Newcastle Emlyn,
Carmarthenshire SA38 9AJ
Tel: 01239 711356

Teifi Tea Rooms is located in the attractive market town of Newcastle Emlyn, surrounded by on all sides by beautiful scenery. A popular place to take a break from exploring the town, the Tearooms attracts many repeat visitors. Jill and Susan Lowry have owned this establishment for nine years now and have created a popular venue renowned for its fabulous home cooking and great array of hot and cold beverages.

A large range of teas and coffees is available and can be enjoyed inside the tea rooms or on the small pavement patio where people watching is the sport of the day. Guests can chose from a variety of hot and cold dishes with specialties including a farmhouse pate, homemade soup and a mixed pepper and bacon quiche. Most dietary needs can be catered for and there are also plenty of vegetarian options. Most tempting however are Jill and Susan's delicious range of home baked Welsh cakes and treats such as homemade scones and traditional Bara brith. Open from 9am-4:00pm Mon-Sat, payment by cash or cheque only please.

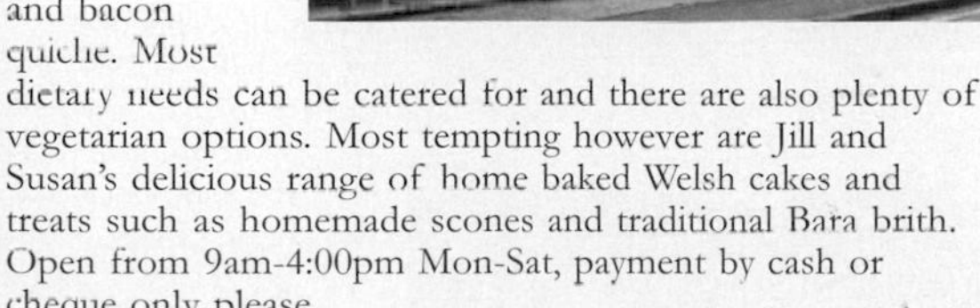

187 THE DROVERS

9 Market Square, Llandovery,
Carmarthenshire SA20 0AB
Tel: 01550 721115
e-mail: jillblud@aol.com
website: www.droversllandovery.co.uk

This exquisitely furnished 18th century town house offers the very best in comfort and cuisine. With a five star rating **The Drovers** is located at the heart of the market town of Llandovery, which is an ideal location for guests wanting to explore the rural beauty of Carmarthenshire. The historic property is extremely eye catching and boasts views overlooking the town square.

Jill and Michael Blud are fantastic hosts and enjoy welcoming guests to stay in one of their five beautifully furnished rooms. The rooms, which are all en-suite and located upstairs, are finished to an extremely high standard and are in keeping with the style of the building. A good quality full British breakfast is served to guests in front of an open fire and evening meals are available on request. The B&B is popular among those attending annual events in the area, including the RAC Rally and the Drovers' Festival. It is also popular with walkers and cyclists and those wanting to explore the surrounding area, including Bethlehem, which is home to Garn Goch, the largest Iron Age hill fort in Wales. Guests can make use of the resident's lounge and computer facilities. There is private parking.

188 PENYGAWSE VICTORIAN TEA ROOMS & GUEST HOUSE

Penygawse, 12 High Street,
Llandovery SA20 0PU
Tel: 01550 721727
e-mail: penygawse@aol.com
website: www.penygawse.com

Located in the centre of the lively town of Llandovery is a coffee lover's dream; **Penygawse**. This Victorian tea room dates back to 1690 and had further additions built in 1751 and 1760, along with the Victorian canopy to the shop front added in 1855. All these additions have provided ample space and charm to create one of the area's best loved tea rooms with a great guest house included.

There are seven three star upstairs guest bedrooms to choose from, all with en suite facilities in a mixture of sizes to suit all budgets. Guests staying can indulge in a hearty cooked breakfast, which is included in the tariff.

The tea rooms themselves are open from 9am-6pm in the summer and 9am-5pm in the winter. Despite the name however, Penygawse is best known for its stunning collection of specialty coffees and home cooked food, all created with local produce. Owners Allan and Lynne pride themselves on serving authentic, high quality food and drink; and even loan their services out to other businesses to train staff in the art of coffee production and blending. The premises also has free wifi and ample off road parking.

189 NEUADD FAWR ARMS

Cilycwm, Llandovery SA20 0ST
Tel: 01550 721644
e-mail: bunty@neuadd-cilycwm.co.uk
website: www.neuadd@cilycwm.co.uk

Located centrally in the charming village of Cilycwm is the fine **Neuadd Fawr Arms**. Sat right on an ancient drovers' road, with glorious views of the picturesque village, this fine country inn has a long and interesting history dating back to the days when weary cattle drovers would take respite from their long journey before the inn's roaring log fire.

Owners Eddie and Bunty have been here for ten years now and work hard to help their guests appreciate the character their inn holds; whilst still maintaining its status as a haven for visitors to the area. Also popular with locals, the Neuadd sports an atmospheric bar and restaurant alongside quality guest accommodation and stabling facilities so that guests can feel free to bring along their horse companions.

In the summer months the inn is open all day every day, closing in the winter on Mondays. Diners here can enjoy a daily changing printed menu that reflects the great Welsh produce that is available season to season. Available from 12-2:30pm and 6-9pm and all day long on Sundays, guests can chose from a variety of mouth watering cuisine that includes dishes such as venison steak, pork tenderloin stuffed with apple and stilton, warm pigeon breast salad or tasty homemade carrot, coriander and orange soup. Children can chose from their own menu or half portions of the main menu. A good selection of soft and alcoholic drinks is also available which includes a choice of two rotating real ales from Welsh only breweries.

For those that choose to stay at the Neuadd, a feeling of comfort and homeliness can be expected at great value for money as guests stay on a generous bed and breakfast rate. There are three upstairs rooms available throughout the year or a quaint self catering cottage also. Totally self contained; the cottage has excellent modern bathroom and kitchen facilities that compliment its olde worlde charm. However if cottage guests don't feel like cooking, Bunty's culinary skills are only a few short steps away at the inn, making the cottage perfect for short breaks away. Please ring for details.

Eddie and Bunty also provide guests with the opportunity for guided horse riding and have their own mountain bike trail.

190 CENNEN ARMS

Trap, nr Llandeilo,
Carmarthenshire SA19 6TP
Tel: 01558 822330
e-mail: cennenarms@aol.com
website: www.cennenarms.com

Cennen Arms is a one of Wales' true hidden gems in an unspoilt location in the picturesque village of Trap, found just south of the more well known Llandeilo. The inn is a real old fashioned country pub meeting and surpassing all expectations. Its fabulous olde worlde décor and cosy atmosphere invite you in, although some guests prefer to relax on the inn's outdoor patio which overlooks the valley on the edge of the Black Mountain and Carreg Cennen Castle.

It is owned and run by Mike and Yvonne Davies who have over 24 years of experience, half of which has been at Cennen. They offer a warm welcome to all who enter and are more than happy to advice visitors to the area the best places to go. They have a small holiday home adjacent to the inn for guests to hire for weekly stays, which is the perfect retreat for families who want to explore this beautifully rural part of Wales. The home has a 5 star rating from the Welsh Tourist board and sleeps up to 8 people in four en suite rooms, all furnished to the highest standards with glorious panoramic views across to the castle.

Food is served up at the inn daily from 12-3pm and 5:30-9pm when guests can choose from the main menu or the daily specials board. Local produce is used to create the dishes here which range from hearty grills, speciality fish dishes, vegetarian options and traditional Welsh pub favourites. Popular dishes include a 10oz Welsh Pork Valentine Steak, steak, mushroom and Guinness pie, Salmon with buttered leeks in a Chardonnay sauce, King Prawn and fish pie and classic Chicken Cymru; chicken breast in a leek, mushroom, cream and Caerphilly cheese sauce. The food here is popular so booking is recommended and essential on weekends.

The well stocked and cosy bar is open every session apart from Monday lunchtime and offers a choice of two fine Welsh ales which includes the regular Rumney Butler and a rotating guest ale. A good collection of other soft and alcoholic drinks is available with a wine selection that can make the perfect accompaniment to your meal.

Children are welcome; all major credit cards are accepted.

191 CAFFI SALVADOR

3 Kings Street, Llandeilo,
Carmarthenshire SA19 6AA
Tel: 01558 822908

Talented chef Sarah Shore-Taylor is the mastermind behind the funky **Caffi Salvador,** located in the heart of Llandeilo on King Street. Sarah used to run the town's local delicatessen before opening here where she serves up the best in local produce and hospitality.

Open every day from 9am-4pm, and from 6:30-8:30pm on Wednesdays and Thursdays, and from 6:30-9:30pm on Fridays and Saturdays, Salvador is a popular place to dine when in Llandeilo; with mosaiced tables, green walls, traditional fireplace and a shocking pink exterior – it's hard to miss! The menu changes twice a day between day times and evenings as it reflects the tastiest local ingredients Sarah has fresh each day to work with. Her specialities are fish dishes which are always made with locally caught fresh fish which can include line caught sea bass with coriander, lime and chilli; stuffed plaice; poached salmon; and hake cutlet with tomato, black olive and caper sauce. Other dishes include a medley of lamb with red wine gravy and parsnip crisps and a vegetable lasagne.

Sarah, her food and her hard working team of staff come highly recommended from both the Western Mail and Independent on Sunday papers. Cash and cheque only please, children welcome.

192 THE ABADAM ARMS

Porthyrhyd, Carmarthenshire SA32 8PL
Tel: 01267 275278
e-mail: melmorgans@btconnect.com
website: www.abadamarms.com

The Abadam Arms is situated in the heart of the small village of Porthrhyd, found just of the A48 on the B4310. Once again it is the hub of its community after Melanie Morgans and her parents Margaret and Brian took over here in September 2009. Its small and cosy atmosphere is traditionally styled documenting the inn's history. Guests can relax inside or in the covered outdoor patio area in the summer months.

Open all day every day the Abadam serves a good choice of soft and alcoholic drinks with a choice of two rotating ales. Food is available from 10am-10pm seven days a week, children welcome. All dishes are freshly prepared by Melanie, using local produce whenever possible. The menu includes a selection of homemade favourites such as cottage pie and lasagne, fish dishes and an impressive list of succulent meat dishes which include a range of steaks and chops. A regularly changing specials menu is also to hand which samples dishes such as salmon sweet chilli stir fry. On Sundays Melanie pulls out all the stops with a three course roast offering a choice of four meats.

The family also offer a choice of two lovely upstairs guest rooms with en suite facilities available all year round, perfect for short breaks away.

193 THE HARRY WATKINS

2 Millfield Road, Felinfoel, Llanelli,
Carmarthenshire SA14 8HY
Tel: 01554 776644
e-mail: rowland@cross1.wanadoo.co.uk
website: www.harrywatkins.co.uk

The Harry Watkins used to be known as the Bear but was re-named about 10 years ago in honour of the former captain of Llanelli's Rugby Union team. He played for Wales six times and was known for his great strength. This Harry Watkins however is well known for its welcoming, warm atmosphere and its mouth-watering food.

Since it has been owned and run by local couple Linda and Rowland Cross who took over in 2004, the inn has gone from strength to strength and is now a favourite for locals and visitors to Llanelli alike.

Open all day every day except Mondays, the inn has a fresh, modern feel to it whilst serving up traditional real ales such as Banks Bitter alongside ever rotating guest ales to sample. An extensive wine collection here accompanies a terrific menu created by Linda and her professional chef. The menu is created sing only fresh local produce and offers a collection of old favourites and pub classics as well as the generously portioned Sunday carvery. Food is available from 12-8:30pm Tuesday to Saturday and from 12-2pm on Sundays. It is advised to book on Fridays, Saturdays and Sundays as seats fill up fast. Children's meals are also available.

Guests can benefit from weekly entertainment each Sunday when there is a quiz night for all from 9pm. In warmer weather guests can also enjoy the inn's modern partially covered patio area. Cash and cheque only please.

194 THE SQUARE

Wind Street, Ammanford,
Carmarthenshire SA18 3DN
Tel: 01269 595792

Local couple Peter and Melanie and their children Alex, Kelly-Anne and Jessica offer a warm welcome to all at their new venture **The Square**, located on in the pretty town of Ammanford. Opening in September this year, the family have worked tirelessly to refurbish this great venue into a modern and comfortable pub with comfy leather dining chairs, squishy sofas and its very own pool table.

They place priority on serving good value food and drink with a menu created by professional chefs that uses locally sourced Welsh produce. Food is served from 12-3pm and 6-9pm Monday-Thursday, 12-6pm Fri/Sat and from 12-3pm for a popular Sunday Lunch, when booking is essential. The specialty here is a succulent 6oz pan fried rump steak in garlic and parsley butter, sourced from locally reared cattle, but other favourites include the all day breakfast, chicken Alfredo pasta, chicken Cymru – in leek, mushroom and Welsh Caerphilly cheese sauce, homemade lasagne and the traditional faggots and peas. Vegetarians are also well catered for with a vegetable tikka massala and homemade vegetable lasagne also on offer. All main meals are under £6 and if there are two of you dining, you can get both your meals for just £10, making the Square a great choice in the current financial climate. A good choice of lighter bites is also available including a traditional ploughman's, and a range of filled jacket potatoes and baguettes. Children are welcome and can order half portions from the main menu.

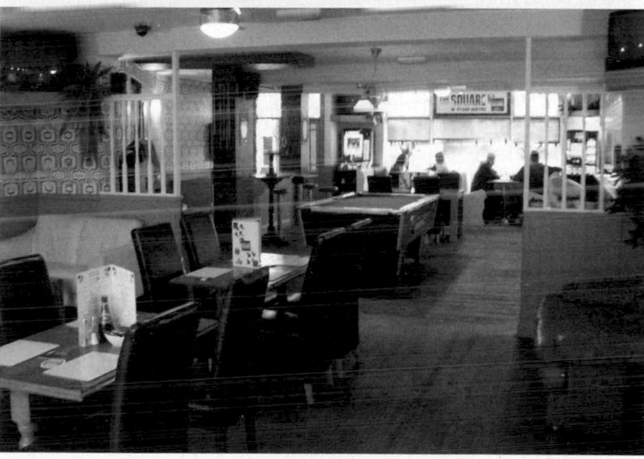

The well stocked bar provides a chilled out place to relax with a range of draught beers, lagers, spirits and wines alongside the regular real ale here; Tomos Watkins. A good selection of soft and hot drinks is also available. Guests can enjoy a livelier atmosphere on Thursday nights however when guests are invited to get out their singing skills for karaoke from 7pm, with a DJ playing every Friday and Saturday night from 8pm and live music from local bands and soloists each Sunday evening.The family also have a stylish function room available for hire, which seats up to 50 guests. Catering is available on request, please ring for details.

195 HALF MOON INN

281 Cwmammam Road, Garnant,
Ammanford, Carmarthenshire SA18 1LS
Tel: 01269 825466
Fax: 01269 822798
e-mail: halfmooninn281@aol.com

Conveniently located on the A474, east of Ammanford, the **Half Moon Inn** was originally three cottages which were converted into an inn during the early 1800s. David and Jean bought the premises in the summer of 2005 and have carried out many improvements which include adding two superb guest bedrooms, both of which have en suite facilities and one has a king size bed. Guests can come on a B&B or room only rate.

The inn is also open all day every day for ale which includes draught keg ales like Worthington, Buckleys and Carling and bottled real ales. Jean and Dave offer up cold and warm bar snacks throughout the day on request which range from breakfast, a selection of filled rolls, to faggots and curries. Guests can relax indoors or take a seat under the inns covered patio area which is heated and well lit throughout the year. A variety of live entertainment is offered every Wed, Fri, Sat and Sunday. Children welcome, cash and cheque only please.

Nearby attractions include the local railway line which is awaiting status for steam trains, and two fabulous golf courses. Also available closeby is hill walking, horse riding and fishing.

197 TAFARN HALFWAY INN

Pontantwn, B4309, Kidwelly,
Carmarthenshire SA17 5HY
Tel: 01269 860941
e-mail: halfway.inn@hotmail.co.uk

Easy to spot with its baby blue painted exterior, the **Tafarn Halfway Inn** sits right on the B4309 in the charming village of Pontantwn, just south of Carmarthen. It is owned and run by business partners Jimmy Jones and Emlyn Davies who have been here for the past two years. The pair have plenty of prior experience in the trade however and have created a real success with locals and visitors alike who enjoy the pair's fine sense of hospitality and Welsh pride.

Open all day every day apart from Mondays, the inn serves a great range of homemade cuisine from 11:30am-9pm Tuesday to Saturday and from 12-2:30pm on Sundays when a fine Sunday lunch is served. Guests can dine in the bar area which offers a good choice of soft and alcoholic beverages along with a rotating guest ale; or they can dine in the pleasant separate restaurant area. In summer months the inn's sunny beer garden can also be taken full advantage of. The dishes served here are created using only the best local produce; with guests raving about the homemade steak and ale pie, the lamb shank and the fish dishes. A smaller snack menu is also available. All major credit cards taken.

196 CORNISH ARMS

1 Gors Road, Burry Port, Llanelli,
Carmarthenshire SA16 OEL
Tel: 01554 833224
e-mail: hugh.d@btconnect.com

Conveniently located just across the road from Burry Port's railway station is the **Cornish Arms**. It is a traditional village pub that has recently undergone a phenomenal makeover. The inn still retains its relaxing ambience and welcoming atmosphere but now does so in a sleeker, more stylish environment. Soft chocolates and warm cream colours compliment the comfy rustic leather dining chairs, low lighting and gorgeous wooden flooring that stretches throughout.

It is owned and run by Hugh and Elaine Davies who pride themselves on providing a quality service to all who step through the door. Their hard work over the last year has seen the creation of a new 70 seater restaurant in the inn which is so popular, booking a table is a necessity. The restaurant serves food from 12-9:30pm Monday to Saturday and from 6:30-9pm on Sundays when a handsome Sunday lunch is also served between 12-3pm. All the food served here is cooked fresh to order and is created using the best local produce around Wales. The menu is created by the skilled hands and creative mind of the Cornish Arm's chef who specialises in fresh fish dishes such as sea bass, plaice, skate, Dover and lemon sole, salmon, hake and haddock. Some fish dishes also make their way onto the ever changing specials board which includes Burry Port mussels in cider and ginger sauce, swordfish and a tuna steak with lemon and tarragon sauce. The menu is not just about fish though with a great selection of grills, poultry, vegetarian dishes and salads also on offer. Popular dishes include a Celtic Pride fillet steak, the Cajun chicken mango melt and mushroom stroganoff. The lunchtime menu also covers all the old time classics including cod and chips, burgers, chilli, chicken Kiev and good old ham, egg and chips. A separate children's menu is available. Guests who come from 12-6:30pm Monday to Saturday can also benefit from the inn's credit crunch deal where main meals are just £4.95 each.

The inn also welcomes guests for drinks only, serving a good range of real ales with the Reverend James being the regular alongside two more rotating guest ales. The new but relaxing atmosphere makes the perfect retreat after a day exploring the surrounding area. All major credit cards accepted apart from Diners.

198 THE WHITE LION HOTEL

The Square, Ferryside,
Carmarthenshire SA17 5RW
Tel: 01267 267214

Over 200 years ago when Ferryside was once and old fishing and cockling port, **The White Lion Hotel** acted as its main customs house. Today it stands between the village's railway station and the stunning shoreline. Found just off the A484, Ferryside is a popular place to visit to enjoy a taste of quiet rural village life. The White Lion fully supports this as its guests can enjoy the relaxing atmosphere created by its owners; the Martin family.

Janet and David and their daughter Sarahjane have been running the show for the past year and have a wealth of experience behind them which they have put into giving the village back its pub. They open all day every day, working hard to ensure their guests satisfaction with whatever they choose. Guests can enjoy lazy afternoon drinks in the inn's large beer garden, or enjoy one of two real ales in the cosy bar areas; where Double Dragon and Best Bitter are the regulars from the Felinfoel Brewery.

Guests can dine throughout the inn or upstairs in the intimate 18 seater restaurant that overlooks the inn's tranquil gardens. It is the father and daughter team that pair up to offer guests a great choice of food with a menu that gets its inspiration mainly from British and French palettes. All dishes here are cooked fresh to order using the best local produce around. Popular dishes include lamb chop, stuffed chicken breast and the mighty carpet bag steak; a large blue steak cooked with mussels! There is also a good choice for vegetarians and those with lighter appetites who can chose from a variety of filled sandwiches and baguettes, jacket potatoes or a homemade soup and roll. Although all the meals here are reasonably priced, the family also offer a credit crunch deal where all meals such as scampi, liver, bacon and onion, lasagne, chicken curry, omelettes and a chicken and bacon wrap are just £4 with a choice of chips, mash, jacket rice or salad to go with them; so every budget can be met. If nothing on the menu takes your fancy but David and Sarahjane have the ingredients in their store cupboard then they are more than happy to cook it up for you. A great children's menu is also available. To avoid disappointment it is recommended to book at all times. Cash and Cheque only please.

199 THE FOUND OUT INN AND BISTRO

8 Killan Road, Dunvant, Gower SA2 7TD
Tel: 01792 203596
e-mail: ebenezerbre@googlemail.com
thefoundoutinn@googlemail.com
website: www.thefoundoutinn.co.uk

The Found Out Inn is found in the charming village of Dunvant on the famous Gower Peninsula. Known best locally for its welcoming, family atmosphere and the great range of food it served throughout the day, it makes a pleasant place to stop off for a meal after seeing some of the sights the peninsula has to offer which include winding rural coastal paths and miles of long sandy beaches. The Gower celebrated its 50th year as the country's first area of outstanding national beauty in 2006 and continues to live up to this high standard.

The Found Out is run by Colin and his partner Leanne in June 2009. Colin has over 20 years experience as a head chef and is ably assisted by the Found Outs own head chef Chris. Together, Chris and Colin have created a menu for the inn that reflects some of the best local produce from the Gower. Guests can choose from the main menu or the daily specials board. Food is served daily from 11am until close and samples a range of fine fish and meat dishes. To start you might enjoy king prawns in garlic and chilli cream sauce, or king scallops with black pudding, orange and bacon salad, or for your main you can choose from Normandy style pork valentine steak, succulent char grilled Welsh sirloin, Cajun rubbed duck breast or a fillet of plaice with lemon butter sauce. Owing to the popularity of the food here it is heavily recommended to book, especially on weekends and on Sunday lunch times when a hearty Sunday roast is served up for all the family to enjoy. The bar is open all day every day and keeps a good selection of draught lagers, wines and spirits along with two real ales, Flowers Original and Green King IPA. Guests can relax inside, enjoying the light and modern décor, or outside on the inn's patio, adjacent to its own large off road car park. Children are very welcome and can enjoy the pubs pool table. All major credit cards accepted.

200 THE BAY BISTRO, COFFEE HOUSE AND SAM'S SURF SHACK

Rhossilli, Gower, Swansea SA3 1PL
Tel: 01792 390519
Fax: 01792 390522
e-mail: rhossillileisure@hotmail.com
website: www.rhossillileisure.co.uk

With panoramic views over popular Rhossilli Bay, guests are assured of a warm and friendly welcome from Sue and Paul at **The Bay Bistro and Coffee House**. Within easy walking distance of the shore, this fine family run business is ideal for ramblers, food lovers and surfers alike who come together to enjoy this particularly beautiful part of the Gower Peninsula.

The Bay Bistro opens every day in the summer months serving up a great range of speciality teas and coffees, hearty breakfasts, baguettes, ciabattas, Paninis, jackets, sandwiches and toasties from 10:30am-5pm. Those with a sweet tooth however can indulge with a choice from the tempting selection of homemade cakes and gateaux on offer, or relax with a cream tea on the sheltered terrace to catch some rays. Each evening the bistro opens from 7-10pm for fine dining with a menu created using the best local produce and fresh fish from the bay. There is something for every taste with succulent Welsh Black steaks, delicious sea bass and mackerel or something from the extensive vegetarian and gluten free menu which includes Glamorgan sausages, curried chickpea, coriander and coconut burgers, and vegetarian lasagne to name a few. Meals can be rounded off with a real Welsh cheese board or melt in your mouth blackberry and apple crumble. The bistro is fully licensed and offers a range of wines, ciders and beers. Owing to the unrivalled location and high quality of food on offer, in the evenings it is essential to book. In winter months the Café is closed on Mondays and Tuesdays, and the bistro is closed from October to Easter.

Next door to the bistro is Sue's son Sam's Surf Shack which is open every day of year providing quality surf gear for hire and sale for all, whether you're an experienced surfer or if it's your first time wriggling into a wetsuit. Sam also offers surf lessons for those who want to learn with a friendly and experienced teacher; which make great gifts for a fun weekend away. The shop also stocks beautiful handmade jewellery that can serve as a timeless reminder of your special break away on the Peninsula which is full of opportunities for exploring the miles of unspoilt beaches and secluded coves that surround Rhossilli.

201 THE KINGS HEAD INN

Llangennith, Gower, Swansea SA3 1HX
Tel: 01792 386212
Fax: 01792 386477
e-mail: info@kingsheadgower.co.uk
website: www.kingsheadgower.co.uk

Located on the north east side of the Gower Peninsula, just a short drive from the busy city of Swansea is **The Kings Head Inn**. It's comprised of a row of three glorious 17th century buildings which stand opposite the picturesque church in the small coastal town of Llangennith. The beach is just a short walk away, making the inn the ideal spot to stop for a meal or drink after a fine days surfing, or a convenient base for a holiday exploring the peninsula's other offerings.

The inn has been owned and run by the Steven's family since the 1980s, who do a terrific job of creating a chilled out and friendly atmosphere for all their guests. The inn itself retains many original features such as exposed stone walling, original wooden beams giving it true olde worlde character.

Guests can enjoy an impressive variety of food throughout the day beginning with breakfast at 9am-11am and from then on main meals are served until 9:30pm. Where possible the food here is created using only the best local produce from the Gower and around Wales so ingredients like butter, milk beef and even custard is Welsh through and through. Despite this, home cooked Thai food is somewhat of a speciality here, along with Indian dishes and pizzas which are particularly popular amongst the locals. Good old fashioned British cooking is also championed here with some excellent pies such as steak and kidney; chicken, leek and asparagus; and Welsh venison, mushroom and blueberries amongst some on offer.

The bar at the Kings Head is equally well stocked, offering a range of soft and alcoholic beverages including a fine choice of three real ales from local Welsh breweries which includes the now famous Felin Foel Brewery. The bar is also proud to hold the largest collection of malt whiskies outside of Scotland, each collected personally from the distilleries where they were made.

Four star accommodation here is available all year round with a choice of 27 en suite rooms ranging from singles to family rooms; some are fully fitted for disabled clients. All rooms were recently refurbished to the highest standard in the finest Gower stone and lie within the Tan House adjacent to the pub, or in the nearby converted Stables.

Children and dogs are welcome. All major credit cards accepted.

202 THE BRITANNIA INN

Llanmadoc, Gower, Swansea SA3 1DB
Tel: 01792 386624
e-mail: enquries@britanniainngower.co.uk
website: www.britanniainngower.co.uk

Boasting awe inspiring views over the Loughor Estuary, **The Britannia Inn** is situated in the picturesque village of Llanmadoc on the North Coast of the famous Gower Peninsula. The Inn dates back to the 17th century and many of the original features have been preserved; in the bar there is the original bread oven, while in the restaurant the beams are thought to have come from ships that were 'lanterned' ashore by wreckers.

Martin and Lindsay Davies who took over here in 2006 are both chefs with a wealth of experience from across the globe. The menu reflects the Davies' experience sampling great local Welsh produce which includes dishes like Welsh Black rump steak, roast suckling pig, pan fried local wild bass Zarzuela, crayfish and saffron risotto and roast Mediterranean vegetable tagliatelle. Lunch menu is available Monday to Saturday in the summer and Tuesday to Saturday in the winter (12.00 to 2.30) Sunday lunch is available 12.00 to 2.30. Evening meals are served 6.00 to 8.30 (a la carte and light meals) Please ring for exact information on menus as they change to reflect the produce available.

The bar itself is well stocked to make the perfect accompaniment to your meal with a range of cask conditioned ales, lagers, stouts and wines. Guests can relax within the rustic interior or soak up the sun in one of the inn's two beer gardens complete with plenty of ducks, rabbits and guinea-pigs to keep the kids entertained. The inn also offers one upstairs guest bedroom with en suite facilities.

203 THE GREYHOUND INN

Oldwalls, Llanrhidian, Swansea SA3 1HA
Tel: 01792 391027

The Greyhound Inn is a handsome 19th century traditional roadhouse inn with a cheerful and welcoming atmosphere. Its young and enthusiastic hosts, Chris and Emily, arrived here in the autumn of 2006 although Emily had worked at the pub for some years before taking over. Emily is an accomplished cook who has made the Greyhound the eating place of choice for many locals and visitors. Her extensive menu ranges from traditional home cooked pub favourites which include steak and ale pie, fish and chips or chicken and leek pie; to fish dishes such as Trout Belle Menuiere and salmon fillet in a balsamic glaze; to pasta dishes; to meat and poultry dishes which include a range of succulent steaks, chicken and rib combos, and lamb shank, not forgetting Emily's speciality homemade curries which are Indian and Thai inspired. Vegetarians are also well catered for with tasty broccoli and stilton pie, Shabzi Balti curry and vegetarian lasagne amongst the dishes on offer. A great range of baguettes, sandwiches, jacket potatoes and burgers are also on offer for those with a lighter appetite. Children can choose from their own menu or have half portions from the main menu. Food is served from 12-9pm Monday to Saturday. On Sundays the whole family can enjoy Emily's traditional 1, 2 or 3 course roast served between 12:30-2:30pm, and then bar meals are served from 3pm onwards. Seasonal desserts are listed on the blackboard. Booking is strongly recommended.

The well stocked bar includes a choice of three real ales with London Pride, Bass and Hancocks H.B being the regular brews, with many other guest ales on rotation. In the summer months guests can choose from up to six real ales which can be enjoyed in the pub's large enclosed beer garden complete with fantastic play area for the children.

The Greyhound is a regular meeting place for the local Folk club which gathers every Sunday at 8pm and also invites a guest folk singer every third Sunday of the month.

The Greyhound accepts all major credit cards, has good disabled access throughout and has meeting and function rooms available for hire.

Located at the most westerly tip of the Gower Peninsula, this fine pub is popular with walkers and lovers of nature's beauty as the region provides splendid views along the coast.

204 CEFN COED COLLIERY MUSEUM

Crynant, Neath SA10 8SN
Tel: 01639 750556

Cefn Coed Colliery museum is situated in the heart of the picturesque Dulais Valley and tells the story of colliery life from Victorian times to the 1950s and how important the coal industry was to the local community. This unique museum is housed in the colliery's existing building, which closed in 1968, and is one out of four collieries in Wales with headframes still in existence.

Experience the harsh, damp and dark conditions that the colliers went through in the very authentic simulated underground gallery, which is equipped with various aspects of mining, such as the stalls, pit props, tramways and other equipment used underground. Or visit one of the many highlights of the museum, such as the distinctive boiler house with its suite of six Lancashire steam boilers or see the magnificent 1927 Worsley Mesne Steam winding engine which is now electrically driven.

As well as exhibiting many fascinating artefacts from the mining industry such as tools and equipment, the museum also houses a restored and unique gas tram, which ran in Neath until 1920 and the model of which can be seen in Neath Museum.

The gift shop sells a wide selection of coal figures, Welsh souvenirs and a vast selection of books based on the coal industry, as well as some of the best genuine and reproduction mining lamps in South Wales.

205 THE CARNE PARK HOTEL

1 Hill Street, Abercynon,
Mid-Glamorgan CF45 4PF
Tel: 01443 740258
website: www.TheCarnePark.com

Situated on the outskirts of the village of Abercynon, found just off the main A470 is the **Carne Park Hotel**. Known locally for having the longest bar in Wales, it is a popular venue to dine or drink throughout the year. Its hosts Derrick and Karen took over 3 years ago and have put the place back on the map, creating a fabulous restaurant and bringing in two rotating ales for guests enjoyment.

The restaurant serves food from 4-9pm Wed/Thurs, 2-9pm Fri/Sat and from 12-3pm on Sundays for a hearty Sunday lunch. The menu comprises great dishes such as Spanish chicken, rack of lamb, beef stroganoff, special surf and turf (medallions of steak with sautéed tiger prawns), and a good selection of vegetarian dishes which include lentil and mushroom hotpot and the chefs special herb pancake. A lighter menu is available for bar snacks and a sumptuous Christmas menu is available throughout the festive period. Owing to popularity it's best to book for the Sunday lunch. Children are welcome and can dine from their own menu or take half portions from the main menu.

Entertainment is the big crowd drawer here with something 5 nights of the week to include Monday night Quiz, Bingo on Tuesday, Wednesday Poker night, Karaoke

206 THE NEW INN

Smiths Avenue, Rhigos,
Aberdare CF44 9YU
Tel: 01685 811071
Fax: 01685 814696

Situated off the main A465 via Glynneath on the outskirts of the village of Rhigos is **The New Inn**. It is owned and run by local couple Chris and Jan who have been here for 5 years now. Chris has an impressive 21 year history in the brewing business so ale and beer drinkers will not be disappointed with the good choice of brews on offer here, which include Brains SA, Worthington and Carling. Guests relax inside amongst the warm but contemporary décor or relax outside in the summer months in the inn's large rear beer garden.

The inn is open all day every day except Mondays and bank holidays, but otherwise offers a warm welcome to all who come to enjoy the friendly environment and tasteful menu.Each day from 12-2:30pm and 6:30-9pm, guests can choose from a carefully selected menu comprised of delicious dishes such as pan fried fillet steak, chicken wrapped in bacon in a creamy white wine and mushroom sauce, grilled plaice with capers and lemon butter or minted lamb steak in a fine honey, mint and brandy sauce. Vegetarians are well catered for with a choice which included caramelised red onion and Goats cheese tart and spinach and mushroom filo pastry parcels with a roast pepper coulis. Children are also well looked after and can dine from their own menu or take half portions from the main menu. Each lunch time a good choice of filled baguettes is on offer for those with a lighter appetite. The majority of produce used in the dishes here is sourced fresh from within Wales itself. This includes the spectacular Sunday roast served up each Sunday lunchtime with a range of meats and a vegetarian option also.

On Friday nights Chris and Jan invite guests to their live entertainment evening which starts at 9:30pm, great fun for all the family. If you enjoy their entertainment evenings, why not book a party at the New Inn, fully catered for by the team. The Christmas Party menu this year samples some fine festive treats such as turkey crown and Christmas pudding alongside other dishes such as poached salmon, brie and beetroot tart and a zingy lime and ginger crunch cheesecake.

207 THE OLD HOUSE INN

Llangynwyd, Maesteg CF34 9SB
Tel: 01656 733310
Mobile: 07703 002165
e-mail: k3rsd@yahoo.co.uk
website: www.oldhousellan.com

The Old House Inn is situated in the Llynfi valley overlooking the rolling hills of Mynydd Baiden, just 6 miles from the Sarn services on the M4 and 10 miles from Port Talbot. The inn is one of the oldest pubs in Wales dating back to 1147 AD and oozes history as it is believed to be the calling place of local Baird William Hopkin from the famous love story "The Maid of Cefn Ydfa" who wrote the story's most popular song in one of the upstairs rooms now affectionately known as Wills room.

Run and owned by the same family since 1967, this olde worlde inn opens its doors all day everyday to locals and visitors to the area alike who come to enjoy the olde worlde feel and unbeatable hospitality that have won the inn its many awards and appearance on ITV's Great Pubs of Wales Programme.

Richard Stephens-David and his family have been running the show for the last two years and provide a stunning restaurant and bar festooned with hundreds of collectable jugs before an impressive original inglenook fireplace. Guests can dine inside or al fresco in the pub's well maintained rear decked beer garden which has a glorious view of the surrounding countryside and the pubs charming thatched roof.

Food is served from 11:30-9pm Monday to Thursday, 11:30-10pm Fridays and Saturdays and from 11:30-8pm on Sundays. The family employ a professional chef who has created a fantastic menu that comprises sharers, fresh fish, grills, healthy or vegetarian options and lighter bites such as jacket potatoes. The choice is vast, but some favourites include homemade classics like steak and ale pie or lasagne Verdi, the 10oz fillet steak, spinach and ricotta cannelloni, pan fried trout, juicy prawn salad and the chicken delight sharer meal which includes BBQ chicken wings and chicken strips in sweet chilli sauce with onion rings and garlic dough balls. The family buy almost all their supplies from other local families who specialise in fresh local produce. Children can choose from their own menu and are welcome throughout. On Sundays a popular Sunday lunch menu is employed for all the family with a choice of courses and options to include the usual meats alongside more unusual mains like cod, scampi and jumbo sausages! Those on a diet or with vegetarian preferences are also well catered for. A fine wine list accompanies your meal along with a real ale on rotation from local breweries. All major credit cards taken.

208 THE GLOBE INN

2 Bridgend Road, Newotn,
Porthcawl CF36 5RN
Tel: 01656 773344
e-mail: nevilleleese@msn.com

The Globe Inn is situated in the picture postcard village of Newton which is just a short drive from the more well known seaside town of Porthcawl. The village itself dates back to the 12th century when it was founded as 'New Town' next to the Norman settlement of Nottage. By the 17th century the village had become a thriving port specialising in exporting and importing wheat, oats, fruit and salad and today stands a tribute to its long and varied history with sights such as Candelstone Castle; a 15th century fortified manor house that was owned by the infamous de Cantelupe family and the fascinating 3000 year old iron age tombs known as the Newton Burrows.

The Globe is within easy walking distance of all this, making it the perfect spot to take a break en route. It is owned and run by Neville and Lisa Leese who have been here for just under 2 years. Neville has been in the trade now for over 26 years and together with Lisa's fine eye, they have created a fantastic inn that the village can be proud of. It's not just locals who love it here though, the inviting and jovial atmosphere combined with quality service and food draws many people in from further afield, making the team here busy most days.

The bar is well stocked with a fine choice of wines, spirits and lagers and offers three real ales for ale lovers; the regular brews being Hancocks HB, Tribute and a rotating guest ale.

The food served up here ranges from light bites and mains, to hearty grills, salads and sides. All the food here is cooked using as much local produce as possible, and all the meat is reared within Wales itself. Popular dishes include the mighty 12oz rump steak, Tipsy steak pie, salmon and crayfish salad and of course the sizzling Fajitas which come with a choice between beef, chicken and vegetables. Food is served from 12-8pm Monday to Thursday; 12-9pm Friday to Saturday and from 12-8pm on Sundays. Wednesday nights are curry nights with a tasty choice of specialty curries to go along with a pint or glass of house wine. Options include classic korma, tikka massala, balti, jalfrezi, madras and a vindaloo for the brave! On Sundays a generous roast is added to the menu, which is particularly popular with families; children are welcome throughout. Owing to popularity, it's recommended to book Saturday nights and Sunday lunchtimes.

In the lifetime of this book, Neville and Lisa plan to open some guest accommodation at the inn, so please ring for details. All major credit cards taken.

209 CARDIFF CASTLE

Cardiff Castle Grounds, Cardiff, South Glamorgan CF10 3RB
Tel: 02920 878100
website: nationaltrust.org.uk

Cardiff Castle is an unusual blend of Roman fort, medieval castle and fanciful Victorian gothic mansion. The Romans established a fort on the site in the 1st century AD, but the square 8 acre fort that remains today was built in the 4th century. When the Normans built their castle in the late 11th century what remained of the Roman walls was buried under earth ramparts. The walls were revealed during excavations in 1889, and were rebuilt on the original foundations - clearly visible in places -between 1922 and 1925.

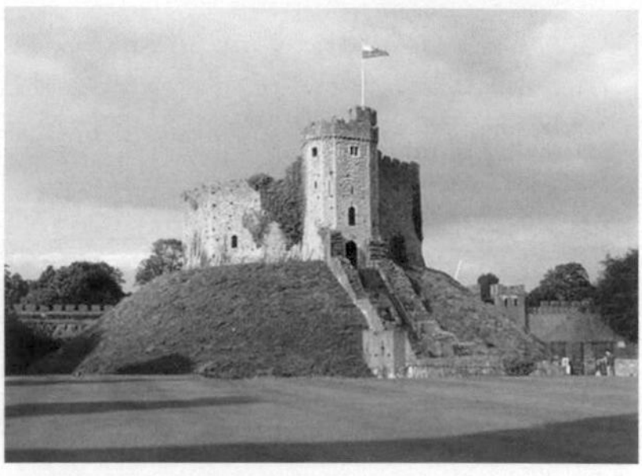

In the late 16th century the Herbert family onverted it into a luxurious and well appointed house. For most of the 17th and 18th centuries the house was left empty and fell into disrepair. In 1766 the house came into the possession of Lord Mountstuart, Marquess of Bute. His son gained immense wealth through the exploitation of mineral resources on his Glamorgan estates and his development of Cardiff as a centre for industrial trade. On his death he left an infant son, John Patrick Crichton Stuart, as "the richest baby in Britain"who lavished money on building projects at many of his properties. In 1869 work began to remodel Cardiff Castle to the designs of the Gothic Revival architect William Burges. A visit to Cardiff Castle without viewing the interiors would mean missing out on some of the most remarkable rooms ever created during the Victorian era.

210 THE WHEATSHEAF INN

The Square, Magor,
Monmouthshire NP26 3HN
Tel: 01633 880608
e-mail: wheatsheaf inn@msn.com

Offering the very best in accommodation, food and drink, **The Wheatsheaf Inn** dates in part to the 14th century and was formerly known as the Princess of Wales. A complete refurbishment was carried out in the autumn of 2007 which has upgraded the inn's facilities while retaining all of its charm and character and more recently the outside has had a repaint.

Mine hosts at the Wheatsheaf are Clare and Dave Hennah who took over here in 2001but have some 13 years experience of the hospitality business. Clare is in charge of the kitchen and her expertise has made the inn well known for its excellent home cooked food. Her specialities include lamb and mint suet pudding, homebaked ham, Old English fish pie, Cauliflower Cheese and butternut squash. Particularly popular are Clare's Wheatsheaf curry, homemade lasagne and steak and ale pie – many customers return time and time again to sample the delicious food on offer. For those with lighter appetites, the snack menu offers a selection of dishes including an all day breakfast, burgers, jacket potatoes and sandwiches/ciabattas. On weekdays, from noon until 5pm, there's a Meal Deal menu with a variety of dishes at very reasonable prices. On Sunday lunchtimes, roasts are added to the regular menus. Food is served from noon until 9.30pm, Monday to Saturday, and from noon until 3pm on Sunday. Booking ahead is strongly recommended on Friday, Saturday and Sunday.

In good weather, you can enjoy your meal outside in the beer garden where there is a dining area with heating. To accompany your meal, a full range of beverages is available including four real ales, including Abbot, Flowers Original, Flowers IPA and a guest ale. The dining and bar areas are beautifully laid out in front of an open fire, which creates a warm and relaxing atmosphere.

The Wheatshead also offers quality accommodation in six attractively furnished and well-appointed rooms, all of which have en-suite facilities and are available all year round. The rooms are spacious and the wooden beams really add to the character of the place. The inn has good disabled access and toilet; children are welcome and there's ample off road parking. Located in the large village of Magor, in Monmouthshire, South East Wales, the inn is close to Chepstow and the city of Newport. Providing the very best in comfort The Wheatsheaf Inn is a popular choice for locals and those visiting the area.

211 THE OLD BARN INN

Magor Road, Llanmartin,
Newport NP18 2EB
Tel: 01633 413382
Fax: 01633 412804
e-mail: theoldbarninn@btconnect.com
website: www.theoldbarninn.co.uk
www.theoldbarninn.com

The hamlet of Llanmartin is tucked away in the South Wales countryside, just a short distance from the A48. Apart from the glorious scenery, the major attraction here is the **Old Barn Inn** which is an absolute must for anyone who appreciates outstanding food and accommodation.

Owners Jackie and Phil Moore took over in 2004 and have maintained top class standards in all departments. The inn's reputation comes mainly from its fantastic restaurant which serves up an exciting menu of light bites, grills, fish and poultry dishes and salads, all of which are created using the best local produce around. Menus change regularly to reflect seasonal goods available but a typical menu includes dishes such as an impressive 16oz sirloin steak, pan fried sea bass, classic cottage pie with a 'leeky roof,' and a sizzling rack of baby back ribs smothered in a finger-licking barbeque sauce. Those with a smaller appetite also have plenty to choose from with a menu that shows less is sometimes more. Dishes include mushroom baked in a port and stilton sauce, grilled goat's cheese salad and Loch Fyne oak smoked salmon served with horseradish mayonnaise and brown bread. Food is served Monday to Thursday from 12-2:30pm and 6-9:30pm, Friday and Saturday 12-9:30pm and Sunday 12-8pm, but guests are welcome to enjoy the bars selection of real ales and refined atmosphere throughout the day either within the barn's atmospheric walls or al fresco on the inn's fully lit and heated patio area.

The Old Barn previously had great accommodation, but was recently refurbished to extend to 15 stunning guest bedrooms, all of which have en suite facilities. Each room is tastefully decorated with modern bespoke furniture and great attention to detail with individual styling, silk furnishings and Egyptian cotton bed sheets. Luxury is the word on guests' lips, particularly when staying in the master suite which has its own balcony sporting glorious views across the countryside and a TV in the chic Jacuzzi bathroom.

A truly inspirational venue for events from weddings to functions, Jackie and Phil have established an enviable reputation for surpassing even the highest of standards with a caring and tailored package for all their guests, whether to dine or stay. Children welcome, all major credit cards taken except American Express and Diners.

212 THE ROSE INN

South Row, Redwick near Magor,
Newport NP26 3DU
Tel: 01633 880501
e-mail: webgry@aol.com
website: www.therose.co.uk

The charming **Rose Inn** is situated in the heart of Redwick, just a short drive from Magor and the coastline. It's scenic location and great facilities make it a popular stop off point for visitors exploring the Newport area. It is owned and run by Gary and Sarah who have created a great homely environment for their guests over the last four years. The inn's pretty flower decked frontage disguises its 15th century status, but inside this is showcased with original oak beams and a roaring fire providing the perfect place to relax or dine with friends. The well stocked bar offers a good selection of fine wines and real ales which include Reverend James and S.A Gold from the Brains Brewery, which can be enjoyed every other session and all day on weekends and summer holidays.

Food is served Tuesday to Saturday from 12-2pm and 6-9pm; and on Sundays from 12:30-2:30pm. The majority of produce used here is sourced locally and is whipped up into a fine menu that ranges from starters and mains to fish dishes, grills and hot and spicy food. Dishes include traditional favourites such as Welsh faggots in ale gravy or homemade steak and ale pie or exciting dishes such as zesty lime salmon fillet, chicken with bacon and cranberry in hickory smoked barbeque sauce, duck with a rich fruit sauce and a whole sea bass with grapes and white wine. Those who prefer spicier food however can sample a range of homemade speciality curries and chillies. Throughout the day a bar snack menu is also available with a large selection of filled sandwiches and jacket potatoes to accompany dishes like lasagne, curry and basket meals. Children and families are welcome and children can dine from their own separate menu which includes healthy and homemade options. Owing to popularity, guests are advised that it's essential to book on weekends and recommended at other times to avoid disappointment.

The inn was recently voted best kept pub in Gwent for 2008-2009, providing great facilities and high standards at all times. The inn also has plenty of outdoor seating for the summer months with a large enclosed rear beer garden complete with play area and swing set for children's use.

214 PENLLWYN MANOR

The Grove, Blackwood,
Gwent NP12 2EQ
Tel: 01495 223466
e-mail: thepenllwynmanor@aol.com

Built in the 16th century the **Penllwyn Manor** is a real hidden gem standing in its own grounds. The establishment was built in 1524 for the grandparents of the famous Captain Henry Morgan. There is an olde world atmosphere throughout the inside of the manor and the modern furnishings add to the superb interior.

The leaseholders Jon and Jackie and their daughters Joanne and Janina have run the manor since May 2009. They have certainly put the place back on the map, offering the very best in food, drink, entertainment and hospitality. Drawing people back like a magnet Penllwyn Manor is open all day every day, offering a good selection of draught keg and real ales.

Food is available between 10am-5.30pm and the full restaurant menu is available between 5.30pm-10pm Monday-Saturday. The majority of produce is sourced from within Wales and there is an extensive menu for diners to choose from. Starters include warm goats cheese salad and crispy duck and chorizo salad. Main courses include slow roasted lamb, marinated salmon, slow braised belly pork and captain's catch of the day. If you still have room after your main course, there are several tempting desserts on offer including strawberry and white chocolate cheesecake and chocolate and cointreau mousse. If it is a lighter appetite you have then lite bites are also offered on the main menu and a specials board gives diners additional choices. Sunday lunch is served between 11.30am-4pm and it is advisable to book – such is its popularity. The manor is also home to Morgans Restaurant, which offers a high standard of mouth watering cuisine including roasted breast of Guinea Fowl served with Foie Gras Potatoes and a Pomegrante and Port Jus. Penllwyn Manor is a child friendly establishment, which has a fantastic lawn at the front of the property, where many visitors like to sit when it is good weather.

There is entertainment provided several evenings a week at the manor, and these nights are extremely popular with locals and visitors. Located within the manor is Penllwyn Tea Rooms, which is a new venture for the leaseholders. Filled sandwiches, jacket potatoes, breakfasts, soups and small meals are served alongside a good range of hot and cold drinks.

Penllwyn Manor is an impressive and charming establishment located in the small town of Blackwood in the South Wales Valleys on the River Sirhowy. Cash and cheque only. Ring for information on accommodation.

213 ANGEL HOTEL

Goldcroft Common, Caerleon,
Newport NP18 1BE
Tel: 01633 430082

The **Angel Hotel** is superb inn located in the heart of the historic Caerleon. Its hosts Harry and Rita Dixon open all day everyday serving fine traditional food and drink to all in a warm and welcoming atmosphere. Two real ales are on offer behind the well stocked bar alongside a fine menu carefully created by Head Chef Nicky Bennett. Guests can choose off the specials board or the main menu which comprises a range of light bites, breakfasts and sandwiches with other dishes to include a hearty sirloin steak, lamb stew and dumplings or spicy chilli con carne. All dishes are cooked fresh to order, made mostly with produce from within Wales. Children can dine from their own menu or half portions of the above. On Sundays a spectacular Sunday lunch is served up, when booking is heavily recommended. All other days in summer food is served from 10am-7pm and from 12-3pm on weekdays and 12-6pm in the winter.

Harry and Rita also offer seven comfortable upstairs rooms, which come on either a room only or B&B rate. Two rooms have good en suite facilities, ideal for short breaks away.

216 THE CROSS KEYS INN

53 Five Locks Road, Pontnewydd,
Cwmbran, Gwent NP44 1BT
Tel: 01633 861545

A popular place with walkers, cyclists, pleasure boaters and bird watchers, **The Cross Keys Inn** stands by the Monmouthshire & Brecon Canal a short drive north of Cwmbran. Leaseholders, Chris and Sian Davies have run the inn for seven years and are extremely welcoming and friendly. A good range of drinks is served at the inviting bar and can be enjoyed inside or out in the large beer garden by the canal.

Open all day every day, food is served Monday-Saturday between 11am-9.30pm and Sunday between 12pm-3.30pm. The restaurant seats 40 people and booking is essential for Sunday lunch. Local suppliers are used wherever possible and there are plenty of dishes to choose from on the printed menu and specials board. All are reasonably priced and generously served, prepared by Sian and the cook Sue. Mixed grill, chicken kiev, Rainbow Trout, chicken curry and homemade steak & kidney pie are among the most popular dishes and there is an extensive choice of meal, poultry, fish and vegetarian dishes. Popular draught keg ales here are John Smiths Smooth and Carling.

There are two guest rooms available for those wanting to explore the area, which has a wide range of attractions for visitors. Cash or cheque only.

215 THE LITTLE CROWN INN

Eiled Road, Wainfelin, Pontypool,
Torfaen NP4 6DR
Tel: 01495 763148
e-mail: ajms229@aol.com
website: www.thelittlecrowninn.co.uk

Home cooking and local produce is at the heart of the extensive menu at **The Little Crown Inn**. All of the dishes are cooked fresh to order and that is perhaps why the establishment is so popular with locals and visitors. Alison and Gus Gregory have owned The Little Crown Inn for the past six years and the establishment was once the runner up for Pub Restaurant of the Year by Living Wales.

The Little Crown Inn is hidden away in the village of Wainfelin, a short drive from Pontypool off the A4043. But the traditional hostelry is really worth finding. Open all day, every day, from mid day until close, there is one rotating real ale. The food is reasonably priced and over 60s get 10 per cent off food from 12pm-6pm every Monday and Wednesday. Butterfly prawns, crab & lime fishcake and steak teriyaki are among the starters on offer. The main menu is extremely varied with plenty of grills, fish, game and poultry dishes among the choices. Favourites include minted Barnsley lamb chop, pheasant wrapped in bacon with sage & onion stuffing, steak mushroom & ale pie and pork Dijon. There are plenty of dishes to keep vegetarian diners content, including homemade vegetable curry, stuffed peppers and classic mushroom stroganoff. There is a specials board too, offering plenty more mouth watering dishes. Food is served Monday-Saturday between 12pm-9pm and there is an early bird special menu from 12pm-6pm. A traditional Sunday lunch is served between 12pm-3pm, and such is its popularity it is advisable to book.

The establishment is child friendly and there is a child's play area and stage to keep younger visitors entertained. A specially designed menu has been created for children under 12 and lasagne, 4oz rump steak and spaghetti bolognaise are among the choices. There is a spacious garden area outside where customers can enjoy a drink or meal on brighter days. Within the last few years the establishment has been totally refurbished and if anything this has enhanced the traditional character of this beautiful village inn. The inn is disabled friendly with a ramp and disabled toilet and there is an off road car park. Food themed evenings are extremely popular among those who frequent the inn and are definitely worth experiencing for those visiting the area. All major credit cards taken.

217 THE GOLDEN LION

21 Queens Street, Nantyglo, Brynmawr, Ebbw Vale NP23 4LW
Tel: 01495 291522
Mobile: 07879458539

The Golden Lion is situated in the village of Nantyglo, which is just a short drive south from Brynmawr and the more well known borough of Gwent. Its lofty location provides its guests with spectacular views across the valley and over the nearby golf course – which provides a tempting afternoon activity for golf enthusiasts with official status as the highest golf course in the UK. Its owners James and Christina have been in the trade for 25 years, 20 of which have been spent at the Golden Lion where they have created a friendly and welcoming atmosphere for their guests who rave about the fantastic food on offer. Known to locals as the hub of its community the inn has a traditional but distinctive styling with comfy seating and a pool and darts table for entertainment.

Christina is the chef here and is well established as the best cook in the village, her speciality being the Sunday lunch which packs out the inn, making booking heavily recommended to avoid disappointments. A good selection of other meals is also available from 12-4pm each day which can be enjoyed throughout the traditionally styled inn. Food is also available on request at other times for party bookings.

On Tuesday to Fridays from 7pm until close and on Sundays from 12pm-close the well stocked bar is open, housing a good choice of wines, spirits and draught ales which include Carling and Worthington. The inn is closed on Saturdays, except for private parties, please ring to book.

Owing to the inn's stunning location, it is a popular base for those who enjoy hiking or touring with plenty of trails in the surrounding area which pass many of the areas historical sites which includes the famous Nantyglo Round Towers. There are three double upstairs rooms to choose from, all of which are handsomely decorated, one with en suite facilities. The rooms all come on a hearty bed and breakfast, which Christina assures you will last you the day. Children and families welcome, cash payments only please.

218 PRINCE OF WALES INN

Merthyr Road,
Princetown, Tredegar NP22 3AE
Tel: 01685 844441
e-mail: johnrichardswcu@aol.com
website: www.princeofwales.me.uk

Located just a short distance off the 'Heads of Valleys' road (A465), the **Prince of Wales Inn** is a superb country pub offering the very best in hospitality, food, ale and accommodation. John and Keri Richards and their son Andrew have been here since the spring of 2005 and have made this Free House once of the most popular places to dine in the area.

Keri is an outstanding cook and her menu offers something for every palate. All the ingredients are sourced from within Wales and cooked fresh to order each day. Guests can dine from 10am-9pm seven days a week and choose from an across the board menu that encompasses light bites and lunches, traditional main meals, curries, grills, seafood and vegetarian dishes. Popular dishes include the Prince of Wales chicken; a succulent breast stuffed with brie and wrapped in bacon, the roasted sea bass with rosemary mash and the homemade faggots. Each Sunday Keri serves up a spectacular two course roast from 12:30-3:30pm when booking is strongly recommended. The well stocked bar offers a good selection which includes a rotating ale from the Tomos Watkins Brewery in Llanelli; an ideal accompaniment to a relaxing evening before the roaring fire.

The inn also offers two quality 3-star rooms for guests with en suite facilities that come on a generous breakfast rate. All major credit cards acceptable, children welcome.

219 RAILWAY TAVERN

Dukestown Road, Dukestown,
Tredegar NP22 4QD
Tel: 01495 722616
e-mail: railwaytavern@yahoo.co.uk
website: www.railwaytaverntredegar.co.uk

Sandra and Gwyn Lewis and their friendly Great Dane Gellett have been providing great hospitality for the past 2 years at the **Railway Tavern**. Open every day the pair serves up a great collection of ales from the famous Brains Brewery alongside a fine menu. The menu includes a hearty selection of grills, pub classics and seafood with popular dishes such as Pork and Apple Turret, Celtic Pride Steak or Grandma's recipe traditional corned beef pie. Food is served 11am-3pm and 5-9:30pm Tuesday to Sunday lunchtime. Great value for money also available with the credit crunch menu, children under 5 eat free. Three upstairs rooms are also available on a breakfast tariff.

220 THE ROYAL OAK

134 Hereford Road,
Monmouth NP25 3GA
Tel: 01600 772505
e-mail:
theroyaloakmonmouth@yahoo.co.uk
website: www.royaloakmonmouth.co.uk

The Royal Oak is located on the Hereford Road just two minutes drive from the historic market town of Monmouth, most famous for being the birthplace of Henry V and the composition site of Bohemian Rhapsody. The Royal Oak makes a great place to stop off for a drink or bite to eat after exploring the town's bustling streets with plenty of shops and tranquil riverside walks to amuse all walks of life.

It is owned and run by Doug and Jude Morris who have created a popular venue for both locals and visitors over the past 18 years. The pair is known best for their outstanding hospitality, great food and selection of well kept ales. They open every session and all day on Saturdays, serving a choice of three real ales which include a rotating guest ale with Timothy Taylor Landlord and Bass being the regular brews. Drinks can be enjoyed throughout the inn which sports an olde worlde feel with barrel chairs and a roaring open log fire in the winter months, or in the summer months; guests can take advantage of the great beer garden to the rear of the property which sports excellent views across the town and a fantastic children's play area.

Food is served from 11:30am-2:30pm and 6-10pm Monday to Saturdays and from 12-2:30pm on Sundays when a hearty roast is served up. On Sunday evenings from 7-9:30pm a good range of bar snacks is available. The main menu is created using produce sourced in Wales, and encompasses a range of filled jacket potatoes and rolls, burgers, pies, fish, salads, soups and starters not to mention a succulent selection of grills and classic pub favourites such as homemade cottage pie, lasagne with garlic bread, Moussaka and steak and kidney pie.

Although most guests come for the fine food on offer, some come to camp, as the Royal Oak also has a small caravan and camping park available for up to 5 caravans/tents all year round. With the pub's facilities close to hand, and just a stone's throw from the Forest of Dean it's an ideal way to see this beautiful area on a budget.

221 THE BOAT INN

Lone Lane, Penallt,
Monmouthshire NP25 4AJ
Tel: 01600 712615
e-mail: info@theboatpenallt.co.uk
website: www.theboatpenallt.co.uk

Occupying a superb position on the bank of the River Wye looking across to Gloucestershire, **The Boat Inn** is a traditional Welsh pub with the unusual feature of being built against a solid rock face. Also rather uncommon is the fact that while the inn is in Wales, its car park is in England. Access via the old Rail Bridge.

Shaleen Goodman took over the inn from the 1st February 2009 and has made this olde worlde hostelry a popular venue, especially with walkers and cyclists. The inn is open all day everyday during the summer months (opening times vary during winter months).

Wholesome and appetising food is served every lunchtime (noon until 2:30pm) and evening (7-9pm) except Sunday and Monday nights. The menu offers something for every taste but why not try the speciality dish Pan Haggerty? A traditional Scottish dish with layers of potato, caramelised onions, mature cheddar cheese and garlic, all oven baked and served with a full salad and crispy garlic bread. Other popular dishes include a choice of beef, chicken and spinach, or spinach and basil pesto lasagne, chunky chilli, home-made curry and a traditional ploughman's. Light bites are also available with a range of filled jackets and baguettes alongside dishes such as prawn cocktail and soup.

Lovers of real ale will also be very happy at the Boat with up to five real ales on offer (during summer months) along with largers, stout and no fewer than 15 traditional ciders and perry to sample. Wine lovers are not left out though, with 25 country fruit wines stocked behind the bar.

In the summer months, customers can enjoy their refreshments in the attractive gardens with its own waterfall. Boats can moor here and on the first Sunday in September, a Raft race is held on the river while live music entertains participants and watchers.

Entertainment at the Boat House is another major attraction, with live music every Tuesday and Thursday from 9pm. The inn welcomes children and dogs. Credit cards are accepted.

222 THE BOAT INN

The Back, Chepstow,
Monmouthshire NP16 5HH
Tel: 01291 628192
e-mail: theboatinn1@aol.com
website: www.theboatinnchepstow.co.uk

The Boat Inn is a fantastic pub with a growing reputation for good food and service. Situated in Chepstow overlooking the river, this magnificent property is eye catching both inside and outside. The facilities are of a high standard throughout the delightful premise. The tenants, Lyndon and Tracy Price have run the establishment for the past two years and have really boosted its popularity in the area. Locals and visitors come together to soak up the friendly atmosphere and to enjoy the very best in food and drink.

Food is available daily, both at lunch times and in the evenings. Chefs, Shane and Lydia create some fantastic dishes and there is plenty to choose from off the extensive menu. The menu is very traditional and has a strong focus on local produce. Among the favourite dishes are homemade beer battered cod and chips; homemade beef lasagne; 8oz Rib Eye Steak; and grilled sea bass. Vegetarian options include stilton, peppered mushroom and onion pudding; and brie, pesto and cherry tomato filo tartlet. All of the dishes are reasonably priced and this is perhaps why customers return time and time again to enjoy the friendly hospitality and good food. For those with a lighter appetite there are plenty of filled jacket potatoes, sandwiches and other lite bites to choose from. Desserts include gooseberry and apple treacle crumble tart; and black forest tumble. Such is The Boat Inn's popularity on a Sunday, it is advisable to book. Like the downstairs area, the upstairs area seats around 45 people and customers can enjoy spectacular views over the river. Customers have four real ales to choose from, which include Rev James, Wadsworth 6x, Bass and Flowers IPA.

The inn is in an ideal place to enjoy something to eat for those visiting Monmouthshire. Located in the town of Chepstow, on the border with Gloucestershire, it is located close to the River Wye, which offers some beautiful scenery. The town is approximately 16 miles from Newport and is well known for having the oldest surviving stone castle in Britain and for hosting the Welsh Grand National at Chepstow Racecourse. The inn's quizzes are popular with locals and visitors, with the winning team taking all of the prize money. Food is served between 12pm-3pm and 6pm-9pm Monday to Fridays and all day on Saturdays and Sundays.

223 LIVE AND LET LIVE

Coleford Road, Tutshill, Chepstow NP16 7BN
Tel: 01291 624782
e-mail: zebedee_5@msn.com

Live and Let Live is run by Maureen Hughes, her family and Zoe Evans who offer a chirpy atmosphere for guests to enjoy some fantastic home cooking in the charming village of Tutshill, across the river from Chepstow. With two real ales on offer each session and food served from 12-2:30pm and 6-9pm Mon-Sat and 12-6pm on Sundays it is a popular place to visit with special attention paid to dietary requirements, providing for vegetarians and using only the finest locally sourced produce in its meals. Sunday lunch is extremely popular so booking is essential to avoid disappointment. A range of value for money deals are available throughout the week, with business meetings, coffee mornings, functions and parties all catered for. Please ring for details. Children welcome, all major credit cards taken.

224 THE OLD FERRY INN

Beachley, Chepstow,
Monmouthshire NP16 7HH
Tel: 01291 622474

Set in the quiet, but pretty village of Beachley underneath the magnificent Severn Bridge on the Gloucestershire side is the **Old Ferry Inn**. To find it, follow the brown visitor signs for the Severn viewing point and you'll be there. Sporting truly glorious views across the river, the inn is a popular place for both locals and tourists alike to sit back and admire the scenery.

People don't just come for the view though, as the inn draws in the crowds to sample the fine food and real ale on offer here. Hosts Murray and Linda Hunt offer a warm welcome to all, opening every day apart from Monday, and open on Bank Holidays. The couple have been here since 2002 and have created a fantastic environment with a mix of traditional and modern décor which is complemented by many trinkets from the inn's long and interesting history.

Food is served from 12-2:30pm and 6:30-9pm Tuesday to Saturday and from 12-3:30pm on Sundays. The team here is headed by a professional chef who ensures that all the dishes here are homemade on the premises each day. The menu changes four times a year to reflect the best seasonal produce around and does not disappoint with something to suit everyone. The vast choice comprises starters such as bacon, mushroom and black pudding stir fry, king prawn salad and duck and orange pate, whereas the mains range from hearty winter warmers, succulent grills, international cuisine and good old pub favourites like homemade steak, mushroom and red wine pie or battered haddock and chips. Other favourite dishes include tender lamb and sweet potato casserole, large baked trout stuffed with herbs and chunky Mexican beef chilli. A daily specials board also offers a good choice which might include tempting treats such as game pie or Glamorgan fritters. The bar offers a good selection of drinks to accompany your meal which includes up to two real ales on rotation from the local Wye Valley Brewery.

Murray and Linda also offer a range quality guest bedrooms; four of which have en suite facilities. All rooms are upstairs and some have glorious views, perfect for watching the sunset over the river. Children and dogs are welcome, all major credit cards accepted.

225 CARPENTERS ARMS

Shirenewton, Chepstow,
Monmouthshire NP16 6BU
Tel: 01291 641231
e-mail: colinfurnival@yahoo.co.uk

The Carpenter's Arms is a superb country inn steeped in history, located in the hamlet of Shirenewton found just West of Chepstow. Its picturesque location surrounded by countryside makes the perfect spot to retire after a long walk to curl up before the inn's impressive fireplace. The building itself dates back over 400 years and was once both a carpenters and a blacksmiths and an ale house before it was all combined into the charming pub you see today. The interior is rustic and traditional; the walls are decked with fascinating old tools from the inn's past, but the atmosphere is light and friendly with a lovely mix of locals and tourists alike, children and dogs welcome.

It has been owned and run by Colin and Angela since January 2009, but the pair has a wealth of experience in the trade having worked as a team since 2001. They open for business every session and all day on weekends, but sometimes close a little earlier on Sunday evenings in the winter months. Angela is a qualified chef and has won many awards for her food. At the Carpenter's she serves up a delightful menu created using fresh Welsh produce that ranges from light bites and starters to mains, fish and seafood, with plenty of vegetarian options also. Her speciality is homemade dishes which include a variety of pies made with Angela's own recipe suet pastry. Other popular dishes include a twist on the classic surf and turf with a 10oz rump steak topped with a seafood medley, honey roast duck, Woodland chicken wrapped in pate and bacon in a creamy wild mushroom sauce, Thai cod and prawn fishcakes or Mediterranean vegetable pasta bake. Each Sunday a traditional roast lunch is added to the menu from 12-6pm which includes a choice of lamb, beef or chicken and all the trimmings including Yorkshire puddings. Food is available Monday to Friday 12-2:30pm and 6-9:30pm and on Saturdays from 12-10pm.

The bar is well stocked with wine, spirits and ales which include London Pride, Spitfire and Bass which can be enjoyed inside or out where the inn's picture postcard surroundings can be truly appreciated. All major credit cards accepted.

226 THE HALL INN

Gwehelog, Usk,
Monmouthshire NP15 1RB
Tel: 01291 672381
e-mail: stuart.savidge@btconnect.com

A distinctive old building, **The Hall Inn** is a delightful pub that has associations with the Chartist movement of the mid 1800s. Today, life at this old worlde hostelry is altogether less revolutionary. The interior is very traditional, with flagstone floors, heavy oak beams and roaring open fires. Cosy and comfortable, the inn has two bars with a separate lounge area that provides just the right ambience for a relaxing drink. As a free house, there is always a fine choice of real ales on tap here with Reverend James and Hobby Horse and Rhymney Bitter as the regular brews together with a rotating guest ale. The pub is also the meeting and playing venue for the local darts club.

Mine host, Stuart Savidge who has been here since 2000 and renowned chef Andrew Yoxall pride themselves on serving some of the best food to be found in the area. Everything is prepared fresh from locally sourced ingredients. All steaks are cut to order and fish is delivered 4 times a week. The menu, which features many local specialities, is supplemented by a constantly changing list of daily specials. The regular menu offers appetising dishes such as salmon cod and leek fish cake amongst the starters, along with baked goat's cheese with basil, pesto and mussels with onion and garlic cream. For your main course how about prime Welsh sirloin steak or braised skirt of beef on horseradish and parsley mashed potato with a red wine and redcurrant sauce? Homemade puddings are something of a speciality here with old favourites like the bread and butter pudding with double cream vying for your attention with dishes such as fresh baked apple pie and melt in your mouth raspberry Pavlova. A note on the menu urges vegetarians if they are struggling to find something they like to have a word with the chef – "he is very adaptable and will strive to please!" Food is served every lunchtime and evening, except Sunday evening and all day on Mondays unless it is a bank holiday. Booking ahead is strongly recommended at weekends.

The inn also offers comfortable accommodation in 3 double rooms, all with en suite facilities.

227 THE HORSESHOE INN

Mamhilad, nr Llanover NP4 8QZ
Tel: 01873 880542
e-mail: info@horseshoe_inn.com
website: www.horseshoe-inn.com

Dating back to the 17th century, **The Horseshoe Inn** is nestled in an idyllic rural location. The pub and restaurant, between Abergavenny and Pontypool, has been owned by Phil Thomas for more than four years.

The quality of the food is extremely high and local produce is a strong focus of the extensive and varied menu. The main menu is changed monthly and the dishes are well presented and served to diners efficiently. There is also a daily specials board to tempt the taste buds. Among the favourite dishes are slow roasted belly pork with black pudding, white onion pureé, pork and cider sauce; and braised shoulder of Welsh lamb with creamed cabbage & bacon, confit carrot, fondant potato and rosemary jus.

The Horseshoe Inn serves quality real ales, on hand pump or direct from the barrel; organic ciders and an interesting, progressive list of wines, many by the glass. The new event suite at the inn caters for up to 90 guests and offers spectacular views of the surrounding countryside. Food is served daily between 12pm-3pm and 6.30pm-9.30pm and it is advisable to book ahead. Credit cards, except American Express and Diners taken. Disabled access is not a problem.

229 WARWICKS COUNTRY PUB AND EATERY

Tal-Y-Coed near Llantilio Crossenny,
Abergavenney NP7 8TL
Tel: 01600 780227
website: www.warwickscountrypub.co.uk

The old worlde **Warwicks Country Pub and Eatery** stands on an ancient drover's road between Monmouth and Abergavenny in the picturesque hamlet of Tal-Y-Coed. Claire and Ian and their trusted waitress Sue opened in August this year and have been drawing in food lovers like a magnet ever since.

Open Thursday to Sunday from 12-3pm and 6-11pm and also on Bank Holidays, the inn is an atmospheric place with a lively clientele who comment highly on the food. The menu is created by a team of professional chefs who serve up a fine range of dishes that include a tasty trio of game with crushed garlic potatoes in a red wine sauce; butternut squash and spinach tagliatelle; and the infamous crispy belly pork dish that comes with battered black pudding in a sweet balsamic port sauce with spring onion mash and vegetables. Children are very welcome and can dine from their own large menu or take half portions of the above. The restaurant is fully licensed and serves a wide variety of beers, wines and spirits to accompany your meal alongside a well kept real ale. All major credit cards taken.

228 THE HARDWICK

Old Raglan Road, Abergavenny,
Monmouthshire NP7 9AA
Tel: 01873 854220
Fax: 01873 854623
e-mail: info@thehardwick.co.uk
website: www.thehardwick.co.uk

Standing on the outskirts of Abergavenny with scenic views of open countryside, **The Hardwick** is a fine old inn noted for its excellent food and well-kept real ales. This is very much a family owned business with Stephen and Joanna Terry and their daughters Olivia and Phoebe all involved in the enterprise. Although this is their first venture all together, Stephen has some 22 years experience in the business as a well known professional chef.

Providing top quality food is a major priority at the Hardwick and gastronomes will be in their element here. The chefs bring imagination and flair to creating menus that are fresh and exciting. The menus change regularly to reflect the best in local produce and locally reared meats, but typical menus cross all borders serving a vast selection of starters, mains and puddings to suit every palette. Starters include pan fried scallops, Tuscan style ricotta dumplings, pigeon breast with German style noodles and pan fried chorizo with Halloumi cheese. The choice for main meals is equally as exquisite with grilled rib eye, roast local duck, rare breed middle white pork meatballs, line caught sea bass on Spanish butter beans, and pasta Rotolo of butternut squash, spinach and goats cheese to choose from. If you still have the room, desserts are also in plenty with innovative twists on all your favourites such as Panetonne bread and butter pudding brulee, treacle tart ice cream with candied pecans and golden syrup or peanut butter and jelly parfait with Valrhona chocolate brownie base, chocolate mousse, peanut brittle and salted caramel sauce. The inn also stocks a good range of homemade ice creams, sorbets, truffles and cheeses.

To accompany your meal there's a comprehensive range of beverages including wine half-bottle carafe or glass and two rotating guest ales. Meals are served in the 60 seater restaurant every lunchtime from 12-3pm and in the evenings from 6:30-10pm, except Sunday evenings and all day Monday unless it is a bank holiday when the restaurant is open for lunch. Children are welcome and all major credit cards apart from American Express and Diners are accepted.

The family have recently refurbished the inn to include disabled toilets and eight guest bedrooms with en suite facilities.

230 THE WALNUT TREE

Llandewi Skirrid, Abergavenny,
Monmouthshire NP7 8AW
Tel: 01873 852797
e-mail: mail@thewalnuttreeinn.com
website: www.thewalnuttreeinn.com

The famous **Walnut Tree** stands at Llandewi Skirrid, just a short drive from Abergavenney. Owner Shaun Hill has been here for 2 years but it is his 40 years experience as a head chef which has given the Walnut its name for fine dining. Closed on Sundays and Mondays but open all other days from 12-3pm and 6:30-9:30pm; an across the board menu created with Welsh produce is served up within a contemporary styled restaurant or al fresco with pretty views across the countryside at the foot of the Skirrid Mountain. Throughout the year two charming cottages are also available to hire from the Walnut, both sleeping up to four people, dogs and children welcome. All major credit cards accepted.

231 THE CROWN AT PANTYGELLI

Old Hereford Road, Pantygelli,
Abergavenny, Monmouthshire NP7 7HR
Tel: 01873 853314
e-mail: crown@pantygelli.com
website: www.thecrownatpantygelli.com

The Crown inn is situated in the rural country hamlet of Pantygelli which lies between the impressive Black Mountains and the historic market town of Abergavenny. The inn itself dates back to the late 16th century in parts when it was the main inn on an old cattle drover's road, and today stands steeped in that history, retaining many original features such as stone walling, low beamed ceilings and large open fires. Its rustic architecture is complimented by a contemporary décor and styling which bring together the inn's cosy atmosphere and high quality of food and drink on offer.

The inn has been owned and run by Steve and Cherie Chadwick for the past 5 years, who have created a thriving hub for their community; organising events and charity fundraisers alongside special food nights which showcase all the great food they have to offer. They open every session, excluding Mondays and bank holidays and have created tidy competition for their fare, so it is best to book on weekends.

The snug bar is well stocked throughout the year with a minimum of four real ales to try which include Rhymney Best, Wye Valley, Bass and a rotating guest ale from a local brewery. But the real attraction here is the food. Served from 12-2pm Tues-Sun and from 7-9pm Tues-Sat, the food here samples the best in local produce, all dishes cooked fresh to order by the inn's very own professional chef. The menu is across the board with a selection of dishes to suit every taste with traditional pub classics like Scampi and chips or steak and ale pie to succulent winter warmers like braised lamb shank with roasted squash and rosemary mash, pork tenderloin with caramelised red onion or more exotic dishes from around the world that range from Salmon rice noodles with bok choi and chilli dressing, roasted figs in parma ham, and vegetable tian topped with goats cheese. There is also plenty to choose from for vegetarians and for those on a gluten free diet, just inform the team and they will do their best to meet your needs. Children are also welcome and can choose smaller portions from the main menu if desired.

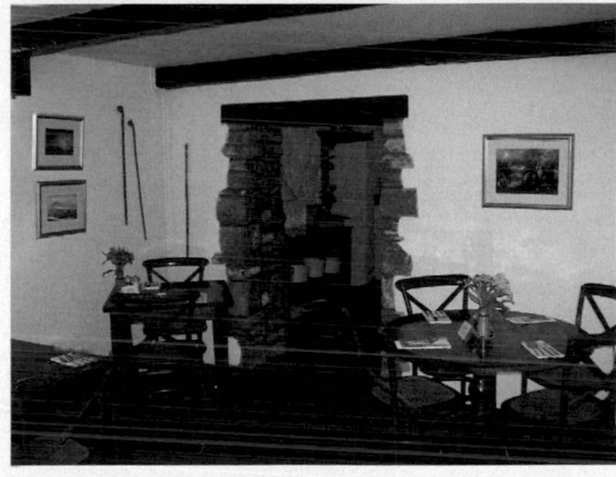

Although guests can enjoy a toasty fire in the winter months, the summertime provides a perfect opportunity to enjoy the inn's flower decked patio which holds breathtaking views of the sunset over the mountains on a clear day.

Tourist Information Centres

BALA
Pensarn Road, Bala LL23 7SR
Tel: 01678 521021
Fax: 01678 521021
e-mail: bala.tic@gwynedd.gov.uk

BANGOR
Town Hall, Deiniol Road, Bangor LL57 2RE
Tel: 01248 352786
Fax: 01248 352786
e-mail: bangor.tic@gwynedd.gov.uk

BARMOUTH
The Station, Station Road, Barmouth LL42 1LU
Tel: 01341 280787
Fax: 01341 280787
e-mail: barmouth.tic@gwynedd.gov.uk

BARRY ISLAND
The Promenade, The Triangle, Barry Island CF62 5TQ
Tel: 01446 747171
Fax: 01446 747171
e-mail: barrytic@valeofglamorgan.gov.uk

BEDDGELERT
Canolfan Hebog, Beddgelert LL55 4YD
Tel: 01766 890615
Fax: 01766 890615
e-mail: tic.beddgelert@eryri-npa.gov.uk

BETWS Y COED
Royal Oak Stables, Betws y Coed LL24 0AH
Tel: 01690 710426
Fax: 01690 710665
e-mail: tic.byc@eryri-npa.gov.uk

BLAENAU FFESTINIOG
Unit 3, High Street, Blaenau Ffestiniog LL41 3ES
Tel: 01766 830360
Fax: 01766 830360
e-mail: tic.blaenau@eryri-npa.gov.uk

BLAENAVON
Blaenavon World Heritage Centre, Church Road,
Blaenavon NP4 9AS
Tel: 01495 742333
Fax: 01495 742332
e-mail: blaenavon.tic@torfaen.gov.uk

BORTH
Cambrian Terrace, Borth SY24 5HY
Tel: 01970 871174
Fax: 01970 871365
e-mail: borthtic@ceredigion.gov.uk

BRECON
Cattle Market Car park, Brecon LD3 9DA
Tel: 01874 622485
Fax: 01874 625256
e-mail: brectic@powys.gov.uk

BRIDGEND
Bridgend Designer Outlet, The Derwen,
Bridgend CF32 9SU
Tel: 01656 654906
Fax: 01656 646523
e-mail: bridgendtic@bridgend.gov.uk

CAERLEON
5 High Street, Caerleon NP18 1AE
Tel: 01633 422656
Fax: 01633 422656
e-mail: caerleon.tic@newport.gov.uk

CAERNARFON
Oriel Pendeitsh, Castle Street, Caernarfon LL55 1ES
Tel: 01286 672232
Fax: 01286 676476
e-mail: caernarfon.tic@gwynedd.gov.uk

CAERPHILLY
The Twyn, Caerphilly CF83 1JL
Tel: 029 2088 0011
Fax: 029 2086 0811
e-mail: tourism@caerphilly.gov.uk

CARDIFF
The Old Library, The Hayes, Cardiff CF10 1AH
Tel: 029 2087 3573
Fax: 029 2023 2058
e-mail: visitor@cardiff.gov.uk

CARDIGAN
Theatr Mwldan, Bath House Road, Cardigan SA43 1JY
Tel: 01239 613230
Fax: 01239 614853
e-mail: cardigantic@ceredigion.gov.uk

CARMARTHEN
113 Lammas Street, Carmarthen SA31 3AQ
Tel: 01267 231557
Fax: 01267 221901
e-mail: carmarthentic@carmarthenshire.gov.uk

CHEPSTOW
Castle Car Park, Bridge Street, Chepstow NP16 5EY
Tel: 01291 623772
Fax: 01291 628004
e-mail: chepstow.tic@monmouthshire.gov.uk

CONWY
Castle Buildings, Conwy LL32 8LD
Tel: 01492 592248
Fax: 01492 573545
e-mail: conwytic@conwy.gov.uk

DOLGELLAU
Ty Meirion, Eldon Square, Dolgellau LL40 1PU
Tel: 01341 422888
Fax: 01341 422576
e-mail: tic.dolgellau@eryri npa.gov.uk

FISHGUARD HARBOUR
Ocean Lab, The Parrog, Fishguard Harbour SA64 0DE
Tel: 01348 872037
Fax: 01348 872528
e-mail: fishguardharbour.tic@pembrokeshire.gov.uk

FISHGUARD TOWN
Town Hall, Market Square, Fishguard Town SA65 9HA
Tel: 01437 776636
Fax: 01384 875582
e-mail: fishguard.tic@pembrokeshire.gov.uk

HARLECH
Llys y Graig, High Street, Harlech LL46 2YE
Tel: 01766 780658
Fax: 01766 780658
e-mail: tic.harlech@eryri-npa.gov.uk

HAVERFORDWEST
Old Bridge, Haverfordwest SA61 2EZ
Tel: 01437 763110
Fax: 01437 767738
e-mail: haverfordwest.tic@pembrokeshire.gov.uk

HOLYHEAD
Stena Line, Terminal 1, Holyhead LL65 1DQ
Tel: 01407 762622
Fax: 01407 761462
e-mail: holyhead@nwtic.com

KNIGHTON
Offa's Dyke Centre, West Street, Knighton LD7 1EN
Tel: 01547 528753
Fax: 01547 529027
e-mail: oda@offasdyke.demon.co.uk

LLANBERIS
41b High Street, Llanberis LL55 4EU
Tel: 01286 870765
Fax: 01286 871924
e-mail: llanberis.tic@gwynedd.gov.uk

LLANDOVERY
Heritage Centre, Kings Road, Llandovery SA20 0AW
Tel: 01550 720693
Fax: 01550 720693
e-mail: llandovery.ic@breconbeacons.org

LLANDUDNO
Library Building, Mostyn Street, Llandudno LL30 2RP
Tel: 01492 577577
Fax: 01492 577578
e-mail: llandudnotic@conwy.gov.uk

LLANELLI
Millennium Coastal Park Discovery Centre,
North Dock, Llanelli SA15 2LF
Tel: 01554 777744
Fax: 01554 757825
e-mail: DiscoveryCentre@carmarthenshire.gov.uk

LLANFAIRPWLLGWYNGYLL
Station Site, Llanfairpwllgwyngyll LL61 5UJ
Tel: 01248 713177
Fax: 01248 715711
e-mail: llanfairpwll@nwtic.com

LLANGOLLEN
Y Chapel, Castle Street, Llangollen LL20 8NU
Tel: 01978 860828
Fax: 01978 861563
e-mail: llangollen@nwtic.com

MERTHYR TYDFIL
14a Glebeland Street, Merthyr Tydfil CF47 8AU
Tel: 01685 379884
Fax: 01685 379884
e-mail: tic@merthyr.gov.uk

MILFORD HAVEN
94 Charles Street, Milford Haven SA73 2HL
Tel: 01646 690866
Fax: 01646 690655
e-mail: milford.tic@pembrokeshire.gov.uk

MOLD
Library Museum & Art Gallery, Earl Road,
Mold CH7 1AP
Tel: 01352 759331
Fax: 01352 759331
e-mail: mold@nwtic.com

MONMOUTH
Market Hall, Priory Street, Monmouth NP25 3DY
Tel: 01600 713899
Fax: 01600 772794
e-mail: monmouth.tic@monmouthshire.gov.uk

MUMBLES
The Methodist Church, Mumbles Road,
Mumbles SA3 4BU
Tel: 01792 361302
Fax: 01792 363392
e-mail: info@mumblestic.co.uk

NEW QUAY
Church Street, New Quay SA45 9NZ
Tel: 01545 560865
Fax: 01545 561360
e-mail: newquaytic@ceredigion.gov.uk

NEWPORT
Museum & Art Gallery, John Frost Square,
Newport NP20 1PA
Tel: 01633 842962
Fax: 01633 222615
e-mail: newport.tic@newport.gov.uk

NEWPORT (PEMBS)
2 Bank Cottages, Long Street,
Newport (pembs) SA42 0TN
Tel: 01239 820912
Fax: 01239 821258
e-mail: NewportTIC@Pembrokeshirecoast.org.uk

OSWESTRY MILE END
Mile End Services, Oswestry Mile End SY11 4JA
Tel: 01691 662488
Fax: 01691 662883
e-mail: tic@oswestry-bc.gov.uk

OSWESTRY TOWN
The Heritage Centre, 2 Church Terrace,
Oswestry Town SY11 2TE
Tel: 01691 662753
Fax: 01691 657811
e-mail: ot@oswestry-welshborders.org.uk

PEMBROKE
Visitor Centre, Commons Road, Pembroke SA71 4EA
Tel: 01437 776499
e-mail: pembroke.tic@pembrokeshire.gov.uk

PENARTH
Penarth Pier, The Esplanade, Penarth CF64 3AU
Tel: 029 2070 8849
e-mail: penarthtic@valeofglamorgan.gov.uk

PORTHCAWL
Old Police Station, John Street, Porthcawl CF36 3DT
Tel: 01656 786639
Fax: 01656 782387
e-mail: porthcawltic@bridgend.gov.uk

PORTHMADOG
High Street, Porthmadog LL49 9LD
Tel: 01766 512981
Fax: 01766 515312
e-mail: porthmadog.tic@gwynedd.gov.uk

PRESTEIGNE
The Judge's Lodging, Broad Street, Presteigne LD8 2AD
Tel: 01544 260650
Fax: 01544 260652
e-mail: presteignetic@powys.gov.uk

PWLLHELI
Min y Don, Station Square, Pwllheli LL53 5HG
Tel: 01758 613000
Fax: 01758 613000
e-mail: pwllheli.tic@gwynedd.gov.uk

RHYL
Rhyl Childrens Village, West Parade, Rhyl LL18 1HZ
Tel: 01745 355068
Fax: 01745 342255
e-mail: rhyl.tic@denbighshire.gov.uk

SAUNDERSFOOT
The Barbecue, Harbour Car Park,
Saundersfoot SA69 9HE
Tel: 01834 813672
Fax: 01834 813673
e-mail: saundersfoot.tic@pembrokeshire.gov.uk

ST DAVIDS
Visitor Centre, Oriel y Parc, St Davids SA62 6NW
Tel: 01437 720392
e-mail: enquiries@stdavids.pembrokeshirecoast.org.uk

SWANSEA
Plymouth Street, Swansea SA1 3QG
Tel: 01792 468321
Fax: 01792 464602
e-mail: tourism@swansea.gov.uk

TENBY
Unit 2, The Gateway Complex, Tenby SA70 7LT
Tel: 01834 842402
Fax: 01834 845439
e-mail: tenby.tic@pembrokeshire.gov.uk

WELSHPOOL
The Vicarage Gardens Car Park, Church Street,
Welshpool SY21 7DD
Tel: 01938 552043
Fax: 01938 554038
e-mail: ticwelshpool@btconnect.com

WREXHAM
Lambpit Street, Wrexham LL11 1WN
Tel: 01978 292015
Fax: 01978 292467
e-mail: tic@wrexham.gov.uk

Image Copyright Holders

Some images in this book have been supplied by **http://www.geograph.org.uk** and licensed under the Creative Commons Attribution-Share Alike 2.0 Generic License. To view a copy of this license, visit **http://creativecommons.org/licenses/by-sa/2.0/** or send a letter to Creative Commons, 171 Second Street, Suite 300, San Francisco, California, 94105, USA.

COPYRIGHT HOLDERS ARE AS FOLLOWS:

Pontcysyllte Aqueduct, Llangollen © Mark Riley	pg 3
St Mary's Church, Mold © Aaron Thomas	pg 4
River Alyn, Mold © Phil Williams	pg 4
St Winefrides Well, Hollywell © Steve Brown	pg 6
Ewloe Castle © Peter Craine	pg 7
Denbigh Castle © Errol Edwards	pg 9
Rhuddlan Castle © George Tod	pg 13
Early Morning, Ruthin © Eirian Evans	pg 15
Llangollen Town & River Dee © Stephen Nunney	pg 17
Valle Crucis Abbey, Llangollen © Robert Edwards	pg 19
Viaduct and Aqueduct, Chirk © Ian Cardinal	pg 20
Holt Castle © Peter Craine	pg 25
War Memorial, Colwyn Bay © Eirian Evans	pg 30
Christ Church, Prestatyn © Tim Heaton	pg 32
Town Walls, Conwy © Mike White	pg 37
Bangor Cathedral © Alan Fryer	pg 39
Caernarfon Castle © Steve Brown	pg 43
Menai Suspension Bridge © Steve F	pg 45
Moelfre Lifeboat Station © Brian Green	pg 49
Old Windmill, Llangefni © Keith Williamson	pg 50
Holyhead War Memorial © Eric Jones	pg 54
Blue Footbridge, Pwllheli © Alan Fryer	pg 61
Criccieth Sea Front © Ken Crosby	pg 63
Hen Bont, Golan © Dewi	pg 62
Llanbedrog Church © Sion Roberts	pg 66
Aberdaron © Colin Park	pg 67
Dolwyddelan Castle © Steve Povey	pg 71
Dolgellau Bridge © Jonathan Billinger	pg 79
Corris © Nigel Brown	pg 83
Clock Tower, Machynlleth © Hayley Green	pg 88
Market Hall, Llandiloes © OLU	pg 90
Montgomery Castle © Derek Harper	pg 93
River Severn, Abermule © Penny Mayes	pg 95
Canal Bridge, Welshpool © John Haynes	pg 96
Wharf, Welshpool © Penny Mayes	pg 97
River Ithon, Llandrindod Wells © Ann Roberts	pg 104
The Lake, Llandrindod Wells © Ann Roberts	pg 105
River Teme, Knighton © Geoff Pick	pg 107
Hay-on-Wye Castle © Humphrey Bolton	pg 109
River Wye, Builth Wells © Ian Medcalf	pg 111
River Usk, Brecon © Pauline Eccles	pg 114
Crickhowell © Keith Salvesen	pg 117
Headland, New Quay © OLU	pg 121
Aberystwyth Marina © Angella Streluk	pg 122
Afon Rheidol, Aberystwth © OLU	pg 123
Fishing Boat, New Quay © Bob Jones	pg 127
Afon Aeron, Aberaeron © Humphrey Bolton	pg 129
Gorsedd Circle, Cardigan © Ceridwen	pg 134
Strata Florida Abbey, Pontrhydfendigaid © Rhys James	pg 131
Teifi Valley Railway, Henllan © Chris Daniels	pg 137
French Stone, Fishguard © Ceridwen	pg 140
Cilgerran Castle © Stephen McKay	pg 142
Entrance to Porthgain © Nigel Callaghan	pg 145
St David's Cathedral © Colin Park	pg 146
Nolton Haven © David Smith	pg 152
Tenby Beach © Diane Morton	pg 156
River Towy, Llansteffan © Ruth Sharville	pg 159
Roman Amphitheatre, Carmarthen © Nigel Davies	pg 160
Laugharne Castle © Humphrey Bolton	pg 163
Llandovery Castle © Philip Halling	pg 166
Llanelli Breakwater © Nick Earl	pg 169
Kidwelly Castle © Colin Park	pg 171
Mumbles Head © Robert Cuthill	pg 173
Maritime Quarter, Swansea © Pam Brophy	pg 174
Mumbles Pier © Pam Brophy	pg 176
Oxwich Castle © Joy Williams	pg 177
Cyfartha Castle, Methyr Tydfil © Ray Jones	pg 183
The Esplanade , Penarth © Mick Lobb	pg 187
Dock Office Building, Barry © Mick Lobb	pg 189
Sunset at Southerndown © Andy Dolman	pg 190
Physic Garden, Cowbridge © Ron Speed	pg 191
Pierhead Building, Cardiff © Philip Halling	pg 194
Friary Gardens, Cardiff © Keith Edkins	pg 195
16th Century Welsh Farmhouse, St Fagans © Roger Cornfoot	pg 196
Transporter Bridge, Newport © Robin Drayton	pg 197
Caerphilly Castle, © Keith Edkins	pg 199
Monnow Bridge, Monmouth © Robin Drayton	pg 204
Round House, Monmouth © Jonathan Billinger	pg 205
Tintern Abbey © Neil Kennedy	pg 206
Castle Dell, Chepstow © Roy Parkhouse	pg 207
Skenfrith Castle © Ray Jones	pg 211

Towns, Villages and Places of Interest

C

L

M

N

O

P

R

S

TRAVEL PUBLISHING ORDER FORM

To order any of our publications just fill in the payment details below and complete the order form. For orders of less than 4 copies please add £1.00 per book for postage and packing. Orders over 4 copies are P & P free.

Name:

Address:

Tel no:

Please Complete Either:

I enclose a cheque for £ ___________ made payable to Travel Publishing Ltd

Or:

Card No: Expiry Date:

Signature:

Please either send, telephone, fax or e-mail your order to:

Travel Publishing Ltd, Airport Business Centre, 10 Thornbury Road, Estover, Plymouth PL6 7PP

Tel: 01752 697280 Fax: 01752 697299 e-mail: info@travelpublishing.co.uk

HIDDEN PLACES REGIONAL TITLES	Price	Quantity
Cornwall	£8.99	....
Devon	£8.99	....
Dorset, Hants & Isle of Wight	£8.99	....
East Anglia	£8.99	....
Lake District & Cumbria	£8.99	....
Lancashire & Cheshire	£8.99	....
Northumberland & Durham	£8.99	....
Peak District and Derbyshire	£8.99	....
Yorkshire	£8.99	....
HIDDEN PLACES NATIONAL TITLES		
England	£11.99	....
Ireland	£11.99	....
Scotland	£11.99	....
Wales	£11.99	....
OTHER TITLES		
Off the Motorway	£11.99	....
Garden Centres & Nurseries	£11.99	....

COUNTRY LIVING RURAL GUIDES	Price	Quantity
East Anglia	£10.99	....
Heart of England	£10.99	....
Ireland	£11.99	....
North East	£10.99	....
North West	£10.99	....
Scotland	£11.99	....
South of England	£10.99	....
South East of England	£10.99	....
Wales	£11.99	....
West Country	£10.99	....

TOTAL QUANTITY:

POST & PACKING:

TOTAL VALUE:

READER REACTION FORM

The *Travel Publishing* research team would like to receive reader's comments on any visitor attractions or places reviewed in the book and also recommendations for suitable entries to be included in the next edition. This will help ensure that the *Hidden Places series of Guides* continues to provide its readers with useful information on the more interesting, unusual or unique features of each attraction or place ensuring that their visit to the local area is an enjoyable and stimulating experience. To provide your comments or recommendations would you please complete the forms below and overleaf as indicated and send to:

The Research Department, Travel Publishing Ltd,
Airport Business Centre, 10 Thornbury Road, Plymouth PL6 7PP

Your Name:

Your Address:

Your Telephone Number:

Please tick as appropriate:

Comments ☐ Recommendation ☐

Name of Establishment:

Address:

Telephone Number:

Name of Contact:

READER REACTION FORM

COMMENT OR REASON FOR RECOMMENDATION:

READER REACTION FORM

The *Travel Publishing* research team would like to receive reader's comments on any visitor attractions or places reviewed in the book and also recommendations for suitable entries to be included in the next edition. This will help ensure that the *Hidden Places series of Guides* continues to provide its readers with useful information on the more interesting, unusual or unique features of each attraction or place ensuring that their visit to the local area is an enjoyable and stimulating experience. To provide your comments or recommendations would you please complete the forms below and overleaf as indicated and send to:

The Research Department, Travel Publishing Ltd,
Airport Business Centre, 10 Thornbury Road, Plymouth PL6 7PP

Your Name:

Your Address:

Your Telephone Number:

Please tick as appropriate:

Comments ☐ Recommendation ☐

Name of Establishment:

Address:

Telephone Number:

Name of Contact:

READER REACTION FORM

COMMENT OR REASON FOR RECOMMENDATION:

Index of Advertisers

ACCOMMODATION

FOOD AND DRINK

PLACES OF INTEREST